Communication Yearbook 29

Communication Yearbook 29

PAMELA J. KALBFLEISCH
EDITOR

Published Annually for the
International Communication Association

LAWRENCE ERLBAUM ASSOCIATES, PUBLISHERS
2005   Mahwah, New Jersey   London

Copyright © 2005 by The International Communication Association

Lawrence Erlbaum Associates, Inc., Publishers
10 Industrial Avenue
Mahwah, NJ 07430

Library of Congress:
ISSN: 0147-4642
ISBN: 0-8058-5581-5 (hardcover)

Cover design by Kathryn Houghtaling-Lacey

Books published by Lawrence Erlbaum Associates are printed on acid-free paper, and their bindings are chosen for strength and durability.

Printed in the United States of America
10 9 8 7 6 5 4 3 2 1

Managing Editor: Barbara Stooksberry, ICA Headquarters
Copy & Production Editor: Matthew Katz, ICA Headquarters

CONTENTS

THE INTERNATIONAL COMMUNICATION ASSOCIATION

The International Communication Association (ICA) was formed in 1950, bringing together academics and other professionals whose interests focus on human communication. The Association maintains an active membership of more than 3,000 individuals, of whom some two thirds are teaching and conducting research in colleges, universities, and schools around the world. Other members are in government, law, medicine, and other professions. The wide professional and geographic distribution of the membership provides the basic strength of the ICA. The Association is a meeting ground for sharing research and useful dialogue about communication interests.

Through its divisions and interest groups, publications, annual conferences, and relations with other associations around the world, the ICA promotes the systemic study of communication theories, processes, and skills. In addition to *Communication Yearbook,* the Association publishes the *Journal of Communication, Human Communication Research, Communication Theory, Journal of Computer-Mediated Communication, A Guide to Publishing in Scholarly Communication Journals*, and the *ICA Newsletter*.

For additional information about the ICA and its activities, visit online at www. icahdq.org or contact Michael L. Haley, Executive Director, International Communication Association, 1730 Rhode Island NW, Suite 300, Washington, DC 20036 USA; phone (202) 530-9855; fax (202) 530-9851; email: ica@icahdq.org.

Editors of the *Communication Yearbook* series:

Volumes 1 and 2, Brent D. Ruben
Volumes 3 and 4, Dan Nimmo
Volumes 5 and 6, Michael Burgoon
Volumes 7 and 8, Robert N. Bostrom
Volumes 9 and 10, Margaret L. McLaughlin
Volumes 11, 12, 13, and 14, James A. Anderson
Volumes 15, 16, and 17, Stanley A. Deetz
Volumes 18, 19, and 20, Brant R. Burleson
Volumes 21, 22, and 23, Michael E. Roloff
Volumes 24, 25, and 26, William B. Gudykunst
Volumes 27, 28, and 29, Pamela J. Kalbfleisch

CONSULTING EDITORS

The following scholars have kindly shared their time and talents in consulting with the editor and in refereeing manuscripts for this volume of the *Communication Yearbook.*

COMMUNICATION AND THE FUTURE: AN INTRODUCTION

This volume of the *Communication Yearbook* centers on the theme of Communication and the Future. Authors in this volume address the future as they review 12 diverse areas of communication research. There have been many changes in the world, and this volume addresses questions such as: Has the discipline of communication kept up with change? Have we adapted to new technology and moved forward in our thinking? What do we as a discipline have to say about the future? Are there new areas in which we should be making a contribution? Are there new ways of looking at long-standing lines of communication research? The focus of this volume is on what we can do as communication scholars to make a difference in everyday life and in the future.

No one is more a part of our future than our children. *Communication Yearbook 29* begins with a chapter by Wendy M. Morgan and Steven R. Wilson reviewing research on nonphysical child abuse. These authors emphasize that we as communication scholars can make a difference in the welfare of our children and in society as a whole. In their chapter, Morgan and Wilson establish research on nonphysical child abuse as a communication issue because children may be verbally abused by those who should be protecting them. Morgan and Wilson place communication front and center as a field that could truly make a difference in the future lives of children. From this chapter it becomes clear that communication scholars are uniquely suited to address this child abuse concern. These authors encourage the communication discipline to turn more of its research endeavors toward the issue of verbal abuse of children.

Children are also a concern to Jan Van den Bulck and Bea Van den Bergh. Their chapter focuses on the child effect in media and communication research. Van den Bulck and Van den Bergh observe that the child effect has been an undervalued approach to researching how children play a part in influencing the media consumption of their parents. Theses authors suggest that children may be socializing their parents to media usage in a family—and that future researchers should consider this effect. In their chapter, Van den Bulck and Van den Bergh describe how communication scholars could make a significant impact in our knowledge of the child effect, which has been overlooked by other disciplines studying child behavior.

Judee K. Burgoon then turns our interest from the future of children toward the future study of motivated deception and its detection. As we are now in an era of Homeland Security and fears of terrorism, deception detection research has new applications in our world. In her chapter, Burgoon reviews research and theory regarding motivated deception and deceit when the stakes are high. In reading this chapter, we can see how scholarly interest in studying deceptive communication has reemerged as communication researchers look toward a not too friendly future.

How do we resist persuasion in a world where others may not have our best interests at heart? Joshua A. Compton and Michael W. Pfau address this concern in their comprehensive review of inoculation theory. If we can inoculate ourselves against future disease, can we be inoculated against the future persuasive attempts of others? In this time of fear and uncertainty, Compton and Pfau review inoculation theory and research and the implications of this research for our future world.

New innovations in research technology have changed the way we do our research and how we advance the frontiers of knowledge. Nicholas A. Palomares and Andrew J. Flanagin examine the potential of electronic communication and information technologies as research tools for future communication research. In their chapter, these authors highlight both the promise and the peril of using new communication technology to advance communication research.

Electronic communication and new communication technology mediate and affect our interactions across several venues and contexts. In their chapter, Stacey L. Connaughton and John A. Daly expand our knowledge of how leaders communicate across temporal, spatial, and geographical boundaries. From their review, it is clear that leadership takes on new dimensions when physical presence is not necessarily an expectation.

This chapter is followed by Zizi Papacharissi's examination of the consequences for using new communication technology. Papacharissi suggests that human needs to manage time, express identity, and establish social contact are central to understanding how people use communication technology to interact with others. Debates on whether one needs to be face to face to communicate are remarkably antiquated when considered in the technological age of the new millennium.

This volume next turns consideration to the ways that public relations research can and is developing in the future. Betteke van Ruler and Dejan Vercic propose a new definition of communication and management for the future that is drawn from four historical approaches to public relations. Their chapter suggests communication scholars consider a new practical view of public relations in which previous models of public relations are combined as strategies.

This examination of the future of public relations is followed by Betty Kaman Lee's examination of crisis communication. In her chapter, Lee suggests that future communication research consider the role that culture plays in crisis communication. Several examples of crisis communication within the culture of Hong Kong emphasize the need for communication scholars to look beyond their traditional research populations and toward the population of the world for future research endeavors.

Raul Roman also considers culture in his examination of development communication. In this chapter, Roman argues that future development communication research consider the central role of theory in building this line of communication inquiry. In his review of the literature, Roman presents the current and future need for theory in the study of applied communication on practical problems such as those encountered in the study of development communication.

In the next chapter, Robert Wicks applies theory to the study of mass communication research. Wicks suggests that message framing and construction of meaning are important for future researchers to fully understand the media and the ongoing role they plays in our lives.

Bryan C. Taylor, William J. Kinsella, Stephen P. Depoe, and Maribeth S. Metzler close this volume on Communication and the Future with an examination of the future legacy of nuclear weapons production in the United States. These authors argue that the normalization of communication regarding nuclear weapons production has created a milieu in which communication scholars have ignored the study of conflict and controversy surrounding this issue. In their chapter, Taylor, Kinsella, Depoe, and Metzler bring our attention back to the communication legacy and future communicative response to nuclear weapons production in an uncertain future.

As editor of *Communication Yearbook 29*, I hope these chapters illuminate what we as a discipline with diverse interests can do to advance our knowledge of communication in the future. We as scholar educators in the communication discipline can make a difference in the lives of people living today and in the future.

ACKNOWLEDGMENTS

Communication Yearbook 29 is the concluding volume of the three volumes of *Communication Yearbook* I have edited on the themes of Communication and Empowerment (*CY 27*), Communication and Community (*CY28*), and Communication and the Future (*CY29*). These volumes were designed to help unify the discipline and move us forward in addressing issues of concern to society as a whole.

The editorial process of peer review for the *Communication Yearbook 27–29* was one in which many dedicated scholar educators unselfishly gave their time to lend their perspectives to the quality of the manuscripts submitted for review. I thank these talented individuals for their contributions to the quality of each volume. They are a vital part of the scholarly credibility of these volumes.

The creativity and hard work of authors published in these volumes are also greatly appreciated. I value that these authors submitted quality manuscripts to *Communication Yearbook* and that they were willing and able to quickly respond to my feedback and that of the reviewers.

An excellent editorial assistant makes all the difference in the world as far as having fun and enjoying the process of bringing excellent scholarship into the public sphere. Organized, talented, and bright, Anita L. Herold was a great editorial assistant and wonderful junior colleague. She was one of two editorial assistants bringing *Communication Yearbook 28* to publication and the sole editorial assistant for *Communication Yearbook 29*. She is definitely someone I would want on my team for future editorial projects. I also appreciate the contributions that editorial assistants Nathan C. MacLean and Valina K. Eckley made on the earlier volumes in this thematic series of *Communication Yearbook.*

Barbara Stooksberry and Matthew Katz in the office of the International Communication Association are careful production editors who added significantly to the quality of this volume. I also appreciate working with the editorial staff at Lawrence Erlbaum Associates Publishers.

Most of all I appreciate the love and support I have received from my family. My husband, Jan Gierman, mother, Marian Kalbfleisch, and sister, Karen Kalbfleisch Lind, have all been a great help to me in their own way. My mother, Marian Kalbfleisch, died during the editing of *Communication Yearbook 29.* Born on March 10, 1921, in Galesburg, Illinois, and died February 28, 2004, in Twin Falls, Idaho, my mother has always been a source of great inspiration to me as someone who always saw the best in others. Even when she was most ill, my mother always asked how others were doing rather than talking about her own concerns. It is perhaps these qualities, seeing the best in others and putting others first, that have the best chance for guiding us to a more peaceful future.

Pamela J. Kalbfleisch
Grand Forks, North Dakota

CHAPTER CONTENTS

1   Nonphysical Child Abuse: A Review of Literature and Challenge to Communication Scholars

WENDY M. MORGAN
STEVEN R. WILSON
Purdue University

To understand nonphysical child abuse better, the authors argue, scholars must provide thorough conceptualization and theoretically grounded operationalization. To illustrate this argument, the authors explicate the terms (a) verbal aggression, (b) psychological aggression, and (c) psychological maltreatment (stemming from communication, sociology, and psychology respectively) and review, for each term, the theoretical conceptualization, operationalization, and implications for intervention. They discuss the importance of and the challenges inherent in developing any theoretically grounded conceptualization and operationalization of nonphysical child abuse and highlight criteria with which to assess both. The authors also argue that scholars of communication are well situated to help fill the gaps in abuse research.

Abigail is a 13-year-old girl. For the past 5 years, her mother has whipped her with a belt on the legs and buttocks as a punishment for any type of misbehavior. At this time, the lacerations from the last whipping have healed, so she can wear shorts in public again. Has Abigail been abused? If so, what type of abuse has taken place? What is the lasting damage?

Michael is a 9-year-old boy. He has never been hit by his parents, but his father routinely tells him that he is stupid and lazy, sometimes in front of his friends. His mother has never said a word about it. Has Michael been abused? If so, what type of abuse has taken place? What is the lasting damage?

Even though these two hypothetical cases differ in terms of physical injury or abuse, both can be viewed as instances of nonphysical abuse.[1] Bones and bruises heal more quickly than memories fade; as a result, nonphysical child abuse can

---

Correspondence: Wendy M. Morgan, Department of Communication, Purdue University, Beering Hall 2114, 100 N. University St., West Lafayette, IN 47907-2098; email: morganw@purdue.edu

Communication Yearbook 29, pp. 1–33

be conceptualized not only as a particular type of abuse different from physical forms of abuse but also as one consequence of physical abuse. In cases such as Abigail's, the nonphysical outcomes may be more damaging in the long term than the physical injuries sustained; it is the meaning of physical abuse that haunts victims (Hart, Brassard, Binggeli, & Davidson, 2002; Vissing, Straus, Gelles, & Harrop, 1991).

Practically speaking, state agencies such as Child Protective Services (CPS) are unlikely to address cases that involve only nonphysical child abuse (i.e., cases such as Michael). This is true for several reasons: The concept of psychological or emotional harm is somewhat vague, it is difficult to prove harm without physical evidence, nonphysical child abuse often accompanies other forms of abuse that are more readily evidenced, and individuals are reluctant to report children experiencing nonphysical child abuse to a system that is already overloaded (National Center on Child Abuse and Neglect [NCCAN], 2002). Low reporting and CPS substantiation rates should not be taken as evidence that nonphysical child abuse fails to cause enough damage to require intervention. Intervention must, however, for the most part take the form of family therapy, parent education, or support programs. Such programs may target families dealing with other types of CPS-substantiated forms of abuse, or they may be intended for families who seek assistance because they recognize the need for help on their own.

One end goal of research in this area is to inform and direct these intervention efforts. To inform intervention, researchers must first understand the phenomenon itself. So far, the concept of nonphysical child abuse has been nebulous, although there are at least three existing ways in which it has been conceptualized. Each body of literature provides useful insights, but each stops short of providing a coherent account of what constitutes nonphysical child abuse, why it happens, and how it happens. These are important questions—not just for intervention but also for developing theories and research findings that have the potential to inform intervention.

Finding answers to these questions is a future task for which communication scholars are uniquely qualified. The field of communication is tuned in to the concept of meaning in a way that few other fields are at this time. Communication theory can help explain how perceptions arising in the moment influence the possibilities for how an interaction may unfold (e.g., Sanders & Fitch, 2001; Tracy, 1991). Questions about the consequences of interaction patterns for identities and relationships lie at the heart of our field (e.g., Baxter & Montgomery, 1996; Burleson, Delia, & Applegate, 1995; Millar & Rogers, 1987).

Communication theory may be just the thing to help sort out that important and yet complicated question surrounding nonphysical abuse: What happened? Even though child abuse has traditionally been addressed within fields such as psychology, sociology, and social work, communication scholarship is clearly relevant and may be necessary if the snarl of issues surrounding nonphysical abuse is to be acknowledged and eventually untangled. What is more, the future application of communication theory and research to such a practically useful matter as

TABLE 1
Overall Comparison of Terms by Major Definitional Issues

	Term reviewed		
Definitional issue	*Verbal aggression*	*Psychological aggression*	*Psychological maltreatment*
Underlying theoretical conceptualization	Personality trait or inherited neurobiology	Conflict theory	Various
Operationalization	Verbal Aggressiveness Scale	Conflict Tactics Scales	Various
Implications for intervention	Identification of persons at risk for abusing	Understanding of U.S. frequencies of psychological aggression	Screening: identification of general patterns that indicate abuse

nonphysical abuse may not only help clarify the phenomenon itself but also raise the level of public awareness regarding communication scholarship.

We argue that, to understand nonphysical child abuse better, and to ask more insightful and practically useful research questions, at least two things must be accomplished in the future: thorough conceptualization and theoretically grounded operationalization. To illustrate our argument, we explicate the following terms, stemming from communication, sociology, and psychology disciplines, respectively: (a) verbal aggression, (b) psychological aggression, and (c) psychological maltreatment. These are not the only existing conceptualizations of nonphysical child abuse one might explore; however, the juxtaposition of these terms reveals the kinds of definitional issues with which any perspective must grapple.

This chapter is divided into four sections. The first three sections are devoted to thorough discussion of each of the three terms listed above. Within each of these three sections, we review the (a) underlying theoretical conceptualization, (b) operationalization, and (c) implications for intervention that are associated with each term. The overall relationship of the chosen terms with the issues covered is reflected in Table 1, and it may be helpful to refer to this table as each term is discussed.

After discussion of each individual term, the fourth section focuses on the importance of and the challenges inherent in developing any theoretically grounded conceptualization and operationalization of nonphysical child abuse. By clarifying relevant issues across terms, we highlight criteria with which to assess any definition, existing or new, and discuss directions for future research. As communication theorists are uniquely qualified to explore the means and nature of harmful symbolic messages, we further argue that scholars of communication should step forth now to help fill the gaps in abuse research in the future.

The terms we review here are rooted in scholarly traditions that deserve high praise for quite literally fashioning something where nothing was before. Before these terms became commonplace, only physical assault of children was considered to be abusive. The very idea that interaction could hurt was born of intuition and personal experience, and the theoretical and methodological foundations were original. Without the work behind the terms reviewed here, the argument we make would not be possible. In this chapter, we will review where these traditions have taken us so far in terms of understanding nonphysical child abuse and argue the need for developments in theory and research, particularly within the field of communication.

VERBAL AGGRESSION

Within this first section, we discuss (a) the underlying theoretical conceptualization of the term verbal aggression, (b) its operationalization, and (c) the implications for intervention highlighted with this perspective.

In a chapter designed to compare and contrast terms often appearing in research on harmful parent–child interaction, an obvious choice is verbal aggression—a very well-known communication concept. As indicated in Table 1, trait verbal aggression has been conceptualized as the predisposition to attack others' self-concepts rather than their arguments, and it has been measured by the Verbal Aggressiveness Scale (Infante & Wigley, 1986)—a widely used scale demonstrating reliability and concurrent validity (Rubin, Palmgreen & Sypher, 1994).

Not originally conceptualized to explore parent-to-child abuse, trait verbal aggression has nonetheless been explored in research on parenting style (Bayer & Cegala, 1992), responses to child noncompliance (Rudd, Vogl-Bauer, Dobos, Beatty, & Valencic, 1998), and physical child abuse (Wilson et al., 2001). The work on verbal aggression introduces the idea that aggressiveness may be an indelible, possibly genetic, part of personality. This is an intriguing but practically and ethically challenging contention.

Conceptualization

Original conceptualization. Infante and colleagues take a personality approach to understanding verbally aggressive communication. In their work, verbal aggression is conceptualized as a psychological trait that predisposes an individual to use verbally aggressive messages, ones that attack the self-concepts rather than (or in addition to) the arguments of others. Trait verbal aggression is contrasted with argumentativeness, a trait that predisposes people to use argumentative messages, ones that attack issues rather than the self-concepts of others (Infante, 1989; Infante & Rancer, 1996; Infante, Riddle, Horvath & Tumlin, 1992; Infante & Wigley, 1986).

Verbal aggression is located within the personality typology of Costa and McCrae (1980). According to their work, personality consists of three major dimensions, each with six facets or subsets. Neuroticism consists of anxiety, depression, self-consciousness, vulnerability, impulsiveness, and hostility. Extraversion consists of attachment, gregariousness, excitement-seeking, positive emotions, activity, and assertiveness. Openness consists of fantasy, aesthetics, feelings, actions, ideas, and values. Infante and Wigley (1986) positioned verbal aggression as a subset of hostility, which is itself a subset of neuroticism.

The term verbal aggression is used in two senses: as a personality trait or predisposition to perform verbally aggressive behavior across a variety of situations and targets, as well as a category of specific behavior stemming from that predisposition, actions that attack the hearer's self-concept. The types of behavior patterns indicative of trait verbal aggression have not been uniformly agreed upon, but scholars are close to achieving this. Infante and Rancer (1996) categorized types of verbally aggressive messages to include character attacks, competence attacks, background attacks, physical appearance attacks, maledictions, teasing, ridicule, threats, swearing, and nonverbal emblems. A 1992 study by Infante et al. found that high verbal aggressives are distinguished from others only in teasing, ridicule, use of profanity and emblems, and their frequency of competence, background, and personal appearance attacks (also see Kinney, 1994).

Regardless of the specific form taken, verbal aggressive behavior is viewed as intentional:

> The trait of verbal aggression involves attacking the self-concepts of others in order to inflict psychological pain, such as humiliation, embarrassment, depression, and other negative feelings about the self. . . . The main reasons high verbal aggressives have given for their use of verbal aggression include having disdain for the target, wanting to be mean to the target, [and] trying to appear "tough." (Infante & Rancer, 1996, p. 323)

Infante (1995) also has suggested that verbal aggression is at once intentional and the result of a lack of skill. In other words, high verbal aggressives may resort to personal attack when they encounter a situation in which they do not know how to counter an argument. Consequently, it has been suggested that skills training may reduce occurrence of verbally aggressive behavior (Infante, 1995).

Even though trait verbal aggression reflects a predisposition toward intentional activity, actual behaviors (verbally aggressive messages) are theoretically caused by an interaction between the trait of verbal aggression and a facilitative situation:

> Verbal aggression may be more likely when the situation involves anger, persons being in a bad mood, a desire for reciprocity, or feigned humor. Furthermore, the likelihood of verbal aggression in the situation may increase when, in addition, the person is a high verbal aggressive . . . and when the two [conversational partners] are in a rational discussion which begins to degenerate into a verbal fight. (Infante et al., 1992, pp. 123–124)

This argument weakens the idea that traits cut across environments; however, the stipulation seems only sensible because some situations, misbehavior or arguments, for instance, are more likely to trigger malicious intent than others.

As much as Infante and colleagues have accounted for situation, intention, and lack of skill, their explanation leaves vague the mechanism causing parents to engage in verbally aggressive messages: Personality simply predisposes them. Do children inherit verbal aggression, or do they learn to engage in aggressive behavior in their own relationships? Is there something (avoidable) about the situations that elicit verbal aggression? Future answers to these questions would be useful keys to understanding nonphysical abuse.

Communibiological perspective. The communibiological perspective modifies and specifies the causal mechanism. The term *communibiology* is used to describe the concept of interpersonal communication as the expression of individual differences in neurobiological functioning that are for the most part genetically determined. Within this framework, verbal aggression is conceptualized as a particular combination of Gray's (1991) three neurobiological systems (fight–flight system, or FFS; behavioral inhibition system, or BIS; and behavioral approach system, or BAS) assumed to underlie temperament, and thus behavior (Beatty & McCroskey, 1997; Valencic, Beatty, Rudd, Dodos, & Heisel, 1998).

These "neurobiological structures underlying temperament traits and individual differences are mostly inherited" (Beatty & McCroskey, 1998, p. 48) and are relatively impervious to environmental or situational influences: "Environment or 'situation' has only a negligible effect on interpersonal behavior" (Beatty & McCroskey, 1998, p. 50). This deterministic position is a bold one considering that scholars adhering to a communibiological perspective have yet to parse genetic triggers of neurobiological functioning from environmental and joint genetic–environmental effects.

All observed outcomes (phenotypes) reflect not only genotype and environment main effects, but also genotype–environment correlations. Environmental similarities co-occur with genetic similarities, be they passive (i.e., when parents provide genes and environment), evocative (i.e., when a child's genetic expression evokes environmental response), or active (i.e., when genetically different children seek out different environments), genotype–environment interactions (just as genetically similar individuals react differently across different environments, genetically different individuals react differently when environment is held constant), and genotype-environment transactions (i.e., genetic expression affects environment, which affects later genetic expression). It is virtually impossible to control for all these factors. The results of any study therefore can usually be attributed to the combination of genetic and environmental influences (see Bronfenbrenner & Ceci, 1994; Bugental & Goodnow, 1998; Coie & Dodge, 1998; Collins, Maccoby, Steinberg, Hetherington, & Bornstein, 2000; Eisenberg, 1998; Rothbart & Bates, 1998).

In sum, at the same time that genetic makeup "mediates reactions to environmental stimuli" (Beatty & McCroskey, 1997, p. 449), environment also moderates genetic expression, from biology to behavior. Neurobiological functions are themselves phenotypic—even beyond infancy and throughout the lifespan—and therefore require the same consideration on the issue of genes versus environment (see Depue, Collins, & Luciana, 1996; Kagan, 1998; Kaufman & Charney, 2001; Sánchez, Ladd, & Plotsky, 2001). The concept of verbal aggression within the communibiological perspective may have to be softened to account for much of the current wisdom surrounding the nature–nurture question.

Even if the conclusions regarding nature versus nurture in respect to verbal aggression within the framework of communibiology are overstated, the perspective at least addresses the issue of genetic inheritance, a line of thought especially important in conjunction with questions regarding intergenerational transmission of abuse. When compared against the other two terms reviewed in this chapter, verbal aggression is unique in this regard.

Operationalization

Until communibiologists introduce genetic or chemical markers of verbal aggression,[2] the Verbal Aggressiveness Scale (VAS; Infante & Wigley, 1986) remains the uncontested standard for measuring verbally aggressive behavior and, theoretically, the standard for measuring trait verbal aggression. On the scale, personality traits are inferred through self-reported patterns of behavior and intent. A good deal of evidence has supported its reliability and concurrent validity (see Rubin et al., 1994); but while scholars accept the validity of the VAS, it must be understood that it cannot indicate a personality type causally prior to social participation. Aggressive behavior is phenotypic and, as discussed above, results from the complex relationship between genetic and environmental factors. That said, past behavior patterns may be our best indicators of future ones. In this regard, the VAS is valuable, but its value could be improved with more detailed theory in the future.

Measurement is always most useful to researchers and practitioners when it is grounded in clear theoretical explanation (Wilson & Sabee, 2003). Three particular questions regarding the nature of trait verbal aggression could be elaborated, allowing the existing scale to become even more useful: What are the importance of particular verbally aggressive behaviors, the role of intent, and the role of facilitative situations?

Preventing damage from verbal aggression requires an understanding of both the link between trait and behavior (discussed above) and the particular behaviors which have the most deleterious effects. Before a list of specific behaviors can become useful, however, researchers must identify how — through what process — these behaviors harm the self-concept. Why are these behaviors most important? What is the mechanism of damage?

Theoretical elaboration on these questions may not only lead to more informative research but also lend greater practical utility to the VAS. Currently, the behaviors measured in the scale seem arbitrary. Two items in the scale (items two and seven) refer specifically to insults, which may be a label for any type of attack. For example, item 2 reads, "When individuals are very stubborn, I use insults to soften the stubbornness." Two items (6 and 16) refer to character attack (item 6 reads, "If individuals I am trying to influence really deserve it, I attack their character"). Item 13 may refer to teasing ("I like poking fun at people who do things which are very stupid in order to stimulate their intelligence"), and item 6 refers to competence attack ("I am extremely careful to avoid attacking individuals' intelligence when I attack their ideas"). The rest are vague (e.g., item 18 reads, "When nothing seems to work in trying to influence others, I yell and scream in order to get some movement from them"). Greater understanding of how verbally aggressive behaviors damage a target's self-concept may not only answer other conceptual questions (Why are particular behaviors considered verbally aggressive while others are not? Do particular types of aggressive behaviors vary in intensity?); they might also lead to greater precision of measurement and therefore greater ability to assess potential damage in any given relationship.

On the issue of intent, there is room for future theoretical consideration. Verbally aggressive people do not always intend harm. They may intend a particular reaction but be unaware of emotional consequences, they may act largely by rote, or they may experience intent only momentarily (Infante & Rancer, 1996). Do these possibilities represent different subtypes of verbal aggression? Are some individuals predisposed toward ignorance of how they hurt others verbally, whereas others are predisposed toward apathy? The answers to these questions may not only tighten the theory, but may also expand the usefulness of the existing scale. Some items comprising the scale clearly tap intent whereas others clearly either do not or are ambiguous. Items such as item 7, which reads, "When people behave in ways that are in very poor taste, I insult them in order to shock them into behaving properly" clearly tap intent, whereas other items (e.g., item 9: "When people simply will not budge on a matter of importance, I lose my temper and say rather strong things to them") are more ambiguous.

At present, though, the scale measures varying degrees of intent from item to item, but does not account for these differences in the final score. As a result, the score is unable to distinguish between parents who use verbally aggressive behavior in a conscious and purposeful manner from parents whose intentions may be more ephemeral. Each case may require different intervention techniques. A conceptualization—and consequently a measure—that accounts for these different situations would be of tangible practical value to individuals charged with intervening.

Another latent dimension of the scale is situation. The VAS asks about the respondent's tendency to perform verbally aggressive behaviors within a variety of situations. This makes sense when thinking about verbal aggression as a general predisposition. However, if verbally aggressive behavior arises from the interplay of predisposition and situational facilitators, it becomes important to reflect on what types of situations are assessed by the VAS. In the scale, items are meant to draw on different kinds of potentially facilitative situations. Item 11 deals with receiving criticism: "When individuals insult me, I get a lot of pleasure out of really telling them off." Item 19 deals with argumentative situations: "When I am not able to refute other people's ideas, I try to make them feel defensive in order to weaken what they say." As with intent, the subdimensions of verbal aggression determined by different situations are not identified; the final score does not account for the types of situations proposed. Theoretical identification of relevant situations (or situations that are likely to trigger verbally aggressive behavior by individuals so predisposed) could potentially allow for more precise measurement, and greater ability to identify the types of situations such individuals should try hardest to avoid or change.

Implications for Intervention

The VAS was not designed with the aim of pointing to nonphysical child abuse requiring intervention. Verbal aggression is an attack on the other's self; damage to the self-concept is implied as a harmful outcome. Hence, verbally aggressive behavior may possibly be abusive if frequent or harsh enough. Both the harmful nature of specific behaviors and the level of verbal aggression that can be labeled "abusive" have yet to be indicated. So far, verbal aggression is seen as an antecedent to abuse—a catalyst for physically abusive behavior—but not as abuse itself (Infante & Rancer, 1996; Roloff, 1996).

It is also important to revisit the fact that as currently conceptualized, the trait of verbal aggression is the focal point of research exploring why people exhibit verbally aggressive behavior. Even though personality or temperament may predispose individuals to act aggressively, there cannot exist abusive levels of a predisposition. No harm can be caused by a predisposition that is not acted upon, and therefore it cannot be used, for instance, to distinguish abusive parents from nonabusive ones.

Identification of an aggressive predisposition does not help identify verbally abusive parents; knowledge of predisposition, however, can still aid intervention. A verbally aggressive person, even when not currently acting on predisposition, may still constitute a risk. The identification of trait verbal aggression may allow practitioners to assess risk status before harm is done, indicating a need for greater attention and skills training (Infante, 1995).

This line of thinking assumes, of course, that skills training is effective. McCroskey and Beatty (Beatty & McCroskey, 1998; McCroskey & Beatty, 2000) have argued that it may not be capable of overriding biological systems. If skills training cannot dampen the predispositions of high verbal aggressives, how can society deal with the knowledge that they may constitute a threat? Communibiologists present no other viable solution. What can be done about high-risk parents if there are no tools to lessen the risk? Trait verbal aggression determines only predisposition, not definite future behavior, and thus society cannot treat parents high in verbal aggression as abusive. Parents cannot be held accountable for behavior they have not enacted, but should the risk posed by verbal aggression be ignored?

For now, there may be no choice but to hope that skills training will be effective. If convincing evidence eventually points to the contrary before another solution presents itself, verbal aggression research may present a tangled ethical dilemma.

PSYCHOLOGICAL AGGRESSION

Whereas Infante's concept of verbal aggression is found in communication literature, psychological aggression hails from sociology—specifically from Straus and colleagues at the University of New Hampshire's Family Research Laboratory. The corresponding Conflict Tactics Scales (CTS) is a measure that has been a crucial step forward for this area of work and is used widely in abuse research. The CTS has been used in three national epidemiological surveys to determine the prevalence and chronicity of a range of conflict behaviors (see Straus & Gelles, 1990). It has contributed information where before there were only questions.

In this second section of our chapter, we review (a) the underlying theoretical conceptualization of psychological aggression, including how the label itself has evolved, (b) its operationalization, and (c) the corresponding implications for intervention. As indicated by Table 1, the term psychological aggression is grounded in conflict theory (discussed below). However, as will be discussed, the theoretical origin of this line of work is not the focus of Straus and colleagues. Instead, the CTS itself has taken the spotlight.

Conceptualization

The theoretical basis for the creation of the CTS is conflict theory (Adams, 1965; Coser, 1956, Dahrendorf, 1959; Scanzoni, 1972). This theory holds that conflict is a basic and inevitable societal function for all human groups, including families. Conflict theories contend that conflict allows change and adaptation to unfolding circumstances and that suppressed conflict can result in stagnation and accumulation of hostility (Straus, 1979). Concerned that researchers and practitioners were advising families to avoid conflict altogether, Straus pointed out that only conflict tactics that do not result in conflict resolution (e.g., aggression) are undesirable:

> A key factor differentiating what the public and many professionals regard as "high conflict families" is not the existence of conflict per se, but rather, inadequate or unsatisfactory modes of managing and resolving the conflicts which are inherent in the family. (Straus, 1979, p.85)

One implication is that the more aggressive the method of dealing with conflict, the less productive it is in resolving that conflict. Straus was especially concerned with physical tactics. If professionals are to discern productive from unproductive conflict tactics within a family, they must have a measurement instrument. Thus, Straus devised the CTS (Straus, 1979).

The behaviors measured in the CTS are arranged into three clusters, or sub-scales, ranging from what Straus (1979) has considered to be least to most aggressive in hierarchical order: reasoning (e.g., item a: "Discussed the issue calmly"), verbal aggression (e.g., item h: "Did or said something to spite the other person"), and (physical) violence (e.g., item p: "Beat up the other person"). The three subscales were originally arranged in this manner to facilitate testing of catharsis theory or leveling (Straus, 1974): the idea that a release of aggression through verbal means may dispel hostility and thus ward off physical assault. Empirical research, including three national epidemiological surveys using two versions of the CTS, has clearly shown a positive correlation between the dimensions of verbal aggression and physical violence, supporting conflict-escalation theory (Berkowitz, 1993) rather than catharsis theory (Straus, Hamby, Finkelhor, Moore, & Runyan, 1998). The opposite of catharsis theory, conflict-escalation theory contends that conflict tends to escalate, and although individuals may begin with less aggressive means (e.g., verbal aggression), aggression may eventually escalate into physical assault.

After development and use of the CTS, the concept behind the verbal aggression subscale of the instrument was itself defined and conceptually analyzed (Vissing et al., 1991). While defining verbal aggression, Vissing et al. initially changed the name to verbal/symbolic aggression in recognition of the difference between this and Infante's work and also to point out the nonverbal elements of aggression. Vissing et al. offered the following definition for verbal–symbolic aggression:

> Verbal/symbolic aggression is a communication intended to cause psychological pain to another person, or a communication perceived as having that intent. The communication act may be active or passive, and verbal or nonverbal. Examples include name calling or nasty remarks (active, verbal), slamming a door or smashing something (active, nonverbal), and stony silence or sulking (passive, nonverbal). (p. 224)

Vissing and Baily (1996) also offer a multifaceted taxonomy of definitional concerns, including whether a message source intended to cause psychological harm, whether the target perceived such intent (present in the definition above), whether verbal–nonverbal acts did cause harm, as well as how such acts were situated in larger interaction patterns, cultural contexts, and situations. Many of these issues (e.g., intent, perception, outcome, and interaction pattern) are not measured in the CTS, the instrument of choice for these scholars. Thus, it is likely that Vissing and Baily offer these definitional concerns to spark further work in the area rather than as definitions of concepts operationally measured in their own work.

Straus and colleagues subsequently renamed the verbal–symbolic aggression subscale of the CTS "psychological aggression" in later versions of the scales (Straus, Hamby, Boney-McCoy, & Sugarman, 1996; Straus et al., 1998). The authors point to Vissing et al. (1991) for the conceptual analysis and definition of the psychological aggression subscale.

Conflict theory (the theoretical foundation of the CTS) and psychological aggression as conceptualized by Vissing and colleagues are not entirely compatible, however, and incorporation of psychological aggression within the CTS is somewhat problematic. Vissing et al. (1991) have indicated that psychological aggression may be more damaging than physical assault. They further have said that even during physical assault, the symbolic meaning of the act may cause more damage than the resulting physical injury. Their research revealed that parental verbal aggression (psychological aggression) as measured by the CTS had a strong association with child aggression toward others, delinquency, and interpersonal problems, above and beyond the effects of parental physical violence. Further, parental psychological aggression accounted for more variance in child aggression than did physical violence by parents (Vissing et al., 1991). Warranted or not, this location of psychological aggression in relation to physical assault is at odds with the basic conceptualization of the CTS as a list of behaviors that increase in level of destructiveness from reasoning to psychological aggression to physical assault. Research indicating that psychological aggression causes as much if not more harm than physical violence may demand future theoretical analysis of the relationship between the CTS subscales.

Such an analysis would need to reconcile another conceptual discrepancy: Vissing et al. (1991) related psychological aggression to physical violence by comparing damage caused, but what constitutes damage in the estimation of Vissing et al. departs from Straus's (1979) original notion. Damage in terms of conflict theory is immediate, unsuccessful conflict resolution, whereas damage according to Vissing et al. is reflected in long-term factors like aggression, delinquency, and interpersonal problems. Perhaps these are not so far removed from each other: Unsuccessful conflict resolution may ultimately lead to aggression, delinquency, and interpersonal problems. The connection, however, has not been explicated. In spite of this conceptual disparity, Straus et al. (1998) declared that the most recent version of the CTS, the Parent–Child Conflict Tactics Scales (CTSPC), is theoretically based in conflict theory.

The fact that this work has been phenomenally successful and has contributed much to the area of scholarship despite potential theoretical contradiction is possibly the best evidence of all for the usefulness of the measure Straus created: the Conflict Tactics Scales (CTS). The CTS is probably his most well recognized and lasting legacy of scholarship.

Operationalization

Practically speaking, the CTS measures prevalence and chronicity of the specific behaviors that are assumed to represent the three subscales of reasoning, verbal (psychological) aggression, and physical violence. In the CTS, frequency of psychological aggression is assessed by asking respondents how frequently they perform actions such as "insulted or swore at the person," "sulked or refused to talk about an issue," and "threw or smashed or hit or kicked something."

Even though the significance of the three subscales can be associated with conflict-escalation theory (Berkowitz, 1993), the conceptual importance of the particular behaviors within each subscale is unclear. Stated simply: Why does the CTS ask about these specific actions to assess psychological aggression as opposed to other possible examples? What exactly do these actions have in common? Are some forms of psychological aggression more severe than other types? As with verbal aggression, psychological aggression may benefit from future attention to theoretical questions regarding the mechanism of damage. The current ambiguity is reflected in the low internal consistency reliability of the subscales. For example, the internal consistency (Cronbach's alpha) of the psychological aggression subscale has an average of .68 and a range of .62 to .77 (Straus & Hamby, 1997). Fortunately, the CTS enjoys concurrent validity with the Child Abuse Potential Inventory (Caliso & Milner, 1992) and construct validity with many theories and previous empirical findings (Straus & Hamby, 1997).

Despite its vague theoretical basis and less than ideal reliability, the CTS has been used in many studies of child abuse: 132 by last count (Straus et al., 1998). Responding to this interest, Straus et al. (1998) created the Parent-Child Conflict Tactics Scales (CTSPC), in an effort to provide a scale that is more adapted to measuring parental behavior.[3] In the process, they have clarified the wording of some items and interspersed the order of the items, to ward off mindless participant responses and avoid the irritation experienced by nonviolent respondents given the original CTS (CTS1). The CTSPC is set up to measure prevalence and chronicity of behaviors that constitute the renamed subscales of nonviolent discipline, psychological aggression, and physical assault, which is itself separated into corporal punishment, physical maltreatment, and severe physical maltreatment. Again, although the significance of the dimensions can be related to conflict-escalation theory, the conceptual importance of the individual behaviors chosen to measure each subscale is vague. Like CTS1, the CTSPC also suffers from low internal consistency reliability. Correlations among CTSPC dimensions demonstrate internal discriminant validity, but construct and concurrent validity have yet to be tested (Straus et al, 1998).

Implications for Intervention

Despite problems with conceptualization and reliability, the CTS1 has been used widely, which allows for comparison of results across studies. According to Barnett, Miller-Perrin, and Perrin (1997), CTS1 is "the most widely used scale in family violence research" (p. 34). The comparison of individuals or individual samples against national statistics may help locate each study within a much larger scope, and either CTS1 or CTSPC can be used for clinical screening. A lack of conceptualization regarding the causal mechanism (i.e., what causes parents to engage in psychological aggression?) or the mechanism of damage (i.e., how does psychological aggression result in harm to children?) limits the usefulness of either scale when it comes to decisions about how to intervene. The scales, however, may provide a good general overview of a family's behavior.

Perhaps the greatest benefit of the research of Straus and colleagues is the knowledge they have generated (with the CTS1) regarding nationwide patterns of behavior. Cultural context is of utmost importance because it helps constitute what can be defined as abuse. If the frequency of a particular type of act lies within or below the average frequency for an entire population, it is arguably socially acceptable, nonabusive. After all, the frequency of a behavior in a culture affects the meaning of that behavior. More common behaviors are likely to have less potential for damaging meaning than less common behaviors. The conceptualization of psychological abuse takes this issue into consideration by defining abuse in relation to the national average of psychologically aggressive attacks (Vissing et al., 1991). Whereas the question of what constitutes abusive levels of the communication construct of verbal aggression is an open one, Vissing et al. have proposed to settle the issue as it relates to psychological aggression.

Vissing et al. (1991) take frequency of aggressive attacks into consideration to distinguish between psychological aggression versus psychological abuse. In the absence of an established standard relying on frequency, Vissing et al. proposed three different thresholds for number of attacks per year that constitute "abuse": 10, 20, and 25 attacks per year.[4] Regardless of the particular number of attacks per year, this way of defining psychological abuse is important to note because it considers differences in social acceptance of various frequencies of behaviors within a culture.

The measurement of behavioral frequency opens the door to measurement of other kinds of national chronicity. A national average of any measurement locus can be assessed. Even a measurement of target perceptions could conceivably provide a similar societal topography of sorts: Large-scale studies could be conducted during which targets of parent-to-child communication would be asked to report on perceptions of harm, and these reports could be compiled to determine averages and the consequent threshold of abuse. If such a study can be conducted in the U.S., it also can be conducted in other countries. Reliable baseline frequencies for samples of various cultural populations would provide a better overall picture of abuse worldwide. The culturally situated distinction between aggression and abuse present in the work of Vissing et al. is a crucial one that is missing for other terms. Their distinction, however, raises its own dilemma—a dilemma the authors do not sufficiently address.

It is quite sensible to allow cultural relativity to determine definitions of abuse, but scholars must also consider possible universals. In the final analysis, abuse must be defined in the midst of a balancing act between consideration of culturally normative frequencies of behavior and ethical judgments regarding individual levels of damage.

Failure to allow for a cultural perspective in defining child abuse and neglect promotes an ethnocentric position in which one's own set of cultural beliefs and practices are presumed to be preferable and superior to all others. On the other hand, a stance of extreme cultural relativism, in which all judgments of humane treatment of children are suspended in the name of cultural rights, may be used to justify a lesser standard of care for some children. (Korbin, 1991, p. 69)

Can scholars define an action as abusive on the merits of the damage it causes even when it is normative within a population? Does the answer to this question differ for physical acts and speech acts? For example, many have persuasively argued that clitoridectomy (or female genital mutilation) is inherently abusive (Dorkenoo, 1994). Can theorists make similar arguments regarding speech acts, or are the symbolic meaning and ethicality of interaction always determined by cultural context?

Given the current theoretical grounding of psychological aggression, this dilemma cannot be taken by the horns. The decision to label a particular level of psychological aggression, or any other concept, as abusive is a difficult one because it involves weighing consideration of cultural context against damage to individuals. In the case of psychological aggression, as with verbal aggression, a worthwhile direction for future research is to generate further explanation regarding the mechanism of damage. The mean number of attacks found by Vissing et al. (1991) was greater than 10 per year (12.6). Does this mean that a stronger case can be made for defining psychological abuse at 20 or 25 attacks per year? Or can the level of damage inflicted at a threshold of 10 per year be considered abusive nonetheless in some cases depending on which specific attacks are performed? Until theory is developed to help answer these questions, the lesson provided by Vissing et al. regarding the distinction between abuse and aggression must remain incomplete.

PSYCHOLOGICAL MALTREATMENT

Unlike the other two terms, psychological maltreatment[5] is not a concept that springs from a particular set of scholars—though it is most often used within the field of psychology. Psychological maltreatment is the term of choice for dozens of different conceptual definitions. Some are based in a larger theoretical framework explaining cause and effect, but most are not. Table 1 only hints at the amorphous quality of the psychological maltreatment literature. That said, the enormous amount of work in the area has done wonders for recognition of the problem. The basic idea of psychological maltreatment is far more accepted now than 20 years ago.

In the third section of this chapter, we discuss (a) the theoretical conceptualizations of psychological maltreatment, (b) some of the possible operational definitions, and (c) the current implications for intervention.

Conceptualization

Theoretical grounding of the concept of psychological maltreatment varies. There are a few theories indicating the mechanism of damage present in psychological maltreatment. These include interference with secure attachment (Crittenden & Ainsworth, 1989; Morton & Browne, 1998), delay or damage to psychological development (Thompson & Kaplan, 1996), denial or frustration of psychological needs (Hart, Germain, & Brassard, 1987), interference with physical growth (Green, Campbell, & David, 1984), alterations in cognitive processes (Sanders & Giolas, 1991; Terr, 1991), and lack of protective factors (Rosenberg, 1987). There is, however, no generally recognized theoretical explanation for why certain interactions may cause harm (Thompson & Kaplan, 1996).

None of these various theories has resulted in specific conceptual or operational definitions of psychological maltreatment. The majority of available definitions are generic, though practically useful. One commonly cited one is the following:

> Psychological maltreatment of children and youth consists of acts of omission and commission which are judged on the basis of a combination of community standards and professional expertise to be psychologically damaging. Such acts are committed by individuals, singly or collectively, who by their characteristics (e.g., age, status, knowledge, organizational form) are in a position of differential power that renders a child vulnerable. Such acts damage immediately or ultimately the behavioral, cognitive, affective, or physical functioning of the child. Examples of psychological maltreatment include acts of rejecting, terrorizing, isolating, exploiting, and missocializing. (Hart, Germain, & Brassard, 1983, p. 2)

There is no explanation of the connection between the various parts of this definition and psychological needs theory (e.g., Hart et al., 1987); rather this is a generic working definition produced by representatives of helping professions and child advocacy groups attending the 1983 International Conference on Psychological Abuse of Children and Youth.

Other definitions provide variations on this theme. For example, Garbarino, Guttman, and Seeley (1986) included intent in their definition. Repetition, or a pattern of parental behavior, is commonly highlighted (e.g., Garbarino et al., 1986; Iwaniec, 1997; O'Hagan, 1995). Child vulnerability, or the degree to which individual children are emotionally susceptible, has also been a factor (see Garbarino et al., 1986; McGee & Wolfe, 1991). In keeping with the 1983 generic working definition, many researchers focus on child outcomes (e.g., Iwaniec, 1997; Kavanagh, 1982; O'Hagan, 1995), and most include behavior in their definitions (e.g., American Professional Society on the Abuse of Children [APSAC], 1995; Barnett et al., 1997; Brassard & Hardy, 1997; Brassard, Hart, & Hardy, 1993; Garbarino et al., 1986; Hart, Brassard, & Karlson, 1996; NCCAN, 1988; O'Hagan, 1995).

Behaviors cited by researchers as examples of psychological maltreatment often are similar; they encompass both verbal and nonverbal interaction and acts of commission and omission. Examples include rejecting (verbal or symbolic acts that express feelings of rejection toward the child), degrading (actions that deprecate a child), terrorizing (actions or threats that may cause extreme fear or anxiety), isolating (preventing the child from engaging in normal social

TABLE 2
Psychological Maltreatment Versus Physical Abuse

Child outcome	Parent behaviors	
	Physical	*Nonphysical*
Physical	Physical abuse	Psychological maltreatment
Nonphysical	Psychological maltreatment	Psychological maltreatment

NOTE: From by McGee, R. A., & Wolfe, D. A. (1991). "Psychological maltreatment: Toward an operational definition." *Development and Psychopathology, 3*, 5. Copyright 1991 by Cambridge University Press. Adapted with permission.

activities), corrupting or exploiting (using a child for the needs, advantages, or profits of the caretaker), denying emotional responsiveness or ignoring (acts of omission whereby a caretaker does not provide necessary stimulation and responsiveness), and close confinement (restricting a child's movement by binding limbs; APSAC, 1995; Barnett et al., 1997; Brassard et al., 1993; Brassard & Hardy, 1997; Garbarino et al., 1986; Hart et al., 1996; NCCAN, 1988; O'Hagan, 1995). McGee and Wolfe (1991) have criticized some of these behaviors for their tautological qualities, arguing that the existence of a behavior must not be determined by its outcome. In response, the term *threatening* has been suggested instead of *terrorizing*, and long lists of specific example behaviors falling into each category have been developed (see Brassard & Hardy, 1997; Hart et al., 1996).

The suggested relationships between psychological and physical maltreatment also vary. As a way to summarize thought in the field, McGee and Wolfe (1991) suggested a 2 x 2 matrix of physical and nonphysical parent behaviors as well as physical and nonphysical child outcomes (see Table 2).

In this definition, physical abuse resides in the cell at the intersection of both physical parent behaviors and physical child outcome, such as when a child sustains a large bruise after being punched by a parent. Psychological maltreatment, on the other hand, resides in all three remaining cells. Thus, psychological maltreatment may be defined as (a) nonphysical child outcomes of physical parent behaviors, such as emotional distress over the relational meaning of a punch; (b) physical outcomes of nonphysical behaviors, such as failure to thrive witnessed in an environment of repetitive threatening; or (c) nonphysical outcomes of nonphysical behaviors, such as low self-esteem occurring as a consequence of frequent insults.

Psychological maltreatment is typically defined in keeping with this definition. Many scholars, howver, narrow McGee and Wolfe's (1991) conceptualization. Psychological maltreatment in some cases is defined in terms of only physical outcomes of nonphysical behaviors (e.g., Kavanagh, 1982), whereas in other cases it is conceived as only nonphysical outcomes of only nonphysical behaviors (e.g., Garbarino et al., 1986), as only nonphysical outcomes of either physical or nonphysical behaviors (e.g., O'Hagan, 1995), or as both physical and nonphysical outcomes of only nonphysical behaviors (e.g., Hart et al., 1996). Taking the opposite tack, Iwaniec (1997) broadened McGee and Wolfe's definition, defining psychological maltreatment as both physical and nonphysical outcomes of either physical or psychological behaviors.

In contrast to the verbal aggression literature in the field of communication, in which there is an absence of discussion regarding abusive levels of interaction, in the psychological maltreatment literature there is an absence of discussion regarding nonabusive levels of interaction. Implicit in the term psychological maltreatment is the assumption of abuse.even lthough many scholars refer to a pattern of behavior when describing psychological maltreatment, the frequency that determines a pattern has not yet been established. Most parents, especially in frustrating situations, occasionally threaten, ignore, or insult their children. Future discussion of when these occasional slips become abusive will need to take place if psychological maltreatment is to be distinguished from an unpleasant but less than abusive construct, as with psychological aggression. As discussed previously, such a discussion must be grounded in a theoretical explanation of the mechanism of damage.

Operationalization

Given the existing diversity of conceptual definitions, it should not be surprising that researchers operationalize psychological maltreatment in numerous ways. Measurement formats include self-report, interview, protective service records, and clinician diagnosis (Barnett et al., 1997; Brassard et al., 1993; Garbarino et al., 1986). Numerous instruments have been developed to measure psychological maltreatment,[6] such as: the Child Abuse and Trauma Scale (CATS; Sanders & Becker-Lausen, 1995), the Child Psychological Maltreatment scale (CPM; Khamis, 2000), the Childhood Trauma Interview (Fink, Bernstein, Handelsman, Foote, & Lovejoy, 1995), the Childhood Trauma Questionnaire (Bernstein et al., 1994), the Children's Perception of Parental Verbal Aggression (CPPVA; Solomon & Serres, 1999), the Comprehensive Childhood Maltreatment Inventory (CCMI; Riddle & Aponte, 1999), the Comprehensive Child Maltreatment Scale (CCMS; Higgins & McCabe, 2001), the Exposure to Abusive and Supportive Environments Parenting Inventory (EASE-PI; Nicholas & Bieber, 1996), the Family Experiences Questionnaire (Briere & Runtz, 1988), the Personal Experiences Survey (Harter, 2000), two different Psychological Maltreatment Inventories (PMI; Engels & Moisan, 1994; Kaisan & Painter, 1992), the Psychological Maltreatment Ratings Scales (PMRS; Brassard et al., 1993), the Psychological Maltreatment Scales (Varia & Abidin, 1999), the Psychological/Verbal Abuse Scale (Pitzner & Drummond, 1997), and the Trauma Symptom Checklist for Children (TSCC; Briere, 1996) and for Young Children (TSYC; Briere et al., 2001). (For review see Carlson, 1997 or Melchert, 1998). None are widely used. Currently, a standard or consensually accepted measurement instrument does not exist.

Most instruments are not grounded in any specific theory of the causes or outcomes of psychological maltreatment. Instead they assess various behaviors assumed to indicate psychological maltreatment. Some instruments are tied to a generic definition of psychological maltreatment whereas others stem from no particular definition at all. Finally, some instruments focus on psychological maltreatment exclusively; others measure psychological maltreatment along with several other types of abuse or neglect. To illustrate, we analyze two examples— Brassard et al.'s (1993) Psychological Maltreatment Ratings Scales (PMRS) and Bernstein et al.'s (1994) Childhood Trauma Questionnaire (CTQ).

The PMRS is a set of rating scales that tap behavioral categories mentioned frequently in prior definitions of psychological maltreatment such as the generic working definition discussed above (Hart et al., 1983; see also Garbarino et al, 1986; NCCAN, 1988). To develop the PMRS, Brassard et al. (1993) compared samples from two populations: abusive and nonabusive mothers. The maltreatment histories of 55 mother–child dyads already substantiated by Child Protective Services (CPS) for physical abuse or neglect were independently confirmed for psychological maltreatment using the criteria developed by NCCAN (1988) for emotional abuse and neglect. These dyads comprised half the participant sample. Fifty-five other mother–child dyads with no CPS-substantiated physical maltreatment history comprised the other half. The nonmaltreatment dyads were not independently confirmed for lack of psychological maltreatment using the NCCAN (1988) criteria.

All participants were visited in their homes and videotaped for 15 minutes as they engaged in an age-appropriate child teaching task. A scale consisting of five behaviors associated with psychological maltreatment (spurning, terrorizing, exploiting or corrupting, denying emotional responsiveness, and isolating) was used to rate the videotapes. In addition to this set of scales, nine other scale sets were administered to assess prosocial aspects of the mother-child relationship. All scales were factor analyzed, resulting in three factors: facilitation of social and cognitive development, psychological abuse, and quality of emotional support. The only factor predicting significant differences in maltreatment status was the psychological abuse factor, which included terrorizing, corrupting or exploiting, spurning, and hostile/controlling touch.

Brassard et al. (1993) did not drop any of the scales from the PMRS. The full measurement instrument correctly classified 82% of cases, with a sensitivity of .92 (proportion of those with maltreatment status correctly identified) and a specificity of .71 (proportion of those without maltreatment status correctly excluded).

To develop the Childhood Trauma Questionnaire (CTQ), Bernstein et al. (1994) conducted an extensive review of literature, after which they wrote 70 items reflecting multiple types of abuse and neglect, including physical, sexual, and emotional abuse, as well as physical and emotional neglect, and related family dysfunction. Examples of items written to tap emotional abuse include "Someone in my family yelled and screamed at me" and "People in my family said hurtful or insulting things to me." All items begin with the phrase "When I was growing up" and are rated on a 5-point Likert scale assessing the frequency of experiences.

To assess measurement reliability and validity, Bernstein et al. (1994) administered the CTQ to 286 patients undergoing treatment for drug addiction in their second or third week of treatment. Sixty-eight patients randomly selected from this group were also given the Childhood Trauma Interview (Fink et al., 1995). Administration and scoring of the Childhood Trauma Interview were carried out blind to the results of the CTQ. Four months later (on average), 40 patients were retested with the CTQ (Bernstein et al., 1994).

Principal components analysis of the CTQ yielded four factors (or subscales), each with its own score, which together accounted for 47.6% of the total variance among items: physical and emotional abuse, emotional neglect, sexual abuse, and physical neglect. After excluding 10 of the 70 items (1 was ambiguous, 3 were included as a validity scale, and 6 exhibited low multiple correlations with the other items in the scale), the four factors displayed high levels of internal consistency ($\alpha = 0.79 - 0.94$) and the entire scale had an alpha of 0.95. Test–retest reliability was also high for the individual factors (ICC = $0.80 - 0.83$) and the entire scale (ICC = 0.88). Partial correlations, controlling for the effects of total score, showed significant association between the physical and emotional abuse factor of the CTQ and the physical abuse factor of the Childhood Trauma Interview. All 70 items are being kept until further validation studies are conducted (Bernstein et al., 1994).

Even though the authors originally intended to assess emotional abuse (psychological maltreatment) as an independent type of abuse among the many types measured, physical and emotional abuse loaded together on the same factor. This result may not be terribly surprising given that physical abuse itself is psychologically and emotionally damaging (Hart et al., 2002). It does, however, raise questions about the meaning of the score for that factor. Does this factor tap the psychological meaning of both physical and nonphysical behavior? Does the physical and emotional abuse factor constitute a measure of psychological maltreatment? Or does this factor reflect two distinct but associated forms of abuse? In part because the CTQ does not reflect any particular definition of psychological maltreatment, and in part because the purpose of the measure is to screen for several types of abuse and neglect, the authors do not address these questions. Instead, they conclude that the CTQ is "an appropriate screening instrument for clinical or research purposes" (Bernstein et al., 1994, p. 1136).

The comparison and contrast between these two scales is typical of relationships between many scales measuring psychological maltreatment. Both instruments were designed to measure psychological maltreatment but started with different ideas of the meaning of that concept: The PMRS is based on a particular definition of psychological maltreatment (Hart et al., 1983; discussed above), whereas the CTQ items did not stem from any particular definition. The PMRS is used for observational coding of psychological maltreatment exclusively, whereas the CTQ is a survey used to screen for abuse and neglect in general. Neither instrument is widely used.

Implications for Intervention

The sheer number of instruments used to measure psychological maltreatment prevents the kind of consistency and opportunity for cross-comparison enjoyed by psychological aggression as measured by the CTS family of instruments. Researchers and clinicians tend to measure psychological maltreatment in different ways. Thus, findings are free to differ by definition and by instrument.

This variation makes comparison across studies difficult: Whereas similarities and differences in findings among studies measuring psychological aggression are sure to reflect differences in behavior in the population sampled (because the measurement instrument is held constant), similarities and differences in findings among studies measuring psychological maltreatment may reflect either differences in conceptualization or differences in population behavior. The measurement instrument varies as much as the population sample from study to study. Even meta-analysis cannot help alleviate this problem until many studies using the same measure can be identified.

The same patterns that allow for that pitfall, however, also allow the greatest benefit of the psychological maltreatment literature: enormous recognition of the problem. Even though different scholars approach the problem in different ways, there is an overwhelming consensus that interaction that is not physical in nature can be immensely damaging. Such attention has helped create similar agreement in society at large. The great number of measurement instruments allows any therapist the opportunity for screening. Theoretically based or not, the majority of measures do identify behavioral patterns that are more likely to occur in troubled families than healthy ones. As a result, psychological maltreatment is much more likely to be diagnosed now than in times past, and it is much more likely to be treated.

Just how practitioners will treat the problem is another issue. In many cases, almost any treatment may be better than no treatment at all. Nonetheless, theoretical explanation for the mechanisms of both cause and damage (why do parents abuse, and how exactly does talk translate to harm) is the best way to direct intervention. This is discussed in more detail below. In the final analysis of these three terms, a common issue is the need for elaborated theories of process in the future, not only in terms of message production on the part of the parent but also in terms of parent–child interaction leading to damage of the child. Below, we argue that this challenge falls squarely on the shoulders of communication researchers.

CHALLENGES AND DIRECTIONS FOR FUTURE RESEARCH

The traditions reviewed form a crucial foundation for the growth of future research in this area. Just as the answer to one question brings on more questions, however, the ground already covered serves to show us where we have yet to go. It is clear after review of these three concepts that any attempt at defining nonphysical child abuse faces similar challenges of conceptualization and operationalization. By reviewing these challenges, we try to highlight lessons learned, for they provide ways of avoiding obstacles on the journey ahead.

In the fourth and final section of this chapter, we discuss lessons drawn from the previous three sections. Specifically, we discuss (a) the importance of thorough conceptualization and the future role that may be played by communication scholars, (b) the importance of theoretically grounded operationalization, and (c) the benefits of a future connection between abuse scholarship and communication scholarship.

Conceptualization

The theoretical underpinning—the conceptualization of abusive interaction—forms the basis for the reasoning behind the operationalization. A clear conceptualization provides a meaningful perspective from which to approach a phenomenon and allows an equally meaningful way to interpret the resulting work. Without a clear conceptualization, the explanatory power of any empirical result is limited. Currently, there is need for elaborated theories to explain the production of abusive messages as well as the processes that link interaction to damage. These issues are at the heart of communication scholarship.

The most basic intervention, healing the child, requires knowledge of at least the nature of the damage sustained by the child. In other words, the "what" question is the barest essential: What happened? Simple awareness of physical injury or verbal behavior is not enough. The most painful wounds of abused children last long after their injuries have healed or the insults have stopped (Brassard & Hardy, 1997). Effective intervention requires comprehension of the symbolic meaning conveyed through parental behaviors, comprehension of the messages children hear. It is this symbolic meaning that affects a child's sense of self and impacts the child's future.

The what question ("what happened?"), which taps the symbolic meaning of nonphysical child abuse, turns out to be a fairly complicated question upon review of verbal aggression, psychological aggression, and psychological maltreatment. In fact, to get at the symbolic meaning of nonphysical child abuse, the umbrella what question must follow from three others: What level of behavior is abusive? How can abuse be defined within the cultural context? How does nonphysical child abuse differ from physical abuse?

These questions are themselves related to the "why" and "how" questions: Why do parents abuse, and through what processes do parental behaviors result in damage to the child? If one of the goals of intervention is to repair and sustain the parent–child relationship when possible, the why and how questions need to be answered. In this case, intervention requires knowledge of the perceptions held by both parent and child regarding themselves and their relationship, as well as an understanding of the kind of physical and verbal behavior patterns that result in and arise from those perceptions. In order to direct intervention efforts adequately,

TABLE 3
Detailed Breakdown Of Conceptual Issues Across Terms

| | Term reviewed | | |
Conceptual issue	*Verbal aggression*	*Psychological aggression*	*Psychological maltreatment*
Level of concept considered abusive— level of damage to child	Abusive levels not discussed	Not explored	Nonabusive levels not discussed
Level of concept considered abusive— cultural context	Not explored	Thresholds of 10, 20, or 25 attacks per year	Not explored
Conceptual location versus physical abuse	Precedes physical assault	Less damaging than physical abuse*	Usually anything other than physical outcome of physical attack
Mechanism of damage	Vague: implied damage to self-concept	Not explored	Various
Causal mechanism	Personality, possibly genetic neurobiology	Not explored	Little discussion

NOTE: * As follows from conflict theory.

abuse research requires sophisticated theory and conceptualization that describe the overall relationship between parent and child (Glaser, 2002).

The future goal of abuse research must be the answer to these questions. A thorough conceptualization is one that not only wrestles with the dilemma of distinguishing an abusive level of behavior situated within cultural context, but also explains the conceptual location of nonphysical child abuse in relation to physical abuse, the mechanism of damage, and the causal mechanism. The analysis of these issues within the conceptualizations of verbal aggression, psychological aggression, and psychological maltreatment is provided in Table 3. (Thorough explanation may be found above in the sections of this paper specific to each term.)

So far, no theory producing a conceptualization of nonphysical child abuse has answered all five questions outlined in Table 3. Current interventions, however, are based on implicit answers to all five questions; hence, the future work of researchers is to wrestle with explicit answers to these questions to better inform intervention. For example, the decision to intervene at all rests on dual considerations of whether parenting behaviors are seriously harmful to children and whether they are considered normative within a cultural context. As a result, if nonphysical child abuse is a phenomenon that differs from physical abuse, the means of intervention may need to be different. Finally, intervention must move toward healing the parent as well as the child if abuse is to stop.

Even though distinction of these issues may be helpful, it must be understood that in practice, they are not discretely separate. For instance, to decide on a definition of abuse, scholars must consider both normative societal activity (cultural context) and individual-level damage caused by that activity (level of damage). Such consideration can take place only within a discussion of the role played by parental behavior in the distinction between psychologically healthy children and children in need of help (mechanism of damage). Of course, the damage caused by any type of behavior (mechanism of damage) will differ according to its prevalence in society (cultural context) because its socially constructed meaning will differ along with its frequency. Thorough and thoughtful conceptualization therefore requires a sophisticated consideration of many individual, family, and societal issues. Scholars will need to address these issues if their future efforts are to aid intervention as much as possible.

In our view, communication scholars are well situated to undertake this challenge. Nonphysical child abuse is a communication issue. Symbolic meaning, message production, and the interplay of interaction and perception fall squarely within the ken of those working within our own field. We can contribute to interdisciplinary work that helps unlock the puzzles and problems that currently exist. Communication scholarship—communication theory—is exactly what is needed in order to move nonphysical child abuse research forward.

Operationalization

Well-formed communication theory would not only help cover intellectual terrain; it would also allow the most productive measurement. Atheoretical instruments have the capacity to measure a broad range of abuse indicators and may assist efforts to screen for abuse; however, they do not suggest a method of intervention. Instruments based in theory are more narrowly focused, and they imply the type of intervention that alleviates the aspect of abuse most crucial to the original theory. For example, the PMRS or CTQ measures many behavioral indicators of abuse, but they are not tied to a theory that points toward a specific solution. On the other hand, the Verbal Aggressiveness Scale (Infante & Wigley, 1986) measures a more narrow range of behavior patterns (those more closely related to the predisposition toward aggression) and carries with it the theoretical position that if there is a solution to be had, it is a particular type of skills training. The usefulness of a theoretically grounded instrument does not stop at the score it produces.

Abuse is not a monolithic phenomenon; it has many dimensions. Any method of intervention is likely to address one dimension of abuse more successfully than another. For instance, both denying emotional responsiveness and aggression are aspects of abusive interaction, but they may be products of different mechanisms requiring different solutions. A broad and generic measure is not able to assess these various co-occurring processes and, as a result, is not able to allow a nuanced approach to intervention. A combination of several theory-based instruments would be far more useful when designing a program of intervention.

A theoretically grounded measure is specific; a clear theoretical conceptualization provides an equally clear placement of measurement locus. Depending on the underlying theory, any number of definitional loci may be relevant. After discussion of verbal aggression, psychological aggression and psychological maltreatment, (at least) three definitional loci deserve closer inspection: outcome, behavior, and perception.

Outcome. If interaction is not causing harm, studies may result in statistical but not practical significance. Implicit in the word abuse is the assumption of harm. Any discussion of abuse therefore must also be a discussion of harmful effects. Examination of behaviors as insulting or threatening must be rooted in a discussion of effects, such as attachment problems or low self-esteem.

Pragmatically speaking, perceptions or behaviors cannot be measured at the same time that outcomes are measured. Outcomes of abuse are often only long term, and the goal is to avoid them by catching the problem early. So any cross-sectional measurement locus such as intent, perception, or behavior is more immediately useful than a definition based on outcome. Such measures can also be used to directly test potential sources of eventual harm. Researchers may have to rely on correlations (e.g., Vissing et al., 1991), longitudinal studies, and memory-based self-reports (e.g. Infante, 1989) to tap the issue of outcome.

Behavior. Regardless of whatever definitional locus may be primary, it is clear that behavior is usually either explicitly or implicitly measured. Traits are implied by behavior patterns, and behaviors denote the presence of abuse. To measure a meaningful concept, every behavior measured must tie directly to a theoretical conceptualization. Without such a tie, the reasoning behind the choice of items measured is unclear.

The issue of conceptual grounding applies to the overall variety of behaviors measured as well. For instance, Infante and colleagues measured only commissive behaviors, Vissing et al. (1991) measured both commissive and omissive behaviors, and Brassard et al. (1993) set out to measure both types when developing the PMRS, although only commissive behaviors performed well. The reasoning behind these choices is not explicitly discussed. Verbal aggressives may theoretically exhibit both types of behaviors, yet only commission is measured. The term psychological aggression also implies inclusion of both commission and omission, but the reasoning behind this choice seems to lie in the fact that they are measured by CTS1 rather than in theory. Researchers must decide what behaviors may be most harmful within the context of a theory that describes the mechanism of harm. Only then will operationalization and measurement of speech acts begin to reveal meaningful results.

Perception. The measurement locus of perception is largely missing from this review of terms. Despite that fact, it deserves consideration. Theories like symbolic interactionism (Blumer, 1969; Mead, 1927/1934, 1927/1982) hold that target perception determines what is seen as reality. The meaning of any behavior is flexible and depends on the existing relational culture, making perception possibly a better indicator of the harmfulness of a situation than concrete behaviors. As a result, perception (e.g., more than intent) may ultimately define whether a behavior causes pain and damage. Perception differs from individual to individual; a focus on target perception therefore may also allow researchers to access differences in experience due to varying developmental stages and levels of child resiliency (see McGee & Wolfe, 1991; Rutter, 1985; Werner & Smith, 1982; Wyman et al., 1992).

Issues such as lack of conscious awareness or refusal to admit actual perceptions may, however, limit the use of perception as a definitional locus. Targets, especially children, may not be consciously aware of any personal damage, or may have reasons to underestimate harm caused; as a result, direct access to target perceptions may in some cases be limited to adolescents, who may be able to self-report current or retrospective accounts, and adults, who may be able to self-report retrospective accounts (e.g., Bernstein et al., 1994).

Despite the tantalizing appeal of accessing the interpretations of the conscious human actors who make up our pools of participants, use of target perception is rare and discussion of its use is rarer still. Researchers may wish to examine use of target perception more closely.

Conclusion

Explication of the terms verbal aggression, psychological aggression, and psychological maltreatment has allowed a larger discussion of the goals of abuse research and of the particular need for communication theory in the future. Child abuse is a new area for communication researchers, but it is a relevant and rich area in which we can and should work (Wilson, 1999). By doing so, we can help make the future brighter for researchers, practitioners, and families alike. Our scholarship can complement abuse literature by helping to ask and answer key questions. Our research findings can eventually make a difference to families through intervention informed by our work. We may even make a difference to the communication field itself by increasing public awareness through the practical application of our research.

All of these visions of the future are related to the answer to one very important question: How can we provide parents, children, and communities with the tools necessary to stop the cycle of abuse? Communication scholars are needed to help find the answer. To do so, our research must begin with strong and comprehensive theories that explain the what, why, and how questions of abuse and employ operational definitions that reflect those theories. Ideally, the construct of nonphysical child abuse will come to practitioners with instruments that both measure the particular theoretical loci of concern and also suggest theoretically relevant courses of intervention. If we undertake the challenge to rigorously engage in both thoughtful conceptualization and conceptually consistent operationalization of nonphysical abuse, our work will matter to scholars and professionals working with families and communities.

NOTES

1. In the absence of an appropriately generic term to use, we have opted for the usage of "nonphysical child abuse." Thus, the term nonphysical child abuse here is meant as an umbrella term, one that refers to any one of the terms (verbal aggression, psychological aggression, and psychological maltreatment) discussed here as well as any other relevant concept not specifically explored here.

2. If the underlying cause of verbally aggressive behavior is genetic, as communibiologists claim, then scholars of communibiology must design an appropriate instrument to measure verbal aggression if they are to facilitate further study of the genetic influences on the neurobiological foundations of personality. Communibiology introduces a physical definition of verbal aggression, but Valencic et al. (1998) measure behavioral rather than biological markers. Specifically, they measure verbal aggression with the Verbal Aggressiveness Scale (Infante & Wigley, 1986) and explore its association to behavioral measures that load on three factors interpreted as the temperament dimensions of extraversion (E), neuroticism (N), and psychoticism (P; Eysenck & Eysenck, 1985). Valencic et al. assumed these dimensions to represent Gray's (1991) neurobiological systems.

Gray himself asserted that the temperamental dimensions of P, E, and N are rooted in the BIS, BAS, and FFS systems, but issued a firm caveat regarding the substitution of behavioral for physical measures:

> It cannot be assumed that a particular dimensional description of personality — e.g., introversion-extraversion (E), neuroticism (N) and psychoticism (P) in the Eysenckian system — embodies a one-to-one correspondence between the dimensions employed and the fundamental emotion systems whose variation between individuals gives rise, ex hypothesis, to personality . . . Analyses of personality such as those offered by Eysenck & Eysenck (1985) or Zuckerman et al. (1988) start from human individual differences measured directly, but in tests whose relation to the postulated underlying emotion systems is unknown. (Gray, 1991, p. 123)

Valencic et al. (1998) did not heed this warning. As a result, they were not able to link behavior to biology in a test of Beatty and McCroskey's (1997) hypotheses regarding the neurobiological roots of verbal aggression.

3. The CTSPC is the third revision of the Conflict Tactics Scales. The second was the CTS2 (Straus et al., 1996). Though the CTS2 is based on the CTS1, the CTS2 was designed specifically to measure partner violence and is not reviewed here.

4. Even the standard of 25 attacks per year yielded in an estimated rate of 113 attacks for every 1,000 children, a rate 38 times greater than the rate of 3.0 per 1000 children estimated from the 1993 National Incidence Study by the National Center on Child Abuse and Neglect (Sedlak & Broadhurst, 1996; Vissing et al., 1991).

5. There is debate surrounding the meaning of the terms *maltreatment* and *psychological*. The National Center on Child Abuse and Neglect (1988) defines abuse as commission (what parents actively do) and neglect as omission (what parents fail to do). Many authors have argued that the term maltreatment subsumes both abuse and neglect (Brassard & Hardy, 1997; Brassard et al., 1993; Garbarino et al., 1986; Hart et al., 1996; McGee & Wolfe, 1991). However, some authors use the terms maltreatment and abuse interchangeably (e.g., Fortin & Chamberland, 1995; Iwaniec, 1997), whereas others seem to arbitrarily pick one or the other with no explanation for their choice of wording (e.g., O'Hagan, 1995; Thompson & Kaplan, 1996).

The terms emotional and psychological have similar definitional misunderstandings. O'Hagan (1995) has attempted to carve out a distinction between the larger terms *emotional abuse* and *psychological abuse*, indicating differences in outcome. He defines emotional abuse as behavior that impairs emotional development, and psychological abuse as "behavior which damages or substantially reduces the creative and developmental potential of crucially important mental faculties and mental processes of a child." (p. 458). Others have contended that psychological maltreatment is a broad category that subsumes emotional maltreatment (APSAC, 1995; Brassard & Hardy, 1997; Hart et al., 1996). Again, some authors treat the terms as synonyms (e.g., Brassard et al., 1993; Iwaniec, 1997; McGee & Wolfe, 1991; Thompson & Kaplan, 1996), while others seem to arbitrarily choose one term or the other (e.g., Fortin & Chamberland, 1995; Mattaini, McGowan, & Williams, 1996).

It is possible that the above arguments for the breadth of both the terms maltreatment and psychological are the reason the combined term psychological maltreatment is popular. They form the basis for our choice of the terminology here.

6. Carlson (1997) estimated the number of instruments to be in the hundreds.

REFERENCES

Adams, B. N. (1965). Coercion and consensus theories: Some unresolved issues. *American Journal of Sociology, 71*, 714–717.
American Professional Society on the Abuse of Children (APSAC). (1995). *Practice guidelines: Psychosocial evaluation of suspected psychological maltreatment in children and adolescents*. Chicago: APSAC.
Barnett, O. W., Miller-Perrin, C. L., & Perrin, R. D. (1997). *Family violence across the lifespan: An introduction*. Thousand Oaks, CA: Sage.
Baxter, L. A., & Mongtomery, B. M. (1996). *Relating: Dialogues and dialectics*. New York: Guilford.
Bayer, C., & Cegala, D. (1992). Trait verbal aggressiveness and argumentativeness: Relations with parenting style. *Western Journal of Communication, 56*, 301–310.
Beatty, M. J., & McCroskey, J. C. (1997). It's in our nature: Verbal aggressiveness as temperamental expression. *Communication Quarterly, 45*, 446–460.
Beatty, M. J., & McCroskey, J. C. (1998). Interpersonal communication as temperamental expression: A communibiological paradigm. In J. C. McCroskey, J. A. Daly, M. M. Martin, & M. J. Beatty, (Eds.), *Communication and personality trait perspectives* (pp. 41–68). Cresskill, NJ: Hampton Press.
Berkowitz, L. (1993). *Aggression: Its causes, consequences, and control*. New York: McGraw-Hill.
Bernstein, D. P., Fink, L., Handelsman, L., Foote, J., Lovejoy, M., Wenzel, K., et al. (1994). Initial reliability and validity of a new retrospective measure of child abuse and neglect. *American Journal of Psychiatry, 151*, 1132–1136.
Blumer, H. (1969). *Symbolic interactionism: Perspective and method*. Englewood Cliffs, NJ: Prentice Hall.
Brassard, M. R., & Hardy, D. B. (1997). Psychological maltreatment. In M. E. Helfer, R. S. Kempe & R. D. Krugman (Eds.), *The battered child* (5th ed.; pp. 392–412). Chicago: University of Chicago Press.
Brassard, M. R., Hart, S. F., & Hardy, D. B. (1993). The psychological maltreatment rating scales. *Child Abuse & Neglect, 17*, 715–729.
Briere, J. (1996). *Trauma symptom checklist for children (TSCC) professional manual*. Odessa, FL: Psychological Assessment Resources.
Briere, J., Johnson, K., Bissada, A., Damon, L., Crouch, J., Gil, E., et al. (2001). The trauma symptom checklist for young children (TSCYC): Reliability and association with abuse exposure in a multisite study. *Child Abuse & Neglect, 25*, 1001–1014.

Briere, J., & Runtz, M. (1988). Multivariate correlates of childhood psychological and physical maltreatment among university women. *Child Abuse & Neglect*, 12, 331–341.

Bronfenbrenner, U., & Ceci, S. J. (1994). Nature-nurture reconceptualized in developmental perspective: A bioecological model. *Psychological Review, 101*, 568–586.

Bugental, D. B. & Goodnow, J. J. (1998). Socialization processes. In W. Damon & N. Eisenberg (Eds.), *Handbook of child psychology, 5ᵗʰ ed., Vol. 3* (pp. 389–462). New York: Wiley.

Burleson, B. R., Delia, J. G., & Applegate, J. L. (1995). The socialization of person-centered communication: Parental contributions to the social-cognitive and communication skills of their children. In M. A. Fitzpatrick & A. L. Vangelisti (Eds.), *Explaining family interactions* (pp. 34–76). Thousand Oaks, CA: Sage.

Caliso, J. A., & Milner, J. S. (1992). Childhood history of abuse and child abuse screening. *Child Abuse & Neglect*, 16, 647–659.

Carlson, E. B. (1997). *Trauma assessments: A clinician's guide*. New York: Guilford Press.

Coie, J. D., & Dodge, K. A. (1998). Aggression and antisocial behavior. In W. Damon & N. Eisenberg (Eds.), *Handbook of child psychology*, Vol. 3 (5th ed., pp. 779–862). New York: Wiley.

Collins, W. A., Maccoby, E. E., Steinberg, L., Hetherington, E. M., & Bornstein, M. H. (2000). The case for nature and nurture. *American Psychologist*, 55, 218–232.

Coser, L. A. (1956). *The functions of social conflict*. Glencoe, IL: Free Press.

Costa, D. T., & McCrae, R. R. (1980). Still stable after all these years: Personality as a key to some issues in adulthood and old age. In P. B. Baltes & O. G. Brim (Eds.), *Life-span development and behavior, Vol. 3* (pp. 63–102). New York: Academic Press.

Crittenden, P. M., & Ainsworth, M. D. S. (1989). Child maltreatment and attachment theory. In D. Cicchetti & V. Carlson (Eds.), *Child maltreatment: Theory and research on the causes and consequences of child abuse and neglect* (pp. 432–463). New York: Cambridge University Press.

Dahrendorf, R. (1959). *Class and class conflict in industrial society*. London: Routledge & Kegan Paul.

Depue, R. A., Collins, P. F., & Luciana, M. (1996). A model of neurobiology-environment interaction in developmental psychopathology. In M. F. Lenzenweger & J. J. Haugaard (Eds.), *Frontiers of developmental psychopathology* (pp. 44–80). New York: Oxford University Press.

Dorkenoo, E. (1994). *Cutting the rose: Female genital mutilation: The practice and its prevention*. London: Minority Rights Group.

Eisenberg, N. (1998). Introduction. In W. Damon & N. Eisenberg (Eds.), *Handbook of child psychology, Vol. 3* (5th ed., pp. 1–24). New York: Wiley.

Engels, M., & Moisan, D. (1994). The psychological maltreatment inventory: Development of a measure of psychological maltreatment in childhood for use in adult clinical settings. *Psychological Reports, 74*, 595–604.

Eysenck, H. J. & Eysenck, M. W. (1985). *Personality and individual differences: A natural science approach*. New York: Plenum Press.

Fink, L. A., Bernstein, D., Handelsman, L., Foote, J., & Lovejoy, M. (1995). Initial reliability and validity of the childhood trauma interview: A new multidimensional measure of childhood interpersonal trauma. *American Journal of Psychiatry, 152*, 1329–1335.

Fortin, A., & Chamberland, C. (1995). Preventing the psychological maltreatment of children. *Journal of Interpersonal Violence, 10*, 275–295.

Garbarino, J., Guttmann, E., & Seeley, J. W. (1986). *The psychologically battered child: Strategies for identification, assessment, and intervention*. San Francisco: Jossey-Bass.

Glaser, D. (2002). Emotional abuse and neglect (psychological maltreatment): A conceptual framework. *Child Abuse & Neglect, 26*, 697–714.

Gray, J. A. (1991). The neuropsychology of temperament. In J. Strelau & A. Angleitner (Eds.), *Explorations in temperament: International perspectives on theory and measurement* (pp. 105–128). New York: Plenum Press.

Green, W. H., Campbell, M., & David, R. (1984). Psychosocial dwarfism: A critical review of the evidence. *Journal of the American Academy of Child Psychiatry, 23*, 39–48.

Hart, S.N., Brassard, M. R., Binggeli, N. J., & Davidson, H. A. (2002). Psychological maltreatment. In J. E. B. Myers, L. Berliner, J. Briere, C. T. Hendrix, C. Jenny, & T. A. Reid (Eds.), *The APSAC handbook on child maltreatment* (2nd ed., pp. 79–104). Thousand Oaks, CA: Sage.

Hart, S. N., Brassard, M. R., & Karlson, H. C. (1996). Psychological maltreatment. In J. Brier, L. Berliner, J. A. Bulkley, C. Jenny, & T. Reid (Eds.), *The APSAC handbook on child maltreatment* (pp.72–89). Thousand Oaks, CA: Sage.

Hart, S. N., Germain, R. B., & Brassard, M. R. (1983). *Proceedings summary of the international conference on psychological abuse of children and youth.* Indiana University, Office for the Study of the Psychological Rights of the Child.

Hart, S. N., Germain, R. B., & Brassard, M. R. (1987). The challenge: to better understand and combat psychological maltreatment of children and youth. In M. R. Brassard, R. B. Germain, & S. N. Hart (Eds.), *Psychological maltreatment of children and youth* (pp. 3–24). New York: Pergamon Press.

Harter, S. L. (2000). Quantitative measures of construing in child abuse survivors. *Journal of Constructivist Psychology,* 13, 103–116.

Higgins, D. J., & McCabe, M. P. (2001). The development of the comprehensive child maltreatment scale. *Journal of Family Studies,* 7, 7–28.

Infante, D. A. (1989). Response to high argumentatives: Message and sex differences. *Southern Communication Journal,* 54, 159–170.

Infante, D. A. (1995). Teaching students to understand and control verbal aggression. *Communication Education,* 44, 51–63.

Infante, D. A., & Rancer, A. S. (1996). Argumentativeness and verbal aggressiveness. In Burelson, B. R. (Ed.), *Communication yearbook, 19* (pp. 319–352).

Infante, D. A., Riddle, B. L., Horvath, C. L., and Tumlin, S. A. (1992). Verbal aggressiveness: Messages and reasons. *Communication Quarterly,* 40, 116–126.

Infante, D. A., & Wigley, C. J. (1986). Verbal aggression: an interpersonal model and measure. *Communication Monographs, 53,* 61–69.

Iwaniec, D. (1997). An overview of emotional maltreatment and failure-to-thrive. *Child Abuse Review, 6,* 370–388.

Kagan, J. (1998). Biology and the child. In W. Damon & N. Eisenberg (Eds.), *Handbook of child psychology, Vol. 3* (5th ed., pp. 177–236). New York: Wiley.

Kaisan, M., & Painter, S. L. (1992). Frequency and severity of psychological abuse in a dating population. *Journal of interpersonal violence, 7,* 350–364.

Kaufman, J., & Charney, D. (2001). Effects of early stress on brain structure and function: Implications for understanding the relationship between child maltreatment and depression. *Development and Psychopathology, 13,* 451–471.

Kavanagh, C. (1982). Emotional abuse and mental injury: a critique of the concepts and a recommendation for practice. *Journal of the American Academy of Child Psychiatry,* 21, 171–177.

Khamis, V. (2000). Child psychological maltreatment in Palestinian families. *Child Abuse & Neglect,* 24, 1047–1059.

Kinney, T. A. (1994). An inductively derived typology of verbal aggression and its relation to distress. *Human Communication Research, 21,* 183–222.

Korbin, J. (1991). Cross-cultural perspectives and research directions for the 21st century. *Child Abuse & Neglect, 15 (Supp. 1),* 67–78.

Mattaini, M. A., McGowan, B. G., & Williams, G. (1996). Child maltreatment. In M. A. Mattaini, & B. A. Thyer (Eds.), *Finding solutions to social problems: Behavioral strategies for change* (pp. 223–266). Washington, DC: American Psychological Association.

McCroskey, J. C., & Beatty, M. J. (2000). The communibiological perspective: Implications for communication in instruction. *Communication Education,* 49, 1–6.

McGee, R. A., & Wolfe, D. A. (1991) Psychological maltreatment. *Development and Psychopathology, 3,* 3–18.

Mead, G. H. (1934). The self and the organism. In C. W. Morris (Ed.), *Mind, self & society: From the standpoint of a social behaviorist* (pp. 135–143). Chicago: University of Chicago Press. (Original lecture 1927).

Mead, G. H. (1982). 1927 Class lectures in social psychology. In D. L. Miller (Ed.), *The individual and the social self: Unpublished work of George Herbert Mead* (pp. 106–175). Chicago: University of Chicago Press. (Original lecture 1927).

Melchert, T. P. (1998). A review of instruments for assessing family history. *Clinical Psychology Review, 18*, 163–187.

Millar, F. E., & Rogers, L. E. (1987). Relational dimensions of interpersonal dynamics. In M. E. Roloff & G. R. Miller (Eds.), *Interpersonal processes: New directions in communication research* (pp. 117–138). Newbury Park, CA: Sage.

Morton, N., & Browne, K. D. (1998). Theory and observation of attachment and its relation to child maltreatment: A review. *Child Abuse & Neglect, 22*, 1093–1104.

National Center on Child Abuse and Neglect. (1988). *Study findings: Study of national incidence and prevalence of child abuse and neglect: 1988*. Washington, DC: NCCAN.

National Clearinghouse on Child Abuse and Neglect Information (2002). *Child abuse and neglect state states series: Issue paper: Current trends in child maltreatment reporting laws*. Washington, DC: U.S. Department of Health and Human Services, National Center on Child Abuse and Neglect.

Nicholas, K. B., & Bieber, S. L. (1996). Parental abusive versus supportive behaviors and their relation to hostility and aggression in young adults. *Child Abuse & Neglect, 20*, 1195–1211.

O'Hagan, K. P. (1995). Emotional and psychological abuse: Problems of definition. *Child Abuse & Neglect, 19*, 449–461.

Pitzner, J. K., & Drummond, P. D. (1997). The reliability and validity of empirically scaled measures of psychological–verbal control and physical–sexual abuse: Relationship between current negative mood and a history of abuse independent of other negative life events. *Journal of Psychosomatic Research, 43*, 125–142.

Riddle, K. P., & Aponte, J. F. (1999). The comprehensive childhood maltreatment inventory: Early development and reliability analyses. *Child Abuse & Neglect, 23*, 1103–1115.

Roloff, M. E. (1996). The catalyst hypothesis: Conditions under which coercive communication leads to physical aggression. In D. D. Cahn & S. A. Lloyd (Eds.), *Family violence from a communication perspective* (pp. 20–36). Thousand Oaks, CA: Sage.

Rosenberg, M. S. (1987). New directions for research on the psychological maltreatment of children. *American Psychologist, 42*, 166–171.

Rothbart, M. K. & Bates, J. E. (1998). Temperament. In W. Damon & N. Eisenberg (Eds.), *Handbook of child psychology, Vol. 3* (5th ed., pp. 105–176). New York: Wiley.

Rubin, R. B., Palmgreen, P. & Sypher, H. E. (1994) *Communication research measures: A sourcebook.* New York: Guilford Press.

Rudd, J. E., Vogl-Bauer, S., Dobos, J. A., Beatty, M. J., & Valencic, K. M. (1998). Interactive effects of parents' trait verbal aggressiveness and situational frustration on parents' self-reported anger. *Communication Quarterly, 46*, 1–11.

Rutter, M. (1985). Resilience in the face of adversity: Protective factors and resistance to psychiatric disorder. *British Journal of Psychiatry, 147*, 598–611.

Sanders, B., & Giolas, M. H. (1991). Dissociation and childhood trauma in psychologically disturbed adolescents. *American Journal of Psychiatry, 148*, 50–54.

Sanders, B., & Becker-Lausen, E. (1995). The measurement of psychological maltreatment: Early data on the child abuse and trauma scale. *Child Abuse & Neglect, 19*, 315–323.

Sanders, R. E., & Fitch, K. L. (2001). The actual practice of compliance seeking. *Communication Theory, 11*, 263–289.

Sánchez, M. M., Ladd, C. O., & Plotsky, P. M. (2001). Early adverse experience as a developmental risk factor for later psychopathology: Evidence from rodent and primate models. *Development and Psychopathology, 13*, 419–449.

Scanzoni, J. (1972). Marital conflict as a positive force. In J. Scanzoni (Ed.), *Sexual bargaining* (pp. 61–102). Englewood Cliffs, NJ: Prentice Hall.

Sedlak, A. J., & Broadhurst, D. D. (1996). *Third national incidence study of child abuse and neglect.* Washington, DC: U.S. Department of Health and Human Services, National Center on Child Abuse and Neglect.

Solomon, C. R., & Serres, F. (1999). Effects of parental verbal aggression on children's self-esteem and school marks. *Child Abuse & Neglect*, 23, 339–351.

Straus, M. A. (1974). Leveling, civility, and violence in the family. *Journal of Marriage and the Family*, 36, 13–29 (plus addendum 442–445).

Straus, M. A. (1979). Measuring intrafamily conflict and violence: The conflict tactics (CT) scales. *Journal of Marriage and the Family, 21*, 75–88.

Straus, M. A., & Gelles, R. J. (1990). *Physical violence in American families: Risk factors and adaptations to violence in 8,145 families*. New Brunswick, NJ: Transaction.

Straus, M. A., & Hamby, S. L. (1997). Measuring physical and psychological maltreatment of children with the Conflict Tactics Scales. In G. Kaufman Kantor & J. L. Jasinski (Eds.), *Out of the darkness: Contemporary research perspectives on family violence* (pp. 119–135). Thousand Oaks, CA: Sage.

Straus, M. A., Hamby, S. L., Boney-McCoy, S., & Sugarman, D. B. (1996). *The revised Conflict Tactics Scales (CTS2): Development and preliminary psychometric data*. Durham, NH: Family Violence Research Laboratory.

Straus, M. A., Hamby, S. L., Finkelhor, D., Moore, D. W., & Runyan, D. (1998). Identification of child maltreatment with the Parent-Child Conflict Tactics Scales: Development and psychometric data for a national sample of American parents. *Child Abuse & Neglect, 22*, 249–270.

Terr, L. C. (1991). Childhood traumas: An outline and review. *American Journal of Psychiatry, 148*, 10–20.

Thompson, A. E., & Kaplan, C. A. (1996). Childhood emotional abuse. *British Journal of Psychiatry, 168*, 143–148.

Tracy, K. (Ed.). (1991). *Understanding face-to-face interaction: Issues in linking goals and discourse*. Hillsdale, NJ: Erlbaum.

Valencic, K. M., Beatty, M. J., Rudd, J. E., Dobos, J. A., & Heisel, A. D. (1998). An empirical test of a communibiological model of trait verbal aggressiveness. *Communication Quarterly, 46*, 327–341.

Varia, R., & Abidin, R. R. (1999). The minimizing style: Perceptions of psychological abuse and quality of past and current relationships. *Child Abuse & Neglect, 23*, 1041–1055.

Vissing, Y., & Baily, W. (1996). Parent-to-child verbal aggression. In D. D. Cahn and S. A. Lloyd (Eds.), *Family violence from a communication perspective* (pp. 85–107) Thousand Oaks, CA: Sage.

Vissing, Y. M., Straus, M. A., Gelles, R. J., & Harrop, J. W. (1991). Verbal aggression by parents and psychosocial problems of children. *Child Abuse & Neglect, 15*, 223–238.

Werner, E. E., & Smith, R. S. (1982). *Vulnerable but invincible: A longitudinal study of resilient children and youth*. New York: McGraw-Hill.

Wilson, S. R. (1999). Child physical abuse: The relevance of language and social interaction research. *Research on Language and Social Interaction, 32*, 173–184.

Wilson, S. R., Brown, V., Sabee, C., Hayes, J. K., Herman, A., & Behl, L. (2001, April). *Mothers' trait verbal aggressiveness and child abuse potential*. Paper presented to the annual meeting of the Central States Communication Association, Cincinnati, OH.

Wilson, S. R., & Sabee, C. M. (2003). Explicating communicative competence as a theoretical term. In J. O. Greene & B. R. Burleson (Eds.), *Handbook of communication and social interaction skills* (pp. 3–50). Hillsdale, NJ: Erlbaum.

Wyman, P. A., Cowen, E. L., Worker, W. C., Raoof, A., Gribble, P. A., Parker, G. R., & Wannon, M. (1992). Interviews with children who experienced major life stress: Family and child attributes that predict resilient outcomes. *Journal of the American Academy of Child and Adolescent Psychiatry, 31*, 904–910.

CHAPTER CONTENTS

2 The Child Effect in Media and Communication Research: A Call to Arms and an Agenda for Research

JAN VAN DEN BULCK
BEA VAN DEN BERGH
Katholieke Universiteit Leuven

This article reviews the literature on the child effect and suggests that it is an underval-ued approach to studying the way families deal with media and the way they commu-nicate. Even young children play an active part in their own socialization and there are many instances in which it is the child who socializes the parent, rather than the other way around. Media and communication research offers excellent opportunities for study-ing this child effect because the introduction of new media or new types of content often provides quasi-experimental settings that allow pre- and posttest research designs. Al-most all research involving parents or their children may benefit from this old but often ignored perspective. Media and communication research could play a pivotal role in the development of the child effect hypothesis because both sociology and psychology have largely ignored the idea.

THE IMPORTANCE OF THE CHILD'S PERSPECTIVE

In order to study children, many researchers have used one of three research strategies. Some have studied what parents report about their children; oth-ers have studied the children directly. A third strategy has been to look at how parents influence their children.

Remarkably, only a very limited number of studies have realized that a fourth strategy exists: to study children to learn about the parents. In other words, in-fluence and effects can go in both directions between all members of a family. Children influence their parents just as parents influence children. Wartella and Jennings (2001) decried that so little research has been done about media and

Correspondence: Jan Van den Bulck, Department of Communication, Katholieke Universitiet Leuven, Van Evenstraat 2 A, 3000 Leuven, Belgium; email: Jan.vandenbulck@soc.kuleuven.ac.be

Communication Yearbook 29, pp. 35–47

family in the past few decades. It is therefore no surprise that only a few studies can be found that apply the "child effect" or "reverse socialization" view. A small number of studies have tried to incorporate this view. Meadowcroft (1986), for instance, found that political discussions in families were influenced by children's motivations and cognitive abilities. McDevitt and Chaffee (2002) went further by examining research showing that parents sometimes changed their political views as a result of confrontation with their children's developing political ideas. They noted that children influenced their parents at several stages of the communication process. Not only did the confrontation between parental views and children's responses have a direct effect, parents were influenced by their children before and after the conversation: they thought about what they went through with their children and tried to anticipate the next conversation. Nichols Saphir and Chaffee (2002) remarked that the lack of interest in the child's effect is remarkable because the very notion of interaction assumes "bidirectional influences" (p. 86). Their study showed that family communication patterns "are constructed mutually by the two generations, rather than dictated unilaterally by parents" (p. 102). Other studies exist, but they are rare, and some require delving into neighboring disciplines: Much psychological research or microsociological research dealing with interactions between people can ultimately be construed as the study of communication between people. Whether and how parents talk to their children about safe sex, for instance, appears to be influenced and even directed by the way in which adolescents deal with and talk about this subject. Adolescents thus initiate indirectly their own sex education. Research has shown that parents talked more about birth control when their children had sex education classes at school (Kirby & Barth, 1991; Levy et al., 1995). As the remainder of this chapter will show, however, even psychology and sociology have largely ignored the child effect perspective.

THE CHILD AS A COGNITIVELY UNDERDEVELOPED PASSIVE RECIPIENT

When studies do look at the relationship between parents and children from the reverse point of view, certain unease with the concept can often be felt. The influence of developmental psychology (and Piaget's theory of stages of cognitive development) appears to have introduced a cognitive bias. Meadowcroft (1986), for instance, referred to Piaget to claim that "Until children develop cognitive skills necessary to understand central messages conveyed within the family communication, they cannot be expected to participate effectively, and their behavior is not expected to conform to demands of the family's communication pattern" (p. 605). McDevitt and Chaffee (2002) used a more careful phrase, believing that as children grow older they become cognitively more complex and "as the parent adjusts to the increasingly sophisticated child, the direction of the influence within the family is almost invariably reversed." The idea of socialization going in the other direction still appeared to make them feel uneasy because they added "to some extent" at the end of the previous quote (p. 285). Their unease showed further on when they called Meadowcroft's assertion that adolescent children, not parents, initiate changes in family communication patterns "counterintuitive" (p. 295).

What little literature there is has been heavily influenced by a cognitive underdevelopment hypothesis that appears to assume that children need to reach a certain level of cognitive development before their actions become understandable and worth studying and before any behaviors can influence them. Whether parent and child attach the same meaning to the same behaviors (either from the parent or the child) is, however, not as important as many researchers implicitly seem to assume. It is assumed too readily that the message delivered ought to be the message received (cf. Austin, 1993). For instance, it has been shown that children's and parents' perceptions of the latter's intentions differ. Koolstra & Lucassen (2004) found large discrepancies between parental perceptions of parental guidance of media use and how much guidance children were actually noticing. The reason for these differences is often not that the children are not able to understand their parents' intentions correctly (as an implicit or explicit cognitive underdevelopment hypothesis would assume) but because they actually choose to perceive them in another way (cf. Alessandri & Wozniak, 1987; Goodnow, 1988; Grusec & Goodnow, 1994; Schwartz, Barton-Henry, & Pruzinsky, 1985; Tein, Roosa, & Michaels, 1994; Van den Bergh & Van Ranst, 1998). Meanings are produced as a result of an active bidirectional negotiation process. If the meaning children attach to parental behaviors differs from the meaning the parents intended to communicate, it does not follow automatically that the child was unable to process the behavior in a meaningful manner and that nothing happened in the child's mind (cf. Krippendorff, 1993). Even if a level of cognitive development has not been reached that will allow the child to interpret parental behaviors in a way which more or less replicates the parent's intentions, some kind of processing still occurs. Even if behaviors are misunderstood, some meaning will still be attached to those behaviors. In other words, a cognitive logic is too narrow. Whether or not children understand what their parents do to, for, or with them, is not the only and maybe not even the most important issue. Even when a child is not able to attach any kind of meaning to a parent's behavior, there may be an emotional side to the interaction. A child may experience the warmth of interaction or suffer from its absence (cf. Austin, 1993). This emotional side of interaction between parent and child "has been shown to correlate positively with, inter alia, cognitive and moral development, independence and with important aspects of the child's self concept, such as global self-worth, social competence or social acceptance and scholastic competence" (Van den Berg & Van den Bulck, 2000, p. 153; see also Clarke-Steward, 1988; Franz, McCleland, & Weinberger, 1991; Harter, 1998; Howes, Hamilton, & Philipsen, 1998; Maccoby & Martin, 1983; Ritchie & Fitzpatrick, 1990; Tein, Roosa, & Michaels, 1994). Things happen inside a child that are worth studying, even if the child does not understand the behavior of the parent on a cognitive level.

BIDIRECTIONAL SOCIALIZATION

As Alanen (1988) remarked Durkheim originally defined the concept of socialization in the context of the *fait social* that is among processes at societal level. Such processes might occur at any age and Nichols Saphir and Chaffee (2002) rightly note how some of the oldest studies of socialization processes looked at adult immigrants (cf. Thomas & Znaniecki, 1927). Gradually, however, the concept was narrowed to describe processes of *internalization* (cf. Parsons, 1951; Parsons & Bales, 1955). Thus it became a psychological rather than sociological concept. As a result, socialization research became a psychological field, focusing on developmental issues. According to Ambert (1992), this domain was further narrowed to a study of the ways in which parents teach their children about the world, with particular emphasis on the mother–child dyad.

Ambert (1992) observed that the concept of socialization as internalization strongly colors this view. It leads to a search for agents that influence the child. The child is seen as an unsocialized entity that has to learn (i.e. internalize) the rules of the social world (Van den Bergh, 1998). Parents, being part of the adult and social world, are already socialized. From this point of view parents can only be agents and children can only be recipients, a perspective that seems to have dominated most research on socialization and childhood, to the extent that "socialization is the more academic term for what childhood processes are" (Alanen, 1988, p. 54).

Some authors have challenged this view. Three types of arguments have been put forward. First, children have been seen as cocreators of their own socialization. This is a way of thinking that must sound familiar to many media and communication theorists. Leadbeater and Raver (1995), for instance, remarked that children engage in active and constructive interpretation of behaviors of socializing agents. What the eventual meaning of those behaviors will be will not be decided by the initiator of the behaviors, but by the interpretation given to them by the receiver. Peterson and Peters (1983), for instance, showed how negative reactions of parents to behaviors children imitate from television will usually teach those children that such behavior is socially unacceptable. In rebellious children, however, it will legitimize and reinforce those behaviors. Even though the message the parent wants to convey in such a case may be clear, the actual meaning attached to it and the way in which it is processed is clearly a result of the child's processing autonomy. Second, it has been shown that children are socialized not only by adult socializing agents. They also socialize themselves. Olesen (2000) showed how children develop individual and very personal strategies for dealing with scary media content on their own, without any intervention by their parents who may not be aware of what is going on. Finally, the relationship between child and parent can also be reversed. There is a lot of developmental research documenting instances in which children influence their parents. Often this influence leads to changes in behavioral patterns and worldviews in the parents, which is obvious evidence of socialization of the parent by the child. Increasingly, children are viewed as producers of their own environment (Eisenberg, 1998) and even as producers of their own development (Ambert, 1992; Belsky, Lerner, & Spanier, 1984; Lerner, 1982).

The child can cause such child effects either actively or passively. Children influence their parents (and thus, indirectly, their own development) passively when their behavior changes the parent, or the behavior of the parent, even though they did not intend to cause any change. For example, a child who does not respond positively when his/her father tries to comfort may thus discourage the father. Any subsequent lack of fatherly involvement therefore finds one of its origins in the behavior of the child (Ambert, 1992). Ambert (1992) provided an overview of research showing how children, including neonates, initiate many (sometimes the majority) of the interactions between child and parent.

Active child effects occur when the child knowingly and willingly tries to influence the parent, which would occur, for instance, when a child tries to persuade an uncooperative parent to buy a particular toy the child saw in a television advertisement (e.g. Buijzen & Valkenburg, 2003). In such a case the child will try to influence attitudes or, failing that, at least the (purchasing) behavior of the parent.

MEDIA AND COMMUNICATION RESEARCH
AND THE SOCIALIZING CHILD

Even developmental psychologists and sociologists of childhood have been accused of ignoring the child effect. It is therefore no surprise that few studies apply this perspective to the field of media or communication research. Widespread societal and academic concern about negative effects of the media on children probably reinforced a paradigm in which children have sometimes been depicted as innocent, powerless, and all too receptive targets in need of protection. Even though many of these concerns are valid, the stress on one-directional influences of the adult world on the child has obscured an entire field of study. This is unfortunate because media and communication studies provide ideal conditions for studying the child effect. The introduction of new media technologies or new types of content offer an objective for studying how parents and children behave towards each other and how new attitudes, cognitions, emotions, or behavioral patterns emerge.

Studying the child effect offers exciting prospects. It suggests, in fact, that the obviousness of the child as passive recipient paradigm has led hundreds of researchers to ignore the old adage that correlation does not imply causation (cf. Kendall & Stuart, 1961). It has been assumed too often that observed changes or innovations could only have been introduced or caused by parents. Nichols Saphir and Chaffee (2002), for instance, remarked that "[a]lthough the causal direction of a significant cross-sectional correlation is ambiguous, scholars have usually assumed that FCP influences adolescents rather than vice-versa" (p. 89). The notion of a child effect suggests that it sometimes pays to look for evidence of a reverse or bidirectional process.

AN AGENDA FOR RESEARCH

It seems difficult to draw up a matrix of all possible questions one might address from the child effect perspective. It is clear, however, that this perspective can be introduced in many areas where extensive (and seemingly exhaustive) research has been done already. Some may be more evident than others, though any research involving parents and children may benefit from the exercise of reversing the causal order. Here are some examples:

The Introduction of New Media

In many cases, children are the active or passive agent of new media and new technology adoption. The children may introduce some media (e.g., computer games, and MP3) into the household; other technologies may be introduced by the parents because of the children (e.g., buying a computer so the child may use it for schoolwork) even if the child does not request it. The first would be an example of the active child effect, the second of its passive form. Evidence of both processes can be found in Van Rompaey, Roe, & Struys (2002), who discuss the adoption of the internet in families. In some families parents decided to get internet access because they believed their children would benefit from it, in other families they delayed or refused getting internet access because they believed this would protect their children. These are examples of passive child effects. Active child effects were evident in families where the children used free trial subscriptions to the internet to persuade the parents to get more permanent internet access.

Equally important are the behavioral issues surrounding the introduction of innovations. New media may lead to new behaviors. Passive child effects occur when parents are forced to introduce new rules and adapt current behaviors or living patterns because of the new media. For instance, if a family has several children or one of the parents enjoys using the new medium as well, some kind of sharing or turn-taking will have to be introduced, as well as ways to resolve ensuing conflicts. Active child effects occur when children teach their parents how to behave with regard to the innovation. This refers to the handling of the technology, as well as what is considered appropriate or embarrassing behavior and the corresponding attitudes. A child may inform (i.e., try to persuade) the parent that the warnings that computer games can cause epilepsy are exaggerated and that there is no need to limit the duration of play.

Research has shown that a correlation exists between intensive use of the VCR by parents and increased use of the VCR by children (Krendl, Clark, Dawson, & Troiano, 1993). Parents' television viewing behaviors are related to their children's viewing habits, and even their sleep habits (Owens et al., 1999). It is worth wondering whether the interpretation of the causal direction of these relationships was made too rapidly and whether parents might start using the VCR more because their children made the use of the apparatus more self-evident and whether parents sometimes end up watching more television and going to bed later because their children persuade them to do so.

The Introduction of New Content

There seem to be two ways in which children introduce new types of media content into the family. One is when new types of content emerge in the media industry (e.g., new TV genres, new magazines, new game formats, and new music styles); the other is when children acquire new tastes by passing from one developmental stage to another. Here, too, a distinction can be made between active and passive child effects. Passive effects occur when parents spending time with their children are involuntarily exposed to the media content their children opt for at that point in their development. Parents of young children may find that a considerable part of their own TV diet consists of cartoons and children's programs. Parents of adolescents may end up spending a lot of time listening to loud music that is part of a subculture of which they understand very little.

Active child effects occur when children actually try to influence the content selection processes or even try to change their parents' style and preferences. They may try to persuade their parents that what they like to listen to, read or watch is, say, old fashioned or out. They may try to influence their parents because they actually want to educate them and improve their preferences, which would be clear evidence that the educational context of socialization can be reversed even in its most literal sense.

Previous research has suggested a correlation between children's patterns of TV viewing and their parents' viewing (cf. Wright, Peters, & Huston, 1990, for an overview). Wright, Peters, and Huston (1990) suggested that the earlier sources overlook the possibility that the viewing patterns of the parents may imitate those of the children, instead of the reverse. Nevertheless even these authors fail to implement the child-effect perspective to its full extent. When discussing correlates of parent–child coviewing, they ask if parents join children in order to share programs suited to the child's tastes and preferences or if parents choose programs suited to their own tastes, allowing the child to join them. In this perspective, parents still appear as the main decision makers and initiators and the actors with the highest level of knowledge and independence. The authors could have taken into account a number of other possibilities. For instance, children may attempt to steer the selection process because they know that a particular choice will either keep (or chase) their parents away. They may attempt to get a program selected to increase the chance of coviewing, particularly when children are better informed about programming than the parents. Even though research has sought to find out whether parents' tastes predicts child viewing at various ages, it would be interesting to see whether and to what extent children's preferences predict parental media use.

Family Rule Making

It has been remarked that media use, and television viewing in particular, is strongly rule-governed, though family members may not always be aware of it (Alexander, 1990). When discussing rules, the temptation is particularly strong to look at the ways in which parents control children's media use. There is, however, no reason why children should not be able to influence the rules or even add some of their own, at least in some families. A typical parental rule might be that the television set cannot be switched on until homework is finished. It is conceivable, however, that in some families a child has to force the other members of the family to help create and respect an atmosphere in which the child can do homework. It may be up to the child to convince some parents to stop watching television in such instances. This would be a rule initiated by the child. Likewise, a child may succeed in introducing the rule that a particular genre of music must be on while they do their homework (claiming, for instance, that any other genre is distracting). Eating arrangements in particular seem to be related to TV viewing habits in families, and it has been shown that some children eat their evening dinner while watching television, even if the rest of the family does not (Van den Bulck, 2000). This suggests at the very least that such children have acquired the right to be exempted from parental dinner rules. Alexander (1990), drawing on Lull (1980), identified three types of media-related rule making. The first type is habitual rules, that is, behaviors that have been repeated so often that they have become an unquestionable right. Examples may be the rule that a child gets to see every next episode of a particular soap opera because they have seen all the previous episodes. In some families this rule might take precedence over parental preferences, and the child may invoke the habit to prove it is a rule. Parametric rules define a range of accepted or permitted behaviors. Parents may limit the types of programs a child is allowed to watch, but the child may exert a similar influence over its parents. If watching the news makes a child frightened, parents may change their own preferences or viewing patterns (passive child effect), but the child may explicitly forbid certain behaviors in such a way that the parent feels forced to comply ("I do not want daddy to watch the news when my favorite show is on"). Finally, Lull identified tactical rules. Here, too, examples can be found of children using all kinds of tactics to force their parents, perhaps without them realizing it, to accept or adapt their preferences or media use. In the context of family communication patterns, Lull shows, for instance, that "when a child is ignored during conversations held by adults, they can gain entry to the discussion by using a television example" (Lull, 1980, p. 202).

Even though it may seem obvious to some that rule making is a parent's prerogative, there are several instances in which this is less obvious than one may think. From a certain age onward, parents lose the evident physical advantage that might allow them to threaten younger children into submission. At any age, of either child or parent, nonviolent means to control family members, such as the threat of withdrawal of affection, can easily work both ways. A strong child may dominate a weaker parent who is worried about losing the child's affection (cf. Ambert, 1992, for a discussion of parents as victims).

Guidance of Media Use

There has been much research about parental guidance of children's media use (see Fujioka & Austin, 2003, Warren, 2003, for recent overviews). Usually, following Bybee, Robinson, and Turrow (1982), three types of guidance are examined. Some studies have analyzed the parental view (e.g., Valkenburg, Krcmar, Peeters, & Marseille, 1999), and others gave the same questions to children (e.g., Van den Bergh & Van den Bulck, 2000), So far, however, there does not appear to have been an attempt to reverse the question by examining the extent to which children attempt to guide the media use of their parents. The same three types of guidance may exist.

Restrictive guidance would occur when children attempt to stop their parents from consuming certain types of content or reduce that consumption. Children might try to convince their parents to stop buying a particular newspaper because of its political views or to stop watching a particular type of television program because their friends despise parents doing so. They may attempt to stop a parent from playing computer games excessively either because it isolates the parent ("You should spend more time with me, so stop playing computer games so much") or because the child believes its effect to be negative ("I get upset if you play those games because you always end up being irritated and edgy"). *Evaluative guidance* implies that the children steer their parents' media use by commenting on the contents of those media. "This kind of music is so silly, only very old people listen to it." *Unfocused guidance* refers to such behaviors as silent coviewing. Existing research has stressed how both parents and children seem to enjoy consuming certain kinds of media together. By showing they enjoy being with them while they watch particular kinds of programs, parents can influence their children's media use. It seems obvious that the reverse might also apply: Children might induce changes in the preferences of their parents by cuddling up on some occasions, but not on others. Parents may start to enjoy certain types of media use because they have learned (though not necessarily consciously) that their children will approve of it and join them. Even if nothing is said, some kind of guidance is present.

Mediating Effects

Those worrying about the effects of media exposure on children have looked at the question of parental mediation of such effects. Some argue that parental intervention reduces or even counteracts the effects of the media. One may wonder whether any child effects of a similar nature occur. Passive child effects might be ordinary media effects that occur as a result of exposure that is caused by the influence or presence of children. Agenda setting effects may occur when a parent watches a news program the child wants to see or when the parent reads a magazine the child brought into the house. Parents may be influenced by toy advertisements they saw while coviewing a children's program. Active child effects might occur when the child plays the role of an intermediary, much like the parent does in the settings studied in previous research. Children might thus negate the effect of an otherwise powerful advertisement ("Come on, dad, all the kids at school think people driving cars like that are silly") or reinforce it ("All cool mums drive cars like that"). Cultivation effects, too, might occur as a result of a child's media consumption behaviors. By adding that certain clothes or a certain way of behaving shown in a movie are cool, the parent may notice elements of storytelling that might otherwise have escaped his or her attention. First-order cultivation effects may be the result of a child's comments ("Look, in this scene you can see the difference in how they do these things in the U.S. and in Canada"). Second-order effects may be the result of political or ideological discussions following exposure to certain themes (McDevitt & Chaffee, 2002; results would apply in this instance, too).

CONCLUSION

It is amazing how much research has been done about parents, children, and the media from, literally, a one-sided point of view. Some people have reversed the direction of the relationships or have used bi- or multidirectional approaches, but there are not many of them (recent examples are McDevitt & Chaffee, 2002, and Nichols Saphir & Chaffee, 2002). In developmental psychology, this perspective has received scant attention, even though it is not a new idea. It has been introduced and reintroduced several times, first by Bell (1968), later by Maccoby and Martin (1983), Belsky, Lerner, and Spanier (1984), and Bell and Chapman (1986) decades ago, but fellow researchers usually have failed to pick up the gauntlet. This observation opens up an exciting avenue for media and communication scholars. There are two reasons why studying reverse socialization or the child effect appears to be important. First, it adds an incredible array of research questions and hypotheses to our field. At the risk of oversimplifying the question, one might argue that any area of research into children and parents would benefit from the question "can the causal relationship be reversed?" It would be interesting to see how classic ideas and theories fare once they are looked at through this prism. Second, the whole field is wide open. Sociologists and psychologists tend to overlook the idea as well; this is an area in which our discipline can really make its mark. No other discipline in the behavioral sciences has a better starting point. We often operate in quasi-experimental conditions. It is possible for us to study the impact of the introduction of new media, new media contents, or new modes of communication and to see how parent–child interaction evolves. Few other fields have such clear pretest–posttest types of situations as readily available. Developing the child-as-socializing-agent perspective is an opportunity for media and communication researchers to influence the entire field of socialization research.

Ambert (1992) argued that the idea is too alien to many people. Children continue to be seen as passive recipients of adults' care, education, and protection. She claimed that there may be institutional reasons for the unwillingness to give up this perspective because an entire child protection industry heavily depends on it. Media research, with its concerns about violence and sexuality and their potential effects on young media consumers, seems to run similar risks. Acknowledging that children are active cocreators of their own reality probably suggests that some of the blame is shifted in cases where the outcome of the process is not what is generally desired. That is not what is advocated here. One should not react to one imbalance by replacing it with another kind. Buckingham (2000), writing in a somewhat different context, rightly warned that:

> There is a significant danger here of simply replacing a view of children as easily impressionable and vulnerable to influence with an opposite view of them as somehow naturally autonomous and competent—as spontaneously "media-literate." Both positions are equally sentimental—and indeed, equally patronizing. (p. 54)

Nevertheless, much media research might benefit from an attempt to reverse the causal direction we tend to look at. After all a discipline that is particularly sensitive to issues about empowerment, differences in interpretation of messages, and so on should realize three things: First, children are active interpreters, second, children initiate some of the parent-child interaction; and finally, children sometimes teach their parents.

REFERENCES

Alanen, L. (1988). Rethinking childhood. *Acta Sociologica, 31*(1), 53–67.

Alessandri, S. M., & Wozniak, R. H. (1987). The child awareness of parental beliefs concerning the child: A developmental study. *Child Development, 58,* 316–323.

Alexander, A. (1990). Television and family interaction. In J. Bryant (Ed.), *Television and the American family* (pp. 211–225). Hillsdale NJ: Erlbaum.

Ambert, A. M. (1992). *The effect of children on parents.* New York: Haworth Press.

Austin, E. W. (1993). The importance of perspective in parent-child interpretations of family communication patterns. *Journal of Broadcasting and Electronic Media, 37*(2), 147–158.

Bell, R. Q. (1968). A reinterpretation of the direction of effects in studies of socialization. *Psychological Review, 75,* 81–95.

Bell, R. Q., & Chapman, M. (1986). Child effects in studies using experimental or brief longitudinal approaches to socialization. *Developmental Psychology, 22,* 595-603.

Belsky, J., Lerner, R. M., & Spanier, G. B. (1984). *The child in the family.* Reading MA: Addison-Wesley.

Buckingham, D. (2000). Studying children's media cultures: A new agenda for cultural studies. In B. Van den Bergh & J. Van den Bulck (Eds.), *Children and media: multidisciplinary approaches.* (pp. 49-66). Leuven, Belgium: Garant.

Buijzen, M., & Valkenburg, P. (2003). The unintended effects of television advertising: A parent-child survey. *Communication Research, 30,* 483-503.

Bybee, C., Robinson, D., & Turow, J. (1982). Determinants of parental guidance of children's television viewing for a special subgroup: mass media scholars. *Journal of Broadcasting and Electronic Media, 26,* 697–710.

Clarke-Steward, K .A. (1988). Parents' effects on children's development: A decade of progress? *Journal of Applied Developmental Psychology, 9,* 41–84.

Eisenberg, N. (1998). Introduction. In W. Damon & N. Eisenberg (Eds.), *Handbook of child psychology. Vol. 3: Social, emotional and personality development.* (pp. 1–24). New York: Wiley.

Franz, C. E., McClelland, D. C., & Weinberger, J. (1991). Childhood antecedents of conventional social accomplishment in midlife adults: A 36-year prospective study. *Journal of Personality and Social Psychology, 60,* 586–595.

Fujioka, Y., & Austin, E. W. (2003). The implications of vantage point in parental mediation of television and child's attitudes toward drinking alcohol. *Journal of Broadcasting & Electronic Media, 47,* 418–434.

Goodnow, J. J. (1988). Parents' ideas, actions and feelings: models and methods from developmental and social psychology. *Child Development, 59,* 286–320.

Grusec, J. E., & Goodnow, J. J. (1994). The impact of parental discipline methods on the child's internalization of values: A reconceptualization of current points of view. *Developmental Psychology, 30*(4), 4–19.

Harter, S. (1998). The development of self-representations. In W. Damon & N. Eisenberg (Eds.), *Handbook of child psychology. Vol. 3: Social, emotional and personality development* (pp. 553–617). New York: Wiley.

Howes, C., Hamilton, C. E., & Philipsen, L. C. (1998). Stability and continuity of child-caregiver and child-peer relationship. *Child Development, 69,* 418-426.

Kendall, M. G., & Stuart, A. (1961). *The advanced theory of statistics.* New York: Charles Griffin.

Kirby, D., & Barth, R. (1991). Reducing the risk: impact of a new curriculum on sexual risk-taking. *Family Planning Perspectives, 23*(6), 253–263.

Koolstra, C. M., & Lucassen, N. (2004). Viewing behavior of children and TV guidance by parents: a comparison of parent and child reports. *Communications, The European Journal of Communication Research, 29,* 179–198.

Krendl, K. A., Clark, G., Dawson, R., & Troiano, C. (1993). Preschoolers and VCRs in the home: a multiple methods approach. *Journal of Broadcasting & Electronic Media, 37,* 293–312.

Krippendorf, K. (1993). The past of communication's hoped-for future. *Journal of Communication, 43*(3), 34–44.

Leadbeater, B., & Raver, C. (1995). Commentary. *Human Development, 38,* 190–199.

Lerner, R. M. (1982). Children and adolescents as producers of their own development. *Developmental Review, 2,* 342–370.

Levy, S. R., Perhats, C., Weeks, K., Handler, A. S., Zhue, C., & Flay, B. R. (1995). Impact of a school-based AIDS-prevention program on risk and protective behavior for newly sexually active students. *Journal of School Health, 65*(4), 145–151.

Lull, J. (1980). The social uses of television. *Human Communication Research, 6,* 197–209.

Maccoby, E. E., & Martin, J. A. (1983). Socialization in the context of the family: parent-child interaction. In P. H. Mussen & E. M. Hetherington (Eds.), *Handbook of child psychology: Vol 4. Socialization, personality and social development* (pp. 1–102). New York: Wiley.

McDevitt, M., & Chaffee, S. (2002). From top-down to trickle-up influence: revisiting assumptions about the family in political socialization. *Political Communication, 19,* 281-301.

Meadowcroft, J. M. (1986). Family communication patterns and political development: the child's role. *Communication Research, 13*(4), 603-624.

Nichols Saphir, M.,& Chaffee, S. H. (2002) Adolescents' contributions to family communication patterns. *Human Communication Research, 28,* 86–108.

Olesen, J. (2000). Childhood, media and viewer positions. In B. Van den Bergh & J. Van den Bulck (Eds.), *Children and media: multidisciplinary approaches* (pp. 67–88). Leuven, Belgium: Garant.

Owens, J., Maxim, R., McGuinn, M., Nobile, C., Msall, M., & Alario, A. (1999). Television-viewing habits and sleep disturbance in school children. *Pediatrics, 104*(3), e27.

Parsons, T. (1951). *The social system.* New York: Free Press.

Parsons, T., & Bales, R. F. (1955). Socialization and interaction process. New York: Free Press.

Peterson, G. W., & Peters, D. F. (1983). Adolescents' construction of social reality: The impact of television. *Youth and Society, 15,* 67–85.

Ritchie, L. D., & Fitzpatrick, M .A. (1990). Family communication patterns: measuring interpersonal perceptions of interpersonal relationships. *Communication Research, 17,* 523–544.

Schwartz, J. S., Barton-Henry, M. L., & Pruzinsky, T. (1985). Assessing child-rearing behaviors: A comparison of ratings made by mother, father, child and sibling on the CRPBI. *Child Development, 56,* 462–479.

Tein, J. Y., Roosa, M. W., & Michaels, M. (1994). Agreement between parent and child reports on parental behaviors. *Journal of Marriage and the Family, 56,* 341–335.

Thomas, W. I., & Znaniecki, F. (1927). *The Polish peasant in Europe and America.* New York: Knopf.

Valkenburg, P. M., Krcmar, M., Peeters, A. L., & Marseille, N. M. (1999). Developing a scale to assess three styles of television mediation: "Instructive mediation," "restrictive mediation," and "social coviewing." *Journal of Broadcasting and Electronic Media, 43*, 52–66.

Van den Bergh, B., & Van den Bulck, J. (2000). Parental media guidance communication and self concept in pre-adolescents. In B. Van den Buergh & J. Van den Bulck (Eds.), *Children and media: Multidisciplinary approaches* (pp. 151–174). Leuven, Belgium: Garant.

Van den Bergh, B., & Van Ranst, N. (1998, July). *LISREL-analysis of factors in the direct family environment that affect the perceived competence of the child.* Poster presented at the 15th biennial ISSBD Meetings, Berne, Switzerland.

Van den Bergh, B. (1998). Kindbeeld in context: Wisselwerking tussen de maatschappelijke en wetenschappelijke benadering van kinderen. *Ethiek & Maatschappij, 1*(4), 92–115.

Van den Bulck, J. (2000). Is television bad for your health? Behavior and body image of the adolescent "couch potato." *Journal of Youth and Adolescence, 29*, 273–288.

Van Rompaey, V., Roe, K., & Struys, K. (2002). Children's influence on internet access at home: adoption and use in the family context. *Information, Communication & Society, 5*(2), 189–206.

Warren, R. (2003). Parental mediation of preschool children's television viewing. *Journal of Broadcasting & Electronic Media, 47*, 394–417.

Wartella, E., & Jennings, N. (2001). New members of the family: the digital revolution in the home. *Journal of Family Communication, 1*, 59–69.

Wright, J. C., Peters, M. St., & Huston, A. C. (1990). Family television use and its relation to children's cognitive skills and social behavior. In J. Bryant (Ed.), *Television and the American family* (pp. 227–251). Hillsdale NJ: Erlbaum.

CHAPTER CONTENTS

3   The Future of Motivated Deception and Its Detection

JUDEE K. BURGOON
University of Arizona

Highly publicized deceptions by spies, terrorists, foreign adversaries, politicians, and corporations occur daily amid fears that the ability to detect such duplicity is far outstripped by the ability to perpetrate it by motivated deceivers. Whether new technologies hold promise for aiding in their detection or instead pose greater risks of vulnerability is the issue addressed in this chapter. Answers to this question lie in considering, (a) humans' general proclivities to detect deceit, (b) features of communication technologies that may abet or deter successful deceit, (c) the role of motivation in deceptive performances, and (d) the potential of information technologies to identify indicators of deceit. This chapter takes up these four issues within the context of a hypothesis called the motivation impairment effect (MIE), which holds that high motivation facilitates deceptive verbal performances but impairs deceptive nonverbal ones and motivation backfires. Examination of empirical evidence expressly testing or directly relevant to the motivation impairment effect reveals that, although modality and motivation frequently emerge as significant influences on deception detectability, effects are not uniform and the modality by motivation interaction needed to substantiate the MIE often fails to materialize or produces patterns incompatible with the hypothesis. Motivation effects sometimes support a choking-under-pressure interpretation and other times support a strategic repair interpretation, leading to the conclusion that the MIE per se may be more illusory than real. If so, the prospect of utilizing new technologies to detect high stakes deception from verbal and nonverbal behavior ironically may show promise.

AUTHOR'S NOTE: Preparation of this essay was partially supported by the U. S. Army Research Institute (Contract #MDA903-90-K-0113) and the Air Force Office of Scientific Research under the U. S. Department of Defense University Research Initiative (Grant F49620-01-1-0394). The views, opinions, and findings in this report are those of the author and should not be construed as an official Department of Defense position, policy, or decision.

Correspondence: Judee K. Burgoon, Center for the Management of Information, Eller College of Management, University of Arizona, Tucson, AZ 85721; email: jburgoon@cmi.arizona.edu

We try harder (Avis Auto Rental).

INTRODUCTION

In today's world, the news landscape is daily littered with incidents involving deception: political misrepresentations, corporate scandals, cases of identity theft, the unmasking of spies, revelations of terrorist plots, battlefield ambushes, sexual predators masquerading on the internet, high profile criminal cases of wives murdered by cheating husbands. Amid such news, Avis's now indelible motto perhaps carries a more cynical and sinister patina than its original tacit pledge of high performance for consumers and financial success for corporate shareholders. One wonders if the slogan better characterizes the exploits of spin-meisters, greedy executives, scam artists, thieves, and adversaries in evading our best efforts to detect their deceits. Does the future hold only bleak prospects for gaining the upper hand against those with ulterior motives and malicious intentions, or might there be means by which the playing field is at least leveled between deceiver and the deceived?

This is the question that this chapter addresses. I begin by examining the premise that it is the nature of human communication to presume truthfulness—and that this presumptive bias, although indispensable to conducting human transactions, leaves us vulnerable to manipulation by the unscrupulous and malevolent. I then consider why this proclivity to believe others' messages may be exacerbated when communication occurs via technology, thus posing an increasing risk as new technologies diffuse to all quarters of contemporary life. This brings me to the central focus of this essay: motivated deception. High stakes lies are motivated lies. Achieving successful deception detection therefore places a premium on understanding how perpetrators' motivation affects their deceptive performances and what implications motivated deception has for future detection of deception under mediated as well as unmediated forms of communication. Germane to this issue is a program of research in psychology on the motivation impairment effect (MIE). If correct, the MIE implies that our best future hope for detecting and thwarting deceptive practices is to focus on identification and interpretation of nonverbal behaviors. I review this program of research in detail, then move to an alternative program of research in communication on interpersonal deception theory (IDT). IDT forecasts a less rosy future but also suggests other avenues for detecting deceit. I conclude by identifying some technological developments that hold promise for recognizing and thwarting deceptive activity.

The Bias Toward Truthfulness

Human communication would not be possible were it not for interlocutors entering encounters with a presumption of some minimum level of common ground and a co-orientation to one another as conspecifics who have the capacity to exchange and understand social signals (Foppa, 1995; Graumann, 1995; Wallbott, 1995), or what Rommetveit described as a mutual commitment to "a temporarily shared social world" (1974, p. 29). This mutuality is foundational to Grice's (1989) cooperative principle, that cointeractants expect one another to engage in cooperative, civil, polite (and presumably truthful) discourse. It doubtless explains one of the most robust findings in the deception literature: a tendency to overestimate the truthfulness of others' communication, dubbed the truth bias (McCornack & Parks, 1986). Research has repeatedly shown that people enter interactions with preconceived expectations for truthfulness and consequently misjudge deceptive communications as truthful (Burgoon, Blair, & Strom, 2005; DePaulo, Zuckerman, & Rosenthal 1980; Levine & McCornack, 1996; Levine, Park, & McCornack, 1999; McCornack, 1997; McCornack & Parks, 1986; Stiff & Miller, 1986; Stiff, Miller, Sleight, Mongeau, Garlick, & Rogan, 1989).

The truth bias may also be attributable to information-processing biases. Gilbert and colleagues have asserted that incoming information and messages are intrinsically and automatically tagged as truthful as the most cognitively efficient means of initially comprehending incoming stimuli and that receivers typically fail to adjust initial judgments unless something alerts them to the need to appraise sender behavior (Gilbert, Krull, & Malone, 1990; Gilbert, Tafarodi, & Malone, 1993; Gilbert & Osborne, 1989; Gilbert, Pelham, & Krull, 1988). Others have argued that humans are cognitive misers who resort to mental shortcuts (heuristics) to base judgments during interactions and, lacking the ability or motivation to engage in deeper appraisals of sender behavior, quickly settle on initial judgments of message veracity, even when such behavior is nonnormative or reveals dishonesty (McCornack, 1997; Stiff, Kim, & Ramesh, 1992; Levine et al., 1999). This "seize and freeze" pattern (Kruglanski, 1989), in which initial biases toward truthfulness persist throughout the conversation, results in an extremely poor accuracy rate in detecting deception, especially when the base rate of deceptive to truthful stimuli is 50–50 (Park & Levine, 2001). An exception is when senders hold a lie bias or are induced to be suspicious from the outset (McCornack & Levine, 1990), but a lie bias can simply result in more false alarms rather than more accurate detection of deceit (Hartwig, Granhag, Stromwall, & Andersson, 2004).

Whatever the explanation, it is this proclivity to believe others' communication that deceivers exploit. The success of that exploitation may be influenced by the medium in which communication is transacted.

Heightened Vulnerability with Electronic Communication

Fears that ability to detect deceit will be further compromised when communication is conducted via electronic means arise from several lines of inquiry. One concerns the relationship between humans and technologies. Work on automation bias (Muir, 1994)—the "tendency to use automation as a heuristic replacement for vigilant information seeking and processing" (Skitka, Mosier, & Burdick, 2000, p 704)—indicates that users of communication and information technologies may place undue trust in such technologies and consequently reduce their own alert-ness, vigilance, and thoughtful analysis (e.g., Biros, Daly, & Gunsch, 2004; Mosi-er, Skitka, Heers, & Burdick, 1997). A second line of inquiry concerns how fea-tures of communication and information technologies affect interactions between people. Research on social presence theory, media richness, and the cues-filtered-out perspective has long held that leaner media—that is, ones with limited band-width for transmitting and receiving the full array of visual, auditory, olfactory, tactile, kinesthetic, and contextual information and ones lacking full feedback capabilities—are impoverished forms of communication that contribute to de-tachment, impersonalization, poorer understanding, inflammatory discourse, less detailed messages, and the like (see, e.g., Daft & Lengel, 1986; Postmes, Spears, & Lea, 1998; Short, Williams & Christie, 1976; Walther & Parks, 2002). A third line of inquiry consonant with interpersonal deception theory (discussed shortly) argues that deceivers are adept at manipulating mediated forms of communica-tion to better serve their aims by making use of the time lags between message transmissions to rehearse, edit, and adapt their messages in response to receiver feedback (Carlson, George, Burgoon, Adkins, & White, 2004; Marett & George, 2004; Woodworth, Hancock, & Goorha, 2005). Whatever the explanation, em-pirical research has confirmed that deception detection is particularly poor when users communicate via text as opposed to audio or face-to-face (FtF) communica-tion (Burgoon, Stoner, Bonito, & Dunbar, 2003; George, Marett, & Tilley, 2004; Woodworth et al., 2005). This finding might actually be consistent with the MIE, to which we turn next.

Detectability Through Nonverbal Cues: The Motivation Impairment Effect

The motivational impairment hypothesis can be traced to theorizing by several scholars (e.g., DePaulo, Zuckerman, & Rosenthal, 1980; Ekman & Friesen, 1969; Ekman & O'Sullivan, 1991; Siegman, 1982, cited in Zuckerman & Driver, 1985) who have proposed that deception is an emotionally charged and arousing activ-ity that produces nonverbal leakage and deception clues—that is, inadvertent and unbidden behavioral indicators that reveal true feelings or signal that deception is taking place. Communicators who are highly motivated to deceive another are expected to try harder than unmotivated communicators to control their perfor-mance so as to produce convincing lies. Paradoxically, though, such effort may be their undoing. The combination of elevated arousal and overcontrol of expressive behaviors is hypothesized to produce insincere and deceptive-looking nonverbal performances that are readily detectable by receivers. In other words, when de-ceivers try harder to cover up their lies, it has the effect of attenuating or reversing the usual relationship between motivation and behavior: "The more people delib-erately try to control their nonverbal cues, the more out-of-control those cues get" (DePaulo & Kirkendol, 1989, p. 60).

This hypothesis is not to be confused with the more general hypothesis of overall impairment (what Baumeister, 1984, called "choking under pressure"), although as will be seen, this is an alternative worthy of consideration and one for which some empirical support exists. Rather, as first defined in DePaulo, Lanier, and Davis (1983), it is a dual hypothesis of nonverbal impairment and verbal improvement:

> In any condition in which nonverbal cues are available, the lies of highly motivated senders will be more readily detected than the lies of less motivated senders. However, if only verbal cues are made available, then the lies of highly motivated senders will be less readily detected. (p. 1097)

Demonstration of support for this hypothesis thus has resided in receiver detection ability. Performance impairment or facilitation is inferred rather than tested directly. That is, the MIE focuses on detection accuracy scores and infers that detectable alterations in nonverbal behaviors must be responsible for the perception of deceit, although nonverbal performance itself has not been examined. Access to nonverbal cues is posited to lead to detection irrespective of which nonverbal modality or set of cues is available to receivers. A further supposition is that motivated deceivers exhibit more of the telltale nonverbal indicators than unmotivated deceivers. A final and crucial part of the MIE is that if only verbal information is available (as in a transcript or text communication), motivated deception performances are less detectable than unmotivated ones.

At first blush, this thesis appeals by virtue of its counterintuitiveness. After all, performers of any complex skills, public speaking included, are routinely exhorted to try harder. The claim that motivated performance is impaired performance bucks up against the received wisdom that higher motivation translates into successful communication and so warrants closer scrutiny on that score alone. In light of the accelerating reliance on computer-mediated communication (CMC), this claim also deserves further scrutiny for its pessimistic implications for future deception detection if in fact motivated deceivers are advantaged by using text-based (i.e., verbal) forms of electronic communication. At the same time, if the MIE is correct, it argues for investing more efforts to perfect detection of telltale nonverbal indicators of deceit.

Such conclusions, however, may be unwarranted. A review of the research that has been adduced to support the MIE suggests that it may be premature to accord this claim the status of fact.

THE MOTIVATION IMPAIRMENT EFFECT: ILLUMINATION OR ILLUSION?

Defining Motivation

An analysis of the MIE must be prefaced with definitions of motivation, performance, and impairment, as these definitions have direct bearing on the status of empirical support for the MIE and the viability of aggregating statistical results meta-analytically.

On its face, the concept of motivation seems fairly straightforward. In real-world circumstances, motivated deceivers are those who have a lot to gain by lying and a lot to lose by being caught. Within the MIE literature, motivation is understood to mean efforts directed toward evading detection: More motivated deceivers try harder to succeed in having their lies accepted as truthful or sincere. This apparently simple interpretation, however, belies the murkiness of what it means to "try harder." In the published deception literature, this problem is typically sidestepped by defining motivation through implicit understandings and informal descriptions or by avoiding definitions altogether. The resultant operationalizations hence reflect diverse and sometimes divergent underlying psychological mechanisms that may exert fundamentally different effects on performance.

For example, in the cheating paradigm pioneered by Exline, Thibaut, Hickey, and Gumpert (1970) and replicated by others, motivation was linked to avoiding negative consequences in that subjects were told they would be expelled if caught cheating. Similarly, in Koper and Sahlman's (1996) analysis of naturally occurring, real-world deceptions by politicians, athletes, military personnel, and the like, motivation was presumed to be operative because of high personal investment and the aversive consequences of detection. In these cases, deceit or fear of detection should evoke highly intense and negative emotional states that are most directly responsible for performance effects.

By contrast, many instantiations of motivation have emphasized positive incentives and rewards, producing sanctioned deceptions that, though ingenious, are game-like and lacking the negative arousal, guilt, or fear associated with more consequential forms of deceit. Prototypical of this approach are Ekman and Friesen's (1969) and Krauss's (1981) classic studies, as well as subsequent investigations building upon their foundation (e.g., Burgoon, Buller, & Guerrero, 1995; Burgoon, Buller, Guerrero, & Feldman, 1994; DePaulo, Lanier, & Davis, 1983; DePaulo, Kirkendol, Tang, & O'Brien, 1988; DePaulo, Stone, & Lassiter, 1985b; DePaulo, LeMay, & Epstein, 1991; Furedy & Ben-Shakhar, 1991; Koper & Miller, 1991), in which motivation was tied to monetary incentives, competitive drives, self-reported desire to succeed, ego needs (e.g., being told that successful lying is relevant to personal and professional success), or some combination thereof. This interpretation, of equating motivation with positive incentives, was employed in Zuckerman and Driver's (1985) meta-analysis of behavioral correlates of lying (subjects were offered a monetary reward for doing well on the deception task or were told that deception was a test of skill). Operationalizing motivation as desire to achieve positive consequences rather than escape aversive ones arguably may induce psychological states devoid of the involuntary high arousal, negative affect, and overcontrol posited to create nonverbal impairment; such an operationalization may create a class of performances that are more amenable to strategic and successful control. Common experience alone suggests that people are quite adept at "running off" such routine deceptions. Thus, any impairment associated with everyday white lies and trivial dissembling may differ markedly from that accompanying more serious deceit. Moreover, when motivation inductions are augmented by self-presentational concerns that potentially heighten public self-consciousness, self-monitoring, or evaluation apprehension (e.g., DePaulo et al., 1983; Krauss, 1981), these latter psychological states, rather than motivation per se, may be the true causal mechanisms for any deleterious or beneficial impact on communication.

Of course, if multimethod operationalizations of motivation produced similar impairment effects, that would be a point in favor of the broad generalizability and method independence of the MIE. Such is not the case, however. Nowhere is the problem of what to "count" as motivation more apparent than in a study by Burgoon and Floyd (2000) in which several candidate operationalizations of motivation (e.g., goal to succeed with deceit, self-presentational concerns, arousal management concerns, self-reported effort, vigilance during the interaction, interacting with a friend versus a stranger) failed to correlate strongly with one another and produced disparate effects on performance and detection accuracy. The argument in behalf of external validity is sound only insofar as various inductions comport with a theoretical model of motivation and produce reliable, replicated patterns. Otherwise, left open to dispute is what actually drives resultant performance.

Apart from the matter of how motivation is defined is its status as a hypothetical or empirical construct. If it is treated as the former, what appears to be a manipulation of motivation may not actually invoke motivation at all. As illustration, one operationalization of high motivation entailed telling lies to an attractive (as opposed to) unattractive target (DePaulo, Stone, & Lassiter, 1985b), the assumption being that deceivers are far more motivated to succeed when lying to attractive targets. Equally plausible arguments could be made that the desire to appear believable is equally relevant with both types of targets or that attractive targets might create more self-consciousness and desire to please than unattractive ones, independent of lying. In the absence of independent corroboration that motivation was induced, anomalous or nonsupportive findings cannot be explained by reference to motivation. When results fail to produce the hypothesized effects and we have no independent evidence that differential motivation was in fact induced during deceit, it remains indeterminate as to whether the failure lies with the MIE hypothesis or with the induction. If motivation is instead treated as an empirical variable, what constitutes an appropriate manipulation check or measure must be resolved. For example, if motivation is regarded as a goal to succeed, then presumably deceivers could be asked prior to or following a deception episode how much it mattered to them to evade detection. If, however, motivation is regarded as behavioral activation or heightened effort (i.e., synonymous with the "trying" part of trying harder), then overt manifestations of more intense effort or perhaps even a physiological indication of heightened arousal and energy output might be required. (A difficulty with this latter approach is the possible tautology of failing to separate motivation, that is, cause, from highly energized performances, or effect). Alternatively, if motivation is regarded as an affective state, such as guilt or fear of embarrassment, then a different form of verification is called for but one which may run the same risk of conflating cause (motivation-induced arousal) with effect (performance impairment).

If magnitude of motivation is also factored into the equation, the problem is compounded further, because some manipulations may have been too anemic to induce high motivation and may have manipulated something else instead, causing "specification error." Miller and Stiff (1993), for instance, criticized much of the extant motivation-related research, and especially studies employing uninterrupted, unidirectional messages and monetary rewards, as likely to produce modest rather than high levels of motivation and to induce task involvement rather than motivation to succeed. Even though it could be argued that finding significant results with modest inductions is evidence of large effect sizes, anomalous findings with verbal behavior have led to speculations that the opposite was the case—that extreme levels of motivation were created and were responsible for both verbal and nonverbal performance being impaired (see DePaulo & Kirkendol, 1989). Such speculations reach a dead-end in the absence of empirical assessments of motivation levels.

Distinguishing Performance Impairment from Detectability

The concept of performance impairment denotes a decrement in the verbal and nonverbal communication of deceivers. However, research on the MIE has focused not on what senders do but rather on judgments receivers make, such as whether lies are detected or senders are judged as sincere, when exposed to truths or lies in a text, audio, visual, or audiovisual modality. (An exception is DePaulo et al., 1988, in which the performance of deceivers was coded). Differential "detectability," though, should be attributed to performance decrements if and only if we can confidently rule out other factors as the cause of receiver judgments. If, for instance, motivated and unmotivated sender performances are judged as equally credible and yet detectability differs, something else must be at stake. The consistent findings of truth biases and leniency errors committed by judges' point to some of the responsibility falling on the receiving side of the equation. For example, receivers read from a transcript when they are in a verbal-only condition; they listen to a videotape or audiotape when they are in an audio channel condition; they watch a videotape in the visual condition; and they watch and listen in an audiovisual condition. These different modes of receiving message information differ in some obvious and perhaps nonobvious ways. Dealing with a dual coding system—symbols and sounds—may require more attentive and deeper processing because readers must first decode the visual symbol then subvocalize it, relative to only listening in the audio mode. Also, different modalities may alter comprehension or the particular linguistic features that are attended to. The addition of visual information may galvanize attention to certain cues while distracting attention from other, potentially more diagnostic ones. Different modalities may affect the degree of suspicion generated or the degree of focus on sender characteristics, both of which can influence the processing of deceptive messages (see Schul & Burnstein, 1998). These possibilities shift the focus from properties of sender performance to properties of receiver information processing. Channel comparisons conflate message delivery systems with receiver modes of processing; as a result, we cannot uncritically assume that modality differences are due to properties of messages (deception displays) rather than of message recipients.

Second, scholars of message production processes have come to realize that verbal and nonverbal codes are inextricably linked, whereas those studying meaning processes have come to realize that interpretations draw in a gestalt fashion upon the constellation of cues that are available. This means that full-channel presentations, in which the nonverbal cues complement and flesh out verbal utterances, do not merely add an independent layer of meaning to that present (e.g., in a transcript-only channel); rather they produce a much richer, nuanced meaning than that available in restricted modalities. It is this fuller representation of the total integrated message that may account for differences in detectability of, say, full-channel versus restricted-channel presentations. Moreover, when multiple channels are present, receivers have the benefit of looking for the goodness of fit among channels. As the work on channel discrepancy highlights (e.g., Zuckerman & Driver, 1985), recognizing that messages "just aren't right" is a key to deception detection. The degree to which different modalities are coordinated or out of sync with one another, as well as the ways in which adding the final piece to a puzzle suddenly reveals its heretofore hidden form, may be all-important in determining a message's sincerity and believability.

Third, participant receivers attend to different cues and process information differently than do observers (Buller & Hunsaker, 1995; Burgoon & Newton, 1991; Burgoon, Buller, Floyd, et al., 1996; Dunbar, Ramirez, & Burgoon, 2003). The fidelity and immediacy of visual and vocal information may be more vivid and potent for participants than observers, for instance. Modality effects that have been found for observer judgments therefore do not necessarily generalize to participant receiver judgments.

These caveats about modality comparisons as a method for understanding verbal and nonverbal cue usage are not meant to invalidate the impressive body of MIE work but rather to point up indeterminacies associated with it and to caution against overinterpretation regarding which nonverbal and verbal cues or modalities are implicated in deceptive encoding and decoding. When significant differences do emerge across modalities, we are still left asking the critical "why" question and left inferring "what" aspect of the communication process accounts for the effect.

Methodologically, yet another possibility is related to the measurement of detectability. In the MIE research, it is commonly calculated as the average

difference in receiver judgments between a sender's truthful and deceptive messages. (The complications associated with this approach are equally applicable
to change scores from, say, a truthful baseline to a deceptive performance or, for
that matter, any use of change scores.) On the surface, this method is appealing
because it is simpler than reporting both sets of means (truthful and deceptive)
for a given condition, and it appears to control for individual differences in the
believability of truthful performances. In essence, the discrepancy scores can be
viewed as adjusted for demeanor or skill differences among senders—but important information is lost in the process. Very different conclusions can be drawn
by ignoring the raw truthful and deceptive ratings because discrepancy or change
scores can be influenced substantially by extreme scores on either the truthful or
deceptive ratings or by lack of comparability in truthfulness across various independent conditions, or both. A very high truthful rating in one condition can make
the difference between truth and deception appear very large in that condition,
even though perceived deceptiveness does not differ across conditions. The MIE
depends on deceptive, not truthful, performances being debilitated or facilitated,
so a fair test of the hypothesis necessitates evidence of differences in those deceptive performances between high motivation and low motivation conditions. Additionally, ceiling and floor effects go undetected yet may account for the large or
small discrepancies that emerge.

These possible drawbacks to using discrepancy and change scores are in
no way original (see, e.g., Cronbach & Furby, 1970; Harris, 1963; Rogosa &
Willett, 1983) nor do they argue for avoiding discrepancy scores altogether.
In most of the MIE tests where only discrepancy scores are reported, though,
information regarding the separate truthful and deceptive judgments is not
recoverable from the tables, leaving open to question what else might be accounting for the patterns that are presented. This becomes particularly problematic as analyses and tables expand into three-way and higher order interactions because, depending on how various cells in a fully saturated design
are combined when decomposing higher order interactions, different conclusions can be reached, conclusions that are spuriously attributed to differences
in performance.

A final methodological problem to be noted in preface is that the audio and
audiovisual modalities are problematic for providing a clean test of the MIE because they simultaneously include the channel purported to benefit from motivation—verbal—with one(s) hypothesized to be harmed—vocal and visual. A pure
test would contrast exclusively nonverbal channels, such as visual-only or content-filtered audio—with text. Even though the MIE merely specifies that impairment will occur in any condition in which nonverbal cues are available, there is
an implicit contradiction here because of the additional part of the hypothesis that
specifies verbal facilitation. Given that facilitated verbal performance could offset
and neutralize any debilitation of nonverbal performance, the clearest test of the
MIE resides in the visual–verbal comparison.

The Nature of Performance Impairment and Facilitation

Separate from the issue of whether impairment should be measured as sender behavior or receiver judgments are the additional issues of what behaviors would qualify as indications of impairment (or facilitation) if they were observed directly and whether all nonverbal (or verbal) behaviors are sufficiently interchangeable and indistinguishable to warrant grouping them all together. The sheer complexity of the task has perhaps discouraged investigations of performance per se, but the challenging nature of the task should not exempt scholars from attempting to designate a priori what behavioral patterns are valid markers of impaired performance. If performance is to be implicated as the cause of ultimate judgments of honesty or deceit, then the true litmus test of the MIE, at least in communication scholarship, would be to examine actual performance. Lacking prior rigorous identification and observation of the crucial features of deception displays that are responsible for successful or failed performances, results become vulnerable to a range of post hoc interpretations that cannot be reconciled.

Deceptive performances entail a constellation of deliberate (strategic) and inadvertent (nonstrategic), static and dynamic, verbal and nonverbal behaviors (see, e.g., Buller & Burgoon, 1994, 1996; DePaulo, Stone, & Lassiter, 1985a; Stiff, Corman, Krizek, & Snider, 1994; Zuckerman & Driver, 1985). Strategic activities include the regulation of verbal content, style, and amount of information delivered (i.e., information management), the regulation of verbal and nonverbal tactics to create desired impressions (image management), and the suppression of behaviors that might reveal deceptive intent or leak true feelings (behavior management). The concept of strategic activity by definition implies that impaired nonverbal performance is not a given. Put differently, nonstrategic indicators of negative arousal, reduced involvement, and performance decrements may be offset by deliberate and successful management of nonverbal as well as verbal behavior. Deciding how many or which ones should show a decrement to warrant declaring a performance impaired is no mean task. Moreover, even if a profile of key indicators could be agreed upon (an issue itself fraught with controversy), not all behaviors need be implicated during any given deception, especially under the more mundane kinds of deceptions pursued in DePaulo's and our own programs of research. It is thus possible for some behaviors to show impairment while others reflect skillful deployment and still others remain unaffected. If impairment is only partial, or if one channel offsets decrements in another—for example, a nervous voice is offset by facial pleasantness and composure—the net amount of impairment may be modest or even imperceptible.

A case in point is the level of involvement and expressivity that deceivers display. MIE proponents have conjectured that highly motivated deceivers become unnaturally stiff, wooden, and inexpressive, a pattern that in the extreme would probably be viewed by most as impaired performance. This principle of overcontrol, which emanates from the four-factor theory (Zuckerman, DePaulo, & Rosenthal, 1981), refers to the well-documented finding that deceivers tend to show reduced expressivity and involvement at the beginnings of interactions (e.g., Burgoon & Buller, 1994; Burgoon, Buller, White, Afifi, & Buslig, 1999; DePaulo et al., 1988; Zuckerman et al., 1981; Zuckerman & Driver, 1985). Short of the extreme, however, a pattern of reduced involvement and expressivity might also be described as subdued but poised, as cautious but self-controlled. The difference between being composed and being overly restrained is one of degree, with the threshold between the former and the latter slight and very difficult to specify. If deceivers intentionally opt for greater self-restraint as a means of inhibiting signs of anxiety and creating a more temperate, modulated presentation (see, e.g., Burgoon, Buller, Floyd, & Grandpre, 1996; Vrij, Semin, & Bull, 1996), their behavior could be judged as a case of successful strategic communication rather than behavioral impairment. In public contexts, for example, minimizing nervousness, nonfluencies, and random movements while maximizing one's intentional communication and self-monitoring would be considered a successful performance. Consequently, it is not immediately obvious what kinds of behaviors qualify as indicators of impairment or, in the case of verbal behavior, facilitation.

These illustrations underscore that all nonverbal channels and behaviors are not the same. To group them together is overly simplistic. Neither the nonverbal channels, nor the cues within them, are isomorphic. Vocalic behaviors differ from visual behaviors, and visual facial cues differ from visual postural ones, especially when it comes to deception and motivation. In particular, cues differ in degrees of controllability and capacity for leaking deceptive intent (an argument elaborated more fully below). Thus, grouping together unlike channels or cues can easily mask significant variability across them.

Possible Explanatory Calculi

Even if it can be demonstrated that motivation backfires, further questions that must be addressed are the conditions under which this principle holds and the underlying explanatory mechanisms accounting for results. The research explicitly testing the MIE has examined a wide range of factors, which makes possible to specify rival hypotheses and explanations generated from other bodies of literature that might account for the same patterns of results. Several alternatives, many of which are taken directly from DePaulo's series of investigations, are examined here; to make the differences more concrete, I have used the approach of assigning contrast codes, which for purposes of statistical comparisons show which conditions or combinations of conditions would be compared to one another.

First, it is important to spell out what constitutes the prototypical set of comparisons to confirm the MIE. It will be recalled that the MIE is a dual hypothesis of impaired nonverbal performance and improved verbal performance under conditions of higher motivation. Operationally, this has usually been tested by employing different modalities that include or exclude verbal and nonverbal information. In the initial test of the hypothesis (DePaulo et al., 1983), four modalities were used: (a) text only, which consists of only verbal information, (b) audio, which

TABLE 1
Contrast Codes for Alternative Tests of Motivation Effects

Hypothesis	Motivation	Verbal	Audio (verbal +vocal)	Visual only	Audiovisual (verbal +vocal +visual)
H1: In any condition, in which non-verbal cues are present, lies of highly motivated senders are more detectable than those of low motivated senders; in conditions containing only verbal cues, lies of high-motivated senders are less detectable than those of low-motivated senders. (Original MIE, all nonverbal modalities weighted equally)	High	-3	+1	+1	+1
	Low	+3	-1	-1	-1
H2: Regardless of modality, detection is higher under high than low motivation. (Main effect for motivation, i.e., choking under pressure)	High	+1	+1	+1	+1
	Low	-1	-1	-1	-1
H3: Under high motivation, detectability increases as channel controllability decreases (verbal+vocal+visual > verbal+vocal > visual > verbal); under low motivation, the opposite rank-order holds. (Motivation x modality interaction, nonverbal modalities differentiated by Ekman & Friesen leakage hierarchy)	High	-3	+1	-1	+3
	Low	+3	-1	+1	-3

consists of both verbal and vocal information (the latter being a nonverbal source of information), (c) audiovisual, which consists of verbal, vocal, and visual information (i.e., it includes both audio and visual nonverbal information), and (d) visual, which excludes any verbal or vocal information and therefore represents a pure nonverbal modality. The appropriate set of contrast codes for testing the MIE, shown in Table 1, is referenced as Hypothesis 1. It specifies a motivation by modality by truth–deception interaction, with no differentiation made among the nonverbal channels. The truth–deception factor is captured in the difference scores that form the detectability dependent measure.

One rival hypothesis is a more general impairment hypothesis, in line with Baumeister's (1984) choking-under-pressure thesis. Such an interpretation, which DePaulo et al. (1983) entertained but dismissed, could be justified by reference to the principle of social facilitation: Moderate arousal is said to facilitate, but excessive arousal to debilitate, performance (Zajonc, 1980). By extension, moderate motivation should optimize all manner of performance, whereas high degrees of motivation should have deleterious effects, a relationship that has been confirmed between arousal change and several facets of communicative performance in non-deceptive contexts (e.g., Burgoon, Kelley, Newton, & Keeley-Dyreson, 1989). Inasmuch as deception has been described as a complex task (Buller & Burgoon, 1996; Buller, Strzyzewski, & Hunsaker, 1991; Gilbert, Pelham, & Krull, 1988), a plausible case could be made that all deceptive performances—verbal and non-verbal—should suffer and detectability should increase, as motivation increases. This alternative appears in Table 1 as Hypothesis 2, which is a main effect for motivation. Even though statistically speaking this main effect is independent of the interaction effect, it cannot be entertained simultaneously with H1 because it contradicts the precise prediction of the MIE that verbal performance will be facilitated. Both H1 and H2 can only obtain if the interaction is ordinal or the simple effect patterns are ignored.

A third, more refined hypothesis can be derived from DePaulo, Zuckerman, and Rosenthal's (1980) principle of controllability and Buller and Burgoon's (1994, 1996) concept of strategic activity in their interpersonal deception theory. The principle of controllability draws upon Ekman and Friesen's (1969; Ekman, 1981) leakage hierarchy, which arrays communication channels from least to most amenable to willful and conscious control and which led to early speculations that motivated senders would try harder to control their self-presentations but would be successful "only in those channels most amenable to willful control" (DePaulo et al., 1983, p. 1096). Involuntary emotional reactions with thought to reside in the nonverbal channels, and nonverbal channels thought to be under less conscious control than the verbal channel, they are regarded as "leakier," that is, more revealing of deceptive intent or "true" feeling states. Within the nonverbal channels, communicators are thought to be more attuned to what they are doing with their faces than their voices (or bodies). Thus, according to the leakage hierarchy proposed by Ekman and Friesen and elaborated by Hocking and Leathers (1980), the verbal channel should be the most controllable, then facial cues, and lastly, vocal ones.[1] Controllability is also related to a channel's sending capacity (e.g., the number of distinctive messages that can be sent and their speed of transmission). The verbal channel is thought to have greater sending capacity, that is, the ability to create a wide range of messages, which not only should facilitate successful deceit but also make it the preferred channel for strategic (deliberate) activity and, hence, the locus of greater self-monitoring. Commitment to the leakage hierarchy and the principle of controllability would therefore result in a rank-ordering of conditions shown in Table 1 as Hypothesis 3. This would constitute the most stringent test of the MIE's explanatory underpinnings because in addition to specifying a motivation by modality by truth–deception interaction, it orders the relationships among nonverbal modalities.

Given that a motivation by modality interaction is open to alternative variants that rearrange the rankings of modalities on detectability and due to differences between high and low motivation within a single modality, Keppel (1991) advocated that significant interactions be followed up by simple effect tests to further isolate the locus of differences. Even though some may find this recommendation unduly stringent, when a design consists of more than a 2 x 2 factorial, the manner in which cells are combined can produce significant effects in line with hypotheses yet mask where the largest differences reside. For example, if detectability is higher in channels containing auditory information than in verbal and visual channels, as some data would suggest (DePaulo et al., 1983),[2] this would place detectability of verbal information on a par with some nonverbal modalities and make the interactions more a function of modality than motivation differences. It is precisely this kind of equivocality in the published MIE literature that invites closer inspection of the patterns of means to discern whether the observed interactions generally conform to the precise MIE prediction or might better conform to rival hypotheses. Though some might question the need for the level of scrutiny that follows, the corpus of data on the MIE is a rich resource for considering the conditions under which motivated deceivers might capitalize on new technologies to perpetrate their deceits and for uncovering the possible moderators of successful detection. A meticulous and exhaustive analysis is therefore needed to allay doubts that the review is selective as well as to arrive at judicious conclusions regarding motivated deception.

EMPIRICAL FINDINGS RELATED TO MOTIVATED DECEPTION

The primary body of MIE research was identified and summarized in DePaulo and Kirkendol (1989). Here, the relevant studies are reviewed chronologically, followed by a synopsis of several other deception studies that are explicitly or tacitly pertinent to motivational impairment or facilitation.

Tests Related to the MIE

Krauss (1981). The earliest relevant investigation, conducted by Krauss (1981), was the precursor for later designs. In Phase 1, half of the deceivers were "aroused" or "motivated" in the following manner: They were told that deception is related to career success and to intellectual and creative ability and that their performance would be evaluated by psychiatrists. Thus, motivation presumably was a matter of "trying harder" when given the "success induction" than when not, although Krauss couched the study in terms of arousal. Tension was rated as a manipulation check but did not differentiate the two conditions. Results of Phase 1 indicated no difference between aroused and unaroused senders' success in deceiving their interviewers. In Phase 2, observers were asked to make deception judgments under one of three modality conditions—visual, auditory (verbal + vocal), or full-channel (verbal + vocal + visual). Observers rated "aroused" liars as less successful than "unaroused" liars in all three nonverbal conditions (i.e., there was a main effect for the motivation manipulation). The audio channel also differed from the full-channel condition for aroused versus unaroused liars.

In light of no significant findings in Phase 1 and significant ones in Phase 2, one possible reading of these results is that detectability differs according to whether judges are participants or observers, that is, modality and motivation may interact with perspective such that participants are less capable of detecting aroused or motivated deceit under certain modalities than are observers, a possibility that surfaces again later. DePaulo et al. (1983) offered an alternative interpretation—that aroused senders "were betrayed by their nonverbal cues" (p. 1097) on the basis of the three conditions all having some form of nonverbal information available. This led to the hypothesis that any time nonverbal cues are available, motivated liars will be more easily detected than unmotivated ones. Because the study did not include a condition that was exclusively verbal, results could not speak definitively to H1 (i.e., the MIE, which requires verbal improvement under motivation). They also did not support H2 or H3 for participants. They could be viewed as congruent with H2 (choking under pressure) as judged by observers.

DePaulo, Lanier, and Davis (1983). This was the first experiment explicitly intended to test the MIE. In Phase 1, senders answered two questions truthfully and two deceptively in front of a panel of peers. Those in the high motivation condition were informed that the ability to lie successfully is very important to career success and were given examples of the importance of deceiving successfully. In addition, they were told that their videotaped responses would be evaluated by a panel of six peers. The low motivation manipulation described the upcoming task as a game, subjects were given examples of innocuous lies, and they were not led to expect that the videotapes would be used later. Thus, the high motivation instructions included many factors—incentive to perform, fear of detection, anticipated negative consequences of failure, heightened self-monitoring and public self-consciousness, communication and evaluation apprehension, and perhaps desire to abbreviate the task so as to alleviate the stress of a public performance—that gained the advantage of a more robust manipulation but lost the ability to ascertain whether motivation per se, its correlates, or other arousal-linked predispositions were responsible for resultant effects. This indeterminancy was compounded by a failed manipulation check. (Like the Krauss investigation, neither self-reported nor observed tension differed between the high and low motivation conditions.) This leaves open the possibility that some of the elements may have worked at cross purposes or neutralized one another or that the low motivation induction created a different mindset and definition of the task while not necessarily eliminating motivation to deceive.[3] In Phase 2, judges saw, heard, or read a subset of the messages and rated them on deceptiveness, planning, and tension. A fourth transcript condition supplied the essential verbal-only condition for comparison to conditions including nonverbal cues. Additional factors—sex of sender, sex of judge, and planning (planned or spontaneous responses)—coupled with motivation, channel, and message type (truth or deception) yielded a 2 x 4 x

TABLE 2

Mean Detectability Scores, by Motivation and Modality,
from DePaulo, Lanier, and Davis (1983)

	Motivation	Verbal	Audio (verbal +vocal)	Visual only	Audiovisual (verbal +vocal +visual)
(a) Across all four modality	High	-.02	.38	.03	.48
conditions	Low	.22	.32	-.23	.19

	Motivation	Verbal only	All nonverbal
(b) Means for original contrast com-	High	-.02	.30
paring verbal modality to average of	Low	.22	.09
all modalities containing nonverbal			
content			

	Motivation	All verbal	Nonverbal only
(c) Means for contrast comparing	High	.28	.03
average of all modalities containing	Low	.24	-.23
verbal content (verbal, verbal+vocal,			
verbal+vocal+visual) to the exclu-			
sively nonverbal modality (visual)			

2 x 2 x 2 x 2 ANOVA design. Despite a failed manipulation check, a comparison between the verbal-only channel and the average of all others (verbal + vocal + visual, verbal + vocal, visual) showed that motivated deceivers were more detectable on average in the three channels containing nonverbal cues than were unmotivated deceivers, whereas the reverse was true in the verbal condition. The means have been arrayed in Table 2, Parts (a) and (b), and labeled according to the kinds of cues available in each channel. These means are detectability scores (i.e., differences between rated deceptiveness while telling the truth and while telling lies, with higher scores representing greater discrepancies and hence, greater detectability). Within columns, the differences between the high and low motivation conditions show positive discrepancies for the visual and AV conditions and a negative discrepancy for the verbal condition.

These results might be interpreted as resounding support for the MIE. On the other hand, because planned comparisons require combining several means into a single estimate, such comparisons may achieve statistical significance even though the individual means depart substantially from the hypothesized pattern. Consequently, such comparisons can be misleading or mask other important patterns, especially when one is decomposing higher order interactions that consist of more than two levels in any given factor. That is the case here. Consider Table 2 more closely. (As a reminder, the audio channel is an amalgamation of one nonverbal channel and one verbal channel.) First, contrary to the prediction that motivated lies should be detectable in any channel in which nonverbal cues are present, highly motivated deceivers were as successful at evading detection in the visual-only as the verbal channel. (Relative to unmotivated senders, motivated senders did show higher detectability in the visual channel, but the near-zero mean gives one pause about concluding that deceit was particularly detectable in that modality, and the low motivation pattern was due to senders' lies being rated as more truthful than their truths.) Second, both high and low motivated deceivers were equally detectable in the audio (verbal + vocal) channel and more so than in the verbal channel alone. This modality effect implies that highly motivated deceivers did not fare worse than those with low motivation in controlling vocal cues. Third, the means can be reconfigured to support the rival hypothesis that verbal performance suffers more impairment. Shown as Part C in Table 2, if the channels containing verbal information are all combined (i.e., verbal + vocal + visual, verbal + vocal, verbal) and contrasted with the visual channel, the pattern implies that conditions in which verbal cues are present are more detectable, regardless of motivation, than ones with only visual information. (The visual condition would still support the conclusion that unmotivated deceivers are less detectable than motivated ones in this nonverbal condition.)

In short, this set of means is amenable to varying conclusions, even drawing upon the same underlying mechanism of controllability to justify them, depending on how cells are combined and compared. Thus, in the absence of follow-up simple effect tests, the array of means could as easily show that (a) motivated and unmotivated senders alike were unsuccessful in controlling their voices, or (b) unmotivated senders did control their faces, but (c) motivated senders controlled their faces and their words. In other words, deceivers successfully controlled their faces, regardless of motivation, but motivation led to additional control of the verbal channel.

DePaulo, Stone, and Lassiter (1985b). Clearly one study does not a generalization make. As DePaulo (personal communication, 1995) rightly observed, the proof lies in the big picture, not the means from any single study. Neither should a principle be judged by the first study in a series; the full body of work and its evolution must be considered. The next MIE investigation included multiple instantiations of presumed motivational differences: sender–target sex combination, telling ingratiating lies (feigning agreement with the receivers) as compared to noningratiating lies (feigning disagreement with receivers),[4] and target attractiveness. The authors hypothesized that senders urged to make a good impression would be more motivated to succeed with their lies and show greater impairment in (a) opposite-sex, (b) ingratiation, and (c) attractive receiver conditions than in same-sex target, unattractive target, and feigned disagreement conditions. However, no manipulation checks were conducted to assess whether any of these factors, separately or in combination, induced differential motivation. The authors also explored the previous unexpected finding of greater detectability in the visual channels, a result that was contrary to the leakage hierarchy, which specifies that facial cues should be more controllable and hence less prone to impairment than vocal cues.

As before, deceptive presentations were contrasted with true agreements and disagreements. However, the target, purportedly seated behind a one-way mirror, did not really exist, so senders no longer addressed physically present receivers nor were they led to anticipate that their videotaped presentations would be viewed later. In another change, the authors abandoned deceptiveness as a dependent measure, instead asking observers to rate how sincere the senders were. These various methodological changes, although gaining the advantages of increased generalizability (by not adhering too narrowly to one set of procedures) and reduced sensitivity to the presence of deception (by avoiding references to honesty or deception in the dependent measures), introduced multiple new factors that could account for any resultant differences among investigations. The change in dependent measures in itself is not trivial. A judgment of another's sincerity arguably is a different order of judgment than one of outright deception. Insincerity not only can be socially acceptable but sometimes is mandated by politeness norms, whereas deceptiveness is typically viewed as reprehensible. (See DePaulo, Rosenthal, et al., 1982, for a similar elaboration of this argument, and DePaulo, Anderson, & Cooper, 1999, for differences resulting from using these implicit as opposed to explicit measures of deceit.) Thus, the results of this and subsequent experiments using the sincerity measure have greater correspondence to studies measuring credibility than actual deceit.

With three operationalizations of motivation in the same experiment, one analytic strategy would have been to contrast the ostensibly maximal motivation condition—telling ingratiating lies to attractive, opposite-sex targets—with the lowest motivation condition—telling noningratiating lies to unattractive, same-sex targets. This, however, was not done. Instead, factors were analyzed separately. The first test supported the MIE (H1). The means, arrayed by condition in Table 3, Part (a), show that senders addressing same-sex receivers ("low motivation") were rated as equally sincere when telling the truth and when deceiving, whereas insincerity by senders addressing opposite-sex receivers ("high motivation") was more detectable in the three conditions containing nonverbal cues than in the verbal condition. If the means are examined as simple effects within each level of motivation, they fit the MIE nicely. If examined within modality so that high and low motivations are contrasted (as DePaulo and colleagues prefer), then the hypothesized nonverbal impairment continues to hold, but the verbal improvement effect disappears.

The visual–verbal contrast, which is not orthogonal to the previous one, was not significant. Not tested was the largest difference—between the audio (verbal + vocal) and verbal conditions—which doubtless was most responsible for the significant interaction effect. Curiously, this comparison would actually support both the verbal facilitation portion of the MIE and the leakage hierarchy's positioning of vocal cues as being most poorly controlled, that is, it supports both H1 and the underlying rationale represented by H3, but the authors chose instead to test the alternative visual-cue impairment hypothesis.

The planned test of ingratiating versus noningratiating lies failed to support H1, but the contrast testing visual impairment did. The pattern of means, shown in Table

TABLE 3

Observed Means for Detectability and Sincerity by Motivation and Modality,
from DePaulo, Stone, and Lassiter (1985b)

	Verbal	Audio (verbal +vocal)	Visual only	Audiovisual (verbal +vocal +visual)
(a) Motivation operationalized as opposite-sex (high motivation) and same-sex (low motivation) target, with detectability scores as the dependent measure				
Opposite sex target	-.04	.32	.25	.20
Same sex target	.04	-.10	.01	.02
(b) Motivation operationalized as ingratiating (high) and noningratiating (low) lies, with detectability scores as the dependent measure				
Ingratiating lies	.01	.12	.39	.30
Noningratiating lies	.00	.10	-.13	-.08
(c) Motivation operationalized as attractive (high) and unattractive (low) targets, with sincerity ratings as the dependent measure				
Attractive targets	5.71	6.41	5.84	6.68
Unattractive targets	5.72	6.68	6.37	6.90

3, Part (b), reveals a different rank-order of modalities. Detectability for those tell-ing ingratiating lies was highest in the visual and audiovisual conditions and much lower in the audio and verbal conditions. Noningratiating lies were least detect-able in the visual channels. These results fit the nonverbal impairment part of the MIE but not the verbal improvement part, and impairment is now more evident in visual than audio modalities.

The third factor of attractiveness failed to produce support for either of the planned contrasts. The authors therefore recast these data in terms of straight sincerity ratings, ignoring the truthfulness or deceptiveness of the performance, which removed an essential factor from the MIE test. It was argued that present-ing self to an attractive other would be more motivating and therefore more sus-ceptible to nonverbal impairment than presenting self to an unattractive other. A failed operationalization thus became transformed: "[O]f all the operational-izations that have been tested thus far, the one that most closely approximates the combination of high motivation and low confidence" (DePaulo, Kirkendol, Tang, & O'Brien, 1988, p. 182). Even though the authors based their claim of support on a modality by motivation interaction, the means [shown in Table 3, Part (c)] reveal that sincerity ratings were lowest in the verbal condition for both attractive and unattractive targets, completely contrary to the MIE prediction of verbal improvement, and highest sincerity ratings obtained in the audio and audio-visual modalities for both attractive and unattractive senders, again contrary to the MIE. Only in the visual condition was a notable difference apparent.[5] Additionally, consistent with H2, insincerity was more readily detected with (a) opposite-sex targets than same-sex ones, (b) ingratiating than noningratiating lies, (c) unattractive than attractive targets, and (d) female than male senders. The main effect for motivation was more consistent across operationalizations than were the motivation by modality by truth/deception interactions, but it was also qualified by some of the interactions. No modality main effects (relevant to Hypothesis 3) were reported.

What should we make of this mix of findings? On the one hand, it might be tempting to gloss the differences among patterns, as well as the unhypothesized main effects and a number of other interactions that further complicate the picture, to conclude that the MIE was at work. On the other hand, the statistical tests and patterns of means neither coincide consistently with the planned contrast specified by Hypothesis 1, nor with the theoretical rankings of controllability of H3, nor, indeed, with each other. What emerges is different orderings with each operationalization plus piecemeal support for other hypotheses. H2 (choking under pressure) garners the most support, but that conclusion is justified only if the various operationalizations represent different degrees of motivation. Consequently, it is difficult to accept the claim that "the consistency of these results with theoretically based predictions, with each other, and [with DePaulo et al., 1983] adds strength to the motivational interpretation" (DePaulo et al., 1985b, p. 1199). Instead, a more accurate construal can be found in the authors' comment that "each of these variables, considered individually, could be alternatively interpreted as indicative of many other constructs besides level of motivation" (DePaulo et al., 1985b, p. 1199).

Still, the numerous significant findings signal that something is going on, but what that is is indeterminate from the varying arrays of means. For example, if motivation is the underlying cause, senders should have appeared sincere to attractive targets when telling the truth in both verbal and nonverbal channels and when lying in the verbal channel, resulting in a main effect favoring greater sincerity with attractive rather than unattractive targets. Instead, the main effect was in the opposite direction. A plausible rival explanation is that senders might have wanted it to be transparent that faked disagreements were just that—faked rather than sincere. From a self-presentational standpoint, this reasoning is as tenable as assuming that motivation would only be high for ingratiating lies. The difference is that deceivers' motivation would be to succeed in achieving their self-presentation aims, not in having the verbal presentation accepted at face value. On this view, the two true agreement and disagreement conditions would generate the least motivation, and senders when pretending to disagree might take advantage of the mixed-message potential available in combined verbal and nonverbal modalities to convey their insincerity. This could explain greater detectability of insincerity with feigned disagreements and transform them from unintended failure to strategic success.

In sum, these results are fraught with inconsistencies among themselves, the prior studies, and the reasoning proffered in their behalf. A number of factors might account for the differences: the shift to sincerity as the dependent measure, sampling or measurement error, or procedural changes that may have inadvertently manipulated other factors to produce specification error (see Pedhazur, 1997). Whatever the explanation, the results probably do not justify treating these variants as clean replications of the previous MIE study.[6]

DePaulo, Kirkendol, Tang, and O'Brien (1988). This next experiment yoked the ingratiation manipulation with the competence-relevance one (making a good impression as a sign of personal, interpersonal, and professional competence). Senders were also informed that they were to make a good impression using only certain cues to which observers would have access, specifically their (a) facial expressions, (b) body movement, (c) combined facial and body activity, (d) tone of voice, (e) words, (f) tone of voice and words, or (g) all four elements. It was hypothesized that motivated senders would try harder to control those cues than the ones to which observers purportedly did not have access and that lies of highly motivated senders would be most detectable when receivers had access to the nonverbal cues senders were intentionally trying to control. The introduction of attempted control of presentation channels was an important innovation and one clearly derived from the reasoning behind the MIE. Another change— dropping the visual-only modality—precluded replication of the visual–verbal contrast and eliminated comparability among the nonverbal condition(s) across studies.

As might be expected, the 2 (conveyed agreement–disagreement) x 2 (truth/ lie) x 7 (channels controlled) x 2 (competence–relevance) x 3 (attractiveness of sender) x 3 (verbal–audio–AV modality for receivers) design produced complex results. The attempted control factor was tested by assigning contrast codes to match the rank-order of the 21 cells on controllability and channel access. The test was not significant ($p = .12$ in one version, $p = .15$ in a second), leaving the authors to draw conclusions from a main effect for channel within the audiovisual condition. Focusing their attention on these three cells (out of 21), the authors suggested that "the means for this condition look just like the motivational impairment effect: Lies were most detectable in the channels that included nonverbal cues" (DePaulo et al., 1988, p. 190). In addition, though, to overlooking all the other means that did not conform to predictions, this conclusion was flawed because it lost the motivation element in the shuffle. To conclude that an MIE was present, a comparison needed to be made between a high motivation and low motivation condition. Instead, the comparison became one of verbal versus nonverbal presentation within one modality. Even had the authors found support, it would have been for a different hypothesis—that when receivers are encouraged to attend specifically to intentionally manipulated cues, they can discern insincerity. (The remaining 18 cells, however, also failed to fit this conclusion.) The authors themselves deemed these findings as merely suggestive and in need of replication.

The competence–relevance effect also failed to produce confirmatory results and so was combined with the third motivation factor, ingratiating versus noningratiating lies. Results were interpreted as supporting the MIE: Ingratiation was seen as more insincere from words than from nonverbal cues of unmotivated (low competence-relevance) senders but more insincere from nonverbal than verbal cues of motivated (high competence–relevance) senders. Examination of Table 4, Part (a), however—where conditions have been ordered from lowest through intermediate to highest degrees of induced motivation—reveals that nonverbal impairment (i.e., detectable insincerity) was greatest at the lowest and highest levels of motivation, producing what would be a curvilinear pattern, whereas the verbal modality shows greatest impairment in an intermediate condition. Effect sizes were also quite small.

Regarding sender attractiveness, moderate and highly attractive senders, whose lies were expected to be the least detectable, instead were the most so. If the 16 means are arrayed in Part (b) of Table 4 in the same fashion as Part A, then they defy locating any consistent pattern. To simplify inspection, consider just the verbal and combined nonverbal modality columns. Unattractive senders show increasing and then decreasing verbal detectability as motivation level increases; a reverse curvilinear pattern appears for nonverbal detectability. Highly attractive senders show linear declines in detectability across motivation levels for both verbal and nonverbal modalities. Even though this latter finding could be interpreted as fitting the predicted benefits of attractiveness in moderating nonverbal impairment, that interpretation is only tenable if the MIE is evident in the unattractive sender condition, which it is not.[7]

Analyzing the combined ingratiation and competence-relevance results also puts the authors on the horns of a dilemma. If they combine the two motivation factors of ingratiation and competence–relevance, the statistical tests fail and the patterns of means do not fit the hypothesis. If they abandon ingratiation as a motivated kind of lie and treat competence–relevance as the main motivation operationalization, then some of the results fit the hypothesis, but the ingratiation manipulation used in previous investigations now fails to replicate. Furthermore, treating competence-relevance as the primary motivation factor is not justified in light of its failure when tested individually. In sum, these intriguing but highly complicated results make it increasingly apparent that sincerity judgments are influenced by a host of factors and that performance is neither uniformly impaired nor improved by factors thought to reflect motivation.

DePaulo, LeMay, and Epstein (1991). In this next, ambitious investigation, the authors crossed importance of succeeding with expectations for success. They hypothesized that those who are most motivated to succeed (because they expect to be evaluated rather than merely questioned) but are least confident of success (because they expect a wary and skilled rather than trusting and unskilled interviewer) should show the most impairment. The women participants were expected to be more motivated to succeed on identity-affirming than identity-repudiating stories.

TABLE 4
Selected Observed Means for Detectability,
from DePaulo, Kirkendol, Tang, and O'Brien (1988)

(a) Three-Way Interaction of Competence-Relevance, Type of Deceit, and Modality

| Condition | Modality judged | | | |
	Transcript (verbal)	Audio (verbal+vocal)	Audiovisual (verbal +vocal+visual)	Combined nonverbals
Low competence-relevance/ Noningratiation	.19	.63	.52	.58
Low competence-relevance/ Ingratiation	.36	.13	.19	.16
High competence-relevance/ Noningratiation	.09	-.07	.31	.12
High competence-relevance/ Ingratiation	.11	.52	.39	.45

(b) Four-Way Interaction of Attractiveness, Competence-Relevance, Type of Deceit, and Modality

	Unattractive sender			
Low competence relevance/ Noningratiation	-.23	.27	.16	.22
Low competence relevance/ Ingratiation	.20	-.36	-.60	-.48
High competence relevance/ Noningratiation	.27	-.38	.14	-.12
High competence relevance/ Ingratiation	.08	.47	.60	.54
	Moderately attractive sender			
Low competence relevance/ Noningratiation	.49	1.00	.94	.97
Low competence relevance/ Ingratiation	.62	.33	.44	.38
High competence relevance/ Noningratiation	-.06	.10	.14	.12
High competence relevance/ Ingratiation	.24	.88	.52	.70

TABLE 4 (continued)
Selected Observed Means for Detectability,
from DePaulo, Kirkendol, Tang, and O'Brien (1988)

(b) Four-Way Interaction of Attractiveness, Competence-Relevance, Type of Deceit, and Modality

	Highly attractive sender			
Low competence relevance/ Noningratiation	.30	.62	.46	.54
Low competence relevance/ Ingratiation	.24	.43	.72	.57
High competence relevance/ Noningratiation	.07	.07	.65	.36
High competence relevance/ Ingratiation	.01	.22	.04	.13

In addition to rating sincerity, judges also rated the plausibility of senders' stories, and participants also rated their own involvement, honesty, and sincerity. These new measures were a useful addition in affording greater insight into perceived performance and participants' own state of mind.

Before considering results, it is important to point out another major departure from prior investigations. No mention is made of nonverbal versus verbal performance, even though modality is included in the experimental design. The MIE is recast as simply a matter of greater motivation producing more detectable insincerity when deceiving, which is actually a variant of H2 applied to deception. The 2 x 2 x 2 x 2 x 3 factorial design created the prospect of highly intricate results, so it is perhaps unsurprising that many higher order interactions did emerge. Several observations could be made, but six findings or conclusions seem particularly noteworthy.

First, as predicted, lies about independence were more detectable than lies about dependence, and identity-affirming lies were especially detectable under conditions of high importance and low success. So far, so good. These patterns, however, held regardless of modality. In other words, the verbal-facilitation and nonverbal-impairment distinction so central to the MIE did not occur.

Second, this report is one of the exceptional instances where mean truth and lie ratings as well as detectability scores were reported. Those means reveal that differences in detectability came about not from the deceptive presentations but from the truthful ones. Truthful stories about independence and dependence, respectively, were rated 5.92 and 5.69. The corresponding ratings for lies were 5.66 and 5.63. When new contrast weights were fitted to deal with this acknowledged problem, the resultant tests on four-way and three-way interactions repeatedly

TABLE 5

Sincerity and Involvement Means for Identity-Affirming and Identity-
Repudiating Truths and Lies, by Importance of and Expectations for Success,
from DePaulo, LeMay, & Epstein (1991)

	Identity-repudiating (dependence)		Identity-affirming (independence)	
	Truths	Lies	Truths	Lies
(a) Sincerity ratings				
Low importance of success				
Low expectations	5.68	5.73	5.74	5.61
High expectations	5.74	5.66	6.10	5.74
High importance of success				
Low expectations	5.58	5.65	6.04	5.53
High expectations	5.78	5.60	5.80	5.64
(b) Involvement ratings				
Low importance of success				
Low expectations	6.77	5.58	6.92	6.27
High expectations	6.46	5.77	6.68	5.82
High importance of success				
Low expectations	5.48	5.84	6.84	5.24
High Expectations	6.13	5.83	6.57	5.39

revealed that the experimental motivation manipulations affected the truthful but not the deceptive stories. Thus, the concerns raised earlier about detectability scores masking differences due to truthful presentations surfaced in this study. The importance of this cannot be overstated. Even though the authors recognized that "it may seem inappropriate to describe participants' communicative performances as impaired" (1991, p. 21) and conceded at the conclusion of the article that "we cannot rule out the interpretation that the results were due to the facilitating effects of effort on both verbal and nonverbal success at truth telling (e.g., participants tried hard when telling their truths in the key conditions)" (1991, p. 23), most of the discussion was devoted to arguing that impairment actually took place because ratings for identity-affirming lies were lower than ratings for truths in key conditions. The validity of this claim therefore revolves around interpretation of the means implicated in the significant three-way and four-way interactions.

If one considers the three-way interaction arrayed in Table 5, Part (a), where the ratings within each row represent scores from the same group of people, it becomes immediately apparent that, with two exceptions, participants received highly similar ratings across their four performances. Clearly, it is truthful rather than deceptive performances that deviate from the group averages. The same conclusion is reached if one instead conducts between-group comparisons. The interactions are a function of the two higher rated identity-affirming truths; there is almost no variance among lies. It is, therefore, invalid to conclude that changes in motivational states produced impairment during deceit. Simply put, the detectability scores are better interpreted as showing exceptional sincerity by senders telling truthful stories when (a) it didn't matter if they succeeded but they expected to succeed anyway or (b) it did matter but they did not expect to succeed in convincing a wary receiver.

Third, the self-report data, which yielded results closely paralleling the observer data, indicate that it was precisely this latter condition in which participants reported being the most involved [see Table 5, Part (b)]. A viable conclusion to draw, then, would be that senders were trying especially hard to be believable when telling real, identity-affirming stories to skeptical receivers who were going to evaluate them. The observer data indicate that senders were also most successful in being perceived as sincere in this condition. In short, motivation facilitated rather than impaired performance.[8]

Fourth, the authors contemplate some alternative explanations for the resultant patterns, one of which is choking under pressure (H2). The tenability of this explanation hinges on which of the manipulated factors increase "pressure." If pressure resides in telling identity-affirming rather than identity-repudiating lies, then the significant truthfulness by identity-relevance interaction that obtained could be regarded as supportive. Ratings showing that identity-relevant stories were less plausible than irrelevant ones would also fit this interpretation, if choking applied more broadly to include truths. If instead, pressure is thought to be highest under conditions of high importance and low expectations of success, then we should see the lowest sincerity ratings in that cell within each column. For the judges' ratings [Part (a)], simple effect tests are unneeded to verify that this is not the case for three of the four columns. In the fourth column (identity-affirming lies), the limited range among the means (5.53 to 5.74) suggests that even if a statistical test achieved significance by taking advantage of the power of the entire design, the magnitude of the effect size would be unimpressive. Thus, this explanation fails to hold up across the board in the judges' data. For the self-report ratings, involvement data are consistent with predictions in the identity-affirming lies and identity-repudiating truths conditions (but not the other two types of stories), but justification would be needed to warrant restricting application of the choking hypothesis to only these two conditions.

Fifth, another proposed explanatory mechanism concerns effort. One could argue that senders may have tried especially hard to appear sincere when expecting low success with skeptical evaluators. This speculation is intuitively sensible and reinforced by high self-reported involvement and sincerity in that condition. What lacks a sensible explanation is why added effort would not also augment the perceived sincerity of lies. Here the authors resurrect the nonverbal impairment argument, but because the experiment failed to produce modality effects, they cannot enlist this explanation. To reiterate, the results are not a case of expressive failure but rather expressive success in conveying sincerity when it mattered most.

That said, a sixth point to be made concerns the issue of overcontrol. Current results are consistent with results elsewhere showing deceivers tend to be less involved and expressive than truth tellers. In an effort to conceal telltale signs of anxiety, negative affect, and deceit, senders often suppress facial, gestural, and bodily animation—sometimes to the point of appearing rigid, unnatural, and over controlled. This behavioral pattern, however, is linked directly to deception rather than to motivation per se. Put differently, it is evidence of deception rather than motivation impairment. Moreover, as noted earlier, a legitimate question is whether such control actually constitutes impairment or strategic communication, in that reduced involvement may also show poise or serve to disassociate senders from messages that do not reflect their true feelings and identities. Thus, an alternative interpretation is that the reduced involvement evident on nearly all the untrue stories, relative to the corresponding truthful ones, was intended to make the lies transparent or at least less compelling than the truthful versions. (The one anomaly under this explanation is the identity-repudiating–high importance–low expectations condition.)

In sum, this investigation is an exemplar of a very rich, labor-intensive, meticulously conducted, and well-powered experiment that yielded provocative findings. It cannot, however, be counted as one supporting the MIE. As with previous investigations, neither the statistical tests nor the arrays of means conform to H1. The essential modality effects were absent in this experiment; therefore, there is also no support for H3. At best, the results might favor H2 (choking under pressure), but that requires post hoc speculations as to which conditions represented the most pressure. Even though one can sympathize with the difficult task the authors faced in trying to make sense of such a complex set of findings, the fact remains that the data will not submit to any one account without forcing and glossing portions of it. And it is the authors' own admirable thoroughness in conducting their statistical tests that paradoxically renders this conclusion.

DePaulo, Blank, Swaim, and Hairfield (1992). In this last investigation by DePaulo and colleagues, self-presentation goals, truth–deception, and degree of scrutiny were manipulated by instructing senders to appear natural, expressive, or inhibited while expressing their attitudes (three truthful and three deceptive) on six issues and under purportedly high or low scrutiny (being observed by five judges versus one). Unlike the previous all-female sample, this sample was all male. Judges were assigned to one of four modalities (verbal, audio, visual, or AV) and rated sender deceptiveness, expressiveness, and attractiveness.

Relevant to the MIE, the analysis of deceptiveness produced only an expressiveness by truth–deception interaction. Senders scoring low on the ACT were judged as more deceptive when lying than when telling the truth; ratings of truths and lies of senders scoring high on the ACT were virtually identical. The crucial modality interactions with deception, goal, and scrutiny that would be needed to test H1 were not reported, presumably because they were not significant. Instead, modality comparisons were made only in regard to judged expressivity. Interestingly, the expressivity results contradicted the DePaulo and Kirkendol (1989) assertion that nonverbal channels are more susceptible to the MIE because they are more difficult to control. Here, senders successfully regulated their visual (and vocal) cues to produce alternative self-presentations of expressivity, naturalness, or inhibition. In other words, senders were capable of controlling their nonverbal behavior in line with their intentions, and those with high trait expressivity were most skilled at doing so. Senders were also most successful in their presentations when asked to be expressive or when under low scrutiny, that is, expressivity and perceived surveillance moderated performance. Thus, once again, the MIE failed to obtain support, as did H3.

Summary

In summarizing the evidence for the MIE, DePaulo and Kirkendol (1989) wrote, "The one-sentence summary of the data I've presented so far is that we've found this motivational impairment effect in almost every place we've looked for it" (p. 60), but closer inspection of those data does not reveal unwavering support. Notwithstanding the substantial thought and effort that have gone into this program of work, a prima facie case for the MIE has yet to be made. The variability across operationalizations of motivation, the number and nature of modalities included, the complexion of the samples, and the measurement of deception detection in itself would preclude drawing unequivocal generalizations about how motivation affects verbal and nonverbal performance during deception. More troublesome, though, is the collective patterns of results. Even though yielding some provocative speculations and highlighting the extent to which communication processes elude simple characterization, they neither comport fully with the MIE hypothesis nor with each other. A summary of which investigations have produced partial or full support for each hypothesis, shown in Table 6, reveals the following:

1. H1, the actual MIE, received unequivocal support in only two instances.

2. H2 (choking under pressure) received more support than any other hypothesis but did not do so across the board and was countered by instances of higher pressure producing facilitation rather than impairment.

3. H3 (the verbal–nonverbal contrast that follows the leakage hierarchy) was supported in only two instances, the same ones supporting H1.

DECEPTION DETECTION IN THE FUTURE

What, then, can be said about future detection of motivated deception? Perhaps the most important implication is that, to the extent that deceivers suffer some impairment due to excessive performance pressure, communication modalities that lessen such pressure should make detection more difficult, whereas modalities that intensify such pressure should produce concomitant intensification of impairment. For example, asynchronous forms of text communication (e.g., email, bulletin boards) that give deceivers ample time to plan, rehearse, or edit their messages should reduce the sense of pressure and thus enhance deceiver performance relative to synchronous (same time) and multimodal forms of communication. The latter require deceivers to manage multiple communication channels simultaneously and to adapt rapidly to receiver feedback. In support of this conjecture,

TABLE 6

Summary of Support or Partial Support for Alternative Hypotheses from the
Motivation Impairment Research Program

	Hypothesis		
Investigation	1	2	3
Krauss (1981)		?	
DePaulo et al. (1983)	+		+
DePaulo et al. (1985), operationalization 1	+	+	+
DePaulo et al. (1985), operationalization 2		+	
DePaulo et al. (1985), operationalization 3		+	
DePaulo & Pfeiffer (1986)			
DePaulo et al. (1988)			
DePaulo et al. (1991)		?	
DePaulo et al. (1992)			

NOTE: Partial support is designated by a question mark.

deceivers report feeling less cognitive taxation and less arousal under text than
FtF communication (Burgoon, Blair, & Moyer, 2003). If motivated deceivers are
in fact capable of strategically and successfully adapting their communication to
evade detection, and if new communication technologies differentially advantage
deceivers in this process, prognostications about future deception detection must
take into account which features of communication technologies aid or deter successful deception. Several lines of deception inquiry, considered next, are informative on this issue.

The Strategic Communication Perspective from Interpersonal Deception Theory

I have already alluded to an alternative characterization of motivated nonverbal and verbal deceptive performances as amenable to successful strategic manipulation. In contrast to the MIE position that nonverbal displays suffer impairment
during motivated deception because of their relatively involuntary and uncontrollable nature, this position, advanced by interpersonal deception theory (IDT;
Buller & Burgoon, 1996) and bolstered by substantial nonverbal and deception literature, posits that senders not only have the capacity to voluntarily and intentionally regulate their deception displays but also do so successfully (although success may vary systematically with a number of preinteractional and interactional
factors). Higher motivation is one of the conditions that should foster success,
at least on some fronts, and by more skilled individuals. A further key premise
of IDT is that deception displays are dynamic, not static, and subject to repairs
based on receiver feedback. Consequently, initial impairment may be transitory,
further diluting any adverse effects on performance. Hence, empirical evidence favoring (a) strategic communication, (b) nonimpairment of nonverbal performances,
(c) impairment of verbal performances, and/or (d) temporal adaptations all pose

challenges to the MIE as well as point to directions for successful deception detection in the future.[9]

Evidence From Experimental Studies Manipulating Motivation

A handful of experiments have manipulated motivation-linked variables and examined their impact on specific behavioral indicators. What makes them especially salient is their direct focus on nonverbal performance, rather than inferring performance impairment from receiver accuracy in detecting deception. One, by Koper and Miller (1991), used a mock poker game as the task. Even though some might question this paradigm because bluffing during card games is expected, the authors argued that "the goal in poker is singularly the selfish, even greedy, accumulation of wealth at the expense of the opponent" and that this self-benefit goal, unlike the typical sanctioned deceit that benefits someone else "clearly simulates unsanctioned deception" (p. 13). Motivational differences were induced via the size of the ante and monetary rewards for successful deceit and/or successful detection during the game. Self-reported involvement, excitement, and value placed on the stakes confirmed that motivation was successfully induced. Deceit was associated with decreased body animation, fewer body adaptors, and increased facial animation, but motivation did not interact with deceit, and higher motivation was associated with more, not less, success. Motivation also failed to correlate with two measures of arousal and did not produce appreciable alterations in nonverbal behaviors. These results conflict with the MIE (H1) and the debilitating impact of heightened motivation (H2).

A second investigation (Furedy & Ben-Shakhar, 1991) measured electrodermal responses while subjects gave deceitful or truthful answers to relevant and neutral items in the guilty knowledge paradigm. Motivation to avoid detection was manipulated by offering half the subjects monetary rewards for an ego-relevant deception task. Results produced no effect for motivation and no interactions with deceit. Thus, motivation did not facilitate verbal performance as the MIE would predict.

A third investigation (Feeley, 1996) is relevant if we can safely assume that liars who voluntarily create their lies after complicity in a cheating incident anticipate more serious consequences and therefore are more motivated than those for whom lying is sanctioned (approved by an experimenter). Eleven measures of sender behavior (e.g., involvement, nervousness) showed virtually no differences between the sanctioned and unsanctioned lie conditions except for less smiling with unsanctioned lies than with sanctioned ones or truth-telling. Feeley concluded that greater motivation to lie had a negligible and nondebilitating impact on performance. Thus, this investigation also failed to support either H1 or H2.

A fourth investigation (Burgoon, Buller, & Floyd, 2001) included two experimental factors that, following the MIE reasoning, should relate to motivation. If senders experience heightened self-presentational concerns when interacting with friends as compared to strangers, and when under extended scrutiny during a monologue as compared to alternating turns at talk during dialogue, deceivers should have experienced elevated motivation in those conditions, resulting in nonverbal impairment and verbal improvement as measured by actual performance or detection accuracy. Friends were more motivated than strangers, as expected, yet managed to create a more pleasant demeanor (based on coder ratings), contrary to the prediction of nonverbal impairment.[10] Motivation did not differ between dialogue and monologue.

Further direct evidence comes from the Zuckerman and Driver (1985) meta-analysis, in which one of the moderator variables was motivation, defined as receipt of incentives to lie. Out of 24 behaviors tested across numerous investigations, 8 differed between low and high motivation. Low motivated communicators exhibited high degrees of blinking, pupil dilation, speech hesitations, adaptors, and changes in body movement; limited smiling and facial movement; nonimmediate (distancing or disassociative) language; and significant discrepancies among verbal and nonverbal channels. From these behavioral profiles, we can characterize low motivated communicators as displaying a high degree of arousal, limited ability to put forward a positive image (through smiling and facial animation), and some performance impairment. Comparatively, high motivated communicators exhibited high degrees of pupil dilation, hesitations, and shrug gestures; little blinking, head movement or postural shifts; higher pitch (another possible marker of arousal); slower and shorter responses; more verbal overgeneralization terms (levelers) and more negative statements. Thus, high motivated communicators showed arousal on some cues but managed to dampen other indicators, to express uncertainty gesturally, and to curtail their verbal output. These patterns largely coincide with Buller and Burgoon's (1994, 1996) portrayal of deceit as entailing strategic behavioral management in the form of suppression of leakage cues and strategic information management in the forms of uncertainty, hesitancy, and reticence. The association between negative statements and deceit among the highly motivated also could be interpreted as motivation having a deleterious rather than propitious effect on the verbal channel.

Finally, two recent experiments manipulated motivation within the context of electronically mediated communication. Unlike all the prior studies, in which judges of truth or deception were not the original recipients of those messages, message senders and message judges interacted with one other. The first, by Woodworth et al. (2005), replicated a previous experiment by Burgoon, Stoner, Bonito, and Dunbar (2003) but with the addition of the "importance of deception skill" as the motivation manipulation. Dyads conducted a get-acquainted conversation either FtF or with text chat. A manipulation check confirmed that motivated receivers placed greater importance on succeeding than did those who did not receive the induction. Consistent with the MIE, receivers in the FtF condition were more suspicious of high motivation deceivers than high motivation truth tellers, whereas receivers in the CMC condition were more suspicious of low motivation deceivers than low motivation truth tellers. Even though access to nonverbal cues (the FtF) condition did not make highly motivated deceivers more detectable than low motivation ones, low motivated deceivers were more detectable in the CMC condition, suggesting a verbal facilitation effect. The authors, however, interpreted their results as consistent with the IDT strategic communication perspective, arguing that the text-based CMC condition made it easier for motivated deceivers to perpetrate deceit. A companion study (Hancock, Curry, Goorha, & Woodworth, 2005), which examined the linguistic behaviors of those in the text condition, showed that deceivers used a variety of maneuvers (e.g., more details, more words) to create coherent and plausible answers. Motivated liars avoided causal terms and negations relative to unmotivated liars. The authors speculated that "this change in linguistic behavior for highly motivated senders may have allowed these senders to avoid some of the traps associated with being specific regarding causal connections during deceptions" (p. 7). Additionally, unmotivated deceivers were subjected to more questions by their partner, a pattern possibly suggestive of low motivation performances eliciting more suspicion.

The second investigation (Burgoon & Blair, 2004) employed interviews regarding a mock theft. Interviews were conducted via text chat, walkie-talkies, or FtF; half the interviewees were given monetary incentives and an "importance" induction to elevate motivation. In preface, deceivers reported being more motivated than truth tellers, as did those in the high motivation condition who interacted FtF or via audio. Consistent with the view that deception can trigger negative arousal and is more cognitively taxing than truth telling, deceivers reported experiencing more negative arousal and cognitive difficulty than truth tellers. When they interacted via text, however, they felt less cognitive difficulty, less negative arousal, and exercised less behavioral control than those interacting FtF or via audio. These results shed some light on the preceding experiments by indicating, first, that deceivers were intrinsically motivated to succeed and second, felt less pressure or discomfort when using text; that is, they were able to overcome the typical experiences of arousal and cognitive taxation when using text. In FtF, far more of the low motivation guilty subjects were accurately detected as deceptive (52%) than were high motivation guilty subjects (37%); in audio communication, there were no differences between high and low motivated guilty subjects; and in text, low motivation guilty subjects were far more accurately detected as deceptive (71%) than were high motivation guilty subjects (27%). These results indicate that motivation did not impair performance in the conditions in which nonverbal information was available to receivers. More generally, motivation aided performance, especially for those in the text condition. Additionally, preliminary linguistic and nonverbal analyses showed that motivation had more impact on truthful than deceptive verbal output: Highly motivated participants talked far more than did low motivation participants, as did those in the audio condition. Also highly motivated deceivers had fewer nonfluencies than did motivated truth tellers, whereas among those with low motivation, deceivers had more nonfluencies than truth tellers. Finally, highly motivated deceivers were more expressive behaviorally and showed fewer adaptor behaviors in the FtF condition, the only one where visual nonverbal cues could be coded. These patterns all show a motivation enhancement effect on both verbal and nonverbal (vocal) performance.

To recap, examining direct evidence of sender performance instead of drawing inferences from receiver judgments leads to the conclusion that motivated deceivers may craft verbal messages that obfuscate some aspects of what they say while also incorporating credibility-enhancing details but avoiding causal claims or negativity that might adversely affect their believability. At the same time, they control leakage, speak fluently, and show higher expressivity, immediacy, and pleasantness than less motivated deceivers, that is, they are more successful at behavior and image management, even though they still experience some performance deficits associated with deception itself. Both the verbal and nonverbal channels show a mix of beneficial and detrimental effects associated with deceit or motivation. It would therefore be inaccurate to attribute a general pattern of impairment or enhancement due to motivated deception.

Evidence From Studies Measuring Motivation

Beyond the above investigations that have explicitly manipulated motivation, other studies have employed explicit measures of motivation. Even though these findings are merely correlational rather than derived from experimental manipulations, and reliance on self-reports is not problem-free, they have the virtue of measuring motivation directly and relating it to specific verbal and nonverbal cues. Burgoon, Buller, and Guerrero (1995; see also Burgoon, Buller, Guerrero, & Feldman, 1994) explored the relationship of self-reported motivation to self-perceived, partner-perceived, and observer-perceived deceptive success during actual interaction. Results showed that motivation had a curvilinear relationship with self-reported success but a linear relationship with observed success: Those who were least and most motivated thought they were most successful in creating credible answers, whereas observers thought those who were most motivated were most successful. Thus, higher motivation was associated with both own and others' perceptions of believability; low motivation was only associated with a perhaps deluded sense of success. If one accepts the MIE reasoning for using detectability scores as a surrogate for measuring performance directly, then the greater success ascribed to motivated senders should be attributable to effective rather than poor performances, inasmuch as overt behavior was the only information available to the observers. Interestingly, the curvilinear relationship on self-reported motivation parallels Ekman, O'Sullivan, Friesen, and Scherer's (1991) claim that moderate motivation may lead to leakage but high motivation may suppress it.

In another investigation (Burgoon, Buller, & Floyd, 2001; Burgoon & Floyd, 2000), candidate measures of motivation included preinteraction assessments of importance placed on succeeding with deceit, projecting a positive image, avoiding embarrassment, creating amicable interpersonal relations, conducting a smooth interaction, and keeping discomfort in check, as well as on expectations for interaction ease. Postinteraction measures included sender effortfulness, sender monitoring of self- and partner behavior, and partner and trained coder ratings of sender behavior. Results were voluminous but not supportive of the MIE. Senders who were more motivated tended to be more successful in evading detection (i.e., receivers were less accurate judging the truth or deceit of motivated senders); they reported more conversational normalcy, control, and dominance under both truth and deception; and their nonverbal performance was likewise rated by trained coders as more normal, dominant, and in control than that of less motivated senders. Those who wanted to succeed put out more effort under truth but not deception. Those who expended more effort and were more vigilant were better able to manage their behavior, image, and information and to produce less impaired verbal and nonverbal performances. Furthermore, motivated senders reduced detectability over time. In short, motivation primarily facilitated success. The only findings that might be construed as consistent with the MIE were that those who expected more difficult interactions reported being less truthful, complete, clear, and direct, that is, they engaged in more information management and were less involved, dominant, and controlling of their nonverbal behavior. This would actually fit the MIE if it were not for the fact that this pattern applied to both truthful and deceptive performances. Consequently, a plausible rival interpretation is that both truth tellers and deceivers who expected difficulty during the interaction were less able to fashion a believable presentation on nonverbal and verbal fronts than those who anticipated an easier time of it.

Evidence from Experiments Testing Strategic Communication Interpretations

Other tangential evidence indicating that senders routinely and effectively modulate their nonverbal deception displays invalidates the MIE premise that deceptive nonverbal behavior is largely reactive and beyond conscious control. Greene, O'Hair, Cody, and Yen (1985), for example, found that deceivers increased laughing and smiling—conceivably to mask negative emotions or to promote a positive image—and, when they had time to plan their deceptions, were able to keep their response latencies short. In Buller, Burgoon, Floyd, Chen, Viprakasit, and Grandpre (2004), deceivers reported attempting to control their nonverbal behavior so as to minimize signs of nervousness and maintain a consistent, normal demeanor. They also attempted to manage the interaction itself by encouraging the receiver to talk more, which not only led to receivers unwittingly assisting in the construction of plausible lies but also afforded senders more time to formulate their answers. Other research has shown that deceivers tune in to the feedback from receivers; calibrate their nonverbal performances over time to present a more involved, pleasant, and normal appearing demeanor (Burgoon, Buller, Dillman, & Walther, 1995; Burgoon, Buller, Ebesu, White, & Rockwell, 1996; Burgoon, Buller, White, et al., 1999; White & Burgoon, 2001); and succeed with such performances (see, e.g., Burgoon, Buller, Ebesu, & Rockwell, 1994; Burgoon, Buller, & Guerrero, 1995; Burgoon, Buller, Guerrero, et al., 1994; Seiter, 1997), thus confirming not only that strategic information, image, and behavior management are possible but also likely to succeed. The DePaulo et al. (1992) experiment itself highlights communicators' ability to strategically manipulate behavior in order to achieve desired self-presentations. Participants instructed to appear natural, expressive, or inhibited were able to do so, especially through nonverbal channels. Moreover, judges were less likely to judge such performances as deceptive when enacted by highly expressive senders.

The low detectability associated with the visual channel comports with the contention that senders are inclined to, and skilled in, controlling facial and other visual cues (see, e.g., Ekman & Friesen, 1969; Keeley-Dyreson, Burgoon, & Bailey, 1991). Many of these cues, even though stereotyped as deceptive, are ones that receivers have been least successful in recognizing (see Buller, Stiff, & Burgoon, 1996; Burgoon, Blair, & Strom, 2005; Burgoon & Buller, 1994; Burgoon, Buller, & Woodall, 1996; Fiedler & Walka, 1993 Levine & McCornack, 1996; Riggio & Friedman, 1983). One reason for deceiver success in visual modalities is that the visual medium promotes a sense of familiarity, personalism, and intimacy (see Biocca, 1997; Hart, 1994; Lehtonen, 1988) that feeds into the well-documented truth bias. To the extent that visual cues are among the most controlled cues and can be used to create pseudo-sincerity and intimacy, they should, at minimum, be relatively impervious to motivational impairment and, at best, may promote rather than hinder deception success. Thus, deceivers may be most successful at evading detection when using visual media and least successful when using auditory media. On the flip side, tools aimed at catching liars may work best when directed toward auditory rather than visual cues.

On the verbal front, evidence that senders betray their fabrications, concealments, and equivocations through their verbal content and linguistic choices implies that some aspects of verbal performance are beyond close monitoring by senders or are not facilitated by motivation. Anolli, Balconi, and Ciceri (2003) examined the linguistic maneuvers of deceivers presenting messages to acquiescent versus suspicious receivers. In the former case, deceivers used more ambiguity and verbosity; in the latter, they displayed more concision and ellipsis. Thus, they strategically modified their verbal output according to their audience. Other research supporting IDT (e.g., Buller, Comstock, Aune, & Strzyzewski, 1989; Buller, Strzyzewski, & Comstock, 1991; Burgoon & Buller, 1994; Burgoon, Buller, Floyd, & Grandpre, 1996; Burgoon, Buller, Guerrero, et al., 1996; Burgoon, Buller, White, & Ebesu, 1994) as well as extant interpersonal deception research (e.g., Greene, O'Hair, Cody, & Yen, 1985; Seiter, 1997; Vrij et al., 1996) implies that aspects of both verbal and nonverbal performances can be facilitated under motivation. At the same time, IDT also posits that some verbal and nonverbal features show initial impairment during extended deceptive exchanges, contrary to using a verbal/nonverbal distinction as the basis for separating what might be impaired from what might be facilitated by motivation. Despite arguments in behalf of verbal messages being subject to close scrutiny, planning, and editing, attempted control has often fallen short of the mark. For example, several studies have shown that deceit is revealed through a variety of linguistic cues (see Anolli, Balconi, & Ciceri, 2003; Buller & Burgoon, 1994; Buller, Burgoon, Buslig, & Roiger, 1994, 1996; Burgoon, Blair, Qin, & Nunamaker, 2003; Seiter, 1997; Vrij, 1999, 2000; Vrij & Akehurst, 1998; Zhou, Burgoon, & Twitchell, 2003; Zhou, Twitchell, Qin, Burgoon, & Nunamaker, 2003). As the previously reviewed modality research also showed, detectability tends to improve when verbal information is available, either alone or in combination with nonverbal information; that is, the verbal channel can be somewhat "leaky." This may be because senders are more prone to control obvious and stereotypic aspects of deceit, such as the amount and plausibility of information that is presented, and are less aware of the telltale signs to be found in nonimmediate, indirect, and obfuscating language or the incongruencies among channels (see, e.g., Bavelas, Black, Chovil, & Mullett, 1990; Buller, Burgoon, Buslig, et al., 1994, 1996). Consequently and ironically, linguistic indices may be more susceptible than many nonverbal features to motivational impairment effects. In fact, if one places any stock in the social facilitation literature, then verbal rather than the nonverbal aspects of deception should have been manifesting the most impairment all along because increased arousal debilitates the performance of novel, difficult, or complex tasks, which verbal deception is purported to be (Seiter, 1997; White & Burgoon, 2001). Conversely, increased arousal is expected to facilitate overlearned behavior. To the extent that the nonverbal aspects of conversational routines are fairly automated, we should expect many nonverbal conversational behaviors to be benefited.

Implications for New Technologies

The last speculation argues for focusing more energy in the future on detecting deceit from text communication. The aforementioned work that has already isolated sets of verbal indicators of deceit demonstrates that higher accuracy in detecting deception is possible if attention is focused on the right cues. The advent of automated analysis of text and advanced statistical and data mining techniques (e.g., Hancock, et al., 2005; Qin, Burgoon, & Nunamaker, 2004; Vrij, 1999; Vrij, Akehurst, Soukara, & Bull, in press; Zhou, Burgoon, Twitchell, & Nunamaker, in press) hold promise for augmenting human detection capabilities with computer-based tools that identify constellations of reliable verbal indicators that distinguish between truthful and deceptive messages (Burgoon & Nunamaker, 2004).

Additionally, technological advances such as automated identification of nonverbal behavior, neural network analyses of multimodal and time series deception indicator data, and psycho-physiological measures such as evoked response potentials may enable better detection of strategic behavior and behaviors that deceivers are disinclined to monitor closely. For example, if deceivers engage in more irregular movements or respiration, or their combined verbal and nonverbal output shows incongruities, or thought processes and associated brain waves differ between imagined events and true ones, then it may be possible for future technologies to at least level the playing field if not counteract deceivers' natural advantages. The trend toward more real-time communication may also reintroduce the time pressure and cognitive difficulty that can lead to deceivers choking under pressure and showing the impairments that will make it easier to separate truths from nontruths.

CONCLUSIONS

The MIE has come to be accorded the status of fact rather than conjecture in much recent deception literature. The current analysis reveals such reification to be premature. The extensive empirical data reviewed here, both from the program of research directly pursuing the MIE and from other investigations of deceptive encoding, might better warrant the conclusion that the MIE is illusory. From a communication perspective, the face validity of the MIE is also in question. If trying harder means that people's deceptions become more transparent by enabling detectors to rely on manifest nonverbal cues as a road map, then paradoxically, only disinterested communicators should succeed, whiereas those who intend to succeed should fail. This conclusion flies in the face of most people's personal experience. Anecdotal and experiential evidence cannot substitute for sound experimental evidence, but ultimately, empirical evidence must be reconciled with common experience, which tells us that motivated deception, occurring routinely under conditions where receivers have access to nonverbal cues, eventuates more often in successful than failed performances. Indeed, the dismal record of accurate deception detection implies that deceivers more often than not have success on their side.

Regarding future research on deception detection, three longstanding speculations merit serious pursuit. Based on the evidence that negative emotions interfere with a wide range of behaviors, we should entertain the possibility that, rather than motivation per se causing facilitation or debilitation, the primary sources of impairment reside in negative and extreme forms of arousal, such as those associated with strong emotions like fear and guilt, and cognitive effort, that is, factors identified 2 decades ago in Zuckerman et al.'s (1981) four-factor theory. This would mean that any communication modalities that mitigate high arousal and negative emotional states would give deceivers a further edge.

Further, given the empirical findings that deception detectability is increased by expectancy violations, incongruencies, and/or discrepancies among nonverbal channels (Bond & Atoum, 1999; Buller & Burgoon, 1994, 1996; Burgoon, 1993; Burgoon, Buller, Dillman, et al., 1995; Hubbell, Mitchell, & Gee, 2001; Zuckerman & Driver, 1985), a strong explanation for apparent impairment effects may be that deceptive performances are susceptible to inadequate coordination among the constellation of verbal and nonverbal cues that comprise them and that it is the deviations from a person's normal communicative patterns that hint at something being amiss.

Finally, if IDT's premises are valid that deception displays are transitory and adaptive, temporal patterns must be examined to determine if motivation more often facilitates than debilitates deceptive success.

NOTES

1. Actually explications of the MIE are inconsistent on whether the specific hierarchy is invoked. For example, in DePaulo and Kirkendol (1989), the authors make the statement "Across the seven replications, it doesn't seem to matter much whether you look at just visual nonverbal cues or just vocal nonverbal cues or both at visual and vocal, though in certain individual studies, sometimes one channel works better than others" (p. 60).

2. This conclusion is based on meta-analyses and summaries presented in DePaulo et al. (1980) and Zuckerman et al. (1981) (see, also, Burgoon, Buller, & Woodall (1996) for further elaboration). The analysis in DePaulo et al. (1980) yielded averaged detection accuracy scores of .98 for audio (verbal+vocal), .78 for text (verbal only), .64 for audiovisual (verbal+vocal+visual), .32 for tone of voice (content-filtered audio), .25 for face, and .15 for body. The Zuckerman et al. (1981) analysis yielded average detectability scores of .35 for audio conditions, .34 for audiovisual conditions, .10 for text and -.10 for visual-only. Also reported was an average $\underline{d}$ of 1.09 for all modalities in which speech was present, .43 for the body, and .05 for the face. DePaulo et al. (1983) concluded that detectability should be highest in channels containing verbal information, which includes the audiovisual and audio conditions, and lowest in visual-only (nonverbal) channels. Certainly, combining all conditions in which verbal information is present could lead to this conclusion. Relative to the audio channel, however, the detectability scores for text alone are lower, suggesting that vocalic information may be responsible for the higher detectability in the audio and audiovisual channels. Even though the score for content-filtered tone of voice does not comport with this conclusion, it is possible that additional relevant vocalic information was filtered out in the process, thereby reducing the diagnostic value of vocal information in that condition (see Gregory & Webster, 1996). The two analyses do support concluding that visual deceit by itself is least detectable.

3. Parenthetically the failed manipulation check is further evidence that deciding what might constitute evidence of motivation is anything but straightforward. The authors apparently escaped this pitfall in subsequent research by omitting any checks on whether measured or manipulated variables had any direct or indirect relevance to motivation. At least, none are reported, although DePaulo et al. (1988) mention collecting checks on two motivation manipulations, channel-controlled and competence-relevance motivation (p. 185), but do not report any statistical tests. Other manipulations, however, are tested. For example, DePaulo et al. (1983) provided evidence of the success of their planning manipulation and showed that lies were clearly more deceptive than truths.

4. This particular manipulation of senders pretending to like or agree with the target, pretending to dislike or disagree, and voicing genuine liking–agreement and disliking–disagreement had been employed in previous deception studies (e.g., DePaulo, Jordan, Irvine, & Laser, 1982; DePaulo, Rosenthal, Green, and Rosenkrantz (1982) and had demonstrated that targets and observers could distinguish lies from truths. As a procedure for inducing deception, its validity and success had already been established.

5. An unanticipated finding that also emerged was that women's lies were more detectable than men's in the nonverbal as opposed to the verbal conditions. In later reports (e.g., DePaulo et al., 1988; DePaulo & Kirkendol, 1989), this factor of sender gender is explored in more detail. Here, post hoc analyses also failed to support the contrast specified by Hypothesis 1; they did produce a significant visual-verbal contrast. Whereas the sex combination operationalization had produced the largest difference in detectability in the audio modality (difference between ingratiating and non-ingratiating lies = .52), and the ingratiating lies manipulation had produced the greatest difference in the visual modality (difference between opposite-sex and same-sex target detectability = .42), this test produced

the greatest difference in the audiovisual modality (difference between female and male detectability = .46; other differences ≤ .24).

6. An investigation by DePaulo and Pfeifer (1986) that focused on detection accuracy has some relevance because it included a motivation induction. In brief, groups of recruits in a federal law enforcement training program, experienced officers, and inexperienced undergraduates were compared on their accuracy and confidence in detecting deception. A footnote indicates that motivation was also manipulated (details are omitted) and produced a sex by motivation interaction and a sex by planning by motivation interaction. Accuracy was higher when judging the lies and truths of highly motivated males but also the planned responses of less motivated females and the unplanned responses of highly motivated females. No modality effects were reported; as a result, this investigation does not test Hypotheses 2 or 3 directly. Still, the results do reveal no uniformity in motivation effects that place qualifications on H2 and, regardless of what modality was utilized, cannot be consistent simultaneously with both the verbal-improvement and nonverbal-impairment portions of H1.

7. Interestingly, in DePaulo and Kirkendol (1989), a subset of these results is reproduced showing that attractive senders experienced the least impairment, verbally and nonverbally, when telling ingratiating lies under the high competence-relevance condition. This was interpreted as confirmation of the hypothesis that attractive people suffer the least impairment. This selective reporting, however, ignores all the preceding factors that qualify or reverse that conclusion. The sex factor also failed to produce results consistent with the MIE. Greatest nonverbal detectability for both women and men occurred in the lowest motivation condition (noningratiating and low competence–relevance), followed by the highest motivation condition (ingratiating and high competence–relevance). Male and female patterns diverged on verbal impairment and did not demonstrate a consistent motivation impairment or improvement effect.

8. It may be informative that another investigation using the same motivation manipulation (De-Paulo, Epstein, & LeMay, 1990), but calling it instead "the prospect of interpersonal evaluation," found that only women scoring above the median on social anxiety showed any inhibition in response to the high importance induction. The finding that only a subset of the total sample experienced any form of impairment due to this manipulation implies either that this operationalization was incapable of inducing consistently high motivation or, more likely in light of the current results, that elevated motivation failed to translate into across-the-board impairment. In either case, the results pose a further challenge to the MIE and/or presage difficulties using importance of success as a motivation manipulation. Also perhaps significant is that the "inhibition" took the form of briefer, less detailed, and more innocuous stories. If inhibition is equated with impaired performance, then impairment occurred in the verbal channel, contrary to the hypothesis of verbal improvement. (These results, however, also can be interpreted as consistent with a strategic communication perspective, such that socially anxious individuals resorted to reticence and vagueness as a form of strategic withdrawal and uncertainty under deception.)

9. The MIE research program itself has identified several moderators thought to attenuate (or exacerbate) the effects of motivation on verbal and nonverbal performance. These directions begin to converge on the IDT position in acknowledging that not all motivated deceptive performances are flawed, nor are all individuals equally affected by motivational factors. Indeed, the authors of the MIE have gone to considerable pains to accommodate the MIE position with the substantial research they themselves have generated (e.g., DePaulo, 1992; DePaulo et al., 1992) regarding the positive impacts of self-presentational motivations, attractiveness, social skills, and other social factors on expressive behavior. The MIE position, then, has not advanced in a vacuum nor has it painted an extremist portrait of nonverbal deception displays as inevitably deteriorating with each new dollop of motivation. That said, to the extent that the MIE becomes increasingly qualified in its scope, its potency as a theoretically viable principle also diminishes.

10. Self-reported and partner-reported image management actually only differed between friends and strangers under truth, from which it might be inferred that both relationship types were equally adept (or inept) at managing their image under deception, i.e., motivation did not differentially affect deceptive performance. Even though I am loathe to draw conclusions from nonsignificant findings, the presence of a pattern under truth is suggestive of any linkage between motivation level and performance being more applicable to truthful behavior.

REFERENCES

Anolli, L., Balconi, M., & Ciceri, R. (2003). Linguistic styles in deceptive communication: Dubitative ambiguity and elliptic eluding in packaged lies. *Social Behavior and Personality, 31,* 687–710.

Bavelas, J. B., Black, A., Chovil, N., & Mullett, J. (1990). *Equivocal communication.* Newbury Park, CA: Sage.

Baumeister, R. F. (1984). Choking under pressure: Self-consciousness and paradoxical effects of incentives on skillful performance. *Journal of Personality and Social Psychology, 46,* 610–620.

Biocca, F. (1997, August). The cyborg's dilemma: Progressive embodiment in virtual environments. *Journal of Computer-Mediated Communication, 3*(2). Available http://www.ascusc.org/jcmc/vol3/issue/biocca2.html

Biros, D., Daly, J., & Gunsch, G. (2004). The influence of task load and automation trust on deception detection. *Group Decision & Negotiation.*

Bond, C. F. Jr., & Atoum, A. O. (1999, October). *Deception judgments: Cue theory and beyond.* Paper presented to the annual meeting of the Society for Experimental Social Psychology, St. Louis, MO.

Buller, D. B., & Burgoon, J. K. (1994). Deception: Strategic and nonstrategic communication. In J. A. Daly & J. M. Wiemann (Eds.), *Strategic interpersonal communication* (pp. 191–223). Hillsdale, NJ: Erlbaum.

Buller, D. B., & Burgoon, J. K. (1996). Interpersonal deception theory. *Communication Theory, 6,* 243-267.

Buller, D. B., Burgoon, J. K., Buslig, A., & Roiger, J. (1994). Interpersonal deception: VIII. Further analysis of nonverbal and verbal correlates of equivocation from the Bavelas et al. (1990) research. *Journal of Language and Social Psychology, 13,* 396-417.

Buller, D. B., Burgoon, J. K., Buslig, A., & Roiger, J. (1996). Testing interpersonal deception theory: The language of interpersonal deception. *Communication Theory, 6,* 268–389.

Buller, D. B., Burgoon, J. K, Floyd, K., Chen, X., Viprakasit, R., & Grandpre, J. (2004). *Strategic behavior during deceptive conversation.* Unpublished manuscript.

Buller, D. B., Burgoon, J. K., White, C., & Ebesu, A. S. (1994). Interpersonal deception: VII. Behavioral profiles of falsification, equivocation, and concealment. *Journal of Language and Social Psychology, 13,* 366–396.

Buller, D. B., Comstock, J., Aune, R. K., & Strzyzewski, K. D. (1989). The effect of probing on deceivers and truthtellers. *Journal of Nonverbal Behavior, 13,* 155–169.

Buller, D. B., & Hunsaker, F. (1995). Interpersonal deception: XIII. Suspicion and the truth-bias of conversational participants. In J. Aitken (Ed.), *Intrapersonal communication processes reader* (pp. 237–257). Westland, MI: McNeil.

Buller, D. B., Stiff, J. B., & Burgoon, J. K. (1996). Behavioral adaptation in deceptive transactions: Fact or fiction? *Human Communication Research, 22,* 589–603.

Buller, D. B., Strzyzewski, K. D., & Comstock, J. (1991). Interpersonal deception: I. Deceivers' reactions to receivers suspicions and probing. *Communication Monographs, 58,* 1–24.

Buller, D. B., Strzyzewski, K. D., & Hunsaker, F. G. (1991). Interpersonal deception: II. The inferiority of conversational participants as deception detectors. *Communication Monographs, 58,* 25–40.

Burgoon, J. K. (1993). Interpersonal expectations, expectancy violations, and emotional communication. *Journal of Language and Social Psychology, 12,* 30–48.

Burgoon, J. K., Blair, J. P. (2004). *Effects of communication modality and motivation on deception and its detection.* Manuscript in preparation.

Burgoon, J. K., Blair, J. P., & Moyer, E. (2003, November). *Effects of communication modality on arousal, cognitive complexity, behavioral control and deception detection during deceptive episodes.* Paper presented at the annual meeting of the National Communication Association, Miami, FL.

Burgoon, J. K., Blair, J. P., Qin, T., & Nunamaker, J. F., Jr. (2003). Detecting deception through linguistic analysis. *Proceedings of the Symposium on Intelligence and Security Informatics.* Berlin: Springer-Verlag.

Burgoon, J. K., Blair, J. P., & Strom, R. (2005, January). *Heuristics and modalities in determining truth versus deception.* Paper presented to the 38th annual meeting of the Hawai'i International Conference on System Sciences, [CD-ROM]. Kona, HI.

Burgoon, J. K., & Buller, D. B. (1994). Interpersonal deception: III. Effects of deceit on perceived communication and nonverbal behavior dynamics. *Journal of Nonverbal Behavior, 18,* 155–184.

Burgoon, J. K., Buller, D. B., Dillman, L., & Walther, J. B. (1995). Interpersonal deception: IV. Effects of suspicion on perceived communication and nonverbal behavior dynamics. *Human Communication Research, 22,* 163–196.

Burgoon, J. K., Buller, D. B., Ebesu, A., & Rockwell, P. (1994). Interpersonal deception: Accuracy in deception detection. *Communication Monographs, 61,* 303–325.

Burgoon, J. K., Buller, D. B., Ebesu, A., White, C., & Rockwell, P. (1996). Testing interpersonal deception theory: Effects of suspicion on nonverbal behavior and relational messages. *Communication Theory, 22,* 243–267.

Burgoon, J. K., Buller, D. B., Floyd, K., & Grandpre, J. (1996). Deceptive realities: Sender, receiver, and observer perspectives in deceptive conversations. *Communication Research, 23,* 724–748.

Burgoon, J. K., Buller, D. B., & Floyd, K. (2001). Does participation affect deception success? A test of the inter-activity effect. *Human Communication Research, 27,* 503–534.

Burgoon, J. K., Buller, D. B., & Guerrero, L. K. (1995). Interpersonal deception: IX. Effects of social skill and nonverbal communication on deception success and detection accuracy. *Journal of Language and Social Psychology, 14,* 289–311.

Burgoon, J. K., Buller, D. B., Guerrero, L. K., Afifi, W., & Feldman, C. (1996). Interpersonal deception: XII. Information management dimensions underlying types of deceptive messages. *Communication Monographs, 63,* 52–69.

Burgoon, J. K., Buller, D. B., Guerrero, L. K., & Feldman, C. M. (1994). Interpersonal deception: VI. Effects of preinteractional and interactional factors on deceiver and observer perceptions of deception success. *Communication Studies, 45,* 263–280.

Burgoon, J. K., Buller, D. B., White, C. H., Afifi, W. A., & Buslig, A. L. S. (1999). The role of conversational involvement in deceptive interpersonal communication. *Personality and Social Psychology Bulletin, 25,* 669–685.

Burgoon, J. K., Buller, D. B., & Woodall, W. G. (1996). *Nonverbal communication: The unspoken dialogue* (2nd ed.). New York: McGraw-Hill.

Burgoon, J. K., & Floyd, K. (2000). Testing for the motivation impairment effect during deceptive and truthful interaction. *Western Journal of Communication, 64,* 243–267.

Burgoon, J. K., Kelley, D. L., Newton, D. A., & Keeley-Dyreson, M. P. (1989). The nature of arousal and nonverbal indices. *Human Communication Research, 16,* 217–255.

Burgoon, J. K. & Newton, D. A. (1991). Applying a social meaning model to relational messages of conversational involvement: Comparing participant and observer perspectives. *Southern Communication Journal, 56,* 96–113.

Burgoon, J. K., & Nunamaker, J. F., Jr. (2004). Toward computer-aided support for the detection of deception. *Group Decision and Negotiation.*

Burgoon, J. K., Stoner, G. M., Bonito, J., & Dunbar, N. (2003, January). *Trust and deception in mediated communication.* Proceedings of the 36th Hawai'i International Conference on System Sciences.[CD-ROM]. Los Alamitos, CA: IEEE.

Carlson, J. R., George, J. F., Burgoon, J. K., Adkins, M., & White, C. H. (2004). Deception in computer-mediated communication. *Group Decision & Negotiation, 13*(1), 5–28.

Cronbach, L. J., & Furby, L. (1970). How should we measure change—or should we? *Psychological Bulletin, 74,* 68–80.

Daft, R. L., & Lengel, R. H. (1986). Organizational information requirements, media richness, and structural design. *Management Science, 32,* 554–571.

DePaulo, B. M. (1992). Nonverbal behavior and self-presentation. *Psychological Bulletin, 111,* 203–243.

DePaulo, B. M., Anderson, E., & Cooper, H. (1999, October). *Explicit and implicit deception detection.* Paper presented to the annual meeting of the Society for Experimental Social Psychology, St. Louis, MO.

DePaulo, B. M., Blank, A. L., Swaim, G. W., & Hairfield, J. G. (1992). Expressiveness and expressive control. *Personality and Social Psychology Bulletin, 18,* 276–285.

DePaulo, B. D., Epstein, J. A., & LeMay, C. S. (1990). Responses of the socially anxious to the prospect of interpersonal evaluation. *Journal of Personality, 58,* 623–640.

DePaulo, B. M., Jordan, A., Irvine, A., & Laser, P.S. (1982). Age changes in the detection of deception. *Child Development, 53,* 701–709.

DePaulo, B. M., Kashy, D. A., Kirkendol, S. E., Wyer, M. M., & Epstein, J. A. (1996). Lying in everyday life. *Journal of Personality and Social Psychology, 70,* 979–995.

DePaulo, B. M., & Kirkendol, S. E. (1989). The motivational impairment effect in the communication of deception. In J. Yuille (Ed.), *Credibility assessment* (pp. 51–70). Deurne, Belgium: Kluwer.

DePaulo, B. M., Kirkendol, S. E., Tang, J., & O'Brien, T.P. (1988). The motivation impairment effect in the communication of deception: Replications and extensions. *Journal of Nonverbal Behavior, 12,* 177–202.

DePaulo, B.M., Lanier, K., & Davis, T. (1983). Detecting the deceit of the motivated liar. *Journal of Personality and Social Psychology, 45,* 1096–1103.

DePaulo, B. M., LeMay, C. S., & Epstein, J. A. (1991). Effects of importance of success and expectations for success on effectiveness at deceiving. *Personality and Social Psychology Bulletin, 17,* 14–24.

DePaulo, B. M., & Pfeifer, R. L. (1986). On-the-job experience and skill at detecting deception. *Journal of Applied Social Psychology, 16,* 249–267.

DePaulo, B. M., Rosenthal, R., Green, C. R., & Rosenkrantz, J. (1982). Diagnosing deceptive and mixed messages from verbal and nonverbal cues. *Journal of Experimental Social Psychology, 18,* 433–446.

DePaulo, B. M., Stone, J. I., & Lassiter, G. D. (1985a). Deceiving and detecting deceit. In B. R. Schlenker (Ed.), *The self and social life* (pp. 323–370). New York: McGraw-Hill.

DePaulo, B. M., Stone, J. I., & Lassiter, G. D. (1985b). Telling ingratiating lies: Effects of target sex and target attractiveness on verbal and nonverbal deceptive success. *Journal of Personality and Social Psychology, 48,* 1191–1203.

DePaulo, B. M., Zuckerman, M., & Rosenthal, R. (1980). Detecting deception: Modality effects. In L. Wheeler (Ed.), *Review of personality and social psychology* (pp. 125–162). Beverly Hills, CA: Sage.

Dunbar, N. E., Ramirez, A., Jr., & Burgoon, J. K. (2003). Interactive deception: Effects of participation on participant-receiver and observer judgments. *Communication Reports, 16,* 23–33.

Ekman, P. (1981). Mistakes when deceiving. *Annals of the New York Academy of Sciences, 364,* 269–278.

Ekman, P., & Friesen, W. V. (1969). Nonverbal leakage and clues to deception. *Psychiatry, 32,* 88–105.

Ekman, P., & O'Sullivan, M. (1991). Who can catch a liar? *American Psychologist, 46,* 913–920.

Ekman, P., O'Sullivan, M., Friesen, W. V., & Scherer, K. (1991). Invited article: face, voice, and body in detecting deceit. *Journal of Nonverbal Behavior, 15,* 125–136.

Exline, R., Thibaut, J., Hickey, C., & Gumpert, P. (1970). Visual interaction in relation to Machiavellianism and an unethical act. In R. Christie & R. Geis (Eds.), *Studies in Machiavellianism* (pp. 53–75). New York: Academic Press.

Feeley, T. H. (1996). Exploring sanctioned and unsanctioned lies in interpersonal deception. *Communication Research Reports, 13,* 164–173.

Fiedler, K., & Walka, I. (1993). Training lie detectors to use nonverbal cues instead of global heuristics. *Human Communication Research, 20,* 199–223.

Foppa, K. (1995). On mutual understanding and agreement in dialogues. In I. Marková, C. Graumann, & K. Foppa (Eds.), *Mutualities in dialogue* (pp. 149–175). Cambridge, UK: Cambridge University Press.

Furedy, J. J., & Ben-Shakhar, G. (1991). The roles of deception, intention to deceive, and motivation to avoid detection in the psychophysiological detection of guilty knowledge. *Psychophysiology, 28,* 163–171.

George, J. F., Marett, K., & Tilley, P. (2004, January). *Deception detection under varying electronic media and warning conditions.* Proceedings of the 37th Hawai'i International Conference on System Sciences.[CD-ROM]. Los Alamitos, CA: IEEE.

Gilbert, D. T., Krull, D. S., & Malone, P. S. (1990). Unbelieving the unbelievable: Some problems in the rejection of false information. *Journal of Personality and Social Psychology, 59,* 601–613.

Gilbert, D. T., & Osborne, R. E. (1989). Thinking backward: Some curable and incurable consequences of cognitive busyness. *Journal of Personality and Social Psychology, 57,* 940–949.

Gilbert, D. T., Pelham, B. W., & Krull, D. S. (1988). On cognitive busyness: When person perceivers meet person perceived. *Journal of Personality and Social Psychology, 54,* 733–740.

Gilbert, D. T., Tafarodi, R. W., & Malone, P. S. (1993). You can't not believe everything you read. *Journal of Personality and Social Psychology, 65,* 221–233.

Graumann, C. F. (1995). Commonality, mutuality, reciprocity—A conceptual introduction. In I. Markovà, C. F. Graumann, & K. Foppa (Eds.), *Mutualities in dialogue* (pp. 1–24). Cambridge, UK: Cambridge University Press.

Greene, J. O., O'Hair, H. D., Cody, M. J., & Yen, C. (1985). Planning and control of behavior during deception. *Human Communication Research, 11,* 335–364.

Gregory, S. W., & Webster, S. (1996). A nonverbal signal in voices of interview partners effectively predicts communication accommodation and social status perceptions. *Journal of Personality and Social Psychology, 70,* 1231–1240.

Grice, P. (1989). *Studies in the way of words.* Cambridge, MA: Harvard University Press.

Hancock, J. T., Curry, L., Goorha, S., & Woodworth, M. (2005). *Automated linguistic analysis of deceptive and truthful synchronous computer-mediated communication.* Paper presented to the 38th Hawai'i International Conference on System Sciences, Kona, HI.

Harris, C. W. (Ed.). (1963). *Problems in measuring change.* Madison, WI: University of Wisconsin Press.

Hartwig, M., Granhag, P. A., Stromwall, L. A, & Andersson, L. O. (2004). Suspicious minds: Criminals' ability to detect deception. *Psychology Crime & Law, 10,* 83–95.

Hocking, J. E., & Leathers, D. G. (1980). Nonverbal indicators of deception: A new theoretical perspective. *Communication Monographs, 47,* 119–131.

Hubbell, A. P., Mitchell, M. M., & Gee, J. C. (2001). The relative effects of timing of suspicion and outcome involvement on biased message processing. *Communication Monographs, 68,* 115–132.

Keeley-Dyreson, M. P., Burgoon, J. K., & Bailey, W. (1991). The effect of stress on decoding kinesic and vocalic communication. *Human Communication Research, 17,* 584–605.

Keppel, G. (1991). *Design and analysis: A researcher's handbook* (3rd ed.). Englewood Cliffs, NJ: Prentice-Hall.

Koper, R. J., & Miller, G. R. (1991, February). *Bluffing as deceptive communication.* Paper presented to the annual meeting of the Western States Communication Association, Phoenix, AZ.

Koper, R. J., & Sahlman, J. M. (1996). *The behavioral correlates of real-world deceptive communication.* Unpublished manuscript.

Krauss, R. M. (1981). Impression formation, impression management, and nonverbal behaviors. In E. T. Higgins, C. P. Herman, & M. P. Zanna (Eds.), *Social cognition: The Ontario symposium* (Vol. 1, pp. 323–341). Hillsdale, NJ: Erlbaum.

Kruglanski, A. (1989). *Lay epistemics and human knowledge: Cognitive and motivational bases.* New York: Plenum.

Lehtonen, J. (1988). The information society and the new competence. *American Behavioral Scientist, 32,* 104–111.

Levine, T. R., & McCornack, S. A. (1996). A critical analysis of the behavioral adaptation explanation of the probing effect. *Human Communication Research, 22,* 575–588.

Levine, T., R., Park, H. S., & McCornack, S. A. (1999). Accuracy in detecting truths and lies: Documenting the veracity effect. *Communication Monographs, 66,* 125–144.

Marett, L. K., & George, J. F. (2004. Deception in the case of one sender and multiple receivers. *Group Decision and Negotiation, 13*(1), 29–44.

McCornack, S. A. (1997). The generation of deceptive messages: Laying the groundwork for a viable theory of interpersonal deception. In J. O. Greene (Ed.), *Message production: Advances in communication theory* (pp. 91–126). Mahwah, NJ: Erlbaum.

McCornack, S. A., & Levine, T. R. (1990). When lovers become leery: The relationship between suspicion and accuracy in detecting deception. *Communication Monographs, 57,* 219–230.

McCornack, S. A., & Parks, M. R. (1986). Deception detection and relationship development: The other side of trust. In M. McLaughlin (Ed.), *Communication yearbook 9* (pp. 377–389). Beverly Hills, CA: Sage.

Miller, G. R., & Stiff, J. B. (1993). *Deceptive communication*. Thousand Oaks, CA: Sage.

Mosier, K. L., Skitka, L. J., Heers, S. & Burdick, M. D. (1997). Patterns in the use of cockpit automation. In M. Mouloua & J. Koonce (Eds.), *Human-automation interaction: Research and practice* (pp. 167–173). Hillsdale NJ: Erlbaum.

Muir, B. M. (1994). Trust in automation: Part I. Theoretical issues in the study of trust and human intervention in automated systems. *Ergonomics, 39,* 1905–1922.

Park, H. S., & Levine, T. R. (2001). A probability model of accuracy in deception detection experiments. *Communication Monographs, 68,* 201–210.

Pedhazur, E. J. (1997). *Multiple regression in behavioral research* (3rd ed.). New York: Holt, Rinehart & Winston.

Postmes, T., Spears, R., & Lea, M. (1998). Breaching or building social boundaries? SIDE-effects of computer-mediated communication. *Communication Research, 25,* 689–715.

Qin, T., Burgoon, J. K., & Nunamaker, J. F., Jr. (2004). An exploratory study on promising cues in deception detection and application of decision trees. *Proceedings of the 37th Hawai'i International Conference on System Sciences.* Los Alamitos, CA: IEEE.

Riggio, R. E., & Friedman, H. S. (1983). Individual differences and cues to deception. *Journal of Personality and Social Psychology, 45,* 899–915.

Rogosa, D. R., & Willett, J. B. (1983). Demonstrating the reliability of the difference score in the measurement of change. *Journal of Educational Measurement, 20,* 335–343.

Rommetveit, R. (1974). *On message structure: A framework for the study of language and communication.* New York: Wiley.

Schul, Y., & Burnstein, E. (1998). Suspicion and discounting: Ignoring invalid information in an uncertain environment. In J. M. Golding & C. M. MacLeod (Eds.), *Intentional forgetting: Interdisciplinary approaches* (pp. 321–348). Mahwah, NJ: Erlbaum.

Seiter, J. S. (1997). Honest or deceitful? A study of persons' mental models for judging veracity. *Human Communication Research, 24,* 216 259.

Short, J., Williams, E., & Christie, B. (1976). *The social psychology of telecommunications.* London: Wiley.

Skitka, L. J., Mosier, K. L., & Burdick, M. (2000). Accountability and automation bias. *International Journal Human-Computer Studies, 52,* 701–717.

Stiff, J. B., Corman, S., Krizek, B., & Snider, E. (1994). Individual differences and changes in nonverbal behavior: Unmasking the changing faces of deception. *Communication Research, 21,* 555–581.

Stiff, J. B., Kim, H. J., & Ramesh, C. (1992). Truth biases and aroused suspicion in relational deception. *Communication Research, 19,* 326–345.

Stiff, J. B., & Miller, G. R. (1986). "Come to think about it . . .": Interrogative probes, deceptive communication, and deception detection. *Human Communication Research, 12,* 339–357.

Stiff, J.B., Miller, G.R., Sleight, C., Mongeau, P., Garlick, R., & Rogan, R. (1989). Explanations for visual cue primacy in judgments honesty and deceit. *Journal of Personality and Social Psychology, 56,* 555–564.

Vrij, A. (1999, October). *Combining verbal and nonverbal measures to detect deceit: An experimental laboratory study and a case study of a convicted murderer.* Paper presented at the annual meeting of the Society for Experimental Social Psychology, St. Louis, MO.

Vrij, A. (2000). *Detecting lies and deceit: The psychology of lying and its implications for professional practice.* Chichester, UK: Wiley.

Vrij, A., & Akehurst, L. (1998). Verbal communication and credibility: Statement validity assessment. In A. Memon, A. Vrij, & R. Bull (Eds.), *Psychology and law: Truthfulness, accuracy and credibility* (pp. 3–26). Maidenhead, UK: McGraw-Hill.

Vrij, A., Akehurst, L., Soukara, S., & Bull, R. (in press). Detecting deceit via analyses of verbal and nonverbal behavior in children and adults. *Human Communication Research.*

Vrij, A., Semin, G., & Bull, R. (1996). Insight into behavior displayed during deception. *Human Communication Research, 22,* 544–562.

Wallbott, H. G. (1995). Congruence, contagion, and motor mimicry: Mutualities in nonverbal exchange. In I. Marková, C. Graumann, & K. Foppa (Eds.), *Mutualities in dialogue* (pp. 82–98). Cambridge: Cambridge University Press.

Walther, J. B., & Parks, M. R. (2002). Cues filtered out, cues filtered in. In M. L. Knapp & J. A. Daly (Eds.), *Handbook of interpersonal communication* (3rd ed.; pp. 529-563). Thousand Oaks, CA: Sage.

White, C. H., & Burgoon, J. K. (2001). Adaptation and communicative design: Patterns of interaction in truthful and deceptive conversations. *Human Communication Research, 27,* 9–37.

Woodworth, M., Hancock, J., & Goorha, S. (2005, January). *The motivational enhancement effect: Implications for our chosen modes of communication in the 21st century.* Paper presented to the 38th Hawai'i International Conference on System Sciences, Kona, HI.

Zajonc, R. B. (1980). Compresence. In P. B. Paulus (Ed.), *Psychology of group influence* (pp. 35-60). Hillsdale, NJ: Erlbaum.

Zhou, L., Burgoon, J. K., & Twitchell, D. (2003). A longitudinal analysis of language behavior of deception in e-mail. *Proceedings of the Symposium on Intelligence and Security Informatics.* [CD-ROM]. Berlin: Springer-Verlag.

Zhou, L., Burgoon, J. K., Twitchell, D., & Nunamaker, J. F., Jr. (2004). Automating linguistics-based cues for detecting deception in text-based asynchronous computer-mediated communication. *Group Decision & Negotiation, 13,* 31–36.

Zhou, L., Twitchell, D., Qin, T., Burgoon, J. K., & Nunamaker, J. F., Jr. (2003). An exploratory study into deception detection in text-based computer-mediated communication. *Proceedings of the 36th Hawai'i International Conference on System Sciences.* [CD-ROM]. Los Alamitos, CA: IEEE.

Zuckerman, M., DePaulo, B. M., & Rosenthal, R. (1981). Verbal and nonverbal communication of deception. In L. Berkowitz (Ed.), *Advances in experimental social psychology* (Vol. 14, pp. 1–59). New York: Academic Press.

Zuckerman, M., & Driver, R. E. (1985). Telling lies: Verbal and nonverbal correlates of deception. In A. W. Siegman & S. Feldstein (Eds.), *Multichannel integrations of nonverbal behavior* (pp. 129–147). Hillsdale, NJ: Erlbaum.

CHAPTER CONTENTS

4   Inoculation Theory of Resistance to Influence at Maturity: Recent Progress In Theory Development and Application and Suggestions for Future Research

JOSHUA A. COMPTON
MICHAEL PFAU
University of Oklahoma

Inoculation theory boasts a dynamic history since McGuire first introduced it in the early 1960s. The last decade, in particular, has been a period of explosive growth for inoculation. Research has offered a more nuanced understanding of how inoculation confers resistance, exploring precise workings of inoculation's core concepts of threat and counterarguing in conjunction with concepts drawn from other theoretical domains, including issue involvement, attitude accessibility, self-efficacy, and affect. Research is also extending practical applications of inoculation, examining new uses in marketing, public relations, politics, and adolescent health campaigns. The purpose of this chapter is to review the classic work on inoculation theory, examine recent developments that inform the workings of inoculation and its applications, and suggest directions for future research. The chapter also suggests extending the application of inoculation into the areas of childhood obesity, body image, gang activity, consumer protection, and employee satisfaction, among others.

It has been more than a decade since Eagly and Chaiken christened inoculation "the grandparent theory of resistance to attitude change" (1993, p. 561). This label could lead one to regard inoculation as an antiquated theory—a wise sage in the legend of persuasion research, but now poised to enter a dormant phase of retirement. On the contrary, perhaps running parallel to the active lifestyles of today's seniors, this "grandparent theory" is not inactive or sedentary. Instead, inoculation theory continues to grow prodigiously. In fact, during the

Correspondence: Joshua A. Compton, Department of Communication, Southwest Baptist University, Bolivar, MO 65613; email: jcompton@sbuniv.edu

Communication Yearbook 29, pp. 97–145

last decade, inoculation scholarship has exploded, taking off in two distinct ways. First, research has ventured further into the inner mechanisms responsible for inoculation's effectiveness, exploring precise workings of inoculation's core concepts of threat and counterarguing in conjunction with concepts drawn from other theoretical domains, including issue involvement, attitude accessibility, self-efficacy, and affect. Findings have contributed to greater nuance about how inoculation works and, therefore, enabled greater precision in its use. Second, research is extending practical applications of inoculation, examining new uses in marketing, public relations, adolescent health campaigns, and politics. More than ever, scholars understand the process of resistance and the viability of inoculation in a number of important realms.

There is much more to understand about how inoculation works. Pfau (1997) called for more research "to enrich the construct, providing greater precision in its use" (p. 134). Even though researchers have heeded these calls, shedding light on once mysterious aspects of the inoculation process and venturing into exciting new domains, the calls continue to inspire future resistance investigations. Inoculation theory may have reached maturity, but research examining the workings of the theory and its applications has, if anything, accelerated. This "grandparent theory" remains spry, and a dormant retirement is not on its horizon.

To explore future possibilities for inoculation research in the communication discipline, we first provide an overview of extant inoculation research, tracing the development of the inoculation construct from its introduction in the early 1960s. Next, we review some of the more important theoretical findings about the basic model of resistance before turning our attention to practical applications of inoculation in commercial advertising, public relations, political campaigns, and adolescent health campaigns. We conclude with recommendations for future inoculation research, including both theoretical development and proposed new applications for inoculation in the contexts of health and consumer behaviors and self-persuasion.

THE INOCULATION EXPLANATION OF RESISTANCE

In the early 1960s, social psychologist McGuire took an about-face. Up to this point, McGuire had worked "on the side of the persuaders" (McGuire, 1970, p. 36). He was not alone. Persuasion research from the 1920s up to this point had looked almost exclusively at how to persuade more effectively (Pfau, 1997), and persuasion had been "treated almost exclusively as a facilitator of change" (Miller & Burgoon, 1973, p. 6). Concerned by this void in persuasion research, McGuire redirected his research program in an attempt to understand how to confer resistance to influence (McGuire, 1970).

According to McGuire's (1964) inoculation theory, individuals can be inoculated against future attitude attacks much the same way individuals can be inoculated against future viral attacks. Just as a biological inoculation injects a weakened version of a virus to enable that person to build resistance against future attack, McGuire (1964) posited that an attitudinal inoculation warns the individual of an impending attitudinal attack (generating explicit threat) against an existing yet vulnerable attitude and presents and then refutes weakened counterattitudinal arguments (triggering implicit threat and providing preemptive refutation) to build attitude resistance.

McGuire's theory had an impressive start, and inoculation was a shot in the arm for persuasion research. The next section reviews the precedence and basic assumptions of the theory.

Origins of Inoculation Theory

Research exploring the relative effectiveness of one-sided versus two-sided persuasive messages was a precursor to the inoculation construct, including a classic study by Lumsdaine and Janis (1953). They found that providing both sides to an issue—counterarguments and refutations of these counterarguments— is comparably effective to a one-sided message in influencing attitudes, but that the two-sided approach confers greater resistance to subsequent persuasive attempts. The authors surmised that the two-sided version offers the recipient "an advance basis for ignoring or discounting the opposing communication and, thus 'inoculated,' the recipient will tend to retain the positive conclusion" (Lumsdaine & Janis, 1953, p. 318). Evidently, presenting both sides of an argument had powerful effects on recipients of these messages. Why?

McGuire's inoculation research program offered an answer. Building on the idea that one can be inoculated against influence attempts, McGuire based his original inoculation theory on the biological analogy of immunization. McGuire (1964) explained:

> In the biological situation, the person is typically made resistant to some attacking virus by pre-exposure to a weakened dose of the virus. This mild dose stimulates his defenses so that he will be better able to overcome any massive viral attack to which he is later exposed, but it not so strong that this pre-exposure will itself cause the disease. (p. 200)

Throughout his research program, McGuire and his colleagues continually referenced this analogic foundation (Anderson & McGuire, 1965; McGuire, 1961a, 1970; McGuire & Papageorgis, 1961, 1962) and called for a closer scrutiny of the biological analogy as a springboard for future inoculation research (McGuire & Papageorgis, 1962).

The biological analogy provides the explanatory underpinning for inoculation theory. McGuire (1961a) not only established it as a point of theoretical origin, but he also invited a careful comparison. For example, in noting the analogous effects of time and subsequent decay (described more thoroughly later in this essay), McGuire (1964) argued, "The parallel is not surprising since the analogy between the mechanisms in the two situations was our theoretical point of departure" (p. 222).

Thus, McGuire argued that the analogy is more than mere decoration; it is a vital, meaningful basis of the inoculation theory. It is, in the words of Eagly and Chaiken (1993), both "clever and valid" (p. 568).

In summary, inoculation theory is both explained and inspired by an analogic comparison with medical inoculation. In contrast with typical persuasion research that offered methods to better influence, inoculation constitutes a preemptive strategy. Indeed, inoculation theory supports the medical adage that "prevention is the best medicine."

Core Elements of Inoculation: Threat and Refutational Preemption

Early in his research program, McGuire surmised that threat played a pivotal role in conferring resistance (McGuire, 1962; McGuire & Papageorgis, 1961). An underlying assumption about the process of inoculation was that a receiver must feel that an existing belief is threatened to motivate the work needed to strengthen an attitude. There must be a catalyst to resistance. McGuire proposed that this catalyst was threat, conceptualized as the recognition of impending challenges to attitudes, which triggers a perception of the vulnerability of attitudes to potential change.

McGuire's early inoculation research assumed threat was initiated by the mere presence of counterarguments in the inoculation pretreatment message. He posited that the realization that there were counterarguments to one's position would be enough to prompt the process of bolstering the attitude (McGuire, 1961a; McGuire & Papageorgis, 1961; Papageorgis & McGuire, 1961), or be "defense-stimulating" (McGuire, 1964, p. 202). This recognition of the vulnerability of attitudes has been described as "shock value" (McGuire, 1961a)—the realization that an existing attitude is not yet immune from attack.

Later, McGuire and Papageorgis (1962) introduced forewarning as additional extrinsic threat, positing that forewarning would work in conjunction with the intrinsic threat of realizing there were counterarguments to one's position, enhancing the process of inoculation. McGuire and Papageorgis (1962) found that the addition of extrinsic threat (i.e., forewarning) did enhance immunity, but that the combination of extrinsic and intrinsic threat was more effective than either one alone (McGuire & Papageorgis, 1962).

Without generated threat, inoculation treatments do not confer optimal resistance (McGuire, 1962, 1964; McGuire & Papageorgis, 1961, 1962; Pfau & Burgoon, 1988; Pfau, Kenski, Nitz, & Sorenson, 1990; Pfau, Van Bockern, & Kang, 1992; Pfau et al., 1997a), whether threat is lessened due to a lack of forewarning (McGuire & Papageorgis, 1962) or by prior reassurance that others are in agreement about the attitude's validity (Anderson & McGuire, 1965). Threat is the key component of inoculation (Pfau et al., 1997a) because inoculation works to build resistance "mostly by increasing people's motivation to defend . . . beliefs" (Petty & Cacioppo, 1986, p. 115). Pfau (1997) considered threat to be "the most distinguishing feature of inoculation" (p. 137). Simply stated, inoculation is impossible without threat (McGuire, 1962; Pfau, 1997; Pfau et al., 1992). Researchers have speculated that threat alone may be enough to confer resistance (Wyer, 1974), and some research has supported this assumption (Freedman & Sears, 1965; Kiesler & Kiesler, 1964). However, McGuire and Papageorgis (1962) found that, although forewarning confers resistance, forewarning alone is not as effective as forewarning accompanied by refutational preemption.

Refutational preemption "provides specific content that receivers can employ to strengthen attitudes against subsequent change" (Pfau et al., 1997a, p. 188). McGuire assumed this process, termed "covert counterarguing," was the active cognitive element in resistance (Eagly & Chaiken, 1993, p. 564). The preemptive refutation component of an inoculation treatment is thought to promote counterarguing in two ways: It provides the specific content to be used in refuting the attitude attack, and it offers guided practice in the act of counterarguing (Wyer, 1974). Insko (1967) insisted that inoculation's ability to generate counterarguments "is crucial for the theory since . . . resistance supposedly results from the accumulation of belief-bolstering material" (p. 302).

McGuire and his colleagues operationalized counterarguing in only one of their inoculation studies. In that study, Papageorgis and McGuire (1961) gave participants 5 minutes to write down as many arguments as they could come up with that supported their beliefs after reading the attack message. Papageorgis and McGuire (1961) found no significant difference in counterarguing output between those receiving a refutational treatment and those in the no treatment (control) condition. This method of operationalizing and assessing counterarguing is questionable, however, in that participants are actually indicating bolstering, not counterarguing, material (Benoit, 1991; Wyer 1974).

No other study in McGuire's research program operationalized counterarguing. "McGuire provided no evidence that his motivational or informational pretreatments . . . increased the ability and willingness of people to counterargue against persuasive attacks" (Smith, 1982, pp. 294–295). However, more contemporary research has found support for the dynamic role of counterarguing in resistance (e.g., Cacioppo, 1979; Petty & Cacioppo, 1986).

The conventional explanation is that inoculation treatments build an arsenal of argumentation, a process motivated by the acceptance of attitude vulnerability. The threat–counterargument conventional explanation has been supported by a series of empirical studies that have operationalized threat and counterarguing output (Pfau, 1992; Pfau & Burgoon, 1988; Pfau et al., 1990, 1992, 1997a, 2001a, 2004a, 2004b; Pfau, Park, Holbert, & Cho, 2001b).

Boundary Conditions for Inoculation Theory

To recreate the "germ free" environment consistent with the medical analogy on which inoculation is based, McGuire elected to limit his research program to issues he termed *cultural truisms*. Cultural truisms "are beliefs that are so widely shared within the person's social milieu that he would not have heard them attacked, and indeed, would doubt that an attack were possible" (McGuire, 1964, p. 201). Early inoculation research therefore, explored such issues as attitudes toward brushing teeth, whether mental illness is contagious, the benefits of the then-new drug penicillin, and use of X-rays to detect tuberculosis (McGuire, 1964). Even though this approach approximated the biological analogy, it also significantly limited the theory's boundaries and its potential applications (Ullman & Bodaken, 1975).

In some respects, it is ironic that inoculation was supposedly limited to noncontroversial topics—a perception that persisted for decades (e.g., Benoit, 1991). The precursor to inoculation, one- versus two-sided message research, often used highly controversial messages, such as the call near the end of World War II for an extended American occupation of Japan (Hovland, Lumsdaine, & Sheffield, 1949). Nonetheless, early inoculation research remained limited to cultural truisms.

McGuire toyed with the idea of framing inoculation more broadly. He reasoned that most beliefs were overprotected because "people tend to defend their beliefs by avoiding exposure to counterarguments rather than by developing positive supports" (1961a, p. 184). Even though cultural truisms were the best exemplar of an overprotected belief, selective exposure insured that most beliefs were overprotected to some degree and, hence, candidates for inoculation. As selective exposure continued to be challenged during the 1960s, however, McGuire viewed a broad conceptualization of inoculation theory as unnecessarily risky. As he explained:

> The questionable empirical status of selective-avoidance as a psychological mechanism made it an unattractively risky assumption on which to base our inoculation studies. If our subjects have not in fact avoided belief-dissonant information on controversial issues, the analogy with biological inoculation would fail. To circumvent this problem, we restricted our experiments on conferring resistance to . . . cultural truisms, with respect to which we would expect the requisite aseptic ideological environment to prevail (Anderson & McGuire, 1965, p. 46).

Later, Pryor and Steinfatt (1978) offered a rationale to extend inoculation beyond just cultural truisms. Their justification for applying inoculation to controversial issues differed from McGuire's original musings, however. When McGuire considered more expansive boundaries for inoculation theory, he reasoned that, because of the tendency of people to invoke selective avoidance in confronting opposing arguments on controversial issues, almost all beliefs are overprotected. By contrast, Pryor and Steinfatt (1978) argued for extending the boundaries of inoculation theory on the grounds that almost no beliefs are overprotected. They maintained that "In the biological case, there are no cultural truisms. . . . What is required is that . . . beliefs in question must not have been attacked by *a particular* virus, not that they must never have been attacked" (1978, p. 219). Therefore, they reasoned that McGuire's biological analogy applied to specific content that might be covered in an inoculation treatment as opposed to the general topic area. Pryor and Steinfatt's (1978) study failed to support the efficacy of inoculation with middle or higher beliefs; however, their rationale that the biological analogy applied to "a *particular* virus" opened the door to inoculation's use with controversial topics.

Subsequent research indicated that inoculation's promise was not limited only to cultural truisms, that the refutational preemption component of inoculation was effective even with highly charged topics. Crane was the first to study the efficacy of inoculation with controversial issues: the treatment of juvenile delinquency and U.S. recognition of "Communist China" (Crane, 1962). This was followed by a spate of studies in the 1970s, all of them featuring controversial issues, including politicians' responsiveness to their constituents (Adams & Beatty, 1977); adopting additional texts for a college class (Burgoon et al., 1976, Burgoon & King, 1974); limiting college admission to juniors and seniors (Burgoon & Chase, 1973); legalizing heroin (Burgoon, Cohen, Miller, & Montgomery, 1978; Miller & Burgoon, 1979); allowing men free entry to women's dorms (Cronen & LeFleur, 1977); an oil company inoculating against U.S. Federal Trade Commission (FTC) attacks (Hunt, 1973); federal control of public education (McCroskey, 1970; McCroskey, Young, & Scott, 1972); commercial advertising (Sawyer, 1973); mandating airbags in cars (Szybillo & Heslin, 1973); and mandating that all students live on campus (Ullman & Bodaken, 1975).

Almost all of inoculation studies since the 1970s have employed controversial issues, including animal testing (Nabi, 2003); banning handguns, legalizing marijuana, legalizing gambling, and restricting television violence (Pfau et al., 1997a, 2001a, 2003, 2004a; Pfau, Holbert, Zubric, Pasha, & Lin, 2000); or have been carried out in controversy-laden contexts like politics (An & Pfau, 2004b; Lin, 2000; Pfau & Burgoon, 1988; Pfau et al., 1990; Pfau, Holbert, Szabo, & Kaminski, 2002); public relations (Burgoon, Pfau, & Birk, 1995; Wan & Pfau, 2004); marketing campaigns (Compton & Pfau, 2004a); academic misconduct (Compton & Pfau, 2004b); adolescent alcohol use (Godbold & Pfau, 2000); commercial advertising (Pfau, 1992); and adolescent smoking (Pfau & Van Bockern, 1994; Pfau, Van Bockern, & Kang, 1992; Szabo, 2000).

If the nature of the content employed in inoculation doesn't impose boundary conditions for inoculation theory, what does? In the next section, under "Individual Differences," we will argue that receiver issue involvement is a precondition for threat and, therefore, determines the boundary conditions for inoculation theory.

Important Research Findings about the Basic Model

Refutational versus supportive defenses. Early research compared the effectiveness of two types of attitude defenses: refutational and supportive. Supportive treatments simply provide reasons for holding an attitude, whereas refutational treatments feature arguments contrary to initial attitudes and refutations of those arguments (McGuire, 1961a, 1962, 1964; McGuire & Papageorgis,

1962; Papageorgis & McGuire, 1961). Supportive treatments constitute a bolstering strategy. Their effectiveness is entirely dependent on whether the recipient was sufficiently motivated to generate more reasons for holding the attitude (McGuire, 1964).

With refutational treatments, however, attitudes are inoculated because the recipient is motivated to generate additional refutations by the mere presence of counterarguments or the explicit forewarning of an impending attitude challenge. Attitudes are also inoculated because of the refutational preemption content, which provides the specific substance a recipient can use to refute arguments opposing attitudes and which provides exemplars of the counterarguing process.

Early research on inoculation found that, although supportive treatments are able to initially bolster attitudes, this effect is short-lived in that these treatments typically are not very effective in protecting attitudes against subsequent attacks. Findings consistently revealed that refutational treatments are superior to supportive treatments in conferring resistance (Anderson & McGuire, 1965; Crane, 1962; McGuire, 1961a, 1962, 1964; McGuire & Papageorgis, 1961; Suedfeld & Borrie, 1978). Subsequently, the refutational treatment became the prototypical inoculation message.

Nonetheless, recent research reveals that people tend to prefer bolstering and are more inclined to use it to protect attitudes. When presented with multiple strategies for safeguarding attitudes, people overwhelmingly chose bolstering over counterarguing, source derogation, negative affect, and other tactics, despite the fact that counterarguing proved to be much more effective in conferring resistance (Jacks & Cameron, 2003). It appears that the primacy of a refutational strategy over a supportive–bolstering approach in protecting attitudes, a finding so overwhelmingly documented in research, has not yet changed the way in which ordinary people attempt to protect their attitudes from change.

Same and Different Treatments

Early research also examined the type of counterarguments employed in an inoculation treatment: refutational same or different–novel. Same inoculation treatments raise and refute the same arguments contained in the subsequent attack message, whereas different, or novel, inoculation treatments bring up and refute different arguments than those featured in a subsequent attack. In this sense, the inoculation-different treatment consists of generic content.

Inoculation research has consistently demonstrated that inoculation works using both same and different inoculation treatments (McGuire, 1961a, 1962, 1964; McGuire & Papageorgis, 1962; Papageorgis & McGuire, 1961; Pfau, 1992; Pfau & Burgoon, 1988; Pfau et al., 1990, 1997a, 2001a, 2003, 2004b). With inoculation-same messages, the content provided in the message carries the load, whereas with inoculation-different treatments, threat motivates the generation of additional supporting reasons for holding the attitude (McGuire, 1962; McGuire, 1964). This ability of inoculation to confer resistance to novel counterarguments is important because it means that inoculation against a limited number of counter-arguments affords protection against all possible counterarguments. As Pfau and Kenski (1990) argued, "If the construct were limited to preemptive refutation, it would afford limited utility since communicators would need to prepare specific preemptive messages corresponding to each and every anticipated attack" (p. 75). Inoculation provides much more utility than this. A single inoculation message confers a blanket of protection against potential attacks.

Active Versus Passive Defenses

Early research also explored how people process inoculation treatments: actively or passively. Researchers' operationalized active treatments as requiring the recipient to write essays explaining their responses to counterarguments presented in the inoculation treatment message and passive defenses as simply asking participants to read an essay that brings up and refutes the counterarguments (Manis & Blake, 1963; McGuire, 1961b, 1964; McGuire & Papageorgis, 1961; Rogers & Thistlethwaite, 1969).

Researchers assumed that active defenses, because they feature participation in attitude defenses, would afford greater resistance.McGuire and Papageorgis (1961), however, found that the passive conditions resulted in stronger immunity against persuasive attacks. They speculated that the active conditions were too difficult because participants were likely unpracticed in defending their attitudes. Additionally, they reasoned that the arguments participants came up with on their own were likely inferior to those prepared by the experimenter and encountered in the attack message (Wyer, 1974).

Other research found that active treatments, passive treatments, and combinations of the two (active–passive, passive–active) all contribute to resistance to influence. There were, however, subtle differences. Passive treatments were superior when a subsequent attack contained the same arguments, whereas active approaches were better when the attack contained different arguments (McGuire, 1961b). Passive treatments were superior in the short term, but they deteriorated and, as a result, active approaches were better following a 2-day interval between treatment and attack (Rogers & Thistlethwaite, 1969). The superiority of active defenses used in conjunction with refutational-different treatments makes sense because they achieve resistance via the motivational catalyst triggered by the threat element of an inoculation treatment rather than by the specific content contained in the refutational preemption component of the message. The superiority of active defenses following a delay between treatment and attack is understandable because delay affords sufficient time for recipients to generate counterarguments, which is essential in eliciting resistance (Insko, 1967).

Role of Time in Resistance

Timing of inoculation treatments and subsequent attacks. There are two issues of timing that are important in the inoculation process: the time required for the generation of counterarguments and the persistence of inoculation's protection over time. The first is treated as a timing issue, whereas the latter is considered an issue of decay. Both issues are relevant to the question of the optimal interval between administration of an inoculation message and exposure to a subsequent persuasive attack.

McGuire (1964) suspected that, once motivated to strengthen an existing attitude in the face of an anticipated persuasive attack, an individual would need time to come up with additional supporting reasons for holding the attitude. As McGuire (1964) noted, this is consistent with the biological analogy because a medical inoculation also requires time after the initial dosage of weakened virulent material for the body to develop the strongest resistance. This explanation is supported by research indicating that resistance requires, or is enhanced by, a delay following the forewarning (Freedman & Sears, 1965; Hass & Grady, 1975; McGuire, 1964; Petty & Cacioppo, 1979, 1986). On the other hand, an inoculation treatment, much like any message, loses effectiveness over time (McGuire, 1962; Pfau, 1997; Pfau et al., 1990; Pryor & Steinfatt, 1978), and a person's motivation to accumulate additional defenses also decays in time (McGuire, 1962). Insko explained the apparent tradeoff. He observed that, in the period following threat, the individual produces attitude-bolstering content, thus facilitating resistance. Eventually, however, as "induced motivation" declines, "the individual ceases to accumulate belief-bolstering material . . . , [dropping] off over time like the ordinary forgetting curve" (1967, p. 316).

These processes appear to work at cross purposes, at least in the intermediate term, suggesting a curvilinear relationship involving the interval between inoculation and subsequent attack and the capacity of an inoculation message to elicit counterarguing and, therefore, to confer resistance. Research, however, has shed very little light on the question about the optimal interval between treatment and attack.

McGuire's own research program manipulated the time between treatment and the subsequent attack to be nearly immediate (e.g., McGuire, 1961a), or a span of a few days (e.g., McGuire & Papageorgis, 1961; McGuire, 1961b, 1966). Later research employed longer durations and found that inoculation's effects were robust, sustaining themselves for weeks (Pfau & Burgoon, 1988; Pfau et al., 1990, 2004a) and even months (Pfau & Van Bockern, 1994). One study that focused specifically on counterarguing reported that counterarguing output elicited by inoculation treatments was "amazingly stable" across time: It did not increase in the days immediately after treatment and it didn't decay for up to 6 weeks following inoculation (Pfau et al., 2004b). The question as to the optimal interval between administration of inoculation treatments and exposure to a subsequent attack is still unresolved.

Another issue relevant to timing is whether there is a difference in the capacity of same or different inoculation treatments to sustain counterarguing effects and, therefore, resistance, across time. This issue has proven less equivocal. Results of early inoculation research revealed that, compared to inoculation-same treatments, inoculation-different messages increased in effectiveness following a modest delay between treatment and persuasive attack (Manis & Blake, 1963; McGuire, 1964) and experienced less decay over time (McGuire, 1962, 1964, 1966; Pryor & Steinfatt, 1978). These studies featured relatively short intervals between treatment and attack, typically 2 to 7 days. Two later studies of inoculation in political campaigns found that inoculation-different treatments uniquely extended resistance effects, but only when the subsequent attack focused on character content (Pfau & Burgoon, 1988; Pfau et al., 1990). Finally, a recent study examined the capacity of inoculation treatments to generate counterarguing output and found inoculation-same messages to be superior immediately following treatment, but because they decayed steadily over time, inoculation-different messages proved to be best at moderate and longer intervals between treatment and attack (Pfau et al., 2004b).

Booster sessions. With medical inoculations, boosters are sometimes used after an initial inoculation to strengthen the bodies' defenses against viral attack. If the medical analogy holds, booster messages should enhance attitude resistance just as they enhance biological inoculation. In the attitudinal inoculation context, a booster session would further bolster the attitude strengthened by the initial inoculation treatment message, presumably by once again raising counterattitudinal arguments and refutations of these arguments. With both medical and attitudinal inoculations, it is reasonable that the initial treatment will decay with time.

Results here have been mixed. McGuire (1961b) found that double defenses only enhance resistance when the same counterarguments are employed in the treatment and booster sessions as appear in the subsequent attitude attack, whereas Tannenbaum, Macaulay, and Norris (1966) found that concept boost messages conferred greater resistance, although the enhancement fell just short of statistical significance. Pfau and colleagues (2004b) found reinforcement messages sustained counterarguing output up to a month-and-a half following exposure to an inoculation treatment, but did not appreciably boost resistance levels. Other studies have found limited impacts, if any, of booster sessions (Pfau et al., 1990, 1992, 1997a; Pfau & Van Bockern, 1994). These studies suggest that additional inoculation treatments, in the form of reinforcement or booster messages, do not enhance resistance, at least not in the form or with the timing employed so far.

However, we should not conclude that reinforcements either are not needed or do not work. This would be counterintuitive because messages decay in time and, therefore, need to be reinforced. The null findings for booster messages reported above likely stem from a failure, at least to date, to identify optimal timing for administration of booster sessions (Pfau et al., 2004b).

Role of Message Source and Communication Modality

Message source and communication form or modality also should impact the capacity of inoculation treatments to confer resistance. Surprisingly, few studies have addressed these factors in resistance.

Message source. Source credibility has been one of the most studied variables in research on persuasion (Eagly & Chaiken, 1993), with its origins in the first treatises on persuasion offered by Aristotle (Solmsen, 1954). Ironically, with the exception of early efforts to use congruity theory as an explanation for inoculation's effectiveness, source credibility has been largely ignored as an active variable in resistance research.

Shortly after McGuire initially formulated inoculation theory, Tannenbaum and colleagues suggested an alternative explanation for resistance effects in proposing congruity theory. Tannenbaum and Norris (1965) reasoned that because incongruity, or inconsistency, between a receiver's perception of a message source and that source's assertion about an attitude object is a precondition for attitude change, that "any means of reducing the degree of incongruity in such a situation [via use of such strategies as source derogation, denial, or prior strengthening of the concept] serves to reduce the degree of attitude change" (p. 147). Tannenbaum and colleagues tested this alternative logic in studies that paralleled McGuire's methodology. These studies found that refutational messages instill resistance to persuasive attacks and offered evidence that source factors were mainly responsible for message effectiveness (Tannenbaum, 1967; Tannenbaum et al., 1966; Tannenbaum & Norris, 1965). Their research suggests message source perception plays a role in resisting persuasive attempts.

Other studies accepted the underlying rationale of inoculation but focused on the role of source factors in resistance. Stone (1969) explored whether perceived credibility of the source of a persuasive attack would impact the efficacy of inoculation strategies with source-oriented participants. Even though he found that source derogation conferred resistance, he did not find the expected differences among source- and message-oriented participants. Whether one is more predisposed to assess persuasive messages based on their source or the content of their messages, when a source's image is derogated, resistance is enhanced.

Pfau and Kenski (1990) reported on the results of inoculation in two political campaigns. The studies featured standard inoculation messages (same and different), but they varied the form of the persuasive attacks, some emphasizing issue content and some stressing character content, thus placing the primary focus of the message on the source of the attacks. Results indicated that inoculation conferred resistance to both issue and character attacks, but that there were subtle differences between the two across time. At shorter intervals between treatment and attack, inoculation-same treatments were more effective in deflecting character as opposed to issue attacks. At longer intervals, however, inoculation-same treatments were better with issue attacks whereas inoculation-different messages were superior with character attacks.

Finally, An and Pfau (2004a) examined the role of source credibility in inducing resistance to candidate attacks in political campaigns during the midterm 2002 U. S. Congressional election campaign. The results indicated that credibility mediated inoculation's effectiveness. More positive perceptions of the credibility of the source of an inoculation message on the dimensions of expertise and trustworthiness enhanced the effectiveness of treatments whereas less positive perceptions on these dimensions undermined effectiveness. The authors concluded that communicators would benefit from concerted efforts to establish a strong base of credibility prior to initiating an inoculation strategy (An & Pfau, 2004a).

Extant research indicates that perceived source credibility impacts resistance to influence, though only a few studies have focused on these variables in inoculation research. There remains much to learn about how the perceptions of source credibility impact the inoculation process of resistance.

Communication modality. Until the 1990s, all inoculation research featured print messages. More recent resistance research has employed other communication forms, or modalities, especially video (e.g., An, 2003; Godbold, 1998; Nabi, 2003; Pfau et al., 1992; Szabo, 2000). The most intricate examination of the effects of communication modality in resistance, however, is provided by the research of Pfau, Holbert, and colleagues (2000).

Pfau, Holbert, et al. (2000) examined whether the form of an inoculation treatment (print versus video) altered the process of resistance. Previous research indicated print is more likely to generate active message processing (Chaiken & Eagly, 1976, 1983; Petty & Cacioppo, 1986), whereas video, a passive medium (Chesebro, 1984; Graber, 1987), is less likely to elicit more passive processing. With this rational, researchers posited that print inoculation treatments would trigger more active cognitive processing in receivers and, therefore, generate more counterarguing output and, as a result, prove more effective in conferring resistance. Contrary to prediction, the researchers found that both video and print inoculation treatments conferred resistance with equal effectiveness. Furthermore, video inoculation treatments elicited more counterarguing output, although differences fell just short of statistical significance.

In addition, researchers posited that, because video stresses images over words (Chesebro, 1984; Meyrowitz, 1985; Salomon, 1987), it would elevate the role and impact of source factors in resistance. This prediction was supported. Indeed, the most important finding of this study was not that video and print inoculation treatments confer resistance, but rather that they go about it in different ways. The process each used to achieve resistance varied significantly. Print inoculation treatments required a number of days for resistance to build and peaked at about the time participants encountered a persuasive attack. Print relied on message content to achieve resistance and, therefore, effects were delayed. By contrast, video treatments triggered an immediate bolstering impact, which was sustained up until the time people encountered a persuasive attack. In addition, video treatments accomplished resistance through source cues, with much less reliance on the specific content of the message to provide resistance.

Individual Differences

A number of individual difference variables have been examined in inoculation research. Some variables, such as issue involvement, play an integral role in the process of resistance and inform the boundaries of the theory. Others, like self-efficacy and gender, simply moderate the extent to which inoculation treatments foster resistance.

Issue involvement. Following up previous research that found involvement may function as a precondition to resistance to influence (Pfau, 1992), Pfau, Tusing, and colleagues (1997a) investigated the role that issue involvement plays in resistance. They conceptualized *issue involvement* as "the importance or salience of an attitude object for a receiver" (p. 190). This definition is consistent with Zaichkowsky's (1985) *personal involvement* construct as it applies to policy issues and embodies what Johnson and Eagly (1989) call *outcome-relevant involvement* and what Petty and Cacioppo (1979) term *issue involvement*.

Pfau et al. (1997a) found that greater involvement promotes resistance and that it functions independently of threat. In contrast to the conventional explanation of threat directly motivating counterarguing, their investigation indicated that only involvement exerted a direct impact on counterarguing. Supporting an earlier finding by Pfau (1992) that involvement was a precondition to resistance, at least in the commercial realm, and other studies suggesting strong associations between involvement and counterarguing (Cacioppo, 1979; Kamins & Asseal, 1987; Papageorgis, 1968; Petty & Cacioppo, 1977; 1979, 1986), Pfau et al. (1997a) argued that "involvement holds the key to inoculation's terrain" (p. 210). They reasoned that, for inoculation to work, issue involvement levels must be optimal. Involvement levels need to be sufficient so that, when people discover in an inoculation treatment that their attitudes are vulnerable to challenges, they will care enough to engage in the active process of counterarguing (Wyer, 1974). Levels cannot be too great, however, or people would already be aware that their attitudes are vulnerable to challenge and alert to opposing messages. In such circumstances, an inoculation message would be unable to motivate them further or to trigger additional counterarguing.

Other studies indicate that involvement plays an active role in resistance (Chen, Reardon, Rea, & Moore, 1992; Petty & Cacioppo, 1977, 1986; Romero, Agnew, & Insko, 1996). Pfau, Compton, and colleagues (2004a) further explored the role of involvement in inoculation. The researchers found that receiver involvement is a dynamic element in resistance, increasing following inoculation and subsequently affecting a number of the other key variables in the process of resistance. Whereas Pfau et al. (2001a) inexplicably detected no significant relationship between initial involvement level and threat, Pfau et al. (2004a) clarified the relationship between threat and involvement. They revealed that elicited threat enhances base involvement levels, thus indicating a synergetic relationship between the two variables. Further, the study revealed that elicited involvement directly enhances counterarguing output, thus facilitating resistance. Together, involvement and threat trigger the process that unleashes resistance. Finally, a study by Pfau et al. (2003) reported that involvement was positively associated with attitude accessibility and that both facilitated resistance.

Self-efficacy. Self-efficacy, or a person's confidence in dealing with challenges, affects responses to threats (Bandura, 1983). Thus, Pfau, Szabo, and colleagues (2001a) posited that self-efficacy would impact the inoculation process of resistance. Their results indicated that self-efficacy does moderate resistance, but the effects depend on the type of inoculation treatment. With affective-anger inoculation messages, self-efficacy enhanced resistance. With cognitive inoculation appeals, however, results revealed a curvilinear pattern, with moderate levels of self-efficacy conferring the most resistance. Inoculation messages that elicit happiness conferred the most resistance when self-efficacy was low.

Gender. Receiver gender has been studied extensively in persuasion, but much less so in resistance. Gender, along with age and self-esteem, was identified as strategic by McGuire (1969, p. 247) because of "the relatively high quantity and quality of research devoted to [it]." Much of the early persuasion research featuring gender emphasized persuasibility. Two meta-analyses (Cooper, 1979; Eagly & Carli, 1981), which statistically combine all relevant experiments in order to integrate their findings, concluded that women are more persuasible than men. Eagly & Carli (1981, p. 10) concluded that "[w]hen probabilities were combined across studies, significant differences were obtained: Males were less influenced than females." Differences in persuasibility, of course, have a direct bearing on the influence of attack messages and, therefore, suggest implications for the ability of inoculation messages to confer resistance.

The few inoculation studies that included gender in their designs suggest subtle differences between men and women. Stone (1969) found on overall differences between men and women in the ability of inoculation messages to confer resistance, although he reported that women were significantly more affected than men by source, as opposed to message, appeals. Also, Dean, Austin, and Watts (1971) reported an interaction involving forewarning and sex. They found that the forewarning of a persuasive message worked to inhibit attitude change for males but to facilitate change with females.

In two studies set in a political context, Pfau and Burgoon (1990) and Pfau et al. (1990) examined the extent to which gender may moderate inoculation effectiveness. Pfau and Burgoon (1990) found that inoculation conferred resistance with both male and female receivers, but treatments rendered males more resistant than females following exposure to a political attack, thus supporting the persuasibility finding described above that men are less susceptible than women to persuasive appeals. An interaction, however, revealed even more nuance. For females, inoculation-same treatments were superior with character as opposed to issue attacks, whereas inoculation-different messages were equal in effectiveness with both attack types. With males, however, different treatments were superior in deflecting character in contrast to issue attacks, whereas same messages were equally effective with both attack approaches. The authors concluded that these findings confirm the greater sensitivity of women to source considerations in inoculation and that it may require more specific information to alter women's, as opposed to men's, perceptions about source credibility.

Pfau and Kenski (1990) confirmed that the influence of source credibility in the process of resistance is more pronounced for female than male receivers. Results did not confirm the triple interaction reported by Pfau and Burgoon (1990), but did affirm part of their findings. Pfau and Kenski (1990) revealed that inoculation-same treatments were superior in conferring resistance with women, whereas inoculation-different messages were better with men. They concluded that, "since women are more sensitive to 'person concerns' (Eagly, 1978; Gilligan, 1982), it requires more specific information to alter their judgments about candidate credibility" (1990, p. 150).

Other receiver considerations. There is limited research in the impact of other individual difference variables in resistance. Pfau and Kenski (1990) reported that age plays a minor role in inoculation. Inoculation-same messages were more effective with middle-aged and older receivers, but results were limited to only one dependent variable, a single dimension of source credibility. Receiver education, by contrast, played a more integral role in resistance. Pfau and Kenski (1990) indicated that inoculation optimizes resistance with more educated receivers, perhaps because they can more effectively use the counterarguing content offered in inoculation treatments. In addition, results revealed subtle differences involving inoculation message type. A double interaction indicated that inoculation-different treatments elicited greater resistance with less educated receivers, whereas inoculation-same messages were superior with moderately educated receivers.

In summary, inoculation research has added useful nuance to the basic model proposed by McGuire and his colleagues, probing supportive and refutational defenses, same and different treatment approaches, active and passive defenses, the role of time in resistance, the influence of source credibility and communication modality in inoculation, and the potentially mediating impact of a various individual-difference variables in the process of resistance. In the next section, we review research that has ventured beyond the basic inoculation model of threat and counterarguing.

Research Expanding the Basic Inoculation Model

This section examines alternative explanations for the way inoculation confers resistance. These explanations are best viewed as expanding the basic model in that they are additive more than competing. They function to enrich inoculation theory, suggesting that the process of resistance is more intricate than had been previously assumed.

Role of affect in resistance. Early inoculation research focused on purported cognitive processes employed during the process of resistance, featuring inoculation treatments that were predominantly rational. An exception was Crane (1962), who warned that "conclusions concerning immunization may need to differentiate between cognition and affect" (p. 449). For the most part, however, early theorizing and research on inoculation simply assumed that the process of resistance was cognitive.

However, more recent research has introduced the role of emotion in the context of inoculation. Lee and Pfau (1997) were the first to explore the relative efficacy of cognitive and affective inoculation messages. They prepared inoculation treatments and attack messages that were designed to elicit both positive and negative emotions as well as messages that were based on reason. Cognitive treatment messages contained facts and rational arguments, whereas affective treatment messages relied on anecdotes and affect-laden language.

They predicted that the cognitive messages would confer the most resistance and that negative inoculation messages would be superior to positive messages in conferring resistance. Their reasoning was based on research findings indicating that negative affect promotes more active, mindful message processing (Bless, Bohner, Schwarz, & Strack, 1990; Schwarz, Bless, & Bohner, 1991), whereas positive affect triggers more passive, less mindful processing (Bohner, Crow, Erb, & Schwarz, 1992; Schwarz, et al., 1991). As predicted, the cognitive treatments promoted the most resistance. They also found that both affective-positive and affective-negative treatments conferred resistance to cognitive attacks. Although Lee and Pfau's (1997) investigation constituted an important first step in understanding the role of affect in resistance, their affect manipulations were weak. Participants receiving affect-based inoculation messages did not report significantly more affect than those receiving cognitive messages.

To follow up Lee and Pfau's (1997) findings, Pfau, Szabo, and colleagues (2001a) compared the relative effectiveness of cognitive, affective-anger, and affective-happiness inoculation treatments. In an attempt to improve on the affect manipulations of Lee and Pfau, these researchers followed Lazarus's (1991) appraisal theory. Appraisal theory is based on goal-attainment. Individuals have a positive response when their environment facilitates goal attainment and a negative response whenever their environment thwarts efforts. Pfau et al. (2001a) constructed affective-happiness messages to suggest to readers that an existing attitude promotes goal attainment and affective-anger messages to imply that the counterarguments contained in anticipated persuasive attacks would impede goal attainment.

All inoculation treatment conditions conferred resistance to subsequent attitude attacks, and all inoculation treatment conditions elicited counterarguing. Additionally, the three treatment conditions also conferred resistance indirectly, with cognitive treatments eliciting threat and enhancing counterarguing and affective-anger and affective-happiness inoculation treatments conferring resistance based more on elicited emotional responses. As predicted, anger-inducing inoculation treatment messages elicited the most threat, generating more counterarguments and greater resistance. "Experienced anger facilitates, whereas experienced happiness undermines, resistance to the influence of persuasive attacks" (Pfau et al., 2001a, p. 244).

In addition to comparing the relative efficacy of cognitive messages versus anger and happiness inoculation messages, Pfau, Szabo, and colleagues (2001a) examined the role and impact of elicited affect in resistance. The resistance process had been assumed to be highly cognitive, in which counterarguing was the lynchpin of resistance. Pfau et al. (2001a), however, found that the process of resistance is also highly emotional. Elicited emotion, particularly anger, made significant contributions to resistance. The cognitive and affective-anger inoculation treatments, working through elicited threat, generated anger, which provided a sizable boost to resistance. No inoculation treatments directly elicited happiness (other variables impacted happiness), and elicited happiness served to undermine resistance to persuasive attacks.

Zuwerink and Devine (1996) and Jacks and Devine (2000) also revealed an active role for affect in resistance. The studies did not inoculate, but employed forewarning in conjunction with a brief delay. Both studies found that, with participants who score low in attitude importance (a dimension of attitude strength), resistance is achieved through both cognitive and affective means. Affect was operationalized in these investigations as irritation, which is akin to elicited anger, as described above.

Building on this foray into the potential impacts of affect in resistance, Nabi (2003) examined the impact of emotionally evocative visuals on the process of resistance. Nabi used the topic of animal research testing, using video-based inoculation treatments and attack messages. Nabi found that the visual treatment messages did elicit emotional responses, and that treatments with consistent affect visual components (those composed of messages with high affect counterargument with corresponding high affect refutation content or low affect counterargument and corresponding low affect refutation content) conferred resistance to a subsequent attack message. However, to the extent that there was inconsistency in the affect visuals (e.g., low affect visuals in the counterargument portion followed by high affect visuals in the refutation portion of the inoculation treatment message), treatments failed to confer resistance.

Nabi's results indicate that both emotion and visuals play important roles in the process of resistance. In addition, her results support the importance of matching affect intensity between counterarguments and refutations contained in inoculation treatments.

Attitude Accessibility as an Explanation for Resistance

Pfau, Roskos-Ewoldsen, and colleagues (2003) posited attitude accessibility as an alternative mechanism for the way inoculation confers resistance. Accessibility, or the retrieval of an attitude from memory (Fazio, 1986, 1995; Fazio, Chen, McDonel, & Sherman, 1982; Fazio, Powell, & Herr, 1983; Roskos-Ewoldsen, 1997), is a product of associative pathways connecting memory nodes. Attitudes that connect objects with evaluations are brought to the surface when a linked node is activated. Pfau et al. (2003) confirmed that inoculation enhances the accessibility of the attitude toward the featured issue, which increases attitude strength, and in time, confers resistance to a subsequent attitude attack.

Pfau, Compton, and colleagues (2004a) further explored the role of attitude accessibility in the process of resistance. As with Pfau et al. (2003), Pfau et al. (2004a) found that attitude accessibility plays in important role in resistance. Results revealed that inoculation treatments elicit threat (and threat enhances base involvements levels) and attitude certainty, and that these variables, over time, contribute to attitude accessibility, which fosters resistance to persuasive attacks. Time is a critical factor in this process in that the attitude accessibility effects do not fully materialize until 3 to 5 weeks following inoculation. Finally, the pattern of results also revealed that counterarguing and attitude accessibility constitute distinct routes to resistance, but that they have a common point of origin in that elicited threat and involvement trigger both. Thus, accessibility is an alternative explanation for the way that inoculation confers resistance, but it is more of an overlapping, than a competing, explanation for resistance.

Research indicating instrumental roles of affect and attitude accessibility in the process of resistance confirm Insko's (1967) premonition, offered nearly 40 years ago, that there is more at work in inoculation than simply the core mechanisms of threat and counterarguing. Furthermore, the structural equation modeling results of recent studies continue to identify unaccounted for, direct paths between inoculation and resistance to persuasive attacks, even after accounting for affect (Pfau et al., 2001a) and accessibility (Pfau et al., 2004a). Clearly, more research needs to be done in order to understand fully the process of resistance to influence unleashed by an inoculation treatment.

Next, we offer an overview of applications of inoculation. The next section examines practical applications of inoculation in the contexts of commercial advertising, public relations, political campaigns, and adolescent health campaigns.

Applications of Inoculation

Commercial advertising. In the early 1990s, inoculation was extended to a new domain: commercial advertising. Specifically, the research looked at inoculation in the context of comparative advertisements—those that explicitly compare the benefits of one product in comparison to another. Levy (1987) estimated in the late 1980s that nearly half of all commercial advertisements were comparative. Even though previous advertising research had examined the effectiveness of two-sided and refutational messages in advertising (Bither, Dolich, & Nell, 1971; Hunt, 1973; Sawyer, 1973; Szybillo & Heslin, 1973), this research failed to assess threat, and threat is a prerequisite for inoculation (McGuire, 1962; Pfau, 1997; Pfau et al., 1992). Pfau (1992) studied comparative advertisements, examining the effects of involvement and message format. Receiver product involvement was conceptualized as the "relevance or salience of the product class for receivers" (Pfau, 1997, p. 144) and format was conceptualized in terms of "style and directionality of the comparative" (p. 144). Pfau found that inoculation confers resistance to comparative advertisements, but only with higher involving products. Pfau (1992), however, reported relatively low levels of elicited threat in this investigation, probably because of the generally low-involving nature of the products featured in the study.

Over a decade later, inoculation was examined in a new commercial advertising domain, predatory marketing. Compton and Pfau (2004a) examined the potential use of inoculation to confer resistance to predatory credit card marketing to college students. Even though the researchers found only minimal impacts of inoculation treatments on college students' attitudes toward credit card debt, they detected significant changes in behavioral intentions, including intent to apply for credit cards and efforts to pay down debt. Also, Compton and Pfau (2004a) reported that inoculation exposure motivated students to talk about credit card issues with one another, thus significantly increasing the likelihood that they would tell others negative things about credit cards. This finding is particularly intriguing, as inoculation may be even more powerful than previously thought. It not only has an impact on those directly exposed to an inoculation message, but also travels through a network of interpersonal interactions.

In summary, inoculation is a powerful strategy in commercial advertising. For advertisers, inoculation can preempt the damage caused by rival campaigns, but it can also aid consumers, acting as a useful strategy for enabling consumers to resist targeted marketing campaigns. Arming consumers with an arsenal of argumentation does not ensure they will resist the pull of advertising, but it does make sure they aren't caught unprepared.

Public relations. Inoculation's first foray into public relations featured an intricate study of Mobil Oil Corporation's ongoing issue advertising campaign (Burgoon et al., 1995). Mobil's campaign was extensive, but little was known about its effectiveness. In this regard, Mobil's issue-advocacy campaign was not unique. Reid, Soley, & Vanden Bergh (1981) concluded that "little is known about the actual effects of advocacy advertising on audience members" (p. 310). Burgoon et al (1995) reasoned that most issue advertising campaigns, and Mobil's campaign in particular, attempt to bolster supporters' attitudes more than to convert opponents. Their investigation supported this assessment. Rather than persuade people, Mobil's issue advocacy campaign inoculated supporters against subsequent attacks. The most successful campaigns are those perceived as other-benefit efforts.

More recently, Wan and Pfau (2004) explored the potential of inoculation in another public relations domain, crisis communication. All organizations are vulnerable to crises (Coombs, 1998); organizations therefore need to take proactive steps to protect their image (Druckenmiller, 1993). Most research on organizational image has stressed post-hoc strategies to repair image damage (e.g., Benoit & Lindsey, 1987; Blaney, Benoit, & Brazeal, 2002; Brinson & Benoit, 1996, 1999). Wan and Pfau (2004) compared preemptive approaches to protect organizations in the event of a crisis. They compared image promotion, a strategy that closely resembles bolstering message in the resistance literature, and inoculation.

An image-promotion approach seeks to foster positive attitudes about an organization, generating a reservoir of good will that can serve as a buffer against attitude slippage in the event of a crisis. In contrast, inoculation would acknowledge an organization's potential vulnerabilities in the context of likely crisis scenarios, and then it would provide preemptive refutation based on what the organization is doing to avert this possibility (Wan & Pfau, 2004). The study predicted that both approaches, in combination, would best protect an organization, but if only one approach were used, inoculation would be superior to image promotion in the event of a crisis. Wan and Pfau (2004) compared these approaches examining public attitudes toward a petroleum company. They compared image promotion, inoculation-same and different, and a combined image-promotion and inoculation approach against a control (no message) condition. Later, some participants were exposed to a hypothetical crisis. Results indicated that all approaches were effective in protecting the organization from attitude slippage following exposure to a crisis. In the absence of a crisis, however, the image promotion approach was slightly superior in maintaining positive organizational image, thus intimating a potential downside to inoculation (Wan & Pfau, 2004).

Political campaigns. Inoculation's effectiveness in protecting attitudes from the influence of persuasive attacks was extended to the political realm for the first time by Pfau and Burgoon (1988).

Candidates tend to rely on three basic strategies in political campaigns: bolstering, which seeks to builds name recognition and image; attack, which attempts to generate negative perceptions of an opponent's record, character, or positions on the issues; and refutation, which consists of a post-hoc answer or refutation of an opponent's attack (see Kaid & Davidson, 1986; Trent & Friedenberg, 1983). Pfau and Burgoon (1988) offered a fourth strategy: inoculation.

In their extensive field experiment during a 1986 U.S. Senatorial campaign, they found that inoculation is an effective political campaign strategy for "undermining the potential influence of the source of political attacks, deflecting the specific content of political attacks, and reducing the likelihood that political attacks will influence receiver voter intention" (1988, pp. 105–106). The results of the study indicated that inoculation is an effective strategy for deflecting the damage that can be done via candidate attacks and that it is the only strategy for preempting attacks initiated late in a campaign.

In 1988, Pfau and colleagues (1990) examined inoculation delivered via direct mail during a presidential campaign. The pattern of results indicated that inoculation was effective in using this communication venue as well, whether the persuasive attack message contained same or different arguments. This investigation also compared inoculation to post-hoc refutation, in which a candidate answers a political attack immediately after it is launched. The results revealed that both approaches were effective, but that inoculation was superior, particularly with strong party identifiers and with nonidentifiers. With weak party identifiers, inoculation's superiority was limited to character attacks.

In short, these studies indicated that inoculation is a viable political campaign strategy. Inoculation hurts candidates who go negative, both in terms of attitudes toward the sponsor and intentions to vote for the sponsor, and it protects supportive attitudes toward the target of the attacks, both in terms of character judgments and issues (Pfau & Burgoon, 1988; Pfau et al., 1990). Inoculation works with all receiver groups, although it is generally more effective with strong party identifiers (Pfau & Burgoon, 1988; Pfau et al., 1990). Inoculation's effectiveness in political contexts is particularly remarkable considering that these studies involved only one inoculation treatment administered during the course of communication-intense political campaigns (Szabo & Pfau, 2002).

Political inoculation research up to this point had been limited to effects about candidates, as opposed to system-based consequences of political advertising, such as people's interest in election campaigns, their knowledge of candidates and their positions, and their likelihood of voting. Recognizing this void, Pfau et al. (2001b) studied whether inoculation could reduce system-based consequences of party- and PAC-sponsored issue advertising. Spending on issue advertising exceeds what is spent on candidate advertising (Wyatt, 2000). The Pfau et al. (2001b) findings were mixed, but encouraging. Those inoculated against party-sponsored advertising were less likely to manifest slippage in awareness and interest in campaigns, exhibited greater knowledge of the candidates, and were more likely to vote. The authors (Pfau et al., 2001b, p. 2395) concluded that inoculation may offer "an antidote to the system-based consequences of issue advertising."

Two recent investigations of inoculation in political campaigns focused on the 2002 midterm election. One study (An & Pfau, 2004a) examined the source credibility of inoculation messages in the previously unexplored context of television advertising. Noting the increasing prevalence of attack advertising (Ansolabehere, Iyengar, Simon, & Valentino, 1994; Jamieson, 1996; Kaid & Johnston, 1991; Kern, 1989; Pfau & Kenski, 1990; Taylor, 1986; West, 1997), and its potential draconian effects, particularly with nonaffiliated voters (Ansolabehere & Iyengar, 1995; Pfau, et al., 2002), An and Pfau (2004a) focused on inoculation's potential to protect candidates from the influence of attacks and to bolster democratic values. The study also explored the impact of source credibility on the inoculation process, a construct that has received limited attention in recent resistance studies. An and Pfau (2004a) found that inoculation protects attitudes against attack advertising, with maximum resistance occurring when the source of the inoculation message is perceived as high credibility. In addition, inoculation protects participatory attitudes. Compared to controls, inoculated participants who later received a political attack ad were more likely to manifest participatory behaviors. They were more inclined to: contribute to campaigns, volunteer for campaigns, proselytize on behalf of candidates, and go to the polls and vote.

In another study, An and Pfau (2004b) examined the viability of inoculation to protect against candidate attacks launched in televised political debates. Results revealed that after viewing a televised political debate, compared to control participants who were not inoculated prior to viewing the debate, inoculated viewers displayed more positive macroattitudes toward their candidate and more positive perceptions of that candidate's competence and character.

Though not explicitly political, Lin's (2000) investigation of inoculation and the spiral of silence theory holds particular promise for enhancing participatory democracy. Spiral of silence theory explains the impact of perception of majority opinion on the expression of minority opinion: Those holding a minority opinion remain silent for fear of isolation. Lin's (2000) study explored whether inoculation could reduce this fear of isolation, thereby freeing people who hold minority views to express them. He found that inoculation was an effective strategy to enhance attitude strength, freeing people from the oppressive constraints described by the spiral of silence.

Inoculation is a particularly viable strategy for political campaigning. It protects candidates from candidate attacks, whether they are launched in televised ads, debates, or other venues. Other strategies are post-hoc and, at best, ameliorate only a small part of the damage that can be inflicted via an attack (Pfau et al., 1990). Hence, Republican political consultant Innocenzi declared, "Inoculation and pre-emption are what win campaigns" (cited in Ehrenhalt, 1985, p. 2563). The promise of inoculation, however, is not limited to winning campaigns. The research of Pfau et al., (2001b), An and Pfau (2004a), and Lin (2000) suggests that inoculation also protects participatory attitudes and behaviors, which underpin democracy.

Adolescent health campaigns. Some of the most impressive applications of inoculation are found in the context of health as a strategy to discourage adolescent smoking and alcohol use. At any early age, children develop healthy attitudes about smoking and drinking, but these attitudes are sorely tested, especially during the transition from elementary to secondary school (Hamburg, 1979), when, for many young adolescents, peer influence replaces parental influence (Evans & Raines, 1982; Friedman, Lichtenstein, & Biglan, 1985; Goldberg & Garn, 1982; Gottlieg & Baker, 1986; McAlister, Perry, & Maccoby, 1979; Sobus, 2003). Health campaigners need to get to students before negative peer pressure does, using a strategy that would "arrest attitude slippage among younger adolescents, rendering them less vulnerable to smoking onset" (Pfau, 1997, p. 148).

One popular smoking prevention strategy has been "social inoculation," a hybrid strategy that incorporates aspects of inoculation theory with Bandura's social learning theory (Wallack & Corbett, 1987). Although effective (Botvin, Baker, Resnick, Filazzola, & Botvin, 1984; Perry, 1987; Perry, Killen, & Slinkard, 1980) Social inoculation differs in a significant way from conventional inoculation in that it features only the refutational preemption component of inoculation, ignoring the crucial threat element. Threat is an instrumental element in inoculation; as a result, social inoculation is not inoculation. Further, because social inoculation usually features a broad array of tactics, it is almost impossible to isolate which tactics are contributing to program effectiveness, which also impedes replication (Flay, 1985).

Pfau and colleagues (Pfau & Van Bockern, 1994; Pfau et al., 1992) posited pure inoculation treatments as a method for combating the influence of peer pressure on young adolescents' smoking attitudes and behaviors. Their longitudinal field study involved South Dakota public school students in their transitory year from sixth grade to seventh grade. Inoculation protected attitudes and behavioral intentions throughout the year, but only for students of low self-esteem. The researchers also incorporated reinforcement treatments, but these booster sessions had no additional effects on attitudes or behavioral intentions. There were several important findings from this study. First, inoculation can protect attitudes against peer pressure to smoke cigarettes. Second, self-esteem moderates the effectiveness of inoculation treatments, an important finding because students with low self-esteem are more likely to smoke (Best, Thomson, Santi, Smith, & Brown, 1988; Elder & Stern, 1986; Foon, 1986; Harken, 1987; Pfau et al., 1992; Pfau & Van Bockern, 1994). Finally, this study found inoculation to have persistent, long-term effects. Eighty-four weeks after participants were exposed to inoculation treatment videos, inoculated students expressed less positive attitudes toward smoking and smokers (Pfau & Van Bockern, 1994).

In 2000, Szabo followed up the Pfau et al. (1992) investigation, examining the potential of inoculation videos to reduce smoking onset among fifth and sixth graders in both urban and rural school systems. Her research also compared efficacy of traditional health-based messages versus normative inoculation anger and happiness messages. Further, Szabo (2000) featured another theoretical perspective, Brehm's reactance theory, to ascertain whether traditional health-based messages carry greater risk than normative inoculation messages in producing boomerang effects—ironically increasing, instead of decreasing, the likelihood that kids will smoke. Reactance theory (Brehm, 1966, 1972) describes a motivational state in which the individual seeks to reclaim a perceived loss of freedom. Szabo found that reactance is a likely response of adolescent students who have had experimental smoking experiences. In addition, Szabo (2000) found that waiting until middle school to dissuade adolescents from smoking may be too late. She advised that antismoking efforts commence as early as third or fourth grade.

As with the onset of smoking, adolescents begin drinking at an early age. Hansen, Graham, Wolkenstein, and Rohrbach (1991) reported that the average alcohol-using teen begins drinking at 13.5 years of age. As with smoking attitudes, younger children have healthy attitudes about drinking (Webb, Baer, & McKelvey, 1995). but also similar to smoking, peer pressure (Hansen et al., 1991; Jessor & Jessor, 1975; U.S. Department of Health & Human Services, 1991; Webb et al., 1995), and overestimation of peer use of alcohol (Aas & Klepp, 1992) change these healthy attitudes and subsequent behaviors.

To date, only one study has explored the efficacy of inoculation to safeguard against adolescent alcohol consumption. Godbold (1998) used informative inoculation videos, normative inoculation videos, and neutral PSAs in an effort to instill resistance to alcohol use. Informative inoculation videos featured rational arguments against drinking whereas normative treatments used social appeals in which peers discouraged alcohol consumption. Godbold (1998) posited that both types of inoculation treatments would work, and that normative appeals would work best.

Normative messages did lower the estimate of peers regarding their acceptance of alcohol use, but did not result in more resistance to the attack message. In fact, neither inoculation treatment message conferred resistance in terms of attitude or behavioral intentions, although the normative appeal did reduce the influence of beer commercials.

Szabo and Pfau (2002) speculated about the reasons for muted resistance effects. First, all groups were already manifesting relatively high levels of threat and, therefore, the treatments failed to elicit greater threat levels. Threat is a precondition for inoculation (McGuire, 1962; Pfau, 1997; Pfau et al., 1992). Second, Godbold's (1998) inoculation and attack messages had unconventional attributes. Inoculation messages were less than 3 minutes in length, which may not have been enough time to elicit threat, and the attack messages employed video format, relying heavily on images and music.

In summary, research suggests that inoculation is a promising strategy in the realms of commercial advertising, public relations, politics, and health. The next section turns to possibilities for future inoculation research: efforts to provide a more nuanced understanding of how inoculation works and to explore new contexts for its application.

FUTURE DIRECTIONS

The next section examines future directions for inoculation research. First, this section explores possibilities for research to further enrich inoculation theory: returning to the underlying medical analogy to see what it implies for further research; exploring cognitive explanations for resistance other than threat and counterarguing; taking a more nuanced, second look at the core constructs of threat and counterarguing; examining non-cognitive explanations for resistance; and probing other issues concerning the process of resistance. Second, this section considers new applications for inoculation.

Beyond the Medical Analogy

Long after McGuire and colleagues posited the theoretical logic of inoculation theory, they continually referenced the biological analogy (Anderson & McGuire, 1965; McGuire, 1970; McGuire, 1961a, 1961b; McGuire & Papageorgis, 1961, 1962). McGuire (1964) encouraged comparison of the biological and attitudinal inoculation mechanisms, noting that the analogy "was our theoretical point of departure" (p. 222). "Using biological innoculation [sic] as a guideline, a number of heuristically attractive hypotheses can be derived about how to confer resistance to persuasion, some of these hypotheses being intriguingly nonobvious" (Anderson &

McGuire, 1965, p. 45). Evidently, McGuire intended for the medical analogy to be more than "clever and valid" (Eagly & Chaiken, 1993, p. 568); it was also intended to serve as the theoretical springboard for further investigations.

In many ways, the medical analogy served the theory well. Several researchers have used the medical analogy as motivation for more nuanced looks at how inoculation confers resistance (e.g., Compton, 2002; Pryor & Steinfatt, 1978). But, much more needs to be done. The analogy suggests a number of directions for future research.

Based on the medical analogy, McGuire posited that weakened counterarguments motivate a bolstering process, much as injection of a weakened virus elicits production of antibodies in a medical inoculation. Notably, the counterarguments must be weakened to the point that they "would stimulate, without overcoming, [one's] defenses" (McGuire & Papageorgis, 1961, p. 327). There is a danger that if counterarguments (or, in the case of the medical vaccination, the virus) were not weakened enough, the inoculation treatment might boomerang. Nevertheless, few studies have explored this weakened version component of inoculation, despite Lumsdaine and Janis's (1953) call for such study in their precursor research to inoculation. They called for further study of counterarguments that vary in terms of "the relative number and cogency of opposing arguments, the context in which they are introduced into the discussion, the extent to which they are explicitly refuted or merely overridden by implication, and so on" (p. 318). McGuire and Papageorgis (1962) made a similar call: "Pursuit of the medical analogy suggests many further questions. How thoroughly weakened should the counterarguments be when the person is pre-exposed to them in order to achieve maximum immunity with the least danger?" (p. 34). Researchers have continued to pose the question but have been provided few answers. Even though studies have varied the number of counterarguments (McGuire, 1964) or the language intensity of treatments (Burgoon et al., 1976), only one study (Compton & Pfau, 2004b) manipulated the strength of the presented counterarguments and refutations in an attempt to more clearly define the stimulate-but-not-overwhelm standard. Compton and Pfau (2004b) found that weak refutations of weak counterarguments were the most effective, yet there is no theoretical explanation for this finding. Clearly, the criterion of stimulate but not overwhelm, suggested by the medical inoculation, needs further examination.

The medical analogy should inspire other studies as well. For example, one promising new medical vaccination is called a *vector vaccine*. With the vectored vaccine—which Nossal (1999) termed the "Trojan Horse" vaccine—specific pathogen-fighting antigens are infused with a live, yet harmless, virus and injected into the body. Nossal (1999) noted that this type of vaccine combines the benefits of the live vaccine with the accuracy of subunit vaccines. Even though it is a promising concept, consistent successful vectoring has not yet occurred. The Trojan Horse vaccine has potentially fascinating applications to inoculation research. Would a more subtle inoculation treatment confer resistance? Indeed, might the resistance be even stronger with this indirect approach? There are numerous possibilities for structuring more subtle vaccinations (disguised inoculation treatments); however, the modes of metaphors, storytelling, and visuals hold particular promise.

In addition, medical vaccines can be enhanced by the presence of substances called *adjuvants,* materials added to vaccinations to prolong or strengthen the conferred resistance (Ertl, Xiang, Pasquini, & Kowalczyk, 1999). One way an adjuvant can confer longer resistance is by slowing down the rate at which the antigen is released into the body. As Nossal (1999) pointed out, capsule vaccines that release antigens at varying times could confer long-term resistance and possibly eliminate the need for booster sessions. Could modifications of an inoculation treatment affect and manipulate the rate at which the counterarguments and refutations confer resistance? For example, a series of refuted counterarguments before the attitude attack would mirror the capsule vaccine technique, as contrasted with the conventional "one-shot" inoculation treatment.

Returning to the medical analogy also offers an alternative to the way attitudinal inoculation researchers are testing booster sessions. Previous work with booster sessions may have used the wrong catalyst. Nossal (1999) pointed out that in a medical inoculation, the second exposure to an antigen, not a repeat inoculation, produces a stronger immune response to the offending antigen. Studies could ascertain whether repeated exposure to the attack, instead of a repeated inoculation treatment, produces a stronger boost.

Finally, although most medical vaccines are prophylactic, building resistance in healthy individuals before exposure to pathogen attack, some vaccines are therapeutic, administered to individuals who are already infected (Nossal, 1999). One example is the rabies vaccine. Whereas this type of vaccine may not completely cure an individual, it can lessen the effects of the disease or condition. Although inoculation is preventative (Pfau, 1997) and works to protect existing attitudes against change, future research could examine effects of inoculation on those already afflicted with a particular harmful belief.

The biological analogy can inspire exciting new inoculation research, but it also has a downside. It limits the theory, particularly in terms of its boundary conditions. As explained previously, one of the reasons early inoculation researchers shied away from exploring uses of inoculation with controversial topics was that the biological analogy suggested it would not work. As Anderson and McGuire (1965) explained:

> As attractive as the innoculation [sic] approach may be, however, the analogy fundamentally assumes that beliefs are maintained in an ideologically, "germ-free" environment, where the believer is seldom exposed to belief-discrepant counterarguments. (p. 45)

This was repeated in Insko's (1967) review of resistance to influence literature, where he noted that the generalizability of inoculation to controversial topics was questionable.

Other attempts to further understand the process of inoculation have clashed with the original medical analogy. Tannenbaum (1967) proposed a third element in inoculation beyond threat and counterarguing: the assertion-weakening component. However, this component quickly disappeared from inoculation research because, according to Rogers and Thistlethwaite (1969), "it does not fit the biological analogy used to describe the theory" (p. 301). Other monumental findings about the process of inoculation also do not closely fit the medical analogy, including the use of explicit forewarning.

The medical analogy on which inoculation is based can either serve as a launching point for continuing research or confound inoculation scholarship. McGuire and other scholars continue to call for a return to the analogy to direct future research, while others decry the limits the analogy places on enhancing attitudinal inoculation constructs with investigations that do not noticeably parallel how biological inoculations confer resistance. Researchers are faced with the decision to treat the analogy as a simple explanatory, or consider a tighter relationship between attitudinal and medical inoculations. Future research should explore the possibility that attitudinal inoculation is more than analogous, but perhaps even isomorphic, to processes of biological inoculation.

Exploring Other Cognitive Explanations for Resistance

Eagly and Chaiken (1993) urged "renewed study [of inoculation] in the context of contemporary theory and methodology" (p. 568). There is still much to discover about the way inoculation works. One of the most pressing quandaries in recent SEM studies of resistance is the puzzling direct path from inoculation treatment to ultimate resistance to persuasive attack. Even though the explanation of threat and counterarguing working in tandem to foster resistance continues to receive strong support in a growing body of research (Pfau, 1992; Pfau & Burgoon, 1988; Pfau et al., 1990, 1992, 1997a, 2001a, 2004a), these elements alone do not provide a complete account of how inoculation confers resistance. The recent SEM studies finding an unexplained, direct path from inoculation to resistance (Pfau et al., 1997a, 2001a, 2004a) suggest either that operationalizations of key elements in inoculation (threat and counterarguing) are not adequately capturing these constructs, or that there remains "unidentified and untested elements in the inoculation process that account for resistance" (Pfau, et al., 2001a, p. 243).

Attitude accessibility is part of the answer. The results of recent studies indicate that inoculation treatments render attitudes more accessible (Pfau et al., 2003) and that accessibility confers resistance via a process that operates independent of counterarguing (Pfau et al., 2004a). Accessibility alone, however, does not completely explain the direct path from inoculation to resistance because, even after attitude accessibility is added to the resistance process, the direct path is still evident.

Another part of the equation may be found in associative networks, or schemas. Associative networks are spider-like structures that reside in long-term memory

(Collins & Loftus, 1975; Fazio, Sanbonmatsu, Powell, & Kardes, 1986; Fazio & Williams, 1986; Higgins, 1996). These structures consist of both cognitive and affective nodes that are connected to each other by associative paths (Anderson, 1983; Forgas, 2001; Greene, 1984; Smith, 1994). The strength of associative paths varies based on the how related specific nodes are (Anderson, 1983; Wyer & Srull, 1989).

Inoculation treatments may affect attitude networks in two ways. Treatments may render networks more accessible, as has been demonstrated (Pfau et al., 2003, 2004a). The inoculation treatment focuses the individual on the content of networks, in essence, priming it. Priming is a spontaneous processing strategy that eschews deliberative processing (Anderson, 1983; Fazio, 1986; Miller & Krosnick, 1996; Sanbonmatsu & Fazio, 1990; Smith & Kirby, 2001), which explains why Pfau et al. (2004a) identified counterarguing and accessibility as independent paths en route to resistance. Priming activates the content of networks. "As a consequence, for some time after a concept is activated, there is an increased probability that it and associated thought elements will come to mind again" (Berkowitz & Rogers, 1986, pp. 58–59). Once an associative network is primed via an inoculation treatment, its content is more readily available for subsequent use (Cappella & Jamieson, 1997).

In addition, the refutational preemption component of an inoculation treatment should produce a more evaporative network by planting additional nodes or by strengthening the perceived salience of existing nodes, or both. If a person is only moderately familiar with an issue, the refutational preemption component of an inoculation treatment is likely to contribute new information nodes, thus updating the associative network. This explanation presupposes that networks are dynamic, always changing, which is consistent with Bartlett's original description of cognitive schema as "complete," but "developing, from moment to moment" (1932, p. 20). When an individual encounters new information that is contained in the refutational preemption component of an inoculation treatment, these new nodes are integrated into an existing network. In this way, inoculation does more than foster attitude accessibility; it also alters the manifest content of associative networks.

In addition, inoculation treatments may alter the relative weight of existing nodes within an associative network. This addresses node strength, which involves the weight of the individual nodes in a network, in contrast to link strength, which consists of the weight of paths that connect the various nodes (Anderson, 1983). It would be expected, for example, that inoculation treatments would weaken content nodes contrary to initial attitudes but strengthen nodes consistent with initial attitudes. As Roskos-Ewoldsen, Ralstin, & St. Pierre (2002) stated: "The initial weak attitude (inoculation) and the (sometimes) concurrent provision of arguments against the position favored by the upcoming attack(s) are thought to strengthen message recipients' evaporative network of supporting beliefs" (p. 27).

In all likelihood, an inoculation treatment does both, but because the refutational preemption element contains more manifest content favoring than opposing existing attitudes, the combination of new content nodes and their relative weight should be greater on behalf of favorable networks than unfavorable ones. Thus, the accessibility explanation may be only part of the "unidentified and untested elements" explaining the way inoculation confers resistance. Associative networks, broadly configured, may hold the key to resistance: Inoculation treatments may prime networks, rendering them more accessible, and they may promote new content nodes or enhance the weighting of existing nodes. Future research needs to operationalize associative networks and test for all three effects.

A More Nuanced Look at Threat and Counterarguing

More than 7 years ago, Pfau urged inoculation researchers to return to basics: "Efforts to enrich inoculation theory require going back to the construct's core assumptions, refining and extending them, and then testing the reformulated logic in laboratory studies" (1997, pp. 151–152). This means refocusing on the concepts of threat and counterarguing.

Threat is purported to be a requisite for inoculation (McGuire, 1962; Pfau, 1997). As a result, threat is an obvious candidate for this type of scrutiny. Although threat was a key element in inoculation theory, it was treated as a primitive term in the theory. Its presence was only assumed in McGuire's inoculation research and in all inoculation studies during the 20 years that followed. In the late 1980s, however, researchers began independently assessing elicited threat in inoculation research (Pfau & Burgoon, 1988; Pfau et al., 1990).

Threat is a requisite for the process of inoculation, but how much threat is optimal to maximize resistance? Pfau et al. (1997) operationalized threat as "forewarning of one or more impending challenges to attitudinal integrity" (p. 189). They found that threat and resistance were positively correlated; however, the amount of threat remains elusive. Elicited threat has been weak in some contemporary inoculation studies (Godbold, 1998; Pfau et al., 1992) and, even when induced threat has been significant, threat levels never rose above middle ranges. Researchers should look at other ways of generating threat in an inoculation treatment. For example, following the lead of Nabi (2003), researchers could use evocative visuals to elicit a stronger affect response to threat.

Thus far, however, little is known about how to vary the degrees of threat experienced by receivers of inoculation treatment messages. Burgoon et al. (1976) found that when an upcoming attack is either certain to happen, or certain not to happen, threat is minimal and resistance is undermined. Burgoon et al. reasoned thus: If an attack is certain to occur, people resign themselves to encounter it; if an attack is certain not to occur, people have no reason to prepare for the attack. However, when there is a 50–50 chance of encountering a persuasive attempt, Burgoon et al. (1976) found resistance to be optimal. The uncertainty of whether an attack will be forthcoming motivates people to bolster an attitude. Future studies should examine varying certainty of an attitude attack, its relation to threat, and the ultimate effect on resistance.

That threat plays a role in the process of inoculation is well supported, but *when* threat unleashes the process of resistance is unclear. In some early studies, threat came from the realization that there were counterarguments to existing beliefs. This suggests that threat might accrue in a cumulative manner, increasing with each encounter with a counterargument. Nevertheless, research has not explored whether this is the case.

Later, inoculation research introduced extrinsic threat with a specific forewarning of an impending attitude attack. This format implies that threat acts at the beginning of the process, an explanation offered by Pfau (1997): "The two components, threat and refutational preemption, work in tandem: *first* threat and *then* refutational preemption" (p. 137, emphasis added). When does threat have its greatest impact—at the beginning of an inoculation treatment message, before the individual encounters counterarguments and refutations; or cumulatively, as the individual encounters each counterargument, one at a time, with each generating greater threat levels? Future research should also investigate when elicited threat dissipates. The conventional explanation that threat motivates the generation of counterarguments during the interim between the treatment and subsequent exposure to a persuasive attack suggests that threat levels persist throughout this interval. At this point, however, this is only an assumption. More study is needed to determine whether threat persists throughout the interval between inoculation and attack and what effects it generates over time. Rogers and Thistlethwaite (1969) noted years ago that "the evidence showing that a threat will stimulate subjects to acquire, through their own efforts . . . belief-bolstering arguments is much less impressive" (p. 301).

Even though the evidence is clear that threat plays an instrumental role in the process of resistance, evidence is not as definitive for counterarguing. Current assessment measures, including the common thought listing technique (Brock, 1967; Greenwald, 1968), have received strong criticism (Eagly & Chaiken, 1993). Furthermore, though some research has confirmed a direct association between elicited counterarguing and resistance (Petty & Cacioppo, 1977, 1986; Pfau et al., 1997a, 2004a), other studies have failed to detect this link (e.g., Pfau et al., 2001a).

Papageorgis and McGuire (1961) were the first to operationalize counterarguing, but they only did it once, and, as was previously discussed, their operationalization was questionable. They had participants list reasons supporting their attitude; however, what is required by counterarguing in a resistance context is that participants generate both counterarguments and refutations (Benoit, 1991; Wyer 1974). This calls for a different approach to assessing counterarguing.

Pfau, Compton, et al. (2004a, 2004b) used an alternative method, employing a recognition check-off procedure. First, participants reviewed a list of 20 arguments, some included in the treatment message, and some that were not. Participants were asked to check those arguments "that other people might have for opposing your position . . . that had entered your mind as you completed the attitude measures." Then, participants rated each argument on a scale from 1 (*weak*) to 7 (*strong*). Next, participants were asked to identify refutations, "arguments that you thought of as to why the opposing arguments were wrong . . . that had entered your mind as you completed the attitude measures." As with the first category of arguments, they were asked to rate each argument on a scale from 1 (*weak*) to 7 (*strong*). Using this method, Pfau, Compton, and colleagues (2004a, 2004b) confirmed a robust presence for counterarguing throughout the process of resistance. Even though this method appears promising, more research is needed to ascertain whether the checklist procedure captures the internal process of covert counterarguing and how it compares to the thought-listing approach.

Regardless of how counterarguing is measured, the conventional time to assess counterarguing is either directly following exposure to an inoculation message, although Pfau et al. (2004a, 2004b) also measured it right after exposure to the persuasive attack. Yet, Miller and Baron (1973) insisted that counterarguing should be during exposure to the persuasive message. If counterarguing is measured immediately after the attack message, we can't rule out the possibility that counterarguing "is a post-persuasion technique used to justify whatever position one finds oneself holding rather than a mechanism for resisting influence" (Miller & Baron, 1973, p. 107). If it is assessed immediately prior to encountering the persuasive message, it may measure anticipatory belief change and not the actual mechanism of counterarguing (Miller & Baron, 1973). These are legitimate concerns that require further attention.

Miller and Baron (1973) offer several recommendations for increasing the validity of counterarguing assessment. When using thought listing, participants should be given limited time to record thoughts. This is more likely to tap into those arguments that were more accessible and were, in fact, used during the reception of the persuasive message. Periods of silence should also be inserted after each major argument of the persuasive message to allow time for the cognitive work of counterarguing. Finally, participants could be asked to record every thought during the reception of the persuasive message, stopping intermittently while reading the message to record thoughts. As an alternative to thought listing, Miller and Baron (1973) suggested use of a counterargument checklist. With this approach, participants are given a list of counterarguments, some that were included in the message and some that were not. Participants are asked to check off those that went through their minds while reading the persuasive message under a time limit. Afterward, the participants could be asked to show where the counterarguments they checked applied to the persuasive message. Researchers could count the number of counterarguments identified to assess the motivation that person had for resisting the persuasive message (Miller & Baron, 1973).

Of these suggestions, to our knowledge, none have been employed in inoculation research with the exception of the counterargument checklist procedure (see Pfau et al., 2004a, 2004b). Of course, Miller and Baron's (1973) list of suggestions is not inclusive. Another option for assessing counterarguing includes using in-depth interviews at different stages of the inoculation process in order to provide a more nuanced view of how threat and counterarguing work in tandem to bolster attitudes against impending persuasive attacks (Compton, 2002).

Noncognitive Explanations for Resistance

Even though inoculation theory posits that resistance is accomplished via an active, cognitive process, three recent inoculation studies offered findings that call into question this assumption. Two of the studies revealed an immediate, as opposed to delayed, resistance effect. In the Pfau et al. (1997a) study, threat triggered immediate bolstering of attitudes in low and moderate involvement conditions. The strengthened attitudes persisted across time, culminating in resistance to persuasive attacks that occurred independent of receiver counterarguing. No theoretical explanation was provided for this result. In retrospect, however, the fact that the immediate effect occurred in low- and moderate-involvement circumstances, but not high involvement conditions, may be instructive. In the Pfau, Holbert, et al. (2000) study, video, but not print, inoculation treatments elicited an immediate bolstering impact, which was sustained until the time people encountered a persuasive attack. Also, the video treatments instilled resistance via source cues and not message content. A third study by Pfau, Szabo, et al. (2001a) revealed that inoculation-happiness treatments elicit resistance completely independent of receiver counterarguing.

What these studies, in common, suggest is that inoculation can confer resistance in ways contrary to the active, cognitive process assumed in inoculation theory. Future studies need to further explore more passive, heuristic processes of resistance, including immediate bolstering of attitudes, the use of source-oriented video treatments, and the role of positive affect. One study (Pfau et al., 1997b) compared the relative effectiveness of central and peripheral inoculation treatments, finding that both fostered resistance but that, contrary to prediction, the two approaches differed little in their effectiveness. The study, however, failed to confirm that the two message approaches actually elicited the message processing that was assumed, and it did not attempt to determine whether the inoculation approaches differed in the way they accomplished resistance.

Clearly, much more needs to be done to incorporate a passive component into the broader explanation of the way inoculation confers resistance. Any number of theories might explain this passive process. For example, the assimilation and contrast constructs of social judgment theory (e.g., Sherif & Hovland, 1961; Sherif, Sherif, & Nebergall, 1965) imply that the threat element of inoculation treatments enhances ego involvement whereas the refutational preemption component "initially triggers assimilation (polarized positive evaluation) in which a receiver's attitude shifts even further toward the position advocated in the pretreatment" (Pfau, 1997, p. 155), and both of these features elicit pronounced contrast effects when individuals eventually encounter subsequent persuasive attacks. Testing the assimilation aspect of this explanation, Ahluwalia (2000) found that biased assimilation contributes to counterarguing and resistance in people when they confront counterattitudinal content.

Another example involves dual-processing theories, the Elaboration Likelihood Model (ELM; Petty & Cacioppo, 1986) and the Heuristic-Systematic Model (HSM; Chaiken, 1987), which posit that, in low involvement conditions, peripheral or heuristic cues play a much more prominent role in influence and, we would suspect, in resistance. One of these more passive cues is the source of an inoculation treatment, as opposed to the treatment's substantive content which, after McGuire's initial studies on inoculation, Freedman and Sears (1965) insisted should receive more attention in resistance research. Similarly, Stone (1969) advocated examining source derogation of the attack message. A final example is affect, whether Lazarus's cognitive-motivational-relational theory (1991) or another perspective, which warrants increased scrutiny in resistance research. Pfau et al. (2001a) found that inoculation treatments elicit anger, and anger significantly fosters resistance; Zuwerink and Devine (1996) and Jacks and Devine (2000) revealed that irritation contributes to resistance, at least with people scoring low in attitude importance.

In addition to the fact that inoculation theory needs to adjust to accommodate the study results noted above, perhaps including a passive, heuristic feature in addition to the traditional cognitive explanation, current methods in inoculation research need to become more innovative as well. Brandt argued that observation of counterarguing is "extremely difficult, if not impossible," instead calling for assessment based more on detecting one's arousal or motivation to counterargue (1979, p. 324). Similarly, Miller and Baron (1973) proposed a method for assessing counterarguing that may prove useful in exploring more passive message processing, arguing:

> Often people seem adept at resisting influence in spite of the fact that they lack concrete reasons for doing so. Consequently, it might be important to assess the extent to which people employ outright evaluative rejection vs. reasoned rejection of persuasion materials. (p. 114)

As participants encountered a message, they would be instructed to indicate whether they "reject outright" or "reject with a reason" each counterargument. This method could shed more light on whether the active process of covert counterarguing is an intrinsic feature of inoculation-induced resistance.

Other Issues Concerning the Process of Resistance

Beyond looking more closely at the inoculation treatment, future research should examine the nature of the persuasive attack. Most resistance studies alter the inoculation treatment messages, but much less is known about impacts of different types of attacks. Nearly all studies have used attacks via print. A few studies have used video. Godbold and Pfau (2000) employed video inoculation and persuasive attack messages, and the attack messages lacked any verbal component, instead relying on images and music. In this study, inoculation failed to confer strong resistance. This failure could be due to the minimal elicited threat; however, the answer may also lay in the visual nature of the attitude attacks (Szabo & Pfau, 2002). Other researchers have successfully used video to confer resistance (Nabi, 2003; Pfau et al., 1992), but these videos also featured a verbal component. Are attack messages composed of only visuals and music impervious to the power of inoculation?

Future research should look at attitude attacks that are less explicit and direct than those used in most contemporary inoculation studies. Implicit influences on attitude are powerful because people fail to resist influences that they don't recognize as persuasion (Mendelberg, 2001). The failure of inoculation to confer resistance in the Godbold and Pfau study (2000) raises important questions about the nature of attack messages.

More needs to be known about booster sessions as well. In reference to booster sessions, Pfau (1997) has suggested that "perhaps it is time to return to the drawing board" (p. 151). Studies of booster sessions must be more inventive to definitively answer whether additional inoculation treatments can enhance resistance. Previous investigations of the effectiveness of reinforcement treatments subjected participants to "multiple exposures to the immunizing messages" (Pfau et al., 1990). One tactic that researchers have yet to use with booster sessions would be to subject people to a series of weakened *attacks* instead of additional inoculation messages. Researchers could also explore the effectiveness of repeated forewarnings during the interim, reminding people that their attitudes will be under attack soon, but not providing any refutational preemption. Cognitive persistence research has suggested that the power of threat lies in the ability to motivation individuals to generate their own thoughts (Love & Greenwald, 1978; Petty, 1977), so using repeated forewarnings for reinforcement has promise.

Another topic that warrants further study is the extent of the blanket protection offered by inoculation. Inoculation evidently spreads a "broad blanket of protection against specific counterarguments raised in refutational preemption and against those counterarguments not raised" (Pfau, 1997, pp. 137–138). The capacity of inoculation treatments to confer resistance beyond the counterarguments explicitly mentioned and then refuted in the inoculation treatment is important. If inoculation were not able to generate resistance beyond the explicit counterarguments and refutations raised in the treatment, individuals would need specific pretreatment messages for any argument they might encounter that runs counter to their existing attitude. Pfau et al. (1990) noted that this umbrella protection is particularly powerful in the political context, when the specific nature of the attacks cannot be anticipated.

How expansive, though, is this blanket of protection? Does it spread beyond content domains? Could individuals be inoculated against a specific classification of attacks: for example, from any attack that is communicated via a television advertisement, or from any attack communicated by a celebrity spokesperson? In an applied setting, could adolescents be inoculated against one undesirable behavior, such as smoking, and the protection afforded extend to other unwanted behaviors like drug or alcohol use? Even though it is indisputable that inoculation confers resistance beyond the arguments explicitly refuted in the treatment, less is known about how far this blanket of protection extends.

Another remaining mystery in inoculation research is time, including optimal timing for treatments and rate of decay. Forty years ago, McGuire (1964) acknowledged, "The theory is not well formed enough quantitatively to specify the exact time parameters" (p. 223). Researchers continue to call for a better understanding of optimal timing during the inoculation process (Pfau et al., 2000). The most specific findings of the optimal timing for inoculation treatments was provided by Pfau et al. (2004b), and yet further specificity is needed.

Finally, research should explore which manifestations of resistance persist the longest and why. Whereas early research indicated that message variables affect decay (McGuire, 1962, 1964, 1966; Pryor & Steinfatt, 1978), less is known about the rate of decay for inoculation effects. Pfau and Burgoon's (1988) finding that attitude decays faster than behavioral intentions (in this study, the likelihood of voting for a particular candidate) suggests that the process of inoculation may be different for its bolstering effects on attitudes and its enhancement of behavioral intentions.

Recent inoculation studies have provided more nuanced views of how inoculation works, but more remains to be learned. The next section explores new applications of inoculation.

New Applications for Inoculation

Health behaviors. The results of previous adolescent health campaign studies encourage further investigations in this domain. Pfau (1995) posited that inoculation could be an effective strategy in reducing adolescent drug alcohol use, reducing violence, improving conflict resolution, and preventing accidents. Researchers have pursued the effectiveness of inoculation in discouraging adolescent alcohol use (Godbold & Pfau, 2000); however, efficacy of inoculation in these other health behaviors remains unexplored.

Adolescent drug use remains a serious national problem (Johnston, O'Malley, & Bachman, 2002). Most children have healthy attitudes about drugs when they are young, but the chances they will try drugs for the first time drastically increases between the ages of 12 and 14 (Johnston, O'Malley, & Bachman, 1991; Oetting & Beauvais, 1990; Segal, 1986) with increasingly strong peer influence (Kreutter, Gerwirtz, Davenny, & Love, 1991). Additionally, students grossly overestimate how many of their peers are using drugs (Hammermeister, Roland, & Page, 2002). McIntosh, MacDonald, and McKeganey (2003) found that one of the most effective strategies in combating peer pressure was to offer reasons not to use drugs. "Not having a good reason for declining an offer leaves the young person exposed to further offers and to attempts at persuasion" (McIntosh et al., 2003, p. 984). Inoculation holds promise as a viable way of giving students reasons to avoid initiating drug use. As retired General Barry McCaffery, director of the Office of National Drug Control Policy (ONDCP) stated, "We're confident that if you can shape youth's attitudes, you can change their drug-taking behavior" (as cited in Marks, 1999, p. 2).

Inoculation also could be an effective strategy in combating childhood obesity. Childhood obesity is a serious problem with significant negative effects on physical and mental health (Ebbeling, Pawlak, & Ludwig, 2002; "Health Implications of Childhood Obesity," 1985). As with smoking and alcohol initiation, peer pressure has an effect on children's health choices (Ebbeling et al., 2002), affecting food choices (American Dietetic Association, Society for Nutrition Education, and American School Food Service Association, 2003). Further, children face an onslaught of television advertisements for unhealthy foods (Borzekowski & Robinson, 2001); however, an effort to foster resistance to negative food choices must start early. Robinson (2000) found that by the time children reach 10 years of age they make about 250 food purchases each year without parental involvement.

At times, it is not actual obesity, but body image, that is the problem. A Centers for Disease Control study found that, although 14% of students were actually "at risk for being overweight," 30% thought they were (as cited in Kowalski, 2003). Often, these negative body images begin in high school, worsened by peer pressure and unrealistic media images (Kowalski, 2003). With findings that inoculation can be successful even in the face of visual attitude attacks (e.g., Nabi, 2003), inoculation treatments could help protect children's healthy images of their appearances before the onslaught of media images and peer pressure.

Inoculation may also be effective in helping adolescents delay sexual activity or encouraging more responsible sexual behaviors (see Pfau, Dillard, & Keller, 2000). Adolescents are having sex at younger ages and with more partners than ever before (Zabin & Hayward, 1993). Conventional abstinence programs designed to reduce the number of young adolescents engaging in sex often fail, illustrating that providing of information alone is not effective (Plotnick, 1993; Zabin & Hayward, 1993). Social inoculation, a preemptive approach featuring a smorgasbord of tactics, is misnamed because it resembles Bandura's social learning theory far more than it does McGuire's inoculation theory. (As we noted previously, social inoculation doesn't include the threat component of inoculation.). Social inoculation has achieved modest short-term success in delaying sexual onset in adolescents (Eisen, Zellman, & McAlister, 1990; Howard & McCabe, 1990; Kirby, Barth, Leland, & Fetro, 1991; Postrado & Nicholson, 1992). The overall impact of social inoculation initiatives is unclear, however, because of the dearth of systematic and rigorous assessment (National Campaign to Prevent Teen Pregnancy, 1998).

In addition, when adolescents do engage in sex, it is often unprotected. Just over half of adolescents report using condoms during sexual relations (Grunbaum et al., 2001). As a result, U.S. rates for adolescent pregnancies, HIV infection, and STDs are alarmingly high (Kirby, 2001). The appropriateness of inoculation in delaying sexual involvement or in enhancing condom use is based on the premise that adolescents need to "learn strategies to avoid having unwanted sexual experiences and find ways to enforce the use of contraception" (Moore & Sugland, 2001, p. 15). This constitutes a fruitful domain for inoculation research and is based on the underlying premise that "all young people deserve access to the information and skills. . . . to aid them in developing responsible decisions about sexuality" (Mabray & Labauve, 2002, p. 31).

Inoculation could also be used to prevent youth violence. At the beginning of this decade, 2.5 million students were victims of school crimes, with 186,000 the victims of serious crimes like rape and assault (Delaney & Puskar, 2003). Many students are acting more aggressively and at earlier ages (McAdams & Lambie, 2003), and children with low self-esteem are particularly prone to this behavior (Lowenstein, 1994). Inoculation is a promising treatment method, especially in light of its proven effectiveness in conferring resistance to smoking for children with low self-esteem (Pfau et al., 1992).

In addition, inoculation might be used as a strategy to reduce teenage involvement in gangs. It is estimated that 3–5% of urban youth are involved in delinquent gangs and that the problem is growing (Esbensen & Huizinga, 1993). Current approaches to this problem are reactive, although strategies designed to keep kids from joining gangs would seem to make more sense (Trojanowicz, 1978). Experts agree that prevention programs need to reach at-risk children before ages 12–14 years, the period when gang recruitment efforts peak.

Inoculation holds much promise for addressing many health issues, particularly those that affect adolescents. The one common theme seems to be that it is important to teach resistance to children early (Stevens & Griffin, 2001), while healthy attitudes remain. Programs aimed at reducing detrimental adolescent behaviors must move beyond merely providing information. Inoculation may be a more effective strategy. It is appropriate that inoculation, inspired by a medical analogy, may make some of its most important contributions in the health context.

Consumer behavior. Compton and Pfau (2004a) reported that inoculation protects college students against predatory credit card marketing campaigns. Further study should examine inoculation's potential to help consumers resist targeted marketing campaigns, especially in instances where consumers are particularly vulnerable. For example, what can be done to better protect the elderly population against unscrupulous telemarketers or fraudulent sweepstakes offers? *Consumers' Research Magazine* warns:

> Elderly people are particularly vulnerable to telemarketing fraud for a variety of reasons. They often are lonely and isolated from their families, and more willing to believe what someone tells them over the telephone. Some suffer mental or physical frailties that leave them helpless against the high-pressure tactics used by telescammers. ("Phone Scam Update," 1996, p. 23)

Inoculation can arm consumers with an arsenal of argumentation, enabling them to resist the pull of targeted marketing appeals that sound too good to be true, but are nonetheless influential.

Another area where inoculation may prove successful is the high cost mortgage industry. Usually, these high interest loans target people with poor credit histories, but they also target the elderly and people with good credit records. Experts "warn potential borrowers to be on guard" (Richey, 1998, p. 1). Inoculation may assist people in resisting these dangerous appeals.

Self-persuasion. One of inoculation's most impressive successes is the broad umbrella of resistance it provides, yet, to date, most inoculation research has looked at specific, concrete, external attitude attacks. Lin's (2000) investigation of inoculation's feasibility of combating the spiral of silence is a notable exception because it looked at conferring resistance to internal self-persuasion. Research should test the limits of inoculation by employing it in areas that fall under the rubric of self-persuasion (see Nienkamp, 2001, for an analysis of self-persuasion).

For example, might inoculation reduce volunteer turnover, protecting against erosion of the motivation and drive of volunteers? Volunteer efforts have high burnout rates (Wilson, 2000), resulting in high turnover. Even though volunteers are not often persuaded to quit by explicit counterarguments, they do become discouraged by a perceived lack of recognition (Gora & Nemerowicz, 1985) and autonomy (Harris, 1996; Holden, 1997). Inoculation treatment messages could be used during volunteer orientation to bolster attitudes against these inevitable internal challenges to their commitments.

Similarly, inoculation could be tested as a way to bolster and protect healthy employee morale. A study conducted by Nabisco Biscuit Company found high employee morale enhances productivity, customer satisfaction, market share, and sales (as cited in Allerton, 1996). Inoculation strategies may be able to bolster the initial commitment to an organization, protecting employee morale against day-to-day challenges of the working environment.

As another example of combating self-persuasion, Compton and Pfau (2004b) examined the use of inoculation to help college students resist temptations to plagiarize. Seemingly, for some students, attitudes upholding academic integrity are not strong enough to withstand the temptation to plagiarize. Inoculation may provide an effective strategy for bolstering attitudes of fairness and academic veracity.

As of yet, the use of inoculation to combat internal persuasion has not been thoroughly tested. Future research is needed to determine whether inoculation is as effective against self-persuasion as it is against external influence.

CONCLUSION

During the past decade, inoculation theory has grown prodigiously. Inoculation research has examined the inner mechanisms responsible for inoculation's effectiveness, exploring precise workings of inoculation's core concepts of threat and counterarguing in conjunction with concepts drawn from other theoretical domains, including issue involvement, attitude accessibility, self-efficacy, and affect. Findings have contributed to greater nuance about how inoculation works and, therefore, much greater precision in its use, including its practical applications in the contexts of advertising, politics, public relations and health. Also, research has expanded the practical applications of inoculation, examining uses in marketing, public relations, politics, and adolescent health campaigns.

As we consider future directions for communication research, and specifically, resistance research, we can benefit from returning to theories that originated in our discipline's early years. Even though Eagly and Chaiken called inoculation the grandparent theory of resistance over a decade ago, the theory continues to inform cutting-edge and exciting scholarship, adding nuance to our understanding of persuasion theory and offering practical applications that can improve health and promote more beneficial political discourse, among others. As evidenced by the recent resurgence of inoculation research, far from retiring, inoculation continues to be academically inspiring.

REFERENCES

Aas, H., & Klepp, K. (1992). Adolescents' alcohol use related to perceived norms. *Scandinavian Journal of Psychology, 33,* 315–325.

Adams, W. C., & Beatty, M. J. (1977). Dogmatism, need for social approval, and the resistance to persuasion. *Communication Monographs, 44,* 321–325.

Ahluwalia, R. (2000). Examination of psychological processes underlying resistance to persuasion. *Journal of Consumer Research, 27,* 217–232.

Allerton, H. (1996). Survey says. *Training & Development, 50*(6), 8.

American Dietetic Association, Society for Nutrition Education, and American School Food Service Association. (2003). Nutrition services: An essential component of comprehensive school health programs. *Journal of Nutrition Education and Behavior, 35,* 57–67.

An, C. (2003). *Efficacy of inoculation strategies in promoting resistance to potential attack messages: Source credibility perspective.* Unpublished doctoral dissertation, University of Oklahoma.

An, C., & Pfau, M. (2004a). *Efficacy of inoculation strategies in promoting resistance to political attack messages: A source credibility perspective.* Manuscript submitted for publication.

An, C., & Pfau, M. (2004b). The efficacy of inoculation in televised political debates. *Journal of Communication, 54,* 421–436.

Anderson, J. R. (1983). *The architecture of cognition.* Cambridge, MA: Harvard University Press.

Anderson, L. R., & McGuire, W. J. (1965). Prior reassurance of group consensus as a factor in producing resistance to persuasion. *Sociometry, 28,* 44–56.

Ansolabehere, S., & Iyengar, S. (1995). *Going negative: How political advertisements shrink and polarize the electorate.* New York: Free Press.

Ansolabehere, S., Iyengar, S., Simon, A., & Valentino, N. (1994). Does attack advertising demobilize the electorate? *American Political Science Review, 88,* 829–839.

Bandura, A. (1983). Self-efficacy determinants of anticipated fears and calamities. *Journal of Personality and Social Psychology, 45,* 464–469.

Bartlett, F. C. (1932). *Remembering: A study in experimental and social psychology.* Cambridge, UK: Cambridge University Press.

Benoit, W. L. (1991). Two tests of the mechanism of inoculation theory. *Southern Communication Journal, 56,* 219–229.

Benoit, W. L., & Lindsey, J. J. (1987). Argument strategies: Antidote to Tylenol's poisonous image. *Journal of the American Forensic Association, 23,* 136–146.

Berkowitz, L., & Rogers, K. H. (1986). A priming effect analysis of media influences. In J. Bryant & D. Zillmann (Eds.), *Perspectives on media effects* (pp. 57–81). Hillsdale, NJ: Erlbaum.

Best, J., Thomson, S. J., Santi, S. M., Smith, E., & Brown, K. S. (1988). Preventing cigarette smoking among school children. *Annual Review of Public Health, 9,* 161–201.

Bither, S. W., Dolich, I. J., & Nell, E. B. (1971). The application of attitude immunization techniques in marketing. *Journal of Marketing Research, 18,* 56–61.

Blaney, J. R., Benoit, W. L., & Brazeal, L. M. (2002). Blowout! Firestone's image restoration campaign. *Public Relations Research, 28,* 379–392.

Bless, H., Bohner, G., Schwarz, N., & Strack, F. (1990). Mood and persuasion: Cognitive response analysis. *Personality and Social Psychology Bulletin, 16,* 331–345.

Bohner, G., Crow, K., Erb, H., & Schwarz, N. (1992). Affect and persuasion: Mood effects on the processing of message content and context cues and on subsequent behaviour. *European Journal of Social Psychology, 22,* 511–530.

Borzekowski, D. L., & Robinson, T. N. (2001). The 30-second effect: An experiment revealing the impact of television commercials on food preferences of preschoolers. *Journal of the American Dietetic Association, 101,* 42–46.

Botvin, G. J., Baker, E., Renick, N. L., Filazzola, D., & Botvin, E. M. (1984). Cognitive behavioral approach to substance abuse prevention. *Addictive Behavior, 9,* 137–147.

Brandt, D. R. (1979). Listener propensity to counterargue, distraction, and resistance to persuasion. *Central States Speech Journal, 30,* 321–331.

Brehm, J. W. (1966). *A theory of psychological reactance.* New York: Academic Press.

Brehm, J. W. (1972). *Responses to loss of freedom: A theory of psychological reactance.* Morristown, NJ: General Learning Press.

Brinson, S. L., & Benoit, W. L. (1996). Dow Corning's image repair strategies in the breast implant crisis. *Communication Quarterly, 44,* 29–41.

Brinson, S. L., & Benoit, W. L. (1999). The tarnished star: Restoring Texaco's damaged public image. *Management Communication Quarterly, 12,* 483–510.

Brock, T. C. (1967). Communication discrepancy and intent to persuade as determinants of counterarguing production. *Journal of Experimental Social Psychology, 3,* 296–309.

Burgoon, M., Burgoon, J. K., Riess, M., Butler, J., Montgomery, C. L., Stinnet, W. D., Miller, M., Long, M., Vaughn, D., & Caine, B. (1976). Propensity of persuasive attack and intensity of pretreatment messages as predictors of resistance to persuasion. *Journal of Psychology, 92,* 123–129.

Burgoon, M., & Chase, L. J. (1973). The effects of differential linguistic patterns in messages attempting to induce resistance to persuasion. *Speech Monographs, 40,* 1–7.

Burgoon, M., Cohen, M., Miller, M. D., & Montgomery, C. L. (1978). An empirical test of a model of resistance to persuasion. *Human Communication Research, 5,* 27–39.

Burgoon, M., & King, L. B. (1974). The mediation of resistance to persuasion strategies by language variables and active-passive participation. *Human Communication Research, 1,* 30–41.

Burgoon, M., Pfau, M., & Birk, T. (1995). An inoculation theory explanation for the effects of corporate issue/advocacy advertising campaigns. *Communication Research, 22,* 485–505.

Cacioppo, J. T. (1979). Effects of exogenous changes in heart rate on facilitation of thought and resistance to persuasion. *Journal of Personality and Social Psychology, 37,* 489–498.

Cappella, J. N., & Jamieson, K. H. (1997). *Spiral of cynicism: The press and the public good.* New York: Oxford University Press.

Chaiken, S. (1987). The heuristic model of persuasion. In M. P. Zanna, J. M. Olson, & C. P. Herman (Eds.), *Social influence: The Ontario symposium* (Vol. 5, pp. 3–39). Hillsdale, NJ: Erlbaum.

Chaiken, S., & Eagly, H. (1976). Communication modality as determinant of message persuasiveness and message comprehensibility. *Journal of Personality and Social Psychology, 34,* 605–614.

Chaiken, S., & Eagly, H. (1983). Communication modality as determinant of persuasion: The role of communicator salience. *Journal of Personality and Social Psychology, 45,* 241–256.

Chen, H. C., Reardon, R., Rea, C., & Moore, D. (1992). Forewarning of content and involvement: Consequences for persuasion and resistance to persuasion. *Journal of Experimental Social Psychology, 28,* 523–541.

Chesebro, J. W. (1984). The media reality: Epistemological functions of media in cultural systems. *Critical Studies in Mass Communication, 1*, 111–130.

Collins, A., & Loftus, E. (1975). A spreading activation theory of semantic memory. *Psychological Review, 82*, 4–7, 407–428.

Compton, J. A. (2002). *Proposing the use of interviews to further understand the impact of threat and counterarguing in the inoculation process of resistance to influence.* Unpublished manuscript, University of Oklahoma.

Compton, J. A., & Pfau, M. (2004a). Use of inoculation to foster resistance to credit card marketing targeting college students. *Journal of Applied Communication Research, 32*, 343–364.

Compton, J. A., & Pfau, M. (2004b). *Using inoculation to mitigate against plagiarism: Confirmation of inoculation's effects on involvement and attitude accessibility, and new insights into rational and affective message approaches.* Paper presented at the Annual Conference of the National Communication Association, Chicago, IL.

Coombs, W. T. (1998). An analytic framework for crisis situations: Better responses from better understanding of the situation. *Journal of Public Relations Research, 10*, 177–191.

Cooper, H. M. (1979). Statistically combining independent studies: A meta-analysis of sex differences in conformity research. *Journal of Personality and Social Psychology, 37*, 131–146.

Crane, E. (1962). Immunization—with and without use of counterarguments. *Journalism Quarterly, 39*, 445–450.

Cronen, V. E., & LaFleur, G. (1977). Inoculation against persuasive attacks: A test of alternative explanations. *Journal of Social Psychology, 102*, 255–265.

Dean, R. B., Austin, J. A., Watts, W. A. (1971). Forewarning effects in persuasion: Field and classroom experiments. *Journal of Personality and Social Psychology, 2*, 210–221.

Delaney, K., & Puskar, K. (2003). Prevention of youth violence: Sustaining our attention and effort. *Journal of Child and Adolescent Psychiatric Nursing, 16*, 39–40.

Druckenmiller, B. (1993). Crises provide insights on image. *Business Marketing, 78*, 40.

Eagly, A. H. (1978). Sex differences in influenceability. *Psychological Bulletin, 85*, 86–116.

Eagly, A. H., & Carli, L. L. (1981). Sex of researchers and sex-typed communications as determinants of sex differences in influenceability: A meta-analysis of social influence studies. *Psychological Bulletin, 90*, 1–20.

Eagly, A. H., & Chaiken, S. (1993). *The psychology of attitudes.* Orlando, FL: Harcourt Brace Jovanovich.

Ebbeling, C. B., Pawlak, D. B., & Ludwig, D. S. (2002). Childhood obesity: Public-health crisis, common sense cure. *Lancet, 360*, 473–482.

Ehrenhalt, A. (1985). Technology, strategy bring new campaign era. *Congressional Quarterly Weekly Report, 43*, 2559–2565.

Eisen, M., Zellman, G. L., & McAlister, A. L. (1990). Evaluating the impact of a theory-based sexuality and contraceptive education program. *Family Planning Perspectives, 22*, 261–271.

Elder, J. P., & Stern, R. (1986). The ABCs of adolescent smoking prevention: An environment and skills model. *Health Education Quarterly, 13*, 181–191.

Ertl, H. C., Xiang, Z. Q., Pasquini, S., & Kowalczyk, D. W. (1999). *Vaccines: Presentation: Encyclopedia of life sciences.* Available: www.els.net. Accessed April 18, 2002.

Esbensen, F., & Huizinga, D. (1993). Gangs, drugs, and delinquency in a survey of urban youth. *Criminology, 31*, 565–587.

Evans, R. I., & Raines, B. E. (1982). Control and prevention of smoking in adolescents: Psychosocial perspective. In T. J. Coates, A. C. Petersen, & C. Perry (Eds.), *Promoting adolescent health: A dialogue on research and practice* (pp. 101–136). New York: Academic Press.

Fazio, R. H. (1986). How do attitudes guide behavior? In R. H. Sorrentino & E. T. Higgins (Eds.), *The handbook of motivation and cognition: Foundations of social behavior* (pp. 204–243). New York: Guilford Press.

Fazio, R. H. (1995). Attitudes as object-evaluation associations: Determinants, consequences, and correlates of attitude accessibility. In R. E. Petty & J. A. Krosnick (Eds.), *Attitude strength: Antecedents and consequences* (pp. 247–282). Mahwah, NJ: Erlbaum.

Fazio, R. H., Chen, J., McDonel, E. C., & Sherman, S. J. (1982). Attitude accessibility, attitude-behavior consistency, and the strength of the object-evaluation association. *Journal of Experimental Social Psychology, 18,* 339–357.

Fazio, R. H., Powell, M. C., & Herr, P. M. (1983). Toward a process model of the attitude-behavior relation: Accessing one's attitude upon mere observation of the attitude object. *Journal of Personality and Social Psychology, 44,* 723–735.

Fazio, R. H., Sanbonmatsu, D. M., Powell, M. C., & Kardes, F. F. (1986). On the automatic activation of attitudes. *Journal of Personality and Social Psychology, 50,* 229–238.

Fazio, R. H., & Williams, C. J. (1986). Attitude accessibility as a moderator of the attitude-perception and attitude behavior relations: An investigation of the 1984 presidential election. *Journal of Personality and Social Psychology, 51,* 505–514.

Flay, B. R. (1985). Prosaic approaches to smoking prevention: Review of findings. *Health Psychology, 4,* 449–488.

Foon, E. (1986). Smoking prevention programs for adolescents: The value of social psychological approaches. *International Journal of the Addictions, 21,* 1017–1029.

Forgas, J. P. (2001). Introduction: The role of affect in social cognition. In J. P. Forgas (Ed.), *Feeling and thinking: The role of affect in social cognition* (pp. 1–28). Cambridge, UK: Cambridge University Press.

Freedman, J. L., & Sears, D. O. (1965). Warning, distraction, and resistance to influence. *Journal of Personality and Social Psychology, 1,* 262–266.

Friedman, L. S., Lichtenstein, E., & Biglan, A. (1985). Smoking onset among teens: An empirical analysis of the initial situations. *Addictive Behaviors, 10,* 1–13.

Gilligan, C. (1982). *In a different voice: Psychological theory and women's development.* Cambridge, MA: Harvard University Press.

Godbold, L. C. (1998). *Conferring resistance to peer pressure among adolescents: Using the inoculation paradigm to discourage alcohol use.* Doctoral dissertation, University of Wisconsin-Madison.

Godbold, L. C., & Pfau, M. (2000). Conferring resistance to peer pressure among adolescents: Using inoculation theory to discourage alcohol use. *Communication Research, 27,* 411–437.

Goldberg, M. E., & Garn, G. J. (1982). Increasing the involvement of teenage cigarette smokers in antismoking campaigns. *Journal of Communication, 32*(1), 75–86.

Gora, J., & Nemerowicz, G. (1985). *Emergency squad volunteers: Professionalism in unpaid work.* New York: Praeger.

Gottlieb, N., & Baker, J. (1986). The relative influence of health beliefs, parental and peer behaviors and exercise program participation on smoking, alcohol use and physical activity. *Social Science and Medicine, 22,* 915–927.

Graber, D. A. (1987). Television news with pictures? *Critical Studies in Mass Communication, 4,* 74–78.

Greene, J. O. (1984). A cognitive approach to human communication: An action assembly theory. *Communication Monographs, 51,* 289–306.

Greenwald, A. G. (1968). On defining attitude and attitude theory. In A. G. Greenwald, T. C. Brock, & T. M. Ostrom (Eds.), *Psychological foundation of attitudes* (pp. 361–388). New York: Academic Press.

Grunbaum, J. A., Kann, L., Kinchen, S. A., Williams, B., Ross, J. G., Lowry, R., & Kolbe, L. (2001). *Youth risk behavior surveillance—United States, 2001.* Washington, DC: Center for Disease Control and Prevention.

Hamburg, D. (1979). Disease prevention: The challenge of the future. *American Journal of Public Health, 69,* 1026–1033.

Hammermeister, J., Roland, M., & Page, R. M. (2002). Are high school students accurate or clueless in estimating substance abuse among peers? *Adolescence, 37,* 567–573.

Hansen, W. B., Graham, J. W., Wokenstein, B. H., & Rohrbach, L. A. (1991). Program intensity as moderator of preventative program effectiveness: Results for fifth grade students in the adolescent alcohol prevention trial. *Journal of Studies on Alcohol, 52,* 568–579.

Harken, L. S. (1987). The prevention of adolescent smoking: Public health priority. *Evaluation & Health Professions, 10,* 373–393.

Harris, M. (1996). An inner group of willing people: Volunteers in a religious context. *Social Policy Administration, 30,* 54–68.

Hass, R. G., & Grady, K. (1975). Temporal delay, type of forewarning, and resistance to influence. *Journal of Experimental Social Psychology, 11,* 459–469.

Health implications of childhood obesity. (1985). *Annals of Internal Medicine, 103,* 1068–1072.

Higgins, E. T. (1996). Knowledge activation: Accessibility, applicability, and salience. In E. T. Higgins & A. W. Kruglanski (Eds.), *Social psychology: Handbook of basic principles* (pp. 133–168). New York: Guilford Press.

Holden, D. (1997). "On equal ground": Sustaining virtue among volunteers in a homeless shelter. *Journal of Contemporary Ethnography, 26,* 117–145.

Hovland, C. I., Lumsdaine, A. A., Sheffield, F. D. (1949). *Experiments in mass communication, 3,* (pp. 201–225). Princeton, NJ: Princeton University Press.

Howard, M., & McCabe, J. B. (1990). Helping teenagers postpone sexual involvement. *Family Planning Perspectives, 22,* 21–26.

Hunt, H. K. (1973). Effects of corrective advertising. *Journal of Advertising Research, 13,* 15–22.

Insko, C. A. (1967). *Theories of attitude change.* New York: Appleton-Century-Crofts.

Jacks, J. Z., & Cameron, K. A. (2003). Strategies for resisting persuasion. *Basic and Applied Social Psychology, 25,* 145–161.

Jacks, J. Z., & Devine, P. G. (2000). Attitude importance, forewarning of message content, and resistance to persuasion. *Basic and Applied Social Psychology, 22,* 19–29.

Jamieson, K. H. (1996). *Packaging the presidency.* New York: Oxford University Press.

Jessor, R., & Jessor, S. L. (1975). Adolescent development and the onset of drinking: A longitudinal study. *Journal of Studies on Alcohol, 36,* 27–51.

Johnson, B. T., & Eagly, A. H. (1989). The effects of involvement on persuasion: A meta-analysis. *Psychological Bulletin, 106,* 290–314.

Johnston, L. D., O'Malley, P. M., & Bachman, G. M. (1991). *Drug use among American high school seniors, college students, and young adults, 1975–1990.* Washington, DC: National Institute on Drug Abuse.

Johnston, L. D., O'Malley, P. M., & Bachman, G. M. (2002). *The monitoring the future national survey results on drug use: Overview of key findings, 2001.* (NIH Publication No. 02-5105). Rockville, MD: National Institute on Drug Abuse.

Kaid, L. L., & Davidson, D. K. (1986). Elements of videostyle: Candidate presentation through television advertising. In L. L. Kaid, D. Nimmo, & K. R. Sanders (Eds.), *New perspectives on political advertising* (pp. 184–209). Carbondale: Southern Illinois University Press.

Kaid, L. L., & Johnston, A. (1991). Negative versus positive television advertising in U.S. presidential campaigns, 1960–1988. *Journal of Communication, 41*(3), 53–64.

Kamins, M. A., & Asseal, H. (1987). Two-sided versus one-sided appeals: A cognitive perspective on argumentation, source derogation, and the effect of disconfirming trial on belief change. *Journal of Marketing Research, 24,* 29–39.

Kern, M. (1989). *30-second politics: Political advertising in the eighties.* New York: Praeger.

Kiesler, C. A., & Kiesler, S. B. (1964). Role of forewarning in persuasive communications. *Journal of Abnormal and Social Psychology, 68,* 547–549.

Kirby, D. (2001). *Emerging answers: Research findings on programs to reduce teen pregnancy.* Washington, DC: The National Campaign to Reduce Teen Pregnancy.

Kirby, D., Barth, R. P., Leland, N., & Fetro, J. V. (1991). Reducing the risk: Impact of a new curriculum on sexual risk-taking. *Family Planning Perspective, 23,* 253–263.

Kowalski, K. M. (2003). Body image. *Current Health 2, 29*(7), 6–12.

Kreutter, K. J., Gerwirtz, H., Davenny, J. E., & Love, C. (1991). Drug and alcohol prevention project for sixth graders: First-year findings. *Adolescence, 26,* 287–293.

Lazarus, R. S. (1991). *Emotion and adaptation.* New York: Oxford University Press.

Lee, W., & Pfau, M. (1997). *The effectiveness of cognitive and affective inoculation appeals in conferring resistance against cognitive and affective attacks.* Paper presented at the annual *conference* of the International Communication Association, Jerusalem, Israel.

Levy, R. (1987). Big resurgence in comparative ads. *Dun's Business Month, 129,* 56–58.

Lin, W-K. (2000). *Humans' internal- and external-oriented cognitions: Inoculation and the spiral of silence—A study of public opinion in democracy.* Unpublished doctoral dissertation, University of Wisconsin-Madison.

Love, R. E., & Greenwald, A. C. (1978). Cognitive responses to persuasion as mediators of opinion change. *Journal of Social Psychology, 104,* 231–241.

Lowenstein, L. F. (1994). Why children kill. *Contemporary Review, 264*(1537), 88–90.

Lumsdaine, A. A., & Janis, I. L. (1953). Resistance to "counterpropaganda" produced by one-sided and two-sided "propaganda" presentations. *Public Opinion Quarterly, 17,* 311–318.

Mabray, D., & Labauve, B. J. (2002). A multidimensional approach to sexual education. *Sex Education, 2,* 31–43.

Manis, M., & Blake, J. B. (1963). Interpretation of persuasive messages as a function of prior immunization. *Journal of Abnormal and Social Psychology, 66,* 225–230.

Marks, A. (1999, August 5). In-your-face ads turn some kids off drugs. *Christian Science Monitor, 91*(175), 2.

McAdams III, C. R., & Lambie, G. W. (2003). A changing profile of aggression in schools: Its impact and implications for school personnel. *Preventing School Failure, 47,* 122–130.

McAlister, A. L., Perry, C., & Maccoby, N. (1979). Adolescent smoking: Onset and prevention. *Pediatrics, 63,* 650–658.

McCroskey, J. C. (1970). The effects of evidence as an inhibitor of counter-persuasion. *Speech Monographs, 37,* 188–194.

McCroskey, J. C., Young, T. J., & Scott, M. D. (1972). The effects of message sidedness and evidence on inoculation against counterpersuasion in small group communication. *Speech Monographs, 34,* 205–212.

McGuire, W. J. (1961a). The effectiveness of supportive and refutational defenses in immunizing and restoring beliefs against persuasion. *Sociometry, 24,* 184–197.

McGuire, W. J. (1961b). Resistance to persuasion conferred by active and passive prior refutation of same and alternative counterarguments. *Journal of Abnormal and Social Psychology, 63,* 326–332.

McGuire, W. J. (1962). Persistence of the resistance to persuasion induced by various types of prior belief defenses. *Journal of Abnormal and Social Psychology, 64,* 241–248.

McGuire, W. J. (1964). Inducing resistance to persuasion: Some contemporary approaches. In L. Berkowitz (Ed.), *Advances in experimental social psychology, 1* (pp. 191–229). New York: Academic Press.

McGuire, W. J. (1966). Persistence of the resistance to persuasion induced by various types of prior belief defenses. In C. W. Backman & P. F. Secord (Eds.), *Problems in social psychology* (pp. 128–135). New York: McGraw-Hill.

McGuire, W. J. (1969). The nature of attitudes and attitude change. In G. Lindzey & E. Aronson (Eds.), *The handbook of social psychology, Vol. 3: The individual in a social context* (2nd ed., pp. 136–314). Reading, MA: Addison-Wesley.

McGuire, W. J. (1970, February). A vaccine for brainwash. *Psychology Today,* 36–39, 63–64.

McGuire, W. J., & Papageorgis, D. (1961). The relative efficacy of various types of prior belief-defense in producing immunity against persuasion. *Journal of Abnormal and Social Psychology, 62,* 327–337.

McGuire, W. J., & Papageorgis, D. (1962). Effectiveness of forewarning in developing resistance to persuasion. *Public Opinion Quarterly, 26,* 24–34.

McIntosh, J., MacDonald, F., & McKeganey, N. (2003). Dealing with the offer of drugs: The experiences of a sample of pre-teenage schoolchildren. *Addiction, 98,* 977–986.

Mendelberg, T. (2001). *The race card: Campaign strategy, implicit messages, and the norm of equality.* Princeton, NJ: Princeton University Press.

Meyrowitz, J. (1985). *No sense of place: The impact of electronic media on social behavior.* New York: Oxford University Press.

Miller, G. R., & Burgoon, M. (1973). *New techniques of persuasion.* New York: Harper & Row.

Miller, G. R., & Burgoon, M. (1979). The relationship between violations of expectations and the induction of resistance to persuasion. *Human Communication Research, 5,* 301–313.

Miller, J., & Krosnick, J. A. (1996). News media impact on the ingredients of presidential evalua-
tions: A program of research on the priming hypothesis. In D. M. Mutz, P. M. Sniderman, & R.
A. Brody (Eds.), *Political persuasion and attitude change* (pp. 79–99). Ann Arbor: University of
Michigan Press.

Miller, W. B., & Baron, R. S. (1973). One measuring counterarguing. *Journal for the Theory of Social
Behavior, 1,* 101–118.

Moore, K. A., & Sugland, B. W. (2001). *Next steps and best bets: Approaches to preventing adolescent
childbearing.* Washington, DC: Child Trends.

Nabi, R. L. (2003). "Feeling" resistance: Exploring the role of emotionally evocative visuals in inducing inoculation. *Media Psychology, 5,* 199–223.

National Campaign to Prevent Teen Pregnancy (1998). *Evaluation abstinence-only interventions.*
Washington, DC: National Campaign to Prevent Teen Pregnancy.

Nienkamp, J. (2001). *Internal rhetorics: Toward a history and theory of self-persuasion.* Carbondale:
Southern Illinois University Press.

Nossal, G. J. (1999). Vaccination. *Encyclopedia of life sciences.* Available: www.els.net. Accessed
April 18, 2002.

Oetting, E. R., & Beauvais, F. (1990). Adolescent drug use: Findings of national and local surveys.
Journal of Consulting and Clinical Psychology, 58, 385–394.

Papageorgis, D. (1968). Warning and persuasion. *Psychological Bulletin, 70,* 271–282.

Papageorgis, D., & McGuire, W. J. (1961). The generality of immunity to persuasion produced by
pre-exposure to weakened counterarguments. *Journal of Abnormal and Social Psychology, 62,*
475–481.

Perry, C. L. (1987). Results of prevention programs with adolescents. *Drug and Alcohol Dependence,
20,* 13–19.

Perry, C. L., Killen, J., & Slinkard, L. A. (1980). Peer teaching and smoking prevention among junior
high school students. *Adolescence, 40,* 275–281.

Petty, R. E. (1977). The importance of cognitive responses in persuasion. *Advances in Consumer Research, 4,* 357–362.

Petty, R. E., & Cacioppo, J. T. (1977). Forewarning, cognitive responding, and resistance to persuasion. *Journal of Personality and Social Psychology, 35,* 645–655.

Petty, R. E., & Cacioppo, J. T. (1979). Issue involvement can increase or decrease persuasion by enhancing message-relevant cognitive responses. *Journal of Personality and Social Psychology, 37,*
1915–1926.

Petty, R. E., & Cacioppo, J. T. (1986). *Communication and persuasion: Central and peripheral routes
to attitude change.* New York: Springer-Verlag.

Pfau, M. (1992). The potential of inoculation in promoting resistance to the effectiveness of comparative advertising messages. *Communication Quarterly, 40,* 26–44.

Pfau, M. (1995). Designing messages for behavioral inoculation. In E. Maibach & R. L. Parrott (Eds.),
Designing health messages: Approaches from communication theory and public health practice
(pp. 99–113). Thousand Oaks: Sage.

Pfau, M. (1997). Inoculation model of resistance to influence. In G. A. Barnett & F. J. Boster (Eds.),
Progress in communication sciences: Advances in persuasion (Vol. 13, pp. 133–171). Greenwich,
CT: Ablex.

Pfau, M., & Burgoon, M. (1988). Inoculation in political campaign communication. *Human Communication Research, 15,* 91–111.

Pfau, M., & Burgoon, M. (1990). Inoculation in political campaigns and gender. *Women's Studies in
Communication, 13,* 1–21.

Pfau, M., Compton, J., Parker, K. A., Wittenberg, E. M., An, C., Ferguson, M., et al. (2004a). The traditional explanation for resistance based on the core elements of threat and counterarguing and an
alternative rationale based on attitude accessibility: Do these mechanisms trigger distinct or overlapping processes of resistance? *Human Communication Research, 30,* 329–360.

Pfau, M., Compton, J., Parker, K. A., An, C., Wittenberg, E. M., Ferguson, M., et al. (2004b). The co-
nundrum of the timing of counterarguing effects in resistance: Strategies to boost the persistence
of counterarguing output. *Communication Quarterly,* in press.

Pfau, M., Dillard, J. P., & Keller, M. L. (2000). *The potential of the inoculation pretreatment strategy to confer resistance to adolescent sexual involvement.* Unpublished manuscript, University of Wisconsin-Madison.

Pfau, M., Holbert, R. L., Szabo, E. A., & Kaminski, K. (2002). Issue-advocacy versus candidate advertising: Effects on candidate preferences and democratic process. *Journal of Communication, 52,* 301–315.

Pfau, M., Holbert, R. L., Zubric, S. J., Pasha, N. H., & Lin, W. (2000). Role and influence of communication modality in the process of resistance to persuasion. *Media Psychology, 2,* 1–33.

Pfau, M., & Kenski, H. C. (1990). *Attack politics: Strategy and defense.* New York: Praeger.

Pfau, M., Kenski, H. C., Nitz, M., & Sorenson, J. (1990). Efficacy of inoculation messages in promoting resistance to political attack messages: Application to direct mail. *Communication Monographs, 57,* 1–12.

Pfau, M., Park, D., Holbert, R. L., & Cho, J. (2001b). The effects of party- and PAC-sponsored issue advertising and the potential of inoculation to combat its impact on the democratic process. *American Behavioral Scientist, 44,* 2379–2397.

Pfau, M., Roskos-Ewoldsen, D., Wood, M., Yin, S., Cho, J., Kerr-Hsin, L., & Shen, L. (2003). Attitude accessibility as an alternative explanation for how inoculation confers resistance. *Communication Monographs, 70,* 39–51.

Pfau, M., Szabo, E. A., Anderson, J., Morrill, J., Zubric, J., Wan, H. (2001a). The role and impact of affect in the process of resistance to persuasion. *Human Communication Research, 27,* 216–252.

Pfau, M., Tusing, K. J., Koerner, A. F., Lee, W., Godbold, L. C., Penaloza, L., et al. (1997a). Enriching the inoculation construct: The role of critical components in the process of resistance. *Human Communication Research, 24,* 187–215.

Pfau, M., Tusing, K. J., Lee, W., Godbold, L. C., Koerner, A., Penaloza, L. J., et al. (1997b). Nuances in inoculation: The role of inoculation approach, ego-involvement, and message processing disposition in resistance. *Communication Quarterly, 45,* 461–481.

Pfau, M., Van Bockern, S., & Kang, J. G. (1992). Use of inoculation to promote resistance to smoking initiation among adolescents. *Communication Monographs, 59,* 213–230.

Pfau, M., & Van Bockern, S. (1994). The persistence of inoculation in conferring resistance to smoking initiation among adolescents: The second year. *Human Communication Research, 20,* 413–430.

Phone scam update. (1996, February). *Consumers' Research Magazine, 79*(2), 23–27.

Plotnick, R. D. (1993). The effect of social policies on teenage pregnancy and childbearing. *Families in Society, 74,* 324–328.

Postrado, L. T., & Nicholson, H. J. (1992). Effectiveness in delaying the initiation of sexual intercourse of girls aged 12–13: Two components of the Girls Incorporated preventing adolescent pregnancy program. *Youth & Society, 23,* 356–379.

Pryor, B., & Steinfatt, T. M. (1978). The effects of initial belief level on inoculation theory and its proposed mechanisms. *Human Communication Research, 4,* 217–230.

Reid, L. N., Soley, L. C., & Vanden Bergh, B. G. (1981). Does source affect response to direct advocacy print advertisements? *Journal of Business Research, 9,* 309–319.

Richey, W. (1998). High-priced loans, high-pressure tactics. *Christian Science Monitor, 90*(142), 1.

Robinson, S. (2000). Children's perceptions of who controls their foods. *Journal of Human Nutrition Dietetics, 13,* 163–171.

Rogers, W. R., & Thistlethwaite, D. L. (1969). An analysis of active and passive defenses in inducing resistance to persuasion. *Journal of Personality and Social Psychology, 11,* 301–308.

Romero, A. A., Agnew, C. R., & Insko, C. A. (1996). The cognitive mediation hypothesis revisited: An empirical response to methodological and theoretical criticism. *Personality and Social Psychology Bulletin, 22,* 651–665.

Roskos-Ewoldsen, D. R. (1997). Attitude accessibility and persuasion: Review and a transactive model. In B. Burleson (Ed.), *Communication yearbook 20* (pp. 185–225). Beverly Hills, CA: Sage.

Roskos-Ewoldsen, D. R., Ralstin, L. A., & St. Pierre, J. (2002). The quick and the strong: Implications of attitude accessibility for persuasion. In J. P. Dillard & M. Pfau (Eds.), *Persuasion: Developments in theory and practice* (pp. 1–45). Thousand Oaks, CA: Sage.

Salomon, G. (1987). *Interactions of media, cognition, and learning: An exploration of how symbolic forms cultivate mental skills and affect knowledge acquisition.* San Francisco: Jossey-Bass.

Sanbonmatsu, D. M., & Fazio, R. H. (1990). The role of attitudes in memory-based decision making. *Journal of Personality and Social Psychology, 59,* 614–622.

Sawyer, A. G. (1973). The effects of repetition of refutational and supportive advertising appeals. *Journal of Marketing Research, 10,* 23–33.

Schwarz, N., Bless, H., & Bohner, G. (1991). Mood and persuasion: Affective states influence the processing of persuasive communications. In M. P. Zanna (Ed.), *Advances in experimental social psychology, 23* (pp. 161–199). San Diego, CA: Academic Press.

Segal, B. (1986). Age and first experience with psychoactive drugs. *International Journal of the Addictions, 21,* 1285–1306.

Sherif, C. W., Sherif, M., & Nebergall, R. E. (1965). *Attitudes and attitude change: The social judgment-involvement approach.* Philadelphia: Saunders.

Sherif, M., & Hovland, C. I. (1961). *Social judgment: Assimilation and contrast effects in communication and attitude change.* New Haven, CT: Yale University Press.

Smith, C. A., & Kirby, L. D. (2001). Consequences require antecedents: Toward a process model of emotion. In J. P. Forgas (Ed.), *Feeling and thinking: The role of affect in social cognition* (pp. 83–106). Cambridge, UK: Cambridge University Press.

Smith, E. R. (1994). Procedural knowledge and processing strategies in social cognition. In R. S. Wyer, Jr., & T. K. Srull (Eds.), *Handbook of social cognition, Vol. 1: Basic processes* (pp. 99–151). Hillsdale, NJ: Erlbaum.

Smith, M. J. (1982). *Persuasion and human action: A review and critique of social influence theories.* Belmont, CA: Wadsworth.

Sobus, K. (2003). Peers and adolescent smoking. *Addiction, 98, Suppl 1,* 37–55.

Solmsen, F. (Ed.). (1954). *The rhetoric and poetics of Aristotle.* New York: Random House.

Stevens, P., & Griffin, J. (2001). Youth high-risk behaviors: Survey and results. *Journal of Addictions and Offender Counseling, 22,* 31–46.

Stone, V. A. (1969). Individual differences and inoculation against persuasion. *Journalism Quarterly, 46,* 267–273.

Suedfeld, P., & Borrie, R. A. (1978). Sensory deprivation, attitude change, and defense against persuasion. *Canadian Journal of Behavioral Science, 10,* 16–27.

Szabo, E. A. (2000). *Inoculation, normative appeals, and emotion as strategies to promote resistance to adolescent smoking.* Unpublished doctoral dissertation, University of Wisconsin-Madison.

Szabo, E. A., & Pfau, M. (2002). Nuances in inoculation: Theory and applications. In J. P. Dillard & M. Pfau (Eds.), *The persuasion handbook: Theory and practice* (pp. 233–258). Thousand Oaks, CA: Sage.

Szybillo, G. J., & Heslin, R. (1973). Resistance to persuasion: Inoculation theory in a marketing context. *Journal of Marketing Research, 10,* 396–403.

Tannenbaum, P. H. (1967). The congruity principle revisited: Studies in the reduction, induction, and generalization of persuasion. In L. Berkowitz (Ed.), *Advances in experimental social psychology, 3* (pp. 271–320). San Diego, CA: Academic Press.

Tannenbaum, P. H., Macaulay, J. R., & Norris, E. L. (1966). Principle of congruity and reduction of persuasion. *Journal of Personality and Social Psychology, 3,* 233–238.

Tannenbaum, P. H., & Norris, E. L. (1965). Effects of combining congruity principle strategies for the reduction of persuasion. *Sociometry, 28,* 145–157.

Taylor, P. (1986). Accentuating the negative: Forget issue; campaign ads this year are heavy on "air pollution." *Washington Post, National Weekly Edition, 3,* 6–7.

Trent, J. S., & Friedenberg, R. V. (1983). *Political campaign communication: Principles and practices.* New York: Praeger.

Trojanowicz, R. C. (1978). *Juvenile delinquency: Concepts and control.* Englewood Cliffs, NJ: Prentice Hall.

U.S. Department of Health & Human Services. (1991). *Too many young people drink and know too little about the consequences.* [Brochure]. Rockville, MD: Author.

Ullman, W. R., & Bodaken, E. M. (1975). Inducing resistance to persuasive attack: A test of two strategies of communication. *Western Speech Communication, 39,* 240–248.

Wallack, L., & Corbett, K. (1987). Alcohol, tobacco and marijuana use among youth: An overview of epidemiological program and policy trends. *Health Education Quarterly, 14,* 223–249.

Wan, H.-H., & Pfau, M. (2004). The relative effectiveness of inoculation, bolstering, and combined approaches in crisis communication. *Journal of Public Relations Research,* in press.

Webb, J. A., Baer, P. E., & McKelvey, R. S. (1995). Development of a risk profile for intentions to use alcohol among fifth and sixth graders. *Journal of the American Academy of Child and Adolescent Psychiatry, 34,* 772–778.

West, D. M. (1997). *Air wars* (2nd ed.). Washington, DC: Congressional Quarterly.

Wilson, J. (2000). Volunteering. *Annual Review of Sociology, 26,* 215–240.

Wyatt, S. (2000, December 12). Gore was biggest spender on TV. *Wisconsin State Journal,* p. B3.

Wyer, R. S., Jr. (1974). *Cognitive organization and change: An information processing approach.* New York: Wiley.

Wyer, R. S., & Srull, T. K. (1989). *Memory and cognition in its social context.* Hillsdale, NJ: Erlbaum.

Zabin, L. S., & Hayward, S. C. (1993). Adolescent sexual behavior and childbearing. Newbury Park, CA: Sage.

Zaichkowsky, J. L. (1985). Measuring the involvement construct. *Journal of Consumer Research, 12,* 341–352.

Zuwerink, J. R., & Devine, P. G. (1996). Attitude importance and resistance to persuasion: It's not just the thought that counts. *Journal of Personality and Social Psychology, 70,* 931–944.

CHAPTER CONTENTS

5 The Potential of Electronic Communication and Information Technologies as Research Tools: Promise and Perils for the Future of Communication Research

NICHOLAS A. PALOMARES
University of California, Davis

ANDREW J. FLANAGIN
University of California, Santa Barbara

Scholars across several disciplines praise the methodological advantages afforded to research endeavors by the use of electronic communication and information technologies. At the same time, however, scholars note several disadvantages stemming from the use of these tools. To assess the utility of electronic communication and information technologies as research tools, we synthesize work on the methodological issues surrounding the use of these technologies for the future of communication research. Our overarching goal is to review prior and current perspectives in order to appropriately assess and critique the use of electronic tools in research pursuits while informing future applications of these tools in the field. Throughout the chapter we articulate the argument that sound theoretical and methodological practices determine the appropriateness of the application of any particular tool. Accordingly, our focus is on the specific methodological concerns that arise with the use of electronic technologies in the conduct of research. We organize our discussion into six major sections: sampling issues; data integrity concerns, including the reliability and validity of research design and measures; the potential afforded by electronic communication and information technologies; contemporary ethical considerations; an explicit assessment of the future of communication research in view of the application of electronic technologies; and a concluding section that establishes the contribution of our review and briefly outlines outstanding issues.

AUTHORS' NOTE: An abbreviated version of this chapter was presented at the annual conference of the National Communication Association, November, 2004, in Chicago, Illinois. The authors thank Miriam Metzger and Ron Rice for their thoughtful comments and suggestions on an earlier version of the chapter.

Correspondence: Nicholas A. Palomares, Department of Communication, One Shields Avenue, University of California, Davis, Davis, CA 95616; email: napalomares@ucdavis.edu

Communication Yearbook 29, pp. 147–185

INTRODUCTION

Scholars across several disciplines praise the methodological advantages provided by electronic communication and information technologies. Espoused benefits include minimizing time spent on mundane tasks such as data entry and participant scheduling (Ilieva, Baron, & Healey, 2002; Reips, 2000, 2002a; Schmidt, 1997; Stanton & Rogelberg, 2002), the ability to acquire large samples quickly (Birnbaum, 2000, 2001; Christians & Chen, 2004; Krantz & Dalal, 2000), and the capacity for novel data capture using technologies such as automated internet data mining (Burton & Walther, 2001) and Web-based observational cameras (Stanton & Rogelberg, 2002). At the same time, however, scholars have noted several disadvantages stemming from the use of electronic technologies, such as a limited ability to acquire representative samples (Brenner, 2002), greater infringement on participants' privacy (Elgesem, 2002), and an increased likelihood of participant fraud (Madge & O'Connor, 2002). Indeed, even the same methods are viewed both positively and negatively. For example, participant self-selection has been framed as both an advantage for (Reips, 2000) and as an obstacle to (Mustanski, 2001; Sills & Song, 2002) sound research.

Nonetheless, the use of electronic communication and information technologies in the conduct of research has increased rapidly over the past decade with the growth of the internet and Web, and many researchers affirm continued use of these tools (Musch & Reips, 2000). In fact, the application of these technologies is evident in the field of communication (e.g., Eveland, Cortese, Park, & Dunwoody, 2004; Flanagin & Metzger, 2003a; Kalyanaraman & Sundar, 2003; Lee, 2004; Lee & Nass, 2002; Lemus, Seibold, Flanagin, & Metzger, 2004; Palomares, 2004; Tidwell & Walther, 2002), and increasing usage seems inevitable in the future. In spite of remarkable growth in the use of these tools in the conduct of research, academic inquiry into their usage has not kept pace. To assess the utility of using electronic communication and information technologies as research tools, in this chapter we synthesize and critically assess work on the methodological issues surrounding the use of these technologies for the future of communication research.

Conceptual Boundaries and Overview

Research and reviews focusing on contemporary technologies range widely in both the terms used to describe these tools [e.g., information and communication technologies (Lievrouw et al., 2001), electronic media (Culnan & Markus, 1987), and advanced information technologies (Huber, 1990)], and their definitions. Based on the ubiquity of specific tools and their prevalence in research endeavors, we focus on electronic communication and information technologies, defined as electronic tools that facilitate communication and information capture, transmission, processing, and storage among people who typically are not co-located. Among the most central electronic communication and information tools used for research today are the internet (i.e., interconnected computers operating as an infrastructure for digital global communication), the Web (i.e., the system of computer servers using a graphical user interface accessed via the internet that includes documents and other files interconnected by hyperlinks), and electronic mail (email). In addition, other internet-based technologies (e.g., newsgroups, chat functions, web logs, and multiuser dungeons, or MUDs) and non–internet-based technologies (e.g., virtual reality, active badges, and mobile telephones) are included in this review when appropriate and informative.

We emphasize research methods that have taken significant advantage of electronic communication and information technologies and to which scholars have dedicated considerable empirical work and discussion. Accordingly, primary attention is devoted to survey research, experimental research, and content analysis, with less attention on other methodologies, such as interaction analysis and focus groups. In this manner, discussion of some research tools is more limited, yet reflects the current use of electronic tools in the conduct of scientific research.

Our overarching goal is to review current research perspectives in order to appropriately assess and critique the use of electronic technologies in research endeavors while informing future applications of these tools in communication research. Throughout the chapter we articulate the argument that sound methodological practices and theoretical concerns determine the rigor and appropriateness of the application of any particular tool(s). Clearly, contemporary technologies offer appealing advantages that have enormous utility for communication scholars. The attractiveness of these tools, however, also creates potential for misuse and abuse and often relies on substantial new skills and resources. Scholars, in other words, may realize benefits when using these technologies, while they may neglect important drawbacks that can potentially surface.

A secondary goal of this chapter, therefore, is to engender a simultaneous appreciation of the utility and potential pitfalls scholars face when invoking electronic communication and information technologies in their research. In this manner, we aim to foster an informed awareness of the methodological issues accompanying the use of electronic technologies for research pursuits. Highlighting ambiguities and unresolved issues, we also hope to spark discussion and continued research on the promise and perils of using these technologies as research tools within and outside the field of communication, so that future research maintains a high level of methodological scrutiny and rigor.

We structure this chapter according to crucial considerations manifest across research methods, rather than by technologies that can aid research endeavors. By so doing, we systematize the literature around major methodological issues integral to most types of research and highlight the bases of sound methods, regardless of the tools invoked in the conduct of research. This structure serves to frame methodological issues in a way that is highly heuristic to scholars' future research endeavors. That is, scholars can use our review by extrapolating the methodological issues we discuss onto specific forms of a wide range of research activities. Accordingly, we organize our discussion into six major sections, focusing on sampling issues; data integrity concerns, including the reliability and validity of research design and measures; the potential afforded by electronic communication and information technologies; ethical considerations; an explicit assessment of the future of communication research in view of the application of electronic technologies; and a concluding section that establishes the contribution of our review and briefly outlines outstanding issues.

SAMPLING

Sampling—the procedure by which researchers acquire their units of analysis—is a primary concern of all sound research (e.g., surveys, experiments, and content analyses).[1] Researchers must weigh several alternatives when determining the best sampling method, including decisions regarding who should be solicited, the necessary number of participants, and the type of sampling required (e.g., probability versus nonprobability). Internet technologies, at times, appear to simplify sampling issues. For instance, different time frames may generate different response rates or different kinds of respondents. Indeed, faster responses from participants can be obtained via the internet (Christians & Chen, 2004; Reips, 2002a): An experiment that randomly assigned individuals to complete the same questionnaire via either email or traditional mail found that email questionnaires were completed and returned in almost half the time (9.22 days versus 16.43; Tuten, Urban, & Bosnjak, 2002), a finding corroborated by a review of 11 studies showing that email surveys were returned in an average of 5.59 days, compared to 12.21 days for mail surveys (Ilieva et al., 2002). Ultimately, reductions in response time can result in differences in response rates. In addition, the internet often affords larger sample sizes compared to non-internet samples, due to decreased costs per respondent (Birnbaum, 2000; Krantz & Dalal, 2000; Reips, 2000), which might yield different kinds of respondents. Nonetheless, in spite of some apparent advantages, such affordances should be framed by an informed awareness of relevant methodological considerations, as detailed next.

Online Participant Recruitment

One of the first considerations for using internet technologies to collect responses from online participants is how to inform individuals about the research study. Several strategies exist. Announcing the study in internet newsgroups (e.g., alt.usenet.surveys) and online communities (such as MUDs), submitting the study's website to search engines (e.g., google.com or yahoo.com) and web portals that list online studies (e.g., the American Psychological Society's listing: http://psych.hanover.edu/Research/exponnet.html), using specialized metatags (i.e., descriptors of a particular webpage used for indexing by search engines), sending email solicitations, submitting messages to an email listserv (such as the

Communication Research and Theory Network accessible at http://lists1.cac.psu. edu/cgi-bin/wa?A0=CRTNET), and other methods have all been suggested and used as means of publicizing studies and soliciting participants (e.g., Batagelj & Vehovar, 1998; Birnbaum, 2000; Buchanan & Smith, 1999; Krantz & Dalal, 2000; Reips, 2001, 2002b; Williams & Robson, 2004).

Even though they can prove useful, these methods for recruiting participants also pose problems.[2] For example, these methods do not guarantee that all participants who know about the study actually participate (Vehovar, Batagelj, Manfreda, & Zaletel, 2002). In fact, the proportion of those who know about a study and those who choose to participate is difficult to determine (Couper, 2000). The use of Web portals, newsgroups, and search engines, for example, does not enable a researcher to determine who read information about a particular study but chose not to participate. There are methods to determine the number of individuals who visit a study's website and choose not to participate (Werner, 2002); however, measuring those who knew about the study but did not visit the study's website remains virtually impossible.

Alternatively, with email solicitations, participant response rates can be assessed based on the number of email messages sent and the number of individuals who participated in the study. Using email solicitations, however, requires a list of current and accurate email addresses, and assumes that individuals check their email accounts on a regular basis. In addition, participants who forward email messages to others, such as their friends or colleagues, can cause problems for determining response rates and adhering to target populations. Overall, although the efficiencies of internet-based tools for sampling are appealing, they are accompanied by their own difficulties.

Online Response Rates

Despite such problems with participant recruitment and the accurate determination of response rates, a great deal of research has focused on accurately determining these rates for online surveys. Reviews of online surveys show response rates of around 30–40%. Cook, Heath, and Thompson (2000), for example, reviewed 68 online surveys and found that the average response rate was 40%. Comley (2000), in a review of 42 Web-based pop-up surveys, showed that response rates ranged from 9% to 48%, with an average of 27%. In each case, these reviews included only surveys in which a specific number of potential participants were available, thus allowing for response rates to be determined highly accurately. Comparisons of online versus mail surveys, however, seem to demonstrate a slightly higher response rate for mail surveys. For example, a review of 10 studies by Ilieva et al. (2002) found that the average response rate for online surveys was 39%, as compared to 46% for mail surveys (for a review with similar conclusions, see Cho & LaRose, 1999).

Two experiments have directly tested response rate differences between online and traditional mail questionnaires (Couper, Blair, & Triplett, 1999; Truell,

Bartlett, & Alexander, 2002). Both experiments randomly assigned individuals to participate in one of two modes of data collection (i.e., traditional mail questionnaire or online questionnaire). Even though Truell et al. found no significant difference between online (51%) and mail (53%) response rates, Couper et al. noted a 71% response rate for the mail questionnaire condition and 43% for the online questionnaire condition—a 28% difference. Potential explanations for this discrepancy include participants' frequency of email use and differences in question numbering between studies. Specifically, not all participants in the Couper et al. study used their employer-assigned email addresses regularly, perhaps exaggerating the difference in response rates between mail and online modes. In addition, a confound in the numbering of questions for Couper et al. might explain differences between the two studies, at least in part: Whereas Truell et al. numbered items identically in both conditions, Couper et al.'s email questionnaire contained 14 subsections with 94 items (numbered from 1–94), but for the mail questionnaire items within each subsection were numbered separately. A potential result is that participants in the email condition of Couper et al.'s study may have been deterred from responding by the large number of questions moreso than those in the mail condition. Further research is necessary to resolve such discrepancies; however, these results raise the possibility that subtle factors can influence online response rates. To date, scholars have focused on three main sources of influence related to online response rates—researcher-based factors, participant-based factors, and technical factors—each of which we cover in turn.

Researcher-based factors. Researchers have examined several factors within their control that can influence response rates online. Similar to non–internet-based research, prenotifications, personalized letters, and follow-up contacts and reminders are associated with higher response rates, according to qualitative and quantitative reviews (Cook et al., 2000; Sheehan, 2001; Tuten et al., 2002). Another method to increase response rates is a promise to share results upon study completion, which is relatively fast, easy, and inexpensive via the internet (Bosnjak & Batinic, 2002; Kleinman, 2004). Using a multimode technique for data collection also increases response rates for online research (Dillman, Phelps, Tortora, Swift, Kohrell, & Berck, 2001; Ilieva et al., 2002; Schaefer & Dillman, 1998). Using this technique, a complete data collection strategy via one mode (e.g., email) is implemented and, after a short amount of time, is followed by another attempt to collect data in a different mode (e.g., mail).

Mixed results regarding response rates exist for other researcher-based factors. Response rate data regarding survey length have been viewed as equivocal by Sheehan (2001) and as a nonfactor by Bosnjak and Batinic (2002), who reported that online participants indicated a willingness to spend at least 10 minutes on a given study. Even though some research has shown no relationship between incentives and response rates (e.g., Frick, Bachtiger, & Reips, 2001), a meta-analysis of 68 online surveys (Cook et al., 2000) revealed that incentives had a negative relation to response rates, perhaps, as the authors speculate, because researchers anticipated low response and, therefore, felt the need to offer incentives. A meta-analysis of mail surveys revealed that up-front incentives (i.e., before survey completion) increased responses by between 8% (for nonmonetary rewards) and 19% (for monetary rewards), whereas incentives contingent upon survey completion did not have an effect (Church, 1993). Perhaps, then, incentives should be given to participants prior to the completion of online studies as well.

Participant-based factors. The effects of individual characteristics also have been examined with regard to online response rates. Participants' curiosity and interest in the research process (Bosnjak & Batinic, 2002), education level (Cook et al., 2000), experience with research participation, and computer literacy levels (Vehovar et al., 2002) are positively associated with participation in research studies. Another important participant-based factor is the research issue's importance (i.e., timeliness, salience) to participants (Cook et al., 2000; Sheehan, 2001; Vehovar et al., 2002). The more interest participants have in the topic, the higher the response rates for online studies. Finally, assurances of confidentiality and anonymity result in higher response rates (Couper, 2000; Couper et al., 1999; Mustanski, 2001; Sassenberg & Kreutz, 2002). Additional individual difference factors that are not currently addressed in the literature but might relate to response rates are the amount of free time that potential participants have, the amount of time they spend on the internet, concerns with online privacy and security, and, perhaps, even participants' outspokenness or eagerness to share ideas online.

Technical factors. Finally, technical factors may affect participants' response rates online. Low modem speeds (or other bandwidth issues), incompatible Web browser versions, internet service provider connection time costs, unreliable connections, and other technical factors have been proposed to decrease response rates (Couper, 2000). A decrease in response rates due to internet service provider costs may be exaggerated in places where flat rates and unlimited connection time for internet access providers are rare, where recipients are charged for receipt of messages, or where internet access is not relatively affordable (e.g., China). In addition, email address errors, firewalls that inhibit message delivery, and anti-spam software all hinder the research process through the resultant nondelivery of messages to potential participants (see, for example, Vehovar et al., 2002). Due to its potential importance in understanding the most efficient use of internet-based technologies for participant solicitation, further research on technical factors is required.

Generalizability

Generalizability refers to the extent to which one is able to infer accurately from a sample to a larger, specified population (Singleton & Straits, 2005). There is a long-standing critique of social scientific research for being too focused on student samples and, therefore, unable to generalize accurately to larger, more diverse populations (see, for example, Smart, 1966). Some scholars, on the other hand, do not consider convenience samples of students to be problematic because certain phenomena span across human behavior and therefore will endure across all types of samples (see, for example, Birnbaum, 2001). Nevertheless, researchers currently have proposed the internet as a tool for sampling nonstudent populations in order to gain more generalizable (i.e., representative) samples (e.g., Buchanan, 2000). Getting a truly representative sample of a large population via the internet, however, is problematic (e.g., Best & Krueger, 2002; Brenner, 2002; Stanton & Rogelberg, 2002).[3]

For a sample to be representative, every unit in the target population (i.e., those to whom one wishes to generalize) must have an equal chance of being included in the sample (Babbie, 1998; Cook & Campbell, 1979; Singleton & Straits, 2005). To achieve this, a reliable and exhaustive list of the target population must exist. Using such lists, means of random selection (such as random digit dialing) are used to select potential respondents, and follow-up techniques (such as incentives) are often employed to gain compliance. In the absence of such ideal lists, researchers have relied on means of communication, such as the telephone, that include a high proportion of the target population (for example, current estimates for telephone saturation in the U.S. are 93%; Best & Krueger, 2002).

Internet-based technologies, however, do not have the equivalent of a telephone directory, nor are webpage uniform resource locators (URLs), email addresses, or other means of identification sufficiently standardized to enable effective means of random selection. Consequently, the frame population (i.e., those for whom one has contact information) of internet users diverges significantly from the target population of internet users (Couper, 2000). Even if random selection of internet users were possible, current internet saturation (both direct and indirect) in the U.S. is approximately 70% (Internet World Stats, 2004), suggesting that a large portion of the population would remain inaccessible to research through this means. These considerations highlight the digital divide that separates those with access to advanced technologies from those who lack such access (bridges.org, 2003). Moreover, internet users are significantly different from nonusers on many demographic, communication, expertise, and attitudinal variables (see Katz & Rice, 2002).

Limitations to generalizability are even more pronounced at the global level (Krantz & Dalal, 2000). Countries across the globe vary drastically in terms of their internet saturation levels and may vary based on economic, social, and cultural factors. The United States Central Intelligence Agency (2003) estimates, for example, that Turkey has almost twice as many internet users as Iran, despite demographically comparable populations. Discrepancies like this can adversely affect a researcher's ability to make accurate generalizations to a global target population.

Internet Versus Non-Internet Sample Comparisons

Researchers have compared demographic characteristics of internet-based samples to non–internet-based samples as a means to assess generalizability. Much of this research, however, has been limited to comparisons between internet samples and non-internet college samples. Nevertheless, compared to college samples, internet samples tend to be more representative of the U.S. as a whole (Bailey, Foote, & Throckmorton, 2000; Birnbaum, 2000; Reips, 2000), yielding older participants (Bailey et al., 2000; Birnbaum, 2000) and providing more equal sex composition (Birnbaum, 2000; sex composition was nearly equal for internet samples, whereas college samples were composed of 73% females). Research also suggests, however, that internet samples are less ethnically diverse than college samples (Bailey et al., 2000), although examination of individuals from various cultures is possible via the internet if they are sought out actively (Reips, 2000). Substantiating these findings, a review of over 30 studies that used internet samples (Krantz & Dalal, 2000) concluded that (a) there is no consensus regarding the sex composition of internet samples, but there is a small trend toward more equal distributions; (b) the large majority of internet samples is ethnically composed of White participants with a tendency to contain North Americans, particularly from the U.S.; and (c) the mean and median ages across studies ranged between 26 and 35 years. internet samples, thus, are fairly representative of the general U.S. population regarding a small set of factors; however, crucial differences exist that call for a need to conduct future research, especially comparing internet samples with non-internet samples composed of nonstudent participants. Katz & Rice (2002) for example, compare demographics between their national random telephone samples and U.S. census data in order to assess the representativeness of their samples.

Improving the Representativeness of Internet Samples

Scholars have suggested and critiqued means to improve the representativeness of internet samples. For example, Best and Krueger (2002) reviewed two common solutions for nonrepresentative samples: weighting and the form-resistant correlation hypothesis. First, data from internet respondents can be weighted by the incidence of known characteristics in the target population using, for instance, census data. Weighting, however, must be conducted with variables that are highly correlated with the key variables under investigation.

The second option is to assert the form-resistant correlation hypothesis by stating that a nonrepresentative sample may shift the means of certain variables but the correlations between variables remain the same. By this logic, the variables measured with internet samples simply shift their positions along their respective axes while maintaining the same correlation among variables. In this manner, although the means of variables measured using internet samples may be unrepresentative of larger populations, the associations between these variables are representative.

The authors critiqued both methods for potentially ignoring the fact that internet and non-internet samples could differ in terms of factors that mediate or moderate responses to the variables measured. Best and Krueger (2002) demonstrated and confirmed this claim empirically, finding that their email and telephone samples were different and that weighting or using the form-resistant correlation hypothesis did not increase the generalizability of the email sample's results. Similarly, Vehovar, Manfreda, and Batagelj (1999) confirmed the limited ability to increase representativeness of internet samples via weighting and Katz and Rice (2002) chose not to weight data because in their assessment costs typically outweigh benefits. In light of these findings, a relevant issue to consider is under what circumstances researchers should use internet samples, an issue we address in the next section.

The Utility of Sampling via the Internet

Despite these participant recruitment, response rate, and representativeness limitations, the internet can be a useful tool for acquiring samples from which accurate generalizations are made. Couper (2000) offered several suggestions to obtain representative samples on the internet. Target populations can be limited to those for whom a list of email addresses is available, thus providing an inclusive frame population from which a probability sample can be drawn. Such a sample would be representative of the individuals included in the list of email addresses. For example, if an email list of every employee from a particular organization were available, then a probability sample could be drawn, and based on those data generalizations could be made to the organization as a whole. The sample of employees from the organization, therefore, would be representative of the organization's employees (although not representative of other organizations).

As another possibility to use the internet to acquire representative samples, random digit dialing of U.S. citizens could be used in conjunction with web or email surveys, such that once called, participants would be asked for their email addresses or to visit a website (e.g., HarrisInteractive.com, 2004, currently employs this technique). This method could cut down personnel costs because telephone calls would be significantly shorter than traditional telephone surveys. In addition, experiments could be conducted with representative samples using this telephone-internet hybrid method. Such a technique, however, would not include those without access to internet technologies. Nonetheless, these methods suggest that there are ways to access samples via the internet and still reap the benefits of the technology while increasing the ability to make accurate generalizations.

Probability sampling is not always the best option (see Shapiro, 2002; Singleton & Straits, 2005). Rather, some research projects call for sampling methods (e.g., purposive, quota sampling) that internet-based tools are well equipped to provide. Indeed, the internet is useful for acquiring samples of individuals from specialized or hard-to-reach populations (e.g., Fortune 500 or volunteer organizations) through purposive sampling (Birnbaum, 2000; Christians & Chen, 2004; Duffy, 2002; Madge & O'Connor, 2002; Mustanski, 2001; Reips, 2002a; Schmidt, 1997; Tuten et al. 2002). Moreover, as noted earlier, internet samples enable researchers who are heavily reliant on university student samples to gain access to a broader range of participants. In this manner, the internet provides a means to access nonstudent samples, potentially bolstering the generalizability of results (see Shapiro, 2002).

Finally, research that focuses on the characteristics and behaviors of only internet users need not attempt to represent the wider population (i.e., those without internet access), although sampling issues still apply if generalizing to all internet users is a research goal. Strategies to capture internet user data include surveys, tracking of online behaviors, and diary methods that record internet usage. In addition, creative strategies for accessing relatively new internet users also exist. For example, in research by Kraut et al. (1998), families received hardware, software, and internet connections in return for access to their internet activities and survey and interview responses. Such quid pro quo arrangements, although expensive, enable researchers to capture extremely comprehensive data on internet use. Nevertheless results obtained in this manner may suffer from limitations to their generalizability.

Unobtrusive Data Obtained via the Internet

A final benefit of internet-based research tools is the ability to acquire data not attained via direct interaction with individuals. Unobtrusive data readily obtained online include (but are not limited to) online postings of text messages, online advertisements, information on websites, online news articles, Web-server activity logs, newsgroup archives, organizational documents, and other units of analysis that do not include human participation in a research study. Rice (1990) discusses the use of computer systems as unobtrusive monitors of data on communication usage, flows, and content, and discusses related issues of sampling, validity, reliability, and ethics. Ramirez, Walther, Burgoon, and Sunnafrank (2002) discuss such "extractive" data collection strategies, noting that ample social information can be obtained in this manner. Analyses of these data could occur through content analysis (Krippendorff, 1980, 2004; Neuendorf, 2002; see, for example, Kleinman, 2004), network analysis of relations (Rice, 1990; Rice & Shook, 1990), or inferential statistics (Flanagin & Spivey, 2004). Limitations to these data collection methods may include sophisticated technical knowledge required to obtain or extract data in some cases and ethical and legal concerns (discussed at greater length later in this chapter). Potential problems regarding the use of messages posted online (e.g., Usenet messages, chat room postings, or online communities) are a lack of knowledge about the demographic characteristics of message senders; interpreting communicators' intended meanings, which can present more difficulty when conversations are text-only (Williams & Robson, 2004); and more effort establishing researcher visibility and intimacy in ethnographic research (LeBesco, 2004).

Scholars have begun to realize the potential of unobtrusive data collection online, and in other venues pre-dating the Web (Burton & Walther, 2001; Foot, Schneider, Dougherty, Xenos, & Larsen, 2003; Kleinman, 2002; Krippendorff, 2004; Majchrzak, Rice, Malhotra, King, & Ba, 2000; McLaughlin, Goldberg, Ellison,

Lucas, 1999; Mitra & Cohen, 1999; Neuendorf, 2002; Rice, 1982, 1990; Rice & Shook, 1990; Rössler, 2002; Stanton & Rogelberg, 2002). Of course, with this potential come myriad issues for researchers to consider. For example, how might researchers systematically sample from among the many millions of websites available (whether seeking a random, purposive, or quota sample), which of the thousands of newsgroups (that date back to 1981 with about 800 million posts via http://groups.google.com/) should one sample, and how does one account for the dynamic nature of the internet, which is constantly undergoing changes (cf., Krippendorff, 2004; Neuendorf, 2002)? Relatedly, scholars conducting computer-aided content analyses to automatically extract certain words or phrases from electronic texts must be aware of potential problems inherent in the programs. For example, computer programs can have difficulty counting typographical errors, misspelled words, words that are not uniformly hyphenated within and across texts (e.g., *e*mail versus email), numbers in numeral versus alphabetic format (e.g., 5 versus five), words differentially conjugated (e.g., run, ran, running), words that are typographically similar but semantically different (e.g., to play a game, to play an instrument, to perform in a play, to play with a toy, to play versus being serious), and words that differ typographically yet are semantically similar (e.g., empty, unfilled, vacant). Krippendorff (2004) presented a thorough discussion of potential problems in this domain, as well as information on computer programs and other means that can potentially resolve such issues.

In sum, although internet-based tools have great potential for aiding research endeavors, researchers must be cognizant of the implications of their sampling method and select the one that is most appropriate for their research goals.

DATA INTEGRITY

Data integrity is a crucial issue when using electronic communication and information technologies as research tools. In short, data integrity refers to the quality of data and the associated results. Data should be both reliable and valid. That is, data should be measured in a way that yields consistent results (i.e., reliable) and should be measured by means that accurately reflect the concept under study (i.e., valid). Even though reliability and validity are core concerns of all research, electronically based methods can create unique problems in these regards. In this section, we focus on some of the major threats to data integrity posed by the use of electronic tools for conducting all types of research. First, we discuss threats to the validity of results, including social desirability, self-selection biases, participant drop-out and mortality, and other threats to validity. Next, we focus on the reliability and validity of concept measurement via technologies. Then, we discuss factors related to item response length and quality. Finally, we consider issues regarding data interdependence based on measuring and observing nonindependent human participants and other units of analysis.

Threats to the Validity of Results

The issue of validity of results focuses on the accuracy of the results obtained. Valid relationships between variables result when the relation does not stem from an unspecified variable, a methodological flaw, or other confound. Several factors can threaten result validity, including social desirability, demand characteristics, participant drop-out and mortality, and other issues, as discussed next.

Social desirability. Social desirability refers to the tendency of research participants to respond to questions or behave in ways that are normatively appropriate (i.e., socially desired), although the term is used under many guises (see, for a review, Richman, Kiesler, Weisband, & Drasgow, 1999). Social desirability can affect the extent to which research results obtained accurately reflect participants' true perceptions and behaviors. Evidence on social desirability in the electronic environment has been mixed. Some research has found less social desirability for online compared to paper-and-pencil studies (Kiesler & Sproull, 1986), whereas other research showed no difference across these modes (Pettit, 2002). Computerized testing has also been shown to lead to more social desirability than paper-and-pencil testing; however, this effect was moderated by computer experience, such that when computer experience was great and questionnaire completion was via computer, individuals had higher social desirability scores than when computer experience was low and survey completion was via computer (Finegan & Allen, 1994). In addition, in a meta-analysis of 61 studies comparing computerized, paper-and-pencil, and face-to-face interviews, Richman et al. (1999) demonstrated that whereas computerized testing versus face-to-face interviews showed lower social desirability effects, several moderating variables were also important, including study design, percentage of women in the sample, mean age of the sample, and type of subject population. Overall, results suggest that social desirability is a complex phenomenon that does not seem to differ simply as a main effect of data collection mode.

An important factor for social desirability is participants' desire for impression management, as demonstrated in several studies. For example, Wilkerson, Nagao, and Martin (2002) found that the mode of administration (computerized versus paper-and-pencil) for a specific questionnaire did not matter, but that the purpose or context of the questionnaire did. Specifically, a job screening context showed higher social desirability effects than did a consumer opinion context. Similarly, Epstein, Klinkenberg, Wiley, and McKinley (2001) found that those completing an internet questionnaire, with peers nearby who could potentially see their responses on the computer screens, rated same-sex targets lower in attractiveness (compared to those completing a paper-and-pencil questionnaire with no overlooking peers). They speculated that this effect was perhaps due to fear of ridicule from peers, although they did not directly assess this claim. Furthermore, research indicates that individuals can treat computers much like they treat other individuals (see, for a review, Reeves & Nass, 1996), suggesting that impression management efforts may be at work when interacting with computers as social agents in the administration of questionnaires. Thus, impression management is one potential reason for social desirability in online environments.

A related factor is participants' sense of anonymity. Anonymity reduces identifiability, leading to reduced social desirability bias because respondents are less likely to be held accountable for behaviors and attitudes that may not correspond with societal norms (Sassenberg & Kreutz, 2002). In fact, participants responding to a questionnaire online have been shown to exhibit the least amount of social desirability bias (regardless of anonymity or lack thereof), whereas those responding via paper-and-pencil anonymously gave more socially desirable responses, and those responding via paper-and-pencil nonanonymously showed even more social desirability in their responses (Joinson, 1999).

In their review of relevant research, Knapp and Kirk (2003) concluded that differences in social desirability biases between data collected online and offline may stem from the fact that confidential data collection techniques (through which participants possibly can be identified) are often employed in online data collection efforts, as opposed to anonymous techniques (through which participants cannot be identified). To assess differences in social desirability, they conducted an experiment in which data collection mode (paper-and-pencil mail questionnaire, online questionnaire, and automated touch-tone phone questionnaire) was randomly assigned to participants who answered the same set of questions ranging in topic sensitivity. In all conditions, a private setting for questionnaire completion was supplied and anonymous response methods were used. They found no significant differences in the social desirability of responses among the three groups, suggesting that anonymity (versus confidentiality) is a crucial factor mitigating social desirability response biases. Based on these findings, although anonymity is a key factor, there also is evidence that data collection mode is important in explaining social desirability response effects, with advantages to electronic means under certain conditions, as compared to other modes (e.g., paper-and-pencil questionnaire conducted in person rather than via the mail). Moreover, some recent research suggests that individuals are better able and more willing to express their "true" selves freely in a computer-mediated context, thus electronic data collection may be superior at reducing socially desirable responses and behaviors (Bargh, McKenna, & Fitzsimons, 2002).

Certain factors affect the existence of socially desirable responses, but they are not inherent to online or computerized data collection methods. Rather, these factors may be related to these data collection modes (e.g., computer-mediated communication tends to offer reduced social cues that can increase anonymity). Future research, therefore, should focus on determining which features of electronic communication and information technologies influence social desirability effects most markedly and the circumstances under which these factors are most likely to occur.

Self-selection bias. Participant self-selection can bias research results because individuals who choose to participate in a particular research project can be different than those who choose not to participate. In this manner, those who self-select to participate may have distinctive characteristics that influence (or bias) results. Depending on the sampling method invoked, this issue may be exaggerated in online studies because online research participants may have to seek out research opportunities more actively than with other forms of data collection (e.g., random digit dialing or student participation pools; Mustanski, 2001; Sills & Song, 2002). For instance, in a sequential sample collected online (whereby every 1000th person who visited MSNBC.com was invited to participate), less online sexual activity and online compulsive behavior were found than in a convenience sample of participants who volunteered for the same topical questionnaire through news and word of mouth reports (Cooper, Scherer, & Mathy, 2001). This finding suggests that individuals are more likely to volunteer for an online study that addresses a topic that is salient to them. Thus, as mentioned earlier, when an issue is important to participants, data integrity may be jeopardized due to self-selection biases.

Reips (2000), nonetheless, has argued that for online experiments, self-selection can be better than less voluntary participation (e.g., college students participating for mandatory course credit). Online participants, he reasoned, are more motivated to participate and provide more thoughtful answers because they can terminate their participation more freely and do not feel forced to take part in research projects. Reips (2000, 2002a) also suggested ways to test if self-selection is a problem for Web-based studies. For example, researchers can use various entry (or "splash") webpages that are advertised in different online locations, all of which lead to the actual study webpage. Reips asserts that results from the different groups of participants can be compared and, if no differences emerge, then self-selection is not an issue. This strategy, however, does not account for the possibility that participants may still differ from nonparticipants, even among those with access to the internet. Importantly, however, self-selection creates greater biases for survey research than for experimental designs, since the random assignment of subjects to conditions helps reduce the effects of self-selection because individuals with varying degrees of motivation to participate become equally distributed across experimental conditions (Cook & Campbell, 1979; Piper, 1998). Nonetheless, high motivation among participants overall may influence results regardless of the methods employed.

Participant dropout or mortality. The third major threat to the validity of online research results is participant drop-out or mortality, which occurs when participants fail to complete their participation in a study, either within one survey or over time in longitudinal panel designs (Knapp & Heidingsfelder, 2001; Piper, 1998). Participant dropout is of particular concern when the premature departure of participants is nonrandom, indicating that some characteristic(s) of those who drop out is meaningful to both their decision to terminate their participation and to relevant independent or dependent variables (Cook & Campbell, 1979). The effect of nonrandom departure is that participants exhibiting certain characteristics are underrepresented in the data collection effort and, therefore, results cannot account for the influence of that characteristic or are influenced disproportionately by participants who lack that characteristic.

Causes of participant dropout take two general forms. First, dropouts can be technically induced, such that electronic communication and information technologies somehow prevent certain participants from continuing with a study (due, for example, to Web browser incompatibilities, slow loading pages or other bandwidth problems, or software malfunctions; Knapp & Heidingsfelder, 2001; Reips, 2000). Second, dropouts can be due to participant-based reasons, such as lack of incentives to continue with a long study, cognitive fatigue, the existence of sensitive topics, a lack of obligation to continue, and other reasons (Frick et al., 2001; Knapp & Heidingsfelder, 2001). For example, Frick et al. (2001) found that although a monetary incentive did not increase initial willingness to participate, it did decrease participants' dropout rates.

Random dropout is typically not a cause for major concern. Dropout is, nonetheless, undesirable and several solutions for reducing dropout rates have been suggested. Reips (2002a) offered three remedies: (a) Researchers can give potential participants information about what the study will entail so that they can accurately assess their willingness to participate before starting; (b) researchers can ask participants to estimate the probability that they are likely to complete the entire study and then only examine data from highly motivated individuals; and (c) researchers can use a warm-up technique, which asks participants a set of questions that is not going to be analyzed, so that only highly motivated individuals participate in the actual study. Even though these solutions may reduce dropout rates for online studies, they also introduce motivational confounds, such that examining only highly motivated participants may induce lower participation rates or biased responses, as discussed earlier.

Additional suggestions to reduce dropout rates include requesting personal information (e.g., age, sex) prior to the study's major tasks and measures, rather than following them, in order to guard against dropout of those who may not wish to share personal information (Frick et al., 2001). Further, participation on the weekend (rather than during the week) tended to reduce dropout rates, perhaps due to reduced time constraints, although asking for participants' email addresses prior to a study increased dropout by 12%, perhaps due to confidentiality concerns (O'Neil & Penrod, 2001). Nonetheless, some features of electronic communication and information tools may help to alleviate dropout rates, given, for example, the reduced cost and increased ease of sending participation reminders via email and automated prompts to participants if they stop responding. In addition, although giving participants a study progress indicator has been suggested to decrease dropout rates (Vehovar et al., 2002), no effect was demonstrated in an experiment that manipulated progress indicator for an online questionnaire (Couper, Traugott, & Lamias, 2001). This particular finding perhaps resulted because webpage download time was greater for the progress indicator condition, which lasted 3–4 minutes longer to complete than the no progress indicator condition. Additional research, without feature-based confounds, is necessary to determine reasons and solutions for participant mortality.

Additional threats to validity. Demand characteristics, such as gender-based expectations revealed by a researcher's sex, are also potential threats to data validity. Scholars have proposed, however, that demand characteristics cause less concern for research using electronic technologies, especially for online research, due to a decrease in the amount of researcher-participant interaction stemming from the ability to automate procedures (Hewson, Laurent, & Vogel, 1996; Piper, 1998; Reips, 2000; Stanton & Rodelberg, 2002). Furthermore, in online research a reduction in evaluation apprehension may result, again possibly due to less researcher-participant interaction (Piper, 1998). Nevertheless, participants at times interact with computers as if they were human (see Reeves & Nass, 1996), which could result in the preservation of these problems. No known data, however, speak to any of these claims.

Maintaining appropriate control over technical factors and participants can be problematic in online studies as well. For example, computer software and hardware specifications can vary from participant to participant (Couper, 2000; Krantz, 2001; Mustanski, 2001; Schmidt, 1997), which might result in unintended variation in experimental stimuli or questionnaire presentation. In addition, contamination effects for online experimental research can create a loss of control because participants can more readily interact with each other and divulge information about the study and its conditions (Buchanan, 2000; Piper, 1998), especially if participants are recruited via newsgroup postings or other means where they may already be in close contact with one another.

Problems of control can be addressed by several means. First, random assignment for experimental research guards against participant control issues to some degree. Moreover, technical specification inconsistencies can be offset by measuring participants' computer configurations, either unobtrusively through computer scripts or directly by asking participants, and then statistically controlling for these variations. Also, technical inconsistencies can be minimized by using client-side (as opposed to server-side) programs that are downloaded by participants and that enable data to be captured and sent to researchers via participants' computers in fixed ways that are not reliant on participants' browsers, bandwidth, or computer configurations (see Reips, 2002a, for a discussion of these technical issues). However, client-side solutions may be inhibited by users' willingness to download software to their personal computers, in view of computer virus and spyware risks.

A final threat to the validity of results is that individuals can participate in the same study multiple times, which is more likely to occur in online data collection efforts (compared to other means) because of the automated nature of much online research (Buchanan, 2000; Mustanski, 2001; Reips, 2000). Duplicate participation can occur intentionally (from participant fraud due to an incentive) or unintentionally (Web browser or other technical malfunction or user error, resulting in a form that is submitted more than once). Even though multiple submissions can be reduced by technical means (e.g., "cookies" or email or internet protocol (IP) address tracking may be implemented), it is extremely difficult to completely eliminate the problem.

Measurement Reliability and Validity

The next major concern regarding data integrity deals with the measurement of concepts or variables. Measurement scales or inventories developed and confirmed as reliable and valid in one mode (e.g., paper-and-pencil) may not be reliable and valid in another mode (e.g., online). When a measure is converted to an online format, the reliability and validity of the scale should, therefore, be assessed before it is used for online research (Buchanan, 2002). Much research has been devoted to assuring the integrity of measurements that were not originally developed and tested using electronic or computerized formats.

A review of the past 3 decades of computerized (but not online) testing of individual difference inventories concluded that most scholars consider computerized administration of these scales to be a valid and reliable alternative to paper-and-pencil methods (Epstein & Klinkenberg, 2001). In addition to assessing the integrity of computerized measurements, research also has examined the validity and reliability of online measures. The majority of this research has found that many existing individual difference inventories maintain their reliability and validity when migrated to an online environment, including a self-monitoring scale (Buchanan, 2000; Buchanan & Smith, 1999; Hertel, Naumann, Konradt, & Batinic, 2002), the Big Five Personality Inventory (Hertel et al., 2002), a sexual jealously scale (Voracek, Stieger, & Gindl, 2001), a social desirability scale, a perfectionist self-presentation scale, a computer anxiety scale (Pettit, 2002), a parental and peer attachment inventory, a negative mood regulation scale, a trait meta-mood scale (Fouladi, McCarthy, & Moller, 2002), and a ruminative response scale (Davis, 1999). A large review of several studies, however, concluded that there is not equivalence for all online and offline personality inventories, noting that those scales exhibiting online-offline similarity tended to be unidimensional constructs and those exhibiting divergence tended to be multidimensional (Buchanan, 2001). For the most part, then, online versions of personality inventories seem to be reliable and valid. Nonetheless, empirical confirmation of this assumption seems prudent, particularly in view of studies indicating relatively low correlations between system-generated versus self-reported email usage data (Rice, Hughes, & Love, 1989).

Comparing online and paper-and-pencil assessments and concluding that no differences exist (i.e., supporting the null hypothesis), however, is not sufficient to say that Web and paper-and-pencil measures are identical, for at least two reasons (Crano & Brewer, 2002). First, small sample sizes may not provide sufficient statistical power to detect differences. Second, different sets of factors may yield the same results for each version of the scale. A preferred method is to use construct validation techniques, which rely on theoretically predicted and empirically confirmed relationships among constructs to determine a scale's integrity (Crano & Brewer, 2002; Krantz & Dalal, 2000).

Online measurement reliability and validity concerns, as reviewed above, focus primarily on personality or individual difference inventories from a psychological perspective. No known research has tested individual difference measures for communication constructs in online contexts. Furthermore, the portability of nonpersonality communication measures into online contexts has yet to be tested. Behavioral measures, such as secondary goal concerns (Dillard, Segrin, & Harden, 1989), relational measures, such as relational closeness (Vangelisti & Caughlin, 1997), and other communication scales, if transported into an online context, will require empirical confirmation of their online reliability and validity via comparative and convergent techniques.

Item Response Length and Quality

The next concern for data integrity centers on the quality or length of participants' responses to open-ended questions and missing responses for closed-ended items. A review of past studies concluded that more detailed response content is provided for open-ended questions in email studies, as compared to paper-and-pencil open-ended items (Tuten et al., 2002), although factors that might contribute to this result (e.g., the size of text input fields) were not examined.

With regard to nonresponse to closed-ended items, data seem to indicate that electronic means of data capture fare slightly better than nonelectronic means. For example, in an experiment in which individuals were randomly assigned to email or mail data collection modes, email items had less nonresponse (36% missing items) compared to mail items (52% nonresponse; Truell et al., 2002). Although Couper et al. (1999) found no difference between data collection mode (email versus mail) with regard to item nonresponse, they did find differences for background measures, such that more missing background items occurred for the mail than for the email condition. Finally, technical means of data capture can serve to eliminate nonresponses entirely, as, for example, when responses are required in data fields. The utility of forced responses, however, should be weighed against its potential hazards, such as the collection of poor quality data or respondent dropout.

Some researchers have speculated that item nonresponse could be due to lack of computer expertise, incompatible Web browsers, and screen resolution differences (Dillman & Bowker, 2001). Additionally, research has shown that greater question nonresponse was observed in a computer-administered questionnaire when using a box entry field into which participants had to type their response values, as compared to a radio button entry condition where participants simply selected the appropriate value to indicate their responses (Couper et al., 2001). Due to the many possible entry formats, and attendant technical considerations, further research is required to address the causes of, and potential solutions for, item nonresponse in electronic research.

Interdependence of Observations

Data interdependence occurs when observations (or measures) of units of analysis are linked in some way, making them similar to each other compared to non-linked units (Anderson & Ager, 1978; Kenny, 1995; Sadler & Judd, 2001). Interdependence problems arise when data from linked units are analyzed as if they are not linked, such as when the interdependence among members of a group within an organization who interact regularly are treated the same as members of the same organization who do not belong to the group. The crucial issue is that interdependence be recognized and accounted for, preferably by avoiding mismatches between levels of theory, measurement, and statistical analysis (see Glick & Roberts, 1984; Klein, Danserau, & Hall, 1994).

Many frequently used statistical tests in social scientific research, such as analysis of variance, are based on the assumption that observations of the units of analysis are independent from one another. Thus, data interdependence violates this assumption and can potentially decrease the integrity of data and associated results unless the problem is appropriately addressed. Importantly, data interdependence is based on two factors: (a) knowledge that the units are linked in some way, and (b) similarities or differences between linked and unlinked units, which require empirical validation. Linked units, therefore, do not automatically create a data interdependence problem because tests can determine if the variation among linked units from the same group is greater or smaller than the variation among unlinked units from different groups. Also, interdependence problems can be controlled through statistical procedures. Examples when interdependence could potentially be problematic include dyadic or group interactions, assessments of communication within couples or families, and other situations in which some participants share commonalities and others do not.

The problem of interdependence of observations is not inherent in any particular mode of research. For example, face-to-face dyadic interactions are just as susceptible to data interdependence issues as are computer-mediated dyadic interactions. Potential problems that are unique to online research are twofold. First, online participants may be linked in ways unknown to researchers. For example, data acquired via participant solicitations in online newsgroups may be at risk for data interdependence due to the connections individuals may have with other individuals via the newsgroup. This situation may not be easily assessed by researchers.

The second potential problem involves data collection of nonhuman units of analysis (e.g., online messages, online advertisements, online news articles, and Web-server activity logs). In this case, the concern is that when sampling these sorts of data they may be differentially linked. For example, messages posted to a particular newsgroup may exhibit different levels of dependence on phenomena within that newsgroup than would messages sampled from a different newsgroup. In this manner, data may be treated as independent observations when in fact they are influenced in meaningful ways by membership in specific groups. In such situations, interdependence of data usually can be tested and statistically controlled, if found. Given these concerns, researchers should be aware of potential interdependence problems in research examining phenomena using electronic communication and information technologies and should take appropriate steps to guard against their deleterious effects.

POTENTIAL BENEFITS OF ELECTRONIC COMMUNICATION AND INFORMATION TECHNOLOGIES AS RESEARCH TOOLS

Appropriate sampling techniques, combined with processes that ensure data integrity, are the bases of all sound research. With this foundation in place, electronic communication and information technologies can provide significant advantages for researchers by increasing the ease with which research tasks are performed and through the addition of novel capabilities offered by these tools.

Mundane and Tedious Tasks Made Easier

The research process can be tedious, complex, and slow. To some degree, the use of electronic communication and information technologies can serve to eliminate or minimize monotonous procedures, simplify intricate elements of the research process, and speed up the entire research cycle. For instance, online data collection can remove the need for data entry and reduce or eliminate data entry errors because data can be captured electronically in fixed formats (Christians & Chen, 2004; Ilieva et al., 2002; Schmidt, 1997). In addition, online signup for laboratory studies via a website, with automated email reminders, can simplify scheduling and alleviate the need for calling each participant individually (Reips, 2000, 2002a; Stanton & Rogelberg, 2002). Web-mediated focus groups may be more readily available and utilized compared to face-to-face focus groups; further, focus groups of special or hard to acquire populations might be easier to gather online (for summaries of several studies using online focus groups, see Williams & Robson, 2004). Studies themselves also can be largely automated, eliminating the need for individuals to oversee every part of a study. Finally, random assignment of participants to experimental conditions can be automated without participants' awareness (Piper, 1998; see Burton & Walther, 2001 for a Web-based random assignment script) and may be easier and less prone to human error than randomized condition schedules or other procedures, such as flipping a coin.

For analyses of online social interactions (e.g., language use or structure), researchers do not need to spend time on transcription, as they would for face-to-face interactions, because interaction transcripts can be generated automatically with perfect accuracy (Christians & Chen, 2004; Stanton & Rogelberg, 2002; see for examples, Rice, 1982; Lemus et al., 2004; Palomares, 2004). Relatedly, although currently not sufficiently accurate, voice recognition software may soon be able to transcribe verbal communications with high fidelity. Finally, electronic communication and information tools enable access to participants from a variety of locations without researchers or participants going anywhere, reducing both time and financial costs.

Electronic technologies also can facilitate mundane and tedious aspects of some content analyses (Krippendorff, 2004). First, Web pages provide an immense data resource for scholars to examine. For example, weblogs (also known as "blogs") are online journals that can be the subject of content analyses (e.g., Trammell & Gasser, 2004). Researchers analyzing Web-based text also are not required to transcribe content, as text is already in electronic format. Having content in electronic format is especially useful when researchers conduct computer-aided content analyses (for a list and description of computer programs used for content analysis see Neuendorf, 2002). These content analysis programs can increase reliability, reducing errors in data. Computers also can help to facilitate the acquisition of representative samples of specified content, notwithstanding the concerns discussed in the previous section on sampling.[4]

Novel Capabilities

New technologies not only offer assistance for typical research tasks, but also allow innovative and distinctive methods of inquiry. More specifically, electronic communication and information technologies enable the presentation of stimuli, the capture of participants' responses, and the performance of content analyses to take on novel forms.

Advances for surveys and experiments. Interviews and surveys can be automated via computerized interview robots (or "bots") that ask individuals questions in seemingly natural conversation (Janetzko, 2002). This tool is extremely useful in reducing the costs of large-scale interviews or surveys and also may be useful for experiments for which control and continuity are high priorities. Further, surveys can be adapted or tailored to participants' previous responses (Epstein & Klinkenberg, 2001; Hertel et al., 2002) offering, for example, follow-up questions based on particular responses to previous questions. In this fashion, interactive exercises with feedback given to participants are more readily available in online contexts (Hertel et al., 2002). Communication educators interested in pedagogical research may find instructor and course assessments less effortful in online contexts with the ability to query students easily and frequently throughout the duration of a course (e.g., Flanagin, 1999).

Moreover, electronically delivered questionnaires can include much more complex structures and are not limited to text (Best & Krueger, 2002). Experiments with photographic or video stimuli (with varying manipulations or conditions) can be more easily presented via electronic technologies (see, for example, Potter, Mahood, & Yao, 2003; Walther, Slovacek, & Tidwell, 2001). This level of interactivity can be extended to online interactive games that can be used to assess different communicative phenomena (Ruppertsberg, Givaty, Van Veen, & Bulthoff, 2001). For example, examinations of group dynamics and leadership emergence could be studied via group-based electronic games or scenarios that are conducted in MUDs. Scholars using diary or log methodologies (e.g., media consumption research) could utilize electronic technologies, such as portable digital assistants (PDAs), to aid participants' entries, with the novel capability to program PDAs to remind participants to input their entries into the PDA-based digital diary/log on a set schedule. Email or Web-based programs could provide a similar function (see, for example, Haridakis, Rubin, & Rubin, 2003; Rubin, Haridakis, Rubin, & Miraldi, 2002).

Major media research firms are capitalizing on advances in electronic communication and information technologies as well. Nielsen, for example, has begun to implement nationwide unobtrusive television rating measures, called the Local People Meter (LPM), with New York as one of the most recent markets (Nielsen Media Research, 2004). The LPM is more accurate than traditional paper-and-pencil diary methods and capable of obtaining data quicker from larger and more diverse samples. Relatedly, Nielsen–NetRatings (2004) uses computer monitoring devices to record participants' Web usage and links these data to participants' consumer purchasing behaviors, collected via in-home universal product code (UPC) scanners. Finally, HarrisInteractive.com (2004) uses a hybrid telephone-email method, whereby potential participants are first called via telephone and asked for their email addresses. Once they supply their email addresses, participants are emailed to participate in the current study and future research.

Advances for social interaction analyses. Observational research of social interactions also can profit from the use of electronic communication and information technologies. Researchers can use Web-based cameras (i.e., web-cams that capture audio and video and transmit these data across the internet) to record individuals in their natural environments without researchers having to visit and set up equipment in many locations (Stanton & Rogelberg, 2002). Interaction analyses of individuals in homes, organizations, and other contexts can be conducted more easily and less obtrusively via these web-cams and other electronic technologies. "Active badges" or "smart cards" can potentially track the whereabouts of participants (Stanton & Rogelberg, 2002), enabling researchers to analyze communication patterns (although when using this methodology the implicit assumption that communication would be operationalized as colocation must be acknowledged). Based on these data, social network analyses (see Monge & Contractor, 2003; Wasserman & Faust, 1994) could be used to explore the nature and form of connection among actors and behaviors (see Garton, Haythornthwaite, & Wellman, 1999). Similarly, mobile telephones, PDAs, and global positioning system (GPS) devices could be used in this way as well.

Computer monitoring devices (Stanton & Rogelberg, 2002) enable individuals' computer usage, online navigation of websites, email messages sent and received, and other forms of communication and interaction to be tracked in a variety of settings (e.g., in participants' homes, organizations, and schools). In addition, a range of variables, such as time spent interacting online or on computer-based work-related activities, are made available through the use of electronic communication and information technologies (Burton & Walther, 2001). Data acquired via mobile telephone technologies similarly could be examined in relation to other variables. These behavioral measures allow for largely unobtrusive observation of participants and could be tested for agreement with attitudinal measures (see, for example, Flanagin & Metzger, 2003b). Researchers also can use these measures as dependent variables for experiments in which independent variables are manipulated and their subsequent effects on these electronic observational measures are determined. These types of data risk a mismatch between conceptual and operational definitions; however, triangulation with other measures, such as self-reports or third-party observations, may provide more robust data. In fact, recent research has indicated that a computer-monitoring program yielded lower levels of internet usage than self-reported diary and survey estimates (Greenberg et al., 2004).

Finally, virtual reality allows researchers to analyze social interactions and observe communicative behaviors in scenarios that take place in simulated, and potentially highly controlled, environments (Stanton & Rogelberg, 2002). Recent research suggests that computers are viewed as more influential than human partners under some conditions and that participant reaction may vary by the degree of anthropomorphism of the virtual partner (Burgoon et al., 2000). In this fashion, virtual reality enables observations in seemingly natural contexts and facilitates observation of situations otherwise difficult to scrutinize or manipulate. Research indicates that under certain conditions individuals interact with media as if they were human (Reeves & Nass, 1996); as a result, these tools can be accurate reflections of how individuals would interact with real people in real situations.

Advances for content analysis. Content analyses also benefit by using electronic technologies. For example, Krippendorff (2004) discussed four types of computer aids for content analyses (i.e., accounts of character strings, text searches, computational content analyses, and interactive-hermeneutic approaches). These four types of computer-assisted content analysis present significant advances on which scholars can capitalize in their research. Content analyses, for example, can be conducted using semantic network analyses to examine the linkages and/or co-occurrences between certain types of content (Rice & Love, 1987). Further, memetic approaches to content analyses—analyses of how content or texts change and evolve over time—are easier with computerized aids (see, for example, techniques such as centering resonance analysis, Corman, Kuhn, McPheee, & Dooley, 2002). Computer programs also improve content analyses by providing researchers with the ability to manage, organize, manipulate, and examine extremely large amounts of content, providing scholars new perspectives they could not obtain without such technologies.

Even though the use of electronic communication and information technologies offers substantial opportunities for researchers, it also raises several ethical concerns, which we address next.

ETHICAL CONCERNS

Ethical issues are an important consideration in the conduct of research. The use of electronic communication and information tools prompts particular ethical concerns within the traditional topics of how to obtain informed consent from research subjects, minimize the possibility of participant harm, guard subjects' privacy, and debrief research participants.

Informed Consent

A major ethical concern when conducting research online is how individuals provide informed consent to participate in research studies (Sharf, 1999). Typically, a physical signature is required to signal informed consent, but this is less feasible when researchers and participants do not meet face-to-face. Methods for acquiring informed consent via the internet include using a telnet application, whereby individuals logon to a secure server and indicate their consent to participate (Smith & Leigh, 1997), or issuing instructions on a webpage that inform participants that they give their informed consent by continuing with the research when they click a hyperlink that takes them to the study's subsequent webpage(s) (Flanagin & Metzger, 2003b; Schmidt, 1997). These methods, however, do not guarantee that participants are at least 18 years of age (unless the frame population ensures this) and are of sound mind, typically requirements for participation in the majority of research studies. In addition, the multilingual nature of the internet can result in potential misunderstandings from participants of different sociolinguistic cultures who may not fully understand the informed consent process. Gaining informed consent from individuals in online groups with fluctuating membership can be difficult, particularly for longitudinal research (Kleinman, 2004). Finally, potential participants can also falsify information (e.g., age) in order to participate in research—particularly if incentives are involved—which can be difficult to detect in online research.

Nonetheless, as Walther (2002) contended, when there is no harm to participants, traditional research conducted face-to-face does not require informed consent, suggesting that online research need not always require informed consent either. That is, regardless of the mode of data collection, if research does not contain significant risks, it should not require participants' informed consent. Walther also argued that the problems of obtaining proper informed consent (e.g., age falsification and participants' lack of competence) are not inherent to online research. Assessing a person's age by inspection, for example, can be difficult in face-to-face contexts, and assessing a person's age vocalically via the telephone is also problematic. Furthermore, assessing competency or judging a person's understanding of informed consent material is not inherently better via face-to-face situations either, as it assumes that potential participants relay relevant signals via verbal and nonverbal cues and researchers are able to detect these cues accurately. Walther concludes that the federally implemented ethical guidelines (by which most U.S. research institutions and universities abide) privilege face-to-face research in terms of the informed consent process. Rather than deeming online research a special circumstance where informed consent must always occur, the informed consent process should depend on the specific research regardless of data collection mode. In other words, one should not claim ipso facto that all online research is problematic with regard to informed consent.

Participant Harm

Another issue is the potential for participant harm when using electronic communication and information technologies as research tools. The ease and speed with which participants can obtain feedback in a study, coupled with the lack of personal debriefing, is one concern. Online research makes it quite simple to provide participants specific results for a study (indeed, this feature may be used as a recruitment technique, as previously discussed). Some scholars warn, however, that information should not be given to participants via the internet if harm may result from such knowledge (Buchanan, 2001, 2002; Kleinman, 2002). For example, in a study examining intelligence or depression levels, the revelation of low intelligence scores or high depression scores can cause psychological harm to participants. Of course, the appropriateness of providing specific feedback is not unique to online research methods, but the potential for participant harm can be magnified given the ease of feedback and the need to supply a qualified individual who is capable of interpreting results and providing necessary counseling when harmful or threatening information is made available.

Another concern regarding participant risk is potential negative effects of interaction with nonhuman agents. Individuals sometimes interact with, and react to, computers as if they had human characteristics (Reeves & Nass, 1996); as a result, researchers should be cautious about the "personalities" imparted to electronic technologies used for research, since participants could be affected by computers' personalities in a negative way. Relatedly, researchers' use of virtual reality and other computer-simulated interactions may also prompt negative events and behaviors, even if participants are told that the simulated "social" interactions are not real. Again, although the interactions themselves may not take place with humans, the experiences of these interactions (e.g., negative responses or unwanted arousals) may affect participants as if the social interaction were real. Harm to participants is a serious concern to which researchers should pay appropriate attention.

Privacy

Electronic communication and information technologies can create new privacy issues for researchers. Some scholars contend that despite the internet's public
nature, public data obtained online differ, for example, from observing individuals on public streets, because the internet is often part of people's homes (Elgesem, 2002). Moreover, some note that privacy may be invaded through intrusive
email messages sent to potential research participants (Cho & LaRose, 1999).
Further, many electronic research devices noted earlier (e.g., active badges, computer monitoring devices, and web-cams) warrant special consideration with regard to potential privacy violations because of their unobtrusive and ubiquitous
capabilities (Stanton & Rogelberg, 2002). These technologies enable less obtru-
sive observation of individuals in many contexts; as a result, some scholars feel
that participants may forget about these monitoring devices and reveal information or behave in ways they would otherwise wish to remain private (Stanton &
Rogelberg, 2002). There also is the potential with these devices (e.g., web-cams)
to collect data from individuals who have not provided their consent to participate in research but are in close proximity to individuals who have provided their
consent. Assuming, however, that participants consent to such unobtrusive observations and have the option to withdraw or remove certain information from the
researcher's database, ethical violations regarding privacy are not likely. Without
participants' informed consent, of course, the use of these observational techniques would most likely result in privacy violations if the situations are not public or the risks to participants are great.

Use of online public data not acquired through participant-researcher interaction (such as content analyses of online message postings, online advertisements,
websites, and other types of nonhuman participant data) is somewhat controversial with regard to privacy concerns. Messages posted online are usually submitted to newsgroups or other online communities that are available to any member
of the public with internet access. Some scholars feel that use of these sorts of data
can be unethical if participants' consent is not formally given because individuals do not intend for their messages to be used for research and have a right to be
able to keep certain information private (Bellotti, 1997; Kleinman, 2002, 2004;
Sharf, 1999). On the other hand, other scholars feel that information posted on
the internet, including online postings in newsgroups, online communities, and
other online discussions, is in the public domain and fair use regulations regarding
copyright dictate that use of these data for research purposes should not be regulated by guidelines that govern the use of human participants (Bruckman, 2002;
Walther, 2002). Use of online communications also does not require researcher-
participant interaction (e.g., participants are not surveyed for the information),
and thus using these data should be exempt from the regulations regarding human
research participation. Bruckman even suggested that online messages should
be linked to particular individuals, because information posted on the internet

is semipublished information and, if no risk is involved, then authors should be given credit for their postings.

Walther (2002), however, argued that messages posted online need not be linked to individuals at all because most social scientific research would merely quantify online messages and report general trends. On the other hand, much qualitative research, such as conversation analysis, would use specific exemplars that, even if pseudonyms are employed, could have the potential to be traced to the corresponding authors through the archival and search capabilities on the internet. Researchers using specific online messages as examples should therefore be aware of the potential to link these messages to participants, especially if links could create a risk for the authors of messages. Observations of online messages that cannot be linked to individuals, and that do not use identifiable examples, on the other hand, should not be considered human participant research.[5]

A final privacy concern in online research is maintaining participant confidentiality. Given the public nature of the internet, keeping information confidential, secure, and private is important when conducting online research. Buchanan (2002) suggested that information transferred between participants' computers and researchers' Web servers should be encrypted to maintain confidentiality, especially when participants' responses are associated with identification information. Participants in online research also should be informed that email messages they send are usually saved on their computers and that Web browsers typically cache webpages they have visited, so that if participants share their computers with others or if they use public computers, their responses could be read by others (Walther, 2002; see also Sharf, 1999). An additional recommendation is that researchers should opt for Web-based as opposed to email-based studies because email-based studies contain participants' email addresses, which could decrease the likelihood of participant confidentiality (Cho & LaRose, 1999; Im & Chee, 2002) and may spawn email viruses. Another method to keep participants' responses confidential is to separate informed consent webpages, which require participants' identification information, from the webpages containing participants' responses, by not linking them in databases (Cho & LaRose, 1999). Additionally, organizations participating in research efforts can randomize user identifications and link them to survey data, so that researchers are unaware of individuals' identities (see, for example, Rice, Hughes, & Love, 1989). A final recommendation to ensure participants' confidentiality is to have the researcher's websites undergo third-party certification, such as that provided by TRUSTe. com. These methods are important to ensure the confidentiality of participants' responses in online research.

Debriefing

A final ethical concern is debriefing participants upon the completion of a research study. Debriefing is particularly important when deception is used, in order for researchers to reveal the true purpose of the study to participants (Singleton

& Straits, 2005). Debriefing also can inform participants of hypothesized relationships, experimental manipulations, and data regarding participants' individual
performance or measures. Typically, debriefing does not pose major problems.
However, online research participants can leave studies more freely before debriefing takes place (Piper, 1998). Debriefing online typically takes the form of
a text-based statement via either a webpage or email; participants (intentionally
or unintentionally), however, can easily ignore these statements online. Suggestions for increasing the likelihood that debriefing occurs successfully in Web-
based research (for participants who complete the study and for those who drop
out early) include emailing a debriefing statement to participants after they leave
the study, making debriefing information available via a hyperlink from a button saying, "click here to leave the study," and automatically providing debriefing information to participants once they leave the study at any stage through
a computer script (Nosek, Banaji, & Greenwald, 2002). Of course, ensuring
that participants are given and actually read the debriefing information is not a
problem limited to online research (Walther, 2002); participants, for example,
can choose to ignore debriefing information in online research just as easily as
in face-to-face research.

Even though the use of electronic technologies in the conduct of research presents particular ethical considerations, scholars should treat all forms of research
equally with regard to ethical guidelines, whether data are collected face-to-face
or electronically. Thus, above all else, researchers should strive to do no harm regardless of the tools invoked. "No harm" research is particularly vital as future
electronic tools reveal unforeseen ethical complexities.

THE FUTURE OF COMMUNICATION RESEARCH AIDED BY
ELECTRONIC COMMUNICATION AND INFORMATION TECHNOLOGIES

As scholars continue to apply electronic communication and information technologies to research endeavors, methodological issues covered in this essay remain important and additional concerns become relevant. Indeed, several of these
concerns are critical to consider for the future of communication research, including (a) the evolving role of advanced electronic technologies in research activities; (b) an informed awareness of the methodological issues associated with the
use of electronic technologies when conducting research; (c) communication-specific issues implied by the use of electronic tools in research; and (d) future applications of electronic technologies, based on current uses and perspectives.

The Evolving Role of Technology in Research Endeavors

To date, electronic communication and information technologies have influenced
scholarly research in at least three ways, each of which has implications for future
applications of these tools. First, researchers have transported traditional methods

and procedures into electronic arenas. The use of technologies in this manner is readily apparent and typically straightforward. Relevant examples include Web-based experiments, online focus groups, email questionnaires, and computerized assessments of face-to-face behaviors. In these instances, traditional methods are transferred to an electronic format, with minimal methodological modifications and typically without embellishment. In many cases, the conversion of methods to electronic means can be achieved without substantial pitfalls, although appropriate methodological vigilance is, of course, critical.

Next, electronic technologies can be used to alter, augment, and expand traditional methods. Researchers can use electronic technologies to generate new or more complex means to assess research questions in novel ways. In such cases, technological advances have the potential for more accurate research methods (e.g., computer-aided content analyses, Web-based questionnaire administration, or online network data collection), new ways to assess phenomena (e.g., adapted or tailored experimental manipulations or computer-captured Web log data), and the exploration of new phenomena that may result (e.g., the use of active badges might prompt the assessment of novel network phenomena). Importantly, such extensions are not new: For example, conversation analytic methodologies did not gain momentum until the advent of the tape recorder, which allowed researchers to capture conversation and make accurate transcripts that served as the basis for systematic analysis (cf. Psathas, 1995). Electronic technologies are similarly capable of ushering in domains of research that have not yet been fully explored because limitations of time, accuracy, expense, and effort.

Third, electronic tools have enabled scholars to direct their research efforts toward understanding electronic technologies themselves. For example, researchers can examine new technology usage via inspection of Web log files and cellular telephone usage. Similarly, research efforts can focus on investigating the methodological issues posed herein, such as the causes of online participant dropout, the convergent validity of a common paper-and-pencil measure administered online, or comparisons of self-report to system-collected usage data.

Informed Awareness

A vital mechanism to maintain the rigor and quality of research using electronic tools is an informed awareness and thorough consideration of the issues outlined in this essay. Anyone conducting electronic-based research must weigh the costs and benefits in order to make informed and thoughtful decisions. Those reading, critiquing, and/or reviewing such research also must pay attention to the issues we have discussed because these issues can influence their appraisal of research. Being cognizant of these issues will help to ensure that future research is sufficiently rigorous to maintain trust in research findings and knowledge claims. Indeed, among our goals in this essay is to prompt discussions among scholars interested in electronic technologies about the conceptual, methodological, and empirical issues surrounding the use of these tools in research endeavors.

Communication-Specific Issues Implied by the Use of Electronic Research Tools

The methodological issues presented in this review are in many respects particularly relevant for communication scholars, given that interindividual interactions are at the core of what communication scientists examine (Chaffee & Berger, 1987). Indeed, many of the methodological issues addressed in this review are fundamentally communicative in nature. For example, reactions to different modes of questionnaire delivery, interaction among individuals online versus in person, and problems with social desirability biases are intrinsically issues of communication delivery, style, intent, and mode. Thus, communication scholars are well equipped to play a major role in assessing the methodological dilemmas we presented. As a consequence, communication scientists should find in this review ideas on research procedures as well as research opportunities.

Future Applications of Electronic Tools in Research

The future presents many possibilities for the use of electronic communication and information technologies as research tools. Many scholars likely will rely increasingly on electronic communication and information technologies in the conduct of their research. Specifically, given the benefits and novel capabilities of using electronic communication and information technologies outlined herein, studies using traditional methodologies will be transferred into electronic environments and existing concepts and measures will be transported into online contexts. Replications of previous findings also will be tested in electronic settings. In addition, novel methodologies will emerge that capitalize on unforeseen features in yet-to-be-realized technologies. Scholars will introduce new concepts and accompanying variables in order to test original ideas and phenomena generated by electronic technologies. Most importantly, however, the future holds an explicit discussion and empirical investigation of relevant issues addressed throughout this essay. Active research directly conceptualizing and testing the methodological issues associated with using electronic tools for research is necessary to inform the rigor and quality of our research endeavors.

CONCLUSION

Rigorous research methods are the foundation of all sound research, regardless of the specific tools invoked. The goal of this chapter has been to explore how the application of electronic tools to the research process provides new possibilities while alerting researchers to specific problems that may arise from this application. On one hand, electronic technologies enable researchers to perform tasks more efficiently while facilitating new forms of data collection and analysis. On the other hand, with these new functions come new obstacles. Only by heeding proper research methods can researchers capitalize on the promise of electronic technologies as research tools while avoiding the perils associated with their use.

Indeed, the promise of these tools is great. Among the most valuable aspects of electronic technologies for research endeavors are their application to make research tasks easier, reach a variety of populations, gather data from a diversity of sources, capture several forms of social interaction, and provide novel ways to conduct experiments, network analyses, surveys, content analyses, and other types of research. Core concerns prompted by these applications are proper sampling, including attention to participant recruitment, response rates, generalizability, and the viability of internet-based samples, and data integrity concerns such as threats to validity, measurement reliability, item response issues, and interdependence among observations. In addition, ethical concerns specific to the use of electronic technologies are crucial in the appropriate use of these tools.

As the use of electronic tools for various research tasks evolves, more research on the tools themselves is required to properly assess their strengths, weaknesses, and appropriateness in research pursuits. Importantly, such examinations should be cognizant of confounds between media and their features and attempt to disentangle the two (for related arguments, see Eveland, 2003; Griffith & Northcraft, 1994; Nass & Mason, 1990; Rice, 1992). For example, a study testing whether social desirability occurs more often in paper-and-pencil surveys versus online surveys also should investigate other feature-based variables, such as anonymity and confidentiality, by fully crossing all variables where possible to avoid confounds. Moreover, conceptual motivations should drive research, as opposed to variable analytic impulses. Doing so will enable researchers to draw conclusions about features and technologies that may signal important distinctions when various tools are employed in future research efforts.

Even though a great deal of research remains to be done to properly assess the utility of electronic technologies as research tools, a first step is an informed awareness of the core issues implied by the use of electronic communication and information technologies in the research process and an attendant understanding of the major methodological issues implied by their use. Our hope is that this essay serves as a preliminary step in outlining these issues, establishing the framework of a research agenda, alerting scholars to the promise and perils associated with the use of electronic technologies as research tools, and sparking an informed and productive discussion on these issues.

NOTES

1. Of course, units of analysis besides individuals, such as television programs, also can be sampled. The focus of the current section, however, is on sampling individuals because that is the primary focus of most research. A discussion of sampling other units of analysis besides individuals, nevertheless, is provided at the end of this section.

2. One potential problem generated is participant self-selection bias; however, we directly address this issue later, when discussing data integrity.

3. Some argue that a representative sample is not necessary with experimental designs, by virtue of the fact that many phenomena under scrutiny do not vary significantly across populations (see Birnbaum,

2001). Consequently, as long as random assignment to experimental conditions is maintained, results adhere unless and until researchers wish to generalize experimental results to wider populations.

4. For additional information, including websites about content analyses, bibliographies on content analyses, message archives, a program that can calculate reliability, information on content analyses programs, and other resources, visit *The Content Analysis Guidebook Online* at http://academic.csuohio.edu/kneuendorf/content/.

5. Researchers should consult their specific institutional regulations before conducting this type of online research because current regulations employed by human participant committees (or internal review boards) at universities and other institutions vary. For a discussion of obtaining approval from internal review boards, see Johns, Hall, and Crowell (2004).

REFERENCES

Anderson, L. R., & Ager, J. W. (1978). Analysis of variance in small group research. *Personality and Social Psychology Bulletin, 4,* 341–345.

Babbie, E. (1998). *The practice of social research* (8th ed.). Belmont, CA: Wadsworth.

Bailey, R. D., Foote, W. E., & Throckmorton, B. (2000). Human sexual behavior: A comparison of college and internet surveys. In M. H. Birnbaum (Ed.), *Psychological experiments on the internet* (pp. 141–168). San Diego, CA: Academic Press.

Bargh, J. A., McKenna, K. Y. A., & Fitzsimons, G. M. (2002). Can you see the real me? Activation and expression of the "true self" on the internet. *Journal of Social Issues. Special Issue: Consequences of the internet for self and society: Is social life being transformed?, 58,* 33–48.

Batagelj, Z., & Vehovar, V. (1998). *Technical and methodological issues in WWW surveys*. Retrieved April 27, 2003, from http://www.ris.org/ris98/stlouis/index.html.

Bellotti, V. (1997). Design for privacy in multimedia computing and communication environments. In P. E. Agre & M. Rotenberg (Eds.), *Technology and privacy: The new landscape* (pp. 63–98). Cambridge, MA: MIT Press.

Best, S. J., & Krueger, B. (2002). New approaches to assessing opinion: The prospects for electronic mail surveys. *International Journal of Public Opinion Research, 14,* 73–92.

Birnbaum, M. H. (2000). Decision making in the lab and on the web. In M. H. Birnbaum (Ed.), *Psychological experiments on the internet* (pp. 3–34). San Diego, CA: Academic Press, Inc.

Birnbaum, M. H. (2001). A web-based program of research on decision making. In U.-D. Reips & M. Bosnjak (Eds.), *Dimensions of internet science* (pp. 23–55). Lengerich, Germany: Pabst Science.

Bosnjak, M., & Batinic, B. (2002). Understanding the willingness to participate in online-surveys: The case of email questionnaires. In B. Batinic & U.-D. Reips & M. Bosnjak (Eds.), *Online social sciences* (pp. 81–92). Toronto, Canada: Hogrefe & Huber.

Brenner, V. (2002). Generalizability issues in internet-based survey research: Implications for the internet addiction controversy. In B. Batinic & U.-D. Reips & M. Bosnjak (Eds.), *Online social sciences* (pp. 93–113). Toronto, Canada: Hogrefe & Huber.

Bridges.org (2003). *Spanning the digital divide: Understanding and tackling the issues*. Retrieved November 23, 2003, from http://www.bridges.org/spanning/download.html.

Bruckman, A. (2002). Studying the amateur artist: A perspective on disguising data collected in human subjects research on the internet. *Ethics and Information Technology, 4,* 217–231.

Buchanan, T. (2000). Potential of the internet for personality research. In M. H. Birnbaum (Ed.), *Psychological experiments on the internet* (pp. 121–140). San Diego, CA: Academic Press.

Buchanan, T. (2001). Online personality assessment. In U.-D. Reips & M. Bosnjak (Eds.), *Dimensions of internet science* (pp. 57–74). Lengerich, Germany: Pabst Science.

Buchanan, T. (2002). Online assessment: Desirable or dangerous? *Professional Psychology: Research & Practice, 33,* 148–154.

Buchanan, T., & Smith, J. L. (1999). Using the internet for psychological research: Personality testing on the World Wide Web. *British Journal of Psychology, 90,* 125–144.

Burgoon, J. K., Bonito, J. A., Bengtsson, B., Cederberg, C., Lundeberg, M., & Allspach, L. (2000). Interactivity in human-computer interaction: A study of credibility, understanding, and influence. *Computers in Human Behavior, 16,* 553–574.

Burton, M. C., & Walther, J. B. (2001). The value of web log data in use-based web design and testing. *Journal of Computer-Mediated Communication, 6*(3). Retrieved April 27, 2003, from http://www.ascusc.org/jcmc/vol6/issue3/burton.html.

Central Intelligence Agency. (2003). *The world factbook.* Retrieved June 10, 2004, from http://www.cia.gov/cia/publications/factbook/.

Chaffee, S. H., & Berger, C. R. (1987). What communication scientists do. In C. R. Berger & S. H. Chaffee (Eds.), *Handbook of communication science* (pp. 99–122). Newbury Park, CA: Sage.

Cho, H., & LaRose, R. (1999). Privacy issues in internet surveys. *Social Science Computer Review, 17,* 421–434.

Christians, C. G., & Chen, S. L. S. (2004). Introduction: Technological environments and evolution of social research methods. In M. D. Johns, S. L. S. Chen, & C. G. Hall (Eds.), *Online social research: Methods, issues, and ethics* (pp. 15–23). New York: Peter Lang.

Church, A. H. (1993). Estimating the effect of incentives on mail survey response rates: A meta-analysis. *Public Opinion Quarterly, 57,* 62–79.

Comley, P. (2000). *Pop-up surveys: What works, what doesn't work and what will work in the future.* Retrieved April 27, 2003, from http://www.virtualsurveys.com/papers/paper_4.html.

Cook, C., Heath, F., & Thompson, R. (2000). A meta-analysis of response rates in Web- or internet-based surveys. *Educational and Psychological Measurement, 60,* 821–836.

Cook, T. D., & Campbell, D. T. (1979). *Quasi-experimentation: Design & analysis issues for field settings.* Chicago: Rand McNally.

Cooper, A., Scherer, C., & Mathy, R. M. (2001). Overcoming methodological concerns in the investigation of online sexual activities. *CyberPsychology & Behavior, 4,* 437–447.

Corman, S. R., Kuhn, T., McPhee, R., & Dooley, K. (2002). Studying complex discursive systems: Centering resonance analysis of communication. *Human Communication Research, 28,* 157–206.

Couper, M. P. (2000). Web surveys: A review of issues and approaches. *Public Opinion Quarterly, 64,* 464–494.

Couper, M. P., Blair, J., & Triplett, T. (1999). Response rate, speed, and completeness: A comparison of internet-based and mail surveys. *Journal of Official Statistics, 15,* 39–56.

Couper, M. P., Traugott, M. W., & Lamias, M. J. (2001). Web survey design and administration. *Public Opinion Quarterly, 65,* 230–253.

Crano, W. D., & Brewer, M. B. (2002). *Principles and methods of social research* (2nd ed.). Mahwah, NJ: Erlbaum.

Culnan, M. J., & Markus, M. L. (1987). Information technologies. In F. M. Jablin, L. L. Putnam, K. H. Roberts, & L. W. Porter (Eds.), *Handbook of organizational communication: An interdisciplinary perspective* (pp. 420–443). Newbury Park, CA: Sage.

Davis, R. N. (1999). Web-based administration of a personality questionnaire: Comparison with traditional methods. *Behavior Research Methods, Instruments & Computers, 31,* 572–577.

Dillard, J. P., Segrin, C., & Harden, J. M. (1989). Primary and secondary goals in the production of interpersonal influence messages. *Communication Monographs, 56,* 19–38.

Dillman, D. A., & Bowker, D. K. (2001). The web questionnaire challenge to survey methodologists. In U.-D. Reips & M. Bosnjak (Eds.), *Dimensions of internet science* (pp. 159–178). Lengerich, Germany: Pabst Science.

Dillman, D. A., Phelps, G., Tortora, R., Swift, K., Kohrell, J., & Berck, J. (2001). *Response rate and measurement differences in mixed mode surveys using mail, telephone, interactive voice response and the internet.* Retrieved April 27, 2003, from http://survey.sesrc.wsu.edu/dillman/papers/Mixed%20Mode%20ppr%20_with%20Gallup_%20POQ.pdf

Duffy, M. E. (2002). Methodological issues in Web-based research. *Journal of Nursing Scholarship, 34,* 83–88.

Elgesem, D. (2002). What is special about the ethical issues in online research? *Ethics and Information Technology, 4,* 195–203.

Epstein, J., & Klinkenberg, W. D. (2001). From Eliza to internet: A brief history of computerized assessment. *Computers in Human Behavior, 17,* 295–314.

Epstein, J., Klinkenberg, W. D., Wiley, D., & McKinley, L. (2001). Insuring sample equivalence across internet and paper-and-pencil assessments. *Computers in Human Behavior, 17,* 339–346.

Eveland, W. P., Jr. (2003). A "mix of attributes" approach to the study of media effects and new communication technologies. *Journal of Communication, 53,* 395–410.

Eveland, W. P., Jr., Cortese, J., Park, H., & Dunwoody, S. (2004). How website organization influences free recall, factual knowledge, and knowledge structure density. *Human Communication Research, 30,* 208–233.

Finegan, J. E., & Allen, N. J. (1994). Computerized and written questionnaires: Are they equivalent? *Computers in Human Behavior, 10,* 483–496.

Flanagin, A. J. (1999) Theoretical and pedagogical issues in computer-mediated interaction and instruction: Lessons from the use of a collaborative instructional technology. *Electronic Journal of Communication / La Revue Électronique de Communication, 9*(1). Retrieved June 11, 2004, from http://www.cios.org/www/ejc/v9n199.htm.

Flanagin, A. J., & Metzger, M. J. (2003a). The perceived credibility of personal web page information as influenced by the sex of the source. *Computers in Human Behavior, 19,* 683–701.

Flanagin, A. J., & Metzger, M. J. (2003b, May). *The role of site features, user attributes, and information verification behaviors on the perceived credibility of web-based information.* Paper presented at the annual conference of the International Communication Association, San Diego, CA.

Flanagin, A. J., & Spivey, E. (2004, May). *Risk mitigation through uncertainty reduction in online auctions.* Paper presented at the annual meeting of the International Communication Association, New Orleans, LA.

Foot, K. A., Schneider, S. M., Dougherty, M., Xenos, M., & Larsen, E. (2003). Analyzing linking practices: Candidate sites in the 2002 US electoral web sphere. *Journal of Computer-Mediated Communication, 8*(3). Retrieved June 25, 2004, from http://www.ascusc.org/jcmc/vol8/issue4/foot.html.

Fouladi, R. T., McCarthy, C. J., & Moller, N. P. (2002). Paper-and-pencil or online? Evaluating mode effects on measures of emotional functioning and attachment. *Assessment, 9,* 204–215.

Frick, A., Bachtiger, M.-T., & Reips, U.-D. (2001). Financial incentives, personal information, and drop out in online studies. In U.-D. Reips & M. Bosnjak (Eds.), *Dimensions of internet science* (pp. 209–219). Lengerich, Germany: Pabst Science.

Garton, L., Haythornthwaite, C., & Wellman, B. (1999). Studying on-line social networks. In S. Jones (Ed.), *Doing internet research: Critical issues and methods for examining the net* (pp. 75–105). Thousand Oaks, CA: Sage.

Glick, W. H., & Roberts, K. H. (1984). Hypothesized interdependence, assumed independence. *Academy of Management Review, 9,* 722–735.

Greenberg, B. S., Eastin, M. S., Skalski, P. D., Cooper, L., Levy, M., & Lachlan, K. A. (2004, May). *"E" for accuracy! Comparing survey, diary, and e-tracking methods of measuring internet use.* Paper presented at the annual conference of the International Communication Association, New Orleans, LA.

Griffith, T. L., & Northcraft, G. B. (1994). Distinguishing between the forest and the trees: Media, features, and methodology in electronic communication research. *Organization Science, 5,* 272–285.

Haridakis, P., Rubin, R. B., & Rubin, A. M. (2003, May). *Reliability and validity of measurers of internet use.* Paper presented at the annual conference of the International Communication Association, San Diego, CA.

HarrisInteractive.com. (2004). *Integrated CATI WAPI: Computer-assisted telephone interviewing/ web-assisted personal interviewing.* Retrieved June 24, 2004, from http://www.harrisinteractive. com/advantages/pubs/HI_Integrated_CATI_WAPI.pdf.

Hertel, G., Naumann, S., Konradt, U., & Batinic, B. (2002). Personality assessment via internet: Comparing online and paper-and-pencil questionnaires. In B. Batinic & U.-D. Reips & M. Bosnjak (Eds.), *Online social sciences* (pp. 115–133). Toronto, Canada: Hogrefe & Huber.

Hewson, C. M., Laurent, D., & Vogel, C. M. (1996). Proper methodologies for psychological and sociological studies conducted via the internet. *Behavior Research Methods, Instruments & Computers, 28,* 186–191.

Huber, G. P. (1990). A theory of the effects of advanced information technologies on organizational design, intelligence, and decision making. In J. Fulk & C. W. Steinfield (Eds.), *Organizations and communication technology* (pp. 237–274). Newbury Park, CA: Sage.

Ilieva, J., Baron, S., & Healey, N. M. (2002). Online surveys in marketing research: Pros and cons. *International Journal of Market Research, 44,* 361–376.

Im, E.-O., & Chee, W. (2002). Issues in protection of human subjects in internet research. *Nursing Research, 51,* 266–269.

Internet World Stats. (2004). *Internet usage stats for America.* Retrieved June 25, 2004, from Internet World Stats: Usage and population statistics website: http://www.internetworldstats.com/.

Janetzko, D. (2002). Artificial dialogues: Dialogue and interview bots for the World Wide Web. In B. Batinic & U.-D. Reips & M. Bosnjak (Eds.), *Online social sciences* (pp. 357–364). Toronto: Hogrefe & Huber.

Johns, M. D., Hall, G. J., & Crowell, T. L. (2004). Surviving the IRB review: Institutional guidelines and research strategies. In M. D. Johns, S. L. S. Chen, & C. G. Hall (Eds.), *Online social research: Methods, issues, and ethics* (pp. 105–124). New York: Peter Lang.

Joinson, A. (1999). Social desirability, anonymity, and internet-based questionnaires. *Behavior Research Methods, Instruments & Computers, 31,* 433–438.

Kalyanaraman, S., & Sundar, S. S. (2003, May). *The psychological appeal of personalized online content: An experimental investigation of customized web portals.* Paper presented at the annual conference of the International Communication Association, San Diego, CA.

Katz, J. E., & Rice, R. E. (2002). *Social consequences of internet use: Access, involvement, and interaction.* Cambridge, MA: MIT Press.

Kenny, D. A. (1995). The effect of nonindependence on significance testing in dyadic research. *Personal Relationships, 2,* 67–75.

Kiesler, S., & Sproull, L. S. (1986). Response effects in the electronic survey. *Public Opinion Quarterly, 50,* 402–413.

Klein, K. J., Danserau, F., & Hall, R. J. (1994). Levels issues in theory development, data collection, and analysis. *Academy of Management Review, 19,* 195–229.

Kleinman, S. S. (2002). Methodological and ethical challenges of researching a computer-mediated group. *Journal of Technology in Human Services, 19,* 49–63.

Kleinman, S. S. (2004). Researching OURNET: A case study of a multiple methods approach. In M. D. Johns & S. L. S. Chen & C. G. Hall (Eds.), *Online social research: Methods, issues, and ethics* (pp. 47–62). New York: Peter Lang.

Knapp, F., & Heidingsfelder, M. (2001). Drop-out analysis: Effects of the survey design. In U.-D. Reips & M. Bosnjak (Eds.), *Dimensions of internet science* (pp. 221–230). Lengerich, Germany: Pabst Science.

Knapp, H., & Kirk, S. A. (2003). Using pencil and paper, internet and touch-tone phones for self-administered surveys: Does methodology matter? *Computers in Human Behavior, 19,* 117–134.

Krantz, J. H. (2001). Stimulus delivery on the Web: What can be presented when calibration isn't possible. In U. D. Reips & M. Bosnjak (Eds.), *Dimensions of internet science* (pp. 113–130). Lengerich, Germany: Pabst Science.

Krantz, J. H., & Dalal, R. (2000). Validity of web-based psychological research. In M. H. Birnbaum (Ed.), *Psychological experiments on the internet* (pp. 35–60). San Diego, CA: Academic Press.

Kraut, R., Patterson, M., Lundmark, V., Kiesler, S., Mukopadhyay, T., & Scherlis, W. (1998). Internet paradox: A social technology that reduces social involvement and psychological well-being? *American Psychologist, 53,* 1017–1031.

Krippendorff, K. (1980). *Content analysis: An introduction to its methodology.* Beverly Hills: Sage.

Krippendorff, K. (2004). *Content analysis: An introduction to its methodology* (2nd ed.). Thousand Oaks, CA: Sage.

LeBesco, K. (2004). Managing visibility, intimacy, and focus in online critical ethnography. In M. D. Johns, S.-L. S. Chen, & C. G. Hall (Eds.), *Online social research: Methods, issues, and ethics* (pp. 63–79). New York: Peter Lang.

Lee, E.-J. (2004). Effects of visual representation on social influence in computer-mediated communication: Experimental tests of the social identity model of deindividuation effects. *Human Communication Research, 30,* 234–259.

Lee, E.J., & Nass, C. (2002). Experimental tests of normative group influence and representation effects in computer-mediated communication: When interacting via computers differs from interacting with computers. *Human Communication Research, 28,* 349–381.

Lemus, D., Seibold, D. R., Flanagin, A. J., & Metzger, M. J. (2004). Argument and decision making in computer-mediated groups. *Journal of Communication, 54,* 302–320.

Lievrouw, L. A., Bucy, E. P., Finn, T. A., Frindte, W., Gershon, R., Haythornthwaite, C., Kohler, T., Metz, J. M., & Sundar, S. S. (2001). Bridging the subdisciplines: An overview of Communication and technology research. In W. Gudykunst (Ed.), *Communication Yearbook 24* (pp. 271–295). Newbury Park, CA: Sage.

Madge, C., & O'Connor, H. (2002). On-line with e-mums: Exploring the internet as a medium for research. *Area, 34,* 92–102.

Majchrzak, A., Rice, R. E., Malhotra, A., King, N., & Ba, S. (2000). Technology adaptation: The case of a computer-supported inter-organizational virtual team. *MIS Quarterly, 24,* 569–600.

McLaughlin, M., Goldberg, S. B., Ellison, N., & Lucas, J. (1999). Measuring internet audiences: Patrons of an on-line art museum. In S. Jones (Ed.), *Doing internet research: Critical issues and methods for examining the net* (pp. 163–178). Thousand Oaks, CA: Sage.

Mitra, A., & Cohen, E. (1999). Analyzing the web: Directions and challenges. In S. Jones (Ed.), *Doing internet research: Critical issues and methods for examining the net* (pp. 179–202). Thousand Oaks, CA: Sage.

Monge, P. R., & Contractor, N. S. (2003). *Theories of communication networks.* Oxford, UK: Oxford University Press.

Musch, J., & Reips, U.-D. (2000). A brief history of Web experimenting. In M. H. Birnbaum (Ed.), *Psychological experiments on the internet* (pp. 61–87). San Diego, CA: Academic Press.

Mustanski, B. S. (2001). Getting wired: Exploiting the internet for the collection of valid sexuality data. *Journal of Sex Research, 38,* 292–301.

Nass, C., & Mason, L. (1990). On the study of technology and task: A variable-based approach. In J. Fulk & C. Steinfield (Eds.), *Organizations and communication technology* (pp. 46–67). Newbury Park, CA: Sage.

Nielsen Media Research. (2004). *Nielsen Media Research to begin offering local people meter data to New York market on June 3rd.* Retrieved June 24, 2004, from http://www.nielsenmedia.com/news-releases/2004/LPMdata_NYmarket_6–04.htm.

Nielsen//NetRatings. (2004). Retrieved June 24, 2004, from http://direct.www.nielsen-netratings.com/mktg.jsp?section=ps_ho.

Neuendorf, K. A. (2002) *The content analysis guidebook.* Thousand Oaks, CA: Sage.

Nosek, B. A., Banaji, M. R., & Greenwald, A. G. (2002). E-research: Ethics, security, design, and control in psychological research on the internet. *Journal of Social Issues, 58,* 161–176.

O'Neil, K. M., & Penrod, S. D. (2001). Methodological variables in web-based research that may affect results: Sample type, monetary incentives, and personal information. *Behavior Research Methods, Instruments & Computers, 33,* 226–233.

Palomares, N. A. (2004). Gender schematicity, gender identity salience, and gender-linked language use. *Human Communication Research, 30,* 556–588.

Pettit, F. A. (2002). A comparison of world-wide web and paper-and-pencil personality questionnaires. *Behavior Research Methods, Instruments & Computers, 34,* 50–54.

Piper, A. I. (1998). Conducting social science laboratory experiments on the World Wide Web. *Library & Information Science Research, 20,* 5–21.

Potter, W. J., Mahood, C., & Yao, M. Z. (2003, November). *Changes in interpretations of violence as a function of changes in narrative characteristics.* Paper presented at the annual conference of the National Communication Association, Miami Beach, FL.

Psathas, G. (1995). *Conversation analysis: The study of talk-in-interaction.* Thousand Oaks, CA: Sage.

Ramirez, A., Walther, J. B., Burgoon, J. K., & Sunnafrank, M. (2002). Information-seeking strategies, uncertainty, and computer-mediated communication. *Human Communication Research, 28,* 213–228.

Reeves, B., & Nass, C. (1996). *The media equation: How people treat computers, televisions, and new media like real people and places.* Cambridge, UK: Cambridge University Press.

Reips, U.-D. (2000). The Web experiment method: Advantages, disadvantages, and solutions. In M. H. Birnbaum (Ed.), *Psychological experiments on the internet* (pp. 89–117). San Diego, CA: Academic Press.

Reips, U.-D. (2001). Merging field and institution: Running a web laboratory. In U.-D. Reips & M. Bosnjak (Eds.), *Dimensions of internet science* (pp. 1–22). Lengerich, Germany: Pabst Science.

Reips, U.-D. (2002a). Standards for internet-based experimenting. *Experimental Psychology, 49*, 243–256.

Reips, U.-D. (2002b). Theory and techniques of conducting web experiments. In B. Batinic, U. D. Reips, & M. Bosnjak (Eds.), *Online social sciences* (pp. 229–250). Toronto, Canada: Hogrefe & Huber.

Rice, R. E. (1982). Communication networking in computer-conferencing systems: A longitudinal study of group roles and system structure. In M. Burgoon (Ed.), *Communication yearbook 6* (pp. 925–944). Beverly Hills, CA: Sage.

Rice, R. E. (1990). Computer-mediated communication system network data: Theoretical concerns and empirical examples. *International Journal of Man-Machine Studies, 32*, 627–647.

Rice, R. E. (1992). Contexts of research on organizational computer-mediated communication: A recursive review. In M. Lea (Ed.), *Contexts of computer-mediated communication* (pp. 113–144). London: Harvester-Wheatsheaf.

Rice, R. E., Hughes, D., & Love, G. (1989). Usage and outcomes of electronic messaging at an R&D organization: Situational constrains, job level, and media awareness. *Office: Technology and People, 5*, 141–161.

Rice, R. E., & Love, G. (1987). Electronic emotion: Socio-emotional content in computer-mediated communication network. *Communication Research, 14*, 85–105.

Rice, R. E., & Shook, D. (1990). Voice messaging, coordination and communication. In J. Galagher, R. Kraut, & C. Egido (Eds.), *Intellectual teamwork: Social and technological foundations of cooperative work* (pp. 327–350). Hillsdale, NJ: Erlbaum.

Richman, W. L., Kiesler, S., Weisband, S., & Drasgow, F. (1999). A meta-analytic study of social desirability distortion in computer-administered questionnaires, traditional questionnaires, and interviews. *Journal of Applied Psychology, 84*, 754–775.

Rössler, P. (2002). Content analysis in online communication: A challenge for traditional methodology. In B. Batinic & U.-D. Reips & M. Bosnjak (Eds.), *Online social sciences* (pp. 291–307). Toronto, Canada: Hogrefe & Huber.

Rubin, R. B., Haridakis, P. M., Rubin, A. M., & Miraldi, P. N. (2002, November). *Comparing methods for assessing internet use.* Paper presented at the annual conference of the National Communication Association, New Orleans, LA.

Ruppertsberg, A., Givaty, G., Van Veen, H., & Bulthoff, H. (2001). Games as research tools for visual perception over the internet. In U.-D. Reips & M. Bosnjak (Eds.), *Dimensions of internet science* (pp. 146–158). Lengerich, Germany: Pabst Science.

Sadler, M. S., & Judd, C. M. (2001). Overcoming dependent data: A guide to the analysis of group data. In M. A. Hogg & R. S. Tindale (Eds.), *Blackwell handbook of social psychology: Group processes* (pp. 497–524). Oxford, UK: Blackwell.

Sassenberg, K., & Kreutz, S. (2002). Online research and anonymity. In B. Batinic, U.-D. Reips, & M. Bosnjak (Eds.), *Online social sciences* (pp. 213–227). Toronto, Canada: Hogrefe & Huber.

Schaefer, D. R., & Dillman, D. A. (1998). Development of a standard email methodology: Results of an experiment. *Public Opinion Quarterly, 62*, 378–397.

Schmidt, W. C. (1997). World Wide Web survey research: Benefits, potential problems, and solutions. *Behavior Research Methods, Instruments & Computers, 29*, 274–279.

Shapiro, M. A. (2002). Generalizability in communication research. *Human Communication Research, 28*, 491–500.

Sharf, B. F. (1999). Beyond netiquette: The ethics of doing naturalistic discourse research on the internet. In S. Jones (Ed.), *Doing internet research: Critical issues and methods for examining the net* (pp. 243–256). Thousand Oaks, CA: Sage.

Sheehan, K. B. (2001). Email survey response rates: A review. *Journal of Computer-Mediated Communication, 6*(2), n.p.

Sills, S. J., & Song, C. (2002). Innovations in survey research: An application of web-based surveys. *Social Science Computer Review, 20*, 22–30.

Singleton, R. A., Jr., & Straits, B. C. (2004). *Approaches to social research* (4th ed.). New York: Oxford University Press.

Smart, R. (1966). Subject selection bias in psychological research. *Canadian Psychology, 7*, 115–121.

Smith, M. A., & Leigh, B. (1997). Virtual subjects: Using the internet as an alternative source of subjects and research environment. *Behavior Research Methods, Instruments, & Computers, 29,* 496–505.

Stanton, J. M., & Rogelberg, S. G. (2002). Beyond online surveys: Internet research opportunities for industrial-organizational psychology. In S. G. Rogelberg (Ed.), *Handbook of research methods in industrial and organizational psychology* (pp. 275–294). Malden, MA: Blackwell.

Tidwell, L. C., & Walther, J. B. (2002). Computer-mediated communication effects on disclosure, impressions, and interpersonal evaluations: Getting to know one another a bit at a time. *Human Communication Research, 28,* 317–348.

Trammell, K. D., & Gasser, U. (2004, May). *Deconstructing weblogs: An analytical framework for researching online journals.* Paper presented at the annual conference of the International Communication Association, New Orleans, LA.

Truell, A. D., Bartlett, J. E., & Alexander, M. W. (2002). Response rate, speed, and completeness: A comparison of internet-based and mail surveys. *Behavior Research Methods, Instruments & Computers, 34,* 46–49.

Tuten, T. L., Urban, D. J., & Bosnjak, M. (2002). Internet surveys and data quality: A review. In B. Batinic, U.-D. Reips, & M. Bosnjak (Eds.), *Online social sciences* (pp. 7–26). Toronto, Canada: Hogrefe & Huber.

Vangelisti, A. L., & Caughlin, J. P. (1997). Revealing family secrets: The influence of topic, function, and relationships. *Journal of Social and Personal Relationships, 14,* 679–705.

Vehovar, V., Batagelj, Z., Manfreda, K. L., & Zaletel, M. (1999). *Web surveys: Can the weighting solve the problem? Proceedings of the Section on Survey Research Methods, American Statistical Association,* pp. 962–967. Retrieved April 27, 2003, from http://www.amstat.org/sections/srms/Proceedings/papers/1999_168.pdf.

Vehovar, V., Batagelj, Z., Manfreda, K. L., & Zaletel, M. (2002). Nonresponse in web surveys. In R. M. Groves, D. A. Dillman, J. L. Eltinge, & R. J. A. Little (Eds.), *Survey nonresponse* (pp. 229–242). New York: Wiley.

Voracek, M., Stieger, S., & Gindl, A. (2001). Online replication of evolutionary psychological evidence: Sex differences in sexual jealously in imagined scenarios of mate's sexual versus emotional infidelity. In U. D. Reips & M. Bosnjak (Eds.), *Dimensions of internet science* (pp. 91–112). Lengerich, Germany: Pabst Science.

Walther, J. B. (2002). Research ethics in internet-enabled research: Human subjects issues and methodological myopia. *Ethics and Information Technology, 4,* 205–216.

Walther, J. B., Slovaceck, C. L., & Tidwell, L. C. (2001). Is a picture worth a thousand words? Photographic images in long-term and short-term computer-mediated communication. *Communication Research, 28,* 105–134.

Wasserman, S., & Faust, K. (1994). *Social network analysis.* Cambridge, UK: Cambridge University Press.

Werner, A. (2002). Contact measurement in the WWW. In B. Batinic, U.-D. Reips, & M. Bosnjak (Eds.), *Online social sciences* (pp. 251–262). Toronto: Hogrefe & Huber.

Wilkerson, J. M., Nagao, D. H., & Martin, C. L. (2002). Socially desirable responding in computerized questionnaires: When questionnaire purpose matters more than the mode. *Journal of Applied Social Psychology, 32,* 544–559.

Williams, M., & Robson, K. (2004). Reengineering focus group methodology for the online environment. In M. D. Johns, S.-L. S. Chen, & C. G. Hall (Eds.), *Online social research: Methods, issues, and ethics* (pp. 25–45). New York: Peter Lang.

CHAPTER CONTENTS

6 Leadership in the New Millennium: Communicating Beyond Temporal, Spatial, and Geographical Boundaries

STACEY L. CONNAUGHTON
Purdue University
JOHN A. DALY
The University of Texas at Austin

Organizations in diverse sectors are utilizing dispersed work groups. Individuals within these organizations now face the challenge of leading others across time and space, a phenomenon known as "distanced leadership." The purpose of this chapter is to provide a comprehensive synthesis and critique of the existing literature on distanced leadership. To this end, we examine the various ways that scholars have conceptualized distance in leadership contexts; we argue that communication is central to leadership in these emergent organizational forms; and we suggest avenues for future communication research to explore that will address organizational trends in the 21st century and beyond.

At the close of the 20th century, several national newspapers, industry journals, and trade magazines reported that thousands of organizations in diverse industries are using distanced work relationships (see Apgar, 1998; Bryan & Fraser, 1999; Hymowitz, 1999; McCune, 1998). Indeed, globalization and recent patterns in organizational restructuring demand that more and more organizations adopt geographically dispersed work groups and utilize advanced technologies to communicate with them (Benson-Armer & Hsieh, 1997; Townsend, DeMarie, & Hendrickson, 1998; Van Aken, Hop, & Post, 1998). In response, organizations in a variety of sectors have transformed many of their traditional offices into global or virtual offices (Davenport & Pearlson, 1998). Individuals within these organizations now face the complex task of leading people who are located in different physical sites than they are.

Correspondence: Stacey L. Connaughton, Purdue University, Department of Communication, Beering Hall of Liberal Arts and Education, Room 2114, 100 North University Street, West Lafayette, IN 47907-1071; email: staceyc@scils.rutgers.edu

Communication Yearbook 29, pp.187–213

Organizations use dispersed work settings in order to maximize productivity, lower costs, serve international customers, and capitalize on globally dispersed talent (Davenport & Pearlson, 1998; Zaccaro & Bader, 2003). Yet distance poses both opportunities and challenges for communication. On one hand, unrestrained geographical, time, and organizational boundaries can lead to greater autonomy, flexibility, and collaboration (Townsend, DeMarie, & Hendrickson, 1998). On the other hand, time zone differences, different communication norms and languages, as well as limited face-to-face contact can complicate interactive and collaborative opportunities.

One challenge relates to leadership. In a recent study of 500 virtual managers, 90% of them perceived managing from afar to be more challenging than managing people on-site. Furthermore, 40% of these virtual managers perceived team members to produce less when physically separated from each other than when colocated (see http://www.3m.com/meetingnetwork/readingroom/gdss_dist_teams.html for study description).

Even a cursory examination of academic and popular press literature reveals that academics and practitioners are just beginning to examine the intricacies of distanced leadership. To date, articles about distanced leadership (or leading from afar) and the uniqueness of these emergent work relationships have appeared in training and development journals (e.g., Geber, 1995; Nelson, 1998), weekly periodicals (e.g., *Fortune* and *Business Week*), and best selling popular management books such as *Virtual Teams* (Lipnack & Stamps, 1997), *Global Work* (O'Hara-Devereaux & Johansen, 1998), and *Mastering Virtual Teams* (Duarte & Snyder, 1999). These forums highlight several challenges to leading from afar, such as building trust, inspiring, managing conflict, preventing feelings of disconnectedness, monitoring and evaluating performance, communicating vision, establishing loyalty to the organization, and maintaining teamwork. Even though these issues are communicative in nature, these works lack rigor in pinpointing the antecedents, processes, and outcomes of this emergent organizational phenomenon. As distanced leadership becomes increasingly common in organizations, understanding the nuances and processes of this phenomenon is critical to organizational and communication research.

The purpose of this chapter is to provide a comprehensive synthesis and critique of the existing literature on distanced leadership. In doing so, we will show why communication is central to leadership in these emergent organizational forms. We begin by arguing that distanced leadership will be ever more present in the future and will be an important issue for communication scholars to investigate; we then present conceptualizations of key terms and argue that communication is central to leadership in dispersed contexts, then critically review existing scholarship on distanced leadership, paying particular attention to the behavioral slant of many of these investigations. We conclude by demonstrating that the topic of distanced leadership merits further attention from communication scholars and suggest avenues for future communication research that will address organizational trends in the 21st century.

DISTANCED LEADERSHIP: AN IMPORTANT AREA
FOR FUTURE LEADERSHIP RESEARCH

Organizations across different sectors and industries are increasingly employing new forms of organizing (Fulk & DeSanctis, 1995). These emergent forms include virtual teams and networks (Rosenfeld, Richman, & May, 2004; Scott, 1997; Scott & Timmerman, 1999), interorganizational mergers and alliances, and offshore outsourcing (DeSanctis & Fulk, 1999; O'Hara-Devereaux & Johansen, 1994). Many virtual teams are knowledge-based teams responsible for developing new products, improving organizational processes, or reconciling customer concerns (Duarte & Snyder, 1999; Lipnack & Stamps, 1997; Townsend et al., 1998). With advances in technology, there has been a growing emphasis on far-flung, distributed, virtual teams as organizing units of work (Bell & Kozlowski, 2002), and it is estimated that 20% of the world's workers will be working virtually by 2005 (Prashad, 2003).

These emergent organizational forms are accompanied by leadership concerns. As Howell and Hall-Merenda (1999) observed:

> Dramatic changes in organizational structures, size, complexity, and work arrangements imply that leaders are increasingly responsible for managing followers who reside in different locations. Leaders in network organizations, multinational companies, or domestic companies with far-flung sites are faced with the challenges of motivating and evaluating followers who [sic] they cannot see. (1999, p. 683)

Hiltz and colleagues have argued that team leadership in distributed settings is critical to team effectiveness (Fjermestad & Hiltz, 1998-1999; Hiltz, Dufner, Holmes, & Poole, 1991; Hiltz & Turoff, 1985). Other organizational scholars have coined the term "e-leadership" to refer to leaders who conduct many leadership processes primarily through electronic channels (see Avolio & Kahai, 2003; Cascio & Shurygailo, 2003; Zaccaro & Bader, 2003).

Even though some virtual–distributed teams may exist in somewhat close geographic proximity, globally dispersed teams are a growing trend (Snow, Snell, Davison, & Hambrick, 1996). Indeed, scholars have called on leadership studies to "stretch its boundaries to match the elastic nature of global work" (Davis, 2003, p. 48). Global teams, in particular, raise compelling future research issues for communication scholars as they are characterized by physical or temporal separation, or both; electronically mediated communication; and multiple national and organizational cultures. One could argue that distanced work relationships, particularly those separated by considerable geographic distance, are defined by the nature of the communication between individuals, given that physical presence is missing. Thus, they offer communication scholars an opportunity to expand what is known about the communicative dimensions of multinational and global organizing, phenomena that will be relevant well into the future (Stohl, 2001).

This area of research contributes to an understanding of communication in the future from the perspective of leadership and organizational communication studies. Consider these trends: (a) the rise of geographically dispersed ad hoc teams assembled for short-term projects; (b) the increasing use of contractors and consultants who do not have loyalty to the organization; and (c) trends in international customer service—how do organizations effectively serve and lead customers from afar? Due to globalization and recent corporate restructuring trends like the ones listed above increasingly demand distanced leadership, the focus of this chapter will be of continuing importance to organizations in the 21st century.

Our Assumptions

To conduct this critical review, we selected scholarly works from communication, management, and psychology that dealt specifically with distanced leadership. Communication scholarship continues to be informed by a growing body of literature on other important issues in virtual environments, such as identification (Pratt, Fuller, & Northcraft, 2000; Scott, 1997), technologies (Biocca, Kim, & Choi, 2001; Browning, Saetre, Stephens, & Sornes, 2004; Leonardi, Jackson, & Marsh, 2004; Scott & Timmerman, 1999), culture (Gibbs, 2002; Grosse, 2002; Stage, 1999), and teams (Majchrzak, Rice, Malhotra, King, & Ba, 2000; Schmidt, Montoya-Weiss, & Massey, 2001). For the purposes of this review, we included only those articles that specifically examined leadership in distanced contexts.

Once we began reviewing these works, we discovered that several of the articles, regardless of disciplinary origin, stated that they examined "communication." Thus, to offer a comprehensive review about leadership and communication in distanced settings, we chose to include all of these articles and consider how they conceptualized communication. As this critical review demonstrates, the literature on distanced leadership tends to (a) include both conceptual pieces and a growing number of empirical studies; (b) be primarily leader- or manager-focused in its inquiry; (c) focus primarily on designated, positional leaders; (d) have a prescriptive tone; (e) examine communication variables; and (f) be concerned with measuring organizational outcomes.

In critically reviewing this literature, we hope to show that communication is central to distanced leadership. We also aim to reveal how this body of research uses communication (or, communications in some cases) and call on communication scholars to conduct additional research in this area in order to enrich our disciplinary and interdisciplinary discussions and understandings of communication in distanced leadership contexts.

CONCEPTUALIZATIONS OF RELATED TERMS

Two terms, *leadership* and *distance,* are, understandably, used often in the work on distanced leadership. This section examines how those terms have been employed.

Leadership

Scholars have employed varying conceptualizations of leadership in research on distanced leadership. As leadership research shows, leadership can be formal or informal, positional or emergent (see Witherspoon, 1997). The majority of scholars have examined distanced leadership that is formal and positional. For instance, Cascio (2000) and Cascio and Shurygailo (2003) focused on managers who have direct reports working remotely and at the primary business location. Cascio discussed the importance of supervisory abilities, delegation, and providing anonymous participation and feedback. Cascio and Shurygailo (2003) noted the characteristics of "effective virtual team leaders" (establish norms early, maintain the appropriate level of control on immediate progress, and encourage and recognize emergent leaders in virtual teams). Davis (2003) based his conceptual piece, "The Tao of Leadership in Virtual Teams," on managers who have direct reports around the world. Fritz and Manheim (1998) conceptualized leadership as management of people, relationships, work, knowledge, and technology in both telecommuting and global project team contexts.

In two descriptive studies, Connaughton and Daly (2003, 2004a) have highlighted the tactics of project leaders, senior managers, and executives of global organizations in communicating with far-flung employees. In an empirical study of geographically dispersed team members' perceptions of their leaders' communication, Connaughton and Daly (2004b) examined leaders who were formal, positional leaders. Also, in an empirical study of LMX relationships between leaders and followers investigating physical distance as a moderating variable, Howell and Hall-Merenda (1999) studied direct reports' perceptions of their leader. Scholars have yet to examine other forms of leadership in geographically distanced settings.

One assumption seems to be shared among these scholars: that distance leadership is more challenging than colocated team leadership. Cascio and Shurygailo (2003), Townsend, DeMarie, and Hendrickson (1998), and Fritz and Manheim (1998) all argued that virtual environments magnify leadership challenges. This assumption is shared by Kayworth and Leidner (2002), who, in their study of 13 culturally diverse global teams (consisting of students from locations in Europe, Mexico, and the United States), argued that virtual team leaders face a fundamentally more complex work environment than traditional team counterparts.

Distance

Scholars have defined distance in various ways, often using the terms "virtual team," "distanced team," and "dispersed team" interchangeably. We believe that it is important for researchers to make some distinctions, however, because there are different degrees of distance (Zigurs, 2003) and various types of distanced teams (Cascio & Shurygailo, 2003).

Degrees of distance. For one, there are various degrees of distance or virtuality (Scott & Timmerman, 1999; Van Aken, Hop, & Post, 1998). Teams range from global (see Connaughton & Daly, 2004b; Jarvenpaa, Knoll, & Leidner, 1998; Jarvenpaa & Leidner, 1998; Maznevski & Chudoba, 2000) to those whose team members are located in different buildings within the same city (Majchrzak, Rice, King, Malhotra, & Ba, 2000). Indeed, distanced or virtual teams exist along a continuum of virtuality, from highly virtual to less virtual (Cohen & Gibson, 2003). Yet work has only begun to examine the extent to which different degrees of virtuality relate to communication among virtual team members.

Types of distanced work relationships. What scholars have coined "virtual teams" are "groups of geographically and/or organizationally dispersed coworkers that are assembled using a combination of telecommunications and information technologies to accomplish an organizational task" (Townsend et al., 1998, p. 17). From this definition we note two characteristics that cut across various types of distanced work relationships: (a) geographic or temporal separation and (b) communication via mediated means (see Cascio & Shurygailo, 2003; Connaughton & Daly, 2003, 2004a, 2004b).

Nevertheless, communication scholars and others have examined various other types of virtual teams. Jackson and colleagues (Leonardi, Jackson, & Marsh, 2004), for instance, examined the telework context. Teleworkers often work remotely part of the time and are considered partially virtual (Davis, 2003). Some may choose to be in the office at the same time, while others may be there at quite different times. Telework is still a form of virtual work because employees are separated physically from each other and meet in person only infrequently. Remote team members, on the other hand, office in multiple locations and sometimes in multiple time zones. At the extreme, a remote team may be globally dispersed, as are the global virtual teams examined by Connaughton and Daly (2003, 2004a, 2004b).

Virtual teams also vary with regard to the amount of face-to-face interaction they have. Some teams have no physical interaction whereas others may have monthly face-to-face team meetings (Lipnack & Stamps, 1997; Townsend et al., 1998). The extent of face-to-face interaction is a variable that has just recently been examined in virtual team research (Kirkman, Rosen, Tesluk, & Gibson, 2004).

After reviewing the literature, we define *dispersed–distanced* teams as teams whose members are generally separated by some degree of time or physical distance, and we conceptualize *distanced leadership* as leadership in those contexts. We believe it is critical to conceive of distanced leadership as being a function of both physical distance and perceived access to the leader.

We also recognize that there are varying degrees of virtuality (Scott & Timmerman, 1999; Zigurs, 2003) and various types of virtual teams (Cascio & Shurygailo, 2003). We contend that virtuality is a matter of degree, and thus teams may be considered highly virtual or less virtual. This may have to do with the richness of the communication media typically used by members to accomplish tasks (Cohen & Gibson, 2003; Townsend et al., 1998) and the extent to which team members are separated by time, space, or both. For instance, a highly virtual team may communicate using only email or instant messenger; contrarily, a less virtual team is likely to meet face-to-face occasionally and use richer media such

TABLE 1
Degree of Virtuality Continuum

	Less virtual	*Highly virtual*
Richness of communication media	Meet face-to-face occasionally	Meet face-to-face rarely or never
	Use (desktop) video-conferencing often	Use email or instant messenger primarily
	Use teleconferencing or telephone often	
Geographical separation	Leaders and members located in different buildings in same city	Leaders and members dispersed globally
Temporal separation	Leaders and members located in same time zone	Leaders and members located in multiple time zones

as videoconferencing or teleconferencing for other interactions. Additionally, a highly virtual team may have members scattered throughout the world, working in different time zones whereas a less virtual team may have members located in the same city. Table 1 visually depicts the dimensions of this continuum.

THE CENTRALITY OF COMMUNICATION IN DISTANCED LEADERSHIP

Communication is central to leadership studies. Using various methodological approaches, relationships between leadership and communication have been advanced in various leadership and management contexts (Fairhurst, 1993; Fairhurst & Chandler, 1989; Fairhurst, Green, & Courtright, 1995; Fairhurst, Jordan, & Neuwirth, 1997; Fairhurst & Sarr, 1996; Lee & Jablin, 1995; Sias & Jablin, 1995; Sypher, 1991; Zorn, 1991). Indeed, communication and management scholars have long studied leadership, typically in colocated settings (e.g., Bass & Avolio, 1994; Burns, 1978; Fairhurst, 2001; Fiedler, 1967; Mintzberg, 1994; 1973; Yukl, 1989). And, scholars have proposed typologies that outline various leadership dimensions (Mintzberg, 1973; Pfeffer, 1981).

Research on leadership in distanced contexts concurs that communication is central to distanced leadership (e.g., Kayworth & Leidner, 2002; Wiesenfeld, Raghuram, & Garud, 1999). Some previous research in distanced organizational contexts has examined how communication relates to trust (Jarvenpaa & Leidner, 1998) and organizational identification (Wiesenfeld, et al., 1999). Other research has examined how communication behaviors of leaders affect the satisfaction employees experience when working far from their leaders (Connaughton & Daly,

2004b). Still other literature has uncovered the communicative choices distanced leaders should make in order to enhance their relationships with distanced individuals (Connaughton & Daly, 2003, 2004a). Underscoring these points, however, is the sometimes implicit, sometimes explicit, argument that virtuality and geographical dispersion strain opportunities for such exchanges (Kraut, Fursell, Brennan, & Siegel, 2001; Kraut & Streeter, 1995; Olson & Olson, 2000; Suchan & Hayzak, 2001).

Distanced leadership is also of interest to communication scholars because much of the leadership work is done via communication technologies. A rich area of communication research continues to expand on traditional and new media in conventional and virtual environments (Lievrouw, 1999; Rice & Gattiker, 2001), although one of the most commonly studied technologies for team processes by communication scholars—group decision support software—has been investigated by examining colocated teams as opposed to virtual ones (see Poole, DeSanctis, Kirsch, & Jackson, 1995; Scott, 1999a; Scott, Quinn, Timmerman, & Garrett, 1999).

Leadership in contemporary organizations is increasingly mediated and virtual in nature. There was a time when much of the work of leadership occurred in face-to-face settings. Today and into the future, however, leaders in many sectors and organizations will interact with team members who are separated by time and space. Communication technologies—cell phones, pagers, email, videoconferencing, listservs, chat rooms, instant messenger, intranets—supplement, and sometimes nearly replace, face-to-face communication.

A key dimension of organizational leadership is building and maintaining relationships with those being led (Bass & Avolio, 1994; Fritz, Narasimhan, & Rhee, 1998; Ring & Van de Ven, 1992; Witherspoon, 1997). These relationships are developed and energized through informal as well as formal interaction. These interactions strengthen cohesion and satisfaction. By providing social context cues, communication helps create shared meaning among team members (Sproull & Kiesler, 1991), which leads to the perception of social presence (Fulk & Boyd, 1991). In the future, these organizational relationships will be increasingly built and maintained through mediated means, thus communication research that examines these issues (Walther, 1992, 1995; Walther & Burgoon, 1992), especially with regard to distanced leadership, will continue to be imperative. Given these circumstances, the use of communication technologies, the accessibility of communication technologies across various sites and functions (e.g., digital divide), the nature of communication across multiple technologies, and the implications of technology use in virtual environments are important considerations for future communication research.

ASSUMPTIONS IN PREVIOUS DISTANCED LEADERSHIP RESEARCH

Certain assumptions about distanced leadership are embedded in the literature. In this review we address three important concerns: (a) the relative importance of physical distance in the distanced leader-member relationship; (b) the impact of early face-to-face contact among leaders and distanced employees, and face-to-face communication in general; and (c) the assumption that distanced work relationships are fundamentally different from colocated work relationships.

Is Physical Distance Crippling to Communication?

The majority of work on distanced work relationships assumes that physical distance is the crucial variable in distanced leadership (see Olson & Olson, 2000). The presumption is that physical distance between leaders and followers makes it difficult for leaders to engage in relational and task-related behaviors (Kerr & Jerimer, 1978) and challenges the quality of the relationship between leaders and far-flung employees (Bass, 1990; Napier & Ferris, 1993). Often, scholars contrast distanced leadership with proximate leadership and claim, as Bass (1990) did, that physical proximity enables more effective communication between leaders and followers.

In studying the moderating effects of physical distance on the relationship between different leadership behaviors and followers' performance, Podsakoff, Todor, Grover, and Huber (1984) found that physical distance negatively moderated the relationship between contingent reward leadership and follower performance. They argued that as physical distance increases, so too do challenges to the leaders' abilities to evaluate performance and provide timely rewards. High-quality leader–follower relationships have been characterized in the literature by followers spending considerable time and energy communicating with the leader (Graen & Scandura, 1987) and on followers' perception that they are receiving high levels of support, confidence, and consideration from the leader (Graen & Uhl-Bien, 1995). Sparrowe and Liden (1997) argued that those types of high-quality relationships are more easily created under conditions of physical proximity and the possibility of face-to-face interactions than they are under geographically distributed conditions.

Whereas prior empirical research and conceptual reviews have typically used physical distance as the presumed critical variable in studying dispersed work relationships, physical distance, per se, may not be the only crucial variable. In addition, the perceived accessibility of people in the distanced relationship may matter in predicting important outcomes (Cascio & Shurygailo, 2003; Fidel & Green, 2004). Accessibility in this context has been defined as the distanced employees' perception that they can reach their leader when desired (see Connaughton & Daly, 2004b). Consider a team spread across the globe that has immediate communication access to one another via different media and has the flexibility to easily travel for face-to-face encounters. Contrast that team to another whose members are physically not that distant from one another but have low immediate access to one another. Which team is more likely to experience difficulties? It may be that the team physically close to each other but with very limited accessibility to each other and to their leader suffers more than the team that has easy accessibility but significant physical distance. This points to the critical role of communication in distanced settings.

Impact of Early Face-to-Face Interaction and Face-to-Face Interaction Generally

Some scholars have argued that, despite the existence of new media, face-to-face communication is still vitally important to achieving organizational outcomes (Cohen & Prusak, 2001). Scholars advancing this argument contend that face-to-face communication enables people to build shared meaning (Zack, 1993), provides people more opportunities to disclose individuating information to each other (Weisband, Schneider, & Connolly, 1995), and allows people to observe each others' responses to situations and to grasp personal nuances revealed through others' facial expressions, gestures, vocal intonations, as well as status markers such as clothing and office size (Daft & Lengel, 1986). The assumption is that face-to-face communication facilitates individuals' familiarity with interactants, thus enhancing communication and performance among team members (Gruenfeld, Mannix, Williams, & Neale, 1996). Face-to-face interactions help managers and subordinates develop personal relationships that are difficult to develop using the leaner media often found in distanced work settings (e.g., email).

It has been argued further that face-to-face communication is imperative for performing particular organizational tasks such as initiating group projects, negotiating issues, and solving problems (Sproull & Kiesler, 1991). In addition to these more planned encounters, face-to-face communication permits unplanned, casual conversation such as greetings before meetings and spontaneous coffee machine chats (Cohen & Prusak, 2001). These unplanned, spontaneous face-to-face encounters can have important organizational results. They give organizational members opportunities to expand their knowledge of each other (Sarbaugh-Thompson & Feldman, 1998), they provide opportunities to give and solicit feedback, and they enhance new organizational members' socialization into the organization (Hage, 1974). The general conclusion of this line of research is that individuals prefer to work in close proximity to their managers so they can engage in face-to-face interaction.

On the other hand, Rice (1984; Rice & Gattiker, 2001) critiqued the presumption made by scholars that face-to-face communication is always preferable and that non–face-to-face communication necessarily involves losses such as lower relationship satisfaction. Zack (1994) found, for example, that initial face-to-face interactions are quite helpful for teamwork, but that as time goes on, and team members come to better understand one another, mediated communication such as email could be used to accomplish tasks. Alge, Wiethoff, and Klein (2003) found that teams with an established history are able to use electronic means of communicating just as effectively as face-to-face.

In the research on distanced leadership, scholars have argued for the importance of face-to-face communication when initially building relationships with remote employees (Connaughton & Daly, 2003, 2004a). This work, however, has reported only perceptions of distanced leaders and has not noted perceptions of distanced organizational members nor has it empirically tested this assumption. This is a critical issue for future research, because for some organizational forms such as temporary project teams, or in cases where travel budgets are tight, face-to-face communication may not be an option. In addition, it may be that some people perform more effectively at a distance, and indeed, some may prefer to work far from their positional leader. Hence, further research that probes leadership and the assumptions and realities around the "necessity" of face-to-face communication in these types of organizational contexts is needed.

Distanced Work Relationships: Are They Necessarily Different from Colocated Relationships?

A common tendency in work on distanced or virtual teams is to compare them to face-to-face, or colocated, teams. This comparison takes a couple of forms. Some scholars contend that virtual teams and face-to-face teams differ along various dimensions. For instance, Bell and Kozlowski (2002) suggested that (a) spatial distance and (b) information, data, and personal communication are the two key dimensions upon which to differentiate virtual and colocated teams. Other scholars have conducted empirical studies that compared virtual and colocated teams across several variables, some of which are communicative. Scott and colleagues (1999), for instance, pinpointed differences in trust, communication satisfaction, and other variables between members of face-to-face teams and virtual teams among students at a large public university. Recent reviews have also acknowledged that the majority of studies on technology use in the group context have compared the use of communication technologies in mediated teams and face-to-face teams (McGrath & Hollingshead, 1994; Scott, 1999b).

Much of the previous leadership work was conducted in situations where leaders and members were colocated. This may be an important distinction, for being colocated with organizational members has been suggested to have potential benefits to leaders. One argument, for instance, is that colocated office settings allow for the development of a corporate culture, frequent and often unplanned communication, immediate access to people for troubleshooting, managerial walkarounds, and direct access to information (Davenport & Pearlson, 1998). In distanced relationships, it has been argued, leaders may experience difficulty in executing these activities.

Even though face-to-face teams can experience these same challenges, these issues are more pronounced in dispersed teams (Zaccaro & Bader, 2003) for two reasons. First, geographic dispersion greatly enhances the complexities of interactions. Connaughton & Daly (2003) uncovered that, conceptually, the major challenges of distanced leadership revolve around issues of isolation and trust, which, in turn, challenge members' sense of identification with the organization and with the leader. On a global level, they also found that these issues are further complicated by cross-cultural communication differences. The second reason these challenges are more pronounced in dispersed teams is that they are likely to be formed for a limited time and then disbanded when tasks are completed. This poses a leadership challenge because the dynamics that help teams become effective often require time to develop (Cramton, 2003).

More research is needed to determine how leadership in colocated settings differs, or does not differ, from leadership in distanced settings. Previous research, however, has concluded that communication is central to distanced leadership. In an empirical study of virtual teams in an international educational setting, for example, Kayworth and Leidner (2002) found that the leaders rated as effective by their members demonstrated a mentoring quality characterized by understanding, empathy, and concern for members. They concluded that a primary difference between leading virtual teams and colocated ones is the limited opportunities for virtual team leaders to project these qualities to their members.

DISTANCED LEADERSHIP AND COMMUNICATION

The literature on communication and distanced leadership can be organized into three groups: (a) literature that examines issues that have been framed as "complexities" of distanced leadership; (b) literature that examines communication variables; and (c) literature that documents relationships between communication variables and organizational outcomes in distanced settings.

Complexities of Distanced Leadership

Leadership of virtual teams is more complex than that of colocated teams for several reasons: (a) Members' identification with the organization, team, and leader may be challenged over distance (Connaughton & Daly, 2003, 2004a, 2004b; Wiesenfeld et al., 1999); (b) trust among leaders and team members may be swift and fleeting (Jarvenpaa, Knoll, & Leidner, 1998); and, (c) communication among leaders and team members may be complicated by diverse ethnic, communication, and organizational backgrounds (Cascio, 1999; Cascio & Shurygailo, 2003). These complexities, all of which are communicative in nature, may affect the satisfaction and productivity of people working in distanced relationships (Hinds & Bailey, 2000; Potter & Balthazard, 2002).

Identification. Identification has been found to be critical to organizational processes, both proximate and distanced (Cheney, 1991; Scott, 1997). Identification is the process in which an individual comes to see an object (e.g., an individual, group, organization) as being definitive of oneself and forms a psychological connection to that object. Even though scholars have offered a variety of conceptual definitions for identification (see Dutton & Dukerich, 1991; Kagan, 1958; Mael & Ashforth, 1992), identification is a communicative process, rooted in discourse (Burke, 1969). Through interaction, or what Cheney and Tompkins (1987) call the "conversation of shared interests" (p. 6), organizational members develop a sense of identification with a target (e.g., with their leader).

Scholars are more frequently investigating multiple targets of identification (Scott, 1997; Scott, Connaughton, et al., 1999). They have most often studied organizational identification and have found that organizational identification leads to several key outcomes: employees' increased commitment to the organization (Sass & Canary, 1991), reduced likelihood of leaving the organization (Saks & Ashforth, 1997; Scott, et al., 1999), increased likelihood of behaving in ways that are aligned with the organization's identity, interests, and beliefs (Cheney, 1983; Dutton, Dukerich, & Harquail, 1994, Simon, 1976; Tajfel, 1981, 1982; Tompkins & Cheney,1983), and increased likelihood of accepting influence attempts (Kelman, 1958; Mowday, Porter, & Steers, 1982; O'Reilly & Chatman, 1986).

Previous research on identification in distanced organizations has found that two identification targets—identification with organization (Wiesenfeld, et al., 1999) and identification with positional boss (Connaughton & Daly, 2004b)—are challenged in distanced contexts. Scholars investigating virtual settings have also tended to focus on team identification, suggesting that distance challenges the ties that bind teams (Scott & Fontenot, 1999). Unlike work done in colocated settings, other identification targets have yet to be examined, and their relationships to organizational outcomes (e.g., job satisfaction, turnover) are just beginning to be explored.

Trust. Trust is of paramount importance in creating and maintaining effective relationships over distance (Lipnack & Stamps, 1997; Nilles, 1998). O'Hara-Devereaux & Johansen (1994) contend that only trust can prevent geographic distance from becoming psychological distance. Trusting relationships promote open, substantive, and influential information exchange (Early, 1986) as well as reduce transaction costs (Cummings & Bromiley, 1996; Handy, 1995). The consequences of limited trust among organizational members can be severe: low organizational commitment (Hart, Caps, Cangemi, & Caillouet, 1986), decreased organizational performance (Cox, 1993), low employee morale (Cangemi, Rice, & Kowalski, 1989), and increased absenteeism and turnover (Cangemi et al., 1989; Mishra & Morrissey, 1990).

Trust between leaders and organizational members is critical to effective distanced leadership (Lipnack & Stamps, 1997; Nilles, 1998; O'Hara-Devereaux & Johansen, 1994) and to successful virtual teams (Jarvenpaa, Knoll, & Leidner, 1998; Jarvenpaa & Leidner, 1998). Across time and space, however, trust has been found to be precarious, swift, and temporal (Geber, 1995; Jarvenpaa, Knoll, & Leidner, 1998; Jarvenpaa & Leidner, 1998). Scholars have explained limited trust in distanced contexts by arguing that the facilitators of trust in face-to-face contexts such as shared norms and experiences (Bradach & Eccles, 1989) and the anticipation of future interactions (Powell, 1990; Walther, 1994) are often unavailable to leaders and members over distance.

Previous research on trust and distanced leadership has found that distanced employees' trust is positively associated with identification with the positional leader (Connaughton & Daly, 2004b; Dutton, et al., 1994; Kramer, 1993).

Connaughton and Daly (2004b) also demonstrated that there is a statistically significant relationship between identification and trust in both distanced and proximate settings.

In reflecting on previous research findings, it is possible that trust is experienced differently in globally remote and virtual organizations than it is in geographically proximate settings. For instance, perhaps instead of emerging from personal relationships as it often does in geographically proximate contexts, trust in some globally remote and virtual organizations (especially those with finite life spans) may emanate from people's shared goals or deadlines. When project teams are under strict timelines, trust must get built quickly or it does not get built at all. This notion, explicated in the theory of swift trust (Meyerson, Weick, & Kramer, 1996), applies to teams whose members have a limited history of working together and are unlikely to work together in the future, yet share an impending deadline that requires their coordination. Whereas traditional theories of trust focus on the construct's interpersonal and relational dimensions, the realities of some globally remote and virtual organizations may call on scholars and practitioners, as Jarvenpaa and Leidner (1998) suggested, wrestling thoughtfully, with slightly different conceptualizations of trust.

Navigating national cultural differences. The more globally dispersed organizations become, the more diversified their members become, representing different national and cultural backgrounds. Cascio (1999) addressed the cross-cultural challenges of distance leadership by positing that individuals raised in low context cultures experience more satisfaction and productivity in virtual teams than those raised in a high context culture. The former might depend more on precise language; the latter on nonverbal and contextual cues that would be unavailable to them in a virtual environment.

Beyond coping with cultural differences concerning the ways people frame their worlds, distanced leaders face more mundane cultural challenges. Working hours and habits may be different; what counts as holidays and as perks may vary; what norms exist for appearance, for entertainment, even for ethical decisions may differ; how important status is and how decisions get made often vary across national cultures. The combination of language differences, national cultural diversity, and varied communication norms presents major challenges to long distance leaders. Making a mistake on any of these can easily foster misunderstandings and, consequently, distrust. Even without an overt error, all of these differences can result in a sense of isolation for people who do not believe their cultural norms are understood or valued (Connaughton & Daly, 2003).

Communication Variables in Distanced Leadership Research

Previous research also has argued that geographical dispersion strains the opportunities for communication between leaders and members. For example, when comparing face-to-face and virtual team members' perceptions, Warkentin, Sayeed, and Hightower (1997) found that face-to-face group members perceived greater team cohesion, more satisfaction with the group interaction process, and more satisfaction with group outcomes than did their distanced counterparts. Other empirical work reveals that communication is challenged in virtual teams (Kraut & Streeter, 1995; Olson & Olson, 2000; Suchan & Hayzak, 2001). Indeed, in an empirical study, Hart and McLeod (2003) concluded that communication is the key constructive property of virtual team relationships.

Communication is examined from a variable-analytic approach in many of the studies we reviewed. The following variables are examined and are reviewed here: (a) frequency, (b) the perceived adequacy of information subordinates receive from managers, (c) the perceived equity of the information subordinates receive, (d) the perceived work versus nonwork focus of managers' communication, and (e) the predictability of interaction.

Frequency. Wiesenfeld, Raghuram, and Garud (1999) found a positive relationship in distanced work settings between the frequency with which employee and manager communicated and employee's organizational identification. Huff, Sproull, and Kiesler (1989) also found that the frequency with which distanced employees communicate with others in the organization leads to greater organizational commitment because frequent communication encourages individuals to feel as though they are actively participating in the organization. In a study of 126 teammates in 7 dispersed teams, Hart and McLeod (2003) found that teams with strong personal relationships communicated more frequently with one another (although messages were shorter) than did team members with weak personal relationships.

Perceived adequacy of information. In studies of distanced teams (e.g., Connaughton & Daly, 2003; Cramton, 2003), distanced employees often report feeling excluded from important conversations, meetings, and even decisions that occur at their managers' locations. They perceive that they are less aware of what is happening because they are located far from the locus of decision making. Prior research has shown a relationship between perceived information adequacy and job satisfaction (Downs, Clampitt, & Pfeiffer, 1988; Rosenfeld, Richman, & May, 2004).

Perceived equity of information sharing. In studies of distanced teams (e.g., Connaughton & Daly, 2003; Cramton, 2000), distanced employees report feeling excluded from important conversations, meetings, and even decisions that occur at their managers' locations. Cramton (2003) made the case that distanced team members are often susceptible to an uneven distribution of information. She argued that people colocated get more information than those at a distance. In an earlier field study, Cramton (2000) also found more conflict in dispersed teams due to an imbalance of information shared, a result she attributed in part to physical distance fostering an erroneous perception that information had been equally shared among distanced and proximate team members. Indeed, colocated team members often neglect to share essential information with those at a distance because they forget distanced employees do not have access to the same information (Cramton & Webber, 2000).

Perceived information equity fosters healthy work relationships. Previous research has demonstrated that this is particularly important in distanced settings. Connaughton and Daly (2003) interviewed a series of global distance leaders across industries and found that distanced leaders believe it is important to ensure that all team members, distant and local, receive the same messages at the same time. For example, they try not to let local people hear about a new policy, initiative, or agenda before distanced individuals. Otherwise, the local group might attain a favored "in" position, creating implied status differences between those working near and far. This is especially the case with the sharing of information. The perception that the leader is sharing the same information with all team members combats the perception of favoritism of one team member over others. In distanced relationships, the sense that the leader is sharing equal information with dispersed and colocated team members may alleviate the creation of in-group or out-group mentalities among proximate and distanced team members.

Work versus nonwork focus. In some research on distanced leadership, employees have complained about the tendency of managers working far from them to limit their communication to work-related issues. In face-to-face environments, communication often incorporates both task and social exchanges. Not only do people talk about work, but they exchange information about family, hobbies, personal issues, and so on. These seemingly mundane exchanges allow people to belong to the organization in a relational sense (Burgoon, et al., 2002). In distance settings, this sort of social interaction may be missing and may contribute to distanced employees' reduced sense of identification with their organization (Connaughton & Daly, 2003; Wiesenfeld et al., 1999). Indeed, research has found that in proximate teams there is greater social connectedness and involvement than in virtual teams (Burgoon et al., 2002). Consequently, one might suspect there is a positive relationship between satisfaction and the degree to which managers are perceived to incorporate both task and nontask information in their interactions with employees. To date, however, researchers have not tested that assumption.

Predictability of interaction. In colocated settings, unplanned communication can be quite easily accomplished. People run into each other in hallways, restrooms, and parking lots and converse; if a meeting needs to happen, people can corral each other to discuss an issue (Davenport & Pearlson, 1998; Kiesler & Cummings, 2002). Contrarily, these spontaneous conversations are not as easy among distanced teams. In distanced settings, managers cannot leave meetings to chance; they need to plan and schedule meetings. Jarvenpaa and Leidner (1998) found that predictable or planned meetings in virtual settings facilitated high trust among global virtual team members.

Communication and Organizational Outcomes in Distanced Settings

Certain communication behaviors have been linked to productivity and performance in colocated organizational settings. For instance, research documents a positive relationship between what the authors deem to be effective communication behaviors and productivity (Hellweg & Phillips, 1980). Moreover, two specific communicative phenomena relate to more positive performance outcomes: successful influence attempts (Kipnis & Schmidt, 1982; Kipnis, Schmidt, & Wilkinson, 1980) and feedback (Cusella, 1987; Fairhurst, Green, & Snavely, 1984; Judge & Ferris, 1993). Communication strengthens cohesion and satisfaction with team outcomes. By providing social context cues, communication helps create shared meaning among team members (Sproull & Kiesler, 1991), which leads to the perception of social presence (Fulk & Boyd, 1991). All are defining characteristics of effective leadership, and all are presumed to be challenged by distance (Lipnack & Stamps, 1997).

Research in distanced settings suggests a positive relationship between some communication variables and organizational outcomes. As noted earlier, Wiesenfeld, Raghuram, and Garud (1999) found a positive relationship in distanced work settings between the frequency with which employee and manager communicated and organizational identification. In addition, Huff, Sproull, & Kiesler (1989) found that the frequency with which distanced employees communicate with others in the organization leads to greater organizational commitment. Frequency and quality of feedback also has been linked to better work relationships and greater task productivity (Potter & Balthazard, 2002).

Considerations

Even though leadership has been conceived of as an interactive process between leaders and followers (Fairhurst, 2001, 1993; Gardner, 1987), the studies of distanced leadership outlined above, as well as others reviewed in this chapter, have tended to focus on leaders, not on distanced employees or the actual talk among them (see Avolio & Kahai, 2003; Cascio & Shurygailo, 2003; Connaughton & Daly, 2003, 2004a; Kayworth & Leidener, 2002; Zaccaro & Bader, 2003).

Previous research of distanced leadership also has tended to examine only distanced work relationships, without comparing them to proximate work relationships (for exceptions, see Connaughton & Daly, 2004b; Howell & Hall-Merenda, 1999). The advantage of using two samples, one proximate and one distant, is that scholars could identify processes and effects distinctively related to distanced leadership. In studies that use only distanced groups, conclusions about leader-member relationships may or may not be a function of distance.

Variation also exists in the ways scholars have measured physical distance. Some studies of distanced teams have measured physical distance on a broad 1 to 5 scale (see Howell & Hall-Merenda, 1999). Employing the "Surface Between Two Points of Latitude and Longitude" program used in geography studies (see http://www.wcrl.ars.usda.gov/cec/java/lat-long.htm), others have calculated the number of miles and the log of those miles between those two locations (Connaughton & Daly, 2004). Still others have used vague measures for distance (Cramton & Webber, 2005). If physical distance is to be considered a critical variable in distanced leadership research, clarity on how scholars are measuring distance is critical for future work to ensure appropriate interpretations of findings.

THE TREATMENT OF COMMUNICATION
IN DISTANCED LEADERSHIP RESEARCH

As is evident in this review, research on distanced leadership research, to date, has tended to adopt a management-centric orientation. The objective of many studies, particularly those from the management tradition, is to pinpoint what constitutes leadership effectiveness and to relate those findings to management-centric organizational outcomes. Perhaps this management orientation helps to explain the somewhat prescriptive tone this literature tends to exude. In this literature, for example, we learn about effective leadership practices (Cascio & Shurygailo, 2003; Connaughton & Daly, 2003, 2004a, Davis, 2003) and our attention is turned to achieving team performance (Howell & Hall-Merenda, 1999; Potter & Balthazard, 2002), enhanced team effectiveness (Kayworth & Leidner, 2002), and other outcomes. Moreover, through in-depth interviews with leaders of global distanced teams, Connaughton and Daly (2003, 2004a) noted several communicative tactics that positional leaders perceive to be effective in leading others from afar. They include (a) utilizing face-to-face communication with distanced employees at the beginning of a distanced work relationship; (b) personalizing communication and employing small talk; (c) overcommunicating with distanced employees; (d) attending to national cultural nuances; (e) choosing certain communication technologies to achieve certain leadership objectives; and, among others, (f) ensuring access to equitable communication technologies. Future researchers can learn much from these literatures and build research programs from them. After all, each of the perceptions reported above constitutes a testable proposition that future research could explore from the perspective of both distanced leaders and distanced employees.

We believe it is also critical to note that many studies consider communication to constitute a set of observable variables. Even though we certainly learn from well-executed variable-analytic studies, we must broaden this research area beyond articulating communication skills and behaviors and communications (plural), as the language of some distanced leadership scholars implies is the current focus (see Cascio, 2000; Kayworth & Leidner, 2002). As we conclude by advancing a future research agenda for this area of research, we hope to open that dialogue further.

DISTANCED LEADERSHIP: A FUTURE RESEARCH AGENDA

The literature on distanced leadership has grown over the past 10 years, as organizations in multiple industries and sectors have adopted dispersed organizational forms. Previous research has given us many important lessons, many of which are of interest not only to scholars, but to practitioners who lead from afar or who work at locations away from their positional leader (see Burtha & Connaughton, 2004). As this review has shown, however, previous research has privileged certain actors' perspectives, methods of inquiry, and considerations of communication, and thus, much work remains.

At the core of future research in this area will be ascertaining the role of actual physical distance in distanced leadership. Implicit in most writings about dispersed teamwork is an assumption that what matters most in determining key outcomes (e.g., productivity, satisfaction) is how physically far apart a leader and employee are from one another (see Olson & Olson, 2000). Thus, two people working in San Diego and Los Angeles are seen as being less distant than two people working in Japan and New York. That physical distance, however, is a critical variable is a testable proposition. Scholars have argued that perceived accessibility to the leader may be more critical to job satisfaction and productivity than physical distance (Connaughton & Daly, 2004b). Crucial to future research will be a fuller explication of the relationship between distanced leader's accessibility, a communicative construct, and other variables.

Other important questions are currently not being asked in research on distanced leadership. For one, what other leadership models, besides behavioral orientations, might inform the study of distanced leadership? Kayworth and Leidner (2002) have contended that the behavioral complexity model of leadership might be applicable to distanced contexts because it allows for, and embraces, paradox and contradiction, topics that are also of interest to organizational communication scholars (Fairhurst, Cooren, & Cahill, 2002; Putnam, 1986; Stohl & Cheney, 2001; Tracy, 2004). Such models underscore the multidimensionality and complexities of leadership and encourage us to move beyond linear, one-way notions of leadership that champion a certain set of behaviors.

Future research may also seek to uncover the political dimensions of distanced leadership. Accompanying many global organizations, particularly those that follow a matrix structure, is the existence of multiple leaders: a host country manager, a functional manager, a manager at headquarters, for example. How are power and control negotiated among multiple leaders? How are distanced organizational members able to negotiate their roles and identities with multiple audiences? What is the relationship between autonomy and control for organizational members separated from great physical distance from their leaders and other team members?

In the 21st century, leadership must be associated with social responsibility. As organizations continue to function globally and to affect individuals' lives around the world, these issues become ever more critical (see Deetz, 2003, 1992; Townsley & Stohl, 2003). Thus, questions that aim to examine the socially responsible distanced leader and distanced organizational member must be addressed. The way scholars frame global issues in their investigations will be important as well. Scholars should attend to the way culture in its many forms (e.g., organizational, national, or functional) exists, functions, may be preserved, may be preserved, and may be championed around the world (see Gibbs's notion of "culture as kaleidoscope"; Gibbs, 2002) instead of framing culture only as something to be navigated to achieve certain outcomes. These are all questions that communication scholars are uniquely positioned to address, and they are important issues that must be integrated into the existing conversations discussed in this critical review.

Future research must also explore different genres of organization beyond the corporate, for-profit collective. Military, government, political parties, associations, and not-for-profit organizations engage in distanced leadership as well. As organizational communication continues to expand beyond the for-profit context (see Ashcraft & Kedrowicz, 2002; Stohl & Cheney, 2001; Trethewey, 1997), research on distanced leadership must as well.

Distanced leadership is a communicative phenomenon. Its proliferation around the world and the issues related to it are too critical to organizational and social processes and to people's lives not to be explored by communication scholars. This is a research context in which our voices should and must be heard.

REFERENCES

Alge, B. J., Wiethoff, C., & Klein, H. J. (2003). When does the medium matter? Knowledge-building experiences and opportunities in decision-making teams. *Organizational Behavior and Human Decision Processes, 91*, 26–37.

Apgar, IV, M. (1998). The alternative workplace: Changing where and how people work. *Harvard Business Review, 76*(3), 121–136.

Ashcraft, K. L., & Kedrowicz, A. (2002). Self-direction or social support? Nonprofit empowerment and the tacit employment contract of organizational communication studies. *Communication Monographs, 69*, 88–110.

Avolio, B. J., & Kahai, S. S. (2003). Adding the "E" to e-leadership: How it may impact your leadership. *Organizational Dynamics, 31*, 325–338.

Bass, B. M. (1990). *Bass and Stodgill's handbook of leadership: Theory, research and management applications* (3rd ed.). New York: Free Press.

Bass, B. M., & Avolio, B. J. (1994). *Improving organizational effectiveness through transformational leadership*. Thousand Oaks, CA: Sage.

Bell, B. S., & Kozlowski, S. W. J. (2002,). A typology of virtual teams: Implications for effective leadership. *Group & Organization Management, 27*, 14–49.

Benson-Armer, R., & Hsieh, T. (1997). Teamwork across time and space. *McKinsey Quarterly, 4*, 18–27.

Biocca, F., Kim, J., & Choi, Y. (2001). Visual touch in virtual environments: An exploratory study of presence, multimodal interfaces, and cross-modal sensory illusions. *Presence, 10*, 247–265.

Bradach, J. L., & Eccles, R. G. (1989). Price, authority, and trust: From ideal types to plural forms. *Annual Review of Sociology, 15*, 97–118.

Browning, L. D., Saetre, A. S., Stephens, K. K., & Sornes, J. (2004). *Information and communication technology in action: Linking theory and narratives of practice*. Herndon, VA: Copenhagen Business School Press

Bryan, L. L., & Fraser, J. N. (1999). Getting to global. *McKinsey Quarterly, 4*, 28–37.

Burgoon, J. K., Bonito, J. A., Ramirez, Jr., A., Dunbar, N. E., Kam, K., & Fischer, J. (2002). Testing the interactivity principle: Effects of mediation, propinquity, and verbal and nonverbal modalities in interpersonal interaction. *Journal of Communication, 52*(4), 657–677.

Burke, K. (1969). *A rhetoric of motives*. Berkeley: University of California Press.

Burns, J. M. (1978). *Leadership*. New York: Harper & Row.

Burtha, M., & Connaughton, S. L. (2004). Learning the secrets of long-distance leadership: Eight principles to cultivate effective virtual teams. *Knowledge Management Review, 7,* 24–27.

Cangemi, J. P., Rice, J., & Kowalski, C. J. (1989). The development, decline and renewal of trust in an organization: Some observations. *Organization Development Journal, 7,* 2–9.

Cascio, W. F. (1999). Virtual workplaces: Implications for organizational behavior. In C. L. Cooper & D. M. Rousseau (Eds.), *Trends in organizational behavior* (pp. 1–14). Chichester, UK: Wiley.

Cascio, W. F. (2000). Managing a virtual workplace. *Academy of Management Executive, 14*(3), 81–90.

Cascio, W. F., & Shurygailo, S. (2003). E-leadership and virtual teams. *Organizational Dynamics, 31,* 362–376.

Cheney, G. (1983). The rhetoric of identification and the study of organizational communication. *Quarterly Journal of Speech, 69,* 143–158.

Cheney, G. (1991). *Rhetoric in an organization society: Managing multiple identities*. Columbia: University of South Carolina Press.

Cheney, G., & Tompkins, P. K. (1987). Coming to terms with organizational identification and commitment. *Central States Speech Journal, 38,* 1-15.

Cohen, S. G., & Gibson, C. B. (2003). In the beginning: Introduction and framework. In C. B. Gibson & S. G. Cohen (Eds.), *Virtual teams that work: Creating conditions for team effectiveness* (pp. 1–13). San Francisco, CA: Jossey-Bass.

Cohen, D., & Prusak, L. (2001). *In good company: How social capital makes organizations work*. Cambridge, MA: Harvard University Press.

Connaughton, S. L., & Daly, J. A. (2003). Long distance leadership: Communicative strategies for leading virtual teams. In D. J. Pauleen (Ed.), *Virtual teams: Projects, protocols, and processes* (pp. 116–144). Hershey, PA: Idea Group.

Connaughton, S. L., & Daly, J. A. (2004a). Leading from afar: Strategies for effectively leading virtual teams. In S. Godar, & S. P. Ferris (Eds), *Virtual & collaborative teams: Process, technologies, & practice* (pp. 49–75). Hershey, PA: Idea Group.

Connaughton, S. L., & Daly, J. A. (2004b). Identification with leader: A comparison of perceptions of identification among geographically dispersed and co-located teams. *Corporate Communication: An International Journal, 9*(2), 89–103.

Connaughton, S. L. & Daly, J. A. (2004, November). *Distanced versus proximate teams: The relationship among perceived communication behaviors of leaders and employee satisfaction*. Paper presented at the annual meeting of the National Communication Association, Chicago, Illinois.

Cox, T. H. (1993). *Cultural diversity in organizations*. San Francisco: Berrett-Koehler.

Cramton, C. D. (2000). *The mutual knowledge problem and its consequences for dispersed collaboration*. Unpublished manuscript. Fairfax, VA: George Mason University.

Cramton, C. D. (2003). Finding common ground in dispersed collaboration. *Organizational Dynamics, 30,* 356–367.

Cramton, C. D., & Webber, S. S. (2000). *The impact of geographic dispersion on work teams: A socio-technical perspective*. Unpublished manuscript. Fairfax, VA: George Mason University.

Cramton, C. D., & Webber, S. S. (2005). Relationships among geographic dispersion, team processes, and effectiveness in software development work teams. *Journal of Business Research, 58*(6), 758–765.

Cummings, L. L. & Bromiley, P. (1996). The organizational trust inventory (OTI): Development and validation. In R. M. Kramer & T. R. Tyler (Eds.), *Trust in organizations: Frontiers of theory and research* (pp. 302–330). Thousand Oaks, CA: Sage.

Cusella, L. P. (1987). Feedback, motivation, and performance. In F. Jablin, L. Putnam, K. Roberts, & L. Porter (Eds.), *Handbook of organizational communication* (pp. 624–678). Newbury Park, CA: Sage.

Daft, R. L., & Lengel, R. H. (1986). Organizational information requirements, media richness and structural design. *Management Science, 32,* 554–571.

Davenport, T. H., & Pearlson, K. (1998). Two cheers for the virtual office. *Sloan Management Review, 39,* 51–65.

Davis, D. D. (2003). The Tao of leadership in virtual teams. *Organizational Dynamics, 33*(1), 47–62.
Deetz, S. (1992). *Democracy in an age of corporate colonization*. Albany: State University of New York Press.
Deetz, S. (2003). Corporate governance, communication, and getting social values into the decisional chain. *Management Communication Quarterly, 16,* 606–611.
DeSanctis, G., & Fulk, J. (Eds.). (1999). *Shaping organizational form: Communication, connection, and community*. Thousand Oaks, CA: Sage.
Downs, C. W., Clampitt, P. G., & Pfeiffer, A. L. (1988). Communication and organizational outcomes. In G. M. Goldhaber & G. A. Barnett (Eds.), *Handbook of organizational communication* (pp. 171–211). Norwood, NJ: Ablex.
Duarte, D. L., & Snyder, N. T. (1999). *Mastering virtual teams: Strategies, tools, and techniques that succeed*. San Francisco: Jossey-Bass.
Dutton, J. E., & Dukerich, J. M. (1991). Keeping an eye on the mirror: Image and identify in organizational adaptation. *Academy of Management Journal, 34*(3), 517–554.
Dutton, J. E., Dukerich, J. M., & Harquail, C. V. (1994). Organizational images and member identification. *Administrative Science Quarterly, 39,* 239–263.
Early, P. C. (1986). Trust, perceived importance of praise and criticism, and work performance: An examination of feedback in the United States and England. *Journal of Management, 12,* 457-473.
Fairhurst, G. T. (2001). Dualisms in leadership research. In F. A. Jablin, & L. L. Putnam (Eds.), *The New Handbook of Organizational Communication* (pp. 379–439). Thousand Oaks, CA: Sage.
Fairhurst, G. T. (1993). The leader-member exchange patterns of women leaders in industry: A discourse analysis. *Communication Monographs, 60,* 321–351.
Fairhurst, G. T., & Chandler, T. A. (1989). Social structure in leader-member interaction. *Communication Monographs, 56,* 215–239.
Fairhurst, G. T., Cooren, F., & Cahill, D. J. (2002). Discursiveness, contradiction, and unintended consequences in successive downsizings. *Management Communication Quarterly, 15,* 501–541.
Fairhurst, G. T., Green, S. G., & Courtright, J. A. (1995). Inertial forces and the implementation of a socio-technical systems approach: A communication study. *Organization Science, 6,* 168–185.
Fairhurst, G. T., Green, S. G., & Snavely, B. K. (1984). Managerial control and discipline: Whips and chains. In R. N. Bostrom (Ed.), *Communication Yearbook 9* (pp. 558–593). Beverly Hills, CA: Sage.
Fairhurst, G. T., Jordan, J. M., & Neuwirth, K. (1997). Why are we here? Managing the meaning of an organizational mission. *Journal of Applied Communication Research, 25,* 243–263.
Fairhurst, G. T., & Sarr, R. A. (1996). *The art of framing: Managing the language of leadership*. San Francisco: Jossey-Bass.
Fidel, R. & Green, M. (2004). The many faces of accessibility: engineers' perception of information sources. *Information Processing & Management 40*(3), 563–581.
Fiedler, F. E. (1967). *A theory of leadership effectiveness*. New York: McGraw-Hill.
Fjermestad, J., & Hiltz, S. R. (1998–1999). An assessment of group support systems experiment research: Methodology and results. *Journal of Management Information Systems, 15,* 7–149.
Fritz, M. B., & Manheim, M. L. (1998, April). Managing virtual work: A framework for managerial action. In P. Sieber and J. Griese (Eds.), *Organizational virtualness, Proceedings of the Vo-Net Workshop*. Bern, Germany: University of Bern.
Fritz, M. B., Narasimhan, S., & Rhee, H. (1998). Communication and coordination in the virtual office. *Journal of Management Information Systems, 14,* 7–28.
Fulk, J., & Boyd, B. (1991). Emerging theories of communication in organizations. *Journal of Management, 17,* 407–466.
Fulk, J., & DeSanctis, G. (1995). Electronic communication and changing organizational forms. *Organization Science, 6,* 337–349.
Gardner, J. W. (1987). Leaders and followers. *Liberal Education, 73*(2), 4–6.
Geber, B. (1995). Virtual teams. *Training, 32*(4), 36–40.
Gibbs, J. L. (2002). *Loose coupling in global teams: Tracing the contours of cultural complexity*. Unpublished doctoral dissertation, University of Southern California.

Graen, G. B., & Scandura, T. A. (1987). Toward a psychology of dyadic organizing. In L. L. Cummings & B. M. Shaw (Eds.), *Research in organizational behavior* (pp. 175–208). Greenwich, CT: JAI Press.

Graen, G. B., & Uhl-Bien, M. (1995). Relationship-based approach to leadership: Development of leader-member exchange (LMX) theory of leadership over 25 years: Applying a multi-level multi-domain perspective. *Leadership Quarterly, 6,* 219–247.

Grosse, C. U. (2002). Managing communication within virtual intercultural teams. *Business Communication Quarterly, 65*(4), 22–38.

Gruenfeld, D. H., Mannix, E.A., Williams, K. Y., & Neale, M. A. (1996). Group composition and decision-making: How member familiarity and information distribution affect process and performance. *Organizational Behavior and Human Decision Processes, 67*(1), 1–15.

Hage, J. (1974). *Communication and organizational control: Cybernetics in health and welfare settings.* New York: Wiley.

Handy, C. (1995). Trust and the virtual organization. *Harvard Business Review, 73*(3), 40–50.

Hart, K. M., Caps, H. R., Cangemi, J. P., & Caillouet, L. M. (1986). Exploring organizational trust and its multiple dimensions: A case study of General Motors. *Organization Developmental Journal 4*(2), 31–38.

Hart, R. K., & McLeod, P. L. (2003). Rethinking team building in geographically dispersed teams: One message at a time. *Organizational Dynamics. 31*(4), 352–361.

Hellweg, S. A., & Phillips, S. I. (1980). Communication and productivity in organizations: A state-of-the-art review. *Proceedings of the 40th Annual Academy of Management Conference* (pp. 188–192), Detroit, Michigan.

Hiltz, S. R., & Turoff, M. (1985). Structuring computer-mediated communication systems to avoid information overload. *Communications of the ACM, 28,* 680–689.

Hiltz, S. R., Dufner, D., Holmes, M., & Poole, M. S. (1991). Distributed group support systems: Social dynamics and design dilemmas. *Journal of Organizational Computing, 2,* 135–159.

Hinds, P. J., & Bailey, D. E. (2000, August). *Virtual team performance: modeling the impact of geographic and temporal virtuality.* Paper presented at the Academy of Management annual meeting, Toronto, Canada.

Howell, J. M., & Hall-Merenda, K. E. (1999). The ties that bind: The impact of leader-member exchange, transformational and transactional leadership, and distance on predicting follower performance. *Journal of Applied Psychology, 84,* 680–694.

Huff, C., Sproull, L., & Kiesler, S. (1989). Computer communication and organizational commitment: Tracing the relationship in a city government. *Journal of Applied Social Psychology, 19,* 1371–1391.

Hymowitz, C. (1999, April 6). Remote managers find ways to narrow the distance gap. *Wall Street Journal,* p. B1.

Jarvenpaa, S. L., & Leidner, D. E. (1998). Communication and trust in global virtual teams. *Journal of Computer-Mediated Communication, 3.* Retrieved from http://www.ascusc.org/jcmc/vol3/issue4/jarvenpaa.html

Jarvenpaa, S. L., Knoll, K., & Leidner, D. E. (1998). Is anybody out there? Antecedents of trust in global virtual teams. *Journal of Management Information Systems, 14,* 29–64.

Judge, T. A., & Ferris, G. R. (1993). Social contexts of performance evaluation decisions. *Academy of Management Journal, 36,* 80–105.

Kagan, J. (1958). The concept of identification. *Psychological Review, 65,* 296–305.

Kayworth, T. R., & Leidner, D. E. (2002). Leadership effectiveness in global virtual teams. *Journal of Management Information Systems, 18,* 7–40.

Kelman, H. C. (1958). Compliance, identification, and internalization: Three processes of attitude change. *Journal of Conflict Resolution, 2,* 51–60.

Kerr, S., & Jerimer, J. M. (1978). Substitutes for leadership: Their meaning and measurement. *Organizational Behavior and Human Performance, 22,* 375–403.

Kiesler, S., & Cummings, J. N. (2002). What do we know about proximity and distance in work groups? A legacy of research. In P. Hinds & S. Kiesler (Eds), *Distributed work* (pp. 57–80). Cambridge, MA: MIT Press.

Kipnis, D., & Schmidt, S. M. (1982). *Profile of organizational influence strategies.* San Diego, CA: University Associates.

Kipnis, D., Schmidt, S., & Wilkinson, I. (1980). Intraorganizational influence tactics: Explorations in getting one's way. *Journal of Applied Psychology, 65,* 440–452.

Kirkman, B. L., Rosen, B., Tesluk, P. E., & Gibson, C. B. (2004). The impact of team empowerment on virtual team performance: The moderating role of face-to-face interaction. *Academy of Management Journal, 47*(2), 175–192.

Kramer, R. M. (1993). Cooperation and organizational identification. In J. K. Murnigham (Ed.), *Social psychology in organizations: Advances in theory and research* (pp. 244–269). Englewood Cliffs, NJ: Prentice Hall.

Kraut, R., E., Fussell, S. R., Brennan, S. E., & Siegel, J. (2001). Understanding effects of proximity on collaboration: Implications for technologies to support remote collaboration work. In P. Hinds & S. Kiesler (Eds), *Distributed work* (pp. 137–162). Cambridge, MA: MIT Press.

Kraut, R. E., & Streeter, L. (1995). Coordination of software development. *Communications of the ACM, 3,* 69–81.

Lee, J., & Jablin, F. M. (1995). Maintenance communication in superior-subordinate work relationships. *Human Communication Research, 22,* 220–257.

Leonardi, P. M., Jackson, M. K., & Marsh, N. (2004). The strategic use of "distance" among virtual team members: A multi-dimensional communication model. In S. H. Godar, & S. P. Ferris (Eds.), *Virtual & collaborative teams: Process, technologies, & practice* (pp. 156–172). Hershey, PA: Idea Group.

Lievrouw, L. A. (1999, May). New media: Deciding what's new about new media. *ICA News,* 10–11.

Lipnack, J., & Stamps, J. (1997). *Virtual teams: Reaching across space, time, and organizations with technology.* New York: Wiley.

Mael, F., & Ashforth, B. E. (1992). Alumni and their alma mater: A partial test of the reformulated model of organizational identification. *Journal of Organizational Behavior, 13,* 103–123.

Majchrzak, A., Rice, R. E., King, N., Malhotra, A., & Ba, S. (2000). Technology adaptation: The case of a computer supported inter-organizational virtual team. *MIS Quarterly, 24,* 569–600.

Maznevski, M. L., & Chudoba, K. M. (2000). Bridging space over time: Global virtual team dynamics and effectiveness. *Organization Science, 11,* 473–492.

McCune, J. C. (1998). Telecommuting revisited. *Management Review, 87,* 10–16.

McGrath, J. E., & Hollingshead, A. B. (1994). *Groups interacting with technology: Ideas, evidence, issues and an agenda.* London: Sage.

Meyerson, D., Weick, K. E., & Kramer, R. M. (1996). Swift trust and temporary groups. In R. M. Kramer & T. R. Tyler (Eds.), *Trust in organizations: Frontiers of theory and research* (pp. 166–195). Thousand Oaks, CA: Sage.

Mintzberg, H. (1973). *The nature of managerial work.* New York: Harper & Row.

Mintzberg, H. (1994). Rounding out the manager's job. *Sloan Management Review 36*(1), 11–26.

Mishra, J., & Morrissey, M. A. (1990). Trust in employee/employer relationships: A survey of West Michigan managers. *Public Personnel Management, 19,* 443–463.

Mowday, R. T., Porter, L. W., & Steers, R. M. (1982), *Employee-organization linkages: The psychology of commitment, absenteeism, and turnover.* San Diego, CA: Academic Press.

Napier, B. J., & Ferris, G. R. (1993). Distance in organizations. *Human Resource Management Review, 3,* 321–357.

Nelson, B. (1998). Recognizing employees from a distance. *Manage, 50*(1), 8–9.

Nilles, J. M. (1998). *Managing telework: Strategies for managing the virtual workforce.* New York: Wiley.

O'Hara-Devereaux, M., & Johansen, R. (1994). *Global work: Bridging distance, culture, & time.* San Francisco: Jossey-Bass.

O'Reilly, C. A., & Chatman, J. (1986). Organizational commitment and psychological attachment: The effects of compliance, identification, and internalization of prosocial behavior. *Journal of Applied Psychology, 71,* 492–499.

Olson, G. M., & Olson, J. S. (2000). Distance matters. *Human Computer Interaction, 15,* 139–178.

Pfeffer, J. (1981). Management as symbolization: The creation and maintenance of organizational paradigms. In L. L. Cummings & R. M. Staw (Eds.), *Research in organizational behavior, 3,* 1–52. Greenwich, CT: JAI Press.

Podsakoff, P. M., Todor, W. D., Grover, R. A., & Huber, V. L. (1984). Situational moderators of leader reward and punishment behaviors: Fact or fiction? *Organizational Behavior and Human Performance, 34,* 21–63.

Poole, M. S., DeSanctis, G., Kirsch, L., & Jackson, M. (1995). Group decision support systems as facilitators of quality team efforts. In L. R. Frey (Ed.), *Innovations in group facilitation: Applications in natural settings* (pp. 299–321). Cresskill, NJ: Hampton Press.

Potter, R. E., & Balthazard, P. A. (2002). Understanding human interactions and performance in the virtual team. *Journal of Information Technology Theory and Application, 4,* 1–23.

Powell, W. W. (1990). Neither market nor hierarchy: Network forms of organizations. *Research in Organizational Behavior, 12,* 295–336.

Prashad, S. (2003, October 23). Building trust tricky for 'virtual' teams. *Toronto Star,* K06.

Pratt, M. G., Fuller, M. A., & Northcraft, G. B. (2000). Media selection and identification in distributed groups: The potential costs of "rich" media. *Research on Managing Groups and Teams, 3,* 231–255.

Putnam, L. L. (1986). Contradictions and paradoxes in organizations. In L. L. Thayer (Ed.), *Organizational communication: Emerging perspectives* (pp. 151–167). Norwood, NJ: Ablex.

Rice, R. E. (1984). Mediated group communication. In R. E. Rice (Ed.), *The new media: Communication, research, and technology* (pp. 129–154). Beverly Hills, CA: Sage.

Rice, R. E., & Gattiker, U. E. (2001). New media and organizational structuring. In F. M. Jablin & L. L. Putnam (Eds.), *The new handbook of organizational communication: Advances in theory, research, and methods* (pp. 544–581). Thousand Oaks, CA: Sage.

Ring, P. S., & Van de Ven, A. H. (1992). Structuring cooperative relationships between organizations. *Strategic Management Journal, 13,* 483–498.

Rosenfeld, L. B., Richman, J. M., & May, S. K. (2004). Information adequacy, job satisfaction and organizational culture in a dispersed-network organization. *Journal of Applied Communication Research, 32,* 28–54.

Saks, A. M., & Ashforth, B. E. (1997). A longitudinal investigation of the relationships between job information sources, application perceptions of fit, and work outcomes. *Personnel Psychology, 50,* 395–426.

Sarbaugh-Thompson, M., & Feldman, M. S. (1998). Electronic mail and organizational communication: Does saying "hi" really matter? *Organization Science, 9,* 685–698.

Sass, J. S., & Canary, D. J. (1991). Organizational commitment and identification: An examination of conceptual and operational convergence. *Western Journal of Communication, 55,* 275–293.

Schmidt, J. B., Montoya-Weiss, M. M., & Massey, A. P. (2001). New product development decision-making effectiveness: Comparing individuals, face-to-face teams, and virtual teams. *Decision Sciences, 32*(4), 1–26.

Scott, C. R. (1997). Identification with multiple targets on a geographically dispersed organization. *Management Communication Quarterly, 10,* 491–522.

Scott, C. R. (1999a). The impact of physical and discursive anonymity on group members' multiple identifications during computer-supported decision making. *Western Journal of Communication, 63,* 456–487.

Scott, C. R. (1999b). Communication technology and group communication. In L. R. Frey (Ed.), *The handbook of group communication theory and research* (pp. 432–472). Thousand Oaks, CA: Sage.

Scott, C. R., Connaughton, S. L., Diaz-Saenz, H. R., Maguire, K., Ramirez, R., Richardson, B., et al. (1999). The impacts of communication and multiple identifications on intent to leave. *Management Communication Quarterly, 12,* 400–435.

Scott, C. R., & Fontenot, J. (1999). Multiple identifications during team meetings: A comparison of conventional and computer-supported interactions. *Communication Reports, 12,* 91–100.

Scott, C. R., Frank, V., Cornetto, K. M., Sullivan, C. & Forster, B. (1999, November). *Communication technology use and key outcomes in novice groups: A comparison of site and virtual teams.* Paper presented at the annual conference of the National Communication Association, Chicago.

Scott, C. R., Quinn, L., Timmerman, C. E., & Garrett, D. (1999). Ironic uses of group communication technology: Evidence from meeting transcripts and interviews with group decision support system users. *Communication Quarterly, 46,* 353–374.

Scott, C. R., & Timmerman, C. E. (1999). Communication technology use and multiple workplace identifications among organizational teleworkers with varied degrees of virtuality. *IEEE Transactions on Professional Communication, 42,* 240–260.

Sias, P. M., & Jablin, F. M. (1995). Differential superior-subordinate relations, perceptions of fairness, and coworker communication. *Human Communication Research, 22,* 5–38.

Simon, H. A. (1976). *Administrative behavior* (3rd ed.). New York: Free Press.

Snow, C. C., Snell, S. A., Davison, S. C., & Hambrick, D. C. (1996). Use transnational teams to globalize your company. *Organizational Dynamics, 24,* 50–67.

Sparrowe, R. T., & Liden, R. C. (1997). Process and structure in leader-member exchange. *Academy of Management Review, 22,* 522–552.

Sproull, L., & Kiesler, S. (1991). *Connections: New ways of working in the networked organization.* Cambridge, MA: MIT Press.

Stage, C. W. (1999). Negotiating organizational communication cultures in American subsidiaries doing business in Thailand. *Management Communication Quarterly, 13*(2), 245–280.

Stohl, C. (2001). Globalizing organizational communication. In F. A. Jablin & L. L. Putnam (Eds.), *The new handbook of organizational communication* (pp. 323–375). Thousand Oaks, CA: Sage.

Stohl, C., & Cheney, G. (2001). Participatory processes/paradoxical practices: Communication and the dilemmas of organizational democracy. *Management Communication Quarterly, 14,* 349–407.

Suchan, J., & Hayzak, G. (2001). The communication characteristics of virtual teams: A case study. *IEEE Transactions on Professional Communication, 44*(3), 174–186.

Sypher, B. D. (1991). A message-centered approach to leadership. In J. A. Anderson (Ed.), *Communication Yearbook 14* (pp. 547–559). Newbury Park, CA: Sage.

Tajfel, H. (1981). *Human groups and social categories.* Cambridge, UK: Cambridge University Press.

Tajfel, H. (1982). Social psychology of intergroup relations. In M. R. Rosenzweig & L. W. Porter (Eds.), *Annual Review of Psychology, 33,* 1–39, Palo Alto, CA: Annual Reviews.

Tompkins, P. K., & Cheney, G. (1983). Account analysis of organizations: Decision-making and identification. In L. L. Putnam & M. E. Pacanowsky (Eds.), *Communication and organizations: An interpretive approach* (pp. 123–146). Beverly Hills, CA: Sage.

Townsend, A. M., DeMarie, S. M., & Hendrickson, A. R. (1998). Virtual teams: Technology and the workplace of the future. *Academy of Management Executive, 12,* 17–29.

Townsley, N. C., & Stohl, C. (2003). Contracting corporate social responsibility. *Management Communication Quarterly, 16,* 599–605.

Tracy, S. J. (2004). Dialectic, contradiction, or double bind? Analyzing and theorizing employee reactions to organizational tensions. *Journal of Applied Communication Research, 32,* 119–146.

Trethewey, A. (1997). Resistance, identity, and empowerment: A postmodern feminist analysis of clients in a human service organization. *Communication Monographs, 64,* 281–301.

Van Aken, J. E., Hop, L., & Post, G. J. J. (1998). The virtual organization: A special mode of strong interorganizational cooperation. In M.A. Hitt, R. D. Nixon, & J. E. Ricart (Eds.), *Managing strategically in an interconnected world* (pp. 301-320). Chichester, UK: Wiley.

Walther, J. B. (1992). Interpersonal effects in computer-mediated interaction: A relational perspective. *Communication Research, 19,* 52–90.

Walther, J. B. (1994). Anticipated ongoing interaction versus channel effects on relational communication in computer-mediated interaction. *Human Communication Research, 20,* 473–501.

Walther, J. B. (1995). Relational aspects of computer-mediated communication: Experimental observations over time. *Organization Science, 6,* 186–203.

Walther, J. B., & Burgoon, J. K. (1992). Relational communication in computer-mediated interaction. *Human Communication Research, 19,* 50–88.

Warkentin, M. E., Sayeed, L., & Hightower, R. (1997). Virtual teams versus face-to-face teams: An exploratory study of a web-based conference system. *Decision Sciences, 28,* 975–996.

Weisband, S. P., Schneider, S. K., & Connolly, T. (1995). Computer-mediated communication and social information: Status salience and status differences. *Academy of Management Journal, 38,* 1124–1151.

Wiesenfeld, B. M., Raghuram, S., & Garud, R. (1999). Communication patterns as determinants of organizational identification in a virtual organization. *Organization Science, 10,* 777–790.

Witherspoon, P. D. (1997). *Communicating leadership: An organizational perspective.* Boston: Allyn & Bacon.

Yukl, G. (1989). Managerial leadership: A review of theory and research. *Journal of Management, 15,* 251–289.

Zaccaro, S. J., & Bader, P. (2003). E-leadership and the challenges of leading e-teams. *Organizational Dynamics, 31,* 377–387.

Zack, M. H. (1993). Interactivity and communication mode choice in ongoing management groups. *Information Systems Research, 4,* 207–238.

Zack, M. H. (1994). Electronic messaging and communication effectiveness in an ongoing work group. *Information and Management, 26,* 231–241.

Zigurs, I. (2003). Leadership in virtual teams: Oxymoron or opportunity? *Organizational Dynamics, 31,* 339–351.

Zorn, T. E. (1991). Construct system development, transformational leadership, and leadership messages. *Southern Communication Journal, 56,* 178–193.

CHAPTER CONTENTS

7   The Real–Virtual Dichotomy in Online Interaction: New Media Uses and Consequences Revisited

ZIZI PAPACHARISSI
Temple University

This synthesis of literature examines conflicting and overlapping conclusions on the uses and consequences of new media and finds that approaches in interpreting these results are frequently guided by the belief that online and offline interactions somehow take place on separate social planes. Rather than viewing this as a real versus virtual question, this review suggests these results be viewed as indicative of the human need to fine-tune social contact, manage time, and express identity in a manner that combines present and future technologies. As online media mature and newer technologies develop, an overview of the contributions and shortcomings of relevant communication research could inform scholarly investigation in the future.

In a critical evaluation of online technology potential titled, "Virtual Geographies: The New Worlds of Cyberspace," Gunkel and Gunkel (1997) argued that definitions, expectations and experiences with previous media can restrict the promise of a new medium, determining its future by the words used to refer to it. Specifically, they concluded that "naming is always an exercise of power. . . . The future of cyberspace, therefore will be determined not only through the invention of new hardware and software, but also through the names we employ to describe it (p. 133). Applied to communication research in new media, one could argue that scholarly attention to online technologies has been simultaneously enhanced and restrained by the tendency to compare online communication to other types of communication, especially mass and interpersonal. Not only has this influenced the language employed to describe online communication, but it has frequently predisposed conclusions drawn on the use and impact of online media.

For example, research on the effects of internet use is occasionally divided along the lines of the now well-known "internet paradox," which identifies the

Correspondence: Zizi Papacharissi, Broadcasting, Telecommunications and Mass Media, Temple University, Annenberg Hall Rm. 6, Philadelphia, PA 19122; email: zpapacha@temple.edu

Communication Yearbook 29, pp.215–237

internet as a medium that connects people virtually while further alienating them in real time and space (Kraut et al., 1998). Despite subsequent research that reversed the causality of those data (Kraut et al., 2002), quantitative and qualitative research on the internet is similarly divided, revealing evidence of the internet as a social revitalizer on the one hand and as an alienating agent on the other. Recent new media research has demonstrated the tendency to move ahead in a different direction, examining the integration of multiple communication channels toward manifold purposes (e.g., Katz & Rice, 2002a, b, c; Matei & Rokeach, 2002). Nevertheless, because any forward movement requires looking back, this literature review offers a retrospective look into communication research in new media, guided by the attempt to identify advances and limitations in research.

This synthesis of literature examines conflicting and overlapping conclusions on the uses and consequences of new media and finds that approaches in interpreting these results are frequently guided by the belief that online and offline interactions somehow take place on separate social planes. Researchers often highlight the fact that avid internet users neglect their offline friends and family, as if these users are not pursuing social contact with "real" and perhaps the same people online. Similarly, other researchers focus on the social bonds created online, overlooking those that are sacrificed offline. Rather than viewing this as a real versus virtual question (engaging in never ending comparisons of face-to-face (FtF) versus electronically mediated interaction), this review suggests these results are viewed as indicative of the human need to fine-tune social contact, manage time, and express identity in a manner that combines present and future technologies. New media have always generated popular enthusiasm over the communicative capabilities they enable for the future (e.g., Marvin, 1988). As online media mature and newer technologies develop, an overview of the contributions and shortcomings of relevant communication research could inform scholarly investigation in the future.

This chapter therefore provides an overview of research on new media uses and consequences and traces how the imposition of a perhaps false dichotomy between real and virtual interaction has influenced the design and interpretation of relevant research. It should be noted that the imposition of this real–virtual dichotomy, does not stem out of scholarly ignorance, but rather should be interpreted as an essential step in learning how to study the social capital of new technologies that blur our conventional understandings of time and space. This study is conceptualized as a comprehensive review of research on new media uses and consequences with the goals of (a) establishing what we do know about new media effects, (b) exposing methodological advances and inadequacies in previous research, (c) identifying errors in the interpretations of quantitative and qualitative data, and (d) suggesting theoretical directions and approaches that might be more fruitful for future research. Whereas the presentation of relevant research is organized with a chronological objective in mind, several of the research trends presented obviously overlap and influence each other. The following sections, therefore, attempt to tentatively group together different research interests that have marked the development of online communication research. These studies are broadly divided in the following three areas: (a) research defining and understanding computer-mediated communication, characterized by the attempt to assert the information and interactive capabilities of new media, (b) scholarly work focusing on online community and identity, and (c) studies investigating uses and consequences of new media. This division merely aids the organized presentation of research and is not designed to overlook the obvious commonalities among the researchers and work contained within these three areas. Rather, it is constructed to trace shifts in the past and current prevalent research interests. This review presents work completed within these three areas and then addresses how the imposition of a real–virtual dichotomy may have influenced the direction or interpretation of research.

COMPUTER-MEDIATED COMMUNICATION: INFORMATIONAL AND INTERACTIVE

Early computer-mediated communication (CMC) research was characterized first by an attempt to understand how the informative capabilities of this new medium compared to those of traditional communication channels and second by the need to assert that the interactive capabilities of this new medium could facilitate communication. New media researchers employed the umbrella term "computer-mediated communication" to refer to all types of communication facilitated by computer technologies. CMC has been defined as "synchronous or asynchronous electronic mail and computer conferencing, by which senders encode in text messages that are relayed from senders' computers to receivers" (Walther, 1992, p. 52). Walther's definition, although frequently used, is somewhat limiting and does not include future communicative applications of computers. December's (1996) more appropriate definition of CMC as "a process of human communication via computers, involving people, situated in particular contexts, engaging in *processes* to shape media for a variety of purposes," is also frequently employed because of the emphasis it places on individuals, context, purposes, and human-computer interaction. The present review adopts the latter definition and employs the terms *online communication, CMC,* and *new media research* interchangeably to refer to processes of communication facilitated by information technologies, involving people in online and offline contexts.

CMC research initially focused on the informational dimension of new technologies and explored how these newer media might differ from traditional face-to-face communication and how they might provide additional communication channels (e.g., Culnan & Markus, 1987; Hiltz & Turoff, 1978; Rice, 1984; Rice & Love, 1987; Sproull & Kiesler, 1986). Several attributes of CMC distinguished it from face-to-face and other mediated communication, including problems in coordination owing to the lack of informational feedback, the absence of social cues in discussion, and depersonalization because of the lack of nonverbal involvement

(Kiesler, Siegel, & McGuire, 1984). This research focused on how poorly virtual interactions compared to the nonverbal rich interchanges of FTF communication. The cues-filtered-out approach, for example, addressed how CMC's limited numbers of nonverbal cues affect online communication by altering the means available for social regulation or context (Culnan & Markus, 1987). Based on such nonverbal cues, media vary in their social presence (Short, Williams, & Christie, 1976) or media richness (Daft & Lengel, 1984). Social presence, "the feeling that other actors are jointly involved in communicative interaction" (Short et al., 1976, p. 65), captured the ability of the medium to support communication exchanges that are warm, personal, sensitive, and active. Lacking nonverbal cues in comparison to other media, computers were found to possess less social presence or media richness than other media, such as the telephone or voice mail (Perse & Courtright, 1993; Rice, 1993). Perceptions of social presence were perceived as influential on uses of and satisfaction with CMC. For example, Perse, Burton, Kovner, Lears, and Sen (1992) found that college students who rated computers as more socially present tended to use them more often and to find them more helpful in learning.

Similarly, media richness theory posited that people distinguish among communication media based on the intrinsic properties (e.g., personalness and warmth) of these media (Daft & Lengel, 1984). These properties influence people's perceptions and selection of media to fulfill communication needs (Fulk, Steinfield, Schmitz, & Power, 1987). The ways in which media richness is applied to communication research are similar to those found in social presence work. Different media are ranked on how rich they are, usually in the following order (starting with the richest): face-to-face, telephone, electronic mail, personal written communication, and formal written communication (Steinfield & Fulk, 1987; Trevino, Lengel, & Daft, 1987).

Even though this line of research spotlighted the immense capabilities of information technologies, it simultaneously encouraged comparisons with established communication channels, especially within organizations. This was not intentional in the sense that researchers primarily investigated what, at the time, were prevalent uses of online communication within organization. It is possible, however, that these comparisons may have restricted our understanding of information technologies not in terms of what they could accomplish, but mostly in terms of what they could or could not perform in relation to different communication channels. Studying CMC as a substitute or a complement to previous channels enabled the discussion of the informational capabilities of new media, but also imposed a framework restricted by the capabilities of previous media, thus establishing the definition of a new medium in old terms.

Research that followed asserted the interactive and informational capabilities of the medium and established the uniqueness of this new communication channel, arguing that it created a sociocultural network where people could fulfill informational and interactive needs (Sproull & Faraj, 1997). As internet use became more popular, other researchers documented the existence of computer-mediated interaction. Walther (1992), for example, found that as computer-mediated communication evolves over time, communicators adapt their language and textual displays to enhance immediacy and to manage relationships they develop through computer-mediated communication. He proposed a social information-processing perspective that embodied relational motivators and the decoding of textual cues that may substitute for nonverbal ones. Walther's (1992) rationale stems out of individuals' fundamental need to affiliate and expend considerable social energy trying to get others to like and appreciate them. As a result, CMC users—just as communicators in any context—should desire to transact personal, rewarding, complex relationships. CMC users should exhibit relational indicators and communicate to do so.

Drawing on concurrent work, which also documented the presence of social cues in CMC (e.g., Daft & Lengel, 1984; Rheingold, 1993; Sproull & Kiesler, 1986), Walther (1993) extended this research to include impression management of individuals through CMC and how relational and personal indicators of CMC vary and change over time (Walther, 1994). He noted that FtF groups did not express greater intimacy than computer-mediated groups (Walther, 1995). Walther (1996) concluded that (a) mediated interaction is rarely impersonal, (b) CMC is interpersonal when users have the time and interest to interact on a relational level, and (c) CMC is hyperpersonal when users can manage relationships and impressions in ways more effective than with FtF communication or other mediated channels. Walther's research documented and theorized on the existence of social cues in CMC and revealed that this communication channel could be used to fulfill socially oriented needs. This contribution was significant because it helped steer potential applications of internet-related technologies away from a strictly organizational setting and revealed how CMC could be integrated into daily social routines and practices. Even though the research recognized CMC as a unique channel for communication, there was still a marked tendency to compare it to face-to-face and other channels for communication, which, at this stage, helped focus the research and suggest some ways of looking into this new medium.

On a parallel research tenant, the socially interactive elements of CMC were further asserted by organizational communication scholars. Regarding new media, organizations are continually agenda setting, that is, surveying the organizational environment adopting information technologies that might increase productivity (Rogers, 1983), often producing mixed reactions, ranging from enthusiasm to alienation, in different groups within the organization (Dutton, 1984; Markus, 1981; Zuboff, 1988). Researchers have documented differences in groups using FtF and CMC for decision making or to brainstorm in organizational settings. The findings typically have indicated that differences in medium use are associated with the presence of personal elements of communication, including audio and visual content. An early study by Ochsman and Chapanis (1974) compared conversations carried on in 10 different modes of communication, including various combinations of handwriting, typewriting, and audio–video content and found the most significant factor in medium choice lay in the inclusion or exclusion of a voice channel. Subsequent studies, focused on electronic communication and including the use of computers and the internet, compared communicative differences within organizations.

Several studies relied on experiments to document communicative differences across channels (Johansen, DeGrasse, & Wilson, 1978; Johansen, Miller, & Vallee, 1975; Johansen, Vallee, & Spangler, 1979), which revealed that individuals within organizations tended to align with those for whom they possessed the most audiovisual cues. For instance, in a teleconferencing setting, individuals were more likely to support the opinions of those with whom they shared the most teleconferencing equipment. Nevertheless, relevant research concluded that effectiveness of the communication channel involved always relies on context; that is, face-to-face communication can provide too many nonverbal cues that can distract from effective decision making as much as enlighten it (Short et al., 1976). Specifically, computer conferencing might increase the amount of time and volume of communication required to achieve consensus and, on occasion, hinder agreement (Hiltz & Turoff, 1978; Kiesler et al., 1984). Still, additional research has shown that as users become more experienced and adept at these systems, they develop screening skills and strategies for enhancing agreement and managing the communication overload (e.g., Hiltz, 1982, 1983; Hiltz & Turoff, 1978; 1981).

Nevertheless, within the organizational setting, CMC groups outperformed groups using verbally oriented media to communicate (e.g., Valacich, Dennis, & Connolly, 1994; Valacich, George, Nunamaker, & Vogel, 1994; Valacich, Paranka, George, & Nunamaker, 1993). Valacich and colleagues argued that computer mediation can support unlimited parallel and distinct communication episodes, whereas traditional (e.g., verbal) media support serial communication. Straus (1997), however, found that although computer-mediated groups exhibited more supportive and less attacking communication than face-to-face groups, computer-mediated groups were less cohesive and satisfied about group outcomes. Similarly, Straus (1996, 1997) concluded that electronic communication was not inherently more depersonalized than face-to-face communication, and that patterns of performance and interaction are similar in computer-mediated and face-to-face groups. In addition, employees who extensively used electronic mail (email) in their organization were more committed to the goals of and better informed about their companies than those who used email less often (Kraut & Attewell; 1997), while FtF discussion contained more argumentation than computer-mediated discussion in decision-making groups (McGuire, Kiesler, & Siegel, 1987).

As research progressed, CMC was appreciated as a functional and appealing alternative to FtF and other communication channels, with researchers studying how individuals adapt it to fulfill their own needs. Despite their textuality, the features of internet-related technologies were reconfigured by early users to convey social information, and this line of research, despite its comparative focus, documents just that. The tendency to compare the internet to FtF venues is an understandable starting point, especially because social interaction online involves the adaptation of several FtF interactional routines and conventions. This early research was a significant contribution because, despite the tendency to compare CMC to other channels of communication, scholars focused on how CMC was used to manage offline (or "real") relationships, at home and in the workplace, online. The tendency to view CMC in comparative mode, and primarily as a supplement or substitute to other media, underestimates the potential and scope of this new medium.

Subsequent work moved beyond comparative accounts in group and organizational communication, examining computer-mediated communication from a perspective that recognized the overlap between online and offline relationships and thus steering away from enforcing a real–virtual dichotomy. Specifically, Poole and DeSanctis (1992) employed structuration theory to understand how members of a given social collective simultaneously liberate and constrain themselves by creating the structures that facilitate and restrict future action. They found that in group communication, "the technology alone cannot guarantee improvements but that these are tied to how groups appropriate the technology in to the interaction system" (p. 43). This less deterministic approach was further implemented in a further study of computerized group decision systems by Poole, Holmes, Watson, and DeSanctis (1993), which concluded that the technological component rendered the discussions more organized but occasionally detracted from thorough and critical discussion. Poole and Holmes (1995) further analyzed how new computer technologies impacted group decision making over time, to find that consensus change, perceived decision quality, and decision scheme satisfaction were determining factors in decision making over time and that to conclude that "new, ill-understood technologies are 'magic wands' is too simple" (p. 123).

On a parallel tenant, Burgoon, Bonito, Ramirez, Dunbar, Kam, and Fischer (2002) recognized the shortcomings of such comparisons across communication channels and focused on overall presence of nonverbal and verbal cues to establish how technologies may augment interaction. Burgoon et al. (2002) also incorporated interactivity to understand mediation, proximity, and verbal and nonverbal modalities in interpersonal interaction and found that nonverbal (especially audio) properties of technologies, rather than the technologies themselves, are key contributors to communication efficacy.

As technology progressed, therefore, researchers corresponded to prevalent uses of CMC within organizations by focusing on the integration of offline and online interaction, as opposed to comparing the two. This shift in scholarly attention marked a departure from the organization realm and allowed the examination of other uses of online technology involving the study of online community and identity presented in the following section. Moreover, it paved the road for research that linked technological benefit or detriment to social and psychological variables at work, a direction to be picked up by later work on the uses and consequences of the internet.

ONLINE IDENTITY AND COMMUNITY

Appreciation for the social potential of CMC led to studies that examined how structural features of the internet and related technologies affected social interaction online. This body of work is characterized by a focus, frequently qualitative, on the community and identity creation online. Resting on the similar assumption that social cues permeate online communication, this group of studies nonetheless tended to mostly feature an ethnographic influence and trace descriptive elements of online behavior. It should be noted that the rise of online communities prompted scholars to refocus attention to this new phenomenon, although parallel CMC studies that documented the social character of CMC lent support to the study of social activity online. More socially oriented uses of CMC were not as prevalent in the early days, so naturally they may have eluded scholarly attention. Nevertheless, online identity management and community formation have fascinated researchers from many fields, and they usually approached this subject from an ethnographic or other qualitative perspective.

The social appeal of information technology was not lost on early technological enthusiasts, who used it much like the telegraph, telephone, radio and television to do old things in new ways (Marvin, 1988; Rheingold, 1993). Rheingold (1993) observed, through studies of the WELL and other online communities, that whenever CMC technology becomes available, people inevitably build social colonies around it. Turkle (1984), one of the pioneers in this area, examined computer culture, identity, the computer, and the creation of computer communities. By focusing on children's interactions with computers and on artificial intelligence, Turkle wrote extensively on how computers change the ways that individuals perceive themselves, pointing out computers present companions without emotional demands, allowing one to be a loner, but never alone.

Turkle's later work (1995, 1996, 1997) focused on identity reinvention and community in cyberspace, noting that users are constantly "dreaming cyborg dreams" of fluid identities and minds that are downloadable to computers. It is no surprise that people should sometimes prefer virtual to real life interaction: In cyberspace, they are allowed to overcome physical appearance and become the person they truly want to be. Turkle articulated this argument by tracing the history of artificial intelligence, but primarily by focusing on her own research of multiuser domainss, or MUDs. In describing MUD involvement, she metaphorically posited that MUD users put their online personae to sleep when exiting a MUD and returning to their real-life personae, thus cycling through different environments and identities. She contrasted this with the traditional notions of identity, which imply oneness, whereas "life on the screen" implies multiplicity and heterogeneity (Turkle, 1997).

The role of the computer as a prosthetic device that catapults one into "cyberspatial interaction" has been examined by Haraway (1991a, 1991b), who approached the question from a postmodern perspective. According to Haraway, the advent and diffusion of new communication technologies can eradicate or blur distinctions between human–animal, human–machine, and physical–nonphysical dimensions, and cyberspace presents an inviting environment for communication and identity exploration. It is the anonymous and textual nature of cyberspace that allows one to overcome identity fixes, such as gender, looks, and disabilities. People choose to explore certain sides of their personalities (e.g., assertiveness) more extensively, or even invent virtual life personae different from their real–life personality (Barnes, 1996; Bolter, 1996). For certain researchers, the striking point is that the individual and computer function as one, and it is because of the machine that the individual is able to reinvent the self online (Stone, 1996).

MUDs are symbolic environments, often game based, in which players are free to alter and reinvent their identities as they please and present another incarnation of online community. The existence of codes of conduct among MUD users and unfortunate disruptions of those codes (the so-called "rape" in LambdaMOO in which a more experienced computer user took over another's MOO identity and character name and used it to express obscene and offensive remarks, hence the "rape," is such an example) further attest to the social nature of these communities (Beaubien, 1996). Not only do MUDs provide opportunities for social interaction, but they allow members to play out real-life fantasies in a manner similar to that of reading romance novels (Ito, 1997).

In extending social interaction and offering additional avenues for expression, online communities also allow individuals to replicate or even reinvent their identities online. MUD members frequently adopt characters, and players in virtual worlds choose avatars through which they interact and communicate. Castells (1997) predicted that people will adopt flexible personalities to adapt and exist in a postpatriarchal world and that, as a result, societies will transform from public-based to self-based. Roles and identity are negotiated through meaning, interaction, and discourse online. Nevertheless, the communities that we inhabit online influence the parts of our personalities that become more prevalent online, as well as how we choose to present ourselves.

Several studies have documented community creation and identity expression online. Reid (1991) studied primarily identity construction and social interaction through internet relay chat (IRC) and traced the transformation of cultural and behavioral tools online by IRC users. Conventional modes of interaction were deconstructed or refashioned online, so as to create new shared cultural codes, which were then adopted to enforce a new type of hegemony (Reid,1991). Baym's (1995, 1997) seminal work on community revealed that soap opera newsgroup members developed their own forms of expression, used the group to develop and reaffirm their own senses of self and identity, developed relationships online, and shared behavioral norms that guided interaction. She found that the members of rec.arts.tv.soaps adapted features of electronic communication, such as subject lines and punctuation marks, to demark subgroups, define genres, and express emotion. These individuals in particular valued opinions that are humorous, insightful, individualistic, and considerate, and they presented a community that, although dispersed in time and space, sustained relationships and kept members interested, even when the soaps themselves were boring.

The behavioral norms adopted by online communities were further explored by McLaughlin, Osborne, and Smith (1995), who studied Usenet discussion groups and compiled a taxonomy of reproachable conduct on Usenet. The taxonomy consisted of the following seven categories: (a) incorrect or novice use of technology (message with header but no lines, confusing the "reply privately" and "reply to group" options, (b) bandwidth waste (excessively long signatures, posting excessively long articles), (c) violation of networkside conventions (inappropriate subject line, failing to encrypt offensive material), (d) violation of newsgroup-specific conventions (failing to use "spoiler" warnings, failing to observe groups conventions for subject lines), (e) ethical violations (reposting private email without permission, playing pranks), (f) inappropriate language (flaming, ridicule), and (g) factual errors (spelling errors, errors in summarizing others' posts). This taxonomy attested to the social nature of the discussion groups that often echo the norms, rules, and discussion topics of real life groups.

Several pieces have traced similar online community successes and failures. These studies trace the activities of both online communities, as well as offline communities that employ the internet to enhance communication among their members. Mitra (1997) described a network community that brought together the Indian diaspora to discuss issues of national concern. Even though this community allowed people to develop and strengthen social and national ties, it often hosted conflict among members who disagree, rendering it a threatening and unpleasant environment,where the hostilities of the outer world are carried on instead of being abandoned. Similar events take place in the Public Electronic Forum (PEN) for the homeless in Santa Monica (Schmitz, 1997). This community was started by the city to provide a free and accessible electronic public forum for the city residents. Homeless people were able to form a strong alliance through it, however, utilizing it to find jobs and better their circumstances. PEN is frequently praised for its success, but Schmitz noted that it has not been immune to conflict, which intimidated several users. Similar early interactive communication systems also included the Berkeley Community Memory Project, established in 1978; the Blacksburg Electronic Village, Inc. (BEV) in Blacksburg, Virginia put in place in 1993; and the La Plaza Telecommunity in Taos, New Mexico, established in 1995 (Rogers & Malhotra, 2000).

The study of electronic community discourse has been undertaken by several researchers who have traced behavioral patterns and adaptations in the online setting. Watson (1997) studied textual discourse on the community for the band Phish and found evidence of bonding and conflict. When conversation got too crowded or too tense, members learned to flock to other groups, in order to participate in a community that was more fulfilling and less threatening. Kolko and Reid (1998) tracked several such communicative failures online and argued that

the fluidity of space combines with the fluidity of identity in cyberspace, further imperiling the ability to talk with any sense of familiarity, with any commitment to codes of the world we know and move through daily in real space. (p. 225)

The authors suggested that this multiplicity of the self contradicted fluidity, as MUD or MOO players viewed the ability to create different selves as the reason to not integrate different kinds of actions and reactions into the same self. It seems that both the online behavior of users, and not just the research approaches, reinforces the presence of dichotomy between online and offline interaction by refusing to integrate the offline and online personas.

This rather individualistic preference for a multiple over an integrated self was also highlighted by Clark (1998) in her studies of teenage online dating. She observed that teen chat rooms provide the setting for the ideal "pure" relationship of the contemporary age in that they offer "imagined intimacy but no need for trust or commitment; thus one that is fulfilling and liberating, ultimately and primarily, to the self" (p. 182). The irony of employing a fluid and the ultimately postmodern technology to escape the trappings of what is known as the postmodern condition is pondered by Bromberg (1996) in her study of MUDs, who remarked that "claims that virtual reality will provide meaning and reveal the secrets of ancient wisdoms and truths otherwise unknowable are appealing when faced with the postmodern notion that there are no universal truths" (p. 147).

Within this environment of simulation, typed text enables identity experimentation, providing the masks participants can don online (Danet, 1998). The modes, synchronous or asynchronous, through which internet-related technologies display text, together with whether text is complemented with audiovisual features, may limit or enhance the possibility for identity experimentation. The conflict between the so-called "real" space the body occupies online and the permutations through which it comes to exist online are explored, but obviously not resolved, by several descriptive studies of behavior in MUDS, MOOs, and other virtual environments (Argyle, 1996; Argyle & Shields, 1996; Lajoie, 1996). Specifically, Lajoie (1996) argued that the "seduction of cyberspace is that it will obscure or silence the problems involved in material existence," which may lead to a more acutely individualistic mode of existence, neglect of material circumstances and reluctance to form collectivities on that basis (p. 169).

These studies, among others, have revealed how online conversations are often subject to rules of behavior modeled after offline interaction, constructed to communicate online effectively. Thus, computer technologies allow individuals to overcome the boundaries of our offline identities and engage in personality play while observing etiquette designed to ensure equality of opinion expression. Even though a few researchers do stop short of unnecessarily glorifying the fluidity of online identity and actually consider the offline ramifications of the "liberating" online experience, the majority of this body of work has focused on descriptive community elements and rhetorical analysis. This was a necessary first step to analyzing the meaning and potential of online communities, which could, however, be enhanced by more frequent acknowledgment of the complexity and occasional irony of identity separation and reinvention online.

As a natural next step, scholarly attention could turn to these remaining issues. For instance, how are offline communities and physical existence affected while

new possibilities in cyberspace are explored? Even though this is potentially liberating, there is an inherent irony in the need to isolate oneself in front of the
computer screen and alienate from others in the offline world in order to be able
to meet each other again in cyberspace. To this point, Willson (1997) argued that
a critical examination of online communities revealed "a 'thinning' of the complexities of human engagement to the level of one-dimensional transactions and
a detaching of the user from the political and social responsibilities of the 'real
space' environment" (p. 159). This observation has not escaped most of this body
of work, but it has also not been critically examined at length.

The social impact of online interaction presents a research agenda, left unexplored by this group of studies, that would help assess the social consequences of
online use. Whereas the documentation of online behaviors and social routines
presented a necessary first step for communication researchers, it frequently
inadvertently emphasized the liberating effects of online expression without
adequately examining the interplay between an individual's offline and online
existence. Focusing primarily on the liberating effects online anonymity exerted on personal expression, several studies neglected to discuss the declining
importance of personal responsibility in online interaction. Moreover, several
studies overlooked additional intricacies of online behavior that involved the
manifestation of social power and status online, thus producing accounts of
online behavior that are deceptively egalitarian (Haythornthwaite & Wellman,
2002). This tendency would actually suffice were the online experience to be
treated as an adventure. In reality, glorification of the liberating potential of online expression needs to be accompanied with a discussion of the social capital
this expression generates, both online and offline. The tendencies reflect the imposition of a forced dichotomy between the real–virtual or online–offline spheres
of interaction.

Moreover, studies have frequently zoomed in on online interaction, overlooking how the online communication is integrated within an individual's daily existence. This is a direction worth pursuing, for, as Kolko and Reid (1998) observed,
"[T]he individual virtual persona is at once too committed to the particularity of
the self it projects and too uncommitted to the continuity of that self" (p. 220). It
would be beneficial to understand exactly how liberating online experiences influence one's personality and lifestyle more directly. Now that a generation is getting
close to having grown up with online access, it would be worthwhile to study the
development of several online communities overtime, quantitatively and qualita-
tively. The development and modification of community membership, etiquette,
behavioral norms, volume and tone of communication, and other factors could be
studied over time.

Finally, an issue of importance lies in how the commercialization of the internet influences community membership and identity expression online. Several of
the studies that highlighted the liberating impact of the internet were conducted
during the early days of the medium. Nowadays, the internet presents more of a
commercial sphere, and perhaps a much less inspiring cultural terrain, littered

with pop-up ads. The concept of community is routinely employed to attract and retain online traffic (Fernback, 2002; Papacharissi, 2002). Additional research that addresses these questions should help clarify the online experience and assess the social capital of online interaction.

Identity exploration and manipulation online also need to be considered more closely. While recognizing that the ability to experiment with different aspects of one's personality can be gratifying, researchers need to move beyond glorifying this feature of the internet and examine other aspects of identity reinvention. For instance, identity expression in MUD environment frequently involves the use of real-life stereotypes and the translation of real-life conventions to a virtual space. Frequently influenced by the fantasy novels or context that are the basis for several MUDs, the people involved do not necessarily discover or recreate new aspects of their personas, but rather, repurpose and experiment with tired real-life stereotypes. In essence, participation in online environments allows those involved to try on different social roles, or rather, considering the lack of personal responsibility online anonymity affords, to try on the costumes for these roles. That can be fun—but does not deserve scholarly attention unless some of the questions underneath the surface are addressed. To this point, in a review of relevant research, Postmes, Spears, and Lea (1998) found that, despite the opportunity for freedom from social influences, people did not always necessarily choose to liberate themselves from these influences. They concluded that:

> Cyberspace may provide the ideal opportunity to create a new virtual society, but if people fall back on the tried and trusted categories of the old world and actively carry over the constraints of their own everyday identities, this new world will rapidly resemble the old one (p. 708).

The pivotal question in this case lies in the human tendency, when afforded the opportunity to reinvent identity with no relative consequences, to resort to the same tired old stereotypes that restrict our offline existence. These stereotypes were the restricting factor of the offline existence, motivating the so-called escape into the online world in the first place. Those engaging in role-play online nonetheless find it meaningful to try on personas structured on conventional and limiting interpretations of masculinity and femininity. Whereas it may be true that these stereotypes offer a familiar and stable context from which to construct a liberating performance, scholarly attention should be drawn to the limitations of an online performance that relies on redressing elements of the dominant ideology. Even though such action could be interpreted as a challenge to the hegemonical context of stereotypical references, it remains embedded in the cultural language of the status quo.

The offline consequences of identity transformation, the development of this behavior overtime, and the connections between virtual and real personalities need to be further explored. Even though some work (Stone, 1996; Turkle, 1996) has examined what happens to the real body when the virtual one metastacizes online, these questions afford additional attention. The presence of a real–virtual dichotomy within this body of work allows research to zoom in on the online experience and study norms and patterns of online behavior in greater depth. At the same time, however, inordinate focus on the virtual effectively separates the offline and online spheres of interaction, thus neglecting to address the offline consequences or antecedents of online behavior. This particular direction is examined by the group of studies presented in the following section.

INTERNET EFFECTS AND THE INTERNET PARADOX

The qualitative body of work on identity expression and community formation online additionally affirmed and documented the originally disputed ability of the internet to foster social communication. The same body of work also provided the context and set up important research questions about the interplay between online and offline behavior. Several were taken up by the mostly quantitative body of work addressing internet uses and consequences that we presented in this last section.

Within this particular group of studies, researchers focused on how new media technologies are used and with what particular consequences. Parks and Floyd (1996) were among the first to quantitatively study levels of friendship formation in cyberspace, building on Walther's social information-processing perspective. They found more developed personal relationships for those who posted (i.e., mailed messages to newsgroups) more often and who had been posting for a longer time. Two-thirds of the relationships that developed online, however, did not remain there. People used the audiovisual capacities of the World Wide Web and then moved on to FtF and telephone communication. Katz and Aspden (1997) supported the positive consequences of online social communication by documenting through surveys that the internet offered additional avenues of social interaction by freeing people from many of the constraints of geography, appearance, or schedule. They found no evidence of people dropping out of social networks because of increased internet use; on the contrary, they concluded that the internet augmented involvement in existing communities. To this point, Constant, Sproull, and Kiesler (1996) added that weak online ties were especially useful for linking people to information and social resources unavailable in people's closest, local groups.

A longitudinal study by Kraut et al. (1998) was one of the first to investigate the lingering question of causality and potential internet effects, which had been hinted at by both qualitative and quantitative work focusing on online community, identity, and online–offline social contact. Focusing on amount of nternet use, personality characteristics, and behavioral and attitudinal effects, and using longitudinal data across 73 households, Kraut et al. (1998) found that greater internet use related to reduced communication in the household, smaller social circles, and greater senses of depression and loneliness. The findings of the study were striking because the researchers involved were able to apply a panel design, equip their respondents with computers, and study online and offline behavior for the first 12–18 months of use. The results were somewhat compromised by the lack of a control group and the novelty of the technology to the study subjects involved. It is possible that more mature users are less overwhelmed with the technology and better able to integrate it with their daily offline routines more smoothly. In addition, although the quantity of internet use was extensively measured and associated with personality characteristics and social communication patterns, the nature of internet use was not adequately investigated so as to be able to distinguish between more solitary uses, like Web surfing and more social uses, like emailing friends or creating a family homepage.

Nevertheless, the results confirmed concerns other scholars (e.g. Putnam, 1996) had raised about the negative effect media could have on social communication and further underlined the distinction between the so-called virtual and real spheres of social contact. These assertions were corroborated by survey findings offered by Nie and Erbring (2000), who concluded that "the more hours people use the Internet, the less time they spend with real human beings" (p. A1). These correlational but not causal claims appeared not to be inclusive of time spent online with physical, therefore, "real" human beings. As other critics argued, these claims were based on only 4.3% of the original sample, implying that over 95% of the sample did not report spending any less time with friends and family because of the internet, and even among the heaviest users, 88% reported no change in the amount of time spent with family and friends (McKenna, Green, & Gleason, 2002).

Additional survey findings attempted to connect online use with personality characteristics and attitudes toward the internet. For example, Papacharissi and Rubin (2000) found that those who considered interpersonal communication less rewarding and were anxious when communicating with others used the internet for interpersonal utility. At the same time, those who were mobile, satisfied with their lives, and were less anxious with FtF communication, used the internet as a convenient means of seeking information and entertainmen, rather than for interpersonal utility or to fill time. People who used the internet to gather information reported that they were greatly satisfied with it, while those who used it primarily for interpersonal interaction developed greater affinity with it (i.e., considered the internet a significant aspect of their everyday existence), but did not report similar levels of satisfaction (Papacharissi & Rubin, 2000). Likewise, Mickelson (1997) documented those parents of children with special needs who sought social support through electronic communities perceived their family and friends less favorably than did other parents. The results did not specify, however, whether the electronic groups increased the isolation or the weak real-life ties led people to seek support online. Similarly, LaRose, Eastin, and Gregg (2001) highlighted the importance of experience as a mediator of potential internet effects, in that novice users might be more likely than experienced ones to immerse themselves in online use and thus sacrifice or temporarily fall behind with offline social contacts.

In the same vein, Morahan-Martin and Schumacher (2000) surveyed 277 undergraduate internet users and found that almost two thirds reported one to three symptoms of pathological internet use. Pathological users were more likely to be male and technologically sophisticated, use real-time interactive activities such as online games and chat lines, and feel comfortable and competent online. These users also scored higher on the UCLA loneliness scale and were socially disinhibited online. Working with a much smaller sample, Hamburger and Ben-Artzi (2000) found that for men, extraversion was positively related to the use of online leisure services and neuroticism was negatively related to information services, whereas for women, extraversion was negatively related and neuroticism positively related to the use of online social services. In contrast, Robinson, Kestnbaum, Neustadtl and Alvarez (2000) compared the mass media use and social life of heavy, light, and nonusers of the internet, and found no significant survey evidence of time displacement, with internet users actually showing signs of more active social lives than nonusers. Along the same lines, Wastlund, Norlander, and Archer (2001) found no significant relationship between internet use and psychological well-being, although they partially confirmed the general response pattern found by Kraut et al. (1998), which indicated that younger individuals tended to use the internet to a higher degree, experiencing a lesser degree of psychological well-being. Shah, Kwak, and Holbert (2001) further specified that informational uses of the internet were positively related to individual differences in the production of social capital, whereas social-recreational uses were relatively related to civic indicators. Additional analyses revealed that production of social capital through internet use was higher among Generation X, tied to television use among baby boomers, and to newspaper use among members of the "civic generation."

At best, these results indicated use of the internet as a functional alternative, suggesting that individuals with different predispositions and needs used the medium to add or make up for something lacking in their offline existence. The variety of methodologies, concepts, and interpretive approaches used, however, prohibits consensus on the nature of internet effects. Additional research reports complicate the picture even further. A group of studies conducted by the Pew Internet and American Life Project revealed a nation becoming increasingly more comfortable with internet use and more adept at integrating online and offline social routines. Rainie and Kohut (2000) reported that, based on survey findings, internet users had more robust social lives than nonusers and that the most fervent internet users were more likely to admit that email use had improved their bonds with relatives. In the same report, internet use for women had the opposite of an isolating effect, helping female users improve their connections to relatives and friends.

Using Pew data, Howard, Rainie, and Jones (2001), found that usage patterns and consequences depended on the individual's orientation toward the medium, and that the more experienced users were more likely to find that the online access had improved different aspects of their personal lives. Similar analysis of the same survey data revealed no evidence of a link between social isolation and internet use

(Lee & Anderson, 2001). In a research report on time spent online, Fox and Rainie (2001) added that online veterans were more likely than new users to weave the internet into their lives at all levels, indicating that as comfort levels with a medium changed, online access had varying consequences for an individual's daily social interaction. Other surveys of teen online access revealed teenagers who were savvy technology users and who used the internet to manage both social and school obligations. Even though the majority of those surveyed enjoyed this experience, they also admitted that it might take away time spent with families (Lenhart, Rainie, & Lewis, 2001).

In an overview of survey results, Horrigan, Rainie, and Fox (2001) concluded that many internet users enjoyed being socially active in online communities, employed the internet to intensify their connection to their local community, and used the internet to deal with the devastating aftermath of the September 11 attacks. Specifically relating to how Americans used the internet after the September 11 attacks, Rainie (2001) reported that most used the internet for informational purpose and for contact and reassurance. In a follow-up report, Rainie and Kalsnes (2001) found that (a) internet use in general decreased in the days after the attack, (b) internet use for getting news rose, (c) fewer people used the internet for fun activities or anything nonattack related matters, and (d) many used discussion groups and email to express frustration, anger, and grief. These results indicated that, instead of an escapist medium, the internet was emerging as a way of remaining connected to the world, and especially friends and relatives.

To summarize, following decades of scholarly endeavor, researchers now recognize that people find ways to communicate with each other online and that they find ways to make up for the lack of nonverbal cues and make this communication more fulfilling. In addition, people socialize and gather information online, using the internet to extend their real-life capabilities. At the same time, increased levels of internet use have been linked to loneliness and depression, but the direction of causality is not entirely clear. Those who are less satisfied with the quality of the social interaction in their own lives are more likely to use the internet for interpersonal contact. More research on the real-life habits of people and how they correspond to their virtual lives is needed before we determine the effects of CMC technologies. Research does seem to indicate that people turn to the internet to make up for and obtain things that they do not possess in real life, however. Nevertheless, when it comes to establishing the impact of the internet social capital, results are mixed, although all point to individual differences and orientations toward the medium as mediating variables.

Certain recent studies have employed several of these suggestions, and revealed that as individuals grow more comfortable with this new technology, they find more meaningful ways of integrating it into their social routines. In a 3-year follow-up of the original Homenet study, Kraut, Kiesler, Boneva, Cummings, Helgeson, and Crawford (2002) found that the negative effects of internet use on social involvement and psychological well-being dissipated as participants grew more comfortable with the medium. Individual characteristics still mediated this experience, so that using the internet predicted better outcomes for extraverts and those with more social support but worse outcomes for introverts and those with less support. In a survey of internet use and well-being in adolescence, Gross, Juvonen, and Gable (2002) found that time spent online was not associated with well-being, but the closeness of instant message communication partners was associated with daily social anxiety and loneliness in school.

Alternatively, Katz and Rice (2002a; 2002b; 2002c), based on survey results from 1995, 1996, 1997, and 2000 argued for a "syntopian" perspective, wherein "the Internet has allowed individuals and groups to find common interests, engage in various types of exchange and create bonds of concern, support, and affection that can unite them for both good and ill" (p. 167). An assortment of recent research has situated the internet within everyday life and considered uses and consequences. For instance, studies have verified that the place and impact of the internet vary depending on the context and use (e.g., Anderson & Tracey, 2002; Boneva & Kraut, 2002; Copher, Kanfer, & Walker, 2002; Wagner, Pischner, & Haisken-DeNew, 2002), indicating that "people are not doing anything particularly new, they are doing old things in new ways and finding that some of those new ways suit their lifestyles better" (Anderson & Tracey, 2002, p. 160)

FUTURE DIRECTIONS

Scholarly attention should now turn to the growing individuation of online activity, which tends to reflect the dominant trend in how individuals employ technologies. As online users develop greater comfort with this medium, they acquire a more individuated mode of interaction and sustain more transient and flexible ties with online and offline communities. Haythornthwaite and Wellman's (2002) recognition of networked individualism can be applied here as a way of understanding that, for the growing majority of online interaction, "the person has become the portal" (p. 40). Blogs, for example, present such a form of self-oriented online activity in that they serve the primary purpose of personal expression while allowing bloggers the secondary options of staying in touch with offline and online social circles as they choose. Recent adaptations of the technology appear to facilitate more self-involved uses of new technologies. A more updated model, then, for new media studies in the future rests on research that focuses on the individual as the hub of online interaction, aptly incorporating social, economic, and psychological concepts that further clarify the motivation and consequence of online activity. The comparison or dichotomization of the offline and online spheres of interaction led to the occasional mischaracterization of online behaviors and consequences. Future research, as well as research on communication media of the future, should benefit from the insights contributed by previous research.

REFERENCES

Anderson, B., & Tracey, K. (2002). Digital living: The impact (or otherwise) of the internet on everyday British life. In C. Haythornthwaite & B. Wellman (Eds.), *The internet in everyday life* (pp. 139–163). Oxford, UK: Blackwell.

Argyle, K. (1996). Life after death. In R. Shields (Ed.), *Cultures of internet: Virtual spaces, real histories, living bodies* (pp.133–142). Thousand Oaks, CA: Sage.

Argyle, K., & Shields, R. (1996). Is there a body in the net? In R. Shields (Ed.), *Cultures of internet: Virtual spaces, real histories, living bodies* (pp. 58–69). Thousand Oaks, CA: Sage.

Barnes, S. (1996). Cyberspace: Creating paradoxes for the ecology of self. In L. Strate, R. Jacobson, & S. B. Gibson (Eds.), *Communication and cyberspace: Social interaction in an electronic environment* (pp. 193–216). Cresskill, NJ: Hampton Press.

Baym, N. (1995). The emergence of community in computer-mediated communication. In S. G. Jones (Ed.), *Cybersociety: Computer-mediated communication and community* (pp. 138–163). Thousand Oaks, CA: Sage.

Baym, N. (1997). Interpreting soap operas and creating community: Inside an electronic fan culture. In S. Kiesler (Ed.), *Culture of the internet* (pp. 103–120). Mahwah, NJ: Erlbaum.

Bolter, J. D. (1996). Virtual reality and redefinition of self. In L. Strate, R. Jacobson, & S. B. Gibson (Eds.), *Communication and cyberspace: Social interaction in an electronic environment* (pp. 105–120). Cresskill, NJ: Hampton Press.

Boneva, B., & Kraut, R. (2002). Email, gender, and personal relationships. In C. Haythornthwaite & B. Wellman (Eds.), *The internet in everyday life* (pp. 372–403). Oxford, UK: Blackwell.

Bromberg, H. (1996). Are MUDs communities? Identity, belonging and consciousness in virtual worlds. In M. Shields (Ed.), *Culture of internet: Virtual spaces, real histories, living bodies* (pp. 143–52). London: Sage.

Burgoon, J. K., Bonito, J. A., Ramirez, A., Jr., Dunbar, N. E., Kam, K., & Fischer, J. (2002). Testing the interactivity principle: Effects of mediation, propinquity, and verbal and nonverbal modalities in interpersonal interaction. *Journal of Communication, 52,* 657 677.

Castells, M. (1997). *The information age, vol. II: The power of identity.* Malden, MA: Blackwell.

Clark, L. S. (1998). Dating on the net: Teens and the rise of "pure" relationships. In S. G. Jones (Ed.), *Cybersociety 2.0* (pp. 159–183). Thousand Oaks, CA: Sage.

Constant, D., Sproull, L., & Kiesler, S. (1996). The kindness of strangers: On the usefulness of electronic weak ties for technical advice. In S. Kiesler (Ed.), *Culture of the internet* (pp. 303–322). Mahwah, NJ: Erlbaum.

Copher, J. I., Kanfer, A. G., & Walker, M. B. (2002). Everyday communication patterns of heavy and light email users. In C. Haythornthwaite & B. Wellman (Eds.), *The internet in everyday life* (pp. 263–290). Oxford, UK: Blackwell.

Culnan, M. J., & Markus, M. L. (1987). Information technologies. In F. Jablin, L. Putnam, K. H. Roberts, & L. W. Porter (Eds.), *Handbook of organizational communication* (pp. 420–444). Thousand Oaks, CA: Sage.

Daft, R. L., & Lengel, R. H. (1984). Information richness: A new approach to managerial behavior and organization design. In B. M. Staw & L. L. Cummings (Eds.), *Research in organizational behavior 6* (pp. 191–233). Greenwich, CT: JAI Press.

Danet (1998). Text as mask: Gender, play, and performance on the Internet. In S. G. Jones (Ed.), *Cybersociety 2.0* (pp. 129–158). Thousand Oaks, CA: Sage.

December, J. (1996). Units of analysis for internet communication. *Journal of Computer-mediated Communication* (online), *1*(4). Retrieved from http://www.cwis.usc.edu/dept/annenberg/vol1/issue4/vol1no.4.html.

Dutton, W. (1984). The rejection of an innovation: The political environment of a computer-based model. *Systems, Objectives and Solutions, 1,* 179–201.

Fernback, J. (2002, October). *Using community to sell: The commodification of community in retail web sites*. Paper presented at the 2002 annual conference of the Association of Internet Researchers, Maastricht, The Netherlands.

Fox, S., & Rainie, L. (2001). *Time online: Why some people use the Internet more than before and why some use it less*. Retrieved from Pew Internet & American Life Project, http://www.pewinternet.org.

Fulk, J., Steinfield, C. W., Schmitz, J., & Power, J. G. (1987). A social information processing model of media use in organizations. *Communication Research, 14,* 529–552.

Gross, E., F., Juvonen, J., & Gable, S. L. (2002). Internet use and well-being in adolescence. *Journal of Social Issues, 58*(1), 75–90.

Gunkel, D. J., & Gunkel, A. H. (1997). Virtual geographies: The new worlds of cyberspace. *Critical Studies in Mass Communication, 14,* 123–137.

Hamburger, Y. A., & Ben-Artzi, E. (2000). The relationship between extraversion and neuroticism and the different uses of the internet. *Computers in Human Behavior, 16,* 441–449.

Haraway, D. J. (1991a). *Simians, cyborgs, and women: The reinvention of nature*. New York: Routledge.

Haraway, D. (1991b). The actors are cyborg, nature is coyote, and the geography is elsewhere: Postscript to "Cyborgs at large." In C. Penley & A. Ross (Eds.), *Technoculture* (pp. 21–26). Minneapolis: University of Minnesota.

Haythornthwaite, C., & Wellman, B. (Eds.). (2002). *The internet in everyday life*. Oxford, UK: Blackwell.

Hiltz, S. R. (1982). Experiments and experiences with computerized conferencing. In R. Landau, J. Bair, & J. Siegman (Eds.), *Emerging office systems* (pp. 182–204). Norwood, NJ: Ablex.

Hiltz, S. R. (1983). *Online communities: A case study of the office of the future*. Norwood, NJ: Ablex.

Hiltz, S. R., & Turoff, M. (1978). *The network nation: Human communication via computer*. Reading, MA: Addison-Wesley.

Hiltz, S. R., & Turoff, M. (1981). The evolution of user behavior in a computerized conferencing system. *Communications of the ACM, 24,* 739–751.

Horrigan, J. B., Rainie, L., & Fox, S. (2001). *Online communities: Networks that nurture long-distance relationships and local ties*. Pew Internet & American Life Project, http://www.pewinternet.org.

Howard, E. N., Rainie, L., & Jones, S. (2001). Days and nights on the internet: The impact of a diffusing technology. *American Behavioral Scientist, 45,* 1–31.

Ito, M. (1997). Virtually embodied: The reality of fantasy in a multi-user dungeon. In D. Porter (Ed.), *Internet culture* (pp. 87–109). New York: Routledge.

Johansen, R., DeGrasse, R., Jr., & Wilson, T. (1978). *Effects on working patterns. Group communication through computers, 5*. Menlo Park, CA: Institute for the Future.

Johansen, R., Miller, R., & Vallee, J. (1975). Group communication through electronic media: Fundamental choices and social effects. In H. Linstone & M. Turoff (Eds.), *The Delphi method: Techniques and applications* (pp. 527–534). Reading, MA: Addison-Wesley.

Johansen, R. Vallee, J., & Spangler, K. (1979). *Electronic meetings: Technical alternatives and social choices*. Reading, MA: Addison-Wesley.

Katz, J. E., & Aspden, P. (1997). A nation of strangers? *Communications of the ACM, 40*(12), 81–86.

Katz, J. E., & Rice. R. E. (2002a). *Social consequences of Internet use: Access, involvement and interaction*. Cambridge: MIT Press.

Katz, J. E., & Rice, R. E. (2002b). Project syntopia: Social consequences of internet use. *IT & Society, 1,* 166–179.

Katz, J. E., & Rice, R. E. (2002c). Access, civic involvement, and social interaction on the Net. In C. Haythornthwaite & B. Wellman (Eds.), *The internet in everyday life* (pp. 114–138). Oxford, UK: Blackwell.

Kiesler, S., Siegel, J., & McGuire, T. W. (1984). Social psychological aspects of computer-mediated communication. *American Psychologist, 39,* 1123–1134.

Kolko, B., & Reid, E. (1998). Dissolution and fragmentation: Problems in on-line communities. In S. G. Jones (Ed.), *Cybersociety 2.0* (pp. 212–230). Thousand Oaks, CA: Sage.

Kraut, R. E., & Attewell, P. (1997). Media use in a global corporation: Electronic mail and organizational knowledge. In S. Kiesler (Ed.), *Culture of the internet* (pp. 323–342). Mahwah, NJ: Erlbaum.

Kraut, R., Kiesler, S., Boneva, K., Cummings, J., Helgeson, J., & Crawford, A. (2002). Internet paradox revisited. *Journal of Social Issues, 58,* 49–74.

Kraut, R., Patterson, M., Lundmark, V., Kiesler, S., Mukophadhyay, T., & Scherlis, W. (1998). Internet paradox: A social technology that reduces social involvement and psychological well-being? *American Psychologist, 53,* 1017–1031.

Lajoie, M. (1996). Psychoanalysis and cyberspace. In R. Shields (Ed.), *Cultures of internet: Virtual spaces, real histories, living bodies* (pp. 153–169). Thousand Oaks, CA: Sage.

LaRose, R., Eastin, M. S., & Gregg, J. (2001). Reformulating the Internet paradox: Social cognitive explanations of Internet use and depression. *Journal of Online Behavior, 1*(2). Available at: http://www.behavior.net/JOB/v1n2/ paradox.html.

Lee, B., & Anderson, J. Q. (2001, August). *Current attitudes of internet users: An analysis of assimilators, hoppers and sensors.* Paper presented at the Association for Education in Journalism and Mass Communication annual convention, Washington, DC.

Lenhart, A., Rainie, L., & Lewis, O. (2001). *Teenage life online: The rise of the instant-message generation and the internet's impact on friendships and family relationships.* Pew Internet & American Life Project, http://www.pewinternet.org.

Markus, M. (1981). Implementation politics: Top management support and user involvement. *Systems, Objectives and Solutions, 1,* 203–216.

Marvin, C. (1988). *When old technologies were new: Thinking about electronic communication in the end of the nineteenth century.* New York: Oxford University Press.

Matei, S., & Ball-Rokeach, S. (2002). Belonging in geographic, ethnic and internet spaces. In C. Haythornthwaite & B. Wellman (Eds.), *The internet in everyday life* (pp. 404–430). Oxford, UK: Blackwell.

McGuire, T. W., Kiesler, S., & Siegel, J. (1987). Group and computer-mediated discussion effects in risk decision making. *Journal of Personality and Social Psychology, 52,* 917–930.

McKenna, K. Y. A., Green, A. S., & Gleason, M. E. J. (2002). Relationship formation on the Internet: What's the big attraction? *Journal of Social Issues, 58,* 9–31.

McLaughlin, M. L., Osborne, K. K., & Smith, C. M. (1995). Standards of conduct on Usenet. In S. G. Jones (Ed.), *Cybersociety* (pp. 57–72). Thousand Oaks, CA: Sage.

Mickelson, K. D. (1997). Seeking social support: Parents in electronic support groups. In S. Kiesler (Ed.), *Culture of the internet* (pp. 157–178). Mahwah, NJ: Erlbaum.

Mitra, A. (1997). Virtual community: Looking for India on the internet. In S. G. Jones (Ed.), *Virtual culture: Identity and communication in cybersociety* (pp. 55–79). Thousand Oaks, CA: Sage.

Morahan-Martin, J., & Schumacher, P. (2000). Incidence and correlates of pathological internet use among college students. *Computers in Human Behavior, 16,* 13–29.

Nie, N., & Erbring, L. (2000). *Internet and society: A preliminary report.* Retrieved from http://www.stanford.edu/group/siqss

Ochsman, R. B., & Chapanis, A. (1974). The effects of 10 communication modes on the behaviour of teams during so-operative problem-solving. *International Journal of Man-Machine Studies, 6,* 579–619.

Papacharissi, Z. (2002). The self online: The utility of personal home pages, *Journal of Broadcasting & Electronic Media 46,* 346–368.

Papacharissi, Z., & Rubin, A. M. (2000). Predictors of internet use. *Journal of Broadcasting & Electronic Media, 44,* 175–196.

Parks, M. R., & Floyd, K. (1996). Making friends in cyberspace. *Journal of Communication, 46*(1), 80–97.

Perse, E. M., Burton, P. I., Kovner, E. S., Lears, M. E., & Sen, R. J. (1992). Predicting computer-mediated communication in a college class. *Communication Research Reports, 9,* 161–170.

Perse, E. M., & Courtright, J. A. (1993). Normative images of communication media: Mass and interpersonal channels in the new media environment. *Human Communication Research, 19,* 485–503.

Poole, M. S., & DeSanctis, G. (1992). Microlevel structuration in computer-supported group decision making. *Human Communication Research, 19,* 5–49.

Poole, M. S., & Holmes, M. (1995). Decision development in computer-assisted group decision making. *Human Communication Research, 22,* 90–127.

Poole, M. S., Holmes, M., Watson, R., & DeSanctis, G. (1993). Group decision support systems and group communication: A comparison of decision making in computer-supported and nonsupported groups. *Communication Research, 20,* 176–213.

Postmes, T., Spears, R., & Lea, M. (1998). Breaching or building social boundaries? SIDE-effects of computer-mediated communication. *Communication Research, 25,* 689–715.

Putnam, R. D. (1996). The strange disappearance of civic America. *American Prospect, 24*(1), 34–48.

Rainie, L. (2001). *How Americans used the internet after the terror attack.* Pew Internet & American Life Project, http://www.pewinternet.org.

Rainie, L., & Kalsnes, B. (2001). *The commons of the tragedy.* Retrieved from Pew Internet & American Life Project, http://www.pewinternet.org.

Rainie, L., & Kohut, A. (2000). *Tracking online life: How women use the internet to cultivate relationships with family and friends.* Pew Internet & American Life Project, http://www.pewinternet.org.

Reid, E. (1991). *Electropolis: Communication and community on internet Relay Chat.* Honors thesis, University of Melbourne.

Rheingold, H. (1993). *The virtual community: Homesteading on the electronic frontier.* Reading, MA: Addison-Wesley.

Rice, R. E. (1984). *The new media: Communication, research and technology.* Beverly Hills, CA: Sage.

Rice, R. E. (1993). Media appropriateness: Using social presence theory to compare traditional and new organizational media. *Human Communication Research, 19,* 451–484.

Rice, R. E., & Love, G. (1987). Electronic emotion: Socioemotional content in a computer-mediated communication network. *Communication Research, 14,* 85–108.

Robinson, J. P., Kestnbaum, M., Neustadtl, A., & Alvarez, A. (2000). Mass media use and social life among Internet users. *Social Science Computer Review, 18,* 490–501.

Rogers, E. M. (1983). *Diffusion of innovations* (3rd ed.). New York: Free Press.

Rogers, E. M., & Malhotra, S. (2000). Computers as communication: The rise of digital democracy. In K. L. Hacker & J. van Dijk (Eds.), *Digital democracy: Issues of theory and practice* (pp. 10–29). Thousand Oaks, CA: Sage.

Schmitz, J. (1997). Structural relations, electronic media, and social change: The Public Electronic Network and the homeless. In S. G. Jones (Ed.), *Virtual culture: Identity and community in cybersociety* (pp. 80–101). Thousand Oaks, CA: Sage.

Shah, D. V., Kwak, N., & Holbert, R. L. (2001). "Connecting" and "disconnecting" with civic life: Patterns of internet use and the production of social capital. *Political Communication, 18,* 141–162.

Short, J., Williams, E., & Christie, B. (1976). *The social psychology of telecommunications.* London: Wiley.

Sproull, L., & Faraj, S. (1997). Atheism, sex, and databases: The net as a social technology. In S. Kiesler (Ed.), *Culture of the internet* (pp. 35–51). Mahwah, NJ: Erlbaum.

Sproull, L., & Kiesler, S. (1986). Reducing social context cues: The case of electronic mail. *Management Science, 32,* 1492–1512.

Steinfield, C. W., & Fulk, J. (1987). On the role of theory in research on information technologies in organizations: An introduction to the special issue. *Communication Research, 14,* 479–490.

Stone, A. R. (1996). *The war of desire and technology at the close of the mechanical age.* Cambridge, MA: MIT Press.

Straus, S. G. (1996). Getting a clue: The effects of communication media and information distribution on participation and performance in computer-mediated and face-to-face groups. *Small Group Research, 27,* 115–142.

Straus, S. G. (1997). Technology, group processes, and group outcomes: Testing the connections in performance in computer-mediated and face-to-face groups. *Human-Computer Interaction, 12,* 227–266.

Trevino, L. K., Lengel, R. H., & Daft, R. L. (1987). Media symbolism, media richness, and media choice in organizations. *Communication Research, 14,* 553–574.

Turkle, S. (1984). *The second self: Computers and the human spirit.* New York: Simon & Schuster.

Turkle, S. (1995). *Life on the screen: Identity in the age of the internet.* New York: Simon & Schuster.

Turkle, S. (1996). Parallel lives: Working on identity in virtual space. In D. Grodin & T. R. Lindlof (Eds.), *Constructing the self in a mediated world: Inquiries in social construction* (pp. 156–175). Thousand Oaks, CA: Sage.

Turkle, S. (1997). Constructions and reconstructions of self in virtual reality: Playing in the MUDs. In S. Kiesler (Ed.), *Culture of the internet* (pp. 143–155). Mahwah, NJ: Erlbaum.

Valacich, J. S. Dennis, A. R., & Connolly, T. (1994). Idea generation in computer-based groups: A new ending to an old story. *Organizational Behavior & Human Decision Processes, 57,* 448–467.

Valacich, J. S., George, J. F., Nunamaker, J. F., & Vogel, D. R. (1994). Physical proximity effects on computer-mediated group idea generation. *Small Group Research, 25,* 83–104.

Valacich, J. S., Paranka, D., George, J. F., & Nunamaker, J. F. (1993). Communication concurrency and the new media: A new dimension for media richness. *Communication Research, 20,* 249–276.

Wagner, G. G., Pischner, R., & Haisken-DeNew, J. P. (2002). The changing digital divide in Germany. In C. Haythornthwaite & B. Wellman (Eds.), *The internet in everyday life* (pp. 164–185). Oxford, UK: Blackwell.

Walther, J. B. (1992). Interpersonal effects in computer-mediated interaction: A relational perspective. *Communication Research, 19,* 52–90.

Walther, J. B. (1993). Impression development in computer-mediated interaction. *Western Journal of Communication, 57,* 381–398.

Walther, J. B. (1994). Anticipated ongoing interaction versus channel effects on relational communication in computer-mediated interaction. *Human Communication Research, 20,* 473–501.

Walther, J. B. (1995). Relational aspects of computer-mediated communication: Experimental observations over time. *Organizational Science, 6,* 186–203.

Walther, J. B. (1996). Computer-mediated communication: Impersonal, interpersonal, and hyperpersonal interaction. *Communication Research, 23,* 3–43.

Wastlund, E., Norlander, T., & Archer, T. (2001). Internet blues revisited: Replication and extension of an Internet paradox study. *CyberPsychology and Behavior, 4,* 385–391.

Watson, N. (1997). Why we argue about virtual community: A case study of the Phish.Net fan community. In S. G. Jones (Ed.), *Virtual culture: Identity and community in cybersociety* (pp. 102–132).

Willson, M. (1997). Community in the abstract: A political and ethical dilemma? In D. Holmes (Ed.), *Virtual politics: Identity & community in cyberspace* (pp. 145–162). Thousand Oaks, CA: Sage.

Zuboff, S. (1988). *In the age of the smart machine: The future of work and power.* New York: Basic Books.

CHAPTER CONTENTS

8 Reflective Communication Management, Future Ways for Public Relations Research

BETTEKE VAN RULER
University of Amsterdam

DEJAN VERČIČ
University of Ljubljana

In this chapter, we propose a two-by-two-dimensional definition of communication and management deriving four basic models of communication management as a result. These analytical models reveal four historical public relations approaches, and looking at these models, it is striking that all are positioned at the behavioral level, that is, on (members of) organizations and their publics. The societal level remains totally neglected. We argue that this is a fundamental misunderstanding of the organizational legitimacy problem, which is one of the most important problems of the future for organizations. To address this, we will propose a new view of practical public relations called reflective communication management that is derived from social sciences rather than behavioral sciences. In this view of communication management the four existing models are combined as strategies.

INTRODUCTION

In *Communication Yearbook 24*, Deetz and Putnam (2001, p. 12) argued "that communication scholars and teachers should direct their attention to the significant problems of our time." In this chapter we will argue that the most important problem in public relations is the societal legitimation of organizations. Because current public relations models are too much oriented at a publics or stakeholders level, they are insufficient to cope with societal issues per se (see also Lauzen & Dozier, 1994).

Correspondence: Betteke van Ruler, Department of Communication Sciences, University of Amsterdam, Kloveniersburgwal 48, 1012 CX Amsterdam, The Netherlands; email: a.a.vanruler@uva.nl

Communication Yearbook 29, pp. 239–273

The *Handbook of Public Relations* (Heath, 2001a), the widely discussed Ledingham and Bruning reader (2000), the textbook of Cutlip, Center, and Broom
(2000) that is used worldwide, the IABC Research Foundation Excellence Study
of the Professors Grunig (Grunig, Grunig, & Dozier, 2002), as well as recent
volumes of the public relations journals, show that the public relations academic community currently defines public relations as a management function concerned with relationship building among publics from a symmetrical perspective
to build trust, preserve or reduce conflict, and build community. Most academic
books do not even comment on the definition-in-use—that is, there seems to be
no discussion any more on what public relations is (see Stacks, 2002). This fits
the conclusion of Vasquez and Taylor (2001, p. 336), who stated in an overview
of current research on public relations that public relations examines the relationships between organizations and publics (see also Hutton, 1999), and it also
shows the strength of the definition of Grunig and Hunt (1984, p. 6) of public relations as "the management of communication between an organization and its
publics," with an emphasis on the word "between." However, as Heath (2001b, p.
2) admits "an evening spent at an awards banquet of the Public Relations Society
of America or the International Association of Business Communicators gives a
much different view of the field." Should we conclude then that most professionals in this field and their clients are unprofessional? Or could it be that this perspective of public relations does not have sufficient empirical force and is, therefore, impossible to establish for practitioners and their clients? If that is the case,
is this because clients are an "obstinate audience" (cf. Bauer, 1963; 1964) and
therefore unwilling to open up to their publics, as many practitioners and scholars
want us to believe? Or is it because the concept itself does not suffice for coping
with current problems?

In this chapter, we argue that a feasible concept of public relations needs more
indicators than relationships alone to reflect the plural nature of its service to organizations and its publics. We will therefore propose a two-by-two-dimensional definition of organization and communication and derive four basic models
of communication management from it. We will propose different indicators for
each of the four models. Then we will argue that the four models are not exclusive, but complementary, and that organizations are best advised to use these simultaneously in various combinations, that is, as strategies. We will argue that
this is necessary because all models are positioned at the behavioral level, that is,
on (members of) organizations and their publics, and are, accordingly, only useful
for daily practice instead of as a concept for a communication policy of an organization. That is because in all models the societal level remains totally neglected.
We will argue that this is a fundamental misunderstanding of the legitimacy problem of organizations, which is to be seen as the key problem of organizations and
of the society in the near future. This needs to be seen from a public view instead
of a public's view, and to address this, we will propose a broader view of practical
public relations called reflective communication management that is derived from
social sciences rather than behavioral sciences. In this view of communication

management, the four existing models are combined as strategies. The broader view is definitely not to be seen as a fifth, new model but has to be considered as an umbrella, under which all four models can be used as daily strategies.

We use the term communication management for several reasons. First of all we use it because it seems to be a common denominator for the field in Europe in both academia and practice (cf. Ruler, Verčič, Bütschi, & Flodin, 2000; Ruler & Verčič, 2002b; Verčič, Ruler, Bütschi, & Flodin 2001), whereas public relations seems to be more common in the U.S., at least in the scholarly community, although we also see that Anglo-American authors often seem to hesitate over which term to use and equate it with public relations (e.g., Dozier, Grunig, & Grunig 1995; Grunig, 1992b; Grunig, et al., 2002; White & Mazur, 1995). However, we will show that the concept of public relations is hardly seen anymore as working in public (cf. Oeckl, 1976) and has therefore lost its public approach, if it ever had it. Hence, we will argue that this concept, because of its connotations of working with and to publics, is no longer sufficient for steering future research in this field. Finally, by using communication management as a concept, we are able to show that it is all about management of communication processes and, therefore, dependent on the definitions of communication-in-use, and consequently of management/organization-in-use. Looking at the field as public relations, the concept of communication is often overlooked. Toth (1992, p. 9) has argued that the concept of communication remains underdefined when it is placed in a systems approach within public relations theorizing, and most current theories are conceptualized from a system approach (although not all, see, for example, Davis, 2002; L' Étang & Pieczka, 1996; Toth & Heath, 1992). The use of communication management as a concept is helpful in steering the focus on communication as the key concept. So, there are practical as well as theoretical reasons for using communication management instead of public relations.

Communication management is an activity of specialists all over the world and a flourishing professional field (Heath, 2001a; Grunig et al., 2002; Mogel, 2002; Ruler & Verčič, 2004; Sriramesh & Verčič, 2003). We nevertheless concur with Long & Hazleton Jr. (1987) in defining it principally as a way to explain and describe how to manage an organization with respect to its communications. Agreeing with Deetz, Tracy, & Simpson (2000) in their argument on organizational communication as a view of organization, we propose to approach the issue of communication management from a general management viewpoint: Managers are the ones who are responsible for the communication policies of an organization and the way in which (members of) an organization communicates. These policies steer the roles of public relations practitioners as well as others who communicate in the context of the organization.

Since 1978, Broom has fathered the debate about roles in public relations practice being abstractions of the everyday activities of public relations practitioners (Broom, 1982; Broom & Smith, 1979; see, for an overview, Dozier, 1992, p. 329). A role can be seen as "the expected behavior associated with a social position" (Banton, 1996, p. 749), and Broom's research was focused on the consultant's roles enacted for senior management by public relations experts. Broom and Smith (1979) conceptualized four dominant roles: the expert prescriber, the communication facilitator, the problem-solving process facilitator, and the communication technician. Research has indicated that the first three roles are highly interrelated, being part of a common underlying manager's role. In addition to conforming that the first three roles were indeed interrelated, Dozier (1984) found two major roles (the manager and the technician) and two minor roles (the media relations specialist and the communication liaison) and concluded that "the manager and technician roles emerge empirically time and again in studies of different practitioners" (Dozier, 1992, p. 334). His manager–technician typology has been tested numerous times in various countries (Grunig et al., 2002; for an overview, see also Dozier, 1992), including the Netherlands (Ruler, 2000). This Dutch research project confirmed the veracity of J. Grunig's lamentation that "in carrying out their duties, those who were both responsible for communication planning and involved in organizational decision-making make little use of data acquired from research" (cited in Dozier, 1992, p. 336). In addition to doing the same kind of operational work as the communication employees, these Dutch public relations professionals took on a wide range of planning activities and other managerial tasks. They showed themselves to be rather overloaded hands on managers. No confirmation was found for Dozier's suggestion (1992, p. 338) that there is a relationship between evaluation activities and participation in management decision making. The latter appeared to be related to hierarchical position rather than to evaluation activities. When "evaluation activities" were used as an indicator of managerial roles, as Dozier suggested, the result was that almost all practitioners (including even those in the upper echelons) had to be classified as technicians (Ruler, 2000).

Another problem with the conceptualization of these roles as manager-technician roles is that there are hardly any specific communication management approaches involved. Any professional could be placed in this dichotomy. It was Grunig (1976, 1989, 1992b) and Grunig and Hunt (1984) who conceptualized public relations roles on a more aggregate level and consequently more with respect to content. Grunig developed four public relations models: publicity, public information, two-way asymmetrical, and two-way symmetrical. All models reveal accompanying roles that are typical of practitioners. In a study among the top 200 companies in the Netherlands, Ruler (1997) concluded that, although these four models did indeed have empirical power in the Netherlands, the practitioners reported to use these models all together. Not part of the research project, it could very well be that they had looked at these models as strategies.

Mintzberg (1973, p. 54–99) showed that general managers themselves are most of the time busy communicating: Most roles of managers are communication roles, and all of these have communication aspects. Furthermore, "long before there was such a field as organizational communication, organization and management theorists incorporated communication as a central concept in their theories" (Tompkins, 1984, p. 71). Today's "information society" (Castells, 1996) views the communication aspects of these roles as even more important than they were when Mintzberg described them, and it changes the communication strategies in use. Nonetheless, communication and public relations textbooks seldom analyze organizational processes and structures and manager's communication policies and tactics. Managers not only play many communication roles, but also use communication with different intentions, goals, objectives, and consequences according to their own basic communicational and organizational principles (cf. Deetz et al., 2000). That is, managers have to manage their communications as they have to manage their budgets, and so on. Without doubt an organization needs specialists to advise and help management execute its communication management properly. We believe, however, that the demands of managers on the specialists and the specialists' own expectations of "good" communication management can be derived from their specific views about how to manage an organization and how to communicate accordingly (Dozier et al., 1995; Grunig et al., 2002; Grunig, 1992a; see also Ruler, 1996, 1997; Zweekhorst, 2001).

Communication management is, therefore, necessarily intertwined with the communication principles and styles of management, which in turn can be derived from specific organization principles and styles. Given that there are many definitions of communication on the one hand—and organization and management on the other—it is impossible to choose a single normative view of communication management without taking into account the related view on organization and management, as most authors do.

DIMENSIONS OF COMMUNICATION MANAGEMENT

Looking over the literature on communication management, we could state that there is one generic principle about communication management: That it is about maximizing, optimizing, or satisfying the processes of meaning creation in order to solve managerial problems. This, however, is accomplished in different ways and guided by different theories and these theories define the different approaches to communication management, as can be found in the literature of the discipline. The scholarly field we describe here is usually divided into "systems, rhetorical and critical approaches" (see Toth, 1992). This has more to do with philosophy of science and accompanying paradigmatic preferences—and so we prefer that conceptual reasons categorize the field according to disciplinary approaches of communication and organization–management.

In a two-dimensional space defined by communication approaches on the one hand and organization and management approaches on the other, we identify four models of communication management: informational, persuasive, relational, and discursive. Following current social sciences, we assume that all social theory is a human construction, "an active effort by communities of scholars to make sense of their social world (cf. Baran & Davis, 2000, p. 4). We will argue that most current approaches of the field of communication management can be positioned in one of these four models in a historical way, and therefore, that they can be used as an historical overview of the field. After that we will argue that these models no longer suffice in the organizational landscape of today.

Approaches to Communication

In this section we will build a categorization of views on communication and will use these views to define a model of communication approaches that are involved in communication management. At the same time this is a rather impossible job, as there are numerous theories of communication, making it is hard to specify the parameters in which to look for theories of communication. The first demarcation we could use is that communication management is on human communication and not on biological or telecommunication. Because it is complex, human communication is difficult to define, hence Littlejohn (1992, p. 6) advised not to seek for a single definition, but rather look at the various concepts behind the term (see also Dance, 1970). According to Rosengren (2000, p. 59), a key aspect of all human communication is meaning, which he explained as the "whole way in which we understand, explain, feel about, and react towards a given phenomenon." This concept of meaning is directed toward "the way individuals make sense of their world through their communicative behaviors" (cf. Putnam, 1983, p. 31), and this point of view begs the question: Who creates whose meaning, and what does this mean for interpreting the world? From this question we can derive two dimensions of communication—the direction of the communication process and the character of meaning—and we will use these two dimensions to structure communication theory.

At first sight the use of the concept of meaning would focus on so-called interpretive theories. That is not necessarily the case; it all depends on what is meant by "meaning" (Preyer, Peter, & Ulkan, 2003). The direction of the communication process is usually operationalized as one-way or two-way, which can be explicated as either one party being active in the communication process or all parties (cf. Grunig, 1989; Heath, 2001c; see also Fearing, 1953; Schramm, 1965; Servaes, Jacobson, & White 1996). Regarding the character of meaning, many theorists differentiate between connotative and denotative meaning by stressing that the connotative meaning steers behavior much more than the denotative (e.g., Berlo, 1960; Langer, 1967; Rosengren, 2000; Thayer, 1987). A denotative meaning of a phenomenon is the dictionary meaning; it is the literal or overt meaning that is shared by most people. The connotative meaning refers to subjective associations. Not all theories stipulate the connotative perspective of meaning, however, and are often (implicitly) oriented on the denotative side of meaning.

Early theory was focused on communication as a one-way process in which a sender does something to a receiver (Gitlin, 2002). When only denotative meaning is involved, transmission of information is enough and the widely cited information theory of communication, developed by Shannon for the Bell Telephone Company to successfully transmit data through communication channels, and likewise made public by Shannon and Weaver (1949), is an example of this view of communication. Their publication warned that this model does not necessarily relate to meaning, but only to transmission of data. In the same year, however, Weaver (1949) proposed that this theory could also work as a general theory of human communication, thereby suggesting that meaning can be transmitted, and many agreed with him.

It was Wiener (1948) who introduced the concept of feedback in his action-reaction model, orientated solely on the denotative side of meaning since communication can be equated with cybernetics. Psychologists like Berlo (1960), however, stipulated that meaning is in the head of people, thereby focusing on the connotative perspective of meaning. Regarding communication management, this would mean that transmission of information is not enough; change of connotative meaning is the important thing (e.g., Miller, 1989). For some authors communication is fundamentally about persuasion of attitudes. According to Perloff (1993), an attitude is a learned, enduring, and affective evaluation of an object (a person, entity, or idea) that exerts directive impact on social behavior.

Looking from the concept of meaning, attitudes can be equated with connotative meanings, and particularly social psychological theories on communication approaches are mostly focused on one-way persuasion (of connotative meaning; cf. Cialdini, 1984; Perloff, 1993; Petty & Cacioppo, 1981). As Pratkanis and Aronson claim, "We humans like to think of ourselves as rational animals. However, it is more true that we are rationalizing animals, that we attempt to appear reasonable to ourselves and to others" (1991, p. 32).

Recent approaches to the concept of communication are much more focused on communication as a fundamental two-way process for creating and exchanging meaning, interactive and participatory at all levels (Servaes, 1999). This can be seen as a paradigmatic change from a sender–receiver orientation to an actor orientation. Paraphrasing Newcomb (1953, 1958), we could say that this is an "A together with B re X orientation" (see also Thayer, 1987).

Again we can find two views of this two-way process. For some, the fundamental key to communication is the ongoing process of creation and revelation of intersubjective meanings (e.g., Putnam & Pacanowsky, 1983); for others it is a process that goes further because it creates a shared meaning, that is, a consensus that can be seen as a new, denotative meaning (Susskind, McKearnan, & Thomas-Larmer, 1999). The latter view is oriented at exchange of information on interests of rational human beings, that is, organizations and their stakeholder groups, in order to negotiate agreement (Ehling, 1992; Grunig, 1989).

This approach to communication is based in the so-called balance models (Littlejohn, 1987, 1992), started by Heider (1946) and developed by Newcomb (1953). The concern is with the degree of consistency or inconsistency, which might exist between two persons in relation to a third person or object. Heider was concerned with the cognitive processes internal to either of the two participants in a relationship, whereas Newcomb focused on the communication process between the two. He made the assumption that communication process is the essential function of enabling two or more individuals to maintain simultaneous orientations to each other and toward objects of an external environment.

Communication is thus a learned response under strain, and we are likely to find more communication activity (information giving, seeking, and exchange) in conditions of uncertainty and disequilibrium (McQuail & Windahl, 1981, p. 21). The key aspect of this model is the relationship between A and B, which is related to a communication process about X (something out there). Newcomb (1953) postulated a strain to symmetry, resulting in a widening of the area of agreement by engaging in communication. That is to say, where there is balance, each participant will resist change, and where there is imbalance, attempts will be made to restore equilibrium.

The premise in all balance models is that people will always search for consistency (Stappers, Reijnders, & Möller, 1990). McLeod and Chaffee (1973) modernized these models into the so-called co-orientation approach, combining balance models and certain aspects of symbolic interactionism, with a focus on interpersonal communication and communication between groups, two-way and interactive. Used by Broom and Dozier, the focus had no longer been on symbolic interactionism but on the accuracy/congruency of the interpretations of issues between stakeholders and organization. If there is no congruency, dialogue should help both parties to develop a congruent (i.e., denotative) interpretation. The former approach follows the idea that communication is based on the sense-making practices of social individuals, as manifested in their use of all kinds of symbolism (Mumby, 1987, p. 113) and can be found in critical, rhetorical, and naturalistic approaches to communication (Putnam, 1983; Toth & Heath, 1992).

The expressed goal of many interpretive studies is to show how particular realities are socially produced and maintained through ordinary talk, stories, rites, rituals, and other daily activities (Deetz, 2001, p. 23). Interpretive scholars assume that reality is socially constructed through worlds and its meanings, symbols, and behaviors (Berger & Luckmann, 1966), and this approach is based in Kant's belief that social reality exists in "spirit of idea" rather than in concrete facts (Putnam, 1983, p. 32).

According to Tompkins and Wanca-Thibault (2001, p. xxix), an interpretive approach is now the dominant view on communication in organizational communication. It is striking that in most two-way communication management approaches, the theories in use stem from interpersonal or group communication. There is hardly any acknowledgment of interpretive two-way mass communication theories, like those of Carey (1975), Servaes et al. (1996), or Mumby (2000). We will therefore not discuss these in this part of our chapter, but rather in the second part of the chapter.

Approaches to Management and Organization

Management can be characterized as the process by which organizational work is done (Stoner & Freeman, 1992). Examination of the various schools of organizational and managerial thought uncovers implications for communication management thinking. It is therefore important to define what is meant by organization and management before viewing definitions of communication in the context of organization and management. In accordance with Scott (1987), we can arrange theories of organization into a cluster of four around two dimensions: the amount of openness in the management processes (closed–open) and the focus on human nature in organizational decision-making (rational–natural).

Scott shows that the closed–rational dimension reveals the field of classical theories such as those of Taylor and Weber, while Taylor concentrated on scientific management and Weber focused on authority structures. The closed–natural dimension is consistent with the human relations school of Mayo and other psychological schools such as Lewin and Likert, who focused on individual and group interaction and relations. They considered people (i.e., employees) primarily as emotional creatures rather than rational ones. The open–rational dimension illustrates the field of contingency theories, of which Katz and Kahn, and Lawrence and Lorsch are typical exponents. The open–natural dimension covers the entire field of modern network or learning theories on organization such as Morgan, Moss, Kanter, and Weick.

These four areas fit the cluster Cole (2000) specified in his widely read book on management theories: classical theories, human relations and other psychological schools, systems and contingency approaches, and modern approaches. Even though Cole does not explicate along the line of theoretical dimensions, the background of these four areas can easily be found in the focus on how people make decisions and in the amount of openness in management processes.

Regarding the dimension of how people (managers) make decisions, March (1994) asked:

> Do decision makers pursue a logic of consequence, making choices among alternatives by evaluating their consequences in terms of prior preferences, or do they pursue a logic of appropriateness, fulfilling identities or roles by recognizing situations and following rules that match appropriate behavior to the situations they encounter? (p. iix)

In other words, is it rational choice by which meaning is logically deduced from "true" facts or an interpretive, limited rational activity through which meaning is constructed?

On the other hand, these approaches also reveal whether management is directive or interactive (e.g., Argyris, 1994), which fits the open–closed dimension of Scott. There is a fundamental distinction in conceptualization of management between control and learning (Argyris & Schön, 1978). Management as control finds its operationalization in managerial intervention as directive intervention, whereas management as learning is operationalized as interactive intervention. Contemporary management authors can be split between those who argue that companies need to be built to perform and those who argue that companies need to be built to last (Collins & Porras, 1998; Foster & Kaplan, 2001). This corresponds to the distinction between shareholder or value management and certain approaches of stakeholder management (Wood, 1991), and with the distinction between hard management and soft management (London, 2002), which in turn corresponds with direction and interaction (Argyris, 1994).

What Communication Management Means

Paraphrasing Peters (1999), to understand communication management is to understand more than just the two concepts and its dimensions. The basic understanding lies in the combination and therefore we should combine the views of communication with the views of organization and management. By doing that, four different theoretical approaches to communication management are discovered: informative, persuasive, relational, and discursive, which are all well-known in literature, and include, in our view, all major approaches to public relations so far.

The Information Model

In this model, dissemination of information about the organization's (i.e.. manager's) plans and decisions, the aim of which is to reduce the uncertainty as knowledge is gained. In recent communication management research, this is seen as a rather naïve concept of communication management, but it is often used as a concept of communication in communication management, and therefore seen as insufficient for this field (c.f. Ledingham & Bruning, 1998). Theoretically, it refers to early theories of how the mass media work (McQuail, 2000), the theoretical field on which communication science has been based. A very influential approach has become the famous Lasswell (1948) formula, "Who says what to whom with what effect" (p. 1), which in practice is often combined with Shannon's information theory of communication (and sometimes referred to as the SMCR model, which is originally from Berlo). The main aspect is the transmission, but the key problem in this model is noise, which can destroy the signal.

The information model of communication management focuses on the dissemination of information, which targets groups to inform (enlighten) them about the plans of the organization and the decisions made (Ruler, 1996). In the former Soviet countries in Europe, it is one of the major topics to educate the organization as well as the public to practice this information model instead of the persuasion model (Lawniczak, 2001; Tampere, 2003). Grunig and Hunt (1984, p. 20–21) argued that in the beginning of the 1980s, about 50% of all organizations in the U.S. practiced a (public) information model. Ledingham & Bruning (2000) assumed that at the turn of the century many organizations still held this as their model, while they "seem to perceive that the production and dissemination of communication messages is the answer to every public relations problem" (p. xi). Successful communication management in this approach is "informing the right people at the right time about the plans and decisions of the organization" (p. xi), but most people are not easy to reach directly, and the most widely used channels to inform the public are the mass media. Thus, informational communication management is primarily broadcasting management. The management of the process of meaning creation—as a generic principle of communication management—in this model is restricted to the revelation of the (denotative) meaning of the sender (e.g., organization) to certain target groups.

The Persuasion Model

Communication management in this model is seen as a means to promote the organization's plans and decisions to important other parties; the aim of this promotion is to enable the organization to continue. The basis for this approach to communication management stems from Bernays (1923; for an overview of his ideas, see Cutlip, 1994; Ewen, 1996), but the expanded introduction of a psychological approach to mass communication instead of a sociological one in the study of communication management gave this model wings. It is to be expected that the increased involvement of social and economic psychology in public relations—corporate communication theory has led this to become a widely used model of communication management in the Western world since the 1980s (L' Étang & Pieczka, 1996). In the former Soviet countries, it was the only model for a long time (Tampere, 2003; Ruler & Verčič, 2004). Theoretically it refers to early theories of rhetoric that were postulated by the Greek philosopher Aristotle, who made a very significant, lasting contribution to persuasion research.

The key aspect in these theories is the seeking of control (Miller, 1989); key problems in this model are the characteristics of the sender (ethos), the audience (pathos), and the message (logos). The persuasion model of communication management focuses on the persuasion of target groups to accept the organization's view on relevant issues (Dolphin, 1999; Foster & Jolly, 1997; Riel, 1995). Grunig (see, e.g., 1989) calls this an asymmetrical approach to communication management in which only the public has to alter its view. As with the information model, in this persuasion model the organization is the sender and the publics are the receiver, but receiving the message (which is key in the information model) is not enough here; the public must also be convinced there is a predefined meaning for the situation. Successful communication management is therefore convinced publics, or ensuring a positive image is held by important target groups.

As it is difficult to convince people, research is thought to be important for discovering what the publics will accept and tolerate. That is why Grunig differentiated between press agentry as one-way and two-way asymmetry, in which model research is done to find out where the publics stand (Grunig & Hunt, 1984, p. 24) and to develop "common starting points" (Riel, 1995) or a "sustainable corporate story" (Riel, 2000). Persuasive communication management is therefore primarily impression management. The management of the process of meaning creation is, in this model, restricted to luring the (connotative) meanings of certain target groups into the meanings of the sender (i.e., the organization).

The Relationship Model

In this model communication management is seen as establishing and maintaining mutually beneficial relationships between an organization and its publics (Cutlip et al., 2000; Ledingham & Bruning, 2000). The aim of the relationship is the creation of consensus, which is a new denotative meaning, on important issues to avoid conflict and assure cooperation (Ehling 1992, p. 633; see also Cutlip et al., 2000; Lesly, 1997, and many other handbooks of public relations; outside the United States, cf. Carty, 1992; Groenendijk, 1997). To accomplish this, it is important not to focus on communication processes toward publics or target groups, but on communication processes between interdependent parties. The premise is that communication between parties will always lead to balance of interests (Grunig, 1992a).

Another premise is that parties are willing to act as involved and rational citizens instead of selfish consumers and producers (David, 2004). Theoretically, this approach is based on the balance theories of communication, which were introduced in public relations theory by Broom and Dozier (see Dozier & Ehling, 1992, p. 179). Key problems in the Broom & Dozier approach are the agreement of corporate views with the public's views of an issue, as well as the perceived agreement of the corporate estimate of the public's views and the public's estimate of corporate views. It is obvious that in the relationship model, the organization, as well as its public is no longer predefined as merely senders and receivers, but each is seen as an actor. In this approach, successful communication management is seen as negotiating with the public for an acceptable meaning of issues, which is a matter of balancing the give and take (Grunig, 1992a). Relational communication management is primarily negotiation management, and in this model, the management of the process of meaning creation is restricted to the cocreation of a new definition of the situation (consensus), that is, a new denotative meaning.

The Dialogue Model

Communication management is seen as the facilitation of dialogic interaction between an organization and its publics (e.g., Burkart, 1996). Heath (2001c) referred to this process as "enactment of meanings" with the aim of these dialogues being the development of learning processes (Deetz et al., 2000, p. xiii). Deetz et al. discussed the process through which people develop their interpretations of an event by focusing on how language, stories, and ritual frame or reframe people's understanding of an event, whereas conversations are useful in creating alternative futures and opening the business to a wider collective learning process (Deetz et al., 2000). Zerfass (1996) called these dialogues "arguments in which new meanings develop" (pp. 31–32). The basis of this view of communication management is contemporary rhetorical theory, which explains discourse tactics as what players use to maneuver in communicative interactions. A key aspect of this view is the creation of as many meanings as possible, which is based more on a battle of interests than on harmony of interests (unlike the relationship model).

Heath (2001c) developed the rhetorical enactment approach of communication management, reasoning that "all of what an organization does and says is a statement. It is a statement that is interpreted idiosyncratically by each market, audience, and public" (p. 4). Wiig (2002, p. 80) developed a mutual learning model of communication management (which she called "corporate communication"), a concept borrowed from Argyris (1994) and his idea of double loop learning. She placed it in the McLeod and Chaffee–Broom and Dozier co-orientation tradition of balancing mutual interests, which shows a relationship approach. In the same book, however, McLain Smith (2002) also developed a mutual learning model under the heading, "Keeping a Strategic Dialogue Moving" (p. 151). Her approach to corporate communication is a typical exponent of the dialogue model because she tackles the ideas that the information people exchange consists of facts and that these facts speak for themselves, that it is possible to take the role of an omniscient observer when giving an account to an actual situation, and that matters of self-interest are illegitimate or inappropriate inputs into a substantive problem. Quality communication management in the discursive model is aimed at finding deliberate and pluralistic solutions for problems. The central perspective of the dialogue model is that by facilitating interactions, new meanings are continually created. This is an open-ended model—a learning process that never stops (Barge & Little, 2002). Discursive communication management is, therefore, mainly dialogue management. In this model, the process of meaning creation is restricted to the cocreation of ongoing learning processes of people who are related organizationally, that is, the cocreation of new connotative meanings (Banks, 1995).

As an overview, we compare the four models on the following levels: organization and management theory and managerial intervention; view of communication management; problem, indicator, and focus of communication management; and the communication intervention strategy (see Table 1).

The Empirical Value of the Four Models

Our assumption is that all major theories of communication management can be subsumed within these four headings, but it is difficult to choose any one model as the best. No research shows any one model will always have better results than any other, and we doubt there will ever be findings that show this. To paraphrase Weick (1987), the question is not: Is the model true? All models are true in themselves. The question is: When and where is the model true?

What makes communication management special for managerial tasks is that its focus is on meaning creation by the actors involved to solve organizational problems per se, and it is realized through various strategies. No manager is really concerned about which strategy is used so long as it supports perceived ways of managerial problem solving. Even though some (European) countries are famous for neocorporatism and their consensus building approach to societal problems (Ruler, 2003), it is unrealistic to say that, even in these countries, management acts

TABLE 1
The Four Models Compared

Model variables	Information	Persuasion	Relationship	Dialogue
Organization and management	classical	human relations	contingency	learning
Managerial intervention	directive	directive	interactive	interactive
Communication	mechanical	psychological	system-interaction	interpretive
CM problem	knowledge	influence	trust	meanings
CM indicator	readability	image/reputation	relationships	understanding of meanings
CM focus	dissemination of information	promotion of plans/ decisions	accuracy of relationships	co-creation of new meanings
CM intervention	informational	persuasive	negotiating	discursive

only interactively and open-mindedly and that everyday organizational communication is restricted to dialogue or negotiation. In practice, it is difficult to choose between directive and purely interactive management, as Hersey & Blanchard (1993) showed. It is also unrealistic to choose between certain communication strategies; all people try to inform and persuade others, and they all engage in dialogues and negotiations now and then (Ruler, 2004a). In environments characterized by uncertainty, uniqueness, and value conflict, "an art of problem framing, an art of implementation, and an art of improvisation" are needed (Schön, 1987, p. 13). In such circumstances, one single normative theory of communication management becomes improbable. We therefore believe that these four models can better be seen as strategies that suit solutions to certain problems, with the aim of long-term survival in society.

If, however, we want to perceive these four models as strategies suitable in certain circumstances, then what is the perspective that determines when these strategies are suitable? For this we need a macro-oriented sociological approach to communication management, which we will develop in the next section of this paper. We call our approach reflective communication management and relate it to the view of people as reflective human beings engaged in a continuous social process of constructing society.

A REFLECTIVE VIEW OF COMMUNICATION MANAGEMENT

Contemporary theories of communication management focus mainly on management–organization as one actor in the communication management process and the publics–target groups–stakeholders–contributors as the other actors. Most of these theories have been developed from (social-) psychological systems or a rhetorical perspective of communication management, and most perceive a relationship between organizations (management) and certain individuals or groups of individuals. Approached from the short-term perspective of managers, the organization needs to survive or expand and needs markets (e.g., members, consumers) for its ideas, services, and products, as well as supportive groups in its environment (e.g., enablers).

The main question, however, is why and how individuals might relate to an organization in a way other than as merely customers. A societal perspective—necessary for long-term survival—can offer a more profound view of communication management. Such a view of communication management is not unusual in German-speaking countries and in Scandinavia, and it can also be found in The Netherlands and in some of the former Soviet countries. This could be because public relations theory in many European countries developed mainly within departments of social sciences, but it could also be because of the specific nature of society (Ruler, 2003: Sriramesh & Verčič, 2003). A societal perspective was also the basis for Olasky's alternative exposition of U.S. public relations history, especially in his differentiation between public and private relations. Referring to the German critical sociologist Habermas, Olasky (1989) claimed that public relations practitioners and academics should approach organizations from a public perspective, as they are concerned with phenomena of reflectivity (of organizational behavior) and societal legitimacy.

From a reflective point of view, public relations is not just a phenomenon to be described and defined, or a way of viewing relationships between parties. It is primarily a strategic process of viewing an organization from the outside, or public view. This approach can also be found in Lauzen & Dozier (1992, 1994), who claimed that public relations should not function so much as obedient to management but rather be more distant from management. The primary concerns of communication management from a reflective approach are an organization's inclusiveness and preservation of the license to operate (Royal Society for the Encouragement of the Arts, Manufacturers, & Commerce [RSA], 1995). As marketing is viewing an organization from a market view, the reflective communication management approach is viewing an organization from a societal or public view.

In the next part of this chapter, we will develop steps for a theory of communication management from a contemporary social sciences perspective of organization and communication. We term this reflective communication management. In this view, all current models of communication management will have a place as strategies of communicative behavior. If theories can be seen as instrumental in putting reality into focus, then concepts can be viewed as the various lenses that help us bring the world into focus (Zijderveld, 2000). For reflective communication management, we will use the lens of organizations as institutions that construct their societal legitimacy in an ongoing reflective communication process.

Organizations as Institutions

In referring to organizational activity, management theory usually focuses on the concept of organization, whereas sociologists view an organization more as an institution. Zijderveld (2000) claimed these two concepts were not alternative explanations but dimensions: All organizations are also institutions. "They have, in effect, organizational and institutional dimensions. In other words, the concepts of organization and institution refer to certain sociological facets of sociocultural reality, not to components or sectors of it" (p. 35). Zijderveld stated that it makes a difference whether a university, a corporation, or a union is seen as an organization or an institution. The concept of organization focuses on functional rationality, the division of staff and line functions, on formal structures of command, on hierarchies of power, and on ways of decision making. The concept of institution, however, shows a different kind of reality that can be labeled as value or substantial rationality. Seeing a corporation or an administration as an institution means there is less concern for careful matching of ends and means and more for definition of the ends to be realized. "The predominance of functional rationality is rather detrimental to the institutional dimensions which are geared towards substantial rationality," Zijderveld argued (p. 95).

The concept of organization is economic and administrative; the concept of institution is social. The organizational dimension gives an organization economic legitimacy and trustworthiness. From the perspective of organization, the focus is on societal values, but only from the perspective of a functional rationality instrumental to economic and administrative reasoning. From the perspective of institution, societal values are the bottom line. That is why only the institutional dimension gives an organization societal legitimation and trustworthiness. In most current communication management theories, only the economic dimension of legitimation is in use. The question is this: Does this economic concept suffice? To address this, we need to differentiate further between the two dimensions.

Institutions are traditional and collective patterns of behavior, ways of acting, thinking, and feeling. "Social behavior is essential for the survival of human beings, while institutions — as traditional patterns of behavior — ensure, by taking for granted the order and security needed for actions to be successful" (Zijderveld, 2000, p. 16). Zijderveld echoed Gehlen, a German sociologist from the beginning of the past century, who claimed that institutions can be seen as universal, perhaps even biologically determined competence structures, while institutes are their specific historical and cultural realizations. "When people live together in groups and set out to divide the labor needed in order to survive, basic institutions will emerge" (2000, p. 37), and they emerge in certain realities, or institutes, that are the empirical realizations of these patterns within a specific history and culture. For example, a corporation is the realization of the institution economy; an administration is the realization of the institution state. Whereas institutes come and go, institutions are more lasting: They are ways of acting, thinking, and feeling, realized in historically and culturally-rooted institutes. From this point of view, we can argue that the organizational dimension is an empirical realization of the more fundamental, societally rooted institutional dimension. For short-term survival, the organizational dimension is important, but for long-term survival, the institutional dimension is more important.

Institutes are thus creations of human beings, established to survive as social entities. As a consequence, they exist only as long as they are seen to be meaningful by their society. What a society considers as meaningful (i.e., socially legitimate) is a social construction itself, based in the dynamic structure of the empirical realizations of its institutions.

Societal Legitimation as an Organizational Constraint

Even though we use the social sciences to define the concept, legitimacy is neither a moral nor an ethical deontological principle, but rather it is related to the empirical issue of what is good and justifiable for (the members of) society. "The legitimacy of an organization is a measure of the extent to which the public and the public sphere at a given time and place find the organization sensible and morally justifiable" (Munck Nielsen, 2001, p. 19). Jensen (1997, p. 228) constructed an empirical model for the societal legitimation of corporations that depends on the construction of economic order. In a liberal economy, corporations are supposed to be economically successful but can act socially innocent. As Friedman (1970, p. 122) stated, "The social responsibility of business is to increase profit." Consequently, the societal legitimacy of corporations is defined by profitability in their markets. As markets are insufficient for distributing goods according to values and qualitative ends in society, government has to repair market insufficiencies thorough legal regulations. In such cases, societal legitimacy is restricted to companies that are legally responsible and do not break the law.

Today, however, corporations are not only confronted with legal regulations, but also with demands by public discourse and nongovernmental organizations that transcend the scope of their markets as well as their legal constraints. Hence, Jensen (2000, p. 64) foresaw "the economically successful, legal and responsible company" as the 21st-century empirical concept of a profitable organization. In this concept, theories of legitimacy must be concerned with the legitimacy of power exercised by corporations and nonprofit organizations. According to Jensen (2000), communication management, from the liberal economic perspective, is restricted to sales promotion, product information, and publicity. From the legal perspective, lobbying is a central focus of communication management. From the public discourse perspective, communication management is to be seen as the basic business condition, whereas public discourse concerns itself with what is good or bad as the constraint.

Holmström (2000) argued that legitimacy must be seen as a precondition for corporate social acceptance and that legitimation is the process that establishes collective perceptions of proper behaviors as the natural way of doing things (i.e., the norms and values in societal culture). She foresaw a new paradigm for

legitimate business conduct that is no longer secured by the conventional economic growth and profit paradigm, but (also) by a public legitimate paradigm by
societal legitimation. This can also be viewed as a decline in the social predominance of functional rationality and an increased emphasis on substantial rationality (i.e., the institutional dimension of organization). In this reasoning, the organizational dimension can be seen as the economic capital of an organization and the
institutional dimension as its cultural capital.

Communication as a Cultural Process

Kückelhaus (1998) described three approaches to communication management: product oriented, marketing oriented, and society oriented. She saw the
predominance of society-oriented approaches in German public relations theory
building and like Holmström, believeed that this is the only possible approach in
the 21st century. The society-oriented approach uses society at large as the unit
of analysis and looks at its social structure and institutions as the basis for quality
communication management. This implies that the orientation is not the corporation or organization itself, but its place in society at large (i.e., in the social structure). It is not a bottom-up but rather a top-down view, or at least it is a macroview
of public relations, which is rather dominant in theory building in German-speaking countries (cf. Signitzer, 1992).

In this respect, society at large is seen from the perspective of what the Ger-
mans call Oeffentlichkeit. Oeffentlichkeit does not mean public (e.g., publics or
audiences); it means public sphere, and more specifically, "what is potentially
known to and can be debated by all" (Hollander, 1988, p. 85). It has to do with
openness and approachability, not in a normative but in an empirical way, and
it is in the public domain that you can find it—in daily speech, on websites, in
newspapers, and so on—having a certain outlook (frame). The moment an organization brings out a certain message, it produces a certain component of public
sphere. Oeffentlichkeit is there as soon as messages have been made public, but at
the same time, Oeffentlichkeit is an activity of human beings who socially interpret and reinterpret these messages (Burkart, 2000). It is an outcome and, therefore, a quality of public communication in society (Ronneberger & Rühl, 1992).
By equating Oeffentlichkeit with the Anglo-American public relations concept
of public, an analytic dimension is lost. An essential aspect of public relations is
its concern with issues and values that are publicly relevant and debated, which
means relating to the public sphere, as Jensen (2000) argued. For this, we need to
see the organization in its institutional dimension, whereas publics are to be seen
more as an aspect of the economic dimension.

This line of public relations thinking was developed in Germany, beginning
with Oeckl (1976) and Hundhausen (Bentele & Wehmeier, 2003, p. 203; see also
Kunczik, 1997, p. 298–301) and in the Netherlands by van der Meiden (1978).
It is also represented in other European countries, and these theorists reason that
public relations is not only about relations with the public(s), but creates a plat-
form for public debate and, consequently, a public sphere. As Ronneberger and

Rühl (1992) argued, public relations is to be measured by the quality and quantity of the public sphere, which it coproduces through its activities. Quality and quantity in the public (sphere) relate to oeffentliche meinung, which can be translated as public opinion. This public opinion, however, is not viewed as an aggregate of individual opinions, conceived in public opinion polling (Price, 1992), which is a psychological approach to public opinion. In the sociological approach, it has a qualitative as well as a quantitative dimension, and the quality is intended as a benchmark for public relations. It is a type of democratic political authority and the foundation on which democracy is built (Habermas, 1962). Thus, its quantity is related to such questions as who is participating in the debate and who is not.

In the societal approach, public relations serves the same kind of (democratic) function as journalism does, as they both contribute to a free flow of information and its meanings. They both contribute to the development of the public sphere in size (how many people are involved in public life?), in level (what is the level at which we discuss public matters?), and in quality (what are the frames used in the debates?). This echoes what Carey (1975) called a cultural approach to communication. Theory building in public relations is closely related to journalism in many European countries, not because the practitioners must deal with journalists, but because of these overlapping functions in society.

Ronneberger and Rühl (1992) stated that in managing the communications of an organization, management cannot avoid having an empirical function in the development of society. Ronneberger (1977) claimed earlier that clarifying the different perspectives in public discourse is the most important role of public relations, thereby furthering the development of public opinion. Faulstieg (1992) saw public relations as interaction in society itself that makes something publicly known and creates public discourse, which is why it has an empirical function in whatever kind of development occurs in a society. Thus, we may argue that communication management is part of the social structure of public meanings through its social construction of community.

In this way, communication management is explicitly defined as a function in the larger societal communication system, much as, for example, journalism and advertising are—not because the professionals work together or the means are alike, but because they all have a function in the larger societal communication system and, consequently, in a certain development of society. Indeed, most of the German and Danish public relations researchers use such a social science paradigm (see Arlt, 1998).

There is another important facet in current European public relations thinking. For many European scholars, public relations produces social reality and therefore, a certain type of society. In this approach, they show an interpretative or constructionist view of reality. Most of them base their thinking on communication management along the constructionist systems theory of the sociologist Luhmann; some are also inspired by Habermas. As Arlt (1998, p. 36) argued, "From Habermas can be learned what is good and bad in communication; from Luhmann, one can learn what communication is."

Even though some normative elements can be found in these sociological approaches, this view differs from the community-building approach developed by Kruckeberg and Starck (1988; see also Starck & Kruckeberg, 2000) and reported by Leeper and Leeper (2000). They defined public relations in a normative way, as the social conscience of an organization that is able to contribute to mutual understanding among groups and institutions and bring harmony to private and public policies. In the European sociological approaches described above, the concept of legitimation is used to describe how an organization, as the exponent of one of the institutions in the social system, coproduces public policies and thereby the empirical realization of institutions. An organization is legitimate as long as there is no public discourse concerning its legitimation, and it is therefore a fundamental empirical approach rather than a normative one. The approach to legitimacy, as explained in the above European communication management theories, is via the development of society itself, thereby revealing a constructionist view of society: constructionism as paradigm by which social reality develops.

In a premodern societal setting, values and norms are concrete and fundamental, even if their truths are not necessarily taken for granted (Zijderveld, 2000). They are institutionally fixed and are closed to reflection and relativization. In the modern world, society is institutionally pluralistic, humanly individualistic, and culturally generalized; that is, things are reversed, and this allows for an empirical foundation of a constructionist view of society. Constructionism is rooted in continental European sociology, but it is certainly not a typical European perspective. It was Dewey in 1916 who argued that society is not only maintained by communication, but also constituted by it (Kückelhaus, 1998, p. 142). Rogers (1994, p. 146) showed in his History of Communication Study how the founding father of social science in Chicago, Small, developed his faculty into the Chicago School, which became famous for its constructionist approach to social science. Despite being strongly influenced by German thinking, they did not simply copy it.

Whereas continental European scholars focused on fundamental thinking and philosophical and rhetorical theory building, U.S. scholars focused on the empirical study of society and thereby were able to develop empirical theories of social life, including the role of communication in it. Nevertheless, the fundamental critical thinking of European scholars at that time was very influential for sociology and communication studies in the U.S. (see Rogers, 1994). It enabled the development of what in 1937 Blumer called symbolic interaction (Ritzer, 2000, p. 58), now known as constructionism (see Bentele & Rühl, 1993), but as far as we can see, it has not yet significantly influenced theories of public relations or communication management like it has influenced theories of organizational communication (cf. Jablin & Putnam, 2001).

The start of sociology can be located in the Enlightenment period, when reasoning was for the first time seen as a fundamental human activity. Traditional authority became unacceptable (i.e., "irrational … contrary to human nature and inhibitive of human growth and development," Ritzer, 2000, p. 12) or, as Krippendorf (1994, p. 102) pointed out, "Social theories must be livable." The roots of sociology are critical to an unbalanced social structure and authority. Sociology has been based on the idea that human beings create society and that society in turn creates its institutions, and thereby the reality for the human beings, in a dynamic process. That is where the roots of symbolic interactionism are located, and this is the basis for constructionism.

The idea that reality is not "something out there," but that human beings construct reality themselves was popularized by one of the most frequently cited works in social sciences, *The Social Construction of Reality*, by Berger and Luckmann (1966, p. 48). For them reality is a quality pertaining to phenomena we recognize as having a being independent of our own volition: We cannot wish them away. Knowledge is the certainty that phenomena are real and that they possess specific characteristics. The sociology of knowledge is therefore concerned with the analysis of the social construction of reality, and social structure can be seen as an essential element of the reality of everyday life.

> At one pole of the continuum are those others with whom I frequently interact in face-to-face situations—my inner circle, as it were. At the other pole are highly anonymous abstractions, which by their very nature can never be available in face-to-face interaction. Social structure is the sum total of these typifications and of the recurrent patterns of interaction established by means of them. (p. 48)

Languages, as the most important system of vocal signs, build up semantic fields or zones of meaning that are linguistically circumscribed (cf. Heath, 1994, 2001b). It is possible to say that man has a nature; it is more significant to say that man constructs his own nature, or simply, that man produces himself. This self-production is always, by necessity, a social enterprise, as Berger and Luckmann (1966) argued. Men together produce a human environment, with the totality of its sociocultural and psychological formations. It may be that a given social order precedes any individual organism's development, but social order is still a human product, or, more precisely, an ongoing human production. By playing roles, the individual participates in a social world; by internalizing these roles, the same world becomes subjectively real to him. Roles represent institutional order, but some of these symbolically represent that order in its totality more than others do. Such roles are of great strategic importance in a society because they represent not only this or that institution, but also the integration of all institutions in a meaningful world. These are the roles that have a special relationship to the legitimating apparatus of society.

Historically, these roles have most commonly been located in political and religious institutions, but this is no longer the case, as it is said that NGOs and corporations now have more power than politics and religion. According to Berger and Luckmann (1966, p. 110), legitimation (the term is from Weber) as a process is best described as a "second-order" objectivization of meaning. Its function is to make objectively available and subjectively plausible the "first-order" objectivizations that have been institutionalized. It embodies the institutional order by ascribing cognitive validity to its objectivized meanings and, in turn, justifies them. In the modern world, however, there is always a rivalry between definitions of reality and social structure can predict its outcome. That is why, in our view, communication management must be studied from a public point of view.

In communication science, as well as in organization science, symbolic interactionism has recently inspired some scholars to take a constructionist view of reality. Analyzing Dewey, who claimed that society does not exist by communication but in communication (Dewey, 1916, p. 5), Carey developed a constructionist approach to mass communication as opposite to a transmission view of communication, which he called "ritual view." "If one examines a newspaper under a transmission view of communication, one sees the medium as an instrument for disseminating news" (1975, pp. 4–5). A ritual view of communication will focus on how the world is portrayed and confirmed in the news. News reading and writing are thus ritual acts. News is not so much information but drama, he claimed. German communication scholars have introduced a constructionist approach to public relations theory (Bentele, 1997; Bentele & Rühl, 1993). The basic premise of this view is that human beings reflect the other to themselves and social reality in a dynamic process. Hence, constructing social reality is a shared process of meanings construction (Bentele & Rühl, 1993). In this view, reflective interpretation and conceptualization of meanings are at the forefront in a constant process of de- and reconstruction (Nistelrooij, 2000, p. 275); they are a reflection. Krippendorf (1994), a constructionist communication scientist, mentioned the recursiveness of communication: It is an ongoing social process of de- and reconstruction of interpretations. Hence, Faulstieg (1992) and other constructionist public relations scholars state that public relations is not so much interaction between human beings, but rather societal action.

REFLECTIVE COMMUNICATION MANAGEMENT

The premise that human beings reflect themselves, the other, and social reality in a constant process of de- and reconstruction is not new. Mead may have been the first to call the attention of the social sciences to the concept of reflexivity. As Ritzer (2000, p. 398) wrote, "The general mechanism for the development of the self is reflexivity or the ability to put ourselves unconsciously into others' places and to act as they act." As a result, people are able to examine themselves as others would examine them. As Mead said:

> It is by the means of reflexiveness—the turning back of the experience of the individual upon himself—that the whole social process is thus brought into the experience of the individuals involved in it; it is by such means, which enable the individual to take the attitude of the other toward himself, that the individual is able consciously to adjust himself to that process, and to modify the resultant process in any given social act in terms of his adjustment to it." (Mead, 1934/1962, p. 134, cited by Ritzer, 2000)

The self allows people to take part in their conversations with others. That is, an individual is aware of what he or she is saying, and as a result, is able to monitor what is being said and to determine what is going to be said next. People cannot experience themselves directly; they can do so only indirectly by putting themselves in someone else's place and viewing themselves from that standpoint. The standpoint people view themselves from can be that of particular individuals or the social group as a whole. As Mead put it, most generally, "It is only by taking the roles of others that we have been able to come back to ourselves" (Mead, 1959, pp. 84–185, cited by Ritzer, 2000)." For Mead, thinking is a silent speaking with oneself (Zijderveld, 2000, p. 54).

Reflectivity is the counterpart of causality: It is an ongoing, interactive process and not a discrete, linear one. Along these lines, reflectivity must be seen as the core concept of social interaction because it provides a better explanation for what happens than causality does. Even though human beings reflect themselves in relation to the other and the social group as a whole, their knowing is reflective knowing. Zijderveld (2000) referred to human beings as a double or a homo duplex. A human being has a private as well as a public life and plays all kinds of social roles in life, and the concept of reflectivity gives mankind the possibility to develop these roles. Roles are defined by society, and in playing certain roles, people develop society. This concept of roles is different from roles theory in public relations so far because it emphasizes the dynamics of it, seeing it from a reflective point of view. The role one takes depends on the situation and the context, as well as on certain societal groups and society on the whole as a role sender.

Enactment, Sense Making, and Framing in Communication Management

Heath (1994) described communication management as an enactment process. The meaning communication managers have of their company, market, environment, customers, themselves, and their jobs affects their job performance. "They enact their jobs as actors enact the scripts in plays" (p. vii), hence, role playing is communication. The focal points of organizational communication analysis, Heath argued, are the acts people perform that are meaningful for themselves and others, along with their thoughts about organizing and working. At the heart of this analysis is an interest in knowing how people in companies create and enact meaning, which is in fact a sense-making approach to the study of organizational performance.

Looking at communication management from this point of view, it is impossible to see communication only as transmission (Foreman-Wernet, 2004) and focus any longer on the traditional logic supporting the idea that the receiver has a deficit (Dervin, 2004a, p. 19). Sense-making involves placing stimuli in some kind of framework and can be seen as a thinking process that uses retrospective accounts to explain and redress surprises, construct meaning, and interact in pursuit of mutual understanding and patterning. "In order to convert a problematic situation to a problem, a practitioner must do a certain kind of work. He must make sense of an uncertain situation that initially makes no sense" (Weick 1995, pp. 6–7). This problem setting is a process in which, interactively, we name the things to which we will attend and frame the context in which we will attend to them (Schön 1983, p. 40). Sense making is grounded as much in deduction from well-articulated theories as it is in induction from specific cases of struggle to reduce ambiguity. Sense making is, however, driven by plausibility rather than accuracy. The concept of organizational sense making is based in action theory, seen as the propositions people have to guide their behaviors (Weick 1995, p. 21), which refers to the basic Thomas theorem that holds that not facts but the interpretation of facts steers people's actions. People, including managers, tend to frame situations so that problems become solvable.

Managers use all kinds of strategies, including manipulation of frames (persuasion), in order to get things done, even if there are conflicting interests that must be resolved. The constraint in this manipulation is public legitimacy, which, because of increased public counteraction, has become increasingly necessary for business to survive. This new, broadened business paradigm requires a larger degree of reflective self-control by management, and this leads to what Schön (1983) called the dilemma of rigor or relevance, which all professionals experience sooner or later. Rigor develops technical rationality, yet depends on internally consistent but normative theories to achieve clearly fixed ends. Relevance develops reflective rationality, focusing on the right solution in the right context. Doubt, therefore, is located more in the situation than in the mind. The task of the professional/manager is to make sense of the situation and construct the appropriate meaning for it; the way to do this is by enacting his or her meanings and reconsidering them, that is, reflection-in-action and reflection on the communication-in-action (cf. Schön, 1983).

Dervin (2004b, p. 83) warned that this is not to be seen as a process of personal relativity, assuming that each person constructs understandings of the world in interaction with his or her own symbolic, social, natural, and physical worlds: "It implies that personal authority will be the exerted power, but since power dynamics do not work through automized individuals, this view in fact leaves the way open for the forces of power anywhere and everywhere." Sense making is always a social process of individuals.

What is seen as appropriate is not random. "Culture defines which act is appropriate and which is not" (Heath, 1994, p. 5). Culture leads people to share a vocabulary that carves reality into meaningful units, but enactments themselves also develop culture, which is why the process in which organizational work is done—management—itself produces culture. Looking at the institutional dimension of organizations, it is obvious that societal culture defines management and is defined by management as well. Sense making comes to life in communication by the way in which people frame the meanings in their heads (Entman, 1993; Goffman, 1974). Hence, framing is basically an interactive cultural process

(D'Angelo, 2002) that in fact shows social reality (Vreese, 2003) and can work as myth (Ruler, 2004b).

Aspects of Reflective Communication Management

What does this all mean for communication management? First, we must differentiate between the societal/institutional and the economic–administrative roles each organization plays in its communication management. The economic role is concerned with the meso- (group) and micro- (interpersonal) level of communications among members of the organization and between the organization and its publics in order to become legitimate in the eyes of specific publics. The societal role is concerned with the macrolevel of societal legitimation. Communication management is concerned with the reproduction of the underlying principles that enable organizations to emerge, develop, and prosper. If we live in an organizational society, this is communicatively enacted (Hassard & Parker, 1993), and it is precisely here that the future of both the theory and practice of communication management come into play. Indeed, it looks like several sectors of industry have lost that element from their perspective with profound effects (e.g., nuclear industry, subsectors of biotechnology like genetic research in both plants and humans).

Second, it means that we must differentiate between the organization as organization and as institute. The reflective model looks at the organization as an empirical realization of an institution in society and the organizational dimension as subordinate to the institutional dimension when it comes to survival. That is why organizational communication is only a strategy, empirically working in and through the social construction of public identity, for which several perspectives (e.g., mechanical, psychological, systems interaction, interpretative) are necessary. Accordingly, communication management is primarily concerned with its public legitimation, and to get public license to operate, it focuses on public opinion (the public sphere) as a quantity as well as a quality. For this, all four existing models of communication management can be used, and all communication management indicators count. The institutional dimension of an organization provokes the reflective umbrella of communication management, whereas the organizational dimension provokes the existing models of communication management, now seen as strategies of the reflective model (see Table 2).

Regarded from this public point of view, the generic principle of communication management can become a more specific one: It is about maximizing, optimizing, or satisfying the process of meaning creation using informational, persuasive, relational, and discursive interventions to solve managerial problems by coproducing societal (public) legitimation.

This is not a specialized management function but a function of management per se. The role of the communication management specialist, however, is to advise

TABLE 2
The Reflective Model of Communication Management
Compared to Existing Models

Model	Information	Persuasion	Relationship	Dialogue	Reflective
Organization and management	classical	human relations	contingency	learning	institutional
Managerial intervention	directive	directive	interactive	interactive	reflection -in-action
Communication	mechanical	psychological	system interaction	interpretive	depends
CM problem	knowledge	influence	trust	meanings	public legitimation
CM indicator	readability	image/ reputation	relationships	understand- ing of mean- ings	public license to operate
CM focus of Management	dissemination of info	promotion of plan/decision	accuracy of relationships	co-creation of new meanings	public sphere
CM intervention	informational	persuasive	negotiating	discursive	depends
Task of CM Specialist	broadcasting of decisions	engineering cooperation to decisions	controlling decision making	mediating decision making	counseling and coaching on reality construction

and coach (the members of) the organization in this process. We will discuss the necessarily changing role of the communication management specialist in the final section of this chapter.

The Role of the Specialist in Communication Management (the Public Relations Professional)

Viewing communication management as primarily an organizational approach and therefore as a function of general management does not explain the flourishing industry of communication management as a specialty. In this last section, we will build a theory of specialist communication management that follows from our approach to communication management as a function of general management.

What distinguishes communication managers from other managers when they sit down at the table is that they contribute special concern for broader societal issues and approaches to problems. Furthermore, they have special concern for the implications of organizational behavior toward and in the public sphere, as well as toward certain stakeholders and target groups. This determines the roles the specialist in communication management can play.

The tasks of the communication manager within an organization, or the consultant who is hired to advise on communication management, can be derived from the four characteristics that were seen as inclusive of communication management by experts on public relations in Europe (see Ruler & Verčič, 2002a). The four characteristics are counseling, coaching, conceptualizing, and executing.

1. Counseling: to analyze changing values, norms, and issues in society and discuss these with members of the organization in order to adjust values, norms, and issue-related points of view in the organization. This role is concerned with organizational guidelines, policies, and standards and aimed at the development of vision or mission, corporate story, and organizational strategies.

2. Coaching: to educate the members of the organization to behave competently in their communications so they can respond to societal demands. This role is concerned with the mentality and behavior of the members of the organization and aimed at internal public groups.

3. Conceptualizing: to develop plans to communicate and maintain relationships with public groups to gain public trust. This role is concerned with commercial and other (internal and external) public groups and with public opinion as a whole. It is aimed at the execution of the organizational mission and strategies.

4. Executing: to prepare the means of communication for the organization (and its members) to help the organization formulate its communications. This role is concerned with services and is aimed at the execution of the communication plans.

To see these roles as inclusive in reflective communication management, we can develop the following parameters of the profession: Communication management as a specialty helps organizations by counseling the deliberations on legitimacy, by coaching its members in the development of their communicative competencies, by conceptualizing communication plans, and by executing communication means, using informational, persuasive, relational, and discursive interventions.

The reflective approach to communication management regards the counseling role as the fundamental one; the other roles follow from it.

CONCLUSION AND DISCUSSION

In this chapter, we have argued that to reflect the plural nature of its service to organizations and society, a feasible managerial concept of public relations requires more indicators than only relationships. This led us to develop a two-by-two-dimensional definition of organization and management as well as communication, and we derived four basic models of communication management from the definition. We argued that these models are not exclusive, but complementary, and that organizations are best advised to use these simultaneously in various combinations, that is, as strategies, because all models operate on the behavioral level—on (members of) organizations and their publics. If taken individually, the societal level, and consequently, the legitimacy problem of organizations, remain totally neglected. To avoid this, we developed the reflective communication management approach, which is related to the view of people as reflective human beings engaged in a continuous social process of constructing society. We also looked at organizations as institutes, thereby focusing on their fundamental rationality in order to develop their societal legitimation. In our approach this legitimation is not based on morality or ethics as a deontological principle, but on the empirical question of what is good and justifiable to (the members of) society. In a premodern social setting, values and norms are concrete and felt to be fundamental, even if they are not true in the sense of being taken for granted, whereas in the modern world, values are plural and dynamic. This allows for a constructionist view of society and communication.

In our societal approach of communication management, society at large is the unit of analysis—the social structure and institutions being the basis for quality communication management. This implies that the point of view is not that of the corporation or organization itself, but the organization's place in society at large (the social structure). Communication management is engaged in constructing society by making sense of situations, creating appropriate meanings out of them, and looking for acceptable frameworks and enactments. This reflective communication management approach sees communication management concerning itself with maximizing, optimizing, or satisfying the process of meaning creation, using informational, persuasive, relational, and discursive interventions to solve managerial problems by coproducing societal (public) legitimation. This means that, for the future research in and of public relations, more emphasis is needed on its societal and communicative antecedents and consequences—that more than how to research is required, that we need research on why and with what effects. Public relations has gained a full recognition within communication science discipline, but to contribute to its full potential, it needs to reflect on its roots in communication.

We believe that management needs a reflective view of its communication management to sustain the license to operate. What communication management specialists offer today, is primarily an unreflected execution, and it is in the gap between demand and supply that the future of communication management is about to grow. If it does not, there will be no future for communication management, and beyond that, management itself.

REFERENCES

Argyris, C. (1994). *On organizational learning*. Cambridge, MA: Blackwell.
Argyris, C., & Schön, D.A. (1978). *Organizational learning: A theory of action perspective*. Reading, MA: Addison-Wesley.

Arlt, H. J. (1998). *Kommunikation, Oeffentlichkeit, Oeffentlichkeitsarbeit. PR von Gestern, PR für Morgen – das Beispiel Gewerkschaft [Communication, public sphere, public relations: PR of yesterday, PR for tomorrow. The example Gewerkschaft]*. Opladen, Germany: Westdeutscher Verlag.

Banks, S. P. (1995). *Multicultural public relations: A social-interpretive approach*. Thousand Oaks, CA: Sage.

Banton, M. (1996). Role. In A. Kuper & J. Kuper (Eds.), *The social science encyclopaedia* (pp. 749–751). London: Routledge.

Baran, S. J., & Davis, D. K. (2000). *Mass communication theory. Foundations, ferment, and future.* Belmont, CA: Wadsworth/Thomson Learning.

Barge, J. K., & Little, M. (2002). Dialogical wisdom, communicative practice, and organizational life. *Communication Theory, 12*, 375–397.

Bauer, R. A. (1963). Communication as a transaction: a comment on the concept of influence. *Public Opinion Quarterly, 27*, 83–86.

Bauer, R.A. (1964). The obstinate audience: The influence process from the point of view of social communication. *American Psychologist, 19*, 319–328.

Bentele, G. (1997). Public relations and reality: A contribution to a theory of public relations. In D. Moss, T. MacManus, & D. Verčič (Eds.), *Public relations research: An international perspective* (pp. 89–109). London: International Thompson Business Press.

Bentele, G., & Wehmeier, S. (2003). From literary bureaus to a modern profession: The development and current structure of public relations in Germany. In K. Sriramesh & D. Verčič (Eds.), *The global public relations handbook: Theory, research, and practice* (pp. 199–221). Mahwah, NJ: Erlbaum.

Bentele, G., & Rühl, M. (Eds.). (1993). *Theorien oeffentlicher Kommunikation [Theories of public communication]*. Munich, Germany: Ölschläger.

Berger, P., & Luckmann, T. (1966). *The social construction of reality: A treatise in the sociology of knowledge*. New York: Penguin Books.

Berlo, D. K. (1960). *The process of communication*. New York: Holt, Rinehart, &Winston.

Bernays, E. L. (1923). *Crystallizing public opinion*. New York: Boni & Liveright.

Broom, G. M. (1982). A comparison of sex roles in public relations. *Public Relations Review, 5*(3), 47–59.

Broom, G. M., & Smith, G. D. (1979). Testing the practitioner's impact on clients. *Public Relations Review, 5*(3), 47–59.

Burkart, R. (1996). Verständigungsorientierte Oeffentlichkeitsarbeit: Der Dialog als PR-Konzeption [Public relations oriented at understanding: The dialogue as concept in public relations]. In G. Bentele, H. Steinmann, & A. Zerfass (Hrsg.), *Dialogorientierte Unternehmenskommunikation. Grundlagen, Praxiserfahrungen, Perspektiven [Dialogoriented business communication. Basics, Praxis, Perspectives]* (pp. 245–270). Berlin: Vistas.

Burkart, R. (2000). *Kommunikationswissenschaft [Communication Science]*. Vienna, Austria: Böhlau.

Carey, J. W. (1975). A cultural approach to communication. *Journal of Communication, 2*(1), 1–22.

Cialdini, R. B. (1984). *Influence*. New York: William Morrow.

Carty, F. X. (1992). *Farewell to hype: The emergence of real public relations*. Dublin, Ireland: Able Press.

Castells, M. (1996). *The information age: Economy, society and culture: Vol. I. The rise of the network society*. Oxford, UK: Blackwell.

Cole, G. A. (2000). *Management: Theory and practice.* (5th ed.). New York: Continuum.

Collins, J. C., & Porras, J. I. (1998). *Built to last: Successful habits of visionary companies*. London: Random House.

Cutlip, S. C. (1994). *The unseen power: Public relations. A history*. Hillsdale, NJ: Erlbaum.

Cutlip, S. C., Center, A. H., & Broom, G. M. (2000). *Effective public relations*. Upper Saddle River, NJ: Prentice Hall.

Dance, F. E. X. (1970). The "concept" of communication. *Journal of Communication, 20*(2), 201–210.

D'Angelo, P. (2002). News framing as a multi-paradigmatic research program: A response to Entman. *Journal of Communication, 52*(4), 870–888.

Davis, A. (2002). *Public relations democracy: Public relations, politics, and the mass media in Britain*. Manchester, UK: Manchester University Press.

David, P. (2004). Extending symmetry: Toward a convergence of professionalism, practice, and prag-
matics in public relations. *Journal of Public Relations Research, 16*, 185–211.

Deetz, S. A. (2001). Conceptual foundations. In F. M. Jablin & L. L. Putnam (Eds.), *The new handbook of organizational communication: Advances in theory, research, and methods* (pp. 3–46).
Thousand Oaks, CA: Sage.

Deetz, S. A., & Putnam, L. L. (2001). Thinking about the future of communications. In W.B. Gudykunst (Ed.), *Communication yearbook 24* (pp. 1–16). Thousand Oaks, CA: Sage.

Deetz, S. A., Tracy, S. J., & Simpson, J. L. (2000). *Leading organizations through transition*. Thousand Oaks: Sage.

Dervin, B. (2004a). Communication gaps and inequities: Moving toward a reconceptualization. In
B. Dervin & L. Foreman-Wernet (Eds.), *Sense-making methodology reader: Selected writings of
Brenda Dervin* (pp. 17–46). Cresskill, NJ: Hampton Press.

Dervin, B. (2004b). Information   democracy: An examination of underlying assumptions. In B. Dervin & L. Foreman-Wernet (Eds.), *Sense-making methodology reader: Selected writings of Brenda
Dervin* (pp. 73–100). Cresskill, NJ: Hampton Press.

Dewey, J. (1916). *Democracy and education*. New York: Macmillan.

Dolphin, R. R. (1999). *The fundamentals of corporate communications*. Oxford, UK: Butterworth
Heinemann.

Dozier. D. M. (1984). Program evaluation and roles of practitioners. *Public Relations Review, 10*(2), 13–21.

Dozier, D. M. (1992). The organizational roles of communications and public relations practitioners.
In J. E. Grunig (Ed.), *Excellence in public relations and communication management* (pp. 327–
355). Hillsdale, NJ: Erlbaum.

Dozier, D. M., & Ehling, W. P. (1992). Evaluation of public relations programs: What the literature
tells us about their effects. In J. E. Grunig (Ed.), *Excellence in public relations and communication
management* (pp. 159–184). Hillsdale, NJ: Erlbaum.

Dozier, D. M., with Grunig, L. A., & Grunig, J. E. (1995). *Manager's guide to excellence in public
relations and communication management*. Mahwah, NJ: Erlbaum.

Ehling, W. P. (1992). Estimating the value of public relations and communication to an organization.
In J. E. Grunig (Ed.), *Excellence in public relations and communication management* (pp. 617–
638). Hillsdale, NJ: Erlbaum.

Entman, R. (1993). Framing: Toward clarification of a fractured paradigm. *Journal of Communication, 43*(4), 51–58.

Ewen, S. (1996). *PR! A social history of spin*. New York: BasicBooks

Faulstieg, W. (1992). *Oeffentlichkeitsarbeit. Grundwissen: kritische Einführung in Problemfelder
[Public relations. Basics: critical introduction into problems]*. Bardowick, Germany: Wissen-
schaftlicher Verlag.

Fearing, F. (1967). Toward a psychological theory of human communication. *Journal of Personality,
22*, 71–78. Reprinted in F. W. Matson & A. Montagu (Eds.), *The human dialogue: Perspectives on
communication* (pp. 179–194). New York: Free Press. (Original work published 1953)

Foreman-Wernet, L. (2004). Rethinking communication: Introducing the sense-making methodology.
In B. Dervin & L. Foreman-Wernet (Eds.), *Sense-making methodology reader: Selected writings
of Brenda Dervin* (pp. 4–16). Cresskill, NJ: Hampton Press.

Foster, R. N., & Kaplan, S. (2001). *Creative destruction: From "built to last" to "built to perform."*
London: Financial Times & Prentice Hall.

Foster, T. R. V., & Jolly, A. (Eds.) (1997). *Corporate communications handbook*. London: Kogan Page.

Friedman, M. (1970, September 13). The social responsibility of business is to increase profit. *New
York Times Magazine*, p. 122.

Gitlin, T. (2002). Media sociology: The dominant paradigm. In D. McQuail (Ed.), *McQuail's reader
in mass communication theory* (pp. 25–35). Thousand Oaks, CA: Sage.

Goffman, E. (1974). *Frame analysis: An essay on the organization of experience*. Boston: Northeastern University Press.

Groenendijk, J. N. A. (1997). Public relations management. In J. N. A. Groenendijk, G. A. T. Haze-
kamp & J. Mastenbroek (Eds.), *Public relations, beleid, organisatie en uitvoering [Public Relations, policy, organization and execution]* (pp. 14–27). Alphen aan den Rijn, Netherlands: Samsom
BedrijfsInformatie.

Grunig, J. E. (1976). Organizations and public relations: Testing a communication theory, *Journalism Monographs*, nr. 46.

Grunig, J. E. (1989). Symmetrical presuppositions as a framework for public relations theory. In C. H. Botan & V. Hazleton Jr. (Eds.), *Public relations theory* (pp. 17–44). Hillsdale, NJ: Erlbaum.

Grunig, J. E. (Ed.). (1992a). *Excellence in public relations and communication management*. Hillsdale, NJ: Erlbaum.

Grunig, J. E. (1992b). Communication, public relations, and effective organizations: An overview of the book. In J. E. Grunig (Ed.), *Excellence in public relations and communication management* (pp. 1–28). Hillsdale, NJ: Erlbaum.

Grunig, J. E., & Hunt, T. (1984). *Managing public relations*. New York: Holt, Rinehart, & Winston.

Grunig, L. A., Grunig, J. E., & Dozier, D. M. (2002). *Excellent public relations and effective organizations: A study of communication management in three countries*. Mahwah, NJ: Erlbaum.

Habermas, J. (1962). *Strukturwandel der Oeffentlichkeit. Untersuchungen zu einer Kategorie der bürgerlichen Gesellschaft* [*Change of the structure of public sphere. Investigation into a category of citizen's society*]. Darmstadt, Germany: Luchterhand.

Hassard, J., & Parker, M. (Eds.). (1993). *Postmodernism and organizations*. London: Sage.

Heath, R. L. (1994). *Management of corporate communication: From interpersonal contacts to external affairs*. Hillsdale, NJ: Erlbaum.

Heath, R. L. (Ed.). (2001a). *Handbook of public relations*. Thousand Oaks: Sage.

Heath, R. L. (2001b). Shifting foundations: Public relations as relationship building. In R. L. Heath (Ed.), *Handbook of public relations* (pp. 1–9). Thousand Oaks: Sage.

Heath, R. L. (2001c). A rhetorical enactment rationale for public relations: The good organization communicating well. In R. L. Heath (Ed.), *Handbook of public relations* (pp. 31–50). Thousand Oaks: Sage.

Heider, F. (1946). Attitudes and cognitive information. *Journal of Psychology, 21*, 107–112.

Hersey, P., & Blanchard, K. H. (1993). *Management of organizational behavior*. Englewood Cliffs, CA: Prentice Hall.

Hollander, E. (1988). *Lokale communicatie en locale openbaarheid. Openbaarheid als communicatiewetenschappelijk concept* [*Local communication and local public sphere: Public sphere as communication scientific concept*]. Nijmegen, Netherlands: Katholieke Universiteit Nijmegen.

Holmström, S. (2000, July). *The reflective paradigm: Turning into ceremony?* Paper presented at the 7th International Public Relations Research Symposium, Bled, Slovenia.

Hutton, J. G. (1999). The definition, dimensions, and domain of public relations. *Public Relations Review, 25*, 199–214.

Jablin, F. M., & Putnam, L. L. (Eds.). (2001). *The new handbook of organizational communication: Advances in theory, research, and methods*. Thousand Oaks, CA: Sage.

Jensen, I. (1997). Legitimacy and strategy of different companies: A perspective of external and internal public relations. In D. Moss, T. MacManus, & D. Verčič (Eds.), *Public relations research: An international perspective* (pp. 225–246). London: ITP.

Jensen, I. (2000, July). *Public relations and the public sphere in the future*. Paper presented at the 7th International Public Relations Research Symposium, Bled, Slovenia.

Krippendorf, K. (1994). A recursive theory of communication. In D. Crowley & D. Mitchell (Eds.), *Communication theory today* (pp. 78–104). Cambridge, UK: Polity Press.

Kruckeberg, D., & Starck, K. (1988). *Public relations and community: A reconstructed theory*. New York: Praeger.

Kückelhaus, A. (1998). *Public relations: die Konstruktion von Wirklichkeit. Kommunikationstheoretische Annäherungen an ein neuzeitliches Phänomen* [*Public relations: The construction of reality. Communication scientific perspectives into a current phenomenon*]. Opladen, Germany: Westdeutscher Verlag.

Kunczik, M. (1997). *Geschichte der Oeffentlichkeitsarbeit in Deutschland* [*History of public relations in Germany*]. Köln, Germany: Bóhlau.

Langer, S. (1967). Mind: An essay on human feeling. Baltimore: Johns Hopkins University Press. Cited in S. W. Littlejohn (1992), *Theories of human communication* (pp. 67–70). Belmont, CA: Wadsworth.

Lasswell, H. D. (1948). The structure and function of communication in society. In L. Bryson (Ed.), *The communication of ideas*. New York: Harper. Also reprinted in W. Schramm, Ed. (1960), *Mass communications* (pp. 117–130). Urbana: University of Illinois Press.

Lauzen, M. M., & Dozier, D. M. (1992). The missing link: The public relations manager role as mediator of organizational environments and power consequences for the function. *Journal of Public Relations Research, 4*, 205–220.

Lauzen, M. M., & Dozier, D. M. (1994). Issues management mediation of linkages between environmental complexity and management of the public relations function. *Journal of Public Relations Research, 6*, 163–184.

Lawniczak, R. (Ed.). (2001). *Public relations contribution to transition in Central and Eastern Europe: Research and practice.* Poznan, Poland: Poznan University of Economics (informal publication,kpr@ae.poznan.pl.)

Ledingham, J. A., & Bruning, S. D. (1998). Relationship management in public relations: Dimensions of an organization-public relationship. *Public Relations Review, 24*, 55–65.

Ledingham, J. A., & Bruning, S. D. (Ed.). (2000). *Public relations as relationship management: A relational approach to the study and practice of public relations.* Mahwah NJ: Erlbaum.

Leeper, K. A., & Leeper, R. V. (2000). *Creating community as social responsibility: A case study.* Paper presented at the 50th International Communication Association Conference, Acapulco, Mexico, June 1–5.

Lesly, P. (1997). *Lesly's handbook of public relations and communications.* Lincolnwood, Ill: NTC Business Books.

L' Étang, J., & Pieczka, M. (1996). *Critical perspectives in public relations.* London: International Thomson Business Press.

Littlejohn, S. W. (1987). *Theories of human communication.* Belmont, CA: Wadsworth.

Littlejohn, S. W. (1992). *Theories of human communication.* Belmont, CA: Wadsworth.

London, S. (2002, February). Corporations with hard and soft centers. *Financial Times, 20*, p. 15.

Long, L. W., & Hazleton, V., Jr. (1987). Public relations: A theoretical and practical response. *Public Relations Review, 13*(3), 3–13.

March, J. G. (1994). *A primer on decision making: How decisions happen.* New York: Free Press.

McQuail, D. (2000). *McQuail's mass communication theory.* Thousand Oaks, CA: Sage.

McQuail, D., & Windahl, S. (1981). *Communication models: For the study of mass communication.* London: Longman.

McLain Smith, D. (2002). Keeping a strategic dialogue moving. In P. Simcic Bronn & R. Wiig (Eds.), *Corporate communication. A strategic approach to building reputation* (pp. 151–176). Oslo, Norway: Gyldendal Akademisk.

McLeod, J. M., & Chaffee, S. H. (1973). Interpersonal approaches to communication research. *American Behavioral Scientist, 16*, 469–499.

Meiden, A. van der. (1978). *Wat zullen de mensen ervan zeggen? Enkele visies op het publiek in de ontwikkelingsgang van de public relations* [*What will people say? Some views on the public in the development of public relations*]. The Hague, Netherlands: NGPR (inaugural lecture).

Miller, G. R. (1989). Persuasion and public relations: Two "ps" in a pod. In C. H. Botan & V. Hazleton Jr. (Eds.), *Public relations theory* (pp. 45–66). Hillsdale, NJ: Erlbaum.

Mintzberg, H. (1973). *The nature of managerial work.* New York: Harper & Row.

Mogel, L. (2002). *Making it in public relations: An insider's guide to career opportunities.* Mahwah, NJ: Erlbaum.

Mumby, D. K. (1987). The political function of narrative in organizations. *Communication Monographs, 54*, 113–127.

Mumby, D. K. (2000). Communication, organization and the public sphere. In P. M. Buzzanell (Ed.), *Rethinking organizational and managerial communication from feminist perspectives* (pp. 3–23). Thousand Oaks, CA: Sage.

Munck Nielsen, J. (2001). *The legitimacy concept and its potentialities: A theoretical reconstruction with relevance to public relations.* Unpublished doctoral dissertation, University of Roskilde, Denmark.

Newcomb, T. M. (1953). An approach to the study of communicative acts. *Psychology Review, 60*, 393–404.

Newcomb, T. M. (1958). Communicative behavior. In R. Young (Ed.), *Approaches to the study of politics* (pp. 244–265). Evanston, IL: Atlantic Books.

Nistelrooij, A. Van. (2000). *Collectief organiseren. Een sociaal-constructionistisch onderzoek naar het werken met grote groepen* [*Collective organizing. A social-constructionistic research project into large scale group work*]. Utrecht, Netherlands: Lemma.

Oeckl, A. (1976). *PR-praxis. Der Schlüssel zur Oeffentlichkeitarbeit* [*Public relations practice: The key to public relations*]. Düsseldorf, Germany: Econ.

Olasky, M. N. (1989). The aborted debate within public relations: An approach through Kuhn's paradigm. In J. E. Grunig & L. A. Grunig (Eds.), *Public Relations Research Annual, Vol. 1* (pp. 87–96). Hillsdale, NJ: Erlbaum.

Perloff, R. M. (1993). *The dynamics of persuasion.* Hillsdale, NJ: Erlbaum.

Peters, J. D. (1999). *Speaking into the air: A history of the idea of communication.* Chicago: University of Chicago Press.

Petty, R. E., & Cacioppo, J. T. (1981). *Attitudes and persuasion: Classic and contemporary approaches.* Dubuque, IA: Wm. Brown.

Pratkanis, A., & Aronson, E. (1991). *Age of propaganda. The everyday use and abuse of persuasion.* New York: W. H. Freeman.

Preyer, G., Peter, G., & Ulkan, M. (2003). *Concepts of meaning: Framing an integrated theory of linguistic behavior.* Dordrecht, Netherlands: Kluwer Academic Publishers.

Price, V. (1992). *Public opinion.* Newbury Park, CA: Sage.

Putnam, L. L. (1983). The interpretive perspective: An alternative to functionalism. In L. L. Putnam & M. E. Pacanowsky (Eds.), *Communication and organizations: An interpretive approach* (pp. 31–54). Beverly Hills, CA: Sage.

Putnam, L. L., & Pacanowsky, M. E. (Eds.). (1983). *Communication and organizations. An interpretive approach.* Beverly Hills, CA: Sage.

Riel, C. B. M. van. (1995). *Principles of corporate communication.* London: Prentice Hall.

Riel, C. B. M. van. (2000). Corporate communication orchestrated by a sustainable corporate story. In M. Schultz, M. J. Hatch, & M. Holten Larsen (Eds.), *The expressive organization: Linking identity, reputation, and the corporate brand* (pp. 157–181). Oxford, UK: Oxford University Press.

Ritzer, G. (2000). *Classical sociological theory.* Boston: McGraw-Hill.

Rogers, E. M. (1994). *History of communication study.* New York: Free Press.

Ronneberger, F. (1977). *Legitimation durch Information* [*Legitimation through information*]. Düsseldorf, Germany: Econ.

Ronneberger, F., & Rühl, M. (1992). *Theorie der Public Relations, ein Entwurf* [*Theory of public relations: A design*]. Opladen, Germany: Westdeutscher Verlag.

Rosengren, K. E. (2000). *Communication: An introduction.* London: Sage.

RSA (1995). *Tomorrow's company.* London: Royal Society for the Encouragement of Arts, Manufactures & Commerce.

Ruler, B. van. (1996). *Communicatiemanagement in Nederland* [*Communication management in the Netherlands*]. Houten, Netherlands: Bohn Stafleu Van Loghum.

Ruler, B. van. (1997). Communication: Magical mystery or scientific concept? Professional views of public relations practitioners in the Netherlands. In D. Moss, T. MacManus, & D. Verčič (Eds.), *Public relations research: An international perspective* (pp. 247–263). London: International Thomson Business Press.

Ruler, B. van. (2000). Communication management in the Netherlands. *Public Relations Review, 26,* 403–423.

Ruler, B. van. (2003). Public relations in the Polder: The case of the Netherlands. In K. Sriramesh & D. Verčič (Eds.), *The global public relations handbook: Theory, research, and practice* (pp. 222–243). Hillsdale, NJ: Erlbaum.

Ruler, B. van. (2004a). The communication grid: An introduction of a model of four communication strategies. *Public Relations Review, 30,* 123–143.

Ruler, B. van. (2004b). Framedoctoring. Het strategisch gebruik van frames in storytelling [Frame doctoring: The strategic use of frames in storytelling]. In G. Rijnja & R. van der Jagt (Eds.), *Storytelling. De kracht van verhalen in communicatie* [*Storytelling: The power of stories in communication*; pp. 39–46]. Alphen aan den Rijn, Netherlands: Kluwer.

Ruler, B. van, & Verčič, D. (2002a). 21st century communication management—the people, the organization. In P. Simcic Bronn & R. Wiig (Eds.), *Corporate communication: A strategic approach to building reputation* (pp. 277–294). Oslo, Norway: Gyldendal Akademisk.

Ruler, B. van, & Verčič, D. (2002b). *The Bled Manifesto on public relations.* Ljubljana, Slovenia: Pristop Communications.

Ruler, B. van, & Verčič, D. (Eds.). (2004). *Public relations and communication management in Europe: A nation-by-nation introduction into public relations theory and practice.* New York: Mouton DeGruyter.

Ruler, B. van, Verčič, D., Buetschi, G., & Flodin, B. (2000). *European body of knowledge on public relations/Communication management: Report of the Delphi Research Project 2000.* Ljubljana, Slovenia: European Association for Public Relations Education and Research.

Schön, D. A. (1983). *The reflective practitioner: How professionals think in action.* New York: Basic Books.

Schön, D. A. (1987). *Educating the reflective practitioner: Toward a new design for teaching and learning in the professions.* San Francisco: Jossey-Bass.

Schramm, W. (1965). How communication works. In W. Schramm (Ed.), *The process and effects of mass communication* (pp. 3–26). Urbana: University of Illinois Press.

Scott, W. R. (1987). *Organizations: Rational, natural, and open systems* (2nd ed.). Englewood Cliffs: Prentice Hall.

Servaes, J. (1999). *Communication for development: One world, multiple cultures.* Creskill, NJ: Hampton Press.

Servaes, J., Jacobson, T. L., & White, S. A. (Eds.). (1996). *Participatory communication for social change.* Thousand Oaks, NJ: Sage.

Signitzer, B. (1992). Aspekte der Produktion von Public Relations-Wissen: PR-Forschung in studentischen Abschlussarbeiten [Aspects of production of public relations knowledge: PR research in student theses]. In H. Avenarius & W. Armbrecht (Eds.), *Ist Public Relations eine Wissenschaft? [Is public relations a science?]* (pp. 171–206). Opladen, Germany: Westdeutscher Verlag.

Shannon, C.E., & Weaver, W. (1949). *The mathematical theory of communication.* Urbana: University of Illinois Press.

Sriramesh, K., & Verčič, D. (Eds.). (2003). *The global public relations handbook: Theory, research, and practice.* Mahwah, NJ: Erlbaum.

Stacks, D. W. (2002). *Primer of public relations research.* New York: Guilford Press.

Stappers, J. G., Reijnders, A. D., & Möller, W. A. J. (1990). *De werking van massamedia. Een overzicht van inzichten [How media work; an overview of insights].* Amsterdam: Arbeiderspers.

Starck, K., & Kruckeberg, D. (2000). Public relations and community: A reconstructed theory revisited. In R. Heath (Ed.), *Handbook of public relations* (pp. 51–59). Thousand Oaks, CA: Sage.

Stoner, J. R. F., & Freeman, R. E. (1992). *Management* (5th ed.). Englewood Cliffs: Prentice Hall.

Susskind, L., McKearnan, S., & Thomas-Larmer, J. (Eds.). (1999). *The consensus building handbook: A comprehensive guide to reaching agreement.* Thousand Oaks, CA: Sage.

Tampere, K. (2003). *Public relations in a transition society 1989–2002.* Unpublished doctoral dissertation, University of Jyväskylä, Finland.

Thayer, L. (1987). *On communication: Essays in understanding.* Norwood, NJ: Ablex.

Tompkins, P. K. (1984). Translating organisational theory: Symbolism over substance. In F. M. Jablin, L. L. Putnam, K. H. Roberts, & L. W. Porter (Eds.), *Handbook of organizational communication: An interdisciplinary perspective* (pp. 70–96). Newbury Park, CA: Sage.

Tompkins, P. K., & Wanca-Thibault, M. (2001). Organizational communication: Prelude and prospects. In F. M. Jablin & L. L. Putnam (Eds.), *The new handbook of organizational communication: Advances in theory, research, and methods* (pp. xvii–xxxi). Thousand Oaks, CA: Sage.

Toth, E.L. (1992). The case for pluralistic studies of public relations: Rhetorical, critical and system perspectives. In E. L. Toth & R. L. Heath (Eds.), *Rhetorical and critical approaches to public relations* (pp. 3–16). Hillsdale, NJ: Erlbaum.

Toth, E. L., & Heath, R. L. (Eds.). (1992). *Rhetorical and critical approaches to public relations.* Hillsdale, NJ: Erlbaum.

Vasquez, G., & Taylor, M. (2001). Research perspectives on "the public." In R. L. Heath (Ed.), *Handbook of public relations* (pp. 139–154). Thousand Oaks: Sage.

Verčič, D., Ruler, B. van, Bütschi, G. & Flodin, B. (2001). On the definition of public relations: A European view. *Public Relations Review 27*(4), 373–387.

Vreese, C. de. (2003). *Framing Europe: Television news and European integration.* Amsterdam: Aksant.

Weaver, W. (1949). The mathematics of communication. *Scientific American, 181,* 11–15.

Weick, K. E. (1987). Theorizing about organizational vommunication. In F. M. Jablin, L. L. Putnam, K. H. Roberts, & L. W. Porter (Eds.), *Handbook of organizational communication: An interdisciplinary perspective* (pp. 97–122). Newbury Park CA: Sage.

Weick, K. E. (1995). *Sensemaking in organizations.* Thousand Oaks, CA: Sage.

White, J., & Mazur, L. (1995). *Strategic communications management: Making public relations work.* Wokingham, UK: Addison-Wesley.

Wiener, N. (1948). *Cybernetics or control and communication in the animal and the machine.* New York: Wiley.

Wiig, R. (2002). Communication models. In P. Simcic Bronn & R. Wiig (Eds.), *Corporate communication: A strategic approach to building reputation* (pp. 151–176). Oslo, Norway: Gyldendal Akademisk.

Wood, D. J. (1991). Corporate social performance revisited. *Academy of Management Review, 16,* 691–718.

Zerfass, A. (1996). Dialogkommunikation und strategische Unternehmensführung [Dialogical communication and strategic management]. In G. Bentele, H. Steinmann, & A. Zerfass (Eds.), *Dialog orientierte Unternehmenskommunikation. Grundlagen, Praxiserfahrungen, Perspektiven [Dialogue-oriented business communication: Basics, praxis, perspectives]* (pp. 23–58). Berlin: Vistas.

Zijderveld, A. C. (2000). *The institutional imperative: The interface of institutions and networks.* Amsterdam: Amsterdam University Press.

Zweekhorst, P. A. M. (2001). *Communicatiemanagers: Visies van topmanagers [Communication managers: Perspectives of top managers].* Amsterdam: Boom.

CHAPTER CONTENTS

9   Crisis, Culture, Community

BETTY KAMAN LEE
City University of Hong Kong

Crisis communication has emerged as a specialized study field for public relations scholars and an empowerment opportunity for practitioners in the past 15 years (Grunig, Grunig, & Dozier, 2002). Several loopholes in current crisis communication writings are noticeable: (a) Organizational crisis lacks a shared definition, (b) a conceptual framework has not yet developed, (c) audience-orientation to crisis communication has not been addressed, (d) current crisis studies lack contextualization, and (e) crisis communication studies are predominantly Western-based. In view of this, this chapter intends to shed some light on the topic of crisis communication and its future directions. The chapter has two parts: In the first, I revisit, refine, and reconceptualize the fundamental concepts related to crisis communication. In part two I discuss the negligence of culture in extant Western-dominated crisis communication. The chapter explains the importance of considering culture in crisis communication and points to a need for international crisis communication research and practice with an audience orientation to serve the international market foreseen in the near future. Below, I review an exemplary case contrasting Hong Kong culture and Western culture to show how the macrosystem of culture affects the microsystem of stakeholders. The contention is that the two-way symmetrical model necessitates the realization of stakeholders as interpretive communities. My suggestion of a co-constructing view to two-way symmetrical communication as a normative model for international crisis communication comes at the end of the chapter.

T he potentially catastrophic consequences and intensive local and international media coverage that a crisis could bring to an organization have aroused the attention of many scholars and practitioners on crisis communication (e.g., Barton, 1993; Benson, 1988; Cheney & Dionisopoulos, 1989; Coombs, 1995, 1998; Coombs & Holladay, 1996; Crable & Vibbert, 1986; Fearn-Banks, 1996; Marcus & Goodman, 1991; Pearson & Mitroff, 1993; Seitel, 1998). To date, crisis communication has emerged as a specialized study field for public relations scholars and an empowerment opportunity for practitioners (Grunig, Grunig, & Dozier, 2002). Extant crisis communication literature is fraught with

---

Correspondence: Betty Kaman Lee, Department of English and Communication, City University of Hong Kong, 83 Tat Chee Avenue, Room No. Y7611, Kowloon Tong, Hong Kong; email: enbetty@cityu.edu.hk

predominantly atheoretical guidelines written by practitioners. Recently, scholars have also developed a number of medium-range theories of crisis communication.

Past efforts are appreciated, but several loopholes in current crisis communication writings are evident: (a) There is a lack of shared definition of organizational crisis; (b) further theoretical conceptualizations on crisis communication are needed to organize scattered concepts into a more meaningful framework; (c) audience-orientation to crisis communication is overlooked; (d) current crisis studies are microminded and incident-specific, lacking contextualization; (e) crisis communication studies in non-Western cultures are scarce; and (f) conception of crisis communication is dominated by and unchallenged in a Western-oriented paradigm.

In part one of this chapter we revisit the fundamental concepts related to crisis communication. They include definitions of organizational crisis, types of crises and crisis categorization, management and communication perspectives to crisis research, and application of the stakeholder theory (Freeman, 1984), the systems theory (von Bertalanffy, 1968), and four public relations models (Grunig, 1989; Grunig & Grunig, 1992; Grunig & Hunt, 1984) to conceptualizing crisis communication. As the force of internationalization is inevitable in the near future, international crisis communication should be a timely topic for both crisis communication scholars and practitioners. Existing frameworks to crisis communication, however, may not be adequate to capture the dynamic mechanisms in international crisis communication. Thus I attempt in part two to expand the fundamental frameworks to better fit the context of crisis communication for the future international markets.

Also in part two, I discuss the negligence of culture in extant Western-dominated crisis communication literature, then explain the importance of culture to crisis communication, which shows a need for international crisis communication research and practice with an audience orientation. This chapter presents an exemplary case that juxtaposes Hong Kong consumers' interpretation of crisis with that of Western consumers to show how the macrosystem of the culture affects the microsystem of individual stakeholders. *Homo narrans* theory (Vasquez, 1993, 1994) expands to view stakeholders as interpretive communities, and, lastly, Deetz's (1994) notion of constitutive codetermination is discussed and integrated into the two-way symmetrical model (Grunig, 1989; Grunig & Grunig, 1992; Grunig & Hunt, 1984) to proffer a normative model for international crisis communication.

THE FUNDAMENTALS

Organizational Crisis Defined

The pool of definitions on organizational crisis (e.g., Aguilera, 1990; Barton, 1993; Coombs & Holladay, 1996; Dutton, 1986; Fearn-Banks, 1996; Fink, 1986; Hermann, 1963; Jackson & Dutton, 1987; Pearson & Clair, 1998; Quarantelli, 1988;

Shrivastava, Mitroff, Miller, & Miglani, 1988; Siomkos & Shrivastava, 1993; Slaikeu, 1990; Weick, 2001; Winter & Steger, 1998) unveils dissenting opinions among scholars on this fundamental task. The following are some definitions on organizational crisis:

> "turning point for better or worse" (Fink, 1986, p. 15);
> "a threat to an organization" (Coombs & Holladay, 1996, p. 280)
> "an unstable or critical time or state of affairs in which a decisive change is pending" (Winter & Steger, 1998, p. 32)

Three core elements characterize an organizational crisis: significant threats, unpredictability or suddenness, and urgency or immediacy (Barton, 1993; Fearn-Banks, 1996; Hermann, 1963; Lerbinger, 1997; Nelkin, 1988; Pearson, Mistra, Clair, & Mitroff, 1997). The nature of significant threat distinguishes a crisis from a problem in magnitude and scope. A crisis threat can result in such things as severe financial losses, sullied reputations, interrupted normal or routine organizational functioning, exhausted resources, loss of stakeholders' support and trust, drastic drop in sales, or extensive damage to human lives, property, natural environments, or various stakeholders, as well as threatened survival of the company (DiMaggio & Powell, 1991; Heath, 1997; Loewendick, 1993; Siomkos & Shrivastava, 1993). Actual, anticipated, or perceived threats are all emerging signs of a crisis (Seeger, Sellnow, & Ulmer, 1998).

Unpredictability or suddenness is another dimension that sounds a siren for crisis. Some scholars (e.g., Murphy, 1996; Pauchant & Mitroff, 1992; Perrow, 1999; Weick, 2001) have argued that crisis is a natural phase of an organization's developmental life cycle—that accidents are "normal" and inevitable consequences notwithstanding organizational precautions, as Perrow (1999) proclaimed. Even though it is highly probable that accidents will occur somewhere at some time in this era of organizational and technological complexity (Perrow, 1999), some aspects are largely unpredictable: (a) crises that involve an external locus of cause such as stakeholder activism, natural disasters, or product tampering; or (b) the specifics of what, when, where, and how a crisis will erupt, as well as public reaction, magnitude, scope of impact, and the like. The unknowns delineate the unpredictable and sudden nature of a crisis.

The outbreak of a crisis also provokes a sense of urgency or immediacy. The advent of new communication technologies can make any crisis that occurs anywhere a nationwide or international news story or cause for heated discussion on the internet (Coombs, 1999). New environmental pressures also draw scrutiny from stakeholders, who are becoming more involved and vocal in organizational matters. Boycotts, scrutiny, and rumor, as well as negative publicity campaigns and internet messages are all possible consequences of dawdling responses to stakeholder demands. Since the dawn of new communication technologies and the rise of stakeholder power, the compelling pressure for an organization to act promptly to contain damage and restore its image in a crisis has intensified.

The synthesis of the three dimensions of a crisis—significant threats, unpredictability or suddenness, and urgency or immediacy—distinguish a crisis from a problem by degree and nature. An organizational crisis is, hence, defined as a nonroutine, unpredictable event that imposes (a) significant threats to an organization and (b) urgency to contain and respond that often interrupts normal organizational functioning.

Types of Crises and Crisis Categorization

There are various kinds of organizational crisis (Coombs, 1999; Pearson & Clair, 1998). The sheer variety suggests the breadth of organizational vulnerabilities while new kinds of organizational crises continually emerge. Several scholars have proffered meaningful categorizations of organizational crises. Dimensions such as severe–normal damage, violent–nonviolent, intentional–unintentional, high–low deniability, and concrete–diffuse victims have been constructed and used to organize various crises (Egelhoff & Sen, 1992; Marcus & Goodman, 1991; Pearson & Mitroff, 1993).

Several scholars have attempted to use three to four categories to classify various crisis types. For instance, Coombs (1995) classified crises into four types based on Weiner's (1986) concept of locus of control: accidents (unintentional and internal), transgressions (intentional and internal), faux pas (unintentional and external), and terrorism (intentional and external). Heath (1997), on the other hand, likened a crisis to an illness in terms of the degree of severity of damage to the organization: bed rest, medication, chronic, and fatal. Lerbinger (1997) categorized various crises into three types based on their cause: crises of the physical world (e.g., natural disasters and technological flaws), crises of the human climate (e.g., labor dispute and consumer boycotting), and crises of management failure (e.g., skewed management value and misconduct).

Crisis Research

A large proportion of crisis research has been written about with the goal of teaching readers the basics of crisis management (e.g., Gottschalk, 1993), for instance, keeping the leader visible, being creative, not wearing sunglasses or chewing gum in media interviews, and the like. A major limitation of these practically oriented writings is the lack of theoretical conceptualization and perspectives to capture the momentum present in the crisis process.

Scholastically-oriented crisis literature has gradually emerged over the past decade. The management perspective first dominated organizational crisis research. Recently, the communication perspective to studying crisis has been in the ascendance. The steadily mounting interest in organizational crisis research signifies its recognized value among scholars in both academic and practical terms: Academically speaking, the distinctive nature of significant threats, suddenness, and immediacy constitutes a unique context into which scholars can delve. In terms of practicality, crisis research guides organizational personnel on crisis prevention, precautions, containment, handling, and recovery. The next section is devoted to reviewing major management approaches to crisis study. Following is a section exploring the communication perspective on crisis research.

Management Perspective to Organizational Crisis Research

Four approaches—psychological, social-political, technological–structural, and comprehensive–integrated—mark the historical development of crisis management research (Pauchant & Douville, 1994; Pearson & Clair, 1998).

The psychological approach to crisis study focuses on three areas: (1) the cognitive biases in expectation, sense making, and information processing of corporate individuals (e.g., Weick, 1988, 1993, 2001); (2) the psychological aspects, such as personality, mental health, and the unconscious elements of corporate individuals (e.g., Pauchant & Mitroff, 1992); and (3) the traumatic experiences of victims and employees (e.g., Janoff-Bulman & Freize, 1983). This approach sets to explore the causes and impact of crises at the individual level. Crisis management adopting the psychological approach would require a variety of managerial backgrounds and perspectives, readjustment of the employees' cognitive orientation and psychological tendency at the precrisis stage, and intensive support of the employee victims at the postcrisis stage (Janoff-Bulman & Freize, 1983; Pauchant & Mitroff, 1992; Weick, 1988, 1993, 2001).

Even though the psychology approach maintains that the cognitive limitations of a few or even a single individual in an organization will cause a crisis, the social–political approach suggests that a crisis results from a collective breakdown in the cultural symbols and ideologies, including shared meaning, sense making, role structuring, legitimization, and institutionalization of socially constructed relationships (O'Connor, 1987; Pearson & Clair, 1998; Weick, 1993, 2001). Crisis management adopting the social-political approach would mean preventing the breakdown in collective meanings, beliefs, and values at the precrisis stage, and reformation of organizational leadership and culture at the postcrisis stage (Hurst, 1995; O'Connor, 1987; Pearson & Clair, 1998; Weick, 1993, 2001).

The technological–structural approach recognizes the power of man-made creations. It refers to technology not only as organizational machines and tools, but also as management procedures, policies, practices, and routines (Pauchant & Douville, 1994). Differing from the psychological and social–political views on crisis, in which the occurrence of a crisis is seen as being caused by one source and is avoidable, a technological–structural approach sees a crisis as being caused by interactive, intertwined, and complex factors and recognizes that catastrophic risk is inherent in the technology and thus unavoidable (Pearson & Clair, 1998; Perrow, 1999). Adopting the technological–structural approach to crisis management would mean enhancing the structural system (e.g., added physical protection, such as retention dikes or reinforcement walls) or organizational system design (e.g., organizational safety training programs) or avoiding high-risk technologies at the precrisis stage, and, in the postcrisis stage, treating damaged individuals and properties (Pearson & Clair, 1998; Perrow, 1999).

Recently, crisis researchers such as Pearson and Clair (1998) and Coombs (1999) have argued that previous approaches to crisis management lack integration, making crisis management writings fragmented and peripheral (Coombs, 1999; Pearson & Clair, 1998). In view of this, Pearson and Clair (1998) provided a descriptive model of the crisis management process. Their integrated model takes into account (a) executive perceptions about risks (organization personnel's concern for or attention to crisis preparations), (b) environmental context (institutionalized practices and industry regulations), and (c) adoption of organizational crisis management preparations at the precrisis stage, and, in the crisis and postcrisis stages, (d) individual and collective reactions, as well as (e) planned and ad hoc responses.

The four approaches (psychological, sociopolitical, technological–structural, and comprehensive–integrated) represent different stages in the development of organizational crisis studies. The psychological approach acknowledges the cause and impact of a crisis at the individual level. Both the social–political and technological–structural approaches see the cause and consequence of a crisis at the organizational level. Despite this difference, these three approaches share a common characteristic in centering attention on the organization, or at least, the members within it. Only the comprehensive–integrated approach recognizes forces outside the organization. The focus, however, is still on the organization's regaining management and control of its environments.

Communication Perspective to Organizational Crisis Research

Fearn-Banks (1996) distinguished crisis communication from crisis management: Crisis management is

> a process of strategic planning for a crisis or negative turning point, a process that removes some of the risk and uncertainty from the negative occurrence and thereby allows the organization to be in greater control of its own destiny. (p. 2)

Crisis communication is "the communication between the organization and its publics prior to, during, and after the negative occurrence. The communications are designed to minimize damage to the image of the organization" (p. 2). Crisis management emphasizes the need to control (Pearson & Clair, 1998); crisis communication stresses the importance of communicating (Fearn-Banks, 1996). In practicality, crisis communication is a pivotal subset of crisis management. In a scholastic viewpoint, nevertheless, a communication perspective carries different underlying assumptions and emphases from a management perspective.

A communication perspective to studying organizational crises would examine the following: (a) communication processes between and among an organization and its stakeholders; (b) the impact of organizational structure and power on communication; (c) the influences of communication on an organization and its stakeholders; (d) the multiple interpretations that symbols might manifest; or (5) the impact of various factors on the communication process in precrisis, crisis, or postcrisis stages.

Research focused on crisis communication has gone through two developmental stages. During stage one, researchers identified and analyzed response strategies used in particular crises (e.g., Allen & Caillouet, 1994; Benoit, 1995), including apologies, excuses, accounts, responses to embarrassment, image restoration, and impression management (Coombs & Schmidt, 2000). At stage two, scholars shifted their attention to identifying the characteristics of crises that predict the selection of appropriate response strategies (e.g., Coombs & Holladay, 1996, 2001).

Elaborate theories have been developed on models of public relations—but public relations roles, gender and public relations, strategic management and public relations, publics, rhetoric and public relations, system theories of public relations critical theories of public relations, global public relations, internal communication, organization-public relationships, and ethics of public relations, theoretical conceptualizations of crisis communication have yet to be exploited.

Stakeholder theory (Freeman, 1984), systems theory (von Bertalanffy, 1968), chaos theory (Murphy, 1996) and excellence theory (Grunig, 1989; Grunig, 2001; Grunig & Grunig, 1992; Grunig et al., 2002: Grunig & Hunt, 1984) are frequently referenced for theoretical conceptualizations in public relations writings.

Freeman (1984) defined a stakeholder as any person or group who has interest, right, claim, or ownership and can affect the achievement of the organization's objective. The advent of the stakeholder concept has geared organizations to reconceptualize their organization–stakeholder relationships. Along with the subtle emergence of literature on corporate planning, systems theory, corporate social responsibility, and organization theory, Freeman's (1984) avowal of the centrality of the stakeholder theory to strategic management has facilitated a conceptual shift in management's perception of its environment. Since its introduction, many organizations have come to realize the danger in underestimating the stakeholder power and acting without regard to stakeholder interests (Coombs, 1999, Freeman, 1984; Post, Frederick, Lawrence, & Weber, 1996). Favorable organization-stakeholder relationships are essential for an organization to survive a crisis; and it is only in and through communication that favorable organization–stakeholder relationships can be restored. That is to say, crisis communication is doomed if (a) important stakeholders are not recognized; and (b) the significance of organization-stakeholder relationships and communication is undervalued.

Systems theory further depicted the relationship and interaction between an organization and its environments. Angelopulo (1990) coined the term *active outward orientation* to describe the degree of openness of boundary spanners of an organization, predicting that the greater the active outward orientation, the greater the organization's potential effectiveness. Grounded on open-systems theory, active outward orientation presupposes a set of basic assumptions of an organization as

(a) an interacting, interrelated whole; (b) an entity striving to maintain an awareness of the nature and potential of its relationship with the environment; (c) an entity permeating all relevant subsystems with relevant information about the environment and the organization; and (d) an entity existing proactively within its environment.

Not necessarily being direct lineages of the systems theory, various theories nonetheless were expanded, extended from, or inspired by the systems perspective (e.g., Aldrich, 1979; Grunig, 1989; Murphy, 1996; Weick, 1988). Aldrich's (1979) dimensions of organizational environments and Murphy's (1996) chaos theory extended the systems framework to describe the turbulent environment in an organizational crisis. Weick's (1988) theory of organizational enactment and Grunig's four models of public relations rendered important implications on crisis management and communication.

Adopting Aldrich's (1979) schemes, the environment of an organization in times of crisis is likely to turn into one characterized by a lean environmental capacity in which resources available in the environment for an organization to deal with the crisis are limited. This limitation of resources in the environment may be due to a crisis affecting or disturbing the environment itself, such as when they display these characteristics:

1. *Environmental heterogeneity,* in which, during a crisis, the differentiation among elements in an organization's environment becomes conspicuous in terms of degree of reactions toward the crisis and expectations on the organizations handling of the crisis. *Environmental instability* in which there is possibility of high degree of turnover in the elements in an organization's environment.

2. *Environmental dispersion,* in which, during a crisis, the resources needed to manage it are dispersed among the environments.

3. *Environmental dissent,* in which an organization's explanation of the crisis, including the causes and the damages, its understanding of its degree of control over the crisis, its way of handling the crisis, and its assessment of its performance are likely to be disputed among other organizations given the nature of environmental heterogeneity in times of crisis.

4. *Environmental turbulence,* in which an organization's environments are highly disturbed by each other given their very nature of interdependence, permeability, and negative entropy.

Murphy's (1996) chaos theory in particular captured the characteristics of postmodern societies as being constituted by forces of disorder, diversity, instability, and nonlinearity (Murphy, 1996). The instability and complexity of constantly changing environments insinuate that (a) issues perceived by the organization in precrisis stage as trivial have the ability to iterate into full-blown crises and (b) stakeholders of interest constantly change. Chaos theory suggests that uncertainty, change, plurality, and loss of control will become central to organized systems and will always dominate relations with publics during volatile times. In view of the possibility that improved research and measurement may not improve outcome in time of unpredictability, chaos theory calls for more sensitive and sophisticated communication at pre- and postcrisis stages vis-à-vis the complex and interactive patterns among the stakeholder systems and the organizational systems and between intrasystems within the organization. In this sense, the nonroutine exigencies of organizational crisis bring about unanticipated outcomes that could be emancipative and threatening.

Both Aldrich (1979) and Murphy (1996) contributed to the conceptualization of the turbulent environment during a crisis. Murphy's (1996) chaos theory particularly captured the nature of increasing environmental complexity of modern times, which calls for increased reflexivity, internal complexity, context sensitivity, patience, and careful timing. Both Aldrich (1979)'s and Murphy's (1996) works helped raise the conceptualization of organizational crises to a more theoretical level. They nevertheless do not address the mechanisms involved in organizational management and communication in times of crisis.

Weick's (1988, 1993, 2001) enactment-based model of organizing went beyond the conventional systems concept of crisis management–communication as reactive activities to suggest an enactment view of seeing crisis management–communication as proactive activities. Seeing that the hazardous events are not necessarily given nor inherent in organized activity, Weick (2001) maintained that the development of crises is indeterminate rather than fixed and that "crisis management can mean quick action that deflects a triggering event as it unfolds rather than delayed action that mops up after the triggering event has run its course" (p. 233).

Weick (1988) also identified three major factors that affect organizational sense making: organizational members' capacity to perceive, their expectations, and public commitments. Given the increasingly diverse environment, Weick (1988) called for the requisite variety (a condition in which a system maintains the internal complexity necessary to cope with external complexity in the environment, von Bertalanffy, 1968) of managerial background and perspective. Weick (1988) also warned that organizational personnel's expectations are subject to self-fulfilling prophecies and that, once public relations responses were made public, especially in the critical moments of precrisis commitments and postcrisis responses, denials of or undoing responses are impossible.

Weick's (1988, 1993, 2001) notion of organizing went beyond the conventional systems thinking of reactive crisis communicative tactics and retrospective accounting, to proactive crisis communicative strategies and prospective thinking. Its contribution notwithstanding, Weick's (1988, 2002) model was management focused and internally oriented and failed to address the communicative essences and dynamic nature of crisis communication between an organization and its external stakeholders. Grunig's (1989) four public relations models, arguably the unique theory of and for public relations, extended the systems perspective to provide a descriptive and normative framework for public relations practice between organization systems and their stakeholder systems in real organizational communication contexts. This chapter attempts to apply these four general models of public relations to the context of organizational crisis.

Four Public Relations Models

Grunig's (1989) four models of public relations supplemented the systems perspective to delineate various communicative mechanisms between organizations and stakeholders in real contexts. Specifically, Grunig's (1989) four models of public relations are further elaborated here to depict in detail: (a) the mindsets of the organization in perceiving the crisis at hand and (b) the organization's perceived solutions to the crisis.

Model 1, the press agentry–publicity model, suggested that organizations that adopt this model in times of crisis would probably underplay the possible damage of its image and reputation due to a crisis. Public relations is a one-way manipulative communication practice; as a result, organizations are likely to disregard the external environment and the reactions of its stakeholders. They are likely to provide their version of stories, even if they are half-true, twisted, incomplete, or false. A sense of responsibility is very low or absent (Grunig, 1989, p.39). The impact of the crisis on the society is not a concern. Hence, organizations are likely to underestimate the destructive potential and consequences of a crisis brought to the stakeholders because the crisis is "their own business," not that of others. With such a mindset, organizations are unlikely to be alert for, or get prepared for, any crises. Organizations adopting the press agentry–publicity model are likely to be the most crisis-prone organizations (Pauchant & Mitroff, 1992).

Model 2, the public information model, is characterized by the mindset that public relations means positive information dissemination. Organizations that adopt the public information model would not deny the significance of crisis. They would, however, attempt to tone it down by avoiding the dissemination of negative information. "No comment" would probably be a frequently used phrase by officials in these organizations. In general, these organizations would prefer to function in a closed system when a crisis strikes and to avoid the media. They would react passively to questions by stakeholders and media. Crisis communication and management may equal the control of the outflow of negative information to the stakeholders. As this model is also one-way, organizations that adopt the public information model effectly disregard stakeholders' reactions in times of crisis—although that may not be their intent.

In Model 3, the two-way asymmetrical model, the main characteristic is that it seeks two-way communication between the organization and its stakeholders because the organization's management intends to persuade its stakeholders. Organizations adopting the two-way asymmetrical model during crisis attempt to produce messages to calm down irate stakeholders. They aim to gauge their stakeholders' reactions toward the crisis in order to take control of the situation. Their priority, then, is to produce persuasive messages to the stakeholders rather than to reduce the impact of the crisis on the stakeholders and on the environment. They are not prepared to make any real behavioral changes to adapt to the demands of the environments. Thinking they know the best, organization management focuses on persuading stakeholders to take its side. Crisis communication is mainly a persuasion task.

Model 4, the two-way symmetrical model, in essence is organizations, by communicating with their stakeholders, seeking ways that are beneficial to both sides. Organizations that use the two-way symmetrical model recognize the interdependent relationships between the organizations themselves and their stakeholders. Realizing the importance of symmetrical communication, they would seek to know stakeholders' expectations and demands of action in times of crisis. They are concerned about the impact of crisis on the stakeholders and on the environment as much as on themselves. It is the belief of the organization that conflicts be resolved through communication, which requires participation of the parties involved through cooperation, not through manipulation or force. These organizations would be willing to change their behavior to adapt to the demands of the crisis. Indeed, these organizations would do their best to reduce the effects of crisis on the stakeholders. Interactive feedback between the organization and their stakeholders would continue in the postcrisis stage. Organizations using this model are likely to obtain stakeholders' acclaim in their handling of the crisis.

The press agentry–publicity model, public information model, and the two-way asymmetrical model are organization-centered approaches to crisis communication that largely ignores possible negative damage to society (Grunig, 1989). Even though these three models may seem to function in normal routine periods, the irresponsible and unsympathetic side of an organization easily manifests itself in times of crisis. From a system perspective, the system of the organization cannot resume when the systems of its stakeholders, upon which the organization is interdependent, are still in a haphazard state, disrupted by the sudden occurrence of a crisis. The two-way asymmetrical model may appear to be effective only when behavioral changes are not required (Grunig, 1989). When the pressing demands of stakeholders are incompatible with the organization's culture, ideologies, practices, or expertise, the organization would disregard the needs and expectations of the environments. Such a response (or rather, lack of response) would have the same negative effects, disappointment from the public and a decrease in organizational image or reputation, as the other two one-way models would. Thus, the two-way asymmetrical model would, in the end, prove to be superficial and deficient in handling crisis.

Grunig and her associates (2002) reported that in some cases, crises stimulate organizations to turn to a symmetrical approach because the CEOs realize that an asymmetrical approach to crisis communication would be too costly. Their research suggests that the two-way symmetrical model (or mixed-motive model of public relations coined by Grunig, 2001 and Grunig, Grunig, & Dozier, 2002) is the only excellence model, in terms of ethical considerations and effectiveness, for crisis communication. They also found that organizations often come to appreciate the value and expertise of public relations practicing two-way symmetrical communication with stakeholders in times of crisis.

In view of the paucity of work in conceptualizing crisis communication, the first part of this chapter encompasses attempts to overview extant literature, identify and define concepts, outline major approaches, and organize literature into a more meaningful conceptual framework. Such retrospective work is meaningful only if it can be geared to prospective directions for crisis communication researchers. It would simply be ironic for crisis communication researchers, who often advocate the value of being proactive and sensitive, not to ask the question of what's next?

In their article, Seeger, Sellnow, and Ulmer (2001) alluded to the following topics for future directions on crisis communication research: (a) the implications of chaos theory (Murphy, 1996) for issue management and post crisis responses; (b) the importance of unanticipated or poorly understood linkages, nonlinear cause-effect relationships, and unconventional patterns in crisis development; (c) the effects of organizational crisis as bifurcation points; (d) the role of stakeholder relationships in crisis development and management; and (e) the role of deep structures or attractors in public relations responses. Culture is left out of the crisis communication sphere as a topic for future studies.

International crisis communication still remains an ill-fated topic in crisis communication literature the fact that the forces driving internationalization are ubiquitous, inevitable, and irresistible. Culbertson and Chen's (1996) criticism that international public relations remains Western-focused and lacks new perspectives, and Grunig et al.'s (2002) advocacy for public relations professionals taking culture into account when they apply the excellence principles raise a stream of questions pertinent to international crisis communication: What kind of theoretical concepts are applicable in conceptualizing international crisis communication? How does culture play a role in crisis communication? How does international crisis communication bring new insights to crisis communication study in the future?

FUNDAMENTAL EXPANDED

Culture Matters

The public relations domain mentions culture, yet it remains largely untouched as a research topic. That international crisis communication is underdeveloped, if not undeveloped, reflects either insensitivity or ethnocentrism in the current crisis communication field. As there are many organizations, businesses, products, and services that have become international, it is just a matter of time before crises will go international as well. In addition to the chaos and havoc comes the unwanted media spotlight. If an organization is dealing with publics of another culture, whose expressions, communications, reactions, and expectations during an organizational crisis are disparate to those of the organization, the organization must deal with both a local crisis and an international crisis. Crisis communication researchers and practitioners nonetheless seem reluctant to envision crisis as being as likely to occur across cultural borders as it is in the domestic territories of international organizations.

The negligence of international crisis communication may also reflect under-lying ethnocentrism among researchers and practitioners. Culbertson and Chen (1996) commented that extant literature on international public relations

> has tended to focus on how those working for western organizations . . . could best practice abroad. While useful, such writings have focused on adaptation of Western approaches, not on development of new ones designed specifically for varied sociocultural settings around the world. (p. 2)

Wakefield (1996) also pointed out that "American organizations often place their own personnel and management techniques into other countries and demand standardization. This approach reflects the 'America knows best' cultural world-view that is harmful in international dealings" (p. 25). The scarcity of internation-al crisis communication writings may reflect a Western-dominated practice both organizationally and ideologically, but international crisis communication is not a simple transfer of Western crisis communication practices to new territories. In such a mindset (Stohl, 2001) insidiously lie a convergence perspective, an ethno-centric worldview, and Western hegemony.

Crisis communication researchers and practitioners may slip into the trap of ethnocentrism without intending to. For instance, are Western practitioners who practice the two-way symmetrical model in the Western style of bargaining, ne-gotiating, and conflict resolving with Asian stakeholders engaging in symmetrical communication? That was not what was intended; nevertheless, Asian stakehold-ers may view the effects as one-way, asymmetrical, and ethnocentric.

Brinkerhoff and Ingle's (1989) theory of structured flexibility introduced the concepts, generic principles, and specific applications to organization manage-ment. Verčič, Grunig, and Grunig (1996) borrowed the concepts and suggested that international public relations practices share generic principles across cul-tures with specific applications varying in the different cultures. Applying Verčič, Grunig, and Grunig's (1996) idea, the two-way symmetrical model should work normatively across cultures as a generic principle. What constitutes symmetrical communication (e.g., the forms and styles of negotiating, bargaining, negotiat-ing, compromising, and conflict resolution), however, should be subject to spe-cific cultural principles. Insensitivity to such specific cultural principles would be perceived as ethnocentrism and result in ineffective strategic communication in international public relations. In times of international crisis, such cultural negli-gence may introduce further complications to an already acute situation.

Culture and Crisis Communication—An Unexploited Sphere

When acknowledging culture, the extant public relations writings regard it as a factor influencing public relations development and practices. Grunig (1992) introduced a model that recognized that a society's culture impacts organization-al culture, which in turn, affects the choice of a public relations model and the worldview of public relations for an organization. This model became an archetype that represented, if not guided, the line of thought of subsequent comparative-analysis research on public relations practices.

Studies have examined how culture influences public relations development and practices outside the United States. Countries and cultures that have been studied include Slovenia (Verčič, Grunig, & Grunig, 1996); Africa, Malaysia, and Singapore (Leuven & Pratt's 1996); India (Newsom, 1996; Sriramesh, 1996); China (Chen, 1996); Thailand (Ekachai, 1995; Ekachai & Komolsevin, 1996); Philippines (Jamais, Navarro, & Tuazon, 1996); Japan (Cooper-Chen, 1996); Saudi Arabia (Alanazi, 1996); Costa Rica (González & Akel, 1996); South and Central America (Sharpe & Simoes, 1996); Finland (Kanso, 1996); Romania (Turk, 1996); Germany (Bentele & Peter, 1996); Europe (Hazleton & Kruckeberg, 1996); Austria and Norway (Coombs, Holladay, Hasenauer, & Signitzer, 1994); and Korea (Kim & Hon, 1998).

This list may create the illusion of adequate cultural divergence in public relations research. The fact that culture has rarely been addressed as an equally dynamic force in influencing stakeholders in times of crisis, though, indicates a confined conceptualization of culture. To date, we know surprisingly little about what stakeholders of other cultures expect and how they evaluate and express themselves during an organizational crisis. If international crisis communication is about communicating with stakeholders of other cultures in times of acute situations, what kind of communication will that be if the cultures of the stakeholders are not in the conscious minds of the public relations practitioners? This sustained neglect has been particularly extraordinary in view of internationalizing forces, the frequent occurrence of organizational crises, the existing aspirations to the two-way symmetrical model, and the potentially prosperous markets in Asia (especially China) in the future (Grunig, 1989; Grunig & Grunig, 1992; Grunig et al., 2002; Grunig & Hunt, 1984). Thus, an audience-oriented approach to international crisis communication is indispensable to the realization of true two-way symmetrical communication. Neglecting the dynamic, interactive momentum between the macrosystem of culture and the microsystem of the stakeholders could beget false interpretations and conclusions, as well as result in crisis mishandling.

The next section is an exemplary case that contrasts Western consumers with Chinese consumers to illustrate how culture is interwoven into stakeholder systems.

Asian Consumers

Schütte (2001) maintained that despite globalization, regional culture remains the strongest influence on consumer behavior. He further challenged the assumption that similar needs and desires drive consumers around the world, and that consumer behaviour is universal. In fact, a study conducted by Lasserre and Probert (2001) showed that Western expatriate managers working in China, Taiwan, Japan, South Korea, Thailand, Singapore, Thailand, Vietnam, Malaysia, and Indonesia all agreed that business rules of the West would not work there.

The prosperous Asian market (especially the China market) foreseen in the future has ignited interest from multinational corporations to understand Asian consumers. Western literature on Asian consumers, however, is sparse. No attempt has been made to understand Asian consumers' evaluation and expectation in an organizational crisis. The few extant studies on Asian consumers are mostly marketing-oriented, focusing on examining Asian consumption attitudes, lifestyle values, consumption trends, and consumption behaviour (e.g., Yasue & Gu, 2001). Some researchers even studied what letters, names, and numbers are favorably perceived by Asian consumers (Ang, 2001; Chan, 1990). Such an asymmetrical, marketing-oriented mindset often leads to a shallow, if not inaccurate, understanding of Asian consumers.

Schütte (2001) pointed out that Asian consumers may buy luxurious brand-name goods for different reasons: For instance, they may buy premium brands more for face reasons and the regard of others than from an individual preference for the product. Further, Asian consumers may appear less active and vocal in a crisis than their Western counterparts because they were less willing to use boycott or protest to express their disappointment (Lee, 2001a). To interpret such behavior as being acquiescent, however, would be a mistake. Lee (2001a) found in her study that Hong Kong consumers were critical and analytical in their evaluation of an organizational crisis. Even though they did not engage in collective boycotts or protests, they expressed strong rejection to organizations that they perceived as problematic and irresponsible. Thus, interpreting consumer behavior without taking into account the underlying cultural factors may lead to erroneous deductions.

Given the drastic political, economic, and sociocultural changes in the past 10 years in the Asian regions, simply characterizing Asian consumers as being collectivistic and "Confucian," as most Western literature does, becomes inadequate to capture the modern Asian cultural essence. Recent studies have identified several major common trends among Asian consumers (Yasue & Gu, 2001).

First, Asian consumers' desire for foreign brands or big brand names has weakened drastically and shifted toward value-oriented brands. French and Crabbe (1998) coined the term "the China brand syndrome" to describe the shift from adoration of Western brands to a gradual acceptance of local brands. Some Chinese consumers have started to perceive some Chinese brands as good and on a par with Western brands. Foreign goods no longer win instant kudos just because they are foreign (French & Crabbe, 1998). Consumers are no longer holding what Sheridan (1999) called in the title of his book, "Asian values, Western dreams." Rather, acceptance of local, mid-market brands is the new Asian consumer sentiment (Speece & So, 1998). Advertising creators have begun to use localization strategy toward becoming less obviously Western but more appealing in tune with local culture (Speece & So, 1998).

Second, Asian consumers have become more cautious and mature in their buying decisions (Yasue & Gu, 2001). Asian consumers were once described as the "most image-conscious consumers in the world," being motivated by the need to gain social recognition (Schütte, 2001, p. 1). They have recently shifted away from pure price consciousness toward a greater value and quality orientation (Speece & So, 1998). Even though many Asian consumers have attained a certain level of affluence, reports indicate that the frantic mood for consumption has cooled down since 1995, partly due to the Asian economic crisis and partly due to an increased demand in product quality (Capon & Ho, 1999; Speece & So, 1998).

The increased acceptance of local–Asian brands and the emphasis of quality over brands suggest an emerging sophistication in Asian consumers. These changes may remain unnoticed to Western researchers and practitioners because most Asian consumers are less vocal of their expectations, demands, and opinions on corporations in public arena than their Western counterparts. Using the Western cultural paradigm to interpret Asian consumers' behavior in a crisis is likely to be doomed to fail.

An Exemplary Case: Hong Kong Consumers Versus Western Consumers

There have been innumerable cases throughout history in which Western consumers' strong emotions and opinions threatened the well-being of organizations.

In contrast, Chinese consumers have demonstrated a quieter and seemingly passive act against organizational crisis (Lee, 2001a, 2002, 2004). Although boycotts and protests are common practices in Western culture, Chinese consumers expressed reluctance in involving in boycotts and protests against organizations. However, Lee's (2001, 2002, 2004) studies showed that such reluctance was not an indication of consumer indifference or acquiescence, but a different sociocultural orientation.

Lee's (2004) study found that Hong Kong consumers are indeed cognitively and emotionally involved in organizational crisis, asserting that as potential customers, they are entitled to know the details of the incident. They tend to engage in in-depth, step-by-step (hierarchical), and active evaluation processing, although their behaviors do not show that. Like their Western counterparts, Chinese consumers express severe and long-term loss in trust and purchase intention in the organization held accountable for a crisis (Lee, 2002). They voice out that an irresponsible organization needs to be punished. Nevertheless, they indicate a reluctance to use boycott or protest as a form of punishment. Instead, they often resort to individual "boycott" rather than collective protest. Chinese consumers' seemingly rational acts contrast with Western consumers' more passionate acts, but all should be viewed in sociocultural contexts.

Western consumers' intense involvement in organizational matters could be traced back to their long history of consumer movement, success in consumer boycotts and protests, and democratic environments (Newsom, Turk, & Kruckeberg, 1998; Winter & Steger, 1998). By 1971, four national consumer organizations had been initiated by American consumers, presenting a potent counterbalance to corporate interests: the Consumer Federation of America, the Nader Organization, the National Consumers League, and the Consumers Union. These organizations are well-structured and organized, encompassing a large number of members. The Consumer Federation of American, for example, currently brings together over 200 groups, representing some 30 million Americans, and defends consumer interests. Formation of these large consumer coalitions signified the emergence of Western consumers into an active consumer–political force engaging the strategy of using the government to reshape corporate affairs.

Since the late 1960s, the Western consumer movement has become stronger, more unified, and more politically significant. Confrontation with businesses proliferated at that time. It was the heyday of consumerism. The sentiment behind consumerism during this period was dissatisfaction and frustration with being cheated by inaccurate and dishonest advertising claims, poor quality or dangerous products, poor after-sales service and repairs, and misleading packaging or labeling. Consumer tactics included media blitzes, class action suits, boycotts, defiant rallies, injunctions, and grassroots lobbying of government agencies (Heath, 1997).

Entering the 1980s, Western consumer movements started to raise concerns about protecting the environment (Newsom, Turk, & Kruckeberg, 1998; Winter & Steger, 1998). Incidents, such as the Three Mile Island nuclear meltdown in 1979, the discovery of Star-Kist's killing of dolphins in 1988, and the Exxon Valdez oil spill in 1989, provoked antagonism from consumers. More and more people joined the movement to save the environment by reacting to the Three Mile Island incident. Consumers started to cancel Exxon credit cards after the Valdez incident because they were disappointed with how Exxon handled the oil spill crisis. A tuna boycott against Star-Kist was initiated after it was publicized that while tuna fishing, Star Kist's supplier killed hundreds of dolphins. Consumers also started to monitor business ethics in the early 1980s. A classic case is the boycott against the Nestle Corporation for its infant formula marketing in less developed countries.

In the 1990s, the consumer movement had come to concentrate its attention on virtually every aspect of human life touched by business. The concern with ethics and environmental protection continued to rise (Heath, 1997). Boycotts, demonstrations, and protests emerged as righteous acts to confront and resist corporate wrongdoing. Examples included PUSH's (People United to Serve Humanity) boycott of Nike shoes due to their exploitation of minorities in 1990; consumers' pressuring Intel to exchange the flawed version of the Pentium chip in 1995; a call for a national boycott against Calvin Klein for possibly engaging in child pornography in advertising its denim line in 1995; a boycott in 1995 on all Gillette products and the products of its subsidiaries (e.g., Oral B) because of its use of animals in product safety tests; and the launching of the McSpotlight website in 1996, accusing McDonald's of promoting ill-health, destroying animal welfare, causing environmental damage, exploiting children through advertising, and paying employees low wages (Fearn-Banks, 1996; Winter & Steger, 1998).

This almost 40 years of effort has rendered Western consumers great power to bring organizations under fire for not taking stands on issues deemed important by the public. Western consumers have evolved from protecting themselves against exploitation and manipulation by fraudulent advertisements and poor quality of products, to a concern for others victimized by organizations' socially irresponsible and unethical practices in such areas as environmental damage, misconduct of personnel, exploitation of minorities, and immoral influence. Today, no organizations would dare to underestimate the power of the Western consumer. The Consumer Union, founded in 1936 to test products across a wide spectrum of industries, publishes a magazine called *Consumer Reports,* which reaches about 3.5 million American consumers per month. Another organization, the Consumer Federation of America, now has more than 260 organizations throughout the U.S., with a combined membership exceeding 50 million people, to lobby for proconsumer legislation.

In many Chinese-based communities, consumerism is still in its infancy stage. Western consumerism had already started to emerge in the 1920s, becoming strong and unified by the early 1960s, but the development of consumerism in Hong Kong showed a different pace and pattern. There has not been one formal consumer-initiated organization in Hong Kong to protect consumer rights. In a U.S. consumer bill of rights from 1962, President Kennedy stated that "every consumer has four basic rights, the right to be informed, the right to safety, the right to choose, and the right to be heard" (Lerbinger, 1997; Newsom et al., 1998). It was not until 1974 that the Hong Kong government founded the Consumer Council.

The Consumer Council became the only official organization for consumer matters in Hong Kong. The Council's main financial source is an annual government subvention. The governor of Hong Kong appoints the chairman, vice chairman, and members. The Council was established at the time of inflationary prices and widespread public concern about profiteering. When it was set up in 1974, its duty was confined to dealing with consumer issues relating to goods, but not services. It wasn't until a year later that the functions of the Council were extended to handle both. In 1992, protection of the interests of purchasers, mortgagors, and lessees of immovable property was added to the function list. In July 1994, the scope of the Council's functions extended to the goods and services provided by public utility and transport companies, broadcasting companies, and statutory bodies. In dealing with consumer complaints, the Council mainly plays a mediating role between the trader and the consumer by examining the causes of the complaint as well as proposing ways to resolve the dispute. When no resolution is reached, the Council will advise the consumer to pursue the case further through legal action. The most the Council can do, when faced with continuous corporate practices that are detrimental to the consumer, is to resort to public censure by naming the trader publicly (Consumer Council, n.d.).

The nature and functions of the Consumer Council reflect the infancy stage of the consumer culture in Hong Kong. The absence of law enforcement and investigative power forces the Consumer Council to play a mild, symbolic role in protecting and promoting the interests of consumers. Even though the Consumer Council has been around for 26 years, Hong Kong is still lagging behind advanced jurisdictions in regard to consumer legal protection against deceptive, misleading, and unfair practices such as bait advertising. Consumer victims often have to rely on themselves to plead for common law action against fraud by proving justifiable or material deceptive representation, including proving evil intent to defraud by the seller.

In contrast, consumer protection laws in Australia, the U.K., and the U.S. provide prohibitions and sanctions against bait-and-switch advertising, failing to supply after accepting payment, and harassment and coercion. Under the laws in these countries, a seller is obliged to have reasonable grounds to be able to supply the goods or services as advertised (Lee, 2001b). Over half of the consumer complaints in Hong Kong would have been prima facie actionable under trade practices laws in Australia, the U.K., and the U.S. (Lee, 2001b).

The inadequacy of consumer protection in Hong Kong has made consumer victims wary to pursue a fraud case. Hong Kong consumers have to depend on the mercy of the sellers on refunds and exchanges. The emergence of consumer forces in a society has to be grounded on a mature and supportive system to protect individual consumers' own economic interest. Consumerism in countries such as Australia, the U.K., and U.S. have already advanced to a mature stage—but Hong Kong, despite proclaiming herself a metropolitan city, remains at the infancy stage in consumer matters (Lee, 2001b).

An unsupportive environment for consumer culture as such explains why Hong Kong consumer activities are still confined to individual complaints on deceptive and unfair trade practices, misleading pricing, false or misleading representation, accepting payment without intention to supply, and bait and switch. Organized and collective actions such as boycotts and protests against corporate wrongdoings are unintelligible and unimaginable to Hong Kong consumers.

Given the almost antithesis of consumer cultures, Hong Kong consumers perceive the functions and effectiveness of boycott differently from their Western counterparts. In Western society, consumers see boycotts and protests as a way to hold business accountable for their activities or inactions (Winter & Steger, 1998). They see boycotting and demonstrating as an organized and effective means of expressing public grievances to a company. As such, boycotts are common and have evolved into more varied forms. In general, there are two common forms of boycotts in Western society: "bargaining chips" and "end-in-itself" (Gelb, 1995). In bargaining chip, boycott consumers advocate pressure to increase the bargaining power of certain social, exploited groups. In the case of the end-in-itself mode, consumers boycott simply to punish an organization or to reduce consumption of a certain product. Here the goal is not to increase the bargaining power of a social group, but to express their anger at some organizational misdeed. The varied forms of boycott in Western society demonstrate the political power and sophistication of Western consumerism. Throughout the history of Western consumerism, boycotts have shown to be an effective means to change organizations' decisions and actions. The success of many consumer boycotts in the West has further reinforced its perceived effectiveness among consumers.

Hong Kong consumers demonstrate a different attitude toward boycotts. From the result of Lee's (2004) study, it was found that Hong Kong consumers see the ultimate purpose of punishment to be the future improvement of the organization rather than the release of anger or disappointment. As such, punishment in the form of monetary fines or boycott is perceived as less meaningful and effective than the resolution of the problem or a guarantee of reform or restructure.

Other societal–cultural factors interplaying with Chinese consumer systems further explain the contrasts with Western systems: (a) Public and collective action of any kind has been subtly, if not openly, guarded against by the Hong Kong government to ensure that it would not become politically threatening; (b) the social climate in Hong Kong discourages large-scale protests and demonstrations; (c) Hong Kong has had several painful experiences throughout her history in which small protests turned into uncontrollable and violent riots; d) Hong Kong consumers have a learned helplessness because they have not experienced a case in which their expression of negative emotions successfully brought about changes in organizational acts; (e) there is no consumer-initiated organization to protect their consumer rights; (f) the Consumer Council, the only formal organization for consumer matters, merely acts as an advisory and information-disseminating entity and does not have investigation and law enforcement power; and (g) Chinese culture values silence and emotional restraint as acts of wisdom.

It is ironic that Hong Kong is often characterized by its consuming culture, but its consumer culture lags far behind her Western counterparts. This is reflected in two levels: firstly, the regulative level, referring to (a) the limited power and (b) the limited scope of the consumer protection laws; and secondly, the societal level—reflected by (a) the low degree of recognition of consumer power as a potential political, economical, and social force; (b) low intention of executing consumer power; and (c) the absence of collective power among Chinese consumers.

Faced with an organizational crisis, Hong Kong consumers display seemingly quieter and more passive behavior than Western consumers. Even so, recent studies (Lee, 2001a, 2002) show that Hong Kong consumers are indeed involved in organizational crisis, asserting that they are entitled to know both as citizens and consumers. When asked to comment on organizational crisis, Hong Kong consumers engaged in in-depth, step-by-step (hierarchical), and active evaluation processes, even when their behavior did not show that. Concern about organizational crisis centers on two main questions: Why did the crisis occur? How did the organization deal with the incident? Their criteria for good crisis handling are (a) promptness of crisis response, (b) detailed explanation and dissemination of information, (c) sincere apology, (d) compensation, (e) proper arrangement for people affected, (f) consistency in response, (g) willingness of the organization to bear crisis responsibility, (h) activity, (i) ability to minimize chaos, (j) high degree of crisis preparedness, and (k) future-oriented mindset and plan (Lee, 2001a).

Like their Western counterparts, Hong Kong consumers hold a standard for organizational crisis-handling and express severe and long-term loss of trust and purchase intention in the organization responsible for a crisis. They often just choose an individual boycott rather than collective protest. It would be a serious mistake for Western crisis communication practitioners to use their Western-cultural paradigm, to decode this seemingly emotionless activity as an absence of consumer grievance and react as such. Without taking into account the macroculture systems of the stakeholders, crisis communication is doomed to fail.

The Western-Hong Kong contrast discussed above demonstrates the dynamic momentum between the macrosystem of culture and the micr system of the stakeholders in a crisis situation. Culture plays a significant role in influencing stakeholders' expectations, communication, reactions, and expressions in a crisis situation. Crisis communication with stakeholders from a different culture necessitates two-way symmetrical communication with an audience orientation. What constitutes "two-way" and "symmetry," however, is subject to cultural influence, hence the need to reconceptualize the two-way symmetrical model to better guide international crisis communication. The subsequent sections are attempts to expand the two-way symmetrical model with an audience orientation and a co-constructing framework for the international crisis communication context in the future.

Stakeholders as Interpretive Communities

McQuail (1997) pointed out that the conception of the audience has evolved in mass communication research from one that characterized the audience as a passive and disconnected mass to one that recognizes audience members as active, resistant to influence, guided by their own concerns, and contextualized individual beings. In the public relations field, scholars have conceptualized audience as publics for more than 20 years, most prominently, in the *situational theory of publics*, which maintains that publics, the segments of stakeholder categories, are the most important components of the environment of an organization (Grunig, 1997; Grunig & Repper, 1992). Notably, the *audience-oriented approach* to crisis communication research and practice is rarely mentioned or conducted.

McLeod (2000) identified two major obstacles that continue to plague progress in audience research for the past 50 years. The first is a lack of concern with audience conceptualization and measurement, with the focus being on the medium rather than the audiences. Consequently, audiences are treated as a clustered, common, passive mass. Second, there is a lack of connection between social structural antecedents. McLeod (2000) attributed such lack of connection to the rigidity of the epistemological and methodological traditions that separate behavioral, critical, and cultural scholars. He contended that behavioral researchers, trained in a social psychology paradigm, often overlook the macrolevels of social networks, community, society, and culture on audience behavioral outcomes. Critical and cultural scholars, on the other hand, bear the underlying assumption that the macroaspects of political, economic, or cultural controls exert an overarching effect that affects everyone in the same manner. McLeod (2002) avowed that efforts to connect the macro- to the microaspects of audience pattern would signify progress in the communication field.

McLeod's (2000) point of view proffers insights to future crisis communication research that (a) the conceptualization of audience needs to be constantly reviewed, challenged, and revised; and (b) the interaction and interactivity of the macrolevels of political, economic, or sociocultural mechanisms with the microlevels of audience patterns need to be recognized.

Echoing McLeod's (2000) point of view, crisis communication scholars are reminded that stakeholders are interpretive communities and that message effects lie as much (or more) in the audiences as in the message. Audience-oriented approach to crisis communication research is scarce, with most of the existing crisis communication research focusing on the identification and analysis of crisis responses adopted by the organization in each crisis case (e.g. Hallahan, 2002; Hearit, 1994; Ice, 1991; Ihlen, 2002). Among the Western-based crisis communication studies (e.g. Coombs, 1998; Coombs & Holladay, 1996, 2001; Coombs & Schmidt, 2000), focus has been on some specific effects such as the effects of crisis types, crisis responsibility, organization performance history, relationship history, or crisis responses to some respondents' perceptions of an organization (e.g., image of an organization, crisis responsibility, reputation), overlooking the activity of the stakeholders as well as the dynamic nature of the crisis communication process. One could reasonably argue that Grunig's (1989) two-way symmetrical model would never come to realization if the activity of the stakeholders is not recognized and acknowledged.

Vasquez's (1993, 1994) homo narrans theory of publics is herein referenced to conceptualize publics as interpretive communities in the context of international crisis communication. Vasquez's (1993, 1994) homo narrans perspective offers a communication-centered view of a public as a rhetorical community that emerges over time though discussion, debate, or argument. These communication interactions cultivate, raise, and sustain a group consciousness developed around an issue of concern. An underlying assumption of this theory is that individuals are motivated to engage in a symbolic communication process to make sense of their world. The public's view of the event represents the symbolic reality resulting from the communication process of message initiation, configuration, and reconfiguration. The homo narrans perspective represents a recent effort to view the public as a communication phenomenon.

The homo narrans perspective contributes to a new view of a public. It expands the view of an individual and goes beyond the traditional view of an individual as an aggregation of social–psychological variables, to address the dynamic and communicative nature of the public. Borrowing Vasquez's (1993, 1994) homo narrans perspective, I suggested herein that stakeholders be conceptualized as interpretive communities in organizational crisis context.

To conceptualize stakeholders as interpretive communities does not negate the communicative nature of a public, but pays more attention to stakeholders' interpreting mechanisms (and abilities), which should arguably precede group communication activities (although new interpretations may be derived after communal exchanges of meanings). At the onset of an organizational crisis, stakeholders' interpretation mechanisms are enacted to make interpretations regarding (a) the event (e.g. locus of cause, crisis responsibility, impact); (b) the organization (e.g. organizational responsibility; crisis handling); and (c) other stakeholders' evaluation and reaction. Stakeholders' interpretations keep evolving and are subject to dynamic influences of culture and accumulated communication activities with stakeholder members. A symbolic crisis reality (crisis, organization, and other stakeholder members' evaluation and reaction) is derived from stakeholders' interpreting activities that guide their own evaluation and reaction.

Conceptualizing stakeholders as interpretive addresses the active, autonomous, and cognitive nature of audiences. Stakeholders also emerge in communities (or imagined communities) rather than in disconnected anonymities. Their sense of community is cultivated by the sense of shared symbolic reality and perceived common interest through rhetorical activities.

Two implications derived from the realization of the more active, autonomous role of the audiences as interpretive communities. First, to study effects concerning just behavior outcomes (e.g., behaviors, attitudes) of stakeholder audiences would become far less meaningful than to look at the process involved in stakeholders' interpretation and construction of the meanings in an organizational crisis. Secondly, stakeholders are no longer individuals, but community members, embedded in the community property of interpretive communities. These community-constituted interpreters would constitute the communal nature of the interpretive act (Fish, 1989). Fish (1989) explained that the reality one knows is indeed the function of the community of which one is a part , that the thoughts one has are conditioned by that community, and one cannot think beyond the limits imposed by the culture.

Culture plays a significant role in defining and constituting community. Community in individualistic cultures contrasts sharply with community in collectivistic culture: Whereas consumer communities in the West are large, political, and organized for a specific (or exclusive) purpose, formal consumer communities are all but nonexistent in Hong Kong. As a collectivistic ethnicity, Chinese function in collective unities that place high priority on social relationships with family, relatives, and friends constituting their core units of community (Bond, 1997; Hampden-Turner & Trompenaars, 1993). This community is the source of rapport and opinions of all kinds. Bonding with this community is strong, sometimes to the extent of being exclusive (Bond, 1997). Communities in Hong Kong are small in size, scattered, exclusive, and apolitical, yet strongly bonded, personal, and multipurpose. The opinions shared, brought out, and solidified in the discursive processes among these community members during an organizational crisis may be no less powerful than those in Western consumer communities.

Hence, boycotts, complaints, and loss of trust could take place within and among the many small circles of community members in Hong Kong without the detection of an organization. In fact, Lee's (2001) study showed that Hong Kong consumers often share and circulate their bad impressions or experiences with corporations within their small circles of social networks. They cease to be consumers of a particular product or service when their social circles circulate negative information about or experience in it. This echoes Olson's (1982) notion that the power of even very small collectivities should not be underestimated. International crisis communication scholars and practitioners should be conscious that the form of stakeholder community is subject to cultural influence.

A Co-Constructing View to Two-Way Symmetrical Model

Deetz (1994) developed a two-dimensional model to delineate two orientations to communication: political practices and decision practices. The political practice dimension deals with what the message is perceived to do in the social world, with expression processes and constitutive processes situated at the two ends. At the expression processes end, messages "represent something that is absent or make public that which is private" (p. 572), that the media of expression are neutral. In the expression conception, messages foster "reproduction of meanings, perceptions or feelings that reside independently somewhere else" (p. 572). On the other hand, the decision practices dimension treats messages as an active part of the reproduction of meanings, perceptions, and feelings. The media of expression--be it making distinctions, attending to the world in particular ways, producing an individual identity, or any other human attempts to interact with the world--is not seen as neutral but active and fundamental. Deetz (1994) explained, "From a constitutive conception, all 'expression' is derived from a more fundamental set of discursive practices in which the things that are to be expressed by messages are 'constitutively' produced through messages" (p.573).

The decision practices dimension addresses the handling of differences in communities. It suggests that differences are resolved in ways ranging from processes of control and domination to processes of coordination and codetermination.

The two dimensions interact to produce four quadrants of communication: quadrant 1—dominating-expression practices a strategy of rewards, propaganda, coercion, and manipulation for control; quadrant 2—codetermining-expression practices involvement, the concept of which is directed by 18th-century notions of the overarching theme of an autonomous individual that embeds self-interests, representational conceptions of language, and free speech in an attempt to influence others; quadrant 3—dominating-constitutive practices consent, which is often invisible through ideological formations, commonsense, routines, and standard practices, naturalization, and discipline; and quadrant 4—codetermining-constitutive practices participation that is based on "giving voice to difference, negotiation of values and decisional premises, and the production of new integrative positions" (Deetz, 1994, p. 574) and that "contestation of dominant position is open" (Deetz, 1994, p. 574).

Deetz (1994) contended that communication is a constitutive process in which meanings are interactively and collaboratively constructed and that only the participation practice (quadrant 4) is truly communicational in this sense. The other three practices conform to the dominant informational perspective that specifies personal expression as political practice and control through influence as decision practice. Deetz's (1994) codetermining-constitutive notion proffers some insight to the reconceptualization of the two-way symmetrical model.

The original two-way symmetrical model specifies that practitioners engage in dialogues (bargaining, negotiating, compromising, and conflict resolving) to bring about symbiotic changes in both the organization and its stakeholders in terms of ideas, attitudes, and behaviors. The concept of dialogue, however, is not a culture-free product. Even though bargaining, negotiating, compromising, and conflict-resolving may be considered two-way, symmetrical dialogues that would foster or indicate equal-footing and fair play with stakeholders in Western culture, (a) they may not be regarded as such in non-Western cultures; or (b) the forms of bargaining, negotiating, compromising and conflict-resolving are understood and practiced in a different way. Especially in an international crisis, where prompt and appropriate actions are called for, and where stakeholders are more sensitive and critical than normal, practicing the Western version of the two-way symmetrical communication may aggravate the already adverse situation.

What one culture understands to be two-way or symmetrical communication, another culture may not see that way. An international crisis can be seen as a cross-cultural critical event for an organization and its stakeholders in which both parties participate to redefine and reconstruct the crisis situation vis-à-vis their own cultural systems. As such, crisis reconstructing is a process of meaning encoding and meaning decoding for both the organization and its cross-cultural interpretive stakeholders. Such a reconstruction process becomes not only a discourse event for both parties, but a dynamic discursive site between two cultures as well. Upon encountering two cultures, what is meant by two-way or symmetrical should be subject to coconstruction and codetermination by the two parties. Without a coconstructing–codetermining process, the presumedly effective Western version of two-way symmetrical crisis communication is doomed to be a vain attempt in an international crisis.

A couple of assumptions underlie the original two-way symmetrical model: (a) bargaining, negotiating, compromising, and conflict-resolving represent two-way symmetrical dialogues; and (b) that the organization and its stakeholders are contesting parties who bargain, negotiate, compromise, and resolve conflict. Applying this original model to the context of international crisis communication may not be adequate or appropriate because the conceptions of symmetrical dialogues are subject to cultural differences and a contesting paradigm to conceptualize stakeholders of other cultures may do more harm than good in the organiza-tion–stakeholder relationships at times of acute crisis.

The coconstructing view to two-way symmetry, on the other hand, sees the in-terface between two cultures and their cultural members not necessarily as a con-test site, but rather an untapped sphere for possible collaborations to coconstruct and codetermine (a) the forms of dialogue, (b) the crisis situation, and (c) crisis handling. A major component in international crisis communication, then, would be to facilitate such coconstructing–codetermining processes prior to, during, and after a crisis.

Practical Implications

Given the inevitable force of internalization, public relations practitioners are urged to prepare for the worst to happen locally and abroad. International crisis communication is not yet a topic in the public relations field, which means no con-ceptual and practical guidelines are available to equip Western practitioners for a crisis occurring outside of Western boundaries. Farinelli (1990) observed that

> public relations has fewer people with international knowledge and experience than any of the other business sectors such as advertising, financial services, and management consulting. We all service the same clients—but public relations has the worst record of all in keeping pace with international changes. (p. 42)

The example shown in this chapter demonstrates that Hong Kong consumers are subject to cultural influence to express, communicate, react, and expect in a disparate way than Westerners during an organizational crisis. It would be a serious error to decode the behavior of these stakeholders by adopting a West-ern paradigm.

Grunig et al. (2002) evidenced a trend toward increasing multiculturalism in public relations firms. Although it may be a good sign for organizational diver-gence (Stohl, 2001), requisite variety (Weick, 1988, 1993, 2001), and third-cul-ture individuals (Featherstone, 1990), they are necessary, but insufficient condi-tions for excellent international crisis communication. After all, using various or third-culture individuals would be futile if it simply meant that more racial-ethnic minority personnel practiced the Western way of public relations.

International crisis communication practitioners should view stakeholders as interpretive communities and should strive for two-way symmetrical communica-tion with their stakeholders from non-Western cultures. They should be reminded, however, that what constitutes two-way and symmetrical is subject to cultural in-fluence. What is appropriate for two-way communication in Western society may not be in other cultures. The best form of dialogue needs to be coconstructed and codetermined by the organization and its stakeholders. One of the roles of inter-national crisis communication practitioners is to facilitate, reinforce, and sustain such coconstructing–codetermining processes at the precrisis, crisis, and postcrisis stages. In addition to being culturally sensitive and culturally competent, a successful coconstructing process requires international crisis communication practitioners to empower the otherwise powerless publics of other cultures (Grunig, Grunig, & Dozier, 2002). This is no easy task. Institutionalized and internalized powerlessness among Hong Kong consumers, for instance, impedes collaborative coconstruction–codetermination to take place. Such a situation requires the power of professionalism from international crisis communication practitioners (Grunig, et al., 2002) to (a) cultivate institutionalized mechanisms across cultural boundaries to remove institutionalized powerlessness; and (b) liberate interpretive communities and prepare or affirm for them an ideal speech situation (Habermas, 1979, 1984).

Theoretical Implications

The conception of audience from passive receivers in the unidirectional models to active participants in two-way models decades ago signified a breakthrough in the communication academy. Despite the fact that criticisms of the early source-channel-message-receiver-effect paradigm are well known among communication scholars, audience-oriented research continues to be overlooked.

To neglect or deny the very nature of audience activity and culture embedded-ness of stakeholders as interpretive communities may lead to poor crisis communication practice and leave crisis communication research as a scholastic-discussion activity in academia only. The cultural element with the unique nature of crisis should make international crisis communication a challenging field to study.

McLeod (2000) posted a challenge to communication scholars to connect the macroaspects of culture to the more microaspects of audience behavior. Contextual analyses of audience behavior are needed, although often overlooked, because macrolevel variables, such as culture, are potential influences on the individual, even if their impact is not readily noticeable to the individuals. Moreover, McLeod (2000) described a general trend of current audience research to shift from the focus of developing universal laws or regularities across time and space to the discovery of conditional scopes of theories in terms of particular locales and situations. With the realization that theories are likely to be conditional to time and space, rather than universal, the need for systematic, comparative research in cultural contexts becomes more salient. This is especially true and pressing for crisis communication, given the inevitable force of globalization of business. What is needed then is a shift from the dominating a Western-based, organization-oriented approach to more culture-specific, audience-oriented crisis communication research and practice that recognize stakeholders as cultural and interpretive communities.

The introduction of culture into existing crisis communication literature forces recognition that crisis communication processes are no longer bounded within a unicultural framework and that constant self-reflections on the prevalent dominant paradigms are needed. Future directions for crisis communication research should be oriented toward examining both macro- and microfactors in the dynamics of the crisis communication process. Here, the dynamic refers not only to the forces involved when two entities interact with each other at the same time. Rather, dynamic alludes to two levels of forces: (a) different forces affecting each other within the microlevel (e.g., organizational crisis response and audience's evaluation of it); and (b) different factors affecting the forces at the macrolevel (e.g., the cultural and societal factors affecting audience's evaluation process of an organizational crisis).

There is an emphasis on studying audience evaluation processes as opposed to evaluation. Evaluation refers to an assessment of an observed phenomenon, whereas evaluation process, on the other hand, takes up a broader meaning that encompasses assessment activity together with its subsequent reactions, as well as factors influencing them. Studying audiences' evaluation of a crisis would stop when the subjects' assessment results reveal. Studying audiences' evaluation process, on the other hand, contextualizes the organization as a system in an environment including the consumers. The process is one in which the consumers, another system in the environment, interact with the sociocultural factors to exercise influence on the organization system.

Organizational crisis context provides a distinctive area for communication research given its unique nature. Topics that call for future research in this unexploited fertile land include (a) Are there any differences between how stakeholders of a particular culture evaluate a local crisis and how they see an international crisis? (b) How are international crisis messages, constructed in certain ways, interpreted by audiences' frames of a particular culture? (c) How do macro- and microfactors interact and affect stakeholders' interpreting process in an international crisis? (d) Are there any differences in this interpreting process across cultures? (e) How do stakeholders of a particular culture interact with their community members in organizational crisis? (f) What and how do community members of a particular culture influence or reinforce others in their interpretations of an international crisis? (g) How the symbolic and metaphoric nuances of dialogue, not necessarily expressed in verbal or explicit action form, are used by the organization and its stakeholders of another culture in an international crisis communication process? (h) How can the best form of dialogue be coconstructed–codetermined by an organization and its stakeholder community of a particular culture culture? And finally, (i) how can the coconstruction–codetermination of the crisis situation and crisis handling be facilitated between an organization and its stakeholders of a particular culture upon an international crisis?

REFERENCES

Aguilera, D. C. (1990). *Crisis intervention: Theory and methodology* (6th ed.). St. Louis, MO: Mosby.

Alanazi A. (1996). Public relations in the Middle East: The case of Saudi Arabia. In H. M. Culbertson & N. Chen (Eds.), *International public relations: A comparative analysis* (pp. 239–256). Mahwah, NJ: Erlbaum.

Aldrich, H. E. (1979). *Organizations and environments*. Englewood Cliffs, NJ: Prentice Hall.

Allen, M. W., & Caillouet, R. H. (1994). Legitimate endeavors: Impression management strategies used by an organization in crisis. *Communication Monographs, 61,* 44–62.

Ang, S. H. (2001). Chinese consumers' perception of alpha-numeric brand names. In S. M. Leoung, S. H. Ang, & C. T. Tan (Eds.), *Marketing in the new Asia* (pp. 272–288). Singapore: McGraw Hill.

Angelopulo, G. C. (1990). The active outward orientation of the organization. *Communicare, 9*(1), 5–20.

Barton, L. (1993). *Crisis in organizations: Managing and communicating in the heat of chaos.* Cincinnati, OH: South-Western.

Benoit, W. L. (1995). *Accounts, excuses, and apologies: A theory of image restoration strategies.* Albany: State University of New York Press.

Benson, J. A. (1988). Crisis revisited: An analysis of the strategies used by Tylenol in the second tampering episode. *Central States Speech Journal, 38,* 49–66.

Bentele, G., & Peter, G. (1996). Public relations in the German democratic republic and the new federal German states. In H. M. Culbertson & N. Chen (Eds.), *International public relations: A comparative analysis* (pp. 349–367). Mahwah, NJ: Erlbaum.

Bond, M. H. (1997). *Beyond the Chinese face: Insights from psychology.* Hong Kong: Oxford University Press.

Brinkerhoff, D. W., & Ingle, M. D. (1989). Integrating blueprint and process: A structured flexibility approach to development management. *Public Administration and Development, 9,* 487–503.

Capon, N., & Ho, M. Y. C. (1999). Jimmy Lai and daily newspapers in Hong Kong. In N. Capon & W. R. Vanhonacker (Eds.), *The Asian marketing casebook* (pp. 140–151). Singapore: Prentice Hall.

Chan, A. K. K. (1990). Localization in international branding: A preliminary investigation on Chinese names of foreign brands in Hong Kong. *International Journal of Advertising, 9,* 81–91.

Chen, N. (1996). Public relations in China: The introduction and development of an occupational field. In H.M. Culbertson, & N. Chen (Eds.), *International public relations: A comparative analysis* (pp. 121–154). Mahwah, NJ: Erlbaum.

Cheney, G., & Dionisopoulos, G.N. (1989). Public relations? No, relations with publics: A rhetorical-organizational approach to contemporary corporate communications. In C. H. Botan & V. Hazleton, Jr. (Eds.), *Public relations theory* (pp. 135–157). NJ: Erlbaum.

Consumer Council (n.d.) *Profile.* Retrieved March 1, 2002, from http://www.consumer.org.hk/website/ws_en

Coombs, W. T. (1995). Choosing the right words: The development of guidelines for the selection of the "appropriate" crisis response strategies. *Management Communication Quarterly, 8,* 447–476.

Coombs, W. T. (1998). An analytic framework for crisis situations: Better responses from a better understanding of the situation. *Journal of Public Relations Research, 10*(3), 177–191.

Coombs, W. T. (1999). *Ongoing crisis communication: Planning, managing, and responding.* Thousand Oaks, CA: Sage.

Coombs, W. T., & Holladay, S. J. (1996). Communication and attributions in a crisis: An experimental study in crisis communication. *Journal of Public Relations Research, 8*(4), 279–295.

Coombs, W. T., & Holladay, S. J. (2001). An extended examination of the crisis situations: A fusion of the relational management and symbolic approaches. *Journal of Public Relations Research, 13,* 32–340.

Coombs, W. T., Holladay, S., Hasenauer, G., & Signitzer, B. (1994). A comparative analysis of international public relations: Identification and interpretation of similarities and differences between professionalization in Austria, Norway, and the United States. *Journal of Public Relations Research, 6,* 23–29.

Coombs, W. T, & Schmidt, L. (2000). An empirical analysis of image restoration: Texaco's racism crisis. *Journal of Public Relations Research, 12,* 163–178.

Cooper-Chen, A. (1996). Public relations practice in Japan: Beginning again for the first time. In H. M. Culbertson & N. Chen (Eds.), *International public relations: A comparative analysis* (pp. 223–238). Mahwah, NJ: Erlbaum.

Crable, R. E., & Vibbert, S. L. (1986). *Public relations as communication management.* Edina, MN: Bellwether Press.

Culbertson, H. M., & Chen, N. (Eds.) (1996). *International public relations: A comparative analysis.* Mahwah, NJ: Erlbaum.

Deetz, S. A. (1994). Future of the discipline: The challenges, the research, and the social contribution. *Communication Yearbook, 17,* 565–600.

DiMaggio, P. J., & Powell, W. W. (1991). The iron cage revisited: Institutional isomorphism and collective rationality in organization fields. In W. W. Powell & P. J. DiMaggio (Eds.), *The new institutionalism in organizational analysts* (pp. 63–82). Chicago: University of Chicago Press.

Dutton, J. E. (1986). The processing of crisis and non-crisis strategic issues. *Journal of Management Studies, 23,* 501–517.

Egelhoff, W. G., & Sen, F. (1992). An information-processing model of crisis management. *Management Communication Quarterly, 5,* 443–484.

Ekachai, D.G. (1995). Applying Broom's role scales to Thai public relations practitioners. *Public Relations Review, 21,* 325–336.

Ekachai, D. G., & Komolsevin, R. (1996). Public relations in Thailand: Its functions and practitioners' roles. In H. M. Culbertson & N. Chen (Eds.), *International public relations: A comparative analysis* (pp. 155–170). Mahwah, NJ: Erlbaum.

Farinelli, J. L. (1990). Needed: A new U.S. perspective on global public relations. Public Relations Journal, 46 (November), 18–19, 42.

Fearn-Banks, K. (1996). Crisis communications: A casebook approach. Mahwah, NJ: Erlbaum Associates.

Featherstone, M. (Ed.). (1990). *Global culture: Nationalism, globalization and modernity.* London: Sage.

Fink, S. (1986). *Crisis management: Planning for the inevitable.* New York: AMACM.

Fish, S. (1989). *Doing what comes naturally: Change, rhetoric, and the practice of theory in literary and legal studies.* Oxford, UK: Clarendon Press.

Freeman, R. E. (1984). *Strategic management: A stakeholder approach.* Boston: Pitman.

French, P., & Crabble, M. (1998). *One billion shoppers: Accessing Asia's consuming passions and fast-moving markets—after the meltdown.* London: Nicholas Brealey.

Gelb, B. D. (1995, March-April). More boycotts ahead? Some implication. *Business Horizons, 38*(2), 70–76.

González, H., & Akel, D. (1996). Elections and earth matters: Public relations in Costa Rica. In H. M. Culbertson & N. Chen (Eds.), *International public relations: A comparative analysis* (pp. 257–272). Mahwah, NJ: Erlbaum.

Gottschalk, J. (1993). *Crisis response: Inside stories on managing image under siege.* Detroit, MI: Gale Research.

Grunig, J. E. (1989). Symmetrical presuppositions as a framework for public relations theory. In C. H. Botan & V. Hazleton, Jr. (Eds.), *Public relations theory* (pp. 17–44). Hillsdale, NJ: Erlbaum.

Grunig, J. E. (1992). What is excellence in management? In J. E. Grunig (Ed.), *Excellence in public relations and communication management* (pp.1–28). Hillsdale, NJ: Erlbaum.

Grunig, J. E. (1997). A situational theory of publics: Conceptual history, recent challenges and new research. In D. Moss, T. MacManus, & D. Verčič (Eds.), *Public relations research: An international perspective* (pp. 3–48). London: International Thomson Business Press.

Grunig, J. E. (2001). Two-way symmetrical public relations: Past, present, and future. In R. L. Health (Ed.), *Handbook of public relations* (pp. 11–30). Thousand Oaks, CA: Sage.

Grunig, J. E., & Grunig, L. A. (1992). Models of public relations and communications. In J. E. Grunig (Ed.), *Excellence in public relations and communication management* (pp. 285–326). Hillsdale, NJ: Erlbaum.

Grunig, J. E., & Hunt, T. (1984). *Managing public relations.* New York: Holt, Rinehart, &Winston.

Grunig, J. E. & Repper, F. C. (1992). Strategic management, publics, and issues. In J. E. Grunig (Ed.), *Excellence in public relations and communication management* (pp. 117–158). Hillsdale, NJ: Erlbaum.

Grunig, L. A., Grunig, J. E., Dozier, D. M. (2002). *Excellent public relations and effective organizations: A study of communication management in three countries.* Mahwah, NJ: Erlbaum.

Habermas, J. (1979). *Communication and the evolution of society* (T. McCarthy, Trans.). Boston: Beacon.

Habermas, J. (1984). *The constitution of society.* Berkeley: University of California Press.

Hallahan, K. (2002). Ivy Lee and the Rockefellers' response to the 1913–1914 Colorado coal strike. *Journal of Public Relations Research, 14*(4), 265–315.

Hampden-Turner, C., & Trompenaars, A. (1993). *The seven cultures of capitalism.* New York: Doubleday.

Hazleton, V., & Kruckeberg, D. (1996). European public relations practice: An evolving paradigm. In H. M. Culbertson & N. Chen (Eds.), *International public relations: A comparative analysis* (pp. 367–380). Mahwah, NJ: Erlbaum.

Hearit, K. M. (1994). Apologies and public relations crises at Chrysler, Toshiba, and Volvo. *Public Relations Review, 20*(2), 113–125.

Heath, R. L. (1997). *Strategic issues management: Organizations and public policy challenges.* Thousand Oaks, CA: Sage.

Heath, R. L. (Ed.). (2001). *Handbook of public relations.* Thousand Oaks, CA: Sage.

Hermann, C. F. (1963). Some consequences of crisis which limit the viability of organizations. *Administrative Science Quarterly, 3,* 143–158.

Hurst, D. K. (1995). *Crisis and renewal.* Boston: Harvard Business School Press.

Ice, R. (1991). Corporate publics and rhetorical strategies: The case of Union Carbide's Bhopal crisis. *Management Communication Quarterly, 4,* 341–362.

Ihlen, O. (2002). Defending the Mercedes A-Class: Combining and changing crisis-response strategies. *Journal of Public Relations Research, 14*(3), 185–206.

Jackson, S. E., & Dutton, J. E. (1987). Categorizing strategic issues: Links to organizational action. *Academy of Management Review, 12,* 76–90.

Jamais, J. F., Navarro, M. J., & Tuazon, R. R. (1996). Public relations in the Philippines. In H. M. Culbertson & N. Chen (Eds.), *International public relations: A comparative analysis* (pp. 191–206). Mahwah, NJ: Erlbaum.

Janoff-Bulman, R., & Frieze, I.H. (1983). A theoretical perspective for understanding reactions to victimization. *Journal of Social Issues, 39,* 1–17.

Kanso, A. (1996). Standardization versus localization: Public relations implications of advertising practices in Finland. In H.M. Culbertson, & N. Chen (Eds.), *International public relations: A comparative analysis* (pp. 299–316). Mahwah, NJ: Erlbaum.

Kim, Y., & Hon, L.C. (1998). Craft and professional models of public relations their relation to job satisfaction among Korean public relations practitioners. *Journal of Public Relations Research, 10,* 155–176.

Lasserre, P., & Probert, J. (2001). Competing in Asian Pacific: Understand the rules of the game. In S. M. Leoung, S. H. Ang, & C. T. Tan (Eds.), *Marketing in the new Asia* (pp. 27–54). Singapore: McGraw Hill.

Lee, B. K. (2001a). *Audience's evaluation process in organizational crisis: A study of consumers in Hong Kong.* Unpublished doctoral dissertation. Hong Kong: Hong Kong Baptist University.

Lee, B. K. (2001b, July). *The development of appropriate crisis response strategies to Chinese-based consumers: Putting message back in its socio-cultural context in crisis communication.* Paper presented at the 8th International Conference of Cross-Culture Communication, Hong Kong.

Lee, B. K. (2002, July). *Audience's evaluation of organizational crisis in Hong Kong.* Paper presented at the 52nd annual conference of the International Communication Association, Seoul, Korea.

Lee, B. K. (2004, May). *Hong Kong consumers' evaluation process in the China Airlines crash.* Paper presented at the 54th annual conference of the International Communication Association, New Orleans, LA.

Leitch, S., & Neilson, D. (2001). Bringing publics into public relations: New theoretical frameworks for practice. In R. L. Heath (Ed.), *Handbook of public relations* (pp. 127–138). Thousand Oaks, CA: Sage.

Lerbinger, O. (1997). *The crisis manager: Facing risk and responsibility.* Mahwah, NJ: Erlbaum.

Leuven, J. K. V., & Pratt, C. B. (1996). Public relations' role: Realities in Asian and in African South of the Sahara. In H. M. Culbertson & N. Chen (Eds*.), International public relations: A comparative analysis* (pp. 93–106). Mahwah, NJ: Erlbaum.

Loewendick, B. A. (1993, November). Laying your crisis on the table. *Training & Development,* pp. 15–17.

Marcus, A. A., & Goodman, R .S. (1991). Victims and shareholders: The dilemmas of presenting corporate policy during a crisis. *Academy of Management Journal, 34,* 281–305.

McLeod, J. M. (2000, April). *Trends in audience research in the United States.* Symposium presentation at the meeting of the International Conference of Chinese Audiences Across Time and Space, City University of Hong Kong, Hong Kong.

McQuail, D. (1997). *Audience analysis.* Thousand Oaks, CA: Sage.

Murphy, P. (1991). The limits of symmetry: A game theory approach to symmetric and asymmetric public relations. In J. E. Grunig & L. A. Grunig (Eds.), *Public relations research annual* (Vol. 3, pp. 115–132). Hillsdale, NJ: Erlbaum.

Murphy, P. (1996). Chaos theory as a model for managing issues and crises. *Public Relations Review, 22,* 95–113.

Nelkin, D. (1988). Risk reporting and the management of industrial crises. *Journal of Management Studies, 25,* 341–351.

Newson, D. (1996). Gender issues in public relations practice. In H. M. Culbertson & N. Chen (Eds.), *International public relations: A comparative analysis* (pp. 107–120). Mahwah, NJ: Erlbaum.

Newsom, D., Turk, J. V, & Kruckeberg, D. (1998). *This is PR: The realities of public relations* (6th ed.). Belmont, CA: Wadsworth.

O'Connor, J. (1987). *The meaning of crisis.* New York: Basil Blackwell.

Olson, M. (1982). *The logic of collective action: Public goods and the theory of groups.* Cambridge, MA: Harvard University Press.

Pauchant, T. C., & Douville, R. (1994). Recent research in crisis management: A study of 24 authors' publications from 1986 to 1991. *Industrial and Environmental Crisis Quarterly, 7,* 43–61.

Pauchant, T. C., & Mitroff, I. (1992). *Transforming the crisis-prone organization.* San Francisco: Jossey-Bass.

Pearson, C. M., & Clair, J. A. (1998). Reframing crisis management. *Academy of Management Review, 23,* 59–76.

Pearson, C. M., Mistra, S. K., Clair, J. A., & Mitroff, I. I. (1997). Managing the unthinkable. *Organizational Dynamics* (Autumn), 51–64.

Pearson, C., & Mitroff, I. (1993). From crisis-prone to crisis-prepared. *Academy of Management Executive, 7,* 48–59.

Perrow, C. (1999). *Normal accidents: Living with high-risk technologies.* Princeton, NJ: Princeton University Press.

Post, J. E., Frederick, W. C., Lawrence, A. T., & Weber, J. (1996). *Business and society: Corporate strategy, public policy, ethics* (8th ed.). Beijing: China Machine Press/McGraw-Hill.

Quarantelli, E. I. (1988). Disaster crisis management: A summary of research *findings. Journal of Management Studies, 25,* 373–385.

Schütte, H. (2001). Asian culture and the global consumer. In S. M. Leoung, S. H. Ang, & C. T. Tan (Eds.), *Marketing in the new Asia* (pp. 115–124). Singapore: McGraw-Hill.

Seeger, M. W., Sellnow, T. L., & Ulmer, R. R. (1998). Communication, organization, and crisis. In M. E. Roloff (Ed.), *Communication Yearbook, 21* (pp. 230–275). Thousand Oaks, CA: Sage.

Seeger, M. W., Sellnow, T. L., & Ulmer, R. R. (2001). Public relations and crisis communication: Organizing and chaos. In R. L. Health (Ed.), *Handbook of public relations* (pp. 155–166). Thousand Oaks, CA: Sage.

Seitel, F. P. (1998). *The practice of public relations* (7th ed.). Beijing: China Machine Press/ Prentice Hall.

Sharpe, M. L., & Simoes, R. P. (1996). Public relations performance in South and Central America. In H. M. Culbertson & N. Chen (Eds.), *International public relations: A comparative analysis* (pp. 273–298). Mahwah, NJ: Erlbaum.

Sheridan, G. (1999). *Asian values, Western dreams.* Sydney, Australia: Allen & Unwin.

Shrivastava, P., Mitroff, I., Miller, D., & Miglani, A. (1988). Understanding industrial crises. *Journal of Management Studies, 25,* 285–303.

Siomkos, G., & Shrivastava, P. (1993). Responding to product liability crises. *Long Range Planning, 26,* 72–79.

Slaikeu, K. A. (1990). *Crisis intervention.* Boston: Allyn & Bacon.

Speece, M. W., & So, S. L. M. (1998). Hong Kong: The consumer market in the 1990s. in A. Pecotich, & C.J. Schultz II (Eds.), *Marketing and consumer behaviour in East and South-East Asia* (pp. 213–250). Sydney, Australia: McGraw-Hill.

Sriramesh, K. (1996). Power distance and public relations: An ethnographic study of southern Indian organizations. In H. M. Culbertson & N. Chen (*Eds.), International public relations: A comparative analysis* (pp. 171–190). Mahwah, NJ: Erlbaum.

Stohl, C. (2001). Globalizing organizational communication. In F. M. Jablin, & L. L. Putnam (Eds.), *The new handbook of organizational communication: Advances in theory, research, and methods* (pp. 323–375).Thousand Oaks, CA: Sage.

Turk, J. V. (1996). Romania: From publicitate past to public relations future. In H. M. Culbertson & N. Chen (Eds.), *International public relations: A comparative analysis* (pp. 341–348). Mahwah, NJ: Erlbaum.

Vasquez, G. M. (1993). A homo narrans paradigm for public relations: Combining Bormann's symbolic convergence theory and Grunig's situational theory of publics. *Journal of Public Relations Research, 5*(3), 201–216.

Vasquez, G. M. (1994). Testing a communication theory-method-message-behavior complex for the investigation of publics. *Journal of Public Relations Research, 6,* 291–316.

Verčič, D., Grunig, L. A., & Grunig, J. E. (1996). Global and specific principles of public relations: Evidence from Slovenia. In H. M. Culbertson & N. Chen (Eds.), *International public relations: A comparative analysis* (pp. 31–66). Mahwah, NJ: Erlbaum.

von Bertalanffy, L. (1968). *General systems theory.* New York: George Braziller.

Wakefield, R. I. (1996). Interdisciplinary theoretical foundations for international public relations. In H. M. Culbertson & N. Chen (Eds.), *International public relations: A comparative analysis* (pp.17–30). Mahwah, NJ: Erlbaum.

Weick, K. E. (1988). Enacting sensemaking in crisis situations. *Journal of Management Studies, 25,* 305–317.

Weick, K. E. (1993). The collapse of sensemaking in organizations: the Mann Gulch disaster. *Administrative Science Quarterly, 38,* 628–652.

Weick, K. E. (2001). *Making sense of the organization.* Oxford, UK: Blackwell.

Weiner, B. (1986). *An attributional theory of motivation and emotion.* New York: Springer-Verlag.

Winter, M., & Steger, U. (1998). *Managing outside pressure: Strategies for preventing corporate disasters.* Chichester, UK: Wiley.

Yasue, M,. & Gu, X.W. (2001). Asian youth and implications for marketing strategies. In S. M. Leong, S. H. Ang, & C. T. Tan (Eds.), *Marketing in the new Asia* (pp. 98–114). Singapore: McGraw-Hill.

CHAPTER CONTENTS

10 The Place of Theory in Development Communication: Retrospect and Prospects

RAUL ROMAN
University of Washington

This chapter analyzes the role of theory in development communication, an area of study conventionally concerned with practical problems and applied research topics. The author provides a review of the theoretical evolution of development communication through the analysis of its three social scientific traditions: the media effects-oriented tradition, the critical theory tradition, and the pragmatic philosophy tradition. Based on this analysis, the author indicates actual prospects for theory building in development communication by discussing opportunities for the formulation of normative theories. This chapter concludes that reaffirming the practical orientation of development communication and supporting intellectual convergence among its intellectual traditions constitute the core tasks that will encourage theoretical creativity in the future.

There are two main difficulties in the attempt to find the place of theory in development communication: (a) its action-oriented nature and (b) the multiple conceptual dissensions within this field of study. Of course, these two interrelated difficulties, the realm of practice and the realm of ideas, are the dual manifestation of the same problem, or just the two faces of the same coin, to use the popular expression. On one side, the work of development communication scholars has always been enthused by a strong rolled-up-sleeves sentiment: willingness (and often a professional responsibility) to do something, a drive for action beyond mere academic reflection. This tendency to actively engage in or depend on project implementation frequently leads to problem-solving and applied research options, often in the form of project evaluation.[1] This proclivity to roll up sleeves and get to work partly explains the way theory is conceived and used by development communication scholars and their prospects for theory building.

Correspondence: Raul Roman, Center for Internet Studies, University of Washington, Box 353055, Seattle, WA 98195-3055; email: rroman@u.washington.edu

Communication Yearbook 29, pp.311–331

On the other side, the search for the place of theory in this field of study may be confused by the variations in the meaning and purpose of development communication itself,[2] an inborn confusion inherited from both the intellectual plurality of the field of communication study and the conceptual disputes about the idea and practice of development.

The unsteady identity of development communication still renders pertinent a question that would likely be perceived as utterly impertinent if it were asked in one of the traditional social sciences. That pertinent question is this: What is development communication? This question is pertinent in the context of this chapter only because there is no precise answer to it. Only a very general definition can encapsulate the diversity of this area of study. We can just contend that what generally holds development communication studies together is a benevolent willingness to study communication phenomena that describe, and also illuminate and help achieve, some kind of (presumably positive) social change, chiefly (and historically) in developing countries — although some scholars consider development communication applications not to be limited to the so-called Third World (Wilkins, 2000). In the concept, there is a broad context, a broad topic of interest, and also an overarching sense of purpose, a kind of moral drive. This overly general description encompasses an array of intellectual approaches to development and to communication. This means that development communication is historically dependent on these two areas of scholarly research and practice: development and communication. Analyzing the roots of this intellectual dependency is the first step to clarifying the place theory occupies in development communication.

First, there is the influence of development. Conceptual revisions of development have framed the way development communication scholars approach their work and think about what they do (Wilkins & Mody, 2001). Since the "invention" of development in the early 1950s (Rist, 1999), development scholars have periodically provided new and revised ideas to guide the economic and social development of the most disadvantaged nations (Peet & Hartwick, 1999). These ideas and ideologies are loosely packaged and labeled, mostly by economists and sociologists, as development theories, models, or paradigms. In this case, theory is understood as the ordinary antonym and complement of practice, a kind of grand theory, or just a paradigm defined in its simplest way: "a basic set of beliefs that guides action" (Guba, 1990, p. 17). Development communication scholars have tended to adhere to one of those paradigms or grand theories. This means that they just position themselves within a general framework of what development is or should be. Servaes (1999) analyzed the evolution of development communication by dividing it according to the chronological evolvement of those grand theories, basically a dichotomy between neo-classical and neo-Marxist models of development. Servaes (1999) concluded with another grand theory, the multiplicity paradigm, a model that paradoxically denies the power of any previous grand theory to generalize about the widely heterogeneous experience of development. The multiplicity paradigm is precisely an antigrand theory framework, a position widely shared today, a time of "epistemological impasse" in development (Escobar, 2000, p. 165), and a time when the concept of development seems to become increasingly blurred[3] (Hulme & Turner, 1990).

The classification of development into general paradigms is a very useful referent for communication scholars. Nonetheless, a fixation with these intellectual schemes can be misleading, at least in three ways. First, the chronological perspective can give the wrong impression that paradigms replace each other over time, as if paradigms were isolated in compartments or as if they could not coexist (Servaes, 1991). Second, these paradigms are often presented as dichotomist or exclusivist, as if they could not mix and influence each other in different ways (Kothari & Minogue, 2002). Third, and probably most importantly, paradigm rhetoric may conceal the relative extent to which those grand generalizations actually influence and are operationalized in reality.

Besides the influence of development just described, the subfield of development communication is a microcosm of the larger field of communication study. The evolution of this subfield has run parallel to changes in the communication field. In the same way, reevaluations of development communication as an area of scholarly research resemble the entrenched discussions about the status, purpose, and functions of the field of communication study.[4] This parallel history witnessed the early predominance of the behavioral sciences in the 1950s and 1960s and the emergence of more pluralistic and exploratory scholarship in the late 1970s and on. Some new trends defied previous conceptions of the role of communication within the social sciences, originating the "epistemological battles of the 1980s" (Monahan & Collins-Jarvis, 1993, pp. 151–152). The result was a more open and eclectic field of study, but also a more fragmented and loose one. The same thing can be said, in a microlevel, about development communication. The same parallelism also applies to the changing conceptions of theory within the field: It is important to underline that communication is "derived eclectically from disciplines with incommensurable intellectual agendas, now often involving radically different conceptions of 'theory'" (Craig, 1999, p. 122). The consideration of this state of affairs is essential in the ongoing identification of theory uses and prospects in development communication.

If we trace a map of the current intellectual options in communication research, we can classify the field in three broad traditions: empirical social research, social philosophy, and critical social theory (Peters, 1993, p. 135). The first tradition "studies influence, the second theorizes participation, the last unmasks domination," and each of these areas corresponds to a "political philosophy and its accompanying mode of social inquiry: liberalism, social democracy, and Marxism" (Peters, 1993, p. 138). Exactly the same map can be used to identify the theoretical trends of development communication today. This three-dimensional map is a useful way to find the place of theory in development communication for two main reasons: (a) It situates the field within the social science tradition, which is the most appropriate framework to analyze its theoretical evolvement and opportunities; and (b) it breaks the dependency chain that ties development communication conceptualizations exclusively with changing fashionable labels of development, a tendency that has obscured and narrowed theoretical thinking in this field of study.

In spite of recognizing the utility of this roadmap for the task at hand, it is nonetheless important to clarify that these three traditions are not absolute, static, and pure entities: They are in constant and open evolution and in mutual dialogue with each other. The different perspectives on social sciences that development communication scholars choose to adopt, or are dragged into adopting, are not emerging from a clinical vacuum either. Social science epistemologies and methods, including different ways of understanding theory, are in complex, constant, and dynamic interaction with development policies and ideologies, historical and social contexts, and politics of academe.

This chapter provides a review of the theoretical evolution of development communication through the analysis of its three social scientific traditions: the media effects-oriented tradition, the critical theory tradition, and the pragmatic philosophy tradition. Based on this analysis, the chapter indicates actual prospects for theory building in development communication by discussing opportunities for the formulation of normative theories. Regarding the above-mentioned difficulties in finding the place of theory in this area of study, this essay concludes that reaffirming the practical orientation of development communication and supporting intellectual convergence among its intellectual traditions constitute the core task that will encourage theoretical creativity in the future.

THE MEDIA EFFECTS-ORIENTED TRADITION

The most salient theoretical influence in development communication, following the pattern of the communication field, comes from the ample territory of communication effects. Development communication scholars in this tradition have used both quantitative and qualitative methods to study a wide range of projects on many different development topics, such as health, nutrition, agriculture, and family planning. The overall characteristic of their research is that they are carried out in naturalistic settings and usually function as auxiliary components of wider projects: They study the behavioral and cognitive effects of public communication strategies. Today, the main theoretical strands that support, legitimize, and frame this research tradition are Bandura's (1977, 2002) social learning or social cognition theory, Rogers's (1995) version of the diffusion of innovations theory, and the long list of health behavior change theories (e.g., see Atkin, 2001). Research in this area includes the study of educational mass media campaigns, social marketing, and entertainment-education initiatives.

This is the oldest and most seasoned social scientific tradition of development communication: Its inception is at the origins of development communication as a scholarly area of research in American universities. In this sense, it is the founding tradition of development communication. A review of the theoretical strands of development communication—and, particularly, a review of this theoretically well-fed tradition—cannot be separated from an appraisal of the historical context that frames its intellectual evolution. For this reason, this section provides a succinct historical review as the introductory linkage to a general analysis of the theories that today guide research in this area.

The Initial Steps of the Founding Tradition of Development Communication

Development communication was born out of a specific conception of development ingrained in a particular historical conjuncture: the modernization paradigm and the start of the Cold War. Most of the early development communication studies were not guided by communication theory, but rather by the pressing imperatives of the modernization theory of economic development. With the invention of the Third World label during the 1950s, "the modernization paradigm became the intellectual property of all the social sciences" (Hulme & Turner, 1990, p. 34). The modernization paradigm was a "model of growth" (Schramm, 1976, p. 45) that advocated top-down national development strategies and centralized macroeconomic plans based on transfer of technology from industrialized nations. It was a one-size-fits-all model of "exogenously induced change" (Golding, 1974, p. 43). Efforts were concentrated on the urban minority of African, Asian, and Latin American countries, with the hope that the effects of development policies would gradually trickle down to the rural and most disadvantaged sectors of society (Rogers, 1976c). The modernization paradigm categorized mass media as one of the independent variables in the neoclassical equation of economic prosperity.

Early development communication studies, which have their clearest examples in Lerner's *The Passing of Traditional Society* (1958) and the special issue of *Public Opinion Quarterly* on international communication, edited by Lowenthal (1952/3), were largely a continuation of academic efforts funded by the U.S. government to understand the persuasive potential of mass media as possible agents of ideology and political propaganda in the first years of the Cold War (Samarajiwa, 1987). This political orientation partly explains the formative influence of mass media effects and warfare psychology on development communication research.[5] The role of mass media was the transmission of messages, charged with Western or modernizing values, with the hope that they would rapidly transform the ideological climate of traditional societies (Rogers, 1976a, 1976c). This change in individual consciousness was believed to be the triggering point of the modernization process (Lerner, 1958). Development communication scholars were therefore interested in studying how contact with mass media was associated with modern knowledge and attitudes, including the diffusion of family planning, health and agriculture innovations.

Generally, the methods used by communication researchers were (a) correlational analyses of mass media and other national development indicators;

(b) survey research, often guided by diffusion of innovations theory, such as the KAP surveys of knowledge (K), attitudes (A), and practice (P) of family planning innovations (Rogers, 1976b); and (c) some field experiments, like the one conducted by Neurath and funded by UNESCO to investigate the role of radio as an "agent in the transmission of knowledge" (Mathur & Neurath, 1959, p. 105).

The early years of the media effects tradition were characterized by a genuine enthusiasm and optimism about the direct effects of media in accelerating development (Schramm, 1964). Nevertheless, by the early 1970s, this approach (a mindset based on hope rather than scientific evidence) started experiencing a dramatic change. The modernization paradigm of development was radically contested. Development communication was severely criticized and self-criticized, mainly on the two habitual (and interrelated) fronts: communication and development. From the standpoint of communication, the effects-oriented tradition was accused of theoretical naïveté, chiefly for reducing the communication process to a technologically deterministic one-way linear model and for ignoring previous media effects research (Beltran, 1976; Melkote, 1991; Mody, 2000). From the point of view of development, communication scholars were accused of applying an ethnocentric and ahistorical approach that simplified the development process and was insensitive to the social contexts of the target countries.

As a result of this crisis, development communication reoriented its course and almost reinvented itself. This ferment in the field (a ferment that, in some sense, still continues today) set the course for more rigorous empirical research in the effects-oriented tradition, while it also opened the door to new epistemologies and new methodological approaches. Regarding this change, Rogers (1982) wrote in the early 1980s: "It is a new ball game for communication research . . . it is indeed an intellectual revolution" (p. viii).

The Theoretical Framework of the Media Effects Tradition

The new ball game in the media effects-oriented tradition basically meant the adoption of an articulated body of behavior change theories and more refined methods of evaluation research. The game was moved by a renovated interest in media campaigns (Rogers & Storey, 1987). This new interest incorporated a "science-based approach" to the design and implementation of communication strategies (Piotrow & Kincaid, 2001). The essence of this tradition, however, remained intact. In fact, "the intuitively appealing idea that media can drive socially significant behavioral change in developing nations persists" (Sherry, 1997, p. 76). Nevertheless this tradition is no more about the self-reliant transmission of prescriptive messages to influence behaviors in a direct way. Purposive media efforts are intended "to influence the knowledge base, or the beliefs, or the social norms underpinning the behaviors rather than just recommending new behaviors" (Hornik, 2002, p. 13).

Most theories used by the effects-oriented tradition come from social psychology. This disciplinary source leads researchers to conceive communication problems as "situations that call for the effective manipulation of the causes of behavior in order to produce objectively defined and measured outcomes" (Craig, 1999, p. 143). Theories in this tradition systematize the social and psychological variables that explain individual disposition to induced change. The increasing sophistication of this theoretical framework tends to reduce the salience of media as agents of social change — although the varying levels of media influence expected certainly depend on the complexity of the intended effects, among other factors. The primary focus of research is the audience: individuals and social networks. The objective is to understand the process by which individuals and communities adopt innovations (Rogers, 1995) or change their behavior (Bandura, 1967) as a result of media and intermedia communication. The typical theoretical mix of public communication campaigns and entertainment–education programs[6] usually blends diffusion theory with some elements of social learning theory (now renamed social cognitive theory). Public health media efforts also include theoretical constructions that complement these two principal theories, most commonly, the health belief model (Rosenstock, Strecher, & Becker, 1988) and the theory of planned behavior (Ajzen, 1991).

The popular diffusion of innovations theory, basically a middle-range theory,[7] describes the social process by which an innovation (an object, idea, or practice perceived as new) is communicated among the members of a community over time. The focus of the theory is not only on awareness and knowledge, but also on attitude change and the decision-making process that leads to the practice or adoption of an innovation (Rogers & Singhal, 1996). The objective is to explain the dynamics of social construction and gradual assimilation of an innovation. The diffusion literature emphasizes that media are instrumental in raising awareness, whereas interpersonal sources are more influential at decision-making stages (Hornik & McAnany, 2001; Vaughan & Rogers, 2000). The theory includes conceptual generalizations about (a) how and through what media an innovation is communicated, (b) the perceived attributes of innovations, (c) the decision process that leads to adoption (or nonadoption), and (d) the characteristics of adopters. Additionally, there is an increasing theoretical concern about the consequences or effects of innovation adoption (Rogers, 1995). One of the key strengths of diffusion theory is its versatile and eclectic nature. Diffusion of innovations is a conceptual meeting point that embraces other theoretical approaches to help illuminate development communication problems (Roman, 2003). For example, theoretical discussions about the consequences of innovations are often connected to the knowledge gap hypothesis (Olien, Donohue, & Tichenor, 1984; Tichenor, Donohue, & Olien, 1970) and the communication effects gap hypothesis[8] (Rogers, 1976c).

Social cognitive theory explains a complex set of psychological processes that must be satisfied before behavior is adopted. Bandura (2002) understood that "most behavior is the product of multiple determinants operating in concert" (p. 139), including cognitive, affective, biological, behavioral, and environmental aspects. Social modeling, or changing through imitation of socially accepted role models' behavior, and self-efficacy, or the personal confidence in one's own capability to perform a certain new proposed behavior, are the two elements of the social cognitive theory that have been most widely applied by effects-oriented tradition researchers in development communication.

Theoretical models around public health media efforts focus on the individual's perception of new behavior, self-efficacy, perception of social pressure to practice or reject new behavior, and individual assessment of barriers and benefits involved in new behavior adoption. The recent "integrative theory of behavior change" (Cappella, Fishbein, Hornik, Ahern, & Sayeed, 2001) summarizes the health belief model and the theory of reasoned action and also adds some elements of social cognitive theory. This new theory estimates that "outcome behaviors are influenced by skills, environmental constraints, and intentions" (Rice & Atkin, 2002, p. 434).

Theoretical Evolution: Review and Renovation

The major criticism of this body of theory comes in two interrelated forms: (a) its concentration on individual variables, with an accompanying individual blame bias (Rogers, 1995), and (b) its omission of sociostructural factors. These perceived conceptual flaws have been partly a cause and a consequence of the research methods employed: The frequent use of survey methods has eventually forced researchers to use the individual response unit as a constrained and limiting research unit.

Studies in the media effects tradition usually assume that "individuals are in volitional control over their behavior" (Melkote, Muppidi, & Goswami, 2000, p. 19). It is argued that:

> an overwhelming focus on individual-level behavior change runs the risk of mistakenly assuming that all individuals (a) are capable of controlling their environment, (b) are on an even playing field, and (c) make decisions of their own free will. Such is seldom the case. (Singhal & Rogers, 2002, p. 127)

The individual blame bias is a predisposition to hold individuals responsible for their problems, ignoring their environmental constraints (Rogers, 1995). The thesis of human deficit or individual ignorance is at the base of the most frequent theory failures in development communication; these failures result from "an incorrect assumption that a particular development problem is amenable to a communication based solution" (Hornik, 1988, p. 14). Even though there are some exceptions,[9] there is a recurrent denunciation of the theoretical gap that fails to account for social structural and cultural factors in the media effects tradition (Melkote et al., 2000)

In any case, it is important to recognize that years of constructive criticism and self-criticism have been well digested, both in entertainment–education and public communication campaigns. On one side, entertainment–education is lean-ing toward "more multilevel, cultural, and contextual theoretical explanations" (Singhal & Rogers, 2002, p. 127), including the use of theories of drama (Kin-caid, 2002), uses and gratifications, agenda setting, knowledge gap, and cultiva-tion (Sherry, 2002). This move is accompanied by a growing "methodological pluralism" (Singhal & Rogers, 2002) that comprises laboratory experiments and the mix of survey and ethnographic methods (Sypher, McKinley, Ventsam, & Valdeavellano, 2002). On the other side, the media effects tradition, principally the branch of public health communication campaigns, is showing a strong theo-retical concern about socio-structural determinants of adoptive behavior (Ban-dura, 2002), such as institutional, infrastructural, and situational factors of change (Cappella et al., 2001; Rice & Atkin, 2002). At the same time, based on lessons learned from practitioners and the array of theoretical perspectives borrowed from social psychology, a kind of informal know-how theory or normative theory for the design and implementation of public health communication campaigns is slowly taking shape (Atkin, 2001). Some scholars, however, point out that there is "a fairly well-developed body of theory *for* campaigns but relatively little theory *of* campaigns" (Salmon & Murray-Johnson, 2001, p. 178). In other words, here is a well-articulated body of theories to help guide campaign strategies, but there is not yet a systematic theorization of campaigns as a social phenomenon.

The media effects tradition uses theory mostly in two ways: (a) to frame studies within a legitimate stream of theory (even in cases when this stream is appropri-ated a posteriori and does not really affect research design), and (b) to derive hy-potheses from it and advance theoretical refinement. That is, theory is mainly used for academic legitimating and theoretical verification purposes. Theory, however, is also used in the design and evaluation of communication interventions (Hornik & Yanovitzky, 2003). In this case, development communication scholars erase the line that conventionally separates theory and practice. In the same way, the pro-gressive development of a normative theory for health communication campaigns would also be a transgression of classical empiricist rules. As indicated before, it is often the case that development communication scholars, besides taking care of evaluation research, are often involved in project implementation.

THE CRITICAL THEORY TRADITION

It would be quite difficult to provide an overview or a unified definition of what critical theory is (Stirk, 2000). It is easier to summarize what critical scholars generally stand for. For scholars in this tradition, the subject of knowledge is no longer disengaged and disembodied, and scientific categories are not timeless, necessary, and unconditioned (Hoy & McCarthy, 1994). Their scholarship is politically explicit. It "subscribes to a Marxist politics and its attendant method of ideology critique" (Peters, 1993, p. 138). Their work is led by a normative stance: The world is unjust and should be changed. The study of power is the overall centerpiece of this tradition (Wilkins, 2000; Wilkins & Mody, 2001). Their general goal is to unveil the invisible apparatus of power that holds the strings of development policy and practices.

Taking into account that critical theory comprises highly diverse and even divergent schools of thought, the influence of this tradition in development communication can still be condensed into two broad points: (a) a primary focus on the systemic analysis of the diverse contexts of its object of study and (b) a general disapproval of positivistic epistemology (understood as value-free research that radically separates the inquirer from a controlled object of study).

On one hand, scholars in this tradition engage in a totalizing scrutiny of the structural, historical, and institutional webs that surround a specific communication strategy. First, as has been pointed out in the previous section, there is an emphasis on the contexts of development communication projects. This approach dates back to the origins of development communication, but became central in the early 1970s with the criticism of the modernization paradigm and the rise of the dependence theory[10] and other alternative models of development, mostly pushed by Latin American scholars (Beltran, 1976; Díaz-Bordenave, 1976). In this sense, critical scholars pay special attention to socioeconomic variables such as education, gender, income, and other factors that may explain differential access to the benefits supposedly facilitated by a communication program. Secondly, these scholars underscore the "futility of examining communication apart from its institutional setting" (Beltran, 1976, p. 118). Their attention goes not only to the effects of communication strategies but to who controls and designs these strategies and for whose benefit. In this line, a proposal for a critical analysis of purposive communication campaigns would look like this: "[R]ather than passively accepting that all social engineering efforts described as in the 'public interest' are actually so, one must examine the underlying assumptions of the campaigners as well as the values they are implicitly and explicitly promoting" (Salmon, 1989, p. 20).

On the other hand, this tradition "challenges commonplace assumptions about the objectivity and moral-political neutrality of science and technology" (Craig, 1999, p. 147). Empirical social science is accused of complying with the establishment and helping maintain the status quo.[11] The critical tradition is concerned with the political nature of scientific knowledge: Who decides what is knowledge, who produces it, for whom, and with what purpose. In relation to this interest in the power dynamics of knowledge creation, there is a recent critical approach to development communication that involves the analysis and disclosure of power structures embedded in institutional discourses of development (Escobar, 2000; Wilkins, 1999). Some scholars argue that the issue is not only communication for development, but communication about development (Wilkins & Mody, 2001). The recent advocacy for a critical content analysis of development discourse as a new task for development communication scholars derives from the poststructuralist theory of development,[12] "a social theory that starts by recognizing that language and discourse are constitutive of social reality" (Escobar, 2000, p. 166). The study of the politics of representation and the power issues involved in the creation and diffusion of utilitarian and development-oriented information by external change agents are also an increasing concern of critical scholars, particularly after the emergence of new communication technologies, such as the internet, that facilitate the creation and diffusion of different kinds of content for community development goals (e.g., Schech, 2002).

It is not rare to get the impression that the critical approach to development communication may have more to do with the political economy of development than with communication itself. The interdisciplinary (or antidisciplinary) approach of critical academics makes them stretch their scholarship to a point from which it is gradually more difficult to justify their inclusion within the communication field. Their mission, however, is clear. The role of the critical theory tradition is to indicate and denounce. It functions as a vigilant lighthouse of development discourse and practice. It is not a specific theory or a theory-oriented tradition in the conventional sense of the testable and falsifiable theory most critical scholars despise. Additionally, it is evident that the critical tradition is not the only stream of social science that produces critical scholarship. This tradition brings a way of looking at things, a perspective, a panoramic focus that points its attention to previously unnoticed objects of study. It tends to present itself in hybrid form, mixed with elements of the other two social science traditions of development communication. The critical perspective has stimulated significant changes in development communication, as proved by the influence it has had on the media effects tradition explained above, at least in three ways: (a) motivating self-reflection about the role of communication in development, (b) helping broaden theoretical endeavors, and (c) encouraging the exploration of different methodological options.

THE PRAGMATIST PHILOSOPHY TRADITION

The pragmatist philosophy tradition corresponds to participatory communication for development; in this sense, it could be renamed the participatory tradition. This social scientific tradition in development communication got its first impulse in the 1970s, when the attention of some communication scholars shifted from large-scale projects to microlevel rural projects. This tradition presents a particular set of ideas about the nature and goals of social science and an accompanying collection of guidelines or tools to put those ideas in practice. As the name pragmatic philosophy indicates, reflection and action are firmly interrelated in this tradition. On the side of reflection, it has a rich philosophical heritage, developed by thinkers such as Dewey (1991), Bernstein (1971), and Rorty (1979), and popularized by social philosophers and activists such as Freire (1970). Pragmatic philosophy conceives social science as an action-oriented form of inquiry that follows the premises of democratic participation (Deetz, 1999; Greenwood & Levin, 1998). Research is understood as a cooperative group effort to solve collectively identified problems.

Scholars in this tradition perceive communication as an end in itself, not a means to an end (Wilkins, 1999). Generally, there is no attention to communication effects; the interest is in the role of communication in the collaborative process of reaching self-help goals. Scholars become research facilitators and development partners. For them communication is not "a descriptive science but a tool of change" (Díaz-Bordenave, 1976, p. 151). Participatory communication is also a "political activity based on changed power equations" (Thomas, 1994, p. 54), in this sense, significantly connected to the critical tradition. There is a wide literature about the strategic application of participation to community development (e.g., see Cohen & Uphoff, 1980). Nevertheless, participatory communication is a very flexible instrument frequently used beyond the confines of academia (Beltran, 1993; Fraser & Restrepo-Estrada, 1998; Gumucio-Dagrón, 2001), with an independent life outside the intellectual endeavors of a social scientific tradition.[13]

There has been a lot of research and theorization about participation, mainly by sociologists and political scientists, but their work "does not represent a systematic theory of participatory communication in development" (Jacobson, 1994, p. 69). Participation has been justified philosophically, and some of the resulting premises of that abstract conceptualization have been translated in reality through the application of different research methods and strategies of participatory communication (Jacobson, 1993). For different reasons, however, there is not enough evaluation research about development projects that purport to be participatory (Frey, 1998; Thomas, 1994) or, in other words, researchers have not shown, in a theoretically integrated way, the role of participatory communication in development (Jacobson, 1994). Partly because of this, and despite the clear epistemological and methodological base of this tradition, the concept and use of participation in development communication are still elastic and loose, debilitated by rhetoric and recurrently manipulated and politicized for different purposes. In any case, although participatory communication "remains under theorized and lacks fundamental definition" (Jacobson & Storey, 2004, p. 99), there are recent signs of change in how development communication researchers in this tradition use and think about theory (e.g., Jacobson, 2003). For example, today we can see how some scholars use Habermas's theory of communicative action to analyze the participatory processes of a communication program in Nepal and to suggest a set of participatory communication indicators for use in the evaluation of development communication projects (Jacobson & Storey, 2004). In other words, there is a current movement in the participatory tradition to use theory as a basis for conceptual clarification, including the development of empirical indicators to evaluate the role of participation in communication projects.

ASSESSING PROSPECT FOR THEORY BUILDING

Two of the central themes that emerge in debates within the communication field are our capacity for creativity, considered as "our ability to generate original theory," and social relevance, or the capacity of our work to "improve the human condition" (Monahan & Collins-Jarvis, 1993, p. 151). These two core values are central for development communication scholars as well. In general, the social relevance of development communication research is rarely questioned, although there is always some dissension mostly coming from postdevelopment and critical scholars (Escobar, 2000). In contrast, after analyzing its three traditions, it can be argued that the creative competence of development communication scholars is rather low. From a conventional standpoint, investment in social relevance seems to be inversely proportional to theoretical creativity. On one side, development communication keeps with the value of social relevance by applying research to particular problems in specific contexts. On the other side, context-bound and applied research "is often at odds with the norms associated with creating useful theory, such as keeping research generalizable to a diversity of situations and perspectives" (Monahan & Collins-Jarvis, 1993, p. 154). One of the biggest challenges in development communication today is preserving the values of social relevance without threatening the opportunities for theoretical creativity. Given the critical interdependence of those two values in development communication, the most relevant aspect at this stage is to understand how its practical orientation (a common thread of its three traditions) has the potential to determine or condition what kind of theories may be generated.[14]

In conventional social science "there is a 'categorical distinction' between research and practice, between the development of scientific theory and applications of this theory to practical problems" (Greene, 1990, p. 228). There is no such distinction in development communication, not even in the media effects tradition, the only tradition that regularly uses theories as an instrument to generate research questions and hypotheses. This is again a manifestation of a larger shift in the field of communication, in which "conventional definitions of theory have lagged far behind practice" and "no longer reflect the actual range of theoretical work in the field" (Craig, 1993, p. 28). Some scholars, who conceive communication as a "practical discipline" (Craig & Tracy, 1995, p. 248), are proposing alternative conceptions of communication theory. These scholars defend the development of what they call practical theory (Barge, 2001; Craig & Tracy, 1995; Petronio, 1999), a kind of normative conceptualization oriented to action. Practical theory (or normative theory) is "centrally concerned with what ought to be; it seeks to articulate normative ideals by which to guide the conduct and criticism of practice" (Craig & Tracy, 1995, p. 249). It is clear that development communication leans toward practical and normative theory. A practical theory is not only an articulated body of knowledge that explains a particular phenomenon; it is also a flexible guide for action. It is not a prescriptive set of indications either; it is a theory that can be tested and refined through consecutive waves of action and reflection. Theory and practice are not separated; they are in dialogue. These scholars understand that "applications should enhance theoretical development and in turn theoretical development should enhance applications" (Cragan & Shields, 1999, p. 102).

The foundations of action research may provide some direction in the definition of criteria for the assessment of the workability and credibility (i.e., the validity) of practical theories of development communication (Greenwood & Levin, 1998). Nevertheless stipulating a clear set of parameters for rigorous evaluation of normative theories is a pressing duty for communication scholars at this point. In addition, although the rationale behind practical theorization spells out its value and usefulness beyond the boundaries of academe (Cissna, 2000), it is obvious that the institutional acceptance of these theories by the mainstream community of scholars constitutes another important challenge.

The three traditions together contribute to determine how these practical theories will look like: (a) The critical theory and the pragmatist philosophy traditions emphasize the need for a systemic conceptualization of problems, preserving the values of locality and specificity; and (b) the effects tradition underscores the importance of generalizability. The intersection of the three traditions demands a subtle balance between practical applicability across different contexts and universal categorization of ideas in the construction of normative theories. In this sense, although the different procedures to formulate, test, and judge practical theories are still to be seen, there are some incipient examples that attest a certain social scientific eclecticism in the way those theories are taking shape in development communication. The clearest example is the integrative theory of behavior change (Cappella et al., 2001) cited above. Another important lead in this direction is the area of organizing for social change (Papa, Auwal, & Singhal, 1995, 1997; Papa, Singhal, Ghanekar, & Papa, 2000). Development communication scholars in this area study the process of personal and community empowerment. They adopt different intellectual perspectives and multimethod approaches that are conducive to a practical theory of organizational communication for community development. These efforts are consonant with research on new social movements,[15] a subject that may serve as a reference for theoretical inspiration in development communication (Huesca, 2001). In addition, new attempts to rigorously conceptualize participatory processes in development communication programs are a very positive contribution to the field (Jacobson & Storey, 2004). In addition, the strategic use of information technologies through the establishment of public access facilities, usually called telecenters, is leading the way to new conceptualizations on the role of new media in rural development by combining different intellectual approaches (Roman & Colle, 2003). Telecenters appear as an opportunity for an integrated study of small media institutions, communication channels, and messages. The intersection of these three elements, a community-based organization that uses different media to create, search, and diffuse locally relevant content, makes telecenters a unique laboratory for researchers interested in studying how communication facilitates the process of economic, social, and cultural change, while presenting a great opportunity for theory testing and theory building (Roman, 2003).

The situation described in this chapter clearly illustrates a call for "theoretical and methodological tolerance" (O'Keefe, 1993, p. 81). This is not a new call or a new hope. In the initial years of this area of study, Lowenthal (1952–1953) envisioned that international communication "may even serve as an integrating force among many branches of the social sciences and humanities" (p. vii). Theoretical creativity in this field is incompatible with strict specialization or exclusivist rejection of different approaches to knowledge and understanding. A reductionist approach to social science, divided into irreconcilable isolated compartments and primitively satisfied with their own limitations, would only impoverish our understanding of the multiple problems and opportunities at stake in this field of study. That is especially the case in the interdisciplinary crossroads of development communication, an area of scholarly reflection that is also an area of social action.

NOTES

1. In this sense, it is worth noticing that "evaluation literature has rarely been concerned with the importance of theory in evaluating a program or with how to incorporate theory into evaluation processes" (Chen, 1990, p. 17). Evaluation research usually focuses on scientific methodological issues, without paying much attention to the theoretical implications of the programs examined.

2. Despite the different names this field of study has received, this paper will refer to it henceforth by the generic title development communication.

3. It is difficult to provide a general or unanimous definitions of development: "For most writers authentic development is perceived as being broadly concerned with the improvement of the conditions of existence of the majority of the population and particularly of the poorest. . . . Any attempt to be more precise than this, in terms of specifying and prioritizing the conditions to be ameliorated and indicating the means of attainment, must be seen as a personal preference reflecting the individual's values, and is unlikely to meet with general approval" (Hulme & Turner, 1990, p. 6). Probably reflecting his personal preference, Rogers (1995) defines development as "a widely participatory process of social change in a society intended to bring about both social and material advancement (including greater equality, freedom, and other valued qualities) for the majority of people through their gaining greater control over their environment" (p. 127).

4. Communication, since its inception as a scholarly field of study in American universities, has endured the habit of discussing convergence and divergence, competing social science traditions, and intellectual separatism (Rogers & Chaffee, 1993). There is a bulky literature about field fragmentation, disciplinary identity crisis, ferment in the field, and every kind of possible criticism and self-criticism from any imaginable perspective, since Berelson (1959) published his pessimistic state of communication research back in the 1950s.

5. Rogers (1994) indicates this Cold War orientation when he explains Schramm's work at Stanford University: "A further reason for Schramm's interest in international communication was his strong sense of patriotism, coupled with a belief that the main post-World War II problems for the United States lay in its Cold War conflict with the Soviet Union and in the related issue of Third World development, which U.S foreign policy at that time defined as a struggle with the Soviet Union for the hearts and minds of people in Latin America, Africa, and Asia" (p. 469).

6. "Entertainment–Education is the process of purposely designing and implementing a media message to both entertain and educate to increase audience members' knowledge about an educational issue, create favorable attitudes, and change overt behavior" (Singhal & Rogers, 2001, p. 343).

7. Theories of the middle range are "theories that lie between the minor but necessary working hypotheses that evolve in abundance during day-to-day research and the all-inclusive systematic efforts to develop a unified theory that will explain all the observed uniformities of social behavior, social organization and social change" (Merton, 1968, p. 39). Theories of the middle range organize a body of findings from replicated studies into a structured system of principles. Theories framed in this way must be amenable to empirical testing and falsifiability (Chaffee & Berger, 1987).

8. The knowledge gap hypothesis states that higher socioeconomic status segments of a population tend to acquire information at a faster rate than lower strata, so that the gap between these sectors tend to increase rather than decrease. The communication effects gap hypothesis is an extension of the knowledge gap: it expands the theory by focusing also on behavioral and attitudinal dependent variables, besides mere knowledge or information gain.

9. Despite the frequent criticism, there is no unanimous agreement about the general oversight of structural explanations in the media effects tradition. For example, Hornik (1989) also considers that, in contrast with the mostly psychological focus of American domestic literature on the effects of public information campaigns, "many scholars concerned with development communication look first to 'system' (or structural) explanations, secondarily to social network explanations and only reluctantly at individual psychological explanations" (p. 114).

10. The dependence theory, in the Marxist tradition of sociological analysis, criticized the early indifference to the historical context of developing countries and the inattention to the imperialistic inertia of the international macroeconomic system. "The myopia of developmental theorists, if not ideological, results from their tendency to view societies in static isolation without an adequate context in the international pattern of relationships" (Eisenstadt, 1976, p. 39).

11. It is important to underline, in any case, that critical theorists occasionally use empirical methods (Rogers, 1994).

12. "The poststructuralist analysis of development shows the ways in which the discourse of development has produced an efficient apparatus that systematically organizes the production of forms of knowledge and types of power, linking one to the other, in the production of Third World social reality" (Escobar, 2000, p. 166).

13. "In spite of participatory communication being a relatively recent topic of interest for academics, its story spans over the last fifty years, from the time Radio Sutatenza started in a remote area of Colombia and the Bolivian miners organized to set up community radio stations in their mining districts" (Gumucio-Dagrón, 2001, p. 8).

14. The issue here is not the multidimensional set of challenges posed to rigorous scholarship by socially relevant projects, although some of these challenges (time and budget constraints, conflicting stakeholder agendas, etc.) may have a significant effect on the way theory is used and the capacity for theoretical creativity in development communication, as indicated before.

15. "In the most general sense, new social movements have been defined as heterogeneous groups forming outside of formal institutions and operating in discontinuous cycles to forge collective meanings and identities that direct action" (Huesca, 2001, p. 421).

REFERENCES

Ajzen, I. (1991). The theory of planned behavior. *Organizational Behavior and Human Decision Processes, 50,* 179–211.

Atkin, C. (2001). Theory and principles of media health campaigns. In R. E. Rice & C. K. Atkin (Eds.), *Public communication campaigns* (pp. 49–68). Thousand Oaks, CA: Sage.

Bandura, A. (1977). *Social learning theory.* Englewood Cliffs, NJ: Prentice Hall.

Bandura, A. (2002). Social cognitive theory of mass communication. In J. Bryant & D. Zillmann (Eds.), *Media effects: advances in theory and research* (pp. 121–153). Mahwah, NJ: Erlbaum.

Barge, J. K. (2001). Practical theory as mapping, engaged reflection, and transformative practice. *Communication Theory, 11,* 5–13.

Beltran, L. R. (1976). Alien premises, objects, and methods in Latin American communication research. *Communication Research, 3*(2), 107–134.

Beltran, L. R. (1993). Communication for development in Latin America: A forty-year appraisal. In D. Nostbakken & C. Morrow (Eds.), *Cultural expression in the global village* (pp. 9–31). Ottawa, Canada: International Development Research Centre.

Berelson, B. (1959). The state of communication research. *Public Opinion Quarterly, 23,* 1–6.

Bersntein, R. (1971). *Praxis and action: Contemporary philosophies of human action.* Philadelphia: University of Pennsylvania Press.

Cappella, J. N., Fishbein, M., Hornik, R., Ahern, R. K., & Sayeed, S. (2001). Using theory to select messages in anti-drug media campaigns. In R. E. Rice & C. K. Atkin (Eds.), *Public communication campaigns* (pp. 214–230). Thousand Oaks, CA: Sage.

Chaffee, S. H., & Berger, C. R. (1987). What communication scientists do. In C. R. Berger & S. H. Chaffee (Eds.), *Handbook of communication science* (pp. 99–122). Newbury Park, CA: Sage.

Chen, H. (1990). *Theory-driven evaluations.* Newbury Park, CA: Sage.

Cissna, K. N. (2000). Applied communication research in the 21st century. *Journal of Applied Communication Research, 28,* 169–173.

Cohen, J. M., & Uphoff, N. T. (1980). Participation's place in rural development: Seeking clarity through specificity. *World Development, 8,* 213–233.

Cragan, J. F., & Shields, D. C. (1999). Translating scholarship into practice: Communication studies reflecting the value of theory-based research to everyday life. *Journal of Applied Communication Research, 27*(2), 92–106.

Craig, R. T. (1993). Why are there so many communication theories? *Journal of Communication, 43*(3), 26–33.

Craig, R. T. (1999). Communication theory as a field. *Communication Theory, 9,* 119–161.

Craig, R. T., & Tracy, K (1995). Grounded practical theory: The case of intellectual discussion. *Communication Theory, 5,* 248–272.

Deetz, S. (1999). Participatory democracy as a normative foundation for communication studies. In T. L. Jacobson & J. Servaes (Eds.), *Theoretical approaches to participatory communication* (pp. 131–167). Cresskill, NJ: Hampton Press.

Dewey, J. (1991). *Logic: The theory of inquiry.* Carbondale: Southern Illinois University Press.

Díaz-Bordenave, J. (1976). Communication of agricultural innovations in Latin America. *Communication Research, 3*(2), 135–154.

Eisenstadt, S. N. (1976). The changing vision of modernization and development. In W. Schramm & D. Lerner (Eds.), *Communication and change: The last ten years — and the next* (pp. 31–44). Honolulu: University Press of Hawaii.

Escobar, A. (2000). Place, power, and networks in globalization and postdevelopment. In K. G. Wilkins (Ed.), *Redeveloping communication for social change: Theory, practice and power* (pp. 163–173). Lanham, MD: Rowman & Littlefield.

Fraser, C., & Restrepo-Estrada, S. (1998). *Communicating for social change.* London: Tauris.

Freire, P. (1970). *The pedagogy of the oppressed.* New York: Herder & Herder.

Frey, L. R. (1998). Communication and social justice research: Truth, justice, and the applied communication way. *Journal of Applied Communication Research, 26*(2), 155–164.

Golding, P. (1974). Media role in national development: Critique of a theoretical orthodoxy. *Journal of Communication, 24*(3), 95–124.

Greene, J. C. (1990). Three views on the nature and role of knowledge in social science. In E. C. Guba (Ed.), *The paradigm dialog* (pp. 227–245). Newbury Park, CA: Sage.

Greenwood, D. J., & Levin, M. (1998). *Introduction to action research: Social research for social change.* Thousand Oaks, CA: Sage.

Guba, E. C. (1990). The alternative paradigm dialog. In E. C. Guba (Ed.), *The paradigm dialog* (pp. 17–27). Newbury Park, CA: Sage.

Gumucio-Dagrón, A. (2001). *Making waves: Stories of participatory communication for social change.* New York: Rockefeller Foundation.

Hornik, R. (1988). *Development communication: Information, agriculture, and nutrition in the Third World.* New York: Longman.

Hornik, R. (1989). The knowledge-behavior gap in public information campaigns: A development communication view. In C. T. Salmon (Ed.), *Information campaigns: Balancing social values and social change* (pp. 113–138). Newbury Park, CA: Sage.

Hornik, R. (2002). Public health communication: Making sense of contradictory evidence. In R. Hornik (Ed.), *Public health communication: Evidence for behavior change* (pp. 1–33). Mahwah, NJ: Erlbaum.

Hornik, R., & McAnany, E. (2001). Theories and evidence: Mass media effects and fertility change. *Communication Theory, 11,* 454–471.

Hornik, R., & Yanovitzky, I. (2003). Using theory to design evaluations of communication campaigns: The case of the National Youth Anti-Drug Media Campaign. *Communication Theory, 13,* 204–224.

Hoy, D. C., & McCarthy, T. (1994). *Critical theory.* Cambridge, MA: Blackwell.

Huesca, R. (2001). Conceptual contributions of new social movements to development communication research. *Communication Theory, 11,* 415–433.

Hulme, D., & Turner, M. M. (1990). *Sociology and development: Theories, policies and practices.* New York: St. Martin Press.

Jacobson, T. L. (1993). A pragmatist account of participatory communication research for national development. *Communication Theory, 3,* 214–230.

Jacobson, T. L. (1994). Modernization and post-modernization approaches to participatory communication for development. In S. A. White (Ed.), *Participatory communication: working for change and development* (pp. 60–75). New Delhi, India: Sage.

Jacobson, T. L. (2003). Participatory communication for social change: The relevance of the theory of communicative action. In P. Kalbfleisch (Ed.), *Communication Yearbook 27* (pp. 87–124). Mahwah, NJ: Erlbaum.

Jacobson, T. L., & Storey, J. D. (2004). Development communication and participation: Applying Habermas to a case study of population programs in Nepal. *Communication Theory, 14,* 99–121.

Kincaid, D. L. (2002). Drama, emotion, and cultural convergence. *Communication Theory, 12,* 136–152.

Kothari, U., & Minogue, M. (2002). Critical perspectives on development: An introduction. In U. Kothari & M. Minogue (Eds.), *Development theory and practice: Critical perspectives* (pp. 1–15). Hampshire, UK: Palgrave.

Lerner, D. (1958). *The passing of traditional society.* New York: Free Press.

Lowenthal, L. (1952/53). Introduction to the special issue on international communication research. *Public Opinion Quarterly, 16*(4), v–x.

Mathur, J. C., & Neurath, P. (1959). *An Indian experiment in farm radio forums.* Paris: UNESCO.

Melkote, S. R. (1991). *Communication for development in the Third World: Theory and practice.* New Delhi, India: Sage.

Melkote, S. R., Muppidi, S. R., & Goswami, D. (2000). Social and economic factors in an integrated behavioral and societal approach to communications in HIV/AIDS. *Journal of Health Communication, 5* (Supplement), 17–27.

Merton, R. K. (1968). *Social theory and social structure.* New York: Free Press.

Mody, B. (2000). The contexts of power and the power of media. In K. G. Wilkins (Ed.), *Redeveloping communication for social change: Theory, practice and power* (pp. 185–195). Lanham, MD: Rowman & Littlefield.

Monahan, J. L., & Collins-Jarvis, L. (1993). The hierarchy of institutional values in the communication discipline. *Journal of Communication, 43*(3), 150–157.

O'Keefe, B. (1993). Against theory. *Journal of Communication, 43*(3), 75–82.

Olien, C. N., Donohue, G. A., & Tichenor, P. J. (1984). Structure, communication and social power: Evolution of the knowledge gap hypothesis. In E. Wartella & D. C. Whitney (Eds.), *Mass communication yearbook 4* (pp. 445–462). Beverly Hills, CA: Sage.

Papa, M. J., Auwal, M. A., & Singhal, A. (1995). Dialectic of control and emancipation in organizing for social change: A multitheoretic study of the Grameen Bank in Bangladesh. *Communication Theory, 5,* 189–223.

Papa, M. J., Auwal, M. A., & Singhal, A. (1997). Organizing for social change within concertive control *systems:* Member identification, empowerment, and the masking of discipline. *Communication Monographs, 64,* 219–249.

Papa, M. J., Singhal, A., Ghanekar, D. V., & Papa, W. H. (2000). Organizing for social change through cooperative action: The [dis]empowering dimensions of women's communication". *Communication Theory, 10,* 90–123.

Peet, R., & Harwick, E. (1999). *Theories of development.* New York: Guilford Press.

Peters, J. D. (1993). Genealogical notes on "the field." *Journal of Communication, 43*(4), 132–139.

Petronio, S. (1999). "Translating scholarship into practice": An alternative metaphor. *Journal of Applied Communication Research, 27*(2), 87–91.

Piotrow, P. T., & Kincaid, D. L. (2001). Strategic communication for international health programs. In R. E. Rice & C. K. Atkin (Eds.), *Public communication campaigns* (pp. 249–266). Thousand Oaks, CA: Sage.

Rice, R. E., & Atkin, C. K. (2002). Communication campaigns: Theory, design, implementation, and evaluation. In J. Bryant & D. Zillmann (Eds.), *Media effects: Advances in theory and research* (pp. 427–451). Mahwah, NJ: Erlbaum.

Rist, G. (1999). *The history of development: From western origins to global faith.* Cape Town, South Africa: ZED Books/University of Cape Town Press.

Rogers, E. M. (1976a). The passing of the dominant paradigm—reflections on diffusion research. In W. Schramm & D. Lerner (Eds.), *Communication and change: The last ten years—and the next* (pp. 49–52). Honolulu: University Press of Hawaii.

Rogers, E. M. (1976b). Where Are We in Understanding the Diffusion of Innovations? In W. Schramm & D. Lerner (Eds.), *Communication and change: The last ten years—and the next* (pp. 204–222). Honolulu: University Press of Hawaii.

Rogers, E, M. (1976c). Communication and development: The passing of the dominant paradigm. *Communication Research, 3,* 213–241.

Rogers, E. M. (1982). Preface to the 1982 edition. In E. M. Rogers (Ed.), *Communication and development: Critical perspectives* (pp. ii–viii). Beverly Hills, CA: Sage.

Rogers, E. M. (1994). *A history of communication study: A biographical approach.* New York: The Free Press.

Rogers, E. M. (1995). *Diffusion of innovations* (4th ed). New York: Free Press.

Rogers, E. M., & Storey, J. D. (1987). Communication campaigns. In C. Berger & S. Chaffee (Eds.), *Handbook of communication science* (pp. 817–846). Newbury Park, CA: Sage.

Rogers, E. M., & Chaffee, S. H. (1993). The past and the future of communication study: Convergence or divergence? *Journal of Communication, 43*(4), 125–131.

Rogers, E. M., & Singhal, A. (1996). Diffusion of innovations. In M. B. Salwen & D. W. Stacks (Eds.), *An integrated approach to communication theory and research* (pp. 409–420). Mahwah, NJ: Erlbaum.

Roman, R. (2003) Diffusion of innovations as a theoretical framework for telecenters. *Information Technologies and International Development, 1*(2), 55–68.

Roman, R & Colle, R. (2003) Content creation for information and communication technology development projects: Integrating normative approaches and community demand. *Journal of Information Technology for Development, 10*(2), 85–94.

Rorty, R. (1979). *Philosophy and the mirror of nature.* Princeton, NJ: Princeton University Press.

Rosenstock I. M., Strecher V. J., Becker M. H. (1988). Social learning theory and the health belief model. *Health Education Quarterly 15,* 175–183.

Salmon, C. T. (1989). Campaigns for social "improvement": An overview of values, rationales, and impacts. In C. T. Salmon (Ed.), *Information campaigns: Balancing social values and social change* (pp. 19–53). Newbury Park, CA: Sage.

Salmon, C. T., & Murray-Johnson, L (2001). Communication campaign effectiveness: Critical distinctions. In R. E. Rice & C. K. Atkin (Eds.), *Public communication campaigns* (pp. 168–180). Thousand Oaks, CA: Sage.

Samarajiwa, R. (1987). The murky beginnings of the communication and development field. In N. Jayaweera & S. Amunugama (Eds.), *Rethinking development communication* (pp. 3–19). Singapore: AMIC.

Schech, S. (2002). Wired for change: The links between ICTs and development discourses. *Journal of International Development, 14,* 13–23.

Schramm, W. (1964). *Mass media and national development.* Stanford, CA: Stanford University Press.

Schramm, W. (1976). End of an old paradigm? In W. Schramm & D. Lerner (Eds.), *Communication and change: The last ten years—and the next* (pp. 45–48). Honolulu: University Press of Hawaii.

Servaes, J. (1991). Toward a new perspective for communication and development. In F. L. Casmir (Ed.), *Communication in development* (pp. 51–85). Norwood, NJ: Ablex.

Servaes, J. (1999). *Communication for development: One world, multiple cultures.* Cresskill, NJ: Hampton Press.

Sherry, J. L. (1997). Prosocial soap operas for development: A review of research and theory. *Journal of International Communication, 4*(2), 75–101.

Sherry, J. L. (2002). Media saturation and entertainment education. *Communication Theory, 12,* 206–224.

Singhal, A., & Rogers, E. M. (2001). The entertainment-education strategy in communication campaigns. In R. E. Rice & C. K. Atkin (Eds.), *Public communication campaigns* (pp. 343–356). Thousand Oaks, CA: Sage.

Singhal, A., & Rogers, E. M. (2002). A theoretical agenda for entertainment-education. *Communication Theory, 12,* 117–135.

Stirk, P. M. R. (2000). *Critical theory, politics and society: An introduction.* London: Pinter.

Sypher, B. D., McKinley, M., Ventsam, S., & Valdeavellano E. E. (2002). Fostering reproductive health through entertainment-education in the Peruvian Amazon: The social construction of Bienvenida Salud! *Communication Theory, 12,* 192–205.

Thomas, P. (1994). Participatory development communication: Philosophical premises. In S. A. White (Ed.), *Participatory communication: Working for change and development* (pp. 49–59). New Delhi, India: Sage.

Tichenor, P. J., Donohue, G. A., & Olien, C. N. (1970). Mass media flow and differential growth in knowledge. *Public Opinion Quarterly, 34*(2), 159–170.

Vaughan, P. W., & Rogers, E. M. (2000). A staged model of communication effects: Evidence from an entertainment-education radio soap opera in Tanzania. *Journal of Health Communication, 5,* 203–227.

Wilkins, K. G. (1999). Development discourse on gender and communication in strategies for social change. *Journal of Communication, 49*(1), 44–64.

Wilkins, K. G. (2000). Accounting for power in development communication. In K. G. Wilkins (Ed.), *Redeveloping communication for social change: Theory, practice and power* (pp. 197–210). Lanham, MD: Rowman & Littlefield.

Wilkins, K. G., & Mody, B. (2001). Reshaping development communication: Developing communication and communicating development. *Communication Theory, 11,* 385–396.

CHAPTER CONTENTS

11 Message Framing and Constructing Meaning: An Emerging Paradigm in Mass Communication Research

ROBERT H. WICKS
University of Arkansas

This chapter analyzes the influence of framing research on the advancement of a meanings paradigm also known as constructionism. Framing models have been useful during the past 2 decades to help explain how people construct meaning by drawing upon stored knowledge or schemas to interpret news and information. Media or message framing refers both to the process of selecting and the manner in which information is presented. News messages may be framed either episodically, as a case study, or thematically, in which general or abstract concepts are presented and emphasized. Schemas, attitudes, and beliefs of professional communicators may influence the ways in which media messages are framed. Journalistic framing involves identifying a problem, assigning responsibility, considering ethical or moral implications, and recommending a solution. Audience or individual framing occurs when people process information in the context of their own schemas. Framing studies often employ multiple methodologies to analyze the messages that are produced and reception processes that occur among audience members. Thus, analysis of the framing literature is important in understanding how both the media and the members of the audience play active and vital roles in the process of constructing social reality. Examples of journalistic and audience framing processes are presented to illustrate how framing operates. Implications for the future are discussed.

Mass communication research is rapidly moving beyond effects research into what has become known as the meanings paradigm. This paradigm challenges the media effects tradition by proposing a more comprehensive and complex explanation of the relationship between how media frames and messages interface with audience frames. Reese (2001) explained media frames "are organizing principles that are socially shared and persistent over time, that work symbolically to meaningfully construct the social world" (p. 11).

Correspondence: Robert H. Wicks, Director, Center for Communication and Media Research, Department of Communication, Kimpel Hall—417, University of Arkansas, Fayetteville, AR 72701; email: rwicks@uark.edu

The concurrent focus on production and reception processes has led to interest in framing by both social scientists and cultural theorists. As such, D'Angelo (2002) has asserted that framing research has taken on a multiparadigmatic character as it attracts the attention of communication researchers from different theoretical and methodological orientations.

Understanding audience framing helps explain how and why different constituencies or individuals develop different attitudes, opinions, and beliefs even if they encounter identical or similar media messages (Morley, 1992). Understanding these framing mechanisms helps to explain how people construct social reality. Bateson (1955, 1972) originally coined the term framing to illustrate and explain how individuals psychologically negotiate levels of abstraction in messages as they communicate. From a communication perspective, framing provides a field of meaning through which messages about people and events may be understood. Rather than studying the effect of media on individuals, framing studies seek to uncover the dynamic relationship between the medium, the issue, and the individual to explain how and why people come to believe and know what they do (Neuman, Just, & Crigler, 1992).

The media serve as a primary conduit through which ideas, attitudes, and beliefs flow. Thus, it is important to understand how we construct meaning as a result of encounters with these messages. Greek philosopher Plato recognized this long ago in his well-known Allegory of the Cave (Plato, trans. 1945, *The Republic,* book 7). In it, Plato described a scenario in which men were chained at the bottom of a cave with a long entrance that allowed only minimal light to enter. These men had been chained since childhood so that they could see only a wall in front of them. Behind them was a parapet with a parallel road behind it. Behind the wall that the men are facing was a fire burning that cast light upon it. People behind the parapet may hold up shapes and objects that cast shadows on the wall. The men may also hear movements or discussions behind them but they may interpret them only through the images cast on the wall in front of them. Plato theorized that such an arrangement would lead the men to construct reality that may be at odds with the true reality that exists behind them. Even though the shadows enabled them to construct a reality, the constructed reality did not accurately represent the true reality of the events taking place behind them.

The Allegory of the Cave is a useful starting point in considering how individuals and media interact. Media effects research originally assumed that powerful effects were exerted on the thought and belief systems of passive audience members. This perspective shifted in the 1960s, as Joseph Klapper (1960) argued that media tended to reinforce rather than alter belief systems. Subsequent work of Noelle-Neumann (1973), McCombs and Shaw (1972), Gerber and Gross (1976), and others signaled the beginning of a period designated as the search for more powerful effects. This important period focused not only on the effects of media, but also considered cognitive processes that occur when audience members interact with media.

Drawing upon cognitive theory, Lowery and DeFleur (1988) asserted that researchers should now consider the interrelationships between message contents and characteristics to develop a meanings paradigm. This new paradigm would be concerned with the "relationship between internal and subjective representations of reality (meanings) and the influence that knowledge had on human conduct" (DeFleur & Ball-Rokeach, 1989, p. 234) to advance our understanding of how people construct social reality. The term commonly given to this is constructionist theory or constructionism (Delia, 1976, 1977). The central feature of the constructionism approach is an understanding of the ways in which people interact with media to construct social reality as opposed to how media influence people.

The emerging meanings paradigm is especially important for the future of communication because it signals the need for greater cross-pollination between communication social science research and cultural studies. Even though social scientists have tended to focus on the outcome of messages such as attitude shifts as the result of debates or the impact of advertising on elections, cultural theorists have tended to try to understand how messages are received and how psychological predispositions may be altered. The combined theoretical and methodological strengths of these approaches will accelerate the evolution of this paradigm leading potentially to a better understanding of how people construct meaning about the world in which they live.

In this chapter, I will argue that the meanings paradigm has begun to produce fruit and is advancing rapidly. In so doing, I will trace the evolution of the media effects tradition to illustrate how media theory and scholarship are shifting to framing and constructionism as a dominant paradigm. Using examples, I will then illustrate how message framing contributes to the construction of social reality. I will conclude with recommendations on how multiple-method research strategies and greater collaboration between social scientists and cultural studies researchers will advance this paradigm in the future.

FROM MEDIA EFFECTS TO MESSAGE FRAMING

McQuail (1994) has asserted that the 20th century was dominated by four paradigm shifts reflecting attitudes toward the potential effects of media. Attitudes constitute the evaluations held toward objects, issues, or other people (Petty & Cacioppo, 1981; Petty, Cacioppo, & Kasmer, 1988; Petty, Priester, & Brinol, 2002). Most of the early research concluded that media messages contributed to the development of attitudes because a passive and unquestioning audience absorbed them. Enhanced understanding of how media messages interacted with human attitudes led to the transition between paradigms.

Phase 1: The Strong Effects Model

The first paradigm from the turn of the century to the early 1930s assumed that effective propaganda campaigns during World War I demonstrated that the media may have strong or powerful effects on shaping attitudes. This early research was inspired by the behaviorist tradition (i.e., stimulus–response theory) in psychology. The basic premise was that people were essentially irrational and that emotional impulses caused them to behave as they did. This perspective was consistent with research in the 1920s, which indicated that media channels could be used for propaganda purposes to alter attitudes and beliefs (e.g., Lasswell, 1927, 1948). Early propaganda researchers, though, also pointed out that such attitude shifting generally occurred over time when carefully constructed ideas and images were developed and presented as part of an overall persuasive campaign intended to change attitudes. Examples of this manipulation were the supposed effectiveness of political advertising campaigns or the ability of politicians to shape public opinion by staging events designed to attract news media coverage (Lazarsfeld & Merton, 1948).

Early media research also endeavored to explain decision-making processes that caused reporters and editors to include or exclude certain stories in newspapers (e.g., Breed, 1955; White, 1950). The significance of this strain of research focused on message salience in which a one-way linear relationship between the message sender and receiver was assumed. Specifically, researchers suspected that if they understood the criteria employed by media gatekeepers in the process of selecting, collecting, and disseminating media information, they would be able to understand something about the opinions, beliefs, and attitudes of the society (Converse, 1964).

Phase 2: The Limited Effects Model

In 1960, Klapper cautioned against assuming that television was capable of having direct and immediate effects on individuals. In his volume, *The Effects of Mass Communication,* Klapper (1960) analyzed the available evidence to offer a more conservative assessment of what was known with respect to media influences over people. To do so, he compiled virtually all of the relevant media effects research produced until the 1960s by social scientists employed at universities as well as that of broadcast industry analysts working in the private sector.

Klapper argued that empirical research does not demonstrate that media are all powerful in influencing behavior. When a media message does produce a direct effect, he suggested, it is a departure from the norm. Klapper also distinguished between the potential for instantaneous and powerful influence of media over individuals and the likelihood that media effects may be subtle and occur over time.

Klapper contended that media effects are mitigated by many variables, including (a) message content; (b) the manner in which communicators construct messages; and (c) the knowledge, attitudes, beliefs, and predispositions an individual held prior to exposure.

Phase 3: The Search for Stronger Effects

The remarkable growth of television in the 1960s led researchers to rekindle the debate on the limited versus powerful effects of media on individuals and society (e.g., Gunter, 1987; Katz, Adoni, & Parness 1977; Neuman, 1976; Robinson & Levy, 1986; Stauffer, Frost, & Rybolt, 1983). Thus began the third phase in the 1970s with an emphasis on a search for stronger effects (Noelle-Neumann, 1973) along with a focus on how media may cognitively influence individuals (Beniger & Gusek, 1995). The 1970s also gave rise to the agenda-setting research tradition (McCombs & Shaw, 1972), the uses and gratifications approach (Rubin, 2002), and cultivation theory (Gerbner & Gross, 1976). Each of these approaches argued from differing perspectives that media must have more than minimal effects.

The problem, some scholars believed, was that the minimal effects perspective advocated by Klapper did not effectively measure what had been retained through the television viewing experience. In a classic article, Bauer (1964) argued that media users are active and goal-oriented. By 1974, Katz, Blumler, and Gurevitch had formulated a statement on media uses and gratifications intended to (a) explain how people use media to gratify their needs; (b) explain motives for media behavior; and (c) identify functions or consequences that follow from needs, motives, and behavior (Rubin, 2002). These researchers argued that ample evidence exists to suggest that people go out of their way to utilize the media to accomplish certain goals and derive specific gratifications. In short, information and entertainment needs significantly drive the behaviors of media audiences. At the same time, McCombs and Shaw (1972) introduced the idea of agenda setting. The media, they argued, were not capable of telling people what to think but were capable of spotlighting topics that caused people to think about certain issues.

Discontent with the limited-effects model continued to produce new streams of research demonstrating more powerful effects. Cultivation researchers reported that fictional crime programs seemed to have the ability to cultivate the beliefs and attitudes of viewers concerning the incidence and type of crime prevalent in society (Gerbner & Gross, 1976; Gerbner, Gross, Morgan, & Signorielli, 1980; Hawkins, Yong-Ho, & Pingree, 1991; Potter, 1991a, 1991b). People may also remain silent when the media present a view contrary to their own because media tend to frame issues in various ways and people may begin to questions their own beliefs (Noelle-Neumann, 1973, 1993). Neither the spiral of silence nor cultivation theory is in complete opposition to the limited-effect perspective; however, both suggest that interaction between the media and people may ultimately produce effects that are not so minimal.

Phase 4: The Cognitive Revolution and Emergence of the Meanings Paradigm

By the middle of the 1980s, rapidly expanding information-processing research in the field of psychology prompted Gardner (1985) to assert that a cognitive revolution had taken place. This revolution profoundly influenced the development of mass communication theory, prompting scholars to consider the relationship between emerging information-processing theory, agenda setting, persuasion, the spiral of silence, uses and gratifications, and cultivation theory. Furthermore, collaborative research between communication scholars and psychologists accelerated leading to significant cross-pollination among the allied fields (e.g., Bryant & Zillmann, 2002; Reeves & Anderson, 1991; Reeves & Thorson, 1986).

Cognitive theory also helped to explain the interaction between dynamic structural variables (e.g., video pacing, type of music, video-editing procedures, gender or race of actors) and content genres (e.g., news, entertainment, or sports programs). Cognitive theory has also been used to evaluate how message content may interact with the viewer's mood or emotional state that may in turn influence message reception and interpretation (Bryant & Zillmann, 1991; Zillmann, 1983a, 1983b, 1991a, 1991b). These studies have generally focused on the internal microlevel psychological processes that take place when people encounter media information. Such inquiries have yielded significant insights as to what causes people to pay attention to media and what they remember from exposure to media information (e.g., Brosius, 1993; Chaffee & Schleuder, 1986; Grimes & Meadowcroft, 1995; Thorson, Reeves, & Schleuder, 1987; Schleuder, White, & Cameron, 1993).

The cognitive revolution also made it clear that earlier research traditions such as uses and gratifications approach, agenda setting, cultivation research, the spiral of silence, as well as other developing theories of persuasion were most beneficial when employed in a complementary fashion. Even though each offered new insights on how people interact with the media, none offered a coherent model that integrated psychological processes and effects of media messages, as well as the influence of broader social, anthropological, and environmental factors. Such a model would require mass communication theorists to evaluate both media content and the psychological composition of the audience members in tandem to explain how people construct social reality by interacting with media content (Shapiro, 1991). Such a model was dubbed the meanings paradigm or constructionism and was dependent upon understanding the components of both message and audience framing.

As Scheufele (1999) explained:

> The description of media and recipients in this stage combines elements of both strong and limited effects of mass media. On the one hand, mass media have a strong impact by constructing social reality, that is, "by framing images of reality ... in a predictable and patterned way" (McQuail, 1994, p. 331). On the other hand, media are limited by an interaction between mass media and recipient. (p. 105)

THE FRAMING CONSTRUCT

Origins of the Framing Construct

Even though four paradigms dominated the 20th century, many of the ideas associated with framing and constructionism actually transcends each. As early as 1922, journalist Walter Lippmann wrote that people are all captives of the pictures in their heads (Lippmann, 1922, p. 3). He explained that "in the buzzing confusion of the outer world, we pick out what our culture has already defined for us, and we tend to perceive that which we have picked out in the form stereotyped for us by our culture" (Lippmann, 1922, p. 81). This statement implied that early theorists recognized that human beings tend to process information in the context of previously stored knowledge for the purpose of reinforcing beliefs and stereotypes, as Klapper (1960) later noted. Lippmann also recognized that the selective portrayal of the world by the newspapers of the 1920s contributed to the construction of social reality by spotlighting certain news items while ignoring others, as McCombs and Shaw (1972) later demonstrated. Hence, to some extent, the roots of framing theory and constructionism can actually to be traced to the 1920s. By the 1980s, the central focus of these ideas had crystallized into asking what people do with media information, rather than how media messages affect people.

To answer this question, theorists began studying the media in the context of message framing (e.g., Burke, 1968; Gitlin, 1980; Goffman, 1974; McLuhan, 1964; Schramm, 1971). Framing theory expands beyond what people talk or think about by examining how they think and talk. It considers message characteristics and how information is crafted. It then goes further by considering the psychological (i.e., cognitive and affective) characteristics of audience members that cause messages to be interpreted in various ways (Maher, 2001). Frames enable people to evaluate, convey, and interpret information based on shared conceptual constructs. As such, media messages contain contextual cues supplied by professional communicators to help people understand information (Reese, Gandy, & Grant, 2001). Framing analysis as an approach to analyzing discourse disseminated by the mass media deals fundamentally with how "public discourse about policy issues is constructed and negotiated" (Pan & Kosicki, 1993, p. 70). It therefore helps to build a more stable theoretical basis of news information processing by focusing on the dynamic interaction among message, source, and receiver (Neuman et al., 1992).

Contemporary media framing theory and research may have begun with theorists such as Goffman (1974), who asserted that individuals must actively classify and interpret their life experiences to make sense of the world around them. These classifications and interpretations are essentially ever-present and ongoing, representing the social constructivism approach (Delia & O'Keefe, 1979). These schemas of interpretation are the frames that enable people to place information in context and make sense of events. Gitlin (1980) expanded upon this by suggesting frames enable journalists to process large amounts of information quickly and enables them to routinely package the information for efficient relay to their audiences. Gamson asserted that the frame is essentially an organizing mechanism that enables communicators to provide meaning (Gamson, 1989, 1992; Gamson & Modigliani, 1989).

The psychological view of framing shares many of the theoretical underpinnings associated with the sociological perspective. Minsky (1975), for example, conceptualized a frame as a template that helps organize knowledge. Iyengar (1991) asserted that framing provides contextual cues to enable people to see where a journalist is going with a story. Journalists utilize schemas (i.e., clusters of knowledge that guide individual's processing of information) to communicate ideas in a shorthand manner. Scripts are schemas in which story lines are organized involving scenarios or routines with agreed-on rules (Rumelhart, 1984; Wicks, 1992). Thus, the interaction between audience member and messages is not necessarily dependent upon issues or aspects of an issue that are being covered. Rather, salience of an issue can produce responses in audiences (Kim, Scheufele, & Shanahan, 2002).

The work of Kahneman and Tversky (e.g., Tversky & Kahneman, 1981; Kahneman & Tversky, 1984) argued that different cognitive frames of the same situations cause different people to arrive at conclusions leading in turn to very different decisions. Media framing, however, can also be influential in shifting public opinion. Later in this chapter, I will provide current examples of framing as they relate to recent events such as the war on terrorism and political communication.

Media–Journalistic Frames

Contemporary framing research is advancing simultaneously across disciplines such as communication (D'Angelo, 2002; Entman, 2003; Entman & Rojecki, 1993; Neuman, et al., 1992; Price & Tewksbury, 1997; Scheufele, 2004), sociology (Gamson, 1988, 1992), political science (Norris, Kern & Just, 2003), journalism (Pan & Kosicki, 1993, 2001; Reese, Gandy, & Grant, 2001), and political psychology (Iyengar, 1991).

Media framing begins when decisions are made on which stories are covered and how they will be treated. It involves selection and salience by placing issues or events within a field of meaning. Professional communicators select particular aspects of reality and then highlight them in the messages that they produce. Entman (1993) viewed the message-framing process in the following way: (a) identify a problem; (b) assess the cause of an event and assign responsibility; (c) consider the issue or problem in the context of legal, ethical, or moralistic principle;, and (d) identify and recommend solutions to the problem. News frames may vary considerably in how they are reported. In one study, Entman (1991) considered differences in portrayal of the Soviet downing of KAL Flight 007 and U.S. downing of Iranian Air Flight 655. Reports in U.S. news magazines devoted more space and coverage and quoted more official sources in reporting the KAL incident than the Iranian Air incident. The tone of coverage was much more accusatory and derogatory in coverage of the KAL incident whereas the Iranian downing was treated more as an unfortunate accident.

Reese (2001) proposed a working definition of media framing that extends Entman's (1993). Reese viewed frames not just as organizing principles, but as a system of exerting power that may influence public opinion. Reese asserted, "The power to frame depends on access to resources, a store of knowledge, and strategic alliances" (2001, p. 20). In other words, taken together, Reese (2001) and Entman (1993) asserted that the concept of framing implies that the way a given piece of information is presented can create different outcomes among different audiences. Furthermore, frames may be manipulated to influence public opinion if proper resources are available.

Media messages also contain contextual cues supplied by professional communicators to help people understand information. Iyengar (1991) suggested that news messages might supply information in the context of either episodic or thematic frames. Episodic framing is event-oriented coverage of breaking news stories. Thematic framing is presenting issues in context with background information. Concrete event-oriented reports, which the news media favor, encourage the production of episodic rather than thematic news stories. Iyengar (1991) explained:

> The episodic news frames take the form of a case study or an event-oriented report and depict public issues in terms of concrete instances (for example, the plight of the homeless person or a teenage drug user, the bombing of an airliner, or an attempted murder). The thematic frame, by contrast, places public issues in some more general or abstract context and takes the form of a timeout, or backgrounder, report directed at general outcomes or conditions. Examples of thematic coverage include reports on changes in government welfare expenditures, congressional debates over the funding of employment training programs, the social or political grievances of groups undertaking terrorist activities, and the backlog in the criminal justice process. (p. 14)

Television news relies most heavily on episodic framing because the medium stresses the recency of the information and the speed of transmission (Postman, 1985; Robinson & Levy, 1986). Given that news stories are presented as discrete items or events, television typically fails to provide relationships among issues, people, and events. One problem with this style of presentation is that if citizens believe that social or political problems are solved as quickly in the real world as they are in movies and on entertaining television programs, they may perceive a sense of powerlessness both as individuals or collectively as members of society (Downs, 1972).

The choice of words and language is also important in the framing process. The Watergate incident that led to the downfall of former President Richard M. Nixon was initially framed by the news media as a partisan issue within an election campaign. Eventually the issue took on broader significance and was framed as widespread corruption within the Nixon White House. Language selected by message producers may also contribute to the framing process. The media initially referred to the Watergate caper denoting political mischief, but that term later gave way to phrases such as the Watergate scandal, with implications of wide-spread corruption (Lang & Lang, 1983).

Influences on Media Message Framing

All mediated messages are constructed by individuals operating within a set of organizational practices or traditions and from their own attitudes, opinions, and beliefs. As a result, mediated messages are representations of reality presented through the prism of the communicator. Media audiences therefore confront the same problems as did the men in Plato's cave. The media produce images, sounds, and other stimuli that enter sensory organs and are converted into coherent messages. Organizational variables, differences in message producers, and reception processes of audience members combine to cause individuals to arrive at very different conclusions following exposure to the same message. These variables that influence frame construction and the construction of social reality may be summarized as follows:

Political or economic orientation of the medium. American magazines and newspapers tend to be either conservative or liberal. *U.S. News and World Report,* for example, has a reputation for being more conservative than *Time* or *Newsweek*. Journalists with conservative or liberal leanings tend to affiliate with news agencies that share their attitudes and predispositions. Thus, although journalists with liberal or conservative leanings may strive for objectivity, they may self-select into organizations and work with colleagues who share political attitudes and beliefs, which may reinforce political orientation (Berkowitz, 1996; Wicks, 2001).

Organizational practices and constraints. Producers of messages work within certain logistical or organizational constraints (Shoemaker & Reese, 1996). Economic concerns can drive what news is covered and what is excluded. Complex information must be compressed to accommodate the structure of media such as television, newspapers, magazines, and the Internet. Because of the institutional nature of journalism organizations and training conventions, these news values would include a set of agreed-on rules defined by media practitioners and handed down to aspiring journalists in college. The rules that govern these strategies normally appear in the first few chapters of any undergraduate textbook on news reporting and include timeliness, prominence of personalities, impact, human interest, conflict, and proximity of an event to the news agency (e.g., Stephens, 1993). Thus packaging and organizational constraints may influence message framing.

Journalistic belief systems. Journalists and editors make unconscious or conscious decisions to explain information based on their belief systems. These belief systems are contained within schemas relating to news values (Wicks, 1992). These messages are colored by their own predispositions, which may influence both the structure and content of the message (Geiger & Reeves, 1991). Personal agendas and biases of news producers further influence how messages are constructed. Objectivity—although a goal of professional communicators—is an unobtainable one.

Techniques to attract audiences. A major objective of media organizations is to attract audiences. Informing audience members often serves as secondary goal. It is true that certain news (e.g., the war in Iraq or the 2004 U.S. presidential race between Bush and Kerry) is capable of both attracting large audiences and informing. It is, however, equally true that dramatic or emotional news with little lasting importance often vies for the lead position in a newscast or a prominent position on the front page. Thus, the desire to present compelling news can drive the framing process (Wicks, 2001).

Message Framing and Media Agenda Setting

Framing theory shares a common foundation with agenda-setting theory in that both focus on issues of public importance presented through the media and whether spotlighting these issues influences perceptions of importance by audience members (McCombs & Ghanem, 2001). Professional communicators are trained to communicate information that unfolds across the timeline of history using standardized selection and presentation criteria (Pan & Kosicki, 1993). The intent of news is to link citizens with occurrences in their environment that they cannot experience firsthand (Bird & Dardenne, 1988). As such, news reporting is intended to provide people with an accurate and realistic snapshot of the world at a specific point in time.

Various scholars (McCombs, Llamas, Lopez-Escobar, & Ray, 1997; McCombs, Shaw, & Weaver, 1997) have argued that agenda setting and framing basically involve the same processes. McCombs, Llamas, et al., (1997) wrote, "The first level of agenda setting is ... the transmission of object salience. The second level of agenda setting involves the transmission of attribute salience" (p. 704). Golan and Wanta (2001) studied second-level agenda setting during the New Hampshire primary elections through a comparison of Gallup poll responses and coverage in three newspapers in the region. Results suggested that McCain was covered much more positively than Bush; however, the results showed less support for media influence on the affective attributes that individuals linked to the two candidates. The processes of the first and second levels of the agenda setting share much in common. The core idea is the same for agendas of attributes as it is for agendas of objects: The salience of elements, objects, or attributes on the media agenda influences the salience of those elements on the public agenda.

Audience Frames

Audience or individual framing focuses on how the receiver interprets messages based upon individual predispositions, attitudes, and beliefs. This is an area where some convergence appears to be taking place between critical theorists and social scientists (D'Angelo, 2002; Scheufele, 1999). Hall (1980) proposed an approach to audience research that has come to be known as *reception analysis*. The basic idea hinges on the premise that to read a text, you must be able to interpret their signs and structure. Thus, audience members will vary widely with respect to interpretation, especially when they encounter media like television with the combination of images, audio, and an array of other production techniques. Audience frames are both cognitive representations of an individual's memory and devices that are communicated through public discourse (Kinder & Sanders, 1990; Pan & Kosicki, 1993). Some of the basic ideas that drive the audience-framing concept can be traced to the writings of Lippmann (1922) on stereotyping, Festinger (1957, 1962) on cognitive dissonance, Heider (1946, 1958) on cognitive balance, and Freedman and Sears (1965) on selective exposure (Lazarsfeld, Berelson & Gaudet, 1968).

Central to the audience-framing concept is the idea that people are more receptive to information that is consistent with previously held beliefs and attitudes. Under certain circumstances, people selectively attend to messages or avoid ones they find unpleasant. Even if people tune out messages, there is no reason to believe that cognitive systems simply shut down entirely. Message salience and the way in which messages are presented may encourage people to rethink previously held attitudes and beliefs. As a result, schemas may be altered, leading to adjustments in the construction of social reality (Shapiro, 1991).

Audience framing is also aligned with media agenda-setting theory (McCombs & Shaw, 1972) because journalists make issues salient through the selection and repetition process. In this respect, Gamson (1992) argued that the different story frames that newsmakers use to construct their messages provide citizens with a basic tool kit of ideas they apply to thinking and talking about politics and public policy issues. Hence, frames connect news media messages to cognitive elements such as thoughts, goals, motivations, and feelings and attitudes held by individuals (Iyengar, 1987; Price, Tewksbury, & Powers, 1997; Shah, Watts, & Fan, 2002; Zaller, 1992). Audience framing effects occur when the media frame interacts with cognitive elements within the viewer, activating particular elements over others (e.g., Iyengar, 1991; Pan & Kosicki, 1993). The cognitive elements that are activated from media coverage of an event are more likely to influence viewers' interpretations, evaluations, and judgments with respect to that event (Gamson, 1992; Iyengar, 1991; Iyengar & Simon, 1994; Lau, Smith, & Fiske, 1991; Neuman et al., 1992; Zaller, 1992).

Audience frames may thus be viewed as an abstract principle, tool, or schemata of interpretation that works through media texts to structure social meaning. The media actively sets the frames of reference that readers or viewers use to interpret and discuss public events. At the same time, people's information processing and interpretation are influenced by preexisting meaning structures, or schemas (Wicks, 1992). When audiences receive media frames, each member makes a conscious or subconscious choice to accept, deny, or mold that frame to fit an existing schema. On the other hand, people may also reject incoming information that is at odds with a preexisting schema.

Strategies to Advance the Future of Framing Theory and Methods

Scheufele (1999) has suggested that if framing as a theory of media effects will advance, researchers should investigate it from four perspectives:

1. Frame building is a journalist-centered approach that involves the construction and structuring of frames to make sense of incoming information. This form of framing involves the ideology and attitudes of the journalist along with professional norms and organizational routines. Political orientation of the news organizations may also play a role, as can various agents such as politicians, interest groups, lobbyists, and other elites.

2. Frame setting is similar to the idea of agenda setting (McCombs, Llamas, et al., 1997; McCombs, Shaw, & Weaver, 1997). Agenda setting, however, is mainly concerned with the salience of issues, while frame setting is concerned with the salience of issue attributes. McCombs and his associates have labeled this second level agenda setting. The distinction is that frame salience refers to the "ease in which instances or associations could be brought to mind" (Tversky & Kahneman, 1973, p. 208) whereas salience of attributes is concerned with cognitive processes related to gathering and processing information.

3. Individual-level effects of framing assume a linkage between media frames and individual-level outcomes. This perspective is similar to cultivation theory (Gerbner & Gross, 1976) in that it allows for theorizing that describes effects of media on behavioral, attitudinal, or cognitive processing; however, studies in this traditional generally provide little insight as to why and how variables are linked.

4. Journalists as audiences assume a position consistent with schema theory in that journalists are cognitive misers. Like audience members, journalists are susceptible to picking up upon and amplifying frames presented in the media. Thus, questions emerge as to whether political elites and other such agents frame issues that are retransmitted by media as opposed to if elite news sources dictate frames that are then retransmitted.

From Message Framing to Constructionism

The concepts of constructivism alluded to earlier and constructionism share common ground but are conceptually different. Many of the principles are adapted from interpersonal constructivist theory.

> Constuctivism defines communication as occurring when two or more people, with a mutually recognized intention to share, exchange messages. Moreover, the sharing process is goal driven. The organization and quality of the verbal and nonverbal behavior employed in that process can be seen fruitfully as a rationally organized means to some end. (Applegate & Sypher, 1988, p. 45)

Constructivism is concerned with communication that is intended to accomplish goals such as persuading, communicating ideas, or comforting people. The intent of the constructivist approach is to understand the influence of the communication process on social and cognitive development (Delia & O'Keefe, 1979).

Constructionism focuses on the relationship among the individual, the medium, and the message (Neuman et al., 1992). Constructionism begins with the assumption that truthful and objective messages do not exist. The messages that are produced by the media are interpretations that have been crafted to reflect the created reality that the writer or producer sees. Audience members then interpret these messages in the context of knowledge that is stored in schemas (Fiske & Taylor, 1991). New information may alter a schema, which in turn may influence the interpretation of future messages. This explains why people may change the way they think about the world as a result of encountering new information.

Neuman et al., (1992) have identified the central features of the emerging constructionism model. Constructionism assumes an active audience that is working to construct meaning from multiple information sources. Studying this audience requires a shift from measuring attitudes to a focus on concepts rooted in cognitive psychology, such as schemas, cognitive maps, and scripts. Attitudes may remain relatively stable whereas constructing meaning represents a dynamic and creative process. As such, the effect of a message on an individual may be quite minimal, but the processes associated with assimilating the message may be much more important. The emphasis, therefore, is on the creation of meaning rather than the degree to which communication may influence behavior.

Constructionism also considers differences in the types of messages presented. Producers and consumers find media messages salient for a wide range of reasons, including prior knowledge, opinions, attitudes, beliefs, and cultural orientation. Constructionism is also sensitive to differences in the information and entertainment media and distribution systems. Significant differences may exist in the ways that people interact with aural, visual, and textual content. The fundamental issue is how effectively these different media engage the audience and whether some of these differences are due to differences in cultural orientation.

Constructionism is concerned with the development of common knowledge rather than public opinion. Neuman and his colleagues (1992) explain that the fundamental issue focuses on

> what people think and how they think about public issues rather than the narrowly defined valence-oriented "opinions" concerning an issue or a candidate. The use of "knowledge" rather than "opinion" emphasizes the need to organize information into meaningful structures. The phrase "common knowledge" emphasizes that the structuring and framing of information is not unique to each individual, but aggregates into the cultural phenomenon of shared perspectives and issue frames. (p. 18)

The constructionism perspective advocates viewing communication as a dynamic and constructive process, the three-way interaction among the individual, the medium and the message. Each member of the audience will use communication to build upon knowledge stored in cognitive schemas in the course of interpreting messages and developing new knowledge. Membership within cultural or social communities may however lead to similarities in the construction meaning.

EXAMPLES OF CONSTRUCTING MEANING

In this section, I consider message and audience framing and how they may lead to the construction of social reality among audience members. Framing research on social movements, terrorism, politics, nuclear power, and social beliefs is reviewed to illustrate how different framing mechanism can influence meaning construction.

Constructing Meaning About Social Movements

Gamson (1995) has focused on how the nature of media discourse influences the construction of collective action frames by social movements. He effectively connected two very different and distinct fields of study through the lens of framing: social movements and the media. Collective action frames are simply action-oriented sets of beliefs and meanings that inspire and legitimate social movement activities and campaigns. They suggest ways of understanding that imply the need and desirability of some form of action (Gamson, 1995, p. 89). Collective action frames can allow media outlets and journalists to heighten a sense of need or urgency about a particular issue presented in the news to the targeted audience; in essence, they provide the media with the tools to bring about a desired effect from the public and its audience. Gamson also suggested the existence of three components of collective action frames: injustice, agency, and identity. Injustice refers to the expression of a moral indignation wheras agency refers to that internal voice that tells us we should participate in some action or movement. Finally, identity refers to the process of defining a problem and typically delineating "us" from "them."

Gamson asserted that often citizens do not feel they can make a difference or bring about change to social, political, or economic conditions. Thus, the collective action frame of the social movement must discover the key element or elements that will resurrect the inherent sense of agency among audience members. The same is true for media when framing an issue. The key, however, is to draw out latent agency without simply pushing buttons; media, like social movements, must find the resonating force within potential followers and viewers to bring them into the fold.

Constructing Meaning About the Middle East and the War on Terror

Message framing with respect to the Middle East is important because many citizens are dependent upon the media for information about this part of the world. The three components of collective action frames—injustice, agency, and identity—can also be applied to media framing of religion and terrorism. First, media often frame stories to illustrate an injustice in a certain way. With regard to issues of terrorism, an injustice is illustrated and portrayed in a way not necessarily to inform an audience, but to appeal to their moral sense of right and wrong; media is then able to identify the we verses them, the good (us) from the bad (terrorists). Gamson's arguments about agency seem to exhibit the greatest link between media framing and audience response in that understanding agency should be crucial to any attempt to grow and bring about cultural, political, or societal change, again the assumption being that such a goal exists.

The Bush administration had a stake in how messages were framed as his bid for reelection got under way. His administration framed the 2003 invasion of Iraq as a defensive measure to protect U.S. interests in the "war on terror." As Norris et al. (2003) observed, various presidential administrations took advantage of the Cold War frame that began to develop after World War II. The framing of good versus evil can produce rally effects that will strengthen support for presidents and other elected officials. This leads to the classic us-versus-them framing dichotomy that Fawaz (1997) believed began in February 1979 when the Ayatollah Khomeini took power in Iran. Images of blindfolded hostages at the U.S. Embassy in Teheran coupled with descriptions of fundamentalist Islamic violence and the introduction of terms like Jihad, holy war, and terrorism produced mental frames that pitted "not only two religions but two civilizations [against each other], even though they have common foundations, not to mention an axiology of common values" (Arkoun, 1995, p. 471).

The late Middle East scholar Edward Said (1978, 1997) went even further, warning that Western media discourse habitually frames Islam and the Middle East as unitary, absolutist, fatalistic, patriarchal, unreasoning, antimodern, punitive, and as synonymous with terrorism and religious hysteria. Wilkins and Downing (2002) contended that the media often portray Muslim Arabs as culturally and psychologically primitive, emotionally unstable, trapped in a patriarchal vise, and obsessed with a bloodthirsty Jihad. Western political, educational, literary, scientific, and military agencies have reinforced these perspectives, assumptions, and rationales. Said (1978, 1997) has repeatedly stressed that Muslims are a religious, not an ethnic, community, but their public homogenization and frequent identification with Arabs and the Middle East can lead to a kind of framing similar to racial stereotyping (Naber, 2000).

Thus, although President Bush, political leaders, and the media have repeated the message that Islam as a faith is not to blame for global unrest, many American Christians and Jews remain suspicious of this religion because of media stereotyping of this faith that appear in media frames. Muslims in the United States also appear to be struggling to find new ways to communicate information about their religion to members of other faiths (Esposito, 1997). To understand framing as it applies to the media messages produced in the West about the Middle East, one must first consider the relationship among the medium, the issue, and the members of the audience. First, the issue of terrorism is highly salient because it contains many of the criteria that define news coverage (e.g., conflict, impact, and timeliness). Second, television as a medium is also important in the framing process, because it tends to present terrorism in a more compelling and emotional way than do print media (Brosius, 1993; Cho et al., 2003). This is because television is dependent upon strong powerful images that stimulate emotions among members of the audience.

Terrorism is perhaps the most important and reported upon issue of the new millennium. The medium of television, which heightens emotional appeal with ongoing coverage of hostilities and acrimony in the Middle East, is also important as a variable for study. Audience members operating from cognitive schemas contribute to the framing process. As a consequence of the constant and repeated linkage between Islam in the context of Muslim extremism over the past several decades, a sizeable portion of the audience has been led to conclude that Islam and terrorism are unitary and inseparable (Said, 1978, 1997).

Constructing Meaning About Politics

Political communication researchers have tended to focus on the construction of political meaning in the context of message packaging, the influence of sponsors such as public relation specialists or politicians, and general practices and norms within a news organization. Framing of candidates is often based on visual imagery rather than issues. Critics often charge that news reporting during the campaign season typically follows the horse race rather than focusing on significant issues. Reasoned analysis is rare because planned visual events are designed to frame candidates in the most favorable light possible (Graber, 1988; Hofstetter, 1976; Kern, 1989; Neuman et al., 1992).

In addition, resources at media companies make rankings in the polls, delegate counts, and the number in attendance at a rally tend to be relatively easy and inexpensive to produce (Kern & Wicks, 1994; Wicks & Kern, 1993, 1995). Eye-catching visuals and emotional or dramatic oratory lead to the presentation of ceremonial images that contain sound bites of marginal substance and little news value (Buchanan, 1991; Hallin, 1992; Just et al., 1996). Much of the information provided during the campaign season reflects the efforts of political handlers to attract the media to locales that will frame a candidate with flattering backdrops but little or no new information. Thus, candidate frames are often created using visuals that are designed to create favorable impressions based on emotional appeals.

During a political campaign, framing also depends on the development of relationships among sources, journalists, and the audience with each player having a role to execute (Patterson, 1980). When candidates do try to frame issues analytically, sources may communicate certain keywords or phrases like "we need to hold the line on taxes," hoping that such rhetoric is noted and reported by journalists. Such phrases are scripted to capture the attention of the audience members to persuade them that they and the candidate are allies. Therefore, the candidate repeats safe phrases about keeping taxes down or the need to improve education to produce a frame emphasizing compassion and concern for the citizen.

Constructing Meaning About Nuclear Power

A classic framing study conducted by Gamson and Modigliani (1989) illustrated how media frames were capable of shifting beliefs about nuclear power. Nuclear power was initially portrayed through the media as economical alternative to polluting power sources such as the burning of fossil fuels. Utility producers and suppliers framed nuclear power as a modern approach to energy needs. Nuclear accidents at Three Mile Island in Pennsylvania in 1979 and Chernobyl in Ukraine in 1986, however, undermined public confidence in nuclear plants as clean, cheap, safe, reliable power producers. The frame changed from nuclear power from futuristic and economical to nuclear power as dangerous and unreliable. As the issue of nuclear power became more salient, journalists and political elites began raising questions about the long-term impact of nuclear power, including what to do with nuclear wastes.

Few people in the 1970s or now have the scientific knowledge to assess the risks versus advantages of nuclear power. People depend on the media to learn new information and knowledge (Ball-Rokeach & DeFleur, 1976). This knowledge about various topics accumulates over time. In the case of nuclear power, information repeated about Three Mile Island and the Chernobyl accident, as well as opposition to nuclear power by the late pediatrician Benjamin Spock and nagging questions about where to store nuclear waste, has contributed to the nuclear power is bad frame. Framing by journalists may have influenced attitude and beliefs systems of audience members. As a result, a commodity that once had a promising future quickly fell into public disfavor.

Constructing Meaning About Social Beliefs

In their study of a local Texas television channel's coverage of the 1991 Gulf War, Reese and Buckalew (1995) demonstrated how the frames used by the journalists contributed to creating a supportive mood for the Gulf policy and the war among the local population. They identified three major frames used by journalists to manage dissent and thereby construct a coherent body of coverage supportive of the Bush Administration's policy toward Iraq: conflict, control, and consensus. The conflict frame highlights the tensions (e.g., antipolicy versus protroops). The control frame presents antiwar protestors as a threat to social order and equivalent to terrorists and criminals. Finally, using the consensus frame led reporters to identify and emphasize expressions of community solidarity. As emphasized by Reese and Buckalew (1995), "the patriotic support-the-troops movement allowed local television to restore the community solidarity threatened by divisive opinion over policy" (p. 53)

Without context between discrete news items, however, audiences fail to make the proper connections and have little information on which to base their understanding of events and occurrences in the news. The most significant issue with respect to framing is not the identification of a problem or issue. Rather, framing is most crucial in the context of assigning responsibility, considering the morality or legality of an issue, or recommending a solution. If media fail on these dimensions, the messages may not resonate with members of the audience.

A study conducted in the Boston area in the late 1980s compared media frames to audience frames by analyzing amount of media contact and tape-recording in-depth interviews of people living in the area (Neuman et al., 1992). The content was drawn from the *Boston Globe, Time, Newsweek, U.S. News and World Report,* and the major network newscasts between 1985 and 1987. Forty-three people were interviewed from 1 to 2 hours by trained interviewers who let the subjects do most of the talking. The idea was to draw on the attitudes, opinions, and beliefs of the respondents rather than force them to react to questioning generated by the researchers.

The frames utilized by the media and the interviewees were then compared. The content analysis revealed that the media framed 29% of the news stories in the context of conflict. Only 6% of the discourse from the interviews, however, focused on conflict. The researchers also found that 36% of the discourse focused on human impact, whereas only 18% of the news stories considered impact. Perhaps most important, 33% of the news reports framed events and issues in the context of powerlessness. Twenty-two percent of the discourse focused on whether citizens had the power to alter their situations. Thus, although the media agenda is important in focusing attention on issues, people identify issues that they find important and pay attention and think about them.

APPROACHES TO STUDYING FRAMING AND THE CONSTRUCTION OF SOCIAL REALITY

Using Multiple Methodologies

Using a combination of methodologies is beneficial in studying how people construct meaning as a consequence of media and audience framing. It is essential to study the communication produced by media institutions with a recognition that differences between individuals and social groups will influence how new information is processed and interpreted. Media practitioners should learn to anticipate how the messages they produce will interact with different members of society in their construction of social reality. As consumers of media, we should realize that our own psychological composition will influence the meanings we construct from media messages.

The range of methodologies available to study constructionism includes surveys, content analyses, correlation data of national surveys, and focus groups (see

Gamson 1992; Gans, 1979; Graber, 1988; Hofstetter, 1976; Iyengar, 1991; Just et al., 1996; Neuman et al., 1992; Patterson, 1980). Approaches often used by cultural theorists, such as field studies and interviewing, will also aid in the evolution of the meanings paradigm. Multiple methodologies enable researchers to understand the dynamics that take place when attitudes, beliefs, and opinions are galvanized and meaning is constructed. The use of multiple methodologies is intended to produce results that contain a high degree of both internal and external validity.

Content analysis. This method enables researchers to investigate the symbols and messages that people encounter. Journalists are trained to find ways of identifying a problem and recommending a solution. Through the use of content analysis, it is possible to investigate the ways in which information was presented to the public. Depending upon the issue, researchers may wish to focus on media messages, including editorials and political cartoons as well as standard news reports. Well-executed content analyses may produce a high degree of external validity if appropriate procedures are employed (see Krippendorff, 1980; Riffe, Lacy & Fico, 1998).

Surveys. These are usually conducted over the telephone, making it possible to include a large and random sample of respondents. The responses are coded using standardized categories that are based on responses to open-ended questions. In some cases, researchers have also employed standard scaling procedures to generate data. The ability to reach a large sample makes it possible to compare the opinion and attitude data to the results of the content analysis. Surveys provide a moderate degree of external validity and "some internal validity from the intercorrelated responses to questions about media usage, knowledge of issues and personal characteristics" (Neuman, et al., 1992, p. 27).

Experiments. This method enables researchers to investigate messages that may produce changes in attitudes, opinions, beliefs, or knowledge. If subjects are randomly assigned to different media stimuli and changes in belief systems take place, then it is reasonable to infer that the communication produced an effect. The unnatural experimental environment, however, may produce attention levels that are higher than might be expected when using media at home. Even though internal validity for experiments is high, external validity is low because of the effects that are attributed to the experimental environment.

Interviews and focus groups. These approaches allow for depth of thought and the prospect of asking follow-up questions. They create an environment that allows people to express themselves in a natural and comfortable setting. The questions are open-ended and recorded for transcription afterward. These sessions provide a sense of flow that may explain underlying thought processes. Interviewing strategies can provide a wealth of information about the processes that take place when people construct meaning. They have a high degree of external validity because they are conducted in naturalistic settings.

Cultural studies. In a classic study, Radway (1984) analyzed the content of popular romance novels. She found that they tended to present characters and plots in which a male-dominated social order is assumed to be natural and fair and one in which feminine identity is achieved through their relationships with strong and heroic men. Radway (1986) then interviewed women who read romance novels regularly. She learned that reading the books actually appeared to represent a social rebellion against male domination and that for the women reading them, the books actually represented an escape from housekeeping chores and child rearing. The women expressed preferences for male characters who demonstrated both strength and kindness. She concluded that readers of romance novels engaged in oppositional decoding or rejecting ideas inconsistent with attitudes and beliefs. Through critically analyzing texts and comparing this to interview data, Radway was able to discern a unique relationship among the text, the message, and the individual.

Undoubtedly, the future of framing research rests upon using quantitative and qualitative strategies together to discern how citizens negotiate meaning about the world in which they live and how media messages contribute to the process of constructing social reality.

CONCLUSIONS

Recommendations for Journalists

Media institutions play an enormous role in our lives by offering products that entertain and inform us. Increasingly, the process of using media involves a reciprocal relationship between the members of the audience and the offerings presented. This relationship requires an understanding of how people negotiate meaning in the course of constructing social reality. It is, therefore, an important and fertile research direction for mass communication scholars and students.

The messages constructed by professional communicators may be considered to be objective because they employ the standard criteria of reporting on who, what, where, when, why, and how. The attitudes, beliefs, and opinions of the communicator, however, shape the actual construction of messages. Furthermore, different journalists or professional communicators may arrive at different conclusions as to who or what is responsible for a problem and what the appropriate solution or course of action may be. Finally, the organizational culture of news agencies may foster a collective set of attitudes or beliefs that may lead to the framing of messages. Journalists should be aware of these influences on message construction and ultimately the frames that they produce.

Recommendations for Audience Members

The audience is also instrumental in the framing process. Audience members interact with information based on their own opinions, attitudes, and beliefs. Individuals do not slavishly absorb the messages as framed by the mass media. They actively filter, sort, and reorganize information in personally meaningful ways in the process of constructing an understanding of public issues (Neuman et al., 1992, p. 77). The challenge for the future is to increase media literacy among audience members (Neuman, 1991). For audiences, the challenge is to better understand the nature of journalistic framing and how the frames created interface with their own schemas and belief systems. This is not an insurmountable task. As Gamson (1992) asserted repeatedly throughout his book: "People are not passive, people are not dumb, and people negotiate with media messages in complicated ways that vary from issue to issue" (p. 4).

Recommendations for Media Researchers

For media researchers, the future has many challenges. First, message framing studies need to go further than simply studying messages and how they influence audience members. One challenge has to do with identifying and articulating media frames. As this chapter has stressed, message frames are not simply topics or categories. They involve systems of communication that place issues and events in a field of meaning. Thus, it is essential to identify recurring frames that can be systematically coded and analyzed.

From a pragmatic standpoint, projects with ambitious goals, such as understanding processes that lead to the construction of meaning, require a significant commitment of personnel and resources. The recent trend of funding agencies is to support projects in which collaboration between scholars and universities is central to the plan. Communication social scientists and cultural theorists should team up to take advantage of reciprocal theoretical and methodological strengths. Communication scholars should network with colleagues in political science, psychology, sociology, and other allied fields to develop elegant research designs that will take advantage of cross-pollination. Such designs will help propel the emerging paradigm of message framing and the construction meaning to the next level.

This chapter has argued that message-framing research and the meanings paradigm are bearing fruit. Recent framing research has considered provocative new topics like media framing of the Columbine school shootings (Chyi & McCombs, 2004), media framing of problems with no cause or solution like pollution, poverty, and incarceration (Kensicki, 2004), and comparisons between the use of episodic versus thematic frames among reporters that were embedded in the 2003 incursion into Iraq (Pfau, Haigh, Gettle, Donnelly, et al., (2004). The use of framing theory provides fertile ground for new and creative mass communication scholarship. Thus, the future of the emerging paradigm appears bright as the framing construct continues to evolve and blossom.

REFERENCES

Applegate, J. L., & Sypher, H. E. (1988). A constructivist theory of communication and culture. In Y. Y. Kim & W. B. Gudykunst (Eds.), *Theories in interpersonal communication* (pp. 41–65). Newbury Park, CA: Sage.

Ball-Rokeach, S. J., & DeFleur, M. (1976). A dependency model of mass media effects. *Communication Research, 3*(3), 21.

Bateson, G. (1955, 1972). A theory of play and fantasy. Reprinted in *Steps to ecology of mind.* (1955/1972). New York: Ballantine Books.

Bauer, R. (1964). The obstinate audience. *American Psychologist, 19,* 319–328.

Beniger, J. R., & Gusek, J. A. (1995). The cognitive revolution in public opinion and communication research. In T. L. Glasser & C. T. Salmon (Eds.), *Public opinion and the communication of consent* (pp. 217–248). New York: Guilford Press.

Berkowitz, D. (1996). Work roles and news selection in TV. Examining the business journalism dialectic. *Journal of Broadcasting and Electronic Media, 37*(1), 67–81.

Bird, S. E., & Dardenne, R. W. (1988). Myth, chronicle, and story: Exploring the narrative qualities of news. In J. W. Carey (Ed.), *Media, myths and narrative: Television and the press* (pp. 67–86). Newbury Park, CA: Sage.

Breed, W. (1955). Social control in the newsroom: A functional analysis. *Social Forces, 33,* 326–355.

Brosius, H. B., (1993). The effects of emotional pictures on television news. *Communication Research, 20,* 105–124.

Bryant, J., & Zillmann, D. (1991). *Responding to the screen: Reception and reaction processes.* Hillsdale, NJ: Erlbaum.

Bryant, J., & Zillmann, D. (2002). *Media effects: Advances in theory and research* (2nd ed.). Hillsdale, NJ: Erlbaum.

Buchanan, B. (1991). *Electing a president: The Markle commission report on campaign '88.* Austin: University of Texas Press.

Burke, J. (1968). *Language as symbolic action: Essays on life, literature, and method.* Berkeley: University of California Press.

Chaffee, S. H., & Schleuder, J. (1986). Measurement and effects of attention to news media. *Human Communication Research, 13,* 76–107.

Cho, J., Boyle, M. P., Keum, H., Shevy, M. D., McLeod, D. M., Shah, D. V., & Pan, Z. (2003). Media, terrorism, and emotionality: Emotional differences in media content and public relations to the September 11th terrorist attacks. *Journal of Broadcasting and Electronic Media, 47,* 309–327.

Chyi, H. I., & McCombs (2004). Media salience and the process of framing: Coverage of the Columbine school shootings. *Journalism and Mass Communication Quarterly, 81*(1), 22–35.

Converse, P. (1964). The nature of belief systems in mass publics. In D. Apter (Ed.), *Ideology and discontent* (pp. 206–261). New York: Free Press.

D'Angelo, P. (2002). News as a multiparadigmatic research program: A response to Entman. *Journal of Communication, 43,* 870–888.

DeFleur, M. L., & Ball-Rokeach, S. (1989). *Theories of mass communication* (5th ed.). New York: David McKay.

Delia, J. G. (1976). The development of functional persuasive skills in childhood and early adolescence. *Child Development, 47,* 1008–1014.

Delia, J. G. (1977). Cognitive complexity, social perspective-taking, and functional persuasive skills in second- to ninth-grade children. *Human Communication Research, 3,* 128–134.

Delia, J. G., & O'Keefe, B. J. (1979). Constructivism: The development of communication in children. In E. Wartella (Ed.), *Children communicating: Media and development of thought, speech, understanding* (pp. 157–186). Newbury Park, CA: Sage.

Downs, A. (1972). Up and down with ecology: The issue attention cycle. *Public Interest, 28,* 38–50.

Entman, R. (1991). Framing U.S. Coverage on international news: Contrasts in narratives of the KAL and Iran Air incidents. *Journal of Communication, 43*(4), 6–27.

Entman, R. (1993). Framing: Toward clarification of a fractured paradigm. *Journal of Communication, 43*(4), 51–58.

Entman, R. M. (2003). Cascading activation: Contesting the White House's frame after 9/11. *Political Communication, 20,* 415–432.

Entman, R., & Rojecki, A., (1993). Freezing out the public: Elite and media framing of the U.S. anti-nuclear movement. *Political Communication, 10,* 151–167.

Esposito, J. L. (1997). Islam and Christianity face to face. *Commonwealth, 124*(2), 11–17.

Fawaz, G. A. (1997). Islam and Muslims in the mind of America. *Journal of Palestine Studies, 26*(2), 68-81.

Festinger, L. (1957). *A theory of cognitive dissonance.* Palo Alto, CA: Stanford University Press.

Festinger, L. (1962). Cognitive dissonance. *Scientific American, 207,* 93.

Fiske, S. T., & S. E. Taylor (1991). *Social cognition* (2nd ed.). New York: McGraw-Hill.

Freedman, J. L., & Sears, D., (1965). Selective exposure. In L. Berkowitz (Ed.), *Advances in experimental social psychology* (Vol. 2, pp. 58–97). New York: Academic Press.

Gamson, W. A. (1988). The 1987 distinguished lecture: A constructionist approach to mass media and public opinion. *Symbolic Interaction, 11*(2), 161–174.

Gamson, W. A. (1989). News as framing: Comments on Graber. *American Behavioral Scientist, 33*(2), 157–161.

Gamson, W. A. (1992). *Talking politics.* Cambridge, UK: Cambridge University Press.

Gamson, W. A. (1995). Constructing social protest. In H. Johnston & B. Klandermans (Eds.), *Social movements and culture* (pp. 85–106). Minneapolis: University of Minnesota Press.

Gamson, W. A., & Modigliani, A. (1989). Media discourse and public opinion on nuclear power: A constructionist approach. *American Journal of Sociology, 95*(1), 1–37.

Gans, H. (1979). *Deciding what's news.* New York: Pantheon.

Gardner, H. (1985). *The mind's new science.* New York: Basic Books.

Geiger, S., & Reeves, B. (1991). The effects of visual structure and content emphasis on the evaluation and memory for political candidates. In F. Biocca (Ed.), *Television and political advertising* (pp. 125–144), Hillsdale, NJ: Erlbaum.

Gerbner, G., & Gross, L. P. (1976). Living with television: The violence profile. *Journal of Communication, 26*(2), 172–199.

Gerbner, G., Gross, L., Morgan, M., & Signorielli, N. (1980). The "mainstreaming" of America: Violence Profile No. 11. *Journal of Communication, 30*(3), 10–29.

Gitlin, T. (1980). *The whole world is watching: Mass media in the making and unmaking of the New Left.* Berkeley: University of California Press.

Goffman, E. (1974). *Frame analysis: An essay on the organization of experience.* New York: Harper & Row.

Golan, G., & Wanta, W. (2001). Second level agenda setting in the New Hampshire primaries: A comparison of coverage in the newspapers and public perceptions of candidates. *Journalism & Mass Communication Quarterly, 78,* 247–259.

Graber, D. E. (1988). *Processing the news: How people tame the information tide.* New York: Longman

Grimes, T., & Meadowcroft, J. (1995). Attention to television and some methods for its measurement. In B. Burleson (Ed.), *Communication Yearbook 18* (pp. 133–161). Thousand Oaks, CA: Sage.

Gunter, B. (1987). *Poor reception: Misunderstanding and forgetting broadcast news.* Hillsdale, NJ: Erlbaum.

Hall, S. (1980). Encoding and decoding in the television discourse. In S. Hall, (Ed.), *Culture, media and language.* London: Hutchinson.

Hallin, D. C. (1992). Sound bite news: Television coverage of elections, 1968–1988. *Journal of Communication, 42*(2), 5–25.

Hawkins, R. P., Yong-Ho, K., & Pingree, S. (1991). The ups and downs of attention to television. *Communication Research, 18*(1), 53–76.

Heider, F. (1946). Attitudes and cognitive organization. *Journal of Psychology, 21,* 107–112.

Heider, F. (1958). *The psychology of interpersonal relations.* New York: Wiley.

Hofstetter, R. C. (1976). *Bias in news: Network television coverage of the 1972 election campaign.* Dayton, OH: Ohio State University Press.

Iyengar, S. (1987). Television news and citizens' explanations of national affairs. *American Political Science Review, 81,* 815–831.

Iyengar, S. (1991). *Is anyone responsible? How television frames political issues.* Chicago: University of Chicago Press.

Iyengar, S., & Simon, A. (1994). News coverage of the Gulf crisis and public opinion: A study of agenda setting, priming, and framing. In W. L. Bennett & D. Paletz (Eds.), *Taken by storm* (pp. 167–185). Chicago: University of Chicago Press.

Just, M. R., Crigler, A. N., Alger, D. E., Cook, T. E., Kern, M., & West, D. M. (1996). *Crosstalk: Citizens, candidates, and the media in a presidential campaign.* Chicago: University of Chicago Press.

Kahneman, D. A., & Tversky, A. (1984). Choices, values and frames. American Psychologist, 39, 341–350.

Katz, E., Adoni, H., & Parness, P. (1977). Remembering the news: What the pictures add to recall. *Journalism Quarterly, 54,* 231–239.

Katz, E., Blumler, J. G., & Gurevitch, M., (1974). Utilization of mass communication by the individual. In J. G. Blumler & E. Katz (Eds.), *The uses of mass communication: Current perspectives on gratifications research.* Beverly Hills, CA: Sage.

Kensicki, L. J. (2004). No cure for what ails us: The media-constructed disconnect between social problems and possible solutions. *Journalism & Mass Communication Quarterly, 81,* 53–73.

Kern, M. (1989). *30-second politics: Political advertising in the eighties.* New York: Praeger.

Kern, M., & Wicks, R. H. (1994). Television news and the advertising-driven new mass media election: A more significant role in 1992. In R. Denton (Ed.), *The 1992 presidential campaign: A communication perspective* (pp. 189–206). Westport, CT: Praeger.

Kim, S., Scheufele, D. A., & Shanahan (2002). Think about it this way: Attribute agenda setting function of the press and the public's evaluation of a local issue. *Journalism & Mass Communication Quarterly, 79,* 7–25.

Kinder, D. R., & Sanders, L. M. (1990). Mimicking political debate with survey questions: The case of white opinion on affirmative action for blacks. *Social Cognition, 8,* 73–103.

Klapper, J. T. (1960). *The effects of mass communication.* New York: Free Press.

Krippendorff, K. (1980). *Content analysis: An introduction to its methodology.* Beverly Hills, CA: Sage.

Lang, G. E., & Lang, K. (1983). *The battle for public opinion: The president, the press, and the polls during Watergate.* New York: Columbia University Press.

Lasswell, H. D. (1927). *Propaganda technique in the World War.* New York: Knopf.

Lasswell, H. D. (1948). The structure and function of communication in society. In L. Bryson (Ed.), *The communication of ideas* (pp. 37–51). New York: Harper.

Lau, R. R., Smith, R. A., & Fiske, S. T. (1991). Political beliefs, policy interpretations, and political persuasion. *Journal of Politics, 53,* 644–675.

Lazarsfeld, P. F., & Merton, R. K. (1948). Mass communication, popular taste and organized social action. In L. Bryson (Ed.), *The communication of ideas* (pp. 95–118). New York: Harper.

Lazarsfeld, P., Berelson, B., & Gaudet, H. (1968). *The peoples' choice.* New York: Columbia University Press.

Lippmann, W. (1922). *Public opinion.* New York: Macmillan.

Lowery, S. A., & DeFleur, M. D. (1988). *Milestones in communication research.* White Plains, NY: Longman.

Maher, T. M. (2001). Framing: An emerging paradigm or a phase of agenda setting. In S. D. Reese, O. H. Gandy, Jr., & A. E. Grant (Eds.), *Framing public life: Perspectives on media and our understanding of the social world* (pp. 83–94). Mahwah, NJ: Erlbaum.

McCombs, M., & Ghanem, S. I. (2001). The convergence of agenda setting and framing.. In S. D. Reese, O. H. Gandy, Jr., & A. E. Grant (Eds.), *Framing public life: Perspectives on media and our understanding of the social world* (pp. 67–82). Mahwah, NJ: Erlbaum.

McCombs, M. E., Llamas, J. P., Lopez-Escobar, E., & Rey, F. (1997). Candidate images in Spanish elections: Second level agenda-setting effects. *Journalism & Mass Communication Quarterly, 74,* 703–717.

McCombs, M. E., & Shaw, D. L. (1972). The agenda-setting function of mass media. *Public Opinion Quarterly, 36,* 176–187.

McCombs, M. E., Shaw, D. L., & Weaver, D. (1997). *Communication and democracy. Exploring the intellectual frontiers of agenda setting theory.* Mahwah, NJ: Erlbaum.

McLuhan, M. (1964). *Understanding media.* New York: American Library.

McQuail, D. (1994). *Mass communication theory: An introduction* (3rd ed.). Thousand Oaks, CA: Sage.

Minsky, M. (1975). A framework for representing knowledge. In P. H. Winston (Ed.), *The psychology of computer vision* (pp. 211–277). New York: McGraw-Hill.

Morley, D. (1992). *Television, audiences and cultural studies.* Routledge: London.

Naber, N. (2000). Ambiguous insiders: an investigation of Arab American invisibility. *Ethnic and Racial Studies, 23,* 37–61.

Neuman, S. B. (1991). *Literacy in the television age: The myth of the TV effect.* Norwood, NJ: Ablex.

Neuman, W. R. (1976). Patterns of recall among television news viewers. *Public Opinion Quarterly, 40,* 115–123.

Neuman, W. R., Just, M. R., & Crigler, A. N. (1992). *Common knowledge: News and the construction of political meaning.* Chicago: University of Chicago Press.

Noelle-Neumann, E. (1973). Return to the concept of powerful media effects. *Studies in Broadcasting, 9,* 67–112.

Noelle-Neumann, E. (1993). *The spiral of silence: Public opinion—Our social skin* (2nd ed.). Chicago: University of Chicago Press.

Norris, P., Kern, M., & Just, M. (2003). *Framing terrorism: The news media, the government and the public.* London: Routledge.

Pan, Z., & Kosicki G. M. (1993). Framing analysis: An approach to news discourse. *Political Communication, 10, 55–75.*

Pan, Z., & Kosicki, G. M. (2001). Framing as a strategic action in public deliberation. In S. D. Reese, O. H. Gandy, Jr., & A. E. Grant (Eds.), *Framing public life: Perspectives on media and our understanding of the social world* (pp. 35–65). Mahwah, NJ: Erlbaum.

Patterson, T. (1980). *The mass media election: How Americans choose their president.* New York: Praeger.

Petty, R. E., & Cacioppo, J. T. (1981). *Attitudes and persuasion: Classic and contemporary approaches.* Dubuque, IA: William C. Brown.

Petty, R. E., Cacioppo, J. T., & Kasmer, J. A. (1988). The role of affect in the elaboration likelihood model of persuasion. In L. Donohew, H. E. Sypher, & E. T. Higgins (Eds.), *Communication, social cognition and affect* (pp. 117–146).

Petty, R. E., Priester, J. R., & Brinol, P. (2002). Mass media attitude change: Implications of the elaboration likelihood model of persuasion. In J. Bryant & D. Zillmann (Eds.), *Media effects: Advances in theory and research* (2nd ed.). Hillsdale, NJ: Erlbaum.

Pfau, M., Haigh, M., Gettle, M., Donnelly, M., Scott, G., Warr, D., & Wittenberg, E., (2004). Embedding journalists in military combat units: Impact on newspaper story frames and tone. *Journalism & Mass Communication Quarterly, 81,* 74–88.

Plato. (1945). *The republic.* New York: Oxford University Press.

Postman, N. (1985). *Amusing ourselves to death.* New York: Viking.

Potter, W. J. (1991a). Examining cultivation from a psychological perspective: component subprocesses. *Communication Research, 18,* 77–102.

Potter, W. J. (1991b). The relationship between first- and second-order measures of cultivation. *Human Communication Research, 18,* 92–113.

Price, V., & Tewksbury, D. (1997). News values and public opinion: A theoretical account of media priming and framing. In G. Barnett & F. J. Boster (Eds.), *Progress in communication sciences* (pp. 173–212). Greenwich, CT: Ablex.

Price, V., Tewksbury, D. & Powers, E. (1997). Switching trains of thoughts: The impact of news frames on readers' cognitive responses. *Communication Research, 24,* 481–506.

Radway, J. (1984). Reading the romance: Women, patriarchy and popular literature. Chapel Hill: University of North Carolina.

Radway, J. (1986). Identifying ideological seams: Mass culture, analytical method, and political practice. *Communication, 9,* 93–123.

Reese, S. D. (2001). Prologue—Framing public life: A bridging model for media research. In S. D. Reese, O. H. Gandy, Jr., & A. E. Grant (Eds.), *Framing public life: Perspectives on media and our understanding of the social world* (pp. 7–31). Mahwah, NJ: Erlbaum.

Reese, S. D., & Buckalew, B. (1995). The militarism of local television: The routine framing of the Persian Gulf War. *Critical Studies in Mass Communication, 12,* 40–59.

Reese, S. D., Gandy, O. H., Jr., & Grant, A. (2001). *Framing public life: Perspectives on media and our understanding of the social world.* Mahwah, NJ: Erlbaum.

Reeves, B., & Anderson, D. R., (1991). Media studies and psychology. *Communication Research, 18,* 597-600.

Reeves, B., & Thorson, E. (1986). Watching television: Experiments on the viewing process. *Communication Research, 13,* 343–361.

Riffe, D., Lacy, S., & Fico, F. G., (1998). *Analyzing media messages: using quantitative content analysis in research.* Mahwah, NJ: Erlbaum.

Robinson, J. P., & Levy, M. (1986). *The main source: Learning from television news.* Beverly Hills, CA: Sage.

Rubin, A. M. (2002). The uses-and-gratifications perspective of media effects. In J. Bryant & D. Zillmann (Eds.), *Media effects: Advances in theory and research* (2nd ed.). Hillsdale, NJ: Erlbaum.

Rumelhart, D. E. (1984). Schemata and the cognitive system. In R. S. Wyer, Jr., & T. K. Srull (Eds.), *Handbook of social cognition* (Vol. 1, pp. 161–188). Hillsdale, NJ: Erlbaum.

Said, E. (1978). *Orientalism.* New York: Pantheon Books.

Said, E. (1997). *Covering Islam: How the media and the experts determine how we see the rest of the world.* New York: Vintage Books.

Scheufele, B. T. (2004, May). *Making frames: Testing a model of news production.* Paper presented at the annual conference of the International Communication Association, New Orleans, LA.

Scheufele, D. A. (1999). Framing as a theory of media effects. *Journal of Communication, 49*(1), 103–122.

Schleuder, J. D., White, A. V., & Cameron, G. T. (1993). Priming effects of television news bumpers and teasers on attention and memory. *Journal of Broadcasting & Electronic Media, 37,* 437–452.

Schramm, W., (1971). The nature of communication between humans. In W. Schramm & D. Roberts (Eds.), *The process and effects of mass communication* (rev. ed., pp. 3–53), Urbana: University of Illinois Press.

Shah, D. V., Watts, M. D., & Fan, D. V. (2002). News framing and cueing of issue regimes: Explaining Clinton's public approval in spite of scandal. *Public Opinion Quarterly, 66,* 339–370.

Shapiro, M. A. (1991). Memory and decision processes in the construction of social reality. *Communication Research, 18,* 3–24.

Shoemaker, P. J., & Reese, S. D., (1996). *Mediating the message: Theories on influences on news content* (2nd ed.). New York: Longman,

Stauffer, J., Frost, R., & Rybolt, W. (1983). The attention factor in recalling network television news. *Journal of Communication, 33*(1), 29–36.

Stephens, M. (1993). *Broadcast news.* Fort Worth, TX: Harcourt, Brace Jovanovich.

Thorson, E., Reeves, B., & Schleuder, J. (1987). Attention to local and global complexity in television messages. In M. L. McGlaughlin (Ed.), *Communication Yearbook 10,* Newbury Park, CA: Sage.

Tversky, A., & Kahneman, D. (1973). Availability: A heuristic for judging frequency and probability. *Cognitive Psychology, 5,* 207–222.

Tversky, A., & Kahneman, D. (1981). The framing of decisions and the psychology of choice. *Science, 211,* 453–458.

White, D. M. (1950). The "gatekeeper": A case study in the selection of news. *Journalism Quarterly, 27,* 383–390.

Wicks, R. H. (1992). Schema theory and measurement in mass communication research: Theoretical and methodological issues in news information processing. In S. Deetz (Ed.), *Communication Yearbook 15* (pp. 115–145). Beverly Hills, CA: Sage.

Wicks, R. H. (2001). *Understanding audiences: Learning to use the media constructively.* Mahwah, NJ: Erlbaum

Wicks, R. H., & Kern, M. (1993). Cautious optimism: A new proactive role for local television news departments in local election coverage? *American Behavioral Scientist, 37,* 262–271.

Wicks, R. H., & Kern, M. (1995). Factors influencing decisions by local television news directors to develop new reporting strategies during the 1992 political campaign. *Communication Research, 22,* 237–255.

Wilkins, K., & Dowing, J. (2002). Mediating terrorism: Text and protest in interpretations of the siege. *Critical Studies in Media Communication, 19,* 419–437.

Zaller, J. (1992). *The nature and origins of mass opinions.* Cambridge, UK: Cambridge University Press.

Zillmann, D. (1983a). Disparagement humor. In P. E. McGhee & J. H. Goldstein (Eds.), *Handbook of humor research, Vol. 1. Basic issues* (pp. 85–107). New York: Springer-Verlag.

Zillmann, D. (1983b). Transfer of excitation in emotional behavior. In J. T. Cacioppo & R. E. Petty (Eds.), *Social psychophysiology: A sourcebook* (pp. 215–240). New York: Guilford.

Zillmann, D. (1991a). Television viewing and physiological arousal. In J. Bryant & D. Zillmann (Eds.), *Responding to the screen: Reception and reaction processes* (pp. 103–134). Hillsdale, NJ: Erlbaum.

Zillmann, D. (1991b). The logic of suspense and mystery. In J. Bryant & D. Zillmann (Eds.), *Responding to the screen: Reception and reaction processes* (pp. 28–304). Hillsdale, NJ: Erlbaum.

CHAPTER CONTENTS

12 Nuclear Legacies: Communication, Controversy, and the U.S. Nuclear Weapons Production Complex

BRYAN C. TAYLOR
University of Colorado at Boulder

WILLIAM J. KINSELLA
North Carolina State University

STEPHEN P. DEPOE
MARIBETH S. METZLER
University of Cincinnati

This chapter engages communication surrounding the history and future of U.S. nuclear weapons production. The authors begin by arguing that these phenomena are normalized, and thus neglected, among citizens and communication scholars, and respond by reviewing the history of the U.S. nuclear weapons production complex and by characterizing communication among its associated organizations and communities. They then examine the material and discursive legacies of this system, emphasizing recent changes that have opened new possibilities for communication between institutions and their stakeholders. The authors next develop three theoretical frames for analyzing communication in this dense and rapidly evolving scene: (a) democracy, participation, and the nuclear public sphere; (b) organizational crisis, change, and stakeholder communication; and (c) nuclear history, memory, and heritage. They conclude by identifying and addressing various challenges associated with adopting this research program. Throughout, the authors foreground and critique the role of communication in responding to the past and creating the future of nuclear weapons production.

INTRODUCTION: RECOVERING THE RELATIONSHIP BETWEEN COMMUNICATION AND NUCLEAR WEAPONS PRODUCTION

This chapter focuses on communication surrounding the organizations and communities involved in the production of nuclear weapons for the U.S. government. In keeping with official discourse, we will use the phrase *nuclear weapons production complex* throughout to describe this

Correspondence: Bryan C. Taylor, Department of Communication, UCB 270, University of Colorado, Boulder, CO 80309-0270; email: taylorbc@colorado.edu

Communication Yearbook 29, pp. 363–409

large sociotechnical system. We emphasize at the outset that this focus differs significantly from traditional studies of nuclear communication as presidential and foreign policy rhetoric.[1] Instead, we focus on the overlapping spheres of organizational and public communication produced in and around the nation's nuclear-industrial infrastructure. This topic may be only vaguely familiar to readers; therfore, we begin with two anecdotes suggesting the opportunities and challenges that it presents for communication research.

The first anecdote is taken from a cartoon published in a 1995 issue of *the Bulletin of the Atomic Scientists*. The cartoon shows a surprised urban pedestrian, paused outside an otherwise innocuous building. There, the figure does a double take at a sign posted outside the building's entrance. Incongruously (and somewhat ominously), the sign reads, "The Bomb, Inc." The reader is left to wonder what the pedestrian will do next.

Our second anecdote is taken from a recent meeting of a nonprofit group seeking to develop a museum on the site of a former nuclear weapons production facility. In this meeting, the group heard a report from one of its members who had just attended a national conference devoted to preserving U.S. nuclear heritage. This member reported that presentations made at the conference indicated that, in U.S. culture, nuclear weapons plants built during the wartime Manhattan Project were more visible and celebrated than others built later during the Cold War. In response, another member, a retired employee of the plant, noted that this difference was "understandable." After all, he said, workers in the Manhattan Project had delivered "a concrete product," the two atomic bombs dropped on the Japanese cities of Hiroshima and Nagasaki. In contrast, at Cold War-era facilities such as this, "We worked hard so that *nothing* would happen."

Together, these two anecdotes suggest how communication contributes to popular understanding of U.S. nuclear weapons development. The cartoon depicting the baffled pedestrian plays on the banality, and hence invisibility, of nuclear weapons as corporate and industrial phenomena. Commonly, nuclear weapons are depicted in the discourse of foreign policy and military elites as a powerful, threatening, and perversely glamorous, technology. As noted above, communication scholars have traditionally engaged this particular genre of nuclear discourse. By emphasizing their prestige, however, this discourse effaces the contingency of nuclear weapons as mundane, organizational products. These weapons always come from somewhere, in other words, and this journey involves a concrete system of materials, locales, personnel, technologies, belief systems, and social practices. Looking directly at this system, even if it requires a double take, broadens our understanding of how communication constitutes and transforms the nuclear condition (Taylor, 1998a).

The second anecdote offers a related lesson. The plant retiree's suggestion that "nothing happened" as a result of Cold War nuclear weapons production signals a key article of faith in post-Cold War culture: that nuclear deterrence "worked" (Schell, 2000). In this dominant narrative, the superpowers are understood to have developed nuclear arsenals because they were deemed necessary to inhibit enemy attack. At the same time, however, these weapons offered their developers no guarantee of military victory if they were actually used; indeed, they promised only destructive retaliation and the escalation of conflict. As a result, the significance of nuclear weapons stabilized during the Cold War around their role as props in a massive theatre of paradox. In this arrangement, the superpowers used nuclear weapons to symbolically display their capabilities and intentions (e.g., as force deployments), precisely in the hope that these intentions would never be realized. This tense, theatrical run ended partly because one of its co-producers, the Soviet Union, was bankrupted by the associated costs of nuclear weapons development and subsequently imploded.

For our purposes, it is significant that the retiree invoked apparent noneventfulness as a measure of his organization's distinctiveness and productivity (i.e., "We worked hard so that *nothing* would happen"). In making this claim about the nature of nuclear weapons production, he joined a legion of speakers who have glossed other, associated legacies: namely, massive, devastating environmental damage, and serious threats to public health and worker safety (Makhijani, Hu, & Yih, 1995). Even though their scope and consequences are highly controversial (Taylor, 1997c), we view these phenomena as the undeniable "something happened" of nuclear weapons production.

These themes—cultural ambivalence, powerful mythology, ambiguous technology, and contested histories—suggest the scope of this chapter. Throughout, we pursue two related goals. The first involves demonstrating the value of a direct focus on communication in adding to scholarly knowledge of the U.S. nuclear weapons production complex. That is, we are concerned with how participants in this system have used discourse to inform and influence each other. Our discussion emphasizes the strategic and creative activities through which they have symbolically constituted this system as a meaningful social reality.

Our focus is not unrelated to those displayed in recent accounts of nuclear weapons production by scholars and journalists (discussed further, below). As a result, and in order to provide necessary context, the scope of literature reviewed in this essay is both historical and interdisciplinary. Our approach is unique, however, in foregrounding how communication expresses participants' identities and interests and affects the intense power relationships surrounding the production of nuclear weapons. As a result, we engage this literature selectively, to review studies published within the communication discipline, and to explicate, thematize, and critique evidence of communication that is presented in other accounts.

This approach offers several advantages, including leveraging communication theory to challenge unreflective claims made about the role of communication in nuclear weapons production. One example of these claims involves frequent charges that a historical lack of communication between nuclear officials and citizens has contributed to the creation of harms (Kauzlarich & Kramer, 1998, p. 115). This claim is certainly true in part; however, its framing obscures an alternate focus on the quality of that communication and implies that a greater quantity is the solution to this problem. This premise is sustained, for example, in well-intended claims that "openness helps create informed [nuclear] citizens and policymakers" (Weeks, 1997, p. 11). Again, this claim has considerable appeal. What it fails to problematize, however, are the discursive codes through which nuclear information is formatted, disseminated, and taken up as a resource by various groups in their local situations (Bazerman, 2001). In these situations, the quantity and clarity of official nuclear discourse are usually problematic, not universal or unambiguous, matters.

Our second goal for this chapter, then, follows from the first: To establish the evolving U.S. nuclear weapons production complex as a relevant case for applying and innovating communication-related theories. To that end, we summarize existing findings, and present an agenda for further inquiry by scholars concerned with nuclear rhetoric, discourse, and symbolism. Specifically, we believe that this essay can help those scholars to consider crucial organizational and institutional dimensions of nuclear communication (Kinsella, 2004a).

In the remainder of this chapter, we elaborate this argument. We first provide a brief history of the U.S. nuclear weapons production complex, emphasizing its characteristics as a communication system. Second, we review the material legacies and institutional conditions created by the dramatic collapse of this system during the late Cold War period. Here, we also identify key stakeholders[2] involved in interpreting and responding to these conditions. Finally, we develop a three-part theoretical framework that engages the uniquely discursive legacies of Cold War nuclear weapons production. Those parts include (a) democracy, participation, and the nuclear public sphere; (b) organizational crisis, change, and stakeholder communication; and (c) nuclear history, memory and heritage. In these sections, we demonstrate how this frameworks can be applied to understanding and critiquing the role of communication in shaping the future of U.S. nuclear weapons production. We conclude by noting specific challenges faced by communication scholars who respond to this call, and proposing some potential solutions.

THE U.S. NUCLEAR WEAPONS PRODUCTION COMPLEX:
A BRIEF HISTORY

Historically, the U.S. production of nuclear weapons has involved a system of more than 300 scientific and industrial sites employing approximately 650,000 people (Zuckerbrod, 2001). Although its operations and effects have been international in scope, the heart of this system involves 17 domestic facilities spread across 3,900 square miles in 13 continental U.S. states. Even though these facilities are owned by the federal government, they have been run by large, prominent industrial contractors (e.g., General Electric) and academic institutions (e.g., the University of California) charged with responsibility for conducting operations and (partly) protected from legal liability for their consequences. The political and economic interests of these organizations are aligned with those of other major defense contractors who build delivery systems for nuclear bombs and warheads (e.g., missiles, submarines, and airplanes) and the technological infrastructure of the nuclear command and control system (e.g., radar, computers, and telecommunications).

The original facilities in this complex were constructed during World War II as part of the Manhattan Project. In this effort, the U.S. successfully produced atomic bombs that were originally envisioned as a deterrent against a feared, comparable Nazi effort, but were ultimately used against the Japanese cities of Hiroshima and Nagasaki. Between 1942 and 1945, a grand drama unfolded throughout three primary sites (Hanford Reservation, Washington; Los Alamos Laboratory, New Mexico; Oak Ridge Reservation, Tennessee) and numerous support sites, as diverse government, scientific, academic, military, and industrial groups collaborated to design and manufacture a weapon of war that, to that point, had been only suggested by theoretical physics and science fiction literature. Faced with daunting technical challenges and cultural conflicts, the workers at each of these sites engaged in highly creative, complex, and risky operations. These included uranium mining, refining, and enrichment; nuclear reactor fuel fabrication and reprocessing; plutonium production; weapons design; production of nuclear and nonnuclear components; weapons testing; and weapons assembly. This effort was unprecedented in its rapid development, immense scale, potential risk of failure, and feverish intensity (Rhodes, 1986). It has since been commemorated as one of the great feats of human organization (Bennis & Biederman, 1997) and a monument of scientific and engineering achievement. As a precedent for federally funded joint ventures in technological research and development, it significantly shaped the political and economic relationships among government, science, industry, and society in the post-WWII era (Martinez & Byrne, 1996).

Following a brief postwar interlude in which its future was undetermined, the nuclear weapons production complex was institutionalized as a durable feature of U.S. society. Three developments contributed to this status. The first involved the failure of former Manhattan Project scientists and their political patrons to propose an acceptable scheme for the international control of atomic energy. As a result, the development and deployment of nuclear weapons remained a sovereign right, accountable only to limited, formal treaties negotiated by the nuclear powers. A second development involved the 1946 passage of the Atomic Energy Act, which formally established the Atomic Energy Commission (AEC) as the governing civilian body for U.S. nuclear weapons development, succeeded from 1975–1977 by the Energy Research and Development Administration, and after 1977 by the Department of Energy (DOE). Structurally, the AEC's group of five commissioners interacted with three internal committees focused on technical, security, and safety matters, and a fourth, Congressional Joint Committee on Atomic Energy (JCAE). Significantly, the AEC was charged with unprecedented, and conflicting, responsibilities to both produce nuclear weapons and protect the public from their hazards (Makhijani 1995, p. 4). The JCAE provided nominal governmental oversight of these activities through its power to consider related bills and resolutions, to hold hearings, and to authorize appropriations. In practice, however, its members typically endorsed the mission of weapons development and exercised only limited oversight. Arguably, this structural containment of regulation inhibited larger Congressional understanding, and thus public debate, of associated policies.

A final development involved growing anticommunist reaction within the U.S. to the expansionism of Stalin's authoritarian regime. In this tense political climate, U.S. officials rationalized nuclear weapons as legitimate solutions to perceived problems of national security. Military strategists subsequently called for increased development and deployment of these weapons, which increased pressure on the nuclear weapons production complex for production output. Following the successful 1949 test of a Soviet fission device, and the discovery of contributions made to that effort by Soviet spies who had infiltrated the Manhattan Project, the Truman administration resolved internal debate in 1950 by authorizing the U.S. development of a vastly more powerful thermonuclear weapon. This hydrogen bomb was successfully tested in 1952, and in 1953 the Soviets responded in kind (Rhodes, 1995).

The overtaxed nuclear weapons production complex rapidly expanded to accommodate these imperatives. Between 1948 and 1960, new scientific research and industrial production facilities were constructed in California (Lawrence Livermore Laboratory), Colorado (Rocky Flats Plant), Florida (Pinellas Plant), Idaho (Idaho National Engineering Laboratory), Kansas (Kansas City Plant), Kentucky (Paducah Gaseous Diffusion Plant), Nevada (Nevada Test Site), New Mexico (Sandia National Laboratory), Ohio (Ashtabula Extrusion Plant; Fernald Feed Materials Production Center; Mound Laboratory; Piketon Gaseous Diffusion Plant), Texas (Pantex Plant), and South Carolina (Savannah River Site). These facilities were designed to increase the capacity, rate, and sophistication of existing operations and to perform new functions required for maintenance of the growing Cold War arsenal. It was not until the 1970s, and only in response to a mounting crisis, that nuclear officials accelerated their progress in developing two permanent repositories for radioactive waste from military production: One recently opened in New Mexico (Waste Isolation Pilot Plant) and another is proposed for Nevada (Yucca Mountain Repository).[3]

Various indicators suggest the extraordinary scope and consequences of Cold War operations in the U.S. nuclear weapons production complex. Between 1945 and 1992, that complex produced in excess of 70,000 nuclear bombs and warheads, at an approximate cost of $370 billion. One thousand and thirty explosive tests of these devices were conducted both above and below ground at facilities in the Pacific Islands and the continental U.S. These operations produced approximately 700,000 metric tons of radioactive metals, 104 million cubic meters of radioactive waste, and 280 million pages of classified documents (Schwartz, 1998). During this period, radioactive and toxic wastes were routinely stored at their sites of generation in improvised and precarious systems or were discharged into the environment. As a result, underground steel tanks holding high-level liquid wastes, buried drums containing contaminated tools, equipment, and clothing, and contaminated liquids discharged into the ground have all posed enduring environmental problems (Alvarez, 2000; Cochran, Arkin, Norris, & Hoenig, 1987).

Throughout the Cold War, cultural awareness and understanding of the nuclear weapons production complex were heavily mediated by hegemonic discourses of secrecy and national security. In their repeated usage by officials, these discourses obscured, moralized and rationalized the existence of these facilities for various audiences. As a result, most workers and community members affiliated with these facilities endorsed (or at least accommodated) their operations and potential consequences as authorized, legitimate, and inevitable (e.g., by attributing an inherent human propensity toward conflict). Nonetheless, these facilities were increasingly blended with nuclear power reactors in the discourse of national and international movements protesting the ethics of nuclear weapons development and the health risks posed by emissions from plant operations and radioactive fallout from nuclear testing (Weart, 1988).[4] Also during this period, officials were increasingly called upon to contain local crises (e.g., fires) caused by inadequate operational controls and by the doubts and resentments of citizens toward perceived threats to their health, safety, and livelihood (e.g., indicated by mysterious increases in livestock deaths; Makhijani & Saleska, 1995; Sumner, Hu, & Woodward, 1995). In responding to these challenges, plant operators and regulators routinely dismissed public concerns and denied responsibility for creating alleged harms. Generally, they were supported in this practice by local news media, community boosters, and land developers who were motivated by patriotic pride and related economic benefits to endorse continued facility operations (Ackland, 1999). From the 1960s through the early 1990s, however, a series of five developments converged to create a legitimation crisis for the U.S. nuclear weapons production complex. Unfolding on several fronts, these developments threatened the operational viability of its facilities and the stakeholder consent their officials had traditionally enjoyed.

The first development resulted from the urgent production schedule maintained by nuclear reactor facilities in the complex during the early Cold War. By the end of the 1960s, those reactors had reached the end of their lifespans and produced a surplus of weapons-grade materials. As a result, the AEC was forced to consider scaling back these operations and either closing the facilities or converting them to new missions such as the generation of electric power. These decisions involved complex technical calculations regarding risk, safety, and economic impacts and were met with strong demands for participation by profacility residents and their elected officials.[5] This process was animated by a larger post-Vietnam and post-Watergate cultural transformation favoring "a greater degree of participatory governance and . . . declining popular trust in experts and scientists" (Carlisle, 1996, p. 133). As a result, decisions that had previously been made behind a curtain of secrecy, and through the relatively simple mechanism of political patronage, shifted irrevocably to forums of conflict among and between political officials, scientific experts, and stakeholder groups.

The second development involved changes in public opinion created by crises at the Three Mile Island (1979) and Chernobyl (1986) nuclear power facilities. These events confirmed popular fears concerning the risks of nuclear reactor technology and the inadequacy of its regulation by overconfident, short-sighted technocrats, who dubiously asserted the infallibility of rationality, industry, and progress as paradigms for policy and operations (Farrell & Goodnight, 1981). Arguably, these events served as surrogates that stimulated and focused latent popular opposition to nuclear weapons and strengthened connections between the peace movement and opponents of nuclear power. In a third development, officials during the first Reagan administration revived bellicose Cold War rhetoric depicting a Soviet "Evil Empire" and enhancing U.S. commitment to actual nuclear war fighting. This trend aggravated nuclear anxiety and contributed to the formation of a briefly popular, but ultimately unsuccessful, movement to freeze nuclear weapons development by halting their production (Bjork, 1992). Fourth was the subsequent negotiation of superpower arms control treaties and the Soviet Union's dramatic disintegration. These events signaled the ending of a stable Cold War mission and funding rationale for the nuclear weapons production complex.

The final development involved the return of repressed consequences from long-standing operational practices at complex facilities. These practices had privileged the interest of weapons production over the health and safety of workers and the public and over the integrity of the environment. Increasingly frequent and undeniable revelations associated with this tradition (e.g., the discovery of contaminated water in wells belonging to the residents surrounding facilities) coincided during this period with the development by state and federal governments of stricter environmental regulations and the failure of decrepit and overextended facilities. Subsequent media coverage, stakeholder litigation, and increased regulatory oversight combined to produce scandalous publicity about this history and generated unprecedented settlements, for example, those paid by the federal government to the owners of contaminated property. The topics of these disturbing revelations included inadequate storage of massive amounts of radioactive and toxic wastes: accidental and deliberate releases of radioactive materials into surrounding communities; medical experimentation by federal researchers with radioactive materials on vulnerable citizens without their informed consent, and the actual extent of contamination at affected facilities. These developments joined moral and political critiques of nuclear deterrence with the more mainstream warrants of environmental integrity, worker health, and public safety. As such, they affected the composition, mission, and rhetoric of existing environmental and antinuclear social movements (e.g., in producing new groups whose members were hostile towards contractor and regulator ineptitude, but otherwise supportive of the weapons production mission).

As a result of growing scandal, heightened investigation, and external criticism, most nuclear weapons production complex facilities were idled and shuttered during this period. Beginning in 1989, the production of new weapons first slowed, and then halted completely. By 1992, several facilities had shifted their mission (at least in part) to environmental remediation. Evolving estimates of the cost to decommission, demolish, and clean up these affected facilities have ranged up to $300 billion. This work will likely require decades for completion and will involve a scale and complexity of operations far exceeding the original Manhattan Project. Requirements for long-term stewardship of these contaminated sites will persist for centuries afterwards, and those deemed irrevocably damaged, or targeted for permanent radioactive waste disposal, may yet be written off as national sacrifice zones (Gray, 1995).

COMMUNICATION SURROUNDING WARTIME AND COLD WAR NUCLEAR WEAPONS PRODUCTION

Over the past 2 decades, a variety of journalists (Bartimus & McCartney, 1991; Broad, 1985; D'Antonio, 1993; Loeb, 1986; Mason, 2000; McCutcheon, 2002; Mojtabai, 1986; Shroyer, 1998) and scholars (Ackland, 1999; Bergeron, 2002; Canaday, 2000; Carlisle, 1996; Cohn, 1987; Dalton, Garb, Lovrich, Pierce, & Whiteley, 1999; Depoe, 2000; Edwards, 1997; Fernlund, 1998; Freer, 1994; Gerber, 1992; Gilles, 1996; Gusterson, 1996; Hales, 1997; Hardert, 1993; Hevly & Findlay, 1998; Katz & Miller, 1996; Kauzlarich & Kramer, 1998; Kinsella, 2001; Lodwick, 1993; Makhijani, Ruttenber, Kennedy, & Clapp, 1995; Metzler, 1997; Pasternak, 1993; Ratliff, 1998; Reed, Lemak, & Hesser 1997; Rosenthal, 1990; Silverman, 2000; Taylor, 1990, 1993a, 1996, 1997a, 1997b; Thorpe, 2004) have examined the cultures of American organizations and host communities associated with nuclear weapons production. Consistently, these accounts emphasize particular belief systems and expressive practices. In summarizing these elements, we do not argue that they were universally distributed, or that they were unquestioned, seamless, or unchanging. Indeed, these studies indicate that relationships among and between stakeholder groups at various weapons production facilities have been marked as much by diversity and conflict as by homogeneity and consensus. Nonetheless, these elements have formed hegemonic boundaries for communication among and between the members of these groups. They have served as enduring frames for the production and interpretation of discourse considered to be normal, legitimate, authoritative, appropriate, and effective (and their opposites).

These elements may be grouped into three clusters. The first cluster involves the uniqueness of cultural ideologies and practices at nuclear weapons production facilities. Here, commentators consistently note several elements. One involves the deep pride, camaraderie, and sometimes bravado, experienced among nuclear workers, based upon their technical expertise and craftsmanship developed in the conduct of complex and risky operations. A related element involves fascination among nuclear scientists and engineers with the compelling intellectual challenges posed by weapons design and testing. These professionals subsequently adhered to a nuclear-technological imperative (e.g., that presumed the necessity of realizing potential technological innovations both for their own sake as well as for national security; Kinsella, 2005). Another element in this cluster involves patriotic dedication and, among some pre-millennial religious groups, theological endorsement of nuclear weapons production as both urgent and righteous. Among workers and community members, this element combined with another—that of economic and psychological dependence on continued operations—to create passionate identification with the weapons production mission and resistance to internal dissent and externally imposed change.

Also contained within this cluster are characteristic beliefs about the risk posed by operations to the health and safety of both workers and the public. Generally, commentators emphasize the relative disregard for those risks displayed by officials and operators (e.g., contractor failure to collect and maintain adequate documentation of worker exposure to radiation). They also emphasize rationalization of that disregard based on the perceived urgency of weapons production, the novel and evolving status of radiation science, and the general standards of the time.

Within weapons production facilities, nuclear workers and professionals were subject to authoritarian principles of organization, such as compartmentalization and encryption. These structures isolated them, constrained their knowledge of the nature and consequences of their work, inhibited their collective ethical reflection, and enforced their conformity to naturalized premises through a numbing discourse of euphemisms, acronyms, assertions, and directives. Commentators also note a dominant, cybernetic view of human communication operating in these facilities, drawn from the contributing cultures of science, engineering, and the military. This view presumed the legitimacy of instrumental imperatives such as efficiency, effectiveness, and conformity by system components to external control. Officially, communicators adopting this viewpoint privileged the objectivity of "facts" as message content. Covertly, they acknowledged the political importance of securing stakeholder consent to operations and developed rhetorical strategies to conceptualize and control the novel and urgent phenomena of nuclear weapons production.

A second cluster of elements includes attitudes held and practices performed toward "outsiders" by the members of these "strong," cohesive cultures. Here, commentators emphasize members' disdain for external surveillance and regulation. Workers and managers, for example, often viewed bureaucratic regulation (e.g., the enforcement of redundant safety procedures, pernicious budgetary "politics," etc.) as rigid, intrusive, and unnecessary. Regulation artificially imposed standardization and conformity on their operations; as a result, many workers also believed that it inhibited their camaraderie and agility (e.g., by commodifying historically informal collaboration between work groups as consultation charged back to internal clients). A related phenomenon involves members moralizing and rejecting criticism by whistleblowers, activists, and news media. Because they were highly identified with the weapons production mission, many facility employees and community residents viewed this criticism as invalid, uninformed, illegitimate, disloyal, and irrelevant. Differences between facility proponents and opponents, as a result, were often moralized and vigilantly policed. There were few possibilities for neutral and dispassionate forms of membership in the affected groups.

A final cluster of elements involves characteristic practices by which officials managed stakeholders. Here, commentators emphasize successful deployment by those officials of formal position, scientific authority, and other mechanisms of exclusion (Kuletz, 1998) to discipline stakeholder dissent. Routinely, for example, those officials asserted national security as a warrant to override local and tribal property rights, to secure exemption from compliance with state regulation, and to establish immunity from prosecution for alleged harms. Additionally, they were able to obstruct, distort, and undermine oversight efforts through the practices of secrecy, deception, and co-optation.

Collectively, these elements suggest the themes and patterns that saturated communication surrounding nuclear weapons production during the Manhattan Project and Cold War eras. Having reviewed this history, we turn in the next two sections to its post-Cold War "legacies." As we will demonstrate, this term encompasses a broad range of phenomena influencing communication among and between stakeholders in that complex.

NUCLEAR WEAPONS PRODUCTION AFTER THE COLD WAR: MATERIAL LEGACIES AND INSTITUTIONAL CHANGES

America's production of nuclear weapons has resulted in a tragic material legacy of damage to human health and the environment, both within the U.S. and elsewhere. These activities have created enormous volumes of hazardous waste products, both radiological and chemical. These hazards include airborne contamination from materials processing and weapons testing, soil contamination at and around production facilities, surface water and groundwater contamination, and massive amounts of stored wastes. The storage and transportation of these wastes create unique hazards, such as criticality, a nonexplosive, high-intensity release of radiation that can result from inadvertent accumulation of critical masses of fissile materials (U.S. DOE, 1997).

U.S. nuclear weapons production facilities are, as a result, some of the most dangerous and polluted sites on the planet. Millions of Americans, ranging from plant workers and neighboring residents to regional residents living downwind and downstream, have all been exposed to increased health risks without their knowledge or consent (Geiger & Rush, 1992; Makhijani, Ruttenber, et. al., 1995). A recent study completed by the U.S. Centers for Disease Control and Prevention has established that radioactive fallout from above-ground nuclear weapons tests conducted between 1951 and 1962 exposed virtually everyone in the United States and contributed to 11,000 excess cancer deaths ("Nuke Testing," 2003). Following the terrorist attacks of September 11, 2001, existing concerns about environmental and human health risks have been joined by increased concerns about the unauthorized diversion of radiological materials by terrorist groups, and the general crisis of international nuclear proliferation.

During most of the Cold War, the environmental and human health impacts of nuclear weapons production were neither fully acknowledged nor openly addressed by the U.S. government. Congress and the executive branch viewed the nuclear weapons production complex as an instrument of military strategy and foreign policy, and concerns for national security trumped all others. For the greater part of the Cold War, federal environmental laws such as the National Environmental Policy Act of 1969, the Comprehensive Environmental Response, Compensation, and Liability Act of 1980 (CERCLA), and the Resource Conservation and Recovery Act of 1976 (RCRA) contained few if any provisions for federal regulation of environmental or hazardous waste practices at federal facilities administered by the Departments of Energy (DOE) or Defense (DOD). This weak regulatory framework, coupled with the traditional sovereign immunity principle that encouraged federal agencies, such as the Environmental Protection Agency (EPA), to refrain from pursuing legal remedies against each other, effectively shielded the DOE from liability for its environmental and waste management practices, even as industries in the private sector faced a growing list of requirements (Applegate, 1999). Two events happened in 1984, however, that dramatically changed the environmental history of the nuclear weapons production complex, and arguably America's environmental history as well.

First, a federal court held in *Legal Environmental Assistance Foundation v. Hodel* (1984) that the DOE's facility in Oak Ridge, Tennessee, was in violation of the Clean Water Act and RCRA. This legal ruling forced the DOE "to acknowledge the applicability of federal environmental laws, as well as certain state and local laws, to its weapons production activities" (National Academy of Sciences [NAS], 1989, p. 35). The impact of this decision was magnified by a second event in late November 1984, when officials in charge of a DOE uranium milling and processing plant located in Fernald, Ohio, announced that the plant had experienced a series of significant dust collector losses, resulting in the release of several hundred pounds of uranium into the atmosphere. Shortly after this incident, Fernald officials informed area residents that production activities had resulted in groundwater contamination affecting the drinking water wells of a number of families who lived next to the site. In the following year, Fernald residents Ken and Lisa Crawford joined 14,000 other Fernald-area residents in a $300 million class action lawsuit against DOE contractor National Lead of Ohio. The suit was settled in 1989 when the DOE agreed to pay $78 million in damages (*Crawford v. National Lead Co.*, 1989). Silverman (2000, p. 265) concluded that Fernald "was thus the first 'domino' in a major process of challenging and ultimately reshaping the American nuclear weapons production system."

As described above, revelations at Fernald led to heightened media coverage of environmental problems at other DOE sites during the rest of the 1980s. Congress attempted to tighten the regulatory requirements on DOE and DOD facilities through the 1986 Superfund Amendments and Reauthorization Act (SARA), which amended CERCLA to include a section specifically pertaining to the cleanup of contaminated sites at federal facilities. In the decade following the passage of SARA, more than 20 DOE facilities were added to the National Priorities List for cleanup, to be paid for from the DOE budget instead of the superfund. Implementation of SARA also produced a number of interagency agreements between the DOE and state and federal environmental agencies concerning cleanup and removal actions at production sites. Finally, the 1992 Federal Facilities Compliance Act codified the applicability of RCRA and related laws to federal facilities (Applegate, 1999; U.S. DOE, 1996). In sum, growing public awareness of the legacy of material damage caused by nuclear weapons production led policy makers to seek greater oversight of the nuclear weapons complex, especially activities related to environmental remediation.

The DOE responded to this heightened scrutiny by instituting a variety of reforms. During the 1980s, it created an Environmental Management (EM) division to oversee cleanup operations and acknowledged in a 5-year plan that the nuclear weapons production complex should operate in compliance with environmental laws and standards that are generally applicable to the private sector (NAS, 1989). During the early 1990s, under the leadership of Secretary Hazel O'Leary, DOE headquarters initiated an ambitious "openness initiative." These reforms included declassifying documents, expanding opportunities for public involvement, competitively rebidding contracts, increasing protections for whistleblowers, and publicly apologizing to victims for harms created by medical experimentation and unsafe working conditions (Alvarez, 2000; "Earning Public Trust," 1993; Gray, 1995; Weeks, 1997). At various locales, these reforms played out with varying success. At Fernald, for example, the Ohio EPA took the DOE to federal court in an effort to force compliance with provisions of RCRA and CERCLA. Throughout this process, the agency was faced with enormous communication challenges. Complying with federal environmental laws would require the agency to modify its entrenched organizational culture of secrecy if interested members of the public were to obtain adequate information about environmental and health hazards and participate in decisions about environmental remediation. In order to tackle new missions to clean up contaminated facilities, DOE personnel would be forced to communicate more openly with new groups of stakeholders with deeply felt concerns.

Early efforts by DOE personnel to interact with representatives of affected communities were largely unsuccessful, reflecting both the structural limitations of federal environmental laws and a high degree of public mistrust of the DOE in

the wake of publicized revelations about agency mismanagement ("Earning public trust," 1993; Office of Technology Assessment, 1991). In 1993, representatives
from DOE's EM office and the EPA participated in a national policy dialogue facilitated by the Keystone Center, a nonprofit environmental conflict management
group. The dialogue was aimed at developing recommendations for improving
the process by which federal facility cleanup decisions are made so that decisions
reflected priorities and concerns of all stakeholders. An important 1993 interim
report generated from this dialogue recommended that Federal agencies such as
the DOE establish community advisory boards to provide independent policy and
technical advice to both regulated and regulating agencies with respect to key
cleanup decisions (Federal Facilities Environmental Restoration Dialogue Committee, 1993).

The DOE responded by obtaining a charter to establish a system of site-specific advisory boards (SSABs), under authority provided by the 1972 Federal Advisory Committee Act (FACA). First obtained in 1994 and renewed biennially
since, the FACA charter contained an umbrella provision that allowed the DOE
to establish local SSABs across the nuclear weapons production complex. Since
their formation beginning in 1994, a dozen SSABs, including boards at Hanford,
Oak Ridge, Fernald, and Rocky Flats, have met more than 120 times annually
(U.S. DOE, 2000). During the 1990s, these local site-specific advisory boards became a key mechanism through which the DOE attempted to regain legitimacy.
The DOE used the SSABs as places to circulate information about environmental
remediation activities and as vehicles for obtaining consensus-based recommendations about clean-up decisions.

How successful these boards have been in informing and involving interested parties in the policies and practices of DOE-EM programs remains an open
question. Some assessments have been positive (Applegate, 1998; Bradbury &
Branch, 1999; Duffield & Depoe, 1997; Williams, 2002). For example, the DOE
reports that since 1994, local SSABs "have provided the Department with literally hundreds of specific recommendations" and have "saved taxpayers hundreds
of millions of dollars" (U.S. DOE, 2000, p. 2). Others, however, have been less
sanguine about the politicized process by which SSABs operate and the substantive impact of their recommendations on DOE decisions (Taylor & Davis, 1999;
Weeks, 2000). Despite these mixed reviews, the DOE has relied on the SSABs as
a centerpiece of its public participation framework.

Following this shift, a number of stakeholder groups have emerged as central
players in negotiating and implementing environmental remediation and waste
management decisions. Three groups in particular have been involved in sanctioned (e.g., local SSABs) and unsanctioned (e.g., lawsuits and protests) public
participation activities.

The first group, affected community members, includes the hundreds of thousands of individuals who have lived in close proximity to nuclear weapons production facilities, as well as those who have lived downwind or downstream of nuclear
test sites in the United States. During the 1980s and 1990s, as environmental and

health risks associated with nuclear weapons production became more apparent, a number of grassroots organizations formed in communities near DOE facilities. At first, organizations such as the Fernald Residents for Environmental Safety and Health (FRESH) and the Hanford Education Action League (HEAL) sought accurate information about levels of environmental contamination and residential exposures to radioactive and other hazardous materials. For these local groups, the agenda quickly expanded to include demands, and in some cases litigation, calling for the DOE to apply existing environmental laws and regulations to site activities, and to expand community participation in environmental decision making.

In 1987, a number of local grassroots groups joined together to form the Military Production Network (subsequently renamed the Alliance for Nuclear Accountability [ANA]). The ANA is a network of more than 30 local, regional, and national peace and environmental groups representing the concerns of communities in the shadows of the U.S. nuclear weapons sites and radioactive waste dumps. For more than a decade, ANA has lobbied Congress and the Executive Branch concerning issues ranging from budget priorities for the DOE (clean-up versus military production) to the continuing role of nuclear weapons in American military policy.

At the local level, ANA-member and other activist organizations have had varying amounts of success in influencing specific DOE cleanup decisions (Ratliff, 1997; Toker, 2002). At some sites, activist leaders have chosen to participate within established institutional frameworks such as SSABs, but only after many years of fighting DOE in the courtroom and in public protests. Other sites have been characterized by disagreements among competing groups, including organizations that support ongoing DOE missions or projects, or by a lack of trust in the local SSAB as a legitimate reflection of community opinions.

The second group—workers—includes in excess of 600,000 men and women who have been employed in the nuclear weapons production complex since its inception. Without full knowledge of overall site operations or their potential health and safety consequences, workers were exposed to a variety of radiological and chemical materials and faced myriad other dangers at sites that manufactured weapons-grade nuclear materials. As the general public discovered more about the hazards associated with nuclear weapons production, America's nuclear workers began to seek their own answers. A federal lawsuit resulted in a landmark 1994 agreement in which the DOE awarded $15 million to Fernald workers, including funds for a lifetime medical monitoring program. In 2000, the DOE acknowledged for the first time a link between occupational exposure and increased cancer rates among DOE production workers (Hebert, 2000). By the end of the year, Congress had enacted the Energy Employees Occupational Compensation Program Act, augmented by Presidential Executive Order 13179 confirming the federal government's commitment "to compensate DOE nuclear weapons workers who suffered occupational illnesses as a result of exposure to the unique hazards of building the nation's nuclear defense" ("Providing Compensation," 2000).

This legislation, which allows workers to file for compensation of up to $150,000 for health problems resulting from exposures to radiation and toxic chemicals, has been implemented slowly and unevenly, leaving many workers' claims unfilled as their conditions deteriorate.

Domestic and international indigenes, such as those contaminated by radioactive fallout from postwar U.S. nuclear testing conducted in the Pacific Marshall Islands, make up the third important affected group. Native Americans in particular have been adversely and disproportionately impacted by nuclear weapons production. Uranium ore for the first atomic bombs was mined on tribal lands in Canada and the southwestern U.S., in many instances by native workers without proper health and safety precautions. Many of the key laboratory and production facilities in the nuclear weapons production complex, including the Los Alamos and Idaho National Labs and the Hanford Reservation, were located on or near lands either held or considered sacred by Native American tribes, a policy identified by critics as nuclear colonialism (Churchill, 1993; Kuletz, 1998). During the Cold War, aboveground nuclear explosions were detonated at the Nevada Test Site in the heart of Western Shoshone country.

For decades, interaction between representatives of the DOE and tribal groups was difficult and ineffectual, echoing historical patterns of miscommunication between the federal government and Native Americans. In 1994, President Clinton sought to improve the situation by issuing a memorandum directing all executive departments to "operate within a government-to-government relationship with federally-recognized Native American Tribes" (Presidential memorandum, 1994). The DOE has since attempted to involve Native Americans more directly in environmental management activities, including the establishment of cooperative agreements, agreements-in-principle, or memoranda of understanding with more than a dozen tribal nations concerned with activities at Hanford, Los Alamos, Idaho National Lab, and the West Valley (New York) Demonstration Project.

Recently, large parcels of land in Utah and Nevada that are considered sacred by Shoshone and other peoples have been earmarked by the DOE for potential nuclear waste disposal sites, including the huge Yucca Mountain project approved by Congress and President George W. Bush in July 2002. The Yucca Mountain project has been vigorously opposed by a number of Native American groups, including the Western Shoshone Defense Project, the Shundahai Network, the Indigenous Environmental Network, Honor the Earth, and the National Environmental Coalition of Native Americans (Indigenous Environmental Network, 2002). A few Native groups, however, have supported the siting of nuclear waste facilities in their communities for economic reasons. For example, a band of the Goshute tribe has, despite internal disagreement, expressed interest in having a repository for commercial reactor waste located on its lands in Skull Valley, Utah.

Over the past 2 decades, then, the DOE has been forced to interact in new ways with affected community members, workers, and indigenes as part of its mandate to remediate contaminated sites within the complex. During this period, all three of these groups have experienced occasional successes in influencing policy decisions. At the same time, all three have experienced ongoing problems with the DOE, stemming from lack of trust, lack of information, and lack of access to decision makers. In many sites, communication problems have been exacerbated by fallout from September 11, 2001, as a number of DOE field offices and contractors have reduced their public affairs budgets, and the DOE has begun to phase out a number of SSABs and related public involvement forums. As a result, the institutional changes toward more openness and accountability described above are both historically significant and precarious.

DISCURSIVE LEGACIES OF NUCLEAR WEAPONS PRODUCTION: A THREE-PART THEORETICAL FRAMEWORK

Thus far, we have used the term "legacy" to describe the material consequences of Cold War nuclear weapons production. As indicated by our review of post-Cold War institutional conditions, however, this term also encompasses a variety of influences that structure the possibilities for communication among and between the stakeholders of nuclear weapons production. One example of these influences is reflexive and involves the way in which DOE officials have utilized the term legacy itself as a powerful trope. In foundational texts of the mid-1990's DOE Openness Initiative (e.g., U.S. DOE, 1995), these officials constructed the material problems of the complex as unavoidable consequences of the Cold War, attributable to choices made by an earlier generation of decision makers under conditions of dire necessity. By employing images such as "closing the circle" on Cold War production through post-Cold War cleanup, DOE officials both contrasted and linked these two historical eras (U.S. DOE, 1995). This discourse simultaneously distanced present DOE managers from the appearance of responsibility for having caused, or for morally judging, the problems they inherited, and positioned them as trustworthy agents for their repair (Kinsella, 2001).[6]

This articulation locates problematic (and ongoing) issues of nuclear ethics and meaning in the past. We therefore stress that both change and continuity characterize the evolving status of the weapons production complex. That is, to be *post-* (as in post-Cold War) is not necessarily to have transcended the organizing principles of an earlier period. It is, instead, to be deeply influenced by those principles even while assessing, interrogating, and transforming them. As we consider communication surrounding nuclear weapons production in the post-Cold War era, then, we share Taylor and Hartnett's (2000, p. 465) goal of "problematiz[ing] this alleged successor by emphasizing how the active residues of its predecessor 'contaminate' its ontological bid for distinctiveness and closure." In this way, we understand the discursive legacies of Cold War nuclear weapons production to be a site of social struggle: They are simultaneously evoked, contested, and reconstructed in communication among and between stakeholders. At stake in this struggle are nothing less than the terms and principles by which the nuclear future will be organized. The quality of our engagement as scholars and citizens with these conditions will determine the legacies, both material and discursive, that we leave to the inhabitants of that future.[7]

In the following section, we review a three-part theoretical framework that we have developed to conceptualize and engage these discursive legacies. This framework configures the interdisciplinary terrain of related scholarship while emphasizing the role of communication. In each case, although space does not permit full review of the relevant literatures,[8] we summarize their central issues and claims, discussing exemplary studies of nuclear weapons production and posing an agenda for future communication research.

Democracy, Participation, and the Nuclear Public Sphere

As much a theoretical construct as an empirical context, the public sphere evokes sharp debate concerning the status of participation, democracy, and deliberation in the late-modern and postmodern eras. Participants in this debate variously orient to Habermas's (1962/1989) history of the modern *bourgeois public lic sphere*. Many commentators, subsequently, have utilized the *critical public sphere* as a normative ideal to evaluate actual public deliberation. This ideal rests upon four conditions. First, all citizens should have access to, and competency in, the available means of expression. Second, citizens should debate openly, democratically, and rationally, deferring their preexisting differences of status and expertise. As a result, speakers should be able to reflect on the intelligibility, truthfulness, and situational appropriateness of offered claims. They should seek to reach consensus through the use of practical reasoning concerned with the quality of a shared lifeworld. Third, citizens should debate matters of general interest. These matters should be accessible to public discourse, and citizens should be sufficiently motivated and informed to engage them. Fourth, deliberation should lead not only to the formation of public opinion, but should also influence official decision making.

Used in this fashion, the critical public sphere clarifies the rhetorical practices by which matters are deliberated in the public interest. Critics utilizing this construct emphasize the ethics and politics that surround the framing of issues, the selection of speakers, and the interpretation of evidence in controversies. Responding to a variety of challenges to this ideal (e.g., concerning the colonization of public discourse by commercial or corporate interests), current public sphere scholars seek to achieve at least three goals. The first involves recovering "a multiplicity of dialectically related public spheres rather than a single, encompassing arena of discourse" (Asen & Brouwer, 2001, p. 6). In so doing, scholars reverse a declinist thesis emphasizing the disruption and fragmentation of traditional deliberation. They reframe the expansion of deliberation created by oppositional counterpublics as a potential benefit to society (e.g., Olson & Goodnight, 1994). Second, critics reconceptualize traditionally opposed entities (e.g., counterpublics and the state; technical and public spheres) to reflect their relative permeability and interdependency (Asen & Brouwer, 2001; Goodnight, 1982). Finally, they examine the tactics used by publics and counterpublics to alternately affiliate and compete with each other and to maintain and transform the mechanisms of deliberation. In this process, critics reveal how standards of decorum and norms of deliberation mistakenly presumed to be transcendent or permanent structures are actually local, contingent accomplishments (Farrell, 1993; Phillips, 1999).

Brought to bear on the history of U.S. nuclear weapons production, this strand of critical theory reveals a public sphere constricted and degraded by technocratic domination (Fisher, 1987, pp. 57–84; Hardert, Reader, Scott, Moulton, & Goodman, 1989; Kinsella, 2002, 2004b; Krasniewicz, 1992; Kuletz, 1998; Metzler, 1997; Nelson & Beardsley, 1987). A wartime climate of urgency led to the secret development of nuclear weapons and to their introduction as a fait accompli rather than their consideration as a potential innovation requiring public ratification. The postwar embrace by U.S. officials of nuclear weapons as a necessary evil legitimated their production under the expansive warrant of national security. Compromised structures of civilian control aligned regulation with the political and economic interests of weapons production and promoted an authoritarian model of nuclear guardianship by scientific, military, and political elites over democratic control practiced by an informed and motivated citizenry (Dahl, 1985; Nolan, 1989). Indeed, this model construed involvement by an unpredictable public as a threat to the high-stakes order of nuclear deterrence (Tannenwald, 1999).

In this context, autonomous, centralized, defensive, secretive, and security-conscious cultures developed and became entrenched at nuclear weapons production facilities. The suppression and distortion of information (e.g., through the use of jargon, euphemism, threat inflation, etc.) precluded informed consent by citizens to the consequences of operations. This process involved officials' use of technical expertise (e.g., of epidemiological science) to colonize public moral argument (Fisher, 1987), and to neutralize alternative (e.g., anecdotal) modes of reasoning. Officials also adopted authoritarian, cynical, superficial, and perfunctory approaches to public participation opportunities (e.g., public hearings). They engineered communication with citizens (e.g., through agenda setting) to minimize perceived irrelevancy and disruption, to discredit unease as irrational perception, and to remove potentially controversial topics and premises from deliberation.

This domination, although powerful, was not monolithic or constant. For example, Dalton, et al. (1999) argued that the strong democracy, weak state structure of U.S. politics (e.g., that mandates agency compliance with Freedom of Information Act requests) has facilitated relative democratization of the post-Cold War nuclear public sphere, at least in comparison to Russia. Similarly, Glass (1993) argued that because the Cold War lifeworld was too complex for total colonization, pockets of critical instability (e.g., created by regional particularity) remained through which citizens could fashion alternate definitions of security and loyalty. They could not supplant the totemic warrant of national security; as a result, these successes were ultimately partial, "fragile, hard to predict, and even harder to repeat" (Glass, 1993, p. 106). Analyses of movements such as the Nuclear Freeze (Bjork, 1992; Hogan, 1994; Rojecki, 1999) and women's peace encampments

(Couldry, 1999; Krasniewicz, 1992) additionally confirm that counterpublics opposing the Cold War nuclear state faced formidable challenges. These challenges included skillful appropriation of their rhetorical visions by officials, ambivalent coverage by news media identified with state power over citizen participation, and inevitable tradeoffs between the adoption of technically substantive and popular-appealing rhetorical strategies.

Here, we are concerned with the transformation of these structures by the controversy surrounding the nuclear weapons production complex. As described above, citizen activism has partly succeeded in revising dominant narratives of the history of the weapons complex, and in restructuring relationships between officials and stakeholders (Blain, 1991; Charles, 1988; Depoe, 2000; Kaplan, 2000; Kinsella, 2001; Metzler, 2001; Ratliff, 1997; Sheak & Cianciolo 1993; Weeks, 1997). Kinsella (2001) conceptualized this moment of instability as one of discursive containment, in which possibilities for citizen participation and deliberation are configured by the rhetorical boundary work of influential actors. During the Manhattan Project and Cold War eras, he argued, officials primarily employed boundaries (e.g., the principle of secrecy) to contain information, restricting its circulation within a narrow community of authorized actors. By the end of the Cold War, however, the effectiveness and perceived legitimacy of secrecy had decreased, and public access to information had increased. Subsequently, officials have shifted tactics to contain the meaning of that information (e.g., by asserting preferred frames of technical expertise over vernacular forms of knowledge).[9] In practice, discursive containment often operates on the premise that public participation is a potential hazard to official interests and should be minimized and controlled. The range and quality of voice in deliberation is, as a result, significantly attenuated.

These conditions suggest a number of topics for further investigation by communication scholars. Here, we outline two related examples of social construction. The first concerns public involvement and participation. The second involves risk as a putatively objective, but in fact, highly selective, organizing principle for public deliberation and institutional decision making.

Public involvement and participation. First, further research is warranted regarding the rhetorical practices by which stakeholders are hailed (both by officials and each other) to participate in policy making (Boiko et al., 1996) and are subsequently enabled and constrained. Crucial here are institutional dynamics that function pragmatically to shape the terms of discussion, the scope of actors' involvement, the legitimacy of particular speakers and speech acts, the rate, sequence, and duration of decision making, and the ways in which technical and nontechnical discourses are articulated (Fiorino, 1996; Kinsella, 2001, 2002, 2004b; Laird, 1993; Mehta, 1998). Research with this focus would engage the micropractices of participants: How do officials manage public meetings and respond to hostile questions (Campbell, Follender, & Shane, 1998; McComas, 2001, 2003a, 2003b)? How appropriately do facilitators summarize the discourse of focus groups? How do opponents succumb to or resist capture and the subversion of their alternate values by expert nuclear discourses (Cohn, 1987)?[10] This focus recovers nuclear democracy as a local, communicative accomplishment, whose forms and practices may vary widely from one scene to another, based on the structures and cultures of particular decision-making and advisory groups (Bradbury & Branch, 1999; Weeks, 2000).

A related issue concerns the integrity of communicative practices suppressed in vernacular criteria used by officials to manage, and by researchers to assess, public participation programs. Stakeholders, for example, commonly perceive particular attributes as necessary for successful programs (e.g., the decision-making process allows full and active stakeholder participation; Carnes, Schweitzer, Peelle, Wolfe, & Munro, 1998; Hanford Advisory Board, 2002). They often lack, however, sufficient resources for understanding how actual (as opposed to hypothetical or idealized) communication accomplishes these outcomes. This focus recovers the practices that saturate nuclear decision making in local, concrete situations (Mehta, 1998) and enables the development of associated practical theory (Cronen, 1995).

Potentially, this research clarifies how affected groups may successfully self-organize to emerge as effective counterpublics, developing and using multipronged, multimodal opposition to engage the complexities of nuclear weapons production and its persistent culture of secrecy. At sites such as Fernald and Hanford, for example (Metzler, 1997; Ratliff, 1998), liminal actors such as whistleblowers, independent scientists, and downwinders (Kinsella, 2001) have effectively challenged the DOE by deploying alternative discourses and forms of knowledge.

Risk as a deliberative organizing principle. Another topic that warrants further examination is the use of "risk" as a key trope in deliberations regarding nuclear policy and operations. As Carlisle (1996) observed, risk has long served as a frame for decision making within the nuclear weapons production complex. Regulatory agencies have also relied heavily on the concept in setting standards for environmental protection and cleanup. Most recently, the DOE has adopted an approach known as Risk-Based End States as a centerpiece of its efforts to determine appropriate levels of environmental remediation for its former weapons production sites (U.S. DOE, 2003). However, there is little clarity within the department or among stakeholders regarding what is meant by risk, or how to operationalize that polysemic term. A representative anecdote comes from a recent experience of one of the authors, who participated in a citizen advisory board workshop on risk at the Hanford site. After a series of presentations on risk models in use at the site, the author learned that none of these models was the same as the one being used by DOE headquarters as the basis for its controversial Risk-Based End States initiative. Furthermore, a member of the consulting organization that produced the model in use at headquarters had expressed concern that this model was not sufficiently developed to serve as a standard. These two points became evident only during a private conversation at lunch and were invisible to many of the meeting participants. This episode illustrates how actors can coordinate in completing tasks without necessarily sharing common goals or understandings. Such conditions can easily lend themselves to the use of strategic ambiguity (Eisenberg, 1984) by officials to preserve privileged positions and foster institutional change agendas without the full awareness of stakeholders.

The academic literature on risk is broad, diverse, and interdisciplinary, spanning perspectives that have been characterized as technical, economic, systems, psychological, organizational, social, cultural, and democratic (Krimsky & Golding, 1992; Renn, 1992). These divergent perspectives are reflected in the literature on risk communication that informs both communication scholarship and standard stakeholder relations practice (e.g., Fischhoff, 1987; Hance, Chess, & Sandman, 1989; Rowan, 1991, 1995). With the exception of a more democratic approach temporarily adopted by the DOE during its 1990s openness initiative, technical and organizational approaches have dominated deliberations regarding the nuclear weapons production complex. These approaches privilege objectives such as legal compliance with regulations, accomplishing tasks efficiently and within budget, and limiting community interference with organizational operations (Fischhoff, 1987). As Needleman (1987) pointed out, such approaches too often "sidestep the public health and human rights goals usually presented as the moral rationale for risk communication-empowering those at risk to make informed decisions" (p. 20). Such empowerment is the goal of the democratic focus, exemplified by calls for an approach to risk communication "that describes the social conditions most likely to secure the best possible technical knowledge about hazards and the best possible methods of addressing stakeholders' concerns" (Rowan, 1995, p. 304). Democratic approaches seek to integrate expert knowledge about risk with values that are important to communities and stakeholders, ideally producing decisions that are superior both technically and socially.

Recent work in European sociology offers a promising foundation for further scholarship on risk communication. This work is largely motivated by the risk society paradigm originated by Beck (1992), in which modernization is inevitably accompanied by the production of hazards. Beck suggested that the distribution of risks has emerged as a central problem for late-modern society, analogous to the more familiar social problem of distributing limited resources. His concept of reflexive modernization incorporates the dual reflexive principles that risk is both a product of social action and a problem to be solved by further social action, and that contemporary societies must examine their own practices in the light of risk. Both principles invite the attention of communication scholars, who are well positioned to consider how such reflexive activities can be accomplished (Kinsella, 2002). Complementary to Beck's paradigm is the work of Luhmann (1993), who placed communication more centrally in the risk problematic. Identifying communication as the autopoetic "operation by which society as a system produces and reproduces itself," Luhmann argued that it is a mistake to attribute risk to technology itself. Instead, he argued, "only communication about technology and—above all—the communication of decisions about the deployment or nondeployment of technology is risky" (Luhmann, 1993, pp. xii–xiii). In this context, Luhmann viewed risk as a time-binding principle that links the future to choices made in the present. Communication scholarship can make important contributions to understanding how such choices are envisioned, articulated, deliberated, and enacted in the evolving nuclear public sphere.

Organizational Crisis, Change, and Stakeholder Communication

Scholars of organizational crisis and change examine how organizations cope with inevitable conditions that threaten the viability of their continued operations and of stakeholder perceptions of their legitimacy and authority (Seeger, Sellnow, & Ulmer, 1998). Although these are both contexts that compel organizational response, crisis may be distinguished from change by its singular, sudden, and severe occurrence (i.e., all crisis is a form of change, but not vice versa). Additionally, whereas they both result from interaction between organizations and their environments, crisis foregrounds the role of organizational mistakes and failures in producing unexpected and traumatic change. Crisis may also be distinguished by the high-stakes organizational responses that its urgency provokes (e.g., apology, justification, excuse, intimidation, ingratiation, and denouncement; Allen & Caillouet, 1994). In this way, crisis and change are not objective conditions, but contested discursive constructs (Hay, 1995, p. 65, in Venette, Sellnow, & Lang, 2003, p. 224). As such, they are inherently compelling to communication scholars because they can dramatically alter how organizations and stakeholders identify each other, conceptualize their respective interests, and represent those interests in various forums of conflict and decision making (Deetz, 1995). This focus emphasizes the politics of voice as a deeply human and moral process through which affected stakeholders develop and perform narratives intended to garner organizational attention and justify their inclusion and consideration in organizational processes.

Scholars distinguish several types of crisis and change (e.g., evolution versus revolution) characterized by the relative pervasiveness, magnitude, rate, and duration of their effects. These effects are created as the triggers and consequences of change ripple across an organization's social reality. Crisis and change thus form dangerous opportunities: Organizational equilibrium is disturbed, stakeholders become anxious and agitated, and the future waits to be born. Much of this literature emphasizes the role played by organizational leaders as they assess the causes of crisis and change, and as they design and implement programs intended to exploit their opportunities and foil their threats. As such, this literature is filled with dramatic stories of heroic success, subcultural obstruction, and disastrous failure (Ulmer, 2001).

These efforts at leadership appear to involve as much art as science. Affected leaders must not only skillfully interpret ambiguous and turbulent environments, but also create (and perform) new narratives. In the case of change, these narratives must adequately bridge a familiar, even if problematic, past and an uncertain and unavoidable future. In the case of crisis, they must remedy immediate harms, resolve to prevent recurrences, and restore compromised legitimacy. In both cases, these narratives must unite and sustain stakeholders, motivating them to change old habits, create new patterns in production and consumption, and, in a very real sense, become new kinds of people. With luck, skill, and resolve, stakeholders may respond to these narratives by collaborating in the development of reflective, ethical, and adaptive organizations (Ross & Benson, 1995).

Communication scholars are uniquely concerned with the discursive dimensions of crisis and change. Their studies depict change agents and stakeholders manipulating symbolic resources (artifacts, metaphors, jargon, genres, rituals, myths, and vision statements) in new ways to express their experience and accomplish their goals (Deetz, Tracy, & Simpson, 2000; Lewis & Seibold, 1998). Crisis and change subsequently become contexts that clarify how discourse constitutes and accomplishes (re-) organization, and does not simply reflect it (Feldman, 1990). One benefit offered by these studies is increased sensitivity to the power of communication as it engages and frames events to create both planned and unplanned consequences. Organizational responses to crisis and change are developed by organizational actors engaged in improvisation, compromise, and imperfect analysis. These actors produce polysemic texts that circulate among diverse subcultures and generate multiple, and potentially conflicting, interpretations. These interpretations in turn produce responses ranging from desired mobilization to confusion and resistance (O'Connor, 1995). In a series of studies conducted at the DOE's Fernald site, for example, Fairhurst and her colleagues (Fairhurst, Cooren, & Cahill, 2002; Fairhurst, Jordan, & Neuwirth, 1997) examined the disorientation and ambivalence experienced by post-Cold War workers as they decommission a core symbol of their identity and by management tasked with motivating this workforce. Contractor downsizing at Fernald has been an especially difficult process, exposing stakeholder differences over appropriate industrial paradigms for conducting operations (e.g., manufacturing vs. construction), organizational politics threatening managers who, in satisfying one group of stakeholders, inevitably alienate others, and lessons from initial downsizing that roll forward uncontrollably to undermine subsequent reorganization.

Regarding the nuclear weapons production complex, then, we see several opportunities for extending these findings. The most obvious involves the unprecedented scale of change efforts directed at organizational entities that have, either actively or by default, created harm. As Kauzlarich and Kramer (1998) argued, these radical efforts seek to change deeply ingrained motivations, opportunities, and control structures that have in the past enabled organizational actors to rationalize the commission of criminal acts. In the process, organizational representatives must also overcome an extraordinary credibility deficit in that they have not historically sought meaningful dialogue with stakeholders.

Additionally, many characteristics of these organizations create contingencies that potentially diffuse and undermine planned change efforts. They are geographically dispersed, for example, and range in type from high-tech, scientific research facilities to unglamorous manufacturing plants. Each organization possesses, in turn, a distinct mixture of regional, professional, and occupational subcultures. Following the end of the Cold War, these organizations experienced increased turnover in membership that, in turn, has affected the coherence and reliability of their collective knowledge and memory. These members (e.g., generational workforce cohorts) have oriented differently to the traditional weapons production mission (Loeb, 1986) and to the apparent ending of the Cold War. They have done so partly by drawing on a volatile mixture of emotions, including relief, denial, nostalgia, resignation, pride, and ironic appreciation (e.g., for predecessors whose mistakes have, at least temporarily, enabled their continued employment). Some of these sites have been targeted for complete closure and cleanup; others have been slated for ongoing weapons development and production; still others will pursue both these missions simultaneously. Some sites were severely constrained in their potential responses to the end of their Cold War mission. Others, such as the DOE's National Laboratories, were encouraged to develop entrepreneurial identities as centers of broad-based research and development. Some sites fashioned relatively deep and consistent support among local stakeholders for the pursuit of these missions; others developed (at best) partial, thin, and fleeting support.

These conditions complicate traditional assumptions about communication surrounding organizational crisis and change. They defy, for example, conventional wisdom that crisis has a discrete, sharp onset. Alternately, we may conceptualize the DOE's legitimation crisis during the late- and post-Cold War period as the result of inexorable convergence between geographically dispersed and initially ambiguous events. This convergence was facilitated by the use of discursive strategies among stakeholders (e.g., displayed in news media coverage) that framed otherwise local and isolated events as elements of a larger, coherent phenomenon. As well, the emergence of this crisis has served for many stakeholders as a (re-) introduction to the existence and operations of these facilities. Those operations were historically obscured by the warrants of security and secrecy. As a result, organizational actors were not able to draw on a history of explicit, undistorted, and consensual relationships with stakeholders to restore legitimacy. Instead, they were required to simultaneously reassert and defend their continued presence.

Additionally, these conditions deflate the romantic myth of unilateral, top-down change imposed by heroic figures. The most likely candidates for this role, the DOE secretaries and their deputies, have consistently expressed humility and frustration with the enormity of their reform charge, the impediments to its implementation, and the resistance it has generated among stakeholders (Lanouette, 1990; Owendorf, 1996). As a large, Byzantine government bureaucracy, the DOE has coped with continuous, turbulent change since its creation in 1977 (Schafer, 1994). Those changes stem from several sources, including the agency's extraordinarily broad mission, which includes the promotion of commercial nuclear power; the geographic dispersal of its operations, which promotes weak centralized control over local fiefdoms; the instability of its associated economic and political environments; and routine turnover among its politically appointed staff. Its frequent restructurings have produced fatigue, anxiety, confusion, and defensiveness among employees and have exacerbated the weakness of DOE's culture relative to the strong cultures of its contractors on whom it depends for achieving operational success (Stelzer, 1996).

Since the end of the Cold War, successive DOE secretaries have attempted to institute multiple planned change programs (Bergeron, 2002, pp. 95–118; Carlisle, 1996, pp. 195–218). Both within and across different administrations, these programs have varied widely in their scope, goals, and ideologies (e.g., in seeking to improve operational effectiveness vs. increasing public accountability). In different sites and moments, these programs have confronted numerous, formidable sources of opposition. These include Cold Warrior staffers intransigently aligned with the ideology of weapons production; field-office employees who identify more with local contractors than with headquarters; regulators who are inadequately trained, thoroughly outnumbered by contractor employees, and challenged by the task of tailoring rigid and competing statutes to the unique needs of specific sites; industrial contractors accustomed to minimal accountability, unqualified and inexperienced in conducting a massive environmental cleanup, and resistant to adopting new performance contracts; Congressional lawmakers with alternate, competing reform agendas that are performed in a high-stakes theater of budgetary politics; and cynical, wary stakeholders unwilling to (re-)invest trust or confidence in DOE and contractor operations. Given these challenges, it is remarkable that the DOE and its contractors have been at least partly successful in increasing the openness, accountability, and perceived legitimacy of their operations.

As we have discussed above, these outcomes resulted in part from the cumulative use by various organizational actors of narrative (Venette, et al., 2003) and impression management strategies (Allen & Caillouet, 1994). These strategies responded to problematic narratives emerging in stakeholder discourse and media coverage of the weapons production complex and addressed the perceived needs of stakeholders. Viewed using Benoit's (1995) scheme, they included *denial* (e.g., shifting responsibility for current conditions to predecessors); *evasion of responsibility* (e.g., claiming to lack information about or control over key elements of situations and that negative consequences were unforeseen and unintended); *reduction of offensiveness* (e.g., minimizing negative consequences, directing audiences to higher values that justified operations, counterattacking accusers, and offering compensation to victims); *corrective action* (e.g., promising to repair damages), and *mortification* (e.g., accepting limited responsibility for specific actions, and apologizing to affected stakeholders).

Collectively, these conditions indicate that we should view any particular nuclear weapons production facility as the site of simultaneous, multilateral change efforts initiated by stakeholders using various influence strategies and pursuing alternately complementary and competitive agendas. Contractor employees engaged in dismantling plant facilities, for example, are subjected to both the resurgent health and safety culture of the post-Cold War DOE and also the unofficial (but no less forceful) culture of efficiency imposed by management attempting to maximize their productivity and profitability. Thus, these organizational scenes are dense with the cognitive, emotional, and discursive labor of stakeholders performing the shifting, tactical identifications that suit their situated, evolving purposes. At the Hanford site, for example, some former critics of its operators, such as environmental and public interest groups, are now vocal advocates for adequate federal funding and oversight to ensure a successful cleanup (Dalton et al., 1999). In this process, new alliances between stakeholders have partly replaced old rivalries.

The DOE and its contractors have achieved some success, then, in changing from insular, arrogant bureaucracies to more engaged and responsible organizational citizens (Reed, et al., 1997). Communication researchers should continue to study, however, the powerful and inertial forces that currently threaten those reforms. Here, we identify five of these forces. The first involves the existence of inadequate and uncertain funding for implementing necessary initiatives. The second involves strong motivation among stakeholders to pursue self-interest at the expense of a common good. Workers, for example, may slow down the cleanup of facilities to extend their employment. Officials may advocate cleanup criteria and end-use scenarios that limit continued responsibility. Congress and the executive branch may seek to fund a rapid, but potentially inadequate, cleanup. A third force involves the development of public participation processes that are nominally designed to produce dialogue and learning, but are actually deployed in ways that preserve existing practices and secure officially preferred decision alternatives (Bergeron, 2002, p. 121; Cheney & Christensen, 2001). A fourth force involves the fatigue, disillusionment, and burnout experienced by organizational change agents (e.g., public involvement specialists) as they trade the permanent emergency of Cold War nuclear weapons production for the permanent controversy of seemingly intractable stakeholder conflict surrounding the decommissioning, demolition, and cleanup of facilities.

A fifth, and perhaps most alarming, force involves the reemergence of national hyper-security and obsessive secrecy as organizing principles following recent allegations of nuclear espionage conducted at Los Alamos and the terrorist attacks of September 11, 2001 (Masco, 2002). The consequences of these events include the reorganization of the DOE's weapons design laboratories under a more restrictive National Nuclear Security Administration and the removal of putatively sensitive documents from public access on agency and contractor websites. Combined with the imminent revival of nuclear weapons production within the U.S.,[11] the mounting pressure on stakeholders to resolve the conflicting priorities of cost and effectiveness in cleaning up contaminated facilities, and the elimination of forums for this deliberation, these developments suggest the persistence of a highly controversial issue (and one that has been largely suppressed in order to preserve the fragile stakeholder coalitions surrounding cleanup of the complex; Taylor & Davis, 1999). That issue is this: To what extent will post-Cold

War reforms instituted by the DOE be sustained? If they are sustained, to what extent will they be contained within the DOE's EM program, thus exempting the agency's defense programs (and their contractors) from significant change and the lasting implications of lessons learned?

Stated another way, we may distinguish here between organizational commitments to taking corrective action for harms committed and to preventing the recurrence of those offensive acts (Benoit, 1995). The former does not necessarily imply the latter, and there is no guarantee that the powerful warrant of national security will not compel future generations of facility operators to repeat their elevation of nuclear weapons production over the values of environment, health, and safety. Bergeron (2002, 2004), for example, argued that the U.S. government has compromised both safety concerns and a precarious international nonproliferation regime in its rush to convert existing civilian power reactors to produce tritium gas allegedly needed to maintain the nuclear arsenal.

In summary, the nuclear weapons production complex represents a compelling opportunity to examine how planned change programs alternately promote, sustain, and defeat effective organizational change and adaptation (Reed, et al., 1997, p. 632). In this case, the overriding issue is whether and how organizations historically steeped in secrecy and deception can ever change their fundamental cultures and traditions of stakeholder management (Dalton et al., 1999). Communication researchers, subsequently, may provide significant and useful knowledge about this process by examining the following four issues.

First, what are the specific elements and processes that characterize communication surrounding planned change in nuclear weapons production organizations?[12] Potential topics here include message design, selection of audiences and channels, designation of sources for the dissemination of information; practices of soliciting and utilizing input; and the active reception, and subsequent use, by stakeholders of organizational messages (Lewis, 1999; Patterson & Allen, 1997). This focus would move beyond summarizing controversial issues (Lowrie & Greenberg, 1999) to foreground the communicative practices through which controversy is produced and resolved. It would also transcend describing the structures of stakeholder involvement (Boiko et al., 1996) to interpret and critique them. Second, what are the impression management strategies used by actors in nuclear weapons organizations to maintain legitimacy in a rapidly changing institutional environment (Allen & Caillouet, 1994; Benoit, 1995)? How do actors perform these strategies in particular scenes? With what consequences? Conversely, how do stakeholders of nuclear weapons production design and perform influence strategies (e.g., by utilizing resources of power, legitimacy, urgency, and network centrality and density) to claim attention from associated organizations (Frooman, 1999; Mitchell, Agle, & Wood, 1997)? How do these organizations subsequently identify, recruit, and prioritize these stakeholders (Boiko et al., 1996)? How should they? Third, how effective and ethical are these organizations in producing secondary- and meta-narration that responds to primary media coverage of crisis (Venette et al., 2003)? Research here should include both organizational responses to immediate crisis and long-term narrative development designed to reestablish legitimacy and authority.

Finally, what are the political dimensions of organizational/stakeholder communication (Deetz, 1992, 1995; Mitchell, et al., 1997) surrounding nuclear weapons production? These elements include the general practices by which stakeholder participation is conceptualized and conducted by organizations (e.g., in selectively defining potential stakeholders as a sign of regard for their relevance and prominence; conducting public meetings in ways indicating either cynical, perfunctory compliance with regulatory requirements, or genuine commitment to mutually transformative dialogue). They may also include the use of specific power tactics by participants, such as allocating resources, controlling agendas, controlling decision-making criteria, rationalization, brinksmanship, co-optation, forming coalitions, using surrogates, and using outside experts (Fairholm, 1993). The use of these tactics may be especially prevalent, for example, among meta-stakeholder groups (e.g., citizens' advisory boards and community reuse organizations), whose mission is to solicit and resolve participation from multiple (and often conflicting) groups.

Nuclear History, Memory, and Heritage

Communication about nuclear weapons production is energized by attempts to define and enforce the legacies of wartime and Cold War-era activities. This process establishes relationships between the discourses of nuclear history, memory, and heritage. These three discourses are similar in that they are all produced when cultural members use symbols to forge meaningful relationships between their experience of the past, present, and future. Because of their apocalyptic potential to rupture the continuity of human experience, nuclear weapons have always posed a radical challenge to these practices (Derrida, 1984; Williams, 1989). Nonetheless, nuclear history, memory, and heritage are unique genres of discourse with important differences. That is, they are each subject to rules that define the legitimacy and authority of their speakers; that specify their appropriate form, content, and meaning; and that constrain the venues of their circulation. These rules shape the potential of each discourse to produce particular effects for the hegemony of nuclear narratives. Cumulatively, these effects shape evolving relationships between the stakeholders of nuclear weapons production facilities.

History is the generic, vernacular term commonly used to designate both past events and the efforts of cultural members to determine their meaning. As a discourse, history is dedicated to exploring and recovering the past as a field of lost, unknown, and perhaps unknowable, events. Represented through historical discourse, past events potentially become "consensually known, open to inspection and proof" (Lowenthal 1998, xi). In this discourse, events are typically considered along an axis of irreversible, linear temporality, with the goal of understanding their causes, natures, and consequences. The discourse produced by historians is inevitably literary and rhetorical. It utilizes discursive conventions to select, emphasize, and interpret the relationships between events in order to produce accounts that inform and influence audiences (Gronbeck, 1998; White, 1980). In its formats and purposes, this discourse serves simultaneously as both a narrative of and argument about past events. The broad genre of historical discourse divides into multiple subgenres, including arcane and specialized academic histories, and more accessible and entertaining popular histories. Academic histories invoke a relatively intellectual, professional, and objectivist discourse, appropriating the rational criteria of argument to support their claims. Their narratives value precision and explanation and are rigorously evaluated by other academic historians for their conformity to these criteria. This process of peer review, and the ongoing competition between academic and popular histories for the allegiance of readers, encourage the production of multiple histories. These accounts circulate continuously within the cultural sphere, auditioning for authority and legitimacy as communally sanctioned accounts of the past. In the field of nuclear history, for example, Krupar (1998) has criticized the complicity of traditional accounts in maintaining (at least until the publication of Hales, 1997) an official Manhattan Project narrative that characterized local lands acquired for the Hanford Reservation as uninhabited and worthless. This narrative effaced the actual history of that region's small but hardy farming culture, which had itself displaced Native Americans, and minimized a variety of burdens created for Hanford, Oak Ridge, and Los Alamos-area residents by the U.S. military's seizure of their property. As its narratives contact, interrogate, and displace each other, history can appear rudely dispassionate in challenging popular, preferred beliefs about the nuclear past.

Memory, alternately, designates partial and interested recollections of the past performed by both individuals and collectives. Although memory is always, to some extent, experienced as an individual phenomenon, it does not necessarily originate in private reflection. Individuals commonly document and interpret their evolving identities through private practices of personal memory (e.g., the use of snapshots and scrapbooks by the members of Manhattan Project communities; Fermi, 1995). These practices alternately parallel and intersect with the public practices through which larger collectives construct, share, and contest their narratives of group identity. In this process, those group narratives are often depicted as if they were derived from a common past (e.g., in commemorative discourse surrounding the dedication of monuments). Ritualistic and populist discourses of memory alternately compete with and complement those of history. For audiences, the claims generated by memory (e.g., in the oral histories of nuclear protestors and workers; Sanger, 1995) are enhanced by the immediacy and authenticity of speakers recounting their lived experience. As a frame for evaluation, the verisimilitude of personal narrative displaces the validity produced by rigorous objectivity. Audiences often value such recollection because it recovers the rich details of personal experience effaced by the grand sweep of historical narrative.

As a vehicle for cultural myth and ideology, memory can also be used to mobilize social and political interests to align in particular ways with dominant institutions (Popular Memory Group, 1982). Potentially, this mobilization can be directed against a dominant regime of history, alleging and prosecuting gaps and distortions in its narratives. This approach was certainly the case, for example, in a recent controversy surrounding a proposed exhibition of the Enola Gay aircraft at the Smithsonian Institution's National Air and Space Museum in Washington, DC. In that controversy, powerful interests pitted the partial, visceral memories of World War II veterans against the more comprehensive and detached narratives of museum curators, with tragic results (Hubbard & Hasian, 1998). Ideally, history evolves as a steady and rational project through the confirmation and revision of explanations. In contrast, memory is both more volatile and obdurate, evolving unpredictably based on the ability of its stewards to recruit and maintain adherents, who need not have directly experienced events in order to support particular, preferred recollections, and to secure and defend sacred sites of its performance (e.g., museums). Like history, memory is inevitably plural and potentially agonistic, as different groups maneuver to privilege their recollections over those of competitors (Zelizer, 1995).

Heritage, finally, designates popular movements that are concerned with preserving and interpreting the past during periods of intensive social, political, and economic change. In such climates, nostalgia and anxiety regarding the integrity of a group's historical roots and preferred myths are particularly high. Heritage movements subsequently operate to collect and exhibit valued knowledge, performances, and artifacts from a group's past to ensure the continued viability of its dominant narratives. In this process, heritage discourse promotes a past that fixes the fluctuation of precarious identities and "enhance[s] the well-being of some chosen individual or folk" (Griffiths, 1996, p. 218). To some extent, heritage reflects the intersection of memory and history. Its movements create

> sites of memory which are charged with a particular persuasive task of representing the past . . . [and] fulfill their rhetorical mission by merging the authenticating force of memory and the objectifying thrust of history in a compelling, culturally legitimate idiom. (Katriel, 1993, p. 75)

Like history and memory, heritage is a promiscuous phenomenon practiced by virtually all nuclear weapons production stakeholders when confronted with traumatic change. It may also be professionalized: DOE contractors occupying former Native American tribal lands, for example, employ cultural resource managers trained in a variety of archaeological and anthropological methods. These personnel are charged with identifying and preserving artifacts from those civilizations and with overseeing their disposition. Heritage may also, finally, be a site of intense political struggle between stakeholders seeking justice for grievances associated with the history of nuclear weapons production. The Nuclear Claims

Tribunal created to adjudicate claims by Pacific Islanders poisoned and displaced by postwar U.S. nuclear testing, for example, was recently forced to consider whether (and how) the lost knowledge and practices of those indigenous groups should be commodified as part of a financial settlement (Kirsch, 2001).

Distinguishing the discourses of nuclear history, memory, and heritage allows us to develop three claims about their role in shaping public understanding of nuclear weapons production. The first is that, as a field of cultural discourse, the history of U.S. nuclear weapons production is extraordinarily dense and agitated (Hubbard, 1998; Kane, 1988; Newman, 1995; Prosise, 1998). It is suffused with public struggle conducted between groups holding widely divergent, and highly moralized, orientations to the related figures, events, organizations, technologies, and policies constituting that actual history. Typically, these orientations pivot around two, deeply opposed, ideological narratives. In the dominant narrative promoted by Cold War patriots and triumphalists, the bomb is depicted as a heroically constructed technology that was justly used against a vicious wartime enemy, that successfully inhibited Soviet expansionism during the Cold War, and that is still required to deter evolving threats to U.S. national security (Engelhardt, 1998). In a second, less popular, but also persistent narrative (e.g., promoted by New Left historians), the bomb is framed as an unnecessary, and perhaps barbarous, device whose wartime use against Japan commenced a profoundly irrational and dehumanizing chapter in the evolution of military strategy and international politics and whose compulsive production has significantly damaged the global economy, public health, and the environment (Makhijani, et al., 1995; Stegenga, 1991).

Even though this characterization obscures a significant middle ground of narratives characterized by ambivalence (e.g., among native peoples modernized by the creation of nuclear weapons production sites; Masco, 1999), it partly maps the heteroglossia of nuclear-cultural history. Because of this condition, visceral conflict frequently erupts around official and popular-cultural sites of nuclear-historical rhetoric, such as Hollywood films and museum exhibitions (Taylor, 1993b; 1998b). In these conflicts, participating groups invoke various, overlapping combinations of historical, memory, and heritage discourses to articulate their interests and discredit their opponents. Frequently, this conflict sustains a history of struggle in which nuclear officials have used and abused the rational discourses of science and bureaucracy in communicating with U.S. citizens. For example, nuclear weapons production officials have employed objectivist discourse in insisting that alternate historical narratives (e.g., those promoted by antinuclear activists) conform to the established (and, implied, self-apparent and consensual) facts of nuclear history. Opponents of orthodox nuclear history, as a result, are most effective (and controversial) when they expose and challenge the taken-for-granted processes by which apparent facts are selected, interpreted, and represented as evidence for historical claims (Taylor, 1996, 1997a).

Secondly, we note the cultural politics through which various elements of the nuclear weapons production complex are selected and emphasized within these controversies. When it is performed as a public affair, nuclear-historical conflict typically invokes the institutional and operational practices through which the Cold War was planned and conducted. These are frequently matters of organizational history. At the same time, however, the unique histories of some weapons production facilities have been minimized by two narrative conventions. These conventions, which may be partly attributed to the conditions of official secrecy and popular anxiety in postwar culture, misrecognize these facilities in two ways. The first convention involves aggregating DOE facilities as an undifferentiated, monolithic apparatus. In this perspective, speakers attribute nuclear weapons to vague and moralized abstractions such as the military-industrial complex, while failing to distinguish the diverse missions and functions of specific agencies and organizations that interact to produce them. The second form of misrecognition involves selectively emphasizing actors within these networks. For example, histories of tribute circulating in popular culture commonly highlight the elite figures (e.g., Robert Oppenheimer), professional communities (physicists), sites (Los Alamos), and events (the Trinity Test) associated with *scientific* research and development of nuclear weapons during World War II. In this process, less glamorous but equally important stories involving the hard hats and smoke-stacks of wartime and Cold War-era production facilities have been neglected. Those elements are frequently minimized in dominant historical narratives as mere vehicles for the attainment of larger policy goals (e.g., maintaining nuclear deterrence; Findlay & Hevly, 1995).

As a result, communication scholars can bear witness to the potential transformation of these conventions in an emerging nuclear heritage and tourism apparatus (Gusterson, 2004; Molella, 2003; Taylor, 2003a). Although this apparatus is not centrally organized or funded, enterprising stakeholders at several nuclear weapons production facilities have responded to the close-out of their Cold War mission by developing projects aimed at these markets (e.g., preserving structures, collecting oral histories of facility workers and community residents; Barnes-Kloth, Depoe, Hamilton, & Lombardo, 1999). Here, practical and ideological purposes converge. At the DOE National Laboratories, for example, preserving the informal, tacit knowledge of aging designers currently deprived of the opportunity to test nuclear weapons is viewed by officials as an urgent, as well as historically rich, project. At another level, preserving documents and artifacts from Cold War weapons production sites may ultimately serve the emerging needs of their long-term stewards several generations hence. As these projects unfold, they become opportunities for stakeholder interaction ranging from enthusiastic collaboration to sharp conflict. This interaction determines the appropriate form, content, and significance of historical narratives as viable commodities in the economies of heritage and tourism.

Further research should consider how these narratives (temporarily) resolve the ambiguity and paradox associated with nuclear history and mediate the ambivalent embrace by traditionally proud and insular communities of unpredictable and critical outsiders (Barnes-Kloth, Depoe, & Hamilton, 1999; Taylor & Freer,

2002). The discursive processes by which these relationships are conceptualized and conducted (and which have grown only more conflicted following the events of September 11, 2001; Molella, 2003, p. 224) should be of particular interest.

Finally, we note the temporal politics surrounding stakeholder representations of the relationship between their Cold War and post-Cold War identities and missions. The discourses of history, memory, and heritage are necessary but volatile resources that are appropriated and performed by stakeholders to depict the past in order to influence present and future conditions (Taylor & Freer, 2002). For example, we have argued above that a discourse of containment suffuses both the material projects of DOE speakers (e.g., in stabilizing and storing radioactive waste) and also their predominant punctuation of the Cold War as a finished operation, whose social, political, and environmental residues are currently problematic but ultimately manageable (e.g., they will eventually be cleaned up; Kinsella, 2001).

Communication scholars can trouble this conventional wisdom by three means. The first is to foreground the unprecedented challenges associated with remediating the harms of Cold War weapons production and with managing radioactive wastes whose risks will endure across truly glacial rates of decay (e.g., the half-life of plutonium is 24 millennia). Significantly, the individuals, organizations, and cultures involved in designing long-term stewardship, and the more recently christened program of legacy management, must confront a renewed nuclear challenge to their mortality: They must rhetorically transcend their own deaths to envision the future. The psychological and logistical challenges associated with producing this kind of long-range planning discourse are widely underestimated (Brand, 1999).

The second means is to establish how the current revival of nuclear weapons production by the U.S. government suggests the continuation and renewal—not the completion or transcendence—of Cold War institutional cultures and operations that have produced the current crisis. Here, it seems urgent that critics examine how the discourses of history, memory, and heritage (e.g., surrounding the detection and prosecution of nuclear spies; Masco, 2002; Taylor, 2002) serve as resources for punctuating the relationship between the first and second nuclear ages (Schell, 2000).

The final means involves clarifying the contingencies surrounding the production and reception of nuclear discourse. This critical practice establishes that stakeholders engaged in periodizing and thematizing nuclear history are involved in a dialectic of remembering and forgetting. It also establishes that, contrary to the discourse of some heritage advocates, the issue is not that the nuclear past will be forgotten, but rather which and whose narratives of that past will be preserved, and how they will be enforced as resources for nuclear citizenship and governance in future generations. In this process, just as scholars have recently challenged official views of space that undergird nuclear hegemony (e.g., as a remote, uninhabited resource readily available for appropriation by authorities; Hales, 1997; Kuletz, 1998), they should also critique the historiography of nuclear weapons production (e.g., in narratives implying that time is a neutral and otherwise empty container for operations). Here, they can consider the following issues: Will the emerging narratives of nuclear history, memory, and heritage encourage accommodation of nuclear hegemony, or heightened resistance (Cable, Shriver, & Hastings, 1999)? Which group's narratives will be privileged as necessary fact? Which will be forgotten, rejected, or marginalized as (mere) nostalgia (Smith, 2000)?

CONCLUSION: FACING THE CHALLENGES OF STUDYING NUCLEAR WEAPONS PRODUCTION

In this chapter, we have pursued several goals. We have recovered a compelling yet understudied site of communication, reviewed its history and culture, and proposed a three-part framework for extending research. In this process, we have pursued the implications of the two anecdotes used to open this essay. We have encouraged communication scholars to perform a double take at the institutions of nuclear weapons production and to explore the discourse waiting behind the door marked "The Bomb, Inc." Beyond that door, we do indeed find that something happened and that a heightened appreciation for the ethics and politics of communication empowers responsible nuclear citizenship and scholarship.

In proposing this research program, however, we have not failed to appreciate the associated challenges. Our own experience has sensitized us to four, specifically. First, the daunting, technocratic complexity of this site discourages researchers through its generation of associated opportunity costs (e.g., the labor of reading dense, legalistic, and technical reports). Second, the inherently morbid aura surrounding the production of nuclear weapons encourages researchers to adopt safer and more pleasant topics. Third, the discourse of nuclear weapons production is often polarized, constricted, agitated, and moralized. These qualities continually challenge scholars to reflect on their own affiliations (e.g., as citizens of a government willing and able to use weapons of mass destruction), to develop more subtle and innovative forms of analysis, and to bear the brunt of stakeholder reaction to analysis that does not conform to preferred scripts. Finally, intradisciplinary specialization has led communication scholars to allocate the study of nuclear communication in a fragmented, partial, and exclusive manner (Taylor, 1998a). We conclude, as a result, by addressing each of these challenges in turn.

First, we hope that we have partly reduced the opportunity costs of this research program by providing this very review. That is, although it cannot serve as a sole or exhaustive account of this site, we hope that this essay has distilled its relevant features and provided an initial resource for formulating and grounding communication research agendas. Second, although we have each wrestled with the frustrating and frightening dimensions of this research topic, we have also experienced significant satisfaction in our related research and service activities.[13] That experience has resonated for us in noting recent calls for communication scholars to move from the relatively protected spheres of academic life to address the messy and compelling needs of citizens engaged in ongoing struggles for dignity and justice. We have found complex and urgent problems associated with this site whose deliberation is potentially enhanced by our sustained attention. As a result, we invite scholars seeking sites for applied communication and social justice research to consider this one. This observation links in turn to the third challenge, in which communication scholars at this site must navigate its stormy waters of visceral emotions, oppressive hierarchies of professional and technical expertise, and morally righteous vernacular. These elements frequently combine to shape the perceived authority and legitimacy of our contributions among stakeholders, who may possess strong affiliations with existing institutions. Nonetheless, we believe that communication scholars are uniquely poised to engage this dilemma in that they are predisposed to both analyze and artfully intervene in scenes of distorted and frozen discourse. Studying the nuclear weapons production complex, in other words, sharpens our practices of observation and rhetorical invention as we seek to produce adequate, ethical, and effective research.

Finally, the very form of this essay reflects what we view as one solution to the fourth problem cited above. That is, we have avoided presenting this site as inherently owned by (only) one of our discipline's subfields. We recognize that there is benefit in pursuing nuclear communication research that neatly conforms to the existing categories and agendas of rhetorical criticism, organizational communication, environmental communication, political communication, or group communication. Nonetheless, our experience with this site has led us to adopt a relatively holistic approach to its analysis. Simply put, we believe that we need all of our tools and voices to make effective claims about communication surrounding nuclear weapons production. As a result, we encourage communication scholars to respond to the complexity of this site by integrating theories and concepts in innovative ways. We do not assume, in this process, that all innovations will be equally effective. Instead, we wish to create the space that is required to make and evaluate these attempts.

We hope that this chapter has succeeded in opening this space and that in coming years a growing number of communication scholars will expand and refine it. In this process, "The Bomb, Inc." may yet become the familiar object of our curious and unflinching gaze. With luck, our research could contribute to reinvigorating the freedom and democracy that, we are told repeatedly, are protected by nuclear weapons. If it can be imagined and represented in new ways, the nuclear future may yet follow a path other than tragic repetition.

NOTES

1. For a review, see Taylor (1998a). More specifically, the study of communication surrounding nuclear weapons production is neglected in, but not incompatible with, rhetorical criticism. In theorizing

identification and consubstantiality, for example, Kenneth Burke observed that the nuclear condition was supported by rhetoric of organization: "Modern war characteristically requires a myriad of constructive acts for each destructive one; before each culminating blast there must be a vast network of operations, directed communally" (quoted in Tietge, 2002, p. 6).

2. We use the term "stakeholder" throughout this chapter in a manner consistent with ongoing development of associated theory in organizational (Clarkson, 1995; Donaldson & Preston, 1995; Frooman, 1999; Mitchell, et al., 1997; Rowley, 1997; Scott & Lane, 2000) and communication studies (Deetz, 1995; Lewis, 1999; Lewis, Richardson, & Hamel, 2003). That theory seeks to adequately conceptualize, identify, and inform communication involving groups, both internal and external to an organization, who are affected (e.g., as a result of claim, ownership, right, or interest) by the outcomes of its past, present, or future operations. We provide a description of principal stakeholders of nuclear weapons production below.

3. Space does not permit adequate treatment of communication surrounding the development of nuclear waste storage facilities. For an overview, see Taylor (2003b). For studies of these two facilities, see Kuletz (1998) and McCutcheon (2002).

4. This blending did not result only from the nuclear symbolism that linked both military production reactors and their technological cousins, commercial power reactors. The two types of facilities are linked at a material level in their production of commonly needed nuclear fuels and a convertible, multipurpose reactor that produced both weapons-grade material and electric power developed at Hanford between 1957 and 1966 (Bergeron, 2002; Carlisle, 1996).

5. It is significant here that the first grassroots movement that transformed official procedures for public involvement in nuclear weapons development was not—as one might expect—antinuclear.

6. An ethnographic anecdote from Taylor and Davis's (1999) study of public involvement at the post-Cold War Rocky Flats facility illustrates how this discourse operates. There, they witnessed an unsettling event that occurred at an annual State of the Flats meeting. In this ritual forum for exchange between DOE officials and stakeholders, a long-time, local antinuclear activist challenged the site's DOE manager publicly to judge the site's previous (and infamous) contractors. "Would you agree that they were evil?" he demanded. The manager, a calm and formidable woman, paused, and looked around the banquet hall filled with the site's current contractors and representatives from local governments. On her face, civility wrestled disdain to a tie. "You know," she said emphatically, "I don't spend a lot of time second-guessing the motives of my predecessors." The room erupted in applause.

7. The bizarre persistence of Cold War-era practices in nuclear weapons strategy has been noted elsewhere (see Taylor, 2003a). Here, we are concerned with associated practices in the sphere of nuclear weapons production. For example, we have observed the persistence of a particular trope of organizational communication dating from the Manhattan Project and Cold War eras: namely, compulsive conformity to arbitrary schedules (e.g., displayed in contractor urgency to meet cleanup project milestones). This observation does not imply that schedules are inherently useless or whimsical. Instead, it foregrounds how they may be enforced in ways that promote unreflective pursuit of preferred means to achieve preferred goals (e.g., securing bonuses) and that minimize collaborative and undistorted reflection about those elements. As a result, the possibilities for ethical dissent to operations and the related interests of health, safety, and the environment potentially are minimized (see Thorpe, 2004).

8. The authors will provide an expanded reference list on request.

9. In practice, nuclear officials have simultaneously contained both the circulation and meaning of information. The nature of those efforts and their relative proportions, however, vary across eras.

10. The term *capture* has also been used to refer to the reverse case, in which regulatory agencies come to be dominated by the groups that they ostensibly oversee.

11. Here, we refer to converging ominous trends involving the conversion of civilian power reactors to produce weapons materials, the design of robust, low-yield nuclear weapons capable of penetrating and destroying hardened, buried targets, the potential resumption of nuclear testing, and the planned construction of a new facility for producing plutonium weapons components (see Ackland, 2003; Bergeron, 2002, 2004; Simon, 2004).

12. Here, it is important to remember that, although they are both a type of organization, the government agencies and industrial contractors involved have very different structures and cultures (see Wilson, 1989). These contexts uniquely shape their respective communicative practices.

13. Three of the authors have served on DOE SSABs.

REFERENCES

Ackland, L. (1999). *Making a real killing: Rocky Flats and the nuclear west.* Albuquerque: University of New Mexico Press.

Ackland, L. (2003, September 14). "Rocky Flats II" in the works. *Denver Post*, p. E1.

Allen, M. W., & Caillouet, R. H. (1994). Legitimation endeavors: Impression management strategies used by an organization in crisis. *Communication Monographs, 61*, 44–62.

Alvarez, R. (2000, May/June). Energy in decay. *Bulletin of the Atomic Scientists, 56*, 24–35.

Applegate, J. S. (1998). Beyond the usual suspects: The use of citizen advisory boards in environmental decision-making. *Indiana Law Journal, 73*, 903–957.

Applegate, J. S. (1999). National security and environmental protection: The half-full glass [review]. *Ecology Law Quarterly, 26*, 350–399.

Asen, R., & Brouwer, D. C. (2001). Introduction: Reconfigurations of the public sphere. In R. Asen & D. C. Brouwer (Eds.), *Counterpublics and the state* (pp. 1–32). Albany: State University of New York Press.

Barnes-Kloth, R., Depoe, S. P., & Hamilton, J. (1999, November). *History in the making: Inside the Fernald Living History Project.* Paper presented at the annual conference of the National Communication Association, Chicago.

Barnes-Kloth, R., Depoe, S., Hamilton, J., & Lombardo, A. (1999, July). *Memories of Fernald: Defining a 'sense of place' through personal narrative.* Paper presented at the conference on Communication and the Environment, Flagstaff, AZ.

Bartimus, T., & McCartney, S. (1991). *Trinity's children: Living along America's nuclear highway.* New York: Harcourt Brace Jovanovich.

Bazerman, C. (2001). Nuclear information: One rhetorical moment in the construction of the information age. *Written Communication, 18*, 259–295.

Beck, U. (1992). *Risk society: Towards a new modernity.* Thousand Oaks, CA: Sage.

Bennis, W., & Biederman, P. W. (1997). *Organizing genius: The secrets of creative collaboration.* Reading, MA: Addison-Wesley.

Benoit, W. L. (1995). *Accounts, excuses, and apologies: A theory of image restoration strategies.* Albany: State University of New York Press.

Bergeron, K. D. (2002). *Tritium on ice: The dangerous new alliance of nuclear weapons and nuclear power.* Cambridge, MA: MIT Press.

Bergeron, K. D. (2004, January–February). Nuclear weapons: The death of no-dual-use. *Bulletin of the Atomic Scientists, 60*, 15–17.

Bjork, R. S. (1992). *The strategic defense initiative: Symbolic containment of the nuclear threat.* Albany: State University of New York Press.

Blain, M. (1991). Rhetorical practice in an anti-nuclear weapons campaign. *Peace and Change, 16*, 355–378.

Boiko, P. E., Morrill, R. L., Flynn, J., Faustman, E. M., van Belle, G., & Omenn, G. S. (1996). Who holds the stakes? A case study of stakeholder identification at two nuclear weapons production sites. *Risk Analysis, 16*, 237–249.

Bradbury, J. A., & Branch, K. M. (1999, February). *An evaluation of the effectiveness of local site-specific advisory boards for U. S. Department of Energy environmental restoration programs.* (Report PNNL-12139). Washington, DC: Pacific Northwest National Laboratory.

Brand, S. (1999). *The clock of the long now: Time and responsibility.* New York: Basic Books.

Broad, W. J. (1985). *Star warriors.* New York: Simon & Schuster.

Cable, S., Shriver, T., & Hastings, D. (1999). The silenced majority: Quiescence and government social control on the Oak Ridge Nuclear Reservation. *Research in Social Problems and Public Policy, 7,* 59–81.

Campbell, K. S., Follender, S. I., & Shane G. (1998). Preferred strategies for responding to hostile questions in environmental public meetings. *Management Communication Quarterly, 11,* 401–421.

Canaday, J. (2000). *The nuclear muse: Literature, physics, and the first atomic bombs.* Madison: University of Wisconsin Press.

Carlisle, R. P. (1996). *Supplying the nuclear arsenal: American production-reactors, 1942–1992.* Baltimore: Johns Hopkins University Press.

Carnes, S. A., Schweitzer, M., Peelle, E. B., Wolfe, A. K., & Munro, J. F. (1998). Measuring the success of public participation on environmental restoration and waste management activities in the U.S. Department of Energy. *Technology in Society, 20,* 385–406.

Charles, D. (1988, January–February). The people vs. the complex. *Bulletin of the Atomic Scientists, 44,* 29–30.

Cheney, G., & Christensen, L. T. (2001). Organizational identity: Linkages between internal and external communication. In F. M. Jablin & L. L. Putnam (Eds.), *The new handbook of organizational communication: Advances in theory, research and methods* (pp. 231–269). Thousand Oaks, CA: Sage.

Churchill, W. (1993). *Struggle for the land: Indigenous resistance to genocide, ecocide, and expropriation in contemporary North America.* Monroe, ME: Common Courage.

Clarkson, M. E. (1995). A stakeholder framework for analyzing and evaluating corporate social performance. *Academy of Management Review, 20,* 92–117.

Cochran, T., Arkin, W., Norris, R., & Hoenig, M. (1987). *Nuclear Weapons Databook: Vol. II: U.S. Nuclear Warhead Production.* Cambridge, MA: Ballinger.

Cohn, C. (1987). Sex and death in the rational world of defense intellectuals. *Signs, 12,* 687–718.

Couldry, N. (1999). Disrupting the media frame at Greenham Common: A new chapter in the history of mediations? *Media, culture, and society, 21,* 337–358.

Crawford v. National Lead Co., 784 F. Supp. 439 (S.D. Ohio, 1989).

Cronen, V. E. (1995). Practical theory and the tasks ahead for social approaches to communication. In W. Leeds-Hurwitz (Ed.), *Social approaches to communication* (pp. 217–242). New York: Guilford Press.

Dahl, R. (1985). *Controlling nuclear weapons: Democracy vs. guardianship.* Syracuse, NY: Syracuse University Press.

Dalton, R. J., Garb, P., Lovrich, N. P., Pierce, J. C., & Whiteley, J. M. (Eds.). (1999). *Critical masses: Citizens, nuclear weapons production, and environmental destruction in the United States and Russia.* Cambridge, MA: MIT Press.

D'Antonio, M. (1993). *Atomic harvest: Hanford and the lethal toll of America's nuclear arsenal.* New York: Crown.

Deetz, S. A. (1992). *Democracy in an age of corporate colonization: Developments in communication and the politics of everyday life.* Albany: State University of New York Press.

Deetz, S. A. (1995). *Transforming communication, transforming business: Building responsive and responsible workplaces.* Cresskill, NJ: Hampton Press.

Deetz, S. A., Tracy, S. J., & Simpson, J. L. (2000). *Leading organizations through transition: Communication and cultural change.* Thousand Oaks, CA: Sage.

Depoe, S. P. (2000, November). *Civic discovery or civic co-optation? Revisiting the Fernald Citizens Advisory Board.* Paper presented at the annual conference of the National Communication Association, Seattle, WA.

Derrida, J. (1984). No apocalypse, not now (full speed ahead, seven missiles, seven missives). *Diacritics, 14*(2), 20–31.

Donaldson, T., & Preston, L. E. (1995). The stakeholder theory of the corporation: Concepts, evidence, and implications. *Academy of Management Review, 20,* 65–91.

Duffield, J. D., & Depoe, S. P. (1997). Lessons from Fernald: Reversing NIMBYism through democratic decision-making. *Inside EPA's Risk Policy Report, 3,* 31–34.

Earning public trust and confidence: Requisites for managing radioactive wastes. (1993, November 1). Final report of the Secretary of Energy Advisory Board Task Force on Radioactive Waste Management. Retrieved January 8, 2000, from http://www.osti.gov/gpo/servlets/purl/10184724-j8WVKp/webviewable/

Edwards, P. N. (1997). *The closed world: Computers and the politics of discourse in Cold War America.* Cambridge, MA: MIT Press.

Eisenberg, E. (1984). Ambiguity as strategy in organizational communication. *Communication Monographs, 51,* 227–242.

Engelhardt, T. (1998). *The end of victory culture: Cold War America and the disillusioning of a generation.* Amherst: University of Massachusetts Press.

Fairholm, G.W. (1993). *Organizational power politics: Tactics in organizational leadership.* Westport, CT: Praeger.

Fairhurst, G. T., Cooren, F., & Cahill, D. (2002). Discursiveness, contradiction, and unintended consequences in successive downsizings. *Management Communication Quarterly, 15,* 501–541.

Fairhurst, G. T., Jordan, J. M., & Neuwirth, K. (1997). Why are we here? Managing the meaning of an organizational mission statement. *Journal of Applied Communication Research, 25,* 243–263.

Farrell, T. B. (1993). *Norms of rhetorical culture.* New Haven, CT: Yale University Press.

Farrell, T. B., & Goodnight, G. T. (1981). Accidental rhetoric: The root metaphors of Three Mile Island. *Communication Monographs, 48,* 271–300.

Federal Facilities Environmental Restoration Dialogue Committee. (1993). *Interim report of the Federal Facilities Environmental Restoration Dialogue Committee.* Washington, DC: U.S. Government Printing Office.

Feldman, S. P. (1990). Stories as cultural creativity: On the relation between symbolism and politics in organizational change. *Human Relations, 43,* 809–828.

Fermi, R. (1995). *Picturing the bomb: Photographs from the secret world of the Manhattan Project.* New York: H. N. Abrams.

Fernlund, K. J. (Ed.). (1998). *The Cold War American West: 1945–1989.* Albuquerque: University of New Mexico Press.

Findlay, J. M., & Hevly, B. (1995). *Nuclear Technologies and nuclear communities: A history of Hanford and the Tri-Cities: 1943-1993.* Seattle: University of Washington, Center for the Study of the Pacific Northwest.

Fiorino, D. J. (1996). Environmental policy and the participation gap. In W. M. Lafferty & J. Meadowcroft (Eds.), *Democracy and the environment: Problems and prospects* (pp. 194–212). Cheltenham, UK: Edward Elgar.

Fischhoff, B. (1987). Treating the public with risk communications: A public health perspective. *Science, Technology, & Human Values, 12*(3–4), 13–19.

Fisher, W. R. (1987). *Human communication as narration: Toward a philosophy of reason, value, and action.* Columbia: University of South Carolina Press.

Freer, B. (1994). Atomic pioneers and environmental legacy at the Hanford site. *The Canadian Review of Sociology and Anthropology, 31,* 305–324.

Frooman, J. (1999). Stakeholder influence strategies. *Academy of Management Review, 24,* 191–205.

Geiger, H. J., & Rush, D. (1992). *Dead reckoning: A critical review of the Department of Energy's epidemiological research.* Washington, DC: Physicians for Social Responsibility.

Gerber, M. S. (1992). *On the home front: The cold war legacy of the Hanford nuclear site.* Lincoln: University of Nebraska Press.

Gilles, C. (1996). No one ever told us: Native Americans and the great uranium experiment. In J. Byrne & S. M. Hoffman (Eds.), *Governing the atom: The politics of risk* (pp. 103–125). New Brunswick, NJ: Transaction.

Glass, M. (1993). *Citizens against the MX: Public languages in the nuclear age.* Urbana: University of Illinois Press.

Goodnight, G. T. (1982). The personal, technical, and public spheres of argument: A speculative inquiry into the art of public deliberation. *Journal of the American Forensic Association, 18,* 214–227.

Gray, P. (1995). *Nuclear weapons "cleanup": Prospect without precedent*. San Francisco: Tides Foundation.

Griffiths, T. (1996). *Hunters and collectors: The antiquarian imagination in Australia*. Cambridge, UK: Cambridge University Press.

Gronbeck, B. E. (1998). The rhetorics of the past: History, argument, and collective memory. In K. J. Turner (Ed.), *Doing rhetorical history* (pp. 47–60). Tuscaloosa: University of Alabama Press.

Gusterson, H. (1996). *Nuclear rites: A nuclear weapons laboratory at the end of the Cold War*. Berkeley: University of California Press.

Gusterson, H. (2004). Nuclear tourism. *Journal for Cultural Research, 8,* 23–31.

Habermas, J. (1989). *The structural transformation of the public sphere: An inquiry into a category of bourgeois society* (T. Burger, Trans.). Cambridge, MA: MIT Press. (Original work published in 1962).

Hales, P. B. (1997). *Atomic spaces: Living on the Manhattan Project*. Urbana: University of Illinois Press.

Hance, B. J., Chess, C., & Sandman, P. M. (1989). *Improving dialogue with communities: A risk communication manual for government*. Trenton, NJ: Dept. of Environmental Protection and Energy.

Hanford Advisory Board. (2002). *White paper on public involvement*. Available at http://www.hanford.gov/boards/HAB

Hardert, R. A. (1993). Public trust and governmental trustworthiness: Nuclear deception at the Fernald, Ohio weapons plant. *Research in Social Problems and Public Policy, 5,* 125–148.

Hardert, R. A., Reader, M., Scott, M. L., Moulton, G. L., & Goodman, A. (1989). A critical theory analysis of nuclear power: The implications of Palo Verde Nuclear Generating Station. *Humanity & Society, 13,* 165–186.

Hebert, H. J. (2000, January 30). U. S. concedes nuke workers likely fell sick. *Las Vegas Review Journal*. Retrieved June 16, 2002, from http://www.lvrj.com/lvrj_home/2000/Jan-30-Sun-2000/news/12857717.html

Hevly, B., & Findlay, J. M. (Eds.). (1998). *The atomic West*. Seattle: University of Washington Press.

Hogan, J. M. (1994). *The nuclear freeze campaign: Rhetoric and foreign policy in the telepolitical age*. East Lansing: Michigan State University Press.

Hubbard, B. (1998). Reassessing Truman, the bomb, and revisionism: The burlesque frame and entelechy in the decision to use atomic weapons against Japan. *Western Journal of Communication, 62,* 348–385.

Hubbard, B., & Hasian, M.A., Jr. (1998). Atomic memories of the Enola Gay: Strategies of remembrance at the National Air and Space Museum. *Rhetoric and Public Affairs, 1,* 363–385.

Indigenous Environmental Network. (2002, May 9). *Nuclear risks for tribes could endanger future generations*. Retrieved June 15, 2002, from http://www.ienearth.org/alerts.html#yucca050902

Kane, T. (1988). Rhetorical histories and arms negotiations. *Journal of the American Forensic Association, 24,* 143–154.

Kaplan, L. (2000). Public participation in nuclear facility decisions: Lessons from Hanford. In D. L. Kleinman (Ed.), *Science, technology, and democracy* (pp. 67–83). Albany: State University of New York Press.

Katriel, T. (1993). Our future is where our past is: Studying heritage museums as ideological and performative arenas. *Communication Monographs, 60,* 69–75.

Katz, S. B., & Miller, C. R. (1996). The low-level radioactive waste-siting controversy in North Carolina: Toward a rhetorical model of risk communication. In C. G. Herndl & S. C. Brown (Eds.), *Green culture: Environmental rhetoric in contemporary America* (pp. 111–139). Madison: University of Wisconsin Press.

Kauzlarich, D., & Kramer, R. C. (1998). *Crimes of the American nuclear state: At home and abroad*. Boston: Northeastern University Press.

Kinsella, W. J. (2001). Nuclear boundaries: Material and discursive containment at the Hanford nuclear reservation. *Science as Culture, 10*(2), 163–194.

Kinsella, W. J. (2002). Problematizing the distinction between expert and lay knowledge. *New Jersey Journal of Communication, 10*(2), 191–207.

Kinsella, W. J. (2004a). Nuclear discourse and nuclear institutions: A theoretical framework and two empirical examples. *Qualitative Research Reports in Communication.*

Kinsella, W. J. (2004b). Public expertise: A foundation for citizen participation in energy and environmental decisions. In S. P. Depoe, J. W. Delicath,& M. Aepli (Eds.), *Communication in environmental decision making: Advances in theory and practice* (pp. 83–95). Albany: State University of New York Press.

Kinsella, W. J. (2005). One hundred years of nuclear discourse: Four master themes and their implications for environmental communication. In S. Senecah (Ed.), *Environmental communication yearbook 2.* Mahwah, NJ: Erlbaum.

Kirsch, S. (2001). Lost worlds: Environmental disaster, "culture loss," and the law. *Current Anthropology, 42,* 167–198.

Krasniewicz, L. (1992). *Nuclear summer: The clash of communities at the Seneca Women's Peace Encampment.* Ithaca, NY: Cornell University Press.

Krimsky, S., & Golding, D. (Eds.). (1992). *Social theories of risk.* Westport, CT: Praeger.

Krupar, J. (1998, August). *Atomic ghost towns: A historiographic review of the Hanford Engineering Works landscape.* Paper presented at the Second Los Alamos Invitational International History Conference, Los Alamos, NM.

Kuletz, V. L. (1998). *The tainted desert: Environmental and social ruin in the American West.* London: Routledge.

Laird, F. N. *(1993). Participatory analysis, democracy, and technological decision making. Science, Technology, & Human Values, 18,* 341–361.

Lanouette, W. (1990, January/February). James D. Watkins: Frustrated admiral of energy. *Bulletin of the Atomic Scientists, 46,* 36–42.

Legal Environmental Assistance Foundation v. Hodel, 586 F. Supp. 1163 (E.D. Tenn. 1984).

Lewis, L. K. (1999). Disseminating information and soliciting input during planned organizational change: Implementers' targets, sources, and channels for communicating. *Management Communication Quarterly, 13,* 43–75.

Lewis, L.K., Richardson, B.K., & Hamel, S.A. (2003). When the "stakes" are communicative: The lamb's and lion's share during nonprofit planned change. *Human Communication Research,* 29, 400-430.

Lewis, L. K., & Seibold, D. R. (1998). Reconceptualizing organizational change implementation as a communication problem: A review of literature and research agenda. In M. E. Roloff (Ed.), *Communication Yearbook 21,* (pp. 93–151). Thousand Oaks, CA: Sage.

Lodwick, D. G. (1993). Rocky Flats and the evolution of mistrust. *Research in Social Problems and Public Policy, 5,* 149–170.

Loeb, P. (1986). *Nuclear culture: Living and working in the world's largest atomic complex.* Philadelphia: New Society.

Lowenthal, D. (1998). *The heritage crusade and the spoils of history.* Cambridge, UK: Cambridge University Press.

Lowrie, K., & Greenberg, M. (1999, Spring). Cleaning it up and closing it down: Land use issues at Rocky Flats. *Federal Facilities Environmental Journal,* 69–79.

Luhmann, N. (1993). *Risk: A sociological theory.* New York: Aldine de Gruyter.

Makhijani, A. (1995). A readiness to harm. In A. Makhijani, H. Hu, & K. Yih (Eds.), *Nuclear wastelands: A global guide to nuclear weapons production and its health and environmental effects* (pp. 1–10). Cambridge, MA: MIT Press.

Makhijani, A., & Saleska, S. (1995). The production of nuclear weapons and environmental hazards. In A. Makhijani, H. Hu, & K. Yih (Eds.), *Nuclear wastelands: A global guide to nuclear weapons production and its health and environmental effects* (pp. 23–64). Cambridge, MA: MIT Press.

Makhijani, A., Hu, H., & Yih, K. (1995). *Nuclear wastelands: A global guide to nuclear weapons production and its health and environmental effects.* Cambridge, MA: MIT Press.

Makhijani, A., Ruttenber, A.J., Kennedy, E., & Clapp, R. (1995). The United States. In A. Makhijani, H. Hu, & K. Yih (Eds.), *Nuclear wastelands: A global guide to nuclear weapons production and its health and environmental effects* (pp. 169–284). Cambridge, MA: MIT Press.

Martinez, C., & Byrne, J. (1996). Science, society and the state: The nuclear project and the transformation of the American political economy. In J. Byrne & S. M. Hoffman (Eds.), *Governing the atom: The politics of risk* (pp. 67-102). New Brunswick, NJ: Transaction.

Masco, J. (1999). States of insecurity: Plutonium and post-Cold War anxiety in New Mexico, 1992-1996. In J. Weldes, M. Laffey, H. Gusterson, & R. Duvall (Eds.), *Cultures of insecurity: States, communities, and the production of danger* (pp. 203–232). Minneapolis: University of Minnesota Press.

Masco, J. (2002). Lie detectors: On secrets and hypersecurity in Los Alamos. *Public Culture, 14,* 441–467.

Mason, B. A. (2000, January 10). Fallout: Paducah's secret nuclear disaster. *The New Yorker,* 30–36.

McComas, K. A. (2001). Theory and practice of public meetings. *Communication Theory, 11,* 36–55.

McComas, K. A. (2003a). Citizen satisfaction with public meetings used for risk communication. *Journal of Applied Communication Research, 31,* 164–184.

McComas, K. A. (2003b). Trivial pursuits: Participant views of public meetings. *Journal of Public Relations Research, 15,* 91–115.

McCutcheon, C. (2002). *Nuclear reactions: The politics of opening a radioactive waste disposal site.* Albuquerque: University of New Mexico Press.

Mehta, M. D. (1998). Risk and decision-making: A theoretical approach to public participation in techno-scientific situations. *Technology in Society, 20,* 87–98.

Metzler, M. S. (1997). Organizations, democracy, and the public sphere: The implications of democratic (r)evolution at a nuclear weapons facility. *Communication Studies, 48,* 333–358.

Metzler, M. S. (2001). The centrality of organizational legitimacy to public relations practice. In R. L. Heath (Ed.), *Handbook of Public Relations* (pp. 321–333). Thousand Oaks, CA: Sage.

Mitchell, R. K., Agle, B. R., & Wood, D.J. (1997). Toward a theory of stakeholder identification and salience: Defining the principle of who and what really counts. *Academy of Management Review, 22,* 853–886.

Mojtabai, A. G. (1986). *Blessed assurance.* Boston: Houghton-Mifflin.

Molella, A. (2003). Exhibiting atomic culture: The view from Oak Ridge. *History and Technology, 19,* 211–226.

National Academy of Sciences. (1989). *The nuclear weapons complex: Management for health, safety, and the environment.* Washington, DC: National Academy of Sciences.

Needleman, C. (1987). Ritualism in communicating risk information. *Science, Technology, & Human Values, 12*(3–4), 20–25.

Nelson, L., & Beardsley, G. L. (1987). Toward an interdisciplinary model of barriers to nuclear arms control. *Social Science Journal, 24,* 375–392.

Newman, R. P. (1995). *Truman and the Hiroshima cult.* East Lansing: Michigan State University Press.

Nolan, J. E. (1989). *Guardians of the arsenal: The politics of nuclear strategy.* New York: New Republic/Basic Books.

Nuke testing killed 11,000, study says. (2003, February 12). *Denver Post,* p. A4.

O'Connor, E. S. (1995). Paradoxes of participation: Textual analysis and organizational change. *Organization Studies, 16,* 769–803.

Office of Technology Assessment. (1991). *Complex cleanup: The environmental legacy of nuclear weapons production* (OTA-O-484). Washington, DC: U.S. Government Printing Office.

Olson, K. M., & Goodnight, G. T. (1994). Entanglements of consumption, cruelty, privacy, and fashion: The social controversy over fur. *Quarterly Journal of Speech, 80,* 249–276.

Owendorf, J. M. (1996). DOE restores trust in post-Cold War era. *Forum for Applied Research and Public Policy, 11,* 110–112.

Pasternak, D. (1993). The Department of Energy's informational black hole. *Research in Social Problems and Public Policy, 5,* 171–177.

Patterson, J. D., & Allen, M. W. (1997). Accounting for your actions: How stakeholders respond to the strategic communication of environmental activist organizations. *Journal of Applied Communication Research, 25,* 293–316.

Phillips, K. R. (1999). A rhetoric of controversy. *Western Journal of Communication, 63,* 488–510.

Popular Memory Group. (1982). Popular memory: Theory, politics, method. In R. Johnson, G. McLennan, B. Schwartz, & D. Sutton (Eds.). *Making histories: Studies in history-writing and politics* (pp. 205–252). London: Hutchinson.

Presidential memorandum. (1994, May 4). Memorandum for the heads of executive departments and agencies. *Federal Register, 59.* Retrieved April 13, 1997, from http://www.em.doe.gov/public/tribal/whletter.html

Prosise, T. (1998). The collective memory of the atomic bombings misrecognized as objective history: The case of the public opposition to the National Air and Space Museum's atom bomb exhibit. *Western Journal of Communication, 62,* 316–347.

Providing compensation to America's nuclear weapons workers. (2000, December 11). Presidential Executive Order 13179. *Federal Register, 65,* 77487.

Ratliff, J. N. (1997). Improving environmental advocacy: How the Hanford Environmental Action League challenged the Department of Energy. *Journal of the Northwest Communication Association, 25,* 42–59.

Ratliff, J. N. (1998). The politics of nuclear waste: An analysis of a public hearing on the proposed Yucca Mountain Nuclear Waste Repository. *Electronic Journal of Communication.* Retrieved April 1, 1999, from http://www.cios.org/getfile\Ratliff_V8N198

Reed, R., Lemak, D. J., & Hesser, W. A. (1997). Cleaning up after the Cold War: Management and social issues. *Academy of Management Review, 22,* 614–642.

Renn, O. (1992) Concepts of risk: A classification. In S. Krimsky & D. Golding (Eds.), *Social theories of risk* (pp. 53–79). Westport, CT: Praeger.

Rhodes, R. (1986). *The making of the atomic bomb.* New York: Simon & Schuster.

Rhodes, R. (1995). *Dark sun: The making of the hydrogen bomb.* New York: Simon & Schuster.

Rojecki, A. (1999). *Silencing the opposition: Antinuclear movements and the media in the Cold War.* Urbana: University of Illinois Press.

Rosenthal, D. (1990). *At the heart of the bomb: The dangerous allure of weapons work.* Reading, MA: Addison-Wesley.

Ross, D. L., & Benson, J. A. (1995). Cultural change in ethical redemption: A corporate case study. *Journal of Business Communication, 32,* 345–362.

Rowan, K. E. (1991). Goals, obstacles, and strategies in risk communication: A problem-solving approach to improving communication about risks. *Journal of Applied Communication Research, 19,* 300–329.

Rowan, K. E. (1995). What risk communicators need to know: An agenda for research. In B. R. Burleson (Ed.), *Communication yearbook 18* (pp. 300–319). Thousand Oaks, CA.: Sage.

Rowley, T. J. (1997). Moving beyond dyadic ties: A network theory of stakeholder influences. *Academy of Management Review, 22,* 887–910.

Sanger, S. L. (1995). *Working on the bomb: An oral history of WW II Hanford.* Portland, OR: Portland State University Continuing Education Press.

Schafer, J. K. (1994). *Organizational theory and federal agency reorganizations: A Department of Energy case study.* Unpublished doctoral dissertation, George Mason University.

Schell, J. (2000, January). The unfinished twentieth century: What we have forgotten about nuclear weapons. *Harper's Magazine,* 41–56.

Schwartz, S. I. (Ed.). (1998). *Atomic audit: The costs and consequences of U. S. nuclear weapons since 1940.* Washington, DC: Brookings Institute.

Scott, S. G., & Lane, V. R. (2000). A stakeholder approach to organizational identity. *Academy of Management Review, 25,* 43–62.

Seeger, M. W., Sellnow, T. L., & Ulmer, R. R. (1998). Communication, organization and crisis. In M. E. Roloff (Ed.), *Communication Yearbook 21* (pp. 230–275). Thousand Oaks, CA: Sage.

Sheak, R. J., & Cianciolo, P. (1993). Notes on nuclear weapons plants and their neighbors: The case of Fernald. *Research in Social Problems and Public Policy, 5,* 97–122.

Shroyer, J. (1998). *Secret mesa: Inside Los Alamos National Laboratory.* New York: Wiley.

Silverman, M. J. (2000). *No immediate risk: Environmental safety in nuclear weapons production, 1942–1985.* Unpublished doctoral dissertation, Carnegie Mellon University.

Simon, R. (2004, June 16). Senate supports funding to study "bunker-buster." *Los Angeles Times.* Retrieved June 20, 2004, from http://www.latimes.com/news/nationworld/nation/la-na-defense16jun16.story

Smith, K. K. (2000). Mere nostalgia: Notes on a progressive paratheory. *Rhetoric and Public Affairs, 3,* 505–527.

Stegenga, J. A. (1991, March). Nuclearism and global economic justice. *Thought, 66,* 14–31.

Stelzer, I. M. (1996). *The Department of Energy: An agency that cannot be reinvented.* Washington, DC: AEI Press.

Sumner, D., Hu, H., & Woodward, A. (1995). Health hazards of nuclear weapons production. In A. Makhijani, H. Hu, & K. Yih (Eds.), *Nuclear wastelands: A global guide to nuclear weapons production and its health and environmental effects* (pp. 65–104). Cambridge, MA: MIT Press.

Tannenwald, N. (1999). The bomb and its discontents [Review Essay]. *International Studies Review, 1,* 105–118.

Taylor, B. C. (1990). Reminiscences of Los Alamos: Narrative, critical theory and the organizational subject. *Western Journal of Speech Communication, 54,* 395–419.

Taylor, B. C. (1993a). Register of the repressed: Women's voice and body in the nuclear weapons organization. *Quarterly Journal of Speech, 79,* 267–285.

Taylor, B. C. (1993b). *Fat Man and Little Boy:* Cinematic representation of interests in the nuclear weapons organization. *Critical Studies in Mass Communication, 10,* 367–394.

Taylor, B. C. (1996). Make bomb, save world: Reflections on dialogic nuclear ethnography. *Journal of Contemporary Ethnography, 25,* 120–143.

Taylor, B. C. (1997a). Home zero: Images of home and field in nuclear-cultural studies. *Western Journal of Communication, 61,* 209–234.

Taylor, B. C. (1997b). Revis(it)ing nuclear history: Narrative conflict at the Bradbury Science Museum. *Studies in Cultures: Organizations and Societies, 3,* 119–145.

Taylor, B. C. (1997c). Shooting downwind: Depicting the radiated body in epidemiology and documentary photography. In M. Huspek & G. Radford (Eds.), *Transgressing scientific discourses: Communication and the voice of other* (pp. 289–328). Albany: State University of New York Press.

Taylor, B. C. (1998a). Nuclear weapons and communication studies: A review essay. *Western Journal of Communication, 62,* 300–315.

Taylor, B. C. (1998b). The bodies of August: Photographic realism and controversy at the National Air and Space Museum. *Rhetoric and Public Affairs, 1,* 331–361.

Taylor, B. C. (2002). Organizing the "unknown subject": Los Alamos, espionage, and the politics of biography." *Quarterly Journal of Speech, 88,* 33–49.

Taylor, B.C. (2003a). "Our bruised arms hung up as monuments": Nuclear iconography in post-Cold War culture. *Critical Studies in Media Communication, 20,* 1–34.

Taylor, B. C. (2003b). Nuclear waste and communication studies [Review of Thomas V. Peterson, *Linked arms: A rural community resists nuclear waste*]. *Review of Communication, 3,* 285–291.

Taylor, B. C., & Davis, S. (1999). Environmental communication and nuclear communication studies: The case of Rocky Flats. In C. B. Short & D. Hardy-Short (Eds.), *Proceedings of the fifth biennial conference on communication and environment* (pp. 286–299). Flagstaff: Northern Arizona University.

Taylor, B. C., & Freer, B. (2002). Containing the nuclear past: The politics of history and heritage at the Hanford Plutonium Works. *Journal of Organizational Change Management, 15,* 563–588.

Taylor, B. C., & Hartnett, S. J. (2000). "National security, and all that it implies…": Communication and (post-) Cold War culture. *Quarterly Journal of Speech, 86,* 465–487.

Thorpe, C. (2004). Against time: Scheduling, momentum, and moral order at wartime Los Alamos. *Journal of Historical Sociology, 17,* 31–55.

Tietge, D. J. (2002). *Flash effect: Science and the rhetorical origins of Cold War America.* Athens: Ohio University Press.

Toker, C. W. (2002). Debating "what ought to be": The comic frame and public moral argument. *Western Journal of Communication, 66,* 53–83.

U.S. Department of Energy (DOE). (1995). *Closing the circle on the splitting of the atom: The environmental legacy of nuclear weapons production in the United States and what the Department of Energy is doing about it.* Washington, DC: DOE-Environmental Management.

U.S. DOE. (1996). *FY 1996 progress in implementing Section 120 of Comprehensive Environmental Response, Compensation, and Liability Act, Tenth annual report to Congress. Office of Environmental Management.* Washington, DC: U.S. Government Printing Office.

U.S. DOE. (1997). *Linking legacies: Connecting the Cold War nuclear weapons production processes to their environmental consequences. Office of Environmental Management.* Washington, DC: U.S. Government Printing Office.

U.S. DOE. (2000). *Environmental management site-specific advisory board (SSAB) guidance.* Office of Environmental Management. Washington, DC: U.S. Government Printing Office.

U.S. DOE. (2003). *Guidance for developing a site specific risk-based end state vision.* Washington, DC: DOE-Environmental Management.

Ulmer, R. R. (2001). Effective crisis management through established stakeholder relationships. *Management Communication Quarterly, 14,* 590–615.

Venette, S. J., Sellnow, T. L., & Lang, P. A. (2003). Metanarration's role in restructuring perceptions of crisis: NHTSA's failure in the Ford-Firestone crisis. *Journal of Business Communication, 40,* 219–236.

Weart, S. (1988). *Nuclear fear: A history of images.* Cambridge, MA: Harvard University Press.

Weeks, J. (1997, October 24). *Democratizing the U.S. Department of Energy: Progress and Policy Impact.* Retrieved May 26, 2002, from http://ksgnotes1.harvard.edu/BCSIA/Library.nsf/pubs/demnrg

Weeks, J. (2000, September). *Advice—and consent? The Department of Energy's site-specific advisory boards.* Retrieved May 26, 2002, from http://ksgnotes1.harvard.edu/BCSIA/Library.nsf/pubs/advice&consent

White, H. (1980). The value of narrativity in the representation of reality. *Critical Inquiry, 7,* 5–27.

Williams, D. C. (1989). Under the sign of (an)nihilation: Burke in the age of nuclear destruction and critical deconstruction. In H. W. Simons & T. Melia (Eds.), *The legacy of Kenneth Burke* (pp. 196–223). Madison: University of Wisconsin Press.

Williams, W. L. (2002). *Determining our environments: The role of Department of Energy citizen advisory boards.* Westport CT: Greenwood Press.

Wilson, J. Q. (1989). *Bureaucracy: What government agencies do and why they do it.* New York: Basic Books.

Zelizer, B. (1995). Reading the past against the grain: The shape of memory studies. *Critical Studies in Mass Communication, 12,* 214–239.

Zuckerbrod, N. (2001, July 28). Compensation to begin for nuclear workers, kin. *Rocky Mountain News,* p. A7.

AUTHOR INDEX

SUBJECT INDEX

A

Access, electronic communication, 168
Accessibility, 195, *see also* Distanced leadership
Accidents, crisis categorization, 278
ACT, 76
Action theory, 262
Active badges, 169
Active child effects, 40, 41, 43, *see also* Child effects
Active defense, 105
Active outward orientation, 281–282
Activism, 382, *see also* Nuclear legacies, nuclear weapons production
Activist organizations, 377
Adjuvants, 123
Adolescents, 119–121, 132–133
AEC, *see* Atomic Energy Commission
Affect, 112–114
Age, 112
Agency component, 347, 348
Agenda-setting effects, 43
Agenda-setting theory, 337, 343
Agreement, 220
Aggressive attacks, 14, *see also* Child abuse, nonphysical
Alcohol abuse, 119, 120–121
Allegory of the cave, 334
Alliance for Nuclear Accountability (ANA), 377
America knows best culture, 287
American scholars, communication management, 258
Americans, meaning construction, 348
ANA, *see* Alliance for Nuclear Accountability
Analysis of variance (ANOVA), 166
design and motivation deception, 64–65
Anger, 113, 130
Anonymity, data validity, 160
Antigrand theory framework, 312–313
Appraisal theory, 113
Argumentation, 220
Argumentativeness, 4, 8–9
Arousal, 52, 63, 81, 130
Artificial intelligence, 222
Asian consumers, 288–290

Assertion-weakening component, 123
Associative networks, 124–125
Atomic bombs, 367, *see also* Nuclear weapons production complex
Atomic Energy Commission (AEC), 367
Attack advertising, 118
Attack messages, 100–101, 131, *see also* Messages
Attitude
    accessibility, 114–115, 124
    inoculation theory of resistance, 103–104, 127
    internet and personality, 229
    message framing to constructivism, 346
    paradigm shift in potential media effects, 335
    parental and child effects, 39
    persuasion and communication, 245
    wartime/Cold War nuclear weapons production, 372–373
Attitudinal inoculation, 99
Attractive targets, 55, *see also* Deception
Audience
    crisis communication, 295, 296, 302
    message framing/meaning construction, 333, 334, 340, 343–344, 346, 351, 353–354
Audiovisual content, 219–220
Authoritarian organization, 372
Automation bias, 51–52
Awareness raising, 317

B

Balance models, 245–246, 250
Bargaining chips boycotts, 293
BAS, *see* Behavioral approach system
Behavior
    leadership and physical distance, 195
    management, 80
    nonphysical child abuse, 14, 25, 37
    norms and online communities, 224
    patterns, 59, 60
Behavior change theories, 316
Behavioral approach system (BAS), 6

ABOUT THE EDITOR

PAMELA J. KALBFLEISCH (Ph.D., Michigan State University, 1985) is professor and director of the School of Communication at the University of North Dakota. Her research reflects an active interest in interpersonal communication and communication in close relationships, covering such topics as social support, mentoring relationships, deceptive communication, and gender issues. Her published research is found in International Communication Association publications *Communication Theory, Human Communication Research* and the *Journal of Communication*, as well as in publications such as *Health Communication, Communication Education, Journal of Applied Communication Research, Howard Journal of Communication*, and the *Journal of Language and Social Psychology*. She edited *Interpersonal Communication: Evolving Interpersonal Relationships* and, with Michael J. Cody, coedited *Gender, Power, and Communication in Human Relationships*, both books published by Lawrence Erlbaum Associates. She authored the *Persuasion Handbook* published by Kendall Hunt, and she has authored and coauthored numerous book chapters and monographs. Kalbfleisch also guest edited a special issue of *Communication Theory* on "Building Theories in Interpersonal Communication," and she serves as associate editor and review board member for nine scholarly publications. She rides quarter horses and competitively paddles outrigger canoes whenever horses or oceans are available.

ABOUT THE CONTRIBUTORS

JUDEE K. BURGOON is professor of communication and director for human communication research, Center for the Management of Information, University of Arizona. She has authored seven books and monographs and over 200 articles, chapters, and reviews related to deception, nonverbal and relational communication, and computer-mediated communication. Her current research, supported by the U.S. Department of Defense and U.S. Department of Homeland Security, centers on issues of human deception and its detection. She is the recipient of the National Communication Association's Distinguished Scholar Award, its highest award for a lifetime of scholarly achievement.

JOSHUA A. COMPTON (M.A., 2000, Southwest Missouri State University) is a doctoral candidate at the University of Oklahoma and instructor at Southwest Baptist University in Bolivar, MO. His research interests include resistance to influence, political communication, media effects, and image restoration. His work has been published recently in *Human Communication Research*.

STACEY L. CONNAUGHTON is an assistant professor in the Department of Communication at Rutgers University. Her published research examines organizational identity, identification, and leadership, particularly as they relate to virtual organizations and political parties. Her published work has appeared in the *Journal of Communication, Management Communication Quarterly, Communication Studies, the Howard Journal of Communications*, and her book, *Inviting Latino Voters: Party Messages and Latino Party Identification*, is under contract with Routledge.

JOHN A. DALY is the Liddell Professor of Communication and the TCB Professor in the Department of Management at the University of Texas at Austin. He has published a number of books and articles on topics related to communication. He has also consulted with a number of companies world-wide on issues tied to improving communication effectiveness.

STEPHEN P. DEPOE (Ph.D., Northwestern University, 1986) is an associate professor in the Department of Communication at the University of Cincinnati. He is also the director of the Center for Health and Environmental Communication Research. His primary research area is environmental communication, with a specific focus on public participation. He is the current editor of *Environmental*

Communication Yearbook, a refereed annual publication of environmental communication scholarship. He is coeditor of *Communication and Public Participation in Environmental Decision Making*, published in 2004 by SUNY Press. He is also a member of the Fernald Citizens Advisory Board, and is president of Fernald Living History, Inc., a nonprofit organization interested in preserving artifacts and stories related to nuclear weapons production and environmental remediation at the Fernald site.

ANDREW J. FLANAGIN (Ph.D., 1996, Annenberg School of Communication, University of Southern California) is an associate professor in the Department of Communication at the University of California, Santa Barbara. His research focuses on communication and information technologies and the ways in which they affect human interaction, including collective action efforts, collaboration, knowledge management, and information sharing. His recent articles have been published in *Communication Monographs, Human Communication Research, Management Communication Quarterly, Communication Research, Journal of Communication, Journalism and Mass Communication Quarterly, Organization Science, New Media and Society*, and *Communication Theory*.

WILLIAM J. KINSELLA (Ph.D., Rutgers University, 1997) is an assistant professor in the Department of Communication at North Carolina State University. His research interests include organizational communication, environmental communication, rhetoric of science and technology, and rhetoric of public policy in scientific and technological settings. His publications include essays in *Management Communication Quarterly, Rhetoric Society Quarterly, The Environmental Communication Yearbook,* and *Qualitative Research Reports in Communication, The New Jersey Journal of Communication*, and *Science as Culture*. He serves on the Department of Energy's Citizens Advisory Board at the (Washington) Hanford site.

BETTY KAMAN LEE (Ph.D., Hong Kong Baptist University, 2001) is an assistant professor in the Department of English and Communication at City University of Hong Kong. Her research interests lie in corporate communication and intercultural communication. Current research has investigated crisis communication and corporate reputation in Chinese-based stakeholder communities with an audience orientation.

MARIBETH S. METZLER (Ph.D., Rensselaer Polytechnic Institute, 1996) is an assistant professor in the Department of Communication at the University of Cincinnati. Prior to doctoral studies, she worked in environmental public affairs for the U.S. Air Force and as an environmental consultant. Her research has appeared in *Communication Quarterly, Communication Studies, the Handbook of Public Relations, the Encyclopedia of Public Relations* (forthcoming), and *Responsible Communication: Ethical Issues in Business, Industry, and the Professions.* Her research focuses on the social implications of organizations.

WENDY M. MORGAN (M.A., Northwestern University, 2000) is a doctoral student in the Department of Communication at Purdue University. Her research focuses on parent–child interaction, and her dissertation proposes a theory of "safe ground" that clarifies parent–child interaction patterns fundamental for establishing child self-esteem and behavioral competence. She has coauthored publications in *Communication Monographs, Communication Yearbook*, and the *Handbook of Family Communication.*

NICHOLAS A. PALOMARES (Ph.D. candidate, University of California, Santa Barbara) is an assistant professor in the Department of Communication at the University of California, Davis. He is interested in conversational behavior and language use, such as the detection and the strategic pursuit of goals in social interaction, computer-mediated communication, and gender, language, and social influence. His recent publications have appeared in *Human Communication Research, Communication Monographs*, and *Journal of Language and Social Psychology.*

ZIZI PAPACHARISSI (Ph.D., University of Texas at Austin) is currently assistant professor in the Department of Broadcasting, Telecommunications, and Mass Media at Temple University. Her research interests include self-presentation online, cybercommunity, and political uses of new media. An earlier version of this paper was presented to the International Association of Mass Communication Researchers (IAMCR) annual conference, Barcelona, Spain, July 2002.

MICHAEL W. PFAU (Ph.D., 1987, University of Arizona) is professor and chair of the Department of Communication at the University of Oklahoma. His research interests include social influence, political communication, and media effects. His research has been published recently in *Human Communication Research* and *Communication Monographs.* He is currently editor of the *Journal of Communication.*

RAUL ROMAN is a research associate at the Center for Internet Studies at the University of Washington in Seattle. Roman's research mostly focuses on the impact of information and communication systems on socioeconomic development in disadvantaged communities of the developing world. He has conducted extensive field research on this and related topics in different countries in Africa, Asia, and Latin America. Roman received his M.S. and Ph.D. degrees in communication and international development at Cornell University.

BRYAN C. TAYLOR (Ph.D., University of Utah, 1991) is an associate professor in the Department of Communication, University of Colorado at Boulder.

His primary research program involves (post-) Cold War culture and rhetoric, particularly surrounding the production of nuclear weapons. His recent publications in this area have appeared in *American Literary History, Critical Studies in Media Communication, Journal of Contemporary Ethnography, Journal of Organizational Change Management, Quarterly Journal of Speech, Rhetoric and Public Affairs, Studies in Cultures, Organizations and Societies*, and *Western Journal of Communication*. He is also coauthor with Thomas R. Lindlof of Qualitative Communication Research Methods. He served from 1998 to 2001 on the Department of Energy's Rocky Flats Citizens Advisory Board and, since 2001, as a member of the Board of Directors of the Rocky Flats Cold War Museum.

BEA R. H. VAN DEN BERGH (Ph.D., Katholieke Universiteit Leuven, Belgium, 1989) is an associate professor at the Department of Psychology, Katholieke Universiteit Leuven, Belgium. Her research interests include child-centered research methods, temperament, stress, self-concept, and living conditions of children and adolescents, and the short- and long-term effects of negative maternal emotions during pregnancy on behavioral outcome and self-regulation problems of the child. Recent articles have appeared in developmental psychology journals such as *Child Development* and in biomedical journals such as *Neuroscience* and *Behavioral Reviews*.

JAN VAN DEN BULCK (Ph.D., Katholieke Universiteit Leuven, Belgium, 1996) is a professor in the Department of Communication, Katholieke Univeristeit Leuven, Belgium, interested in media effects research and in cognitive approaches to cultivation and socialization in particular. Increasingly he is also looking at behavioral effects of media use. His current research projects deal with cognitive approaches to cultivation theory and with medical and psychomedical correlates of media use. Recent articles have appeared in international communication journals such as *Journal of Broadcasting and Electronic Media* and in biomedical journals such as *Emergency Medical Journal, Journal of Sleep Research*, and *The Annals of Pharmacotherapy*.

BETTEKE VAN RULER (Ph.D.) is a professor of communication and organization at the Amsterdam School of Communications Research (ASCoR) and chair of the Department of Communication Science of the University of Amsterdam, The Netherlands. She is doing research on professionalization of public relations and on the relationship between public relations and journalism. She has published in *Public Relations Review, Journal of Public Relations Research*, and *Journal of Communication Management*. She has also written many books. Recently she edited *Public Relations and Communication Management* in Europe, a nation-to-nation introduction into public relations theory and practice, together with Dejan Verčič. She is also editor of the *International Journal of Strategic Communication*, published by Erlbaum.

DEJAN VERČIČ (Ph.D., London School of Economics) is founding partner in Pristop Communications, a communication management consultancy based in Ljubljana, Slovenia, and assistant professor for public relations and communication management at the University of Ljubljana. In 2000 he received a special award by the Public Relations Society of Slovenia, and in 2001 he was awarded the Alan Campbell-Johnson Medal for outstanding service to international public relations by the UK Institute of Public Relations. Recent publications include *The Global Public Relations Handbook*, with K. Sriramesh, and *Public Relations and Communication Management in Europe*, with B. Can Rule.

ROBERT H. WICKS (Ph.D., Michigan State, 1987) specializes in information-processing and political communication research. His work has appeared in many journals, including *Communication Research, Journalism and Mass Communication Quarterly, the Journal of Broadcasting and Electronic Media*, and *American Behavioral Scientist*. Wicks is author of *Understanding Audiences: Learning to Use the Media Constructively* and of many book chapters related to his expertise. He has worked professionally as a newspaper, radio, and television reporter, editor, and manager.

STEVEN R. WILSON (Ph.D., Purdue University, 1989) is a professor and director of graduate studies in the Department of Communication at Purdue University. His research and teaching focus on interpersonal influence and message production in a variety of contexts, from parent-child interaction in abusive families to intercultural business negotiations. He is the author of *Seeking and Resisting Compliance: Why People Say What They Do When Trying to Influence Others*, as well as more than 40 journal articles and book chapters on these topics.

6516